# English Composition and Grammar

BENCHMARK EDITION

Fifth Course

# English Composition and Grammar

BENCHMARK EDITION

**John E. Warriner**

**Fifth Course**

**Harcourt Brace Jovanovich, Publishers**

Orlando San Diego Chicago Dallas

THE SERIES

English Composition and Grammar: Introductory Course
English Composition and Grammar: First Course
English Composition and Grammar: Second Course
English Composition and Grammar: Third Course
English Composition and Grammar: Fourth Course
English Composition and Grammar: Fifth Course
English Composition and Grammar: Complete Course
Annotated Teacher's Edition and Teacher's Resource Book for each above title.

CORRELATED SERIES:

English Workshop: Introductory Course
English Workshop: First Course
English Workshop: Second Course
English Workshop: Third Course
English Workshop: Fourth Course
English Workshop: Fifth Course
English Workshop: Review Course

Composition: Models and Exercises, First Course
Composition: Models and Exercises, Second Course
Composition: Models and Exercises, Third Course
Composition: Models and Exercises, Fourth Course
Composition: Models and Exercises, Fifth Course
Advanced Composition: A Book of Models for Writing, Complete Course

Vocabulary Workshop: Introductory Course
Vocabulary Workshop: First Course
Vocabulary Workshop: Second Course
Vocabulary Workshop: Third Course
Vocabulary Workshop: Fourth Course
Vocabulary Workshop: Fifth Course
Vocabulary Workshop: Complete Course

**John E. Warriner** taught English for thirty-two years in junior and senior high schools and in college. He is chief author of the *English Composition and Grammar* series, coauthor of the *English Workshop* series, general editor of the *Composition: Models and Exercises* series, and editor of *Short Stories: Characters in Conflict*. His coauthors have all been active in English education.

For permission to reprint copyrighted material, grateful acknowledgment is made to the following sources:

*American Mensa Ltd., 2626 E. 14th ST, Brooklyn, NY 11235, and Robert Kunnecke:* "Stop the Killer Air Bags" by Robert Kunnecke from *Mensa Bulletin*, #282, December 1984. Mensa is an organization whose members have scored at, or above, the 98th percentile of the general population on any standardized IQ test.

*Atheneum Publishers, Inc.:* From *The Miracle Worker* by William Gibson. Copyright 1956, 1957 by William Gibson; copyright renewed © 1959, 1960 by Tamarock Productions, Ltd., and George S. Klein and Leo Garel as trustees under three separate deeds of trust. From "Be Careful" in *Happy to Be Here* by Garrison Keillor. Copyright © 1982 by Garrison Keillor.

*The Atlantic Monthly:* From "Pleas for Balance, Responsibility and Judgment" by Jeffrey Goodman in *The Atlantic Contest Booklet, 1961-62*. Copyright © 1962 by The Atlantic Monthly Company, Boston, MA.

*Bowker Magazine Group, Reed Publishing, USA:* From "Roadblock to Bookbuying" by Elmo Roper in *Publisher's Weekly* Magazine, June 16, 1958.

*Brandt & Brandt Literary Agents, Inc. and The New York Times Company:* From *Hers* by Anne Farrar Scott. Copyright © 1985 by The New York Times Company.

*Curtis Brown, Ltd.:* From *Dawn Over Zero* by William L. Laurence. Copyright © 1946 by William Laurence.

*Chicago Tribune Company:* "Ali's Brain and Cruelest Sport" by Joan Beck from the *Chicago Tribune*, September 24, 1984. Copyright September 24, 1984, by the Chicago Tribune Company.

*Henry Steele Commager:* From "Television: The Medium in Search of Its Character" by Henry Steele Commager in *TV GUIDE* Magazine, June 25, 1966.

*Dodd, Mead & Company, Inc.:* From "Trifles" in *Plays* by Susan Glaspell. Copyright 1920 by Dodd, Mead & Company, Inc.; copyright renewed 1948 by Susan Glaspell.

*Doubleday & Company, Inc.:* "Child on Top of a Greenhouse" from *The Collected Poems of Theodore Roethke* by Theodore Roethke. Copyright 1946 by Editorial Publications, Inc. From *Speech Can Change Your Life* by Dorothy Sarnoff. Copyright © 1970 by Dorothy Sarnoff. "Cry Silent" by Donna Whitewing from *The Whispering Wind* by Terry Allen. Copyright © 1972 by The Institute of American Indian Arts.

*Farrar, Straus & Giroux, Inc.:* From "Los Angeles Notebook" in *Slouching Towards Bethlehem* by Joan Didion. Copyright © 1967, 1968 by Joan Didion. From "A Walk to the Getty" in *Annie John* by Jamaica Kincaid. Copyright © 1983, 1984, 1985 by Jamaica Kincaid. Originally published in *The New Yorker*. From "A Summer's Reading" in *The Magic Barrel* by Bernard Malamud. Copyright © 1956, 1958 by Bernard Malamud.

*J. G. Ferguson Publishing Company:* From *The Great Explorers* by Piers Pennington. Copyright 1979 by J. G. Ferguson Publishing Company.

*Harcourt Brace Jovanovich, Inc.:* From the Introduction to "Escape and Interpretation" in *Literature: Structure, Sound, and Sense*, Third Edition by Laurence Perrine. From "Everyday Use" in *In Love & Trouble* by Alice Walker. Published by Harcourt Brace Jovanovich, Inc.

*Harper & Row, Publishers, Inc.:* From *Pilgrim at Tinker Creek* by Annie Dillard. Copyright © 1974 by Annie Dillard. From pp. 25 and 84–85 in *ATOMIC ENERGY: A New Start* by David E. Lilienthal. Copyright © 1980 by David E. Lilienthal. From *Roughing It* by Mark Twain. From p. 18 of "Death of a Pig" in *Essays of E. B. White* by E. B. White. Copyright 1947, 1975 by E. B. White.

*Harvard University Press:* From *One Writer's Beginnings* by Eudora Welty. Copyright © 1983, 1984 by Eudora Welty. Published by Harvard University Press.

*John Hawkins & Associates, Inc.:* From "The Last Bullet" by MacKinlay Kantor.

*Hill and Wang, a division of Farrar, Straus & Giroux, Inc.:* From "The Mother of the Gracchi" in *The Big Sea* by Langston Hughes. Copyright 1940 by Langston Hughes; copyright renewed © 1968 by Arna Bontemps and George Houston Bass.

*Henry Holt and Company, Inc.:* "The Silken Tent" from *The Poetry of Robert Frost*, edited by Edward Connery Lathem. Copyright 1942 by Robert Frost; copyright © 1969 by Holt, Rinehart and Winston; copyright © 1970 by Lesley Frost Ballantine.

*Pantheon Books, a division of Random House, Inc., and Woman's Day:* From "The Moustache" in *EIGHT plus ONE* by Robert Cormier. Copyright © 1975 by Robert Cormier; copyright © 1975 by CBS Magazines, the Consumer Publishing Division of CBS Inc. Originally published in *Woman's Day*, November 1975.

*Peachtree Publishers Ltd.:* From "Are Cheerleaders Really Necessary?" in *Won't You Come Home, Billy Bob Bailey* by Lewis Grizzard. © 1980 by Lewis Grizzard.

*Penguin Books Ltd.:* From *The Personality of Animals* by H. Munro Fox. Copyright © 1940 by H. Munro Fox. Published by Pelican Books.

*G. P. Putnam's Sons:* From *The Outline of Science* by J. Arthur Thompson.

*The Rainbird Publishing Group Limited, London:* From *Mark Twain and His World* by Justin Kaplan. Published by Crescent Books, New York.

*Random House, Inc.:* Entries "student" and "Wilson" from the *Random House College Dictionary*, Revised Edition. Copyright © 1975, 1979, 1980, 1982, 1984 by Random House, Inc. From *The Forest and the Sea: A Look At the Economy of Nature and the Ecology of Man* by Marston Bates. Copyright © 1960 by Marston Bates.

*Rapport Publishing Company, Inc.:* Review of *Smith and Other Events* by Arnold Berman in *The West Coast Review of Books*, Vol. 10, No. 5. Copyright 1984 by Rapport Publishing Company, Inc.

*Simon & Schuster, Inc.:* Entries "annoy," "coyote," "gene," "growth," and "pig," synonyms for "fault," and idioms for "business" from *Webster's New World Dictionary of the American Language*, Second College Edition. Copyright © 1984 by Simon & Schuster, Inc. From *Five Seasons* by Roger Angell. Copyright © 1972, 1973, 1974, 1975 by Roger Angell.

*Smithsonian Institution Press:* From "Animal Shelters Struggle to Keep Up with Millions of Abandoned Pets" by Patricia Curtis in *Smithsonian*, September 1982. From "Roots in China" by Leslie Wong in *Smithsonian*, April 1977.

*TIME:* "In West Virginia: Drive for Life" from *TIME* Magazine, October 6, 1980. Copyright 1980 by Time Inc. All rights reserved.

*Viking Penguin Inc.:* From *Winesburg, Ohio* by Sherwood Anderson. Copyright 1919 by B. W. Huebsch; copyright renewed 1947 by Eleanor Copenhaver Anderson. From *Death of a Salesman* by Arthur Miller. Copyright 1949, renewed © 1977 by Arthur Miller. From "A Book of Great Short Stories" in *The Portable Dorothy Parker*. Copyright 1927, renewed © 1955 by Dorothy Parker. From "Making Science Work" in *Late Night Thoughts on Listening to Mahler's Ninth Symphony* by Lewis Thomas. Copyright © 1981 by Lewis Thomas.

The *H. W. Wilson Company:* From *Readers' Guide to Periodical Literature.* Copyright © 1973, 1974 by The H. W. Wilson Company. From *Readers' Guide to Periodical Literature.* Copyright © 1974, 1975 by The H.W. Wilson Company. From *Readers' Guide to Periodical Literature.* Copyright © 1980 by The H.W. Wilson Company.

## PHOTO CREDITS

**Key:** T, Top; B, Bottom

**Cover:** HBJ Photo

Page 1, M. Thong/H. Armstrong Roberts; 2, Tom Bean; IW1, Werner H. Muller/Peter Arnold, Inc.; IW2, HBJ Photo/Rodney Jones; IW4, Comstock; IW5, Norman Owen Tomalin/Bruce Coleman, Inc.; IW6, Kim Steele Photography; IW8, Scott Ransom/Taurus Photos; IW9T, Eunice Harris/Photo Researchers, Inc.; IW9B, Joseph Nettis/Photo Researchers, Inc.; IW10, Anthony Bannister/Animals Animals; IW12, James Wiley; IW13, Library of Congress; IW14, Mike Kagan/Monkmeyer Press Photo; IW16, Joseph DiChello, Jr.; 319, M. Thonig/H. Armstrong Roberts; 320, D. Winston/H. Armstrong Roberts; 377, Ed Cooper; 378, J. Irwin/H. Armstrong Roberts; 667, Ellis Herwig/Stock, Boston; 668, Foley/H. Armstrong Roberts; 751, D.P.I.; 752, ZEFA/H. Armstrong Roberts.

Printed in the United States of America

ISBN 0–15–311735–4

# To the Student

Travelers who have been abroad several times and are planning yet another trip and a longer one know something about what to expect, but because the next trip will take them to places they have not visited, they know they will encounter much that will be new. So it is with each successive course in English. Because you have studied English before, you have, as you start another English course, a fairly good idea of what lies ahead. However, since each succeeding course is more advanced than the one preceding it, you know that, like the travelers, you will encounter much that will be new. You will learn more of the conventions of standard usage. You will refresh your knowledge of language skills you have already studied and go on to the study of the more advanced skills that must be mastered by anyone who, like you, wishes to speak and write with clarity and force.

Command of one's language comes in two ways. It comes first from everyday experience in using the language—in speaking it, reading it, and writing it—and, second, it comes with the regular practice of skills that a course in English provides. Your teacher and your textbook are your guides in this work. By following their directions, you will improve your competence in self-expression.

As you continue to study English, you will find more and more emphasis on learning to *write* well. This is because the skills involved in writing are harder to master than those involved in speaking. You probably learned to speak English before you went to school, but only in school have you learned to write it and only in English class is direct attention given to how to write. Teachers of other subjects judge your writing, but very few can take the time to help you to improve it. This is the responsibility of the English teacher and the English textbook. If you follow your teacher's instructions carefully and study the textbook on your own, as well as when you are assigned work in it, you will have a greater command of English at the end of this course than you had at the beginning.

The phrase "on your own" in the preceding sentence means literally what it says. This book is not only a guide and storehouse of practice materials. It is also designed for use as a reference book. By referring to the book, you can find out the answer to any question that arises when you are writing a composition, whether the question be about a minor matter like the use of a comma or about a major matter like the organization of a composition. Familiarize yourself with the contents of the book and make full use of the index.

J.W.

# CONTENTS

# Part Two: COMPOSITION: Writing and Revising Sentences

# Part Three: TOOLS FOR WRITING AND REVISING

## GRAMMAR

---

## MECHANICS

# **Part Four:** RESOURCES FOR WRITING AND STUDYING

# Part Five: SPEAKING AND LISTENING

# PART ONE

# COMPOSITION
## The Writing Process

# CHAPTER 1

# Writing and Thinking

## THE WRITING PROCESS

Whenever you write a paragraph or an essay, you are involved in an ongoing process that involves thinking, making decisions, and rethinking. Writing is not something that happens all at one time. Rather, many steps are required from the time that you first think about a piece of writing until the time that you consider yourself finished. In this chapter, you will learn about the stages in the writing process and the many steps that make up each stage.

**PREWRITING**—Considering your purpose, audience, attitude, and tone; choosing and limiting a subject; and gathering and ordering information

**WRITING THE FIRST DRAFT**—Expressing your ideas in sentences and paragraphs

**EVALUATING**—Judging the content, organization, and style of a draft

**REVISING**—Improving the content, organization, and style in a draft

**PROOFREADING**—Checking the revised version to correct errors in grammar, usage, and mechanics

**WRITING THE FINAL VERSION**—Preparing a final version and proofreading it

## PREWRITING

Prewriting involves all the planning and thinking that occurs before you begin a first draft. During this stage, you answer five important questions: Why am I writing? For whom am I writing? What will I write about? What will I say? How will I say it?

### THE WRITER'S PURPOSE

**1a. Have in mind a clear purpose for writing.**

Every piece of writing has a purpose—sometimes more than one. Even with multiple purposes, however, a single one usually guides the writing. In an essay about losing your date at a concert, you may describe the band's music, but your main purpose is to tell a story.

***Techniques for Prewriting.*** As you begin to plan and think about a piece of writing, consider the four basic purposes for writing:

| | |
|---|---|
| • *Narrative* writing relates a series of events. | An essay about a veteran's memories of the bombing of Pearl Harbor |
| • *Expository* writing gives information or explains. | A brochure about a community college's programs |
| • *Descriptive* writing describes a person, place, or thing. | A paragraph describing a bone cell |
| • *Persuasive* writing attempts to persuade or convince. | A pamphlet about the dangers of drinking and driving |

**EXERCISE 1. Identifying Purposes for Writing.** Identify your purpose (to narrate, to explain, to describe, or to persuade) for writing about the following topics. (More than one purpose is possible.)

1. How to balance a checking account
2. What happens before and during a parachute jump
3. Why scientific experiments on animals should be abolished
4. The sights and sounds in the gym before a basketball game
5. Tips on using a lawnmower safely

## CRITICAL THINKING:
### Analyzing How Purpose Affects Writing

*Analysis* involves breaking a whole into smaller parts and deciding how the parts are related. When you narrow a general subject into a limited, more specific topic, you use analysis. During the prewriting stage, you will analyze how one part of your writing—purpose—affects both the content you include and the words you choose.

Consider how purpose affects a paragraph about the Santa Ana wind. If your purpose is to inform, you will include specific details about the wind's origin and effects, and you will write in fairly formal language.

> A Santa Ana is a hot, dry, persistent wind that blows periodically over southern California and makes people behave strangely. The wind comes down from the Santa Ana Mountains, passes through the Santa Ana canyon, and descends to the coastal plain. Like similar dry, hot winds around the world, called *Foehns,* the Santa Ana makes many people feel nauseated and jumpy. It has been blamed for drastic personality changes, headaches, allergies, and depression. When the Santa Ana blows over Los Angeles, some teachers do not even try to teach; they say students cannot concentrate on schoolwork. Scientists speculate that the Santa Ana, and the other malevolent winds, carries an unusual excess of positive electrical charges, and that it is these ions that disturb people.

However, if your purpose in writing is to relate a series of events—to tell a story—you might use less formal language and choose amusing events.

> One Saturday afternoon, when the Santa Ana had been blowing for three days, my brother and I decided to do our long-delayed chores: cutting the overgrown grass and trimming the hedges. We should've known better. The temperature was 105 degrees, and we were both feeling edgy from the constant wind. Ralph mowed what he called his "half" of the lawn and started inside to cool off. I protested, rather more violently than necessary, that he hadn't done his share: I'd already finished trimming all the bushes. We got into a nose-to-nose shouting match—each of us calling the other lazy, stubborn, and selfish. It took our next-door neighbor's spraying us with the garden hose for us to cool down. Next time the Santa Ana blows, I won't start with an outdoor task that involves anyone but myself.

Persuasion and description also combine different details and language. To persuade, you use formal, concise, clear language; you present opinions, reasons, and evidence. To describe, you use less formal, freer language; you include concrete, sensory details and vivid images.

**EXERCISE 2. Analyzing How Purpose Affects Writing.** Two purposes for writing are given for each topic listed below. Consider how each purpose would affect a piece of writing on the given topic. For each purpose, indicate what aspect of the topic you would write about and what kinds of details you would include. Write your answers and be prepared to explain them.

1. *Topic:* The problems of teen-age drinking
   *Purpose:* a. To relate a series of events b. To persuade
2. *Topic:* The character Huck Finn in *The Adventures of Huckleberry Finn* by Mark Twain
   *Purpose:* a. To inform b. To describe

## THE WRITER'S AUDIENCE

**1b. Identify the audience for whom you are writing.**

You always write for an audience, but audiences may vary widely in age, background, and opinion. Like purpose, audience affects both content and language: you will not write the same way for all people. If your topic is "the beginnings of the Chicago-Burlington Railroad," you will write differently for railroad buffs and for third-graders.

**EXERCISE 3. Identifying Purpose and Audience.** List at least seven different pieces of writing that you have read during the past few weeks. (You might include articles, instructions and directions, and stories.) Identify the main purpose and the intended audience for each piece of writing.

---

## CRITICAL THINKING:
### Analyzing How Audience Affects Writing

The following paragraph was written for educated adults familiar with literary criticism and difficult vocabulary.

In his exploration of the literary possibilities of dialect, Mark Twain went far beyond Cable, Joel Chandler Harris, and other local colorists of his time, although he was indebted to them for showing the way. Dialect became naturalized in *Huckleberry Finn* and the English language broadened and invigorated thereby into something altogether new in narrative prose and altogether native, a written, literary medium with the rhythms, freedom, and color of American colloquial speech. (Mark Twain used English, Howells said admiringly, "as if it had come up out of American, out of Missourian ground.") This vernacular shapes the vision and passion of the book, for it is not 'Mr. Mark Twain', the narrator of *Tom Sawyer* ('he told the truth, mainly'), who now tells Huck's story, but Huck Finn himself. As he undergoes an education of his sound heart through his adventures on the river and along its shores, Huck ultimately passes judgment on society and its supporting assumptions of right and wrong. For all his boyishness and generosity Huck is shrewder, and a more adversary and rebellious figure, than even the rapscallion Duke and Dauphin, who reach derisive conclusions of their own—"Hain't we got all the fools in town on our side? and ain't that a big enough majority in any town?"

JUSTIN KAPLAN

If you were to rewrite this paragraph for junior-high students, you would probably explain or omit the names of unfamiliar people (Cable, Joel Chandler Harris, and Howells). You would define unfamiliar terms (*dialect, colloquial speech,* and *vernacular*), shorten sentences, and simplify vocabulary (change *derisive* to *mocking* and *colloquial* to *conversational*).

As you analyze audience, you will also consider purpose, for the two are closely related. In persuasive writing, for example, your audience's beliefs and feelings are particularly important.

***Techniques for Prewriting.*** As you plan a piece of writing, ask yourself the following questions about your audience:

- What does the audience already know about the topic?
- What background or technical information might this audience need to understand the topic?
- What language and style are most appropriate for the audience: simple or complex words and sentences, casual or formal presentation?
- Does the audience have any bias (strong feelings either for or against) toward the topic? If so, what is the bias?

**EXERCISE 4. Analyzing the Effects of Audience.** Read the item that follows, in which four different audiences are given for one topic and purpose. Then write answers to the numbered questions.

*Topic:* The exciting experience you had driving a foreign sports car

*Purpose:* To relate a series of events

*Audiences:* (a) your friends, (b) professional auto racers, (c) American auto workers laid off because of declining sales, (d) people who have never driven a car

1. Which audiences would have greater knowledge of the topic? Less knowledge?
2. For which audiences would terms need to be defined? Which terms?
3. Which audiences would need background information?
4. Which audiences might have strong feelings for or against the subject? How would the feelings affect your writing?
5. For which audience would you choose to write? Why?

**EXERCISE 5. Rewriting a Paragraph for a Different Audience.** Read the following paragraph carefully; then rewrite it for one of the suggested audiences. Define terms, provide background information, and consider the audience's opinions as you rewrite.

a. people who have never seen educational television
b. fifth-graders
c. people who work for an educational television station

It is in the realm of education that the failure of television is most conspicuous. If we compare television with the University, or with an institution almost as new as television itself, the Foundation, we see at once the nature of the failure. Even those departments of television devoted to information have greater resources than most universities or foundations, but what have they to show for these resources? There is "educational television," to be sure, but it is weak and miscellaneous, largely because it lacks the funds and the personnel to make educational television as palatable to the public as commercial television. Now and then television gives us a brief interlude of "culture"—the glory that was Greece, perhaps, or the saga of Columbus, but these are exceptions.

HENRY STEELE COMMAGER

## CHOOSING AND LIMITING A SUBJECT

**1c. Choose a subject that is appropriate for your audience.**

Your subject should be both understandable and interesting to the audience, so you must consider your readers' knowledge and backgrounds. For example, you could conceivably explain the theory of quantum mechanics to fifth-graders, but your paper would have to include extensive background information and definition of terms.

Your subject should also be appropriate to the audience's interest. For instance, people who live in southern Florida will not be as interested in how to save money on heating bills as homeowners in cold climates will be.

**EXERCISE 6. Choosing a Subject Appropriate for an Audience.** By answering *yes* or *no,* indicate whether each subject is appropriate for the audience given. Be prepared to discuss your answers.

1. The physical dangers of Little League baseball—the Parent-Teacher Association of an elementary school
2. Factors in rejection of transplanted organs—high-school anatomy class
3. How to restore wooden furniture—owners of antique stores
4. How to make homemade peanut butter—commercial peanut-butter manufacturers
5. Unusual camera techniques in the movie *Citizen Kane*—the high-school student government

**1d. Limit your subject so that it can be covered in the form of writing you have chosen.**

A *subject* is a broad, general area of knowledge, such as "computers" or "professional sports." A *topic* is a limited, more specific subject, such as "the advantages of a laser printer" or "how the pro football draft works." The briefer your form of writing, the more limited your topic must be. In a paragraph you have only a few sentences in which to develop your ideas. In a composition you may have several pages. You must tailor your topic to the form to cover it adequately.

**EXERCISE 7. Distinguishing Between Subjects and Topics.** Identify each item as either a broad, general subject (*S*) or a suitably limited topic (*T*) for a short composition.

1. Elephants
2. Imagery in Emily Dickinson's poetry
3. Trivia games—a new fad
4. Police-cadet program for teens

5. The United States Senate
6. Law enforcement
7. The advantages of contact lenses
8. A hotline for saving beached whales
9. Rugby—British football
10. Modern education

---

## CRITICAL THINKING:
### Analyzing a Subject

To find topics, a general subject may be analyzed (divided and subdivided) into its smaller parts. Depending on the subject, the basis for the analysis can be time periods, examples, features, uses, causes, history, or types.

EXAMPLES 1. *Subject divided into examples*
*Subject:* American movie classics for children
*Topics:* *Pinocchio*
*The Wizard of Oz*
*Chitty-Chitty Bang-Bang*

2. *Subject divided into features, or aspects*
*Subject:* F. Scott Fitzgerald's *The Great Gatsby*
*Topics:* Point of view
Major characters
Plot
Setting
Themes

3. *Subject divided into time periods*
*Subject:* Pre-Columbian exploration of the New World
*Topics:* Viking settlement and exploration (800–966)
Leif Ericson (c. 1000)
Norse settlement (1014–1015)
Portuguese exploration (1447–1498)
Danish and English exploration (1473–1481)

**EXERCISE 8. Analyzing Subjects to Develop Topics.** From the list below, choose five subjects and divide each one into at least three smaller parts. (Note: For each subject, different analyses are possible and correct.)

1. New fads
2. Careers
3. Ghosts
4. Computers

5. Family history
6. The school newspaper
7. Teen problems
8. Zoos
9. Gymnastics
10. The Great Depression

**EXERCISE 9. Limiting a Subject to Develop Topics Suitable for Paragraphs.** Choose one of the subjects that you analyzed for Exercise 8. Could each of these topics be covered adequately in a paragraph of seven or eight sentences? If not, divide the topics further until you have at least three that could be covered in one paragraph each.

## TONE

**1e. Identify your attitude toward your topic and its expression through tone.**

Your feelings about a topic influence the tone of your writing. Sometimes the topic or purpose dictates your attitude, but sometimes you choose it: positive (favorable) or negative (unfavorable), humorous or serious, angry or enthusiastic. Tone is the expression of that attitude or point of view toward a subject, created through the language and details you choose for your writing.

Consider the tone of the following paragraph. What is the writer's attitude toward the subject? What particular words and details convey his attitude and create the personal, comical tone?

> What is choking like? Those who have experienced it describe it as "the most humiliating thing that ever happened to me." There they are, paying good money for this food and having a wonderful time, talking and joking with close associates, when suddenly, still laughing, they feel the last bite go down the wrong way. Immediately, they sense the foolishness of the situation—to strangle on your own humor!—and they laugh harder and turn red and begin to die, surrounded by people who politely look away. Their obituary flashes before their eyes:
>
> GUY CHOKES ON BEEF, DIES ON FLOOR
>
> Bystander Attempts Back-Pounding Procedure,
> But to No Avail; "He was a Good Eater," Say
> Victim's Friends, "and a Great Kidder"
>
> The only hope is that Dr. Henry J. Heimlich, the discoverer of the famous lifesaving anti-choking embrace, will be dining at the same restaurant and will come running over and perform the maneuver on the spot. And yet, to be

> hugged from behind by a complete stranger while you lie gagging on the floor: Is it worth it? How much better to be smart and not choke at all!
>
> GARRISON KEILLOR

The same topic could be written about with a more formal, serious tone. What changes would you make in the paragraph to alter its tone?

Remember, finally, that while you control tone in your writing, you cannot choose it at random. The tone must be appropriate for your topic and purpose.

**EXERCISE 10. Identifying Tone.** Bring to class three different paragraphs from a variety of sources, such as newspapers, magazines, books, or short stories. Identify the tone of each paragraph and the author's attitude toward the subject.

## GATHERING INFORMATION

**1f. Gather information appropriate to your purpose.**

Your purpose for writing is a key to the kinds of information you must gather. For example, to *describe* a specific place in the hills of Oregon, you need to collect vivid, sensory details: the sights, the sounds, the feel of the weather. By contrast, to *inform* about Harriet Tubman's work in freeing slaves before the Civil War, you would provide dates, statistics, and historical facts.

You can learn techniques for gathering the information you need: the methods in the following pages show you how to tap your own personal resources and how to analyze a topic. You may find one or several techniques that work particularly well for you.

### Direct and Indirect Observation

**(1) Use your powers of observation to note specific details.**

Whenever your observations are firsthand (through your own senses of sight, smell, sound, taste, or touch), they are *direct observations.* In the following paragraph, the writer's direct observation provides vivid, interesting details.

> Last summer we went to the first circus that came to town, or more precisely, came to the parking lot of a suburban shopping mall. Not far beyond the fleet of Sears repair trucks a swaying line of elephants was staked. Snaking his trunk around, one elephant swiped hay from another.

He curled his trunk around a fair-sized clump, shook it and tossed it into the cave that was his mouth. The elephants seemed quite comfortable and not at all surprised to find themselves at a shopping mall. They were bigger than the repair trucks.

ANNE FARRER SCOTT

*Indirect observations* are all those that you do not make through your own senses. When you listen to someone else's experiences or read about them, you are making an indirect observation.

---

## CRITICAL THINKING:
### Observing Specific Details

Observing requires special attention to details of experience. Obviously, you cannot notice everything, but you can improve your powers of observation. You can make a habit of close attention.

**EXERCISE 11. Testing Your Powers of Observation.** Answer each question below from memory.

1. Does the front door of your house or apartment open inward or outward?
2. How many cheerleaders does your school have?
3. Who are the sponsors of your favorite television program?
4. How many checkout counters are there in your favorite supermarket?
5. When you replace a light bulb, which way do you turn the old bulb to unscrew it? Which way do you turn the fresh bulb?

## A Writer's Journal

**(2) Keep a writer's journal to record your thoughts and feelings about your experiences.**

A writer's journal—in which you record your ideas, experiences, and feelings—can be an excellent source of topics and details. You may include anything you like: random thoughts, strong opinions, striking quotations, interesting conversations. A writer's journal should contain only what you feel comfortable sharing with others, so you might consider also keeping a journal for your personal use.

**EXERCISE 12. Using a Journal Entry to Gather Ideas for Writing.** Read the following journal entry and answer the questions that follow it.

November 6

This weekend with my cousin Jenni was great! Saturday night Aunt Mae showed us some Charlie Chaplin and Laurel and Hardy films. What a riot! I laughed so hard my sides ached. Charlie Chaplin, the "Little Tramp," looked the same in all three movies—a bowler hat, baggy trousers, an old-fashioned coat that's too small, floppy shoes, and a cane that he keeps twirling. But Laurel and Hardy were my favorites. I love how they tip their hats and how Hardy flips his tie when he's embarrassed. Neither one is very bright, but the heavy one, Hardy, thinks he is and blames Laurel for everything that goes wrong. Then Laurel takes off his hat, scratches his head till his hair sticks straight up, and grins. All the movies were made in the 1920s, before films had sound, but they're still hilarious.

1. The journal writer has decided to write an essay describing Laurel and Hardy. What information about this topic does the journal entry contain that the writer could use?
2. List at least three other topics, suggested by the entry, that you might write about. Where would you look for information about each topic you listed?

## Brainstorming and Clustering

### (3) Use brainstorming and clustering to find writing ideas.

Both brainstorming and clustering are techniques that generate a free flow of ideas. They can help you find topics for writing as well as specific details for your topic.

To *brainstorm,* write your subject or topic on a piece of paper and begin listing whatever ideas or words come to mind. Work quickly, jotting down every idea that occurs to you. Relax, and do not stop to evaluate the ideas you are listing. Simply write down everything that enters your mind.

Only when you have finished brainstorming should you stop to evaluate the material you have listed. Decide which of the items could be usable topics or details, and circle them. These circled items may stimulate other ideas.

Here are a student's brainstorming notes on the topic "care of floppy computer disks."

Floppy disk (or diskette)—what it is—magnetic coating, paper holder, looks like old 45 rpm record
Diskettes are fragile, easily damaged
Don't touch dark exposed surface—could scratch or mar with oil from fingerprints
Don't put diskette on monitor or near TV—information may be damaged
Static electricity can scramble data: use plastic mat under chair, antistatic spray
Keep away from anything magnetized (some paper clips, scissors)
Avoid excessive cold or heat—keep disk between 60–85 degrees
Write out label before attaching to disk. Never use ballpoint or pencil—soft felt-tip pen best
Store upright in paper sleeves to avoid scratching
Be safe—make a backup disk and store in separate place

Clustering, or making connections, is similar to brainstorming. Unlike brainstorming, however, clustering groups related ideas together in the form of a diagram instead of a list. To cluster, write your subject or topic in the center of the paper, and circle it. Think about the circled item and write around it whatever related ideas come to mind. As you add each new idea, circle it and draw a line connecting it either to the subject in the center or to related ideas already on the paper.

Here is a clustering diagram for the previous topic.

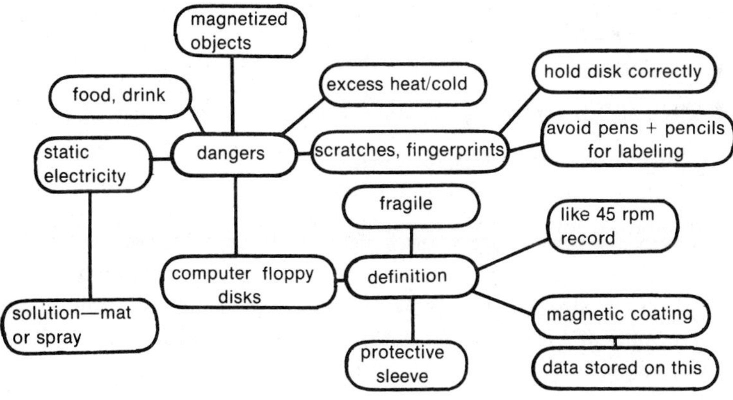


**EXERCISE 13. Using Brainstorming or Clustering to Gather Information.** In this exercise you will generate specific ideas and information to develop a limited topic. Use either brainstorming or clustering to gather information about a topic you developed for Exercise 9 on page 11 or for another topic of your choice.

## Asking the 5 *W-How?* Questions

### (4) Ask the *5 W-How?* questions to gather information.

Asking the basic *Who? When? Where? What? Why?* and *How?* questions can help you gather specific details for your writing. Not every question will apply to every topic.

EXAMPLE *Topic:* Seeing-eye dogs
*Who?* Who can obtain a dog? Who trains the dog?
*What?* What tasks do the dogs perform? What is the cost of training? What breed is best?
*Where?* Where can a blind person obtain a dog?
*When?* When (at what age) is a dog trained?
*Why?* Why are some dogs better than others?
*How?* How long is the training? How is a dog trained?

**EXERCISE 14. Ask the 5 *W-How?* Questions to Gather Information.** Use the *5 W-How?* questions to gather information about one of the following topics or a topic of your own. Write both your questions and the answers. (Do research to find the answers if necessary.)

1. A favorite relative
2. An experience with violent weather
3. A proposal for solving the problem of school vandalism
4. Requirements for voting in an election
5. Modern dance

## Asking Point-of-View Questions

### (5) Use different points of view to gather information.

Asking three basic questions—What is it? How does it change or vary? What are its relationships?—allows you to consider a topic from different points of view. These questions will produce others, all of which will help you generate information and specific details.[1]

1. *What is it?* The first point of view focuses on the topic itself: what it looks like, what it does, and how it differs from others of its kind. The "What is it?" question, because it defines, is useful even when your topic is an abstract idea.

[1] This technique is based on ideas in *Rhetoric: Discovery and Change* by Richard E. Young, Alton L. Becker, and Kenneth E. Pike (New York: Harcourt Brace Jovanovich, 1971).

EXAMPLE *Topic:* Robert Frost's poem "The Death of the Hired Hand" [What is the poem's structure? Who is speaking in the poem? What is the setting? What is revealed in the poem? What is the mood? How is this poem different from other Frost poems?]

2. *How does it change or vary?* The second point of view focuses on a topic's changes over time. Its questions may bring out information about a topic's history or stages. From this point of view, you also consider how the topic keeps its identity even while it varies.

EXAMPLE *Topic:* The evolution of the typewriter [When was the typewriter invented? What were important typewriter developments (portable, electric, memory)? How does an electronic typewriter differ from a word processor? Will word processors and computers eliminate typewriters in the future?]

3. *What are its relationships?* The third point of view focuses on how the topic's parts, or aspects, are related to each other and to the topic as a whole. It may also reveal how the topic is related to similar topics. (Note that this approach is similar to the critical thinking skill of analysis.)

EXAMPLE *Topic:* Animal surgery [What kinds of surgery does a veterinarian perform? How do surgical procedures vary from animal to animal? What kinds of animal surgery are most difficult? How is animal surgery like or unlike surgery on humans?]

**EXERCISE 15. Asking Point-of-View Questions to Gather Information.** Using the three point-of-view questions, gather information about two of the topics below. Write all of the questions that you think of as well as your answers.

1. A type of movie (horror, science fiction, fantasy)
2. A recent scientific development
3. A social problem, such as the punishment of criminals
4. A literary technique (foreshadowing, flashback, irony, imagery, allusion)
5. A craft or hobby (quilting or woodworking)

## CLASSIFYING INFORMATION

**1g. Classify your ideas and information by grouping related items.**

The next step in the writing process is to classify, or group, the ideas and details you have gathered. You must decide how the items are related.

---

## CRITICAL THINKING:
### Classifying Ideas

When you *classify,* you identify details that are similar and group them under a heading that explains what they have in common. What heading could cover the following details?

EXAMPLE Running practice called line runs
Jumping rope
Jogging
Tennis-handle exercise

These items are all exercises used by the tennis team, so they may be grouped under "Tennis Team's Exercise Program."

When classifying yields more than one heading, you must also decide the relationship and relative importance of the groupings. You may even discover information that does not fit in any of your groups and headings and should be discarded.

***Techniques for Prewriting.*** Use the following questions to classify ideas and details you have gathered.

- Which items have something in common? What is it? (Use the common element to write a heading.)
- Are some items or groupings more important than others? If so, which ones?
- Which items are subdivisions (examples, parts, etc.) of the main ideas? (If you have not listed any subdivisions for your main ideas, return to the information-gathering techniques.)

**EXERCISE 16. Classifying Ideas and Information.** Read the following ideas for a composition on the pros and cons of a law requiring use of automobile seat belts. Decide which ideas can be grouped together, and write a heading for each group. (Note: The headings are not in the list.) Then, write the ideas under their proper headings. You may discard items that do not fit.

One study suggests mandatory seat belt law might save 12,000 lives a year.
400,000 moderate-to-serious auto injuries occur per year; 2.8 million minor ones per year.
Government should not infringe on personal freedom.
In Ontario mandatory law led to increased use—24 percent pre-law, 77 percent after.
Mandatory seat belt law will be very difficult to enforce.
Traffic injuries cost society—lost wages, high medical bills, court costs, high insurance premiums.
Almost all cars have seat belts; few have air bags.
Without mandatory law, seat belt use remains unchanged—approximately 12 percent of population voluntarily use seat belts.
Studies in 36 countries and cities with seat belt laws show dramatic reduction in highway deaths and injuries.
Police should spend time fighting crime, not enforcing seat belt law.
Law is not necessary; in time, voluntary use through advertising campaigns and driver's education.

## ARRANGING INFORMATION

**1h. Arrange your ideas in a logical order.**

After you have classified your ideas under main headings, you must decide the order in which to present the information. With this sequence decided, you have an informal outline for your paper.

Often, your purpose suggests an order. For example, to explain how to put out a campfire, you will probably follow chronological (time) order. To persuade unsympathetic readers to support a cause, you will probably begin with the argument least objectionable to them. To explain a technical subject, you will first define terms and give background information. Always present your ideas in the order that you think will be clearest and most interesting to your audience. (You will learn more about types of order in Chapter 2.)

**REVIEW EXERCISE A. Following the Steps for Prewriting.** Prepare to write a paragraph on a topic of your choice. Choose a subject, and limit it to a topic for a single paragraph. Decide on your purpose and audience. Using at least one of the techniques for gathering information dicussed on pages 12–17, list specific details to include. Classify the details under main headings, and arrange the information in an appropriate order.

# WRITING THE FIRST DRAFT

After the prewriting activities, you are well prepared for the second stage in the writing process, writing the first draft, sometimes called *drafting.*

## WRITING THE FIRST DRAFT

**1i. Write a first draft, keeping the audience and purpose in mind.**

When you write a first draft, do not struggle for perfection: you will evaluate, revise, and proofread later. In a first draft it is important that you express your ideas as clearly as possible. As you write, keep in front of you the list of details that you have classified and arranged in order. Remember to choose specific details and language that are appropriate both for your audience and your purpose.

## CRITICAL THINKING:
### Synthesizing

The word *synthesis* comes from two Greek words that mean "to place together." All writing is a synthesis, the creation of a new whole, because writers combine words and ideas in new ways to create letters, compositions, poems, and stories.

The writing process itself often gives you new ideas. During the first draft, you may rethink earlier decisions. You may adjust tone, insert a new detail, order ideas more effectively. You may make whatever changes seem appropriate to you, even while you are shaping each sentence in the first draft.

***Techniques for Writing.*** As you write a first draft, remember to

- write freely, concentrating on expressing your ideas.
- use your prewriting notes or informal outline as a guide.
- choose details and language appropriate to your audience, purpose, and attitude toward the topic.
- include the discoveries that arise from the process.

**EXERCISE 17. Writing a First Draft.** Using the prewriting notes you developed for Review Exercise A, write a first draft of a paragraph. You may want to refer to the Guidelines for Evaluating Paragraphs (page 57) before you begin.

## EVALUATING

A first *draft,* by definition, is not a finished piece of writing. All writers—professionals as well as students—must evaluate their first drafts to improve them. To continue in the writing process, you must be able to recognize the weaknesses, as well as the strengths, of your writing.

### EVALUATING YOUR WRITING

**1j. Evaluate your first draft.**

Evaluation is the process of judging: determining what does and does not work. If you have made changes during a first draft, you have already begun to evaluate. Now, however, you must evaluate the finished draft as a whole, and this step requires distance: you try to see the writing as if it were someone else's. You also judge the writing in its entirety: content, organization, and style. A thorough evaluation requires several rereadings of your first draft, and by using different techniques, you can gain new insights from each review.

***Techniques for Evaluating.*** To gain different perspectives on your draft, use the following techniques:

- Set your draft aside for a while so that you can see it fresh, as though it were not your own writing.
- Read aloud, to "hear" what you have said. Listen for confusing statements, missing details, inappropriate language or tone.
- Have a classmate or someone else read your draft and comment on strengths and weaknesses. (Professional writers almost always rely on a friend or an editor to evaluate their writing.)

## CRITICAL THINKING:
### Evaluating Content, Organization, and Style

When you *evaluate,* you judge your writing on the basis of carefully developed *criteria,* or standards, that can be grouped under three headings:

*Content:* What have you said?
*Organization:* How have you arranged your ideas?
*Style:* How have you used words and sentences?

The following Guidelines for Evaluating apply to almost any form of writing. Using this checklist, you can identify problems in your draft and mark them for later revision.

## GUIDELINES FOR EVALUATING

***Content***

| | |
|---|---|
| Purpose | 1. Do the paper's ideas and details support the primary purpose: to explain, to describe, to persuade, or to tell a story? |
| Audience | 2. Will the intended audience find the paper interesting? Does the paper contain necessary background information and explanations of terms? |
| Topic Development | 3. Is the information sufficiently detailed for the audience's understanding? Is some information unnecessary? |

***Organization***

| | |
|---|---|
| Order | 4. Is similar information presented together, or must the reader jump back and forth among ideas? Does the order of the information clarify the main idea? |
| Transitions | 5. Are sentences smoothly joined by connecting words? Does one idea lead clearly and smoothly to another, or does information seem to be missing? |

***Style***

| | |
|---|---|
| Tone | 6. Do the words and details effectively communicate the writer's attitude toward the topic? Does the paper sound serious enough, or light enough, for its purpose? |
| Sentence Structure | 7. Do the sentences vary in length and structure to avoid monotony? |

Word Choice

8. Are words precise and specific rather than general and vague? Is meaning clear rather than fuzzy? Are descriptive words vivid? Do these words create concrete, sensory images?

---

**EXERCISE 18. Evaluating a First Draft.** Read the following draft, intended for a high-school audience, and evaluate it using the Guidelines for Evaluating on pages 22–23. Number your paper as the guidelines are numbered, 1–8, and write *yes* if the guideline is met and *no* if it is not. Give at least one specific example from the draft to support each answer.

The latest development in contact lenses is extended-wear lenses that you can keep on the eyes overnight. They are made of very soft and bendable plastic. Most people who wear extended-wear lenses say they are more comfortable than thicker lenses or than hard lenses. Extended-wear lenses have some advantages. They are comfortable and can be worn up to 30 days without removing them from your eyes. It is the FDA which made up the 30-day limit. In time you will be able probably to wear them for more than two months without taking them off. Extended-wear lenses with a high water content (and some have low water content) are comfortable to wear. These high-water extended-wear lenses allow oxygen to pass easily to the cornea. Also, you can see well with them.

There are some disadvantages to wearing extended-wear contacts. One is that people take them for granted, and they leave them in the eye too long. When they are not properly cleaned, they get a buildup of protein and other secretions, and this buildup may lead to eye infections or other problems. Also, people with extended-wear contacts need to make many visits to the doctor. Follow-up visits should be done every six months at the longest—better yet, every three months—according to Dr. Lester Caplan, chief of contact lens service.

**EXERCISE 19. Evaluating a First Draft.** Using the Guidelines for Evaluating, evaluate the first draft you wrote for Exercise 17 or any other first draft. Reread your draft several times. Then jot notes on your draft, indicating where changes are needed. Another way to evaluate is to number a paper 1–8 (to follow the guidelines) and to indicate whether each guideline was met. For each that was not, note why. You may also want to exchange papers with another student and evaluate that student's draft.

## REVISING

When you evaluate, you uncover problems; when you revise, you correct them. The revising you do after you evaluate should be thorough; you must decide on specific ways to improve each weakness in the paper.

### REVISING YOUR FIRST DRAFT

**1k. Revise your first draft.**

Four basic revision techniques can correct most problems in writing: adding, cutting, replacing, or reordering.

***Techniques for Revising.*** Use the following techniques to improve your draft:

| TECHNIQUE | EXAMPLE |
|---|---|
| • *Add* Add new information, details, sentences, or words. | Nova Scotia was the site of the first permanent North American settlement north of Florida. |
| • *Cut* Take out information, details, sentences, or words. | To the contention that ~~the use of~~ sunscreen lotions will promote a tan without burning, the experts say that ~~a~~ tanned skin is ~~a~~ damaged skin. |
| • *Replace* Remove information, details, sentences, or words and substitute something else. | A mosaic is made by putting together ~~tesserae.~~ small pieces of colored glass or stone. |
| • *Reorder* Move information, details, sentences, or words to another place in the paper. (tr.) | Pliés are an early exercise in dance classes. Pliés prepare for the more vigorous jumps and leg extensions that come later in class. The slow bending of the knees stretches the calves and ankles and loosens the knee and hip joints. |

These techniques can be used for problems in content, organization, or style. Notice how one writer used the techniques to revise the following paragraphs. (See page 33 for revising and proofreading symbols.)

*Topic:* The sinking of Henry VIII's warship the *Mary Rose*
*Purpose:* To relate a series of events
*Audience:* Classmates and teacher

| | |
|---|---|
| Sunday, July 19, 1545, was a warm and almost | |
| windless day in Portsmouth. Portsmouth was in a festive | replace |
| mood as the British fleet set sail to engage the oncoming | |
| French fleet, and it was swelled with soldiers and offi- | add/cut/reorder |
| cials. No one, though, was more joyful than Henry VIII. | replace/add |
| As he observed the harbor from the battlements of | replace/cut |
| Southsea Castle, his gaze sought out his special pride, the | replace |
| flagship *Mary Rose*. She was truly a landmark ship: very | replace/cut |
| successful in battle since her building in 1509, rebuilt in | |
| 1536 to become one of the first ships built exclusively for | replace |
| war, and fitted with shining bronze cannons in her lower | replace |
| decks. Named after Henry's favorite sister, the *Mary* | reorder/add/replace |
| *Rose* made medieval ramming-and-boarding techniques | add/cut |
| obsolete. | add |
| A slight breeze arose. Suddenly the *Mary Rose* | |
| heeled over. In less than two minutes, she sank before | |
| Henry's eyes. Because of a net laid over the upper deck | replace |
| to prevent enemy boarding, the crew was trapped and | cut/reorder |
| could not jump off. With "one long wailing cry," 660 of | cut/add |
| the 700 men on board went down with their ship. | |

The following chart shows how the revision techniques can be combined with the evaluation guidelines to solve writing problems. The other composition chapters in this book contain revision charts for specific forms of writing.

## REVISING A DRAFT

| PROBLEM | TECHNIQUE | REVISION |
|---|---|---|
| ***Content*** | | |
| The ideas and details do not help to explain, describe, persuade, or tell the story. | Add/Cut | Add explanation, argument, descriptive detail, or narrative detail. Cut information unrelated to the purpose. |
| The reader will not be interested in the paper. | Add/Replace | Add examples, anecdotes, dialogue, or more details. Replace unrelated details with ones that appeal to the audience's interests or background. |
| Unfamiliar terms are not explained. | Add/Replace | Add a definition or explanation. Replace unfamiliar terms with familiar ones. |
| The information is insufficient for the readers' understanding. | Add | Add details, facts, examples, etc. to support the topic. |
| Some information does not support the topic and may confuse or distract the reader. | Cut | Cut out sentences or parts of sentences that do not relate directly to the topic and purpose. |
| ***Organization*** | | |
| The reader cannot follow the ideas. | Reorder | Check the order set in the prewriting plan. Then, move ideas or details to clarify meaning. |

| PROBLEM | TECHNIQUE | REVISION |
|---|---|---|
| Connections between ideas are fuzzy. | Add | Add words that help link sentences: *thus, however, then, first, in addition, as a result,* etc. Add missing information. |
| ***Style*** The tone is unsuitable for the audience and purpose. | Replace | Create a lighter tone by replacing formal words with less formal ones (slang, contractions, etc.). Create a more serious tone by replacing slang and contractions with standard vocabulary. |
| The tone does not convey the writer's intended attitude | Replace/Add | Add words or details that reflect the writer's feelings (angry, approving, comic, etc.), or replace those that do not convey the intended attitude. |
| The sentences are monotonous. | Replace/ Reorder | Combine sentences by joining them with *and, but, for,* or *or;* by making one subordinate to the other; or by making one a modifying phrase. Begin sentences in different ways. |
| The words are dull and vague. Meaning is not clear. | Replace | Replace general terms with precise, exact words. Replace bland descriptions with vivid, sensory details. |

**EXERCISE 20. Revising a First Draft.** Revise the paragraphs you evaluated in Exercise 18 on page 23. For each problem in the draft that you found, identify a technique to correct it, and make the necessary improvement.

EXAMPLE

*Evaluation:* An abbreviation is not explained
*Technique:* *Add* an explanation
*Revision:* It is the FDA which made up the 30-day limit.

**REVIEW EXERCISE B. Revising Your Own First Draft.** Using the evaluation of your first draft from Exercise 19, write a revision. Be sure to refer to the preceding revision chart.

---

## PROOFREADING

---

In the next stage in the writing process, *proofreading,* you reread your revised writing to find and correct errors in grammar, usage, and mechanics (spelling, capitalization, and punctuation.)

### PROOFREADING YOUR WRITING

**1l. Proofread your revised writing.**

Proofreading your own writing requires particularly keen attention. Some hints will help you focus on the task.

***Techniques for Proofreading.*** To improve your proofreading accuracy, use the following techniques:

- Put your paper aside for a while. You will see errors more quickly when you read it again.
- Cover the lines below the one you are proofreading. You will not read ahead and pass over an error.
- Read the paper twice: once sentence by sentence and once letter by letter. You will catch errors in usage and grammar, as well as in mechanics.

---

### CRITICAL THINKING:
### Applying the Standards of Written English

In proofreading, you apply the standards of written English to your writing. These standards, or *conventions,* prevent your readers from being confused by inaccuracies or irritated by errors. The standards are summarized in the Guidelines for Proofreading that follow. They are also explained in greater detail in other parts of this book. Refer to those parts whenever you are unsure about applying the standards of written English.

## GUIDELINES FOR PROOFREADING

1. Is every sentence complete? (pages 321–30)
2. Does every sentence end with a punctuation mark? Are all punctuation marks correct? (pages 603–44)
3. Does every sentence begin with a capital letter? Are all proper nouns and appropriate proper adjectives capitalized? (pages 587–602)
4. Does every verb agree in number with its subject? (pages 476–89)
5. Are verb forms and tenses correct? (pages 515–25, 533–43)
6. Are subject and object forms of personal pronouns correct? (pages 495–504)
7. Does every pronoun agree with its antecedent in number and gender? Are pronoun references clear? (pages 489–93, 340–47)
8. Are frequently confused words (such as *lie* and *lay, fewer* and *less*) used correctly? (pages 525–33, 566–86)
9. Are all words spelled correctly? (pages 645–66)
10. Is the paper neat and free from obvious corrections? (pages 30–33)

**EXERCISE 21. Applying the Conventions of Written English.** In each sentence, find and correct the error in grammar, usage, or mechanics. If you cannot correct an error, use the index of this book to find the appropriate rule, given in parentheses. Then make the correction.

1. Each of the girls have finished the assignment. (subject/verb agreement with indefinite pronouns)
2. The person, who asked you for directions to the convention center, is Bob's youngest sister, Stephanie. (punctuating restrictive adjective clauses)
3. Lauren and me are in charge of ticket sales for the class musical.

(using the subjective case of pronouns that are the subject of a sentence)

4. Of all the paintings in the museum, which do you like best. (punctuating questions)
5. Whenever Larry and Flo have a major disagreement, which is about every other day. (sentence fragments)
6. If you want advice about a summer job, see Mrs. Pettigrew, she's the guidance counselor in charge of employment opportunities. (run-ons)
7. The lettuce had froze in the refrigerator. (past participle of an irregular verb)
8. Allison plays the flute so good that she is first chair. (using adjectives and adverbs correctly)
9. Mitch lay the box of photographs on the kitchen table. (correct use of *lie* and *lay*)
10. Natalie works for the Fairwell electric company on the corner of Grove Street and Madison Avenue. (capitalizing names of specific companies)

EXERCISE 22. **Proofreading a Revised Draft.** Proofread the draft you revised for Review Exercise B or some other writing you have revised. Use the Guidelines for Proofreading and the Revising and Proofreading Symbols (page 33).

---

## WRITING THE FINAL VERSION

---

The last step in the writing process is to prepare a final, clean copy of your revised and proofread paper.

### USING CORRECT MANUSCRIPT FORM

**1m.** Write the final version in correct manuscript form.

Although there is no single correct way to prepare a manuscript, the Guidelines for Correct Manuscript Form that follow are widely accepted standards. Your final recopying of the paper is also the time to correct common errors in abbreviations, number usage, and word divisions. Remember to proofread once again after you recopy to catch any accidental errors or omissions.

## GUIDELINES FOR CORRECT MANUSCRIPT FORM

1. Use lined composition paper or, if you type, $8\frac{1}{2}$ x 11-inch white paper.
2. Write on only one side of the paper.
3. Write in blue or black ink, or typewrite using double-spacing.
4. Leave a one-inch margin at the top, sides, and bottom of the page. The right-hand margin should be as straight as possible.
5. Indent the first line of each paragraph about one-half inch.
6. Follow your teacher's instructions for placing your name, the class, the date, and the title on the manuscript.
7. Number all pages.
8. Write legibly and neatly. If you are typing, do not strike over letters or cross out words. If you have to erase, do it neatly.
9. Before handing in your final version, proofread it carefully to make certain that you have copied accurately.

**(1) Use only customary, accepted abbreviations.**

In most writing, you should spell out words rather than abbreviate them, but some abbreviations are acceptable.

The abbreviations *Mr., Mrs., Ms., Dr., Jr., Sr., Rev.,* and *St.* are used with names. Spell them out in other uses. The college degrees *B.S., Ph.D.,* etc. may be used with or without a name.

EXAMPLES Our family **doctor** and **Mr.** Walker both attended Indiana University.
**Rev.** Richard Longworth, **Jr.,** and his family attend **St.** Luke's Church.
She received her **Ph.D.** just last year.

The abbreviations *A.D., B.C., A.M.,* and *P.M.* are acceptable when used with numbers, and abbreviations for organizations are acceptable if they are generally known. Note that periods are usually omitted in abbreviations of governmental agencies.

EXAMPLES Cleopatra died in 30 **B.C.**
At the **Y.W.C.A.** [or **YWCA**] we have aerobics class at 7:30 **P.M.**
The **UN**'s opening session is today.

**(2) Follow the rules for writing numbers.**

The general rule is to spell out numbers that can be expressed in one or two words and to use numerals for others.

EXAMPLES five million, the forty-first yardline, 342, 1987

Numbers in writing, however, do not easily conform to a single rule, and common usage requires several exceptions. A number beginning a sentence is spelled out. Days of the month and page numbers are written as numerals. A mixture of numbers—some one or two words, some longer—should all be written in the same way, either as words or as numerals. Statistical and technical writing generally expresses all measurements as numerals.

EXAMPLES **Six hundred sixty** people were polled in a survey on **May 3** [either May 3 or the **third of May,** not May 3rd].
Downtown, a **2-story** frame house still stands next to a **110-story** skyscraper.
In the experiment, **50 percent** of the subjects received **3 ounces** of water.

**(3) Divide words correctly at the end of a line.**

When you must divide a word at the end of a line, hyphenate it between syllables. Use the following general rules, but consult a dictionary if you are unsure of a word's syllables.

Do not divide a one-syllable word. Divide a word with double consonants between the consonants. Hyphenate words with prefixes and suffixes between the root and the prefix or suffix. In addition, avoid dividing words so that a single letter ends a line or only two letters begin a line. In these instances, a slightly uneven margin is preferable to an awkward hyphenation.

EXAMPLES climbed [not climb-ed]; com-mittee; trans-mission; hope-ful; idol--ize [not i-dolize]; propa-ganda [not propagan-da]

**EXERCISE 23. Writing the Final Version.** Write the final version of the writing you proofread for Exercise 22. Use the rules for correct manuscript form or those your teacher provides. Be sure to proofread this version carefully before you hand it in.

---

## CHAPTER 1 WRITING REVIEW

**Practicing the Writing Process.** Write a paragraph or short composition on a topic of your choice. Be sure to go through each stage in the writing process: prewriting, writing a first draft, evaluating, revising, proofreading, and writing a final version.

## REVISION AND PROOFREADING SYMBOLS

| *Symbol* | *Example* | *Meaning of Symbol* |
|---|---|---|
| s ≡ | N.E. 175th street | Capitalize a lowercase letter. |
| ø | an Ordinary day | Lowercase a capital letter. |
| ∧ | an exception rule (to the) | Insert missing words, letters, or punctuation marks. |
| / | similer (a) | Change a letter. |
| ℓ | What day is is it? | Leave out a word, letter, or punctuation mark. |
|  | a neccessary step | Leave out and close up. |
| ⁐ | a dis honest person | Close up space. |
| ∿ | beleive | Change the order of the letters. |
| (tr.) | people who travel from England | Transfer the circled words. (Write (*tr.*) in nearby margin.) |
| ¶ | ¶"Hello," she smiled. | Begin a new paragraph. |
| ⊙ | I feel tired | Add a period. |
| ^, | Well here we are. | Add a comma. |
| # | highschool | Add a space. |
| (:) | the following people | Add a colon. |
| ^; | Monday, September 19th Tuesday, September 20th and Wednesday, September 21st | Add a semicolon. |
| = | extended wear contact lenses. | Add a hyphen. |
| ˅' | Maries new boyfriend | Add an apostrophe. |
| (Stet) | The meeting will be held next Monday at | Keep the crossed-out material. (Write (*stet*) in nearby margin.) |

## CHAPTER 2

# Writing Paragraphs

## STRUCTURE AND DEVELOPMENT

A paragraph is a group of closely related sentences that work together to present one main idea. A paragraph may be complete in itself or part of a longer composition.

In this chapter you will review the structure of the paragraph and learn to apply the stages of the writing process to developing the paragraph form.

## THE STRUCTURE OF A PARAGRAPH

### THE MAIN IDEA

**2a. A paragraph is a series of sentences that presents and develops one main idea.**

The main idea of a paragraph is often stated in a single sentence. The other sentences in the paragraph present details that develop, or support, that idea. In the following paragraph, the writer states the main idea in the first sentence, then develops the idea by presenting many specific examples.

> **Some of Manhattan's larger supermarkets now stock a marvelous variety of truly healthful foods—produce.** Counters are laden with almost as many

unusual fruits and vegetables as shoppers find at Oriental produce stands. At the Food Emporium there were vibrant yellow peppers from the Netherlands, American red peppers, sweet melons from Israel, bright orange persimmons, kiwis, celery root, fennel, both red and white sunchokes (once known as Jerusalem artichokes), Kirby cucumbers, plum tomatoes, hydroponically grown tomatoes and even out-of-season asparagus. It is the kind of choice that propels the cook out of the store and into the kitchen.

MARIAN BURROS

## THE TOPIC SENTENCE

**2b. The *topic sentence* states the one main idea of a paragraph.**

In many paragraphs, like the one above by Marian Burros, the main idea is stated directly, in a topic sentence. This sentence controls the entire paragraph: It further limits the topic, and it restricts the content of the other sentences.

The topic sentence is often the first sentence. In this position, it tells the reader immediately what aspect of the topic the writer will discuss, and it reminds the writer to keep to the point. In some cases, the topic sentence may be placed elsewhere in the paragraph—in the middle or at the end. In the following paragraph, the writer concludes with a topic sentence that summarizes the details given.

"I knew him only as a person who worked twenty-four hours a day," Mario Cuomo says of his father. "We never sat down to dinner, or very rarely—on the holidays, in the later years. He never took me for a walk. He never had a man-to-man talk with me. I never saw him relaxed until, in later years, the store had to be closed on Sunday mornings after ten o'clock. On Sunday afternoons, he took us to the movie theatre: the Savoy—always the same theatre. I think of him as being very affectionate, but I don't remember him putting his arm around me. You always had the sense that he had great feeling for you. You saw him providing for you, at enormous pain to himself. You saw him doing nothing for himself—never bought himself anything, never enjoyed himself, never went out alone. He went out with my mother. **So the overwhelming impression we got was that this man was offering us his life; he didn't have to put his arm around you."**

KEN AULETTA—*The New Yorker*

You may occasionally encounter a paragraph in which the main idea is suggested rather than stated directly. In your own writing, however, you will generally find that stating your main idea directly in a single sentence will result in more effective paragraphs.

### Topic and Restriction Sentences

In some paragraphs two sentences work together to state the main idea. The first sentence introduces a general idea, and the second one restricts that idea by focusing on one particular aspect. These two sentences are called the *topic* and *restriction sentences.*

> [Topic] **I believe the guiding emotion in my mother's life was pity.** [Restriction] **It encompassed the world.** During the war (World War II), she heard on a radio broadcast that the Chinese, fearing their great library would be destroyed, took the books up in their hands and put them onto their backs and carried all of them, on foot, over long mountain paths, away to safety. Mother cried for them, and for their books. Almost more than eventual disaster, brave hope that it could be averted undid her. She had had so many of those brave hopes herself. Crying for the old Chinese scholars carrying their precious books over the mountain gave her a way too of crying for herself, with her youngest child, who was serving with the Navy at the battle of Okinawa.
>
> EUDORA WELTY

## SUPPORTING SENTENCES

**2c. Other sentences in the paragraph give specific information that supports the main idea stated in the topic sentence.**

An effective paragraph provides enough details, or specific information, to make the main idea clear. Usually, three or more details, such as facts, statistics, examples, or reasons, are needed to develop a main idea adequately. (In Chapter 3 you will learn more about using the different kinds of details.) Compare the following two versions of a paragraph.

WEAK **A lot of free tourist information is available.** You can get booklets and brochures from state governments. You can also get information about what to see and where to stay.

> **For those planning travel in the United States, one of the biggest bonanzas is the abundance of free tourist information available from almost every state government.** For a 13-cent postcard or, increasingly, at no cost at all but the time it takes to call a toll-free 800 number, you can usually get by

mail at least an overview of the travel opportunities that a state has to offer. Often you get much more, such as booklets and brochures giving all sorts of information on what to see, where to eat and stay, suggested self-guided tours and details on parks, lakes, ski slopes, golf courses, forests and wildlife refuges.

PAUL GRIMES

**EXERCISE 1. Improving Weak Paragraphs.** Each of the following paragraphs is weak because it does not contain enough specific information to develop the main idea clearly and specifically. Revise each paragraph, adding more supporting information. (You may need to do some research to find the information.) You may also revise the topic sentence.

1. You may want to buy a car, but before you do there are many practical matters to consider. One thing is the cost of car insurance. Another is whether or not you can afford to pay for gasoline and maintenance.
   (*Hint:* Provide more specific information about each of the considerations. Separate the cost of gasoline and the cost of maintenance, and try to think of other considerations.)
2. Americans who want to live to a healthy old age had better reconsider their eating habits. People should eat lots of fruit and vegetables and less red meat. Children as young as two should start watching their cholesterol levels.
   (*Hint:* Add information about the relationship of cholesterol to heart disease. Recommend other changes in the American diet.)
3. Deciding on a career is one of the most difficult decisions that young adults face. You need to consider many aspects carefully. One of them is the training required and whether or not you can afford to complete that training.
   (*Hint:* List several more aspects to consider. Be as detailed and specific as you can. Consider giving a specific example for each aspect that you mention.)

## THE CLINCHER SENTENCE

**2d. A paragraph may end with a clincher sentence.**

A *clincher,* or *concluding, sentence* may reemphasize the main idea expressed in the topic sentence, as in the following paragraph:

**Children should not receive pets unless they understand and accept the responsibility involved in caring for them, according to the two organizations.** Before giving a pet as a gift, they warn, decide who will take on the responsibilities of caring for the animal—such as feeding, housebreaking and changing litter pans. Apartment dwellers should be certain pets are allowed. And be sure no one in the family is allergic to them. **Often, the organizations say, animals given as gifts during the holidays must be returned because their owners were not prepared to care for them properly.**

LISA BELKIN

A clincher sentence may instead summarize the information given, suggest a course of action, or reveal an insight the writer has gained. The clincher sentence in the following paragraph reveals the insight the writer gained from contemplating the stars.

Stars shone with a clarity beyond anything I could remember. I was looking into—actually seeing—the past. **By looking up into the darkness, I was looking into time.** The old light from Betelgeuse, five hundred twenty light-years away, showed the star that existed when Christopher Columbus was a boy, and the Betelgeuse he saw was the one that burned when Northmen were crossing the Atlantic. For the Betelgeuse of this time, someone else will have to do the looking. **The past is for the present, the present for the future.**

WILLIAM LEAST HEAT MOON—BLUE HIGHWAYS: A JOURNEY INTO AMERICA

**EXERCISE 2. Writing Clincher Sentences.** For each of the following paragraphs, write several different clincher sentences. Choose the one you think is most effective.

1. After years of searching, astronomers at the University of Arizona believe they may have discovered the first planet outside our solar system. The planet is named Van Biesbroeck 8B and orbits a dim star 21 light years away from Earth. The newly found planet is a huge, gaseous sphere almost the size of Jupiter. It has a surface temperature of 2,000 degrees Fahrenheit —far too hot to support any form of life as we know it.

2. When you are ordering merchandise from a mail order catalog, follow certain precautions to ensure that your order will arrive safely. First, consider checking out the company before you order, by calling your state's Division of Consumer Services. Usually, this is a toll-free number. You can ask if there have been complaints against the company. Also, keep a copy of the order form with the price, description, item number, and date you ordered the merchandise. Make sure that you print the information clearly

on the order blank and fill it out completely. According to the Federal Trade Commission, an order must be shipped within thirty days after receipt of a properly completed order form. If you haven't received your merchandise within thirty days, write promptly to the company. Most important of all, never send cash for a mail order item. Always send a check or money order so that you will have proof of your payment.

THE DEVELOPMENT OF A PARAGRAPH

## PREWRITING

### CHOOSING AND LIMITING A SUBJECT

**2e. Choose a subject and limit it to a topic suitable for a paragraph.**

Planning a paragraph begins with limiting a broad subject to a topic that can be covered clearly and precisely in the space available. Although paragraphs vary in length, most are only about 150 to 200 words long. Thus you must limit a broad subject considerably to find a suitably limited topic. (Review the information on choosing and limiting a subject on pages 8–11.)

**EXERCISE 3. Choosing and Limiting a Subject.** Choose one of the following subjects or another subject that interests you. Analyze the subject by dividing and subdividing it to find at least three suitable topics for a paragraph. Select one topic to write about.

1. Natural wonders
2. Machinery
3. The Civil War
4. Sculpture
5. Track and field sports

### CONSIDERING PURPOSE AND AUDIENCE

**2f. Determine your purpose for writing, and identify your audience.**

A paragraph may contain elements of more than one of the four basic types of writing (exposition, persuasion, narration, and description), but the writer usually has one main purpose. For example, narrative paragraphs often include descriptive details, but their primary purpose is to tell a story. Determining your primary purpose enables you to choose the kinds of details and pattern of organization that will best fulfill that purpose. It also enables you to decide what your attitude is toward your topic and how to express that attitude through the tone of your writing.

Since the needs and interests of audiences vary widely, think carefully about your readers. Although you cannot predict precisely how they will respond to your writing, you can plan to use information and language that is neither too difficult nor too simple for them. You can also choose language that expresses the tone appropriate for your audience. (See pages 4–8, 11–12 for more information on how purpose, audience, and tone affect writing.)

***Techniques for Prewriting.*** In thinking about your purpose and your audience, ask yourself:

- Is my primary purpose to explain or to inform, to persuade, to tell a story, or to describe?
- What topic will interest my audience?
- What details and background information will they need to understand the topic?
- What ideas and language will they be able to understand?

**EXERCISE 4. Identifying Purpose and Audience.** Bring to class three paragraphs from newspapers or magazines. Be prepared to tell what each paragraph's primary purpose is and to identify the audience for which it was written.

## GATHERING INFORMATION

### 2g. Gather information on your limited topic.

Keeping your purpose and audience in mind, use one or more of the information-gathering techniques (see pages 12–17) to collect details on your topic. Be sure to take notes as you gather information, and remember that you will have time later to evaluate the details you assemble.

**EXERCISE 5. Gathering Information.** Gather information on the topic you chose for Exercise 2 or on another suitably limited topic of your choice.

## DEVELOPING A PARAGRAPH PLAN

**2h. Develop a paragraph plan.**

A *paragraph plan* is an informal outline consisting of a topic sentence and a list of supporting details arranged in a logical order.

### Writing an Effective Topic Sentence

An effective topic sentence is one that meets the following three requirements.

**(1) A topic sentence should be neither too limited nor too broad.**

A specific fact is usually too limited to serve as a topic sentence because it cannot be developed. On the other hand, a statement that cannot be developed clearly and precisely in a single paragraph is too broad.

TOO LIMITED Gravity shoes enable the wearer to hang upside-down from his or her feet.
TOO BROAD Sports are good for you.
SUITABLE Physicians have come to view regular exercise as an essential part of a regimen to prevent illness.

**(2) A topic sentence should state the paragraph's main idea directly and precisely.**

An effective topic sentence is neither vague nor wordy. Write several versions of your topic sentence, concentrating on replacing vague words with precise ones and eliminating unnecessary phrases such as "In this paragraph I am going to tell you about. . . ."

VAGUE Some jobs are dangerous.
PRECISE Certain diseases occur more frequently among hairdressers and cosmetologists than among the rest of the population.

WORDY I am going to explain the voluntary measure that has been instituted to cut down on air pollution caused by automobiles in the city of Denver in Colorado.

PRECISE Denver, Colorado, has instituted a voluntary measure designed to reduce air pollution caused by automobiles.

**(3) A topic sentence should arouse the reader's interest.**

Whenever possible, try to catch the reader's attention by including a vivid detail, a clever twist, or by addressing the reader directly to involve him or her in the topic.

WEAK Learning to type is important.

IMPROVED Learning to type will help you in at least three ways.

WEAK There are ways to cope with stress.

IMPROVED The next time you are ready to explode—from anger or exhaustion or any other kind of stress—try these three techniques for relieving stress.

***Techniques for Prewriting.*** To evaluate your topic sentence, ask yourself:

- Is it neither too broad nor too limited?
- Does it state my main idea directly and precisely?
- Will it catch the interest of my audience?

**EXERCISE 6. Improving Topic Sentences.** Revise each of the following topic sentences, adding any information you need to make it more effective.

1. In this paragraph I am going to tell you about something that happened to me one day after school last year.
2. The rules for forming English plurals have many exceptions.
3. Have you ever been bobsledding?
4. *Hoosegow,* a slang word for *jail,* comes from the Spanish word *juzgado,* which means "court of justice."
5. I want to tell you about the interesting ancient Incan civilization in Peru.

**EXERCISE 7. Writing Topic Sentences.** For each list of details, write an effective topic sentence. You would not necessarily use all of the details in a paragraph.

1. *Details:* Building of "great green wall" in northwestern China
   Government-sponsored program to plant trees to serve as a windbreak
   "Green wall" to be 4,600 miles long
   Sandstorms disrupt travel by plane and train; caused by winds up to 80 miles per hour
   Newlyweds urged to plant tree to celebrate wedding
   Chinese Air Force drops tree seedlings from planes, seeding more than 590,000 acres of trees
   Severe penalties for cutting down trees
   Every Chinese citizen 11 and older required to plant at least three trees a year
2. *Details:* Hodson Senior Center in the Bronx, New York
   Founded more than forty years ago with five members; now has eight hundred members
   Activities for members include painting, knitting, ceramics, pool, cards
   Center members have own jazz band; sponsor trips
   Teachers lecture on health care; other courses offered
   Serves breakfast and lunch; open from 8:30 A.M. to 4:30 P.M.

## Selecting and Arranging Details

Analyze the material you have gathered to ensure that each detail is directly related to the main idea stated in your topic sentence. Remove any details that do not support your main idea, and arrange the remaining information in a logical order (see page 19).

***Techniques for Prewriting.*** To determine whether a detail is directly related to your main idea, ask yourself:

- Does the detail strongly support my main idea?
- Will it help my audience understand the main idea rather than confuse or distract them?
- How does the detail function within the paragraph? Is it a fact? An example? A reason? A concrete or sensory detail?

**REVIEW EXERCISE A. Writing Topic Sentences.** Write a topic sentence for the limited topic on which you gathered information for Exercise 5. Then decide which details most effectively support your main idea, and arrange them in a logical order.

# WRITING

## UNITY

**2i. Every sentence in a paragraph should directly relate to the main idea.**

A paragraph in which every sentence helps develop one main idea has *unity*. Any sentence that does not directly support the main idea should be removed; such sentences only confuse the reader.

Find the one sentence that destroys this paragraph's unity:

> **Youth hostels, which provide inexpensive lodging for thrifty tourists, are growing in popularity as the cost of hotel rooms rises.** School groups, families, and individuals are learning that they need not pay thirty-five to forty dollars a night for a hotel room when they can stay in a hostel for less than six dollars. When they began in England over sixty years ago, hostels charged only a shilling, then about twenty-five cents, for a night's lodging. While hotel prices discourage travel, hostel prices encourage it. Millions more American and foreign tourists will be able to afford travel in the United States as soon as enough youth hostels are built to accommodate them.

The sentence that begins "When they began in England . . ." should be omitted. Although it is about the topic of youth hostels, it does not contribute to the paragraph's main idea: the increasing popularity of inexpensive youth hostels.

**EXERCISE 8. Identifying Sentences That Destroy Unity.** Each of the following paragraphs contains one or more sentences that do not directly relate to the main idea in the topic sentence. Find these sentences, copy them onto your paper, and be ready to explain how they destroy the paragraph's unity.

1. **Today's teen-agers have more educational opportunities than their grandparents had.** More and better schools are being built all over the country. Scholarships are available in much greater number for thousands of deserving students. Radio and television bring the finest drama, music, and art to almost every home. The modern college serves better food in its students' cafeteria. Books are more readily obtainable than they once were because of public libraries and the abundance of paperback editions. Compared to the teen-agers of sixty years ago, today's young adults have a much better chance to get a well-rounded education.

2. **Water is an essential part of the human diet—even more important than food.** The body can go a long time without food but not more than two or three days without water. Water provides nutrients, lubricates joints and membranes, and enables you to digest and absorb food and to eliminate wastes. Under normal circumstances, you need about two and a half quarts of water a day, which you take in not only by drinking but also by eating. Most fruits and vegetables are eighty percent water. You should drink lots of water before, during, and after periods of vigorous exercise, especially in hot weather. You need to drink more water than is necessary to quench your thirst because your thirst can be satisfied before you have drunk enough. Another essential nutrient is salt. Too much salt in one's diet, however, can have harmful effects.
3. **People are reading more and more every day.** There is hardly a drugstore in the United States that doesn't sell a line of paperback books. Today the best books in fiction, science, travel, biography, and drama can be purchased for a fraction of their original cost. Magazines with ten million readers per issue are not uncommon. Unfortunately, some magazines, in spite of their increased circulation, have had to suspend publication because of high production costs. Library circulations reach new records each month.

## COHERENCE

**2j. The ideas in a paragraph should be arranged in a logical order and clearly connected.**

A *coherent* paragraph is one in which the ideas flow smoothly from one sentence to the next and the relationships between the ideas are clear. Coherence may be achieved in two ways. First, the ideas in a paragraph may be arranged in a logical order, such as chronological order, spatial order, order of importance, and comparison or contrast. Second, the ideas and sentences may be linked together by means of transitional expressions, pronouns, and references to ideas already mentioned.

### Logical Order

Presenting ideas in a logical order makes a paragraph easy to follow. Four ways of arranging ideas are in chronological order, in spatial order, in order of importance, and in an order that reveals comparison or contrast.

#### Chronological Order

**(1) Ideas may be arranged in chronological order.**

Chronological order is used in narrative writing to relate a series of events. It is also used in expository writing to explain a process, as in the following paragraph.

Later, when Bea has some time, she takes me into the back, into a room about a third the size of a high-school gym, where the tortilla-making machinery and the kitchen are situated. The tortillas are manufactured under the supervision of Jake Montoya, Bea's husband and co-proprietor. The process begins the way it has for centuries, with dried corn kernels soaking in a solution of lime and water. At the M & J, three hundred pounds of white corn at a time are brought to a boil in a chest-high metal bin, drained and thoroughly rinsed, and then shovelled into a hopper and ground into a fine, moist paste called *masa.* (Traditionally, the corn has been ground on a *metate,* a slab of smooth stone, with a *mano,* a sort of stone rolling pin. Although some Indians still do it this way as a daily practice or on ceremonial occasions—corn, especially white and blue cornmeal, is sacred to the Pueblo Indians—people from nearby pueblos often come to the M & J to buy their *masa.*) The *masa* goes into a spreader, which rolls the dough to a thickness of about one-sixteenth of an inch and stamps it into circles about six inches across. These drop onto a conveyor belt that passes over gas flames, flips the tortillas, bakes them once again, and then sends them out onto a mesh conveyor belt to cool. Someone at the end—Lupe Guerrero, his brother Rosolio Guerrero, or Lino Ramirez, longtime employees who double as cooks during restaurant hours—stacks them and puts them into packages.

GWENETH CRAVENS—*The New Yorker*

The following transitional expressions are often used to show chronological order.

| | |
|---|---|
| after | in the beginning (end) |
| afterward | in the meantime |
| as soon as | later |
| at first | meanwhile |
| at last | moments later |
| at the same time | next |
| before | since |
| during | soon |
| earlier | then |
| finally | until |
| first | when |
| formerly | while |

**EXERCISE 9. Writing a Paragraph Using Chronological Order.** Use the following information to write a paragraph in which the ideas are arranged in chronological order. You may combine or reword the sentences in any way that you choose.

*Topic sentence:* The thirty-two-mile bike trip that Mitch, Gary, and I planned last weekend turned out to be a comic disaster.

a. A jagged piece of glass flattened Mitch's back tire.
b. Disgusted with the two accidents, we decided to end the trip.
c. We started out at 6 A.M., laden with lunch and water bottles, but no one had thought to bring tools or a bike repair kit.
d. We bought a patch kit, and I talked the owner into lending us a bicycle wrench, which he asked us to return immediately.
e. Mitch fixed his bike.
f. Gary and I left Mitch with his flat tire while we pedaled furiously to the nearest bicycle store, some six miles away and, of course, not yet open.
g. We waited there till the owner opened the bike store at 9 A.M.
h. We returned the wrench and headed south again toward Coconut Grove.
i. About two miles from the Grove, Gary's pedal fell off completely, and none of us could put it back.
j. We waited for Mom to pick us up in her van, and we sat on the curb and ate our lunches, inhaling fumes from the heavy traffic.
k. It was noon by the time we got home, ready to do something "safe" like going to a movie.

## Spatial Order

**(2) Ideas may be arranged in spatial order.**

Spatial order enables the reader to visualize where details are in relation to one another. The arrangement directs the reader's attention in an orderly way—for example, from left to right, from top to bottom, or from near to far. In the following paragraph, the writer begins by describing the objects on a shelf and then describes the objects in three different corners of her room. Notice the boldfaced transitional expressions, which locate the objects precisely in the room.

> Lying there in the half-dark of my room, I could see my shelf, with my books—some of them prizes I had won in school, some of them gifts from my mother—and with photographs of people I was supposed to love forever no matter what, and with my old thermos, which was given to me for my eighth birthday, and some shells I had gathered at different times I spent at the sea. **In one corner** stood my washstand and its beautiful basin of white

enamel with blooming red hibiscus painted at the bottom and an urn that matched. **In another corner** were my old school shoes and my Sunday shoes. **In still another corner**, a bureau held my old clothes. I knew everything in this room, inside out and outside in. I had lived in this room for thirteen of my seventeen years. I could see in my mind's eye even the day my father was adding it onto the rest of the house. Everywhere I looked stood something that had meant a lot to me, that had given me pleasure at some point, or could remind me of a time that was a happy time. But as I was lying there my heart could have burst open with joy at the thought of never having to see any of it again.

JAMAICA KINCAID—*The New Yorker*

The following transitional expressions are often used to clarify spatial order.

| | | |
|---|---|---|
| above | between | opposite |
| across | beyond | outside |
| against | down | over |
| alongside | facing | throughout |
| among | in a corner | to the side of |
| around | in back of | toward |
| at | in front of | under |
| before | inside | underneath |
| behind | in the middle | up |
| below | near | upon |
| beneath | next to | within |
| beside | on | without |

**EXERCISE 10. Writing a Paragraph Using Spatial Order.** Using the following information, write a paragraph in which the details are arranged in spatial order. You may combine or reword sentences in any way you choose.

*Topic sentence:* In her painting of the outside of a subway car, the artist has captured the exuberance of today's urban graffiti artists.

a. In large blue letters: "Ride a bicycle instead."
b. A chocolate cake with pink candles and the message: "Happy Birthday, Janice"
c. A heart with names written in a foreign-looking alphabet
d. In red letters: "The world is flat.—1491"
e. In huge letters: "This train stops here."

## Order of Importance

**(3) Ideas may be arranged in order of importance.**

Using order of importance enables you to emphasize your more important ideas. In an expository or persuasive paragraph, ideas that provide stronger support for the main idea or that the audience will find more convincing receive emphasis from being placed either first or last. In the following paragraph, the writer gives three reasons to explain his opinion that storing nuclear waste in pools of water is preferable to burying it. The reasons are arranged from least important to most important.

> **Keeping waste fuel in deep pools of water at the reactor sites for at least another twenty years has a number of advantages (in addition to the fact that the safety record of pool storage is a long and unblemished one).** [3] The alternative—choosing some means of waste containment now and burying the material deep in the earth—would preclude a future decision to resume reprocessing. We would lose forever large and valuable amounts of uranium, a commodity that might be in short supply in another few decades. [2] The pool solution, which keeps the wastes on the reactor sites, would also eliminate the controversial waste transportation issue. [1] In addition, wastes stored in pools can be readily monitored from time to time by nuclear technicians, and this would not be possible if the wastes were sealed and buried. I believe we should recognize the fact that we now have a safe and effective means of temporary waste storage that will buy the years of time we need in order to resolve the problem on an enduring basis.
>
> DAVID E. LILIENTHAL

The following transitional expressions are used to indicate order of importance.

| | |
|---|---|
| above all | less (least) important |
| besides | more (most) important |
| finally | moreover |
| first (second, third, etc.) | next |
| for one reason | of greater (greatest) importance |
| furthermore | of less (least) importance |
| in the first place | to begin with |

**EXERCISE 11. Writing a Paragraph Using Order of Importance.** Choose one of the following topic sentences (*should* or *should not*). Then decide which of the reasons given support that topic sentence, list them in order from least important to most important, and write a paragraph. You may combine or reword sentences in any way you choose.

*Topic sentence:* Couples who plan to marry (should, should not) be required to take a psychological test to see whether they are compatible.

*Reasons:*

a. Test would reveal potential problem areas.
b. Couples could work out compromises on problem areas before they marry.
c. Such a test would be too expensive for many people.
d. Many apparently unsuited couples have married and lived happily together.
e. Such a test would infringe on people's personal freedoms.
f. If people approached marriage more cautiously, the divorce rate might not be so high.
g. Marriages that are "destined for failure" would be avoided.
h. A single test can't possibly be accurate enough to reveal all the things that might cause problems in a marriage.

## Comparison and Contrast

### (4) Ideas may be arranged in an order that reveals comparison or contrast.

*Comparison* is used to show how two or more things are alike; *contrast,* how they are different. Facts, incidents, concrete or sensory details, and examples may be used to point out similarities and differences between the topics. A paragraph may include both comparison and contrast.

The following paragraph uses comparison to explain how two plays are alike.

> Shakespeare's *Hamlet* and Maxwell Anderson's *Winterset* are linked not only by the revenge theme and by a rich, lifelike verse but also by common pleas for balance, individual strength and careful judgment. Both Hamlet and Mio show a tragic loss of balance in the face of overpowering emotions, while Claudius and Garth, Gertrude and Esdras reveal and suffer from fear to face and right a known wrong. The misfortunes suffered by Laertes and Gaunt and the pain they cause others are the result of indiscriminate judgments. Both plays, by exposing these human shortcomings, enable a reader to gain insight into his own problems.
>
> JEFFREY GOODMAN

The following paragraph uses contrast to explain how the North Pole and the South Pole are different.

> The two ends of the earth are areas of diametrically opposite natures. An almost landlocked sea covers the North Pole, a vast island contains the South Pole. In the north the polar region is surrounded by inhabited territories and has been the home of the Eskimo peoples for millennia. The Antarctic, unknown until almost two centuries ago, is still uninhabited except for the staffs of various national research stations. Its climate is harsher than that of the Arctic in the north by several degrees.
>
> PIERS PENNINGTON

In this paragraph, the ideas are arranged according to the *point-by-point* or *alternating method.* For each feature that is contrasted, both topics are mentioned. For example, the second sentence contrasts the terrain the two poles occupy.

The ideas in a comparison or contrast may instead be arranged according to the *block method:* All the ideas about one topic are presented first, followed by all the ideas about the second topic. With the block method, the paragraph about the North and South poles might read this way:

> The North and South Poles are markedly different in terrain, population, and climate. The North Pole is covered by a huge, frozen sea. The area surrounding the North Pole has been inhabited for thousands of years by Eskimos, and its climate is cold but not harsh. In contrast, the South Pole is located on a huge, frozen island. Except for scientists doing research, the Antarctic is totally uninhabited, for its climate is extremely harsh and inhospitable.

The following transitional expressions are often used to indicate comparison or contrast.

COMPARISON also, and, besides, both, in the same way, just as, like, similar, similarly

CONTRAST although, but, by contrast, however, on the other hand, though, unlike, whereas

**EXERCISE 12. Writing a Paragraph of Comparison and Contrast.** Using the following information, write a paragraph comparing *and* contrasting the llama and the camel. You may use either the point-by-point method or the block method. You do not have to use all of the information provided.

| FEATURES | LLAMA | CAMEL |
| --- | --- | --- |
| Type of animal | Hoofed mammal | Hoofed mammal |
| Habitat | South America | Arabia, North Africa, Central Asia |

| | | |
|---|---|---|
| Uses | Beast of burden, meat, wool, milk | Beast of burden, meat, cloth, milk |
| Size | Smaller than camel | Larger than llama |
| Hump | No hump | One or two humps (storage places for fat) |
| Color | Brown, white, black piebald | Ranging from dirty white to dark brown |

**REVIEW EXERCISE B. Choosing a Logical Order for Arranging Ideas.** For each of the following topics, tell which kind of order you would use: chronological, spatial, order of importance, or comparison and contrast. (For some topics, more than one order is possible.) Be prepared to discuss your choices.

1. The Appalachian Mountains and the Rocky Mountains
2. Why everyone should learn how to use a computer
3. The layout of a new shopping mall
4. What I like about large cities
5. An airport terminal during a holiday rush
6. Jazz music and the blues
7. The advantages of growing your own herbs
8. The attack on Pearl Harbor on December 7, 1941
9. How to conduct an interview
10. A day I'd like to forget

## Connections Between Ideas

Direct references and transitional expressions are useful for connecting the ideas within and between sentences.

### Direct References

*Direct references* are words and phrases that remind the reader of ideas already mentioned. They may be pronouns, repeated words and phrases, or synonyms.

As you read the following paragraph, notice how the boldfaced words and phrases refer to ideas presented earlier in the paragraph.

> Sometimes when you face a multiple-choice question on a test, you realize that you do not know the correct answer. You may, however, be able to determine **it** by a process of elimination. In **this process,** you consider all the choices one by one, questioning the reasonableness of **each. Some** will be obviously absurd and may be eliminated. The **one** that is left should be a safe guess.

## Transitional Expressions

*Transitional expressions* are words and phrases that indicate the relationships between ideas. Notice in the paragraph that follows how the boldfaced transitional expressions tie the ideas together and show their relative importance.

> Stevenson's choice of telling a large part of *Treasure Island* from Jim's point of view has obvious advantages. **First,** the boy hero's account gives the illusion that we are reading an authentic document—a report of exciting events by someone who participated in them. **Second,** we are spared in Jim's narrative many details that an impersonal description of the action would have to include **but** which would probably contribute little to the unfolding of the story. **In other words,** Jim's adventurous young mind filters out incidents **and** data that a more mature narration would include, in favor of the high points of excitement **and** suspense. **Finally, since** Jim's own discoveries play such an important part in the plot, his account enables us to share the ignorance **and** curiosity that precede them **and** the surprise, fear, **or** delight that they produce.

Transitional expressions can be grouped according to the kind of relationship they indicate.

***Transitional Expressions***

*To link similar ideas or add an idea*

| | | |
|---|---|---|
| again | for instance | likewise |
| also | further | moreover |
| and | furthermore | of course |
| another | in addition | similarly |
| besides | in a like manner | then |
| equally important | in the same way | too |

*To limit or contradict an idea*

| | | |
|---|---|---|
| although | however | on the other hand |
| and yet | in spite of | otherwise |
| as if | instead | provided that |
| but | nevertheless | still |
| conversely | nor | yet |
| even if | on the contrary | |

*To indicate cause, purpose, or result*

| | | |
|---|---|---|
| as | for | so |
| as a result | for this reason | then |
| because | hence | therefore |
| consequently | since | thus |

*To indicate time or position*

| | | |
|---|---|---|
| above | beyond | nearly |
| across | eventually | next |
| afterward | finally | now |
| around | first (second, etc.) | opposite to |
| at once | here | thereafter |
| before | meanwhile | thereupon |

*To indicate an example, a summary, or a conclusion*

| | | |
|---|---|---|
| as a result | in any event | in short |
| consequently | in brief | on the whole |
| for example | in conclusion | to sum up |
| for instance | in fact | therefore |
| in any case | in other words | thus |

**EXERCISE 13. Analyzing a Paragraph for Coherence.** Identify the direct references and transitional expressions in the following paragraph.

No animal has yet been discovered that can "see" infrared light with its eyes. But there are other ways of "seeing" than with eyes alone. Infrared light is actually a form of heat, and certain creatures, notably the rattlesnake and its relatives, have organs that detect it as effectively as though they "saw" it. In front of and slightly below their eyes, the snakes have two pits: each contains a thin membrane, behind which is a cavity filled with air. The membrane is filled with many nerve endings; there are 3,500 in each tiny pit—about 100,000 times as many as humans have on an equal area of skin. Furthermore, these nerve endings are very close to the surface of the membrane. Thus a "pit viper," as such snakes are called, can sense from a foot and a half away a glass of water only a few degrees warmer than the surrounding air. Rattlesnakes will actually strike at such objects, showing that they use this sensitivity to locate warm-blooded prey. These organs not only respond to radiant heat, but they also enable the snakes to detect the direction from which the heat comes. The rims of the pits act to screen out radiation from the sides; they cast heat "shadows," which of course vary with the direction from which the heat reaches the pits. These shadows, falling on the nerves of the membrane, inform the snakes where the heat source is and enable them to strike accurately.

NIKO TINBERGEN—*Time-Life Books Inc.*

**EXERCISE 14. Choosing Appropriate Transitional Expressions.** From the choices given in parentheses in the following sentences, choose the transitional expressions that you think most clearly link the ideas. On a separate sheet of paper, write the expressions after the appropriate item number. Be prepared to explain your choices.

1. In *What Color Is Your Parachute?* the author includes questions to help readers discover what kind of job they want. (As a result, On the other hand, For example), readers are told to ask themselves the following question: "On the last day of my life, what must I have done so that my life will be satisfying to me?"
2. (Because, Although, In spite of the fact that) divers who dive from the 10-meter (33-foot) board strike the water with such force that they could break their fingers, they plunge into the water fists first.
3. Ringing of the ears may be caused by repeated exposure to excessively loud noises. (Nevertheless, For this reason, In short), people who listen to music wearing headphones are advised to keep the volume moderate.
4. In recent years, there has been an increasing number of attacks on human beings by grizzly bears in Yellowstone and Glacier National Parks. (However, For example, As a result), park management officials have closed garbage dumps in both parks and forbidden people to feed the bears. Backpackers are (nevertheless, otherwise, also) advised to hang their food at least ten feet off the ground at night.
5. Scientists used to believe that sharks had very poor eyesight, (and, because, but) in an experiment designed to test their vision, sharks wearing blinders repeatedly crashed into the walls of their tanks. The researchers concluded, (moreover, likewise, therefore), that sharks do depend on their vision to navigate.

## WRITING A FIRST DRAFT

**2k. Write the first draft of your paragraph.**

Your first draft is your first opportunity to shape your ideas into sentences. Write freely, keeping in mind your audience and purpose and adding any related details that you think of. Remember that you will have time later to evaluate, improve and correct your writing.

***Techniques for Writing.*** In writing the first draft of your paragraph

- Use your paragraph plan as a guide.
- Keep your purpose and audience in mind.
- Write freely, and try to express your ideas clearly.
- Add related ideas as you think of them.

**EXERCISE 15. Writing a First Draft.** Using the working plan you prepared for Review Exercise A (page 43), write the first draft of your paragraph. As you write, keep in mind what you have learned about unity and coherence in a paragraph.

## EVALUATING

### EVALUATING YOUR PARAGRAPH

**2l. Evaluate the content, organization, and style of your draft.**

In evaluating, or judging, your writing, try to view it from the point of view of your audience. The following guidelines will help you evaluate any paragraph you write. In Chapter 3 you will find specific guidelines for evaluating the four types of paragraphs (expository, persuasive, descriptive, and narrative).

### CRITICAL THINKING:
**Evaluating**

Whenever you apply standards, or criteria, to judge something, you are using the critical thinking skill of evaluation. The standards with which you judge act like a gauge against which you can measure your own performance. The following Guidelines for Evaluating Paragraphs provide good standards for judging the effectiveness of the paragraphs you write.

## GUIDELINES FOR EVALUATING PARAGRAPHS

| | |
|---|---|
| Topic Sentence | 1. Does the topic sentence identify a suitably limited topic? Does it clearly state one main idea? |
| Topic Development | 2. Is enough specific infomation provided to develop the main idea clearly and precisely? |
| Unity | 3. Is every sentence directly related to the main idea? Is there any irrelevant information? |
| Concluding Sentence | 4. Does the clincher sentence, if there is one, provide a strong ending for the paragraph? |
| Coherence | 5. Are the ideas arranged in a logical order that is appropriate for the purpose? |
| Relationships Between Ideas | 6. Do the ideas flow smoothly from one sentence to the next? Are direct references and appropriate transitional expressions used to link ideas? |
| Word Choice | 7. Is the language specific and vivid? Is it appropriate for the audience? Are technical terms and difficult words defined or explained? |
| Sentence Variety | 8. Are the sentences appropriately varied in structure and length? |
| Tone | 9. Is the tone suitable for the purpose and the audience? Is it consistent? |

**EXERCISE 16. Evaluating a First Draft.** Using the guidelines above, evaluate the following draft of a paragraph. Answer each question on the guidelines in writing, numbering your answers to match the numbers of the guidelines.

> Portable stereo radios and cassette players that are worn with earphones can be dangerous. They do provide wonderful sound, as you may know. People who wear them while they use city streets cannot hear traffic. Drivers cannot hear car horns or sirens. This city has just passed an ordinance that says people who wear them when they ride their bicycles in the streets will be ticketed. The fine is fifty dollars.

**EXERCISE 17. Evaluating Your Paragraph.** Using the guidelines on this page, evaluate the first draft you wrote for Exercise 15. You may also want to use the appropriate guidelines for a specific type of paragraph (see Chapter 3). Save your paper.

# REVISING

## REVISING YOUR PARAGRAPH

**2m. Revise your paragraph to improve the content, organization, and style.**

Once you have evaluated your paragraph to identify areas that need to be improved, you can use four basic techniques to revise the paragraph: adding, cutting, reordering, and replacing. The following chart illustrates how these four revising techniques can be applied to the paragraph form.

### REVISING PARAGRAPHS

| PROBLEM | TECHNIQUE | REVISION |
|---|---|---|
| The paragraph does not have a topic sentence. | Add | Add a sentence that identifies the topic and states the main idea of the paragraph. |
| The topic sentence is too broad. | Cut | Remove words, phrases, or clauses that do not keep to the one main idea of the paragraph. |
| The topic sentence is too narrow. | Add | Add words, a phrase, or a clause that will make the topic sentence adequately cover all of the material in the paragraph. |
| The topic sentence is dull. | Add/Replace | Add vivid, interesting details. Replace general words and phrases with specific ones. |

| PROBLEM | TECHNIQUE | REVISION |
|---|---|---|
| The main idea is not clear. | Add | Add facts, statistics, examples, causes, effects, reasons, or an incident to the paragraph. |
| Material does not directly relate to the main idea. | Cut | Remove the material. |
| The paragraph trails off or ends abruptly. | Add | Add a clincher sentence that brings the paragraph to a logical conclusion: Restate the main idea, summarize the information, emphasize an important point, or suggest a course of action. |
| The ideas are not easy to follow. | Reorder | Rearrange the sentences and the information in a logical order. |
| The ideas do not flow smoothly. | Add/Replace | Add direct references and transitional expressions to the paragraph. Substitute more appropriate transitional expressions. |
| The language is dull. | Add/Replace | Add vivid nouns, verbs, and modifiers. Replace general words and expressions with specific ones. |
| The language is too difficult. | Add/Replace | Add definitions and explanations. Substitute easier words and shorter, simpler sentences. |
| The sentences are monotonous. | Add/Replace | Combine sentences. Vary sentence beginnings. Vary sentence length. |
| The tone is inappropriate or inconsistent. | Replace | Substitute words that are more formal/informal, humorous/serious, etc. |

**EXERCISE 18. Revising a First Draft.** Using your answers for Exercise 16 (page 57), revise the first draft in that exercise. First copy the paragraph as it is printed; then use the paragraph revision chart above to improve it. Copy your revised version on a separate sheet of paper.

**REVIEW EXERCISE C. Revising Your Paragraph.** Using your answers for Exercise 17 (page 57), revise the first draft you wrote for Exercise 15. Refer to the chart on pages 58–59 for revision strategies. Save your paper.

## PROOFREADING AND PREPARING A FINAL COPY

### PROOFREADING YOUR PARAGRAPH AND PREPARING A FINAL COPY

**2n. Proofread your paragraph, prepare a final copy, and proofread again.**

Once you have revised your paragraph, proofread it carefully, using the Guidelines for Proofreading on page 29. Then recopy the paragraph in correct manuscript form (see pages 30–32) and proofread this copy as well.

**EXERCISE 19. Proofreading Your Paragraph.** Use the Guidelines for Proofreading on page 29 to correct your grammar, usage, and mechanics. Then make a final copy of your paragraph and proofread it carefully.

## CHAPTER 2 WRITING REVIEW

**Writing Paragraphs.** Choose three topics from Review Exercise B (see page 52) or three other topics. Develop each topic into a paragraph, using a different order for each one: chronological order, spatial order, order of importance, or comparison and contrast. Concentrate on one paragraph at a time.

**PREWRITING** First, decide whether the topic is limited enough for a paragraph; if not, limit it further. Next, determine your purpose and identify your audience. Then gather information on your topic, select and arrange the details you will use, and write a topic sentence.

**WRITING** As you write your first draft, keep your audience and purpose in mind, and try to make your ideas clear and interesting.

**EVALUATING, REVISING, AND PROOFREADING** Use the Guidelines for Evaluating Paragraphs (page 57) and the appropriate guidelines in Chapter 3 to judge your writing, and refer to the paragraph revision chart on pages 58–59 as you revise. Then proofread your revised draft, using the Guidelines for Proofreading on page 29. Proofread again after you make a final copy.

# CHAPTER 3

# Writing Four Types of Paragraphs

## WRITING FOR DIFFERENT PURPOSES

Most paragraphs can be classified into four types, depending on the writer's purpose: expository, persuasive, descriptive, and narrative.

1. An *expository paragraph* informs or explains.

EXAMPLE A paragraph explaining the function of the cornea

2. A *persuasive paragraph* attempts to convince the reader to agree with an opinion and, sometimes, to perform a specific action.

EXAMPLE A paragraph urging readers to sign cornea-donor cards

3. A *descriptive paragraph* describes a person, place, or object.

EXAMPLE A paragraph describing someone who has had a cornea transplant

4. A *narrative paragraph* tells a story or relates a series of events.

EXAMPLE A paragraph relating how a person's cornea was injured

A paragraph may contain elements of more than one purpose. For example, a paragraph explaining the function of the cornea may include descriptive details. Usually, however, one purpose is primary and largely determines the content and the language.

In this chapter you will learn methods of developing each of these four types of paragraphs. The most appropriate method for a particular paragraph will depend partly on your purpose and partly on your audience.

## THE EXPOSITORY PARAGRAPH

The purpose of an expository paragraph is to inform or to explain. An expository paragraph may be developed with facts and statistics, with examples, by analysis of cause and effect, by definition, or by a combination of these methods. It should be direct and unemotional in tone, avoiding vague words and emotional appeals such as loaded words. It should also be objective; that is, the writer's personality should not intrude.

INAPPROPRIATE TONE — I was flabbergasted to discover that there are single-sided, single density computer diskettes, double-sided, double density diskettes, and other combinations, too.

APPROPRIATE TONE — Computer diskettes vary in the number of usable sides (single or double) and in the density (single or double) of information they can hold.

Any of the four types of order (chronological, spatial, order of importance, or comparison and contrast) may be appropriate for an expository paragraph. Usually, your purpose will suggest a logical order. For example, chronological order is the logical order to use in a paragraph explaining a process. (See pages 45–52 for more information on logical order.)

### Developing with Facts and Statistics

**3a. Develop an expository paragraph with facts and statistics.**

A *fact* is a statement that can be proved to be true; a *statistic* is a numerical fact. In the following paragraph, the writer uses both facts and statistics to develop the main idea.

> Planes of the future may be held together by glue instead of by thousands of rivets, or metal bolts. Experiments conducted by American aircraft manufacturers and the Air Force revealed that a glued aircraft would have several advantages over a riveted one. It would not only weigh 15 percent less but also cost 20 percent less to build and maintain. Structural tests on a glued fuselage showed that it could survive 120,000 hours of flight, which is four times the life of the average riveted aircraft. Furthermore, the glued fuselage proved to be less likely to develop cracks, and the glue even

retarded the growth of cracks cut into the fuselage deliberately. Results from tests of the plane's resistance to environmental stresses such as salt air, high humidity, and freezing temperatures were similarly encouraging.

---

## CRITICAL THINKING:
## Distinguishing Between Facts and Opinions

A *fact* is information that can be proved to be true. An *opinion* is a judgment, which cannot be proved. In order to write effective expository and persuasive paragraphs, you must be able to distinguish between facts and opinions. It is also essential for you to know whether what you hear or read is accurate and verifiable or simply someone's opinion. One way to tell the difference is to watch or listen for the presence of "judgment" words, such as *should* or *should not* and words in comparative and superlative forms.

FACT Volcano National Park is on the island of Hawaii.
OPINION Volcano National Park is America's most beautiful park.
FACT Many elderly residents of nursing homes have no contact with young people.
OPINION Nursing homes should be combined with orphanages so that both generations could benefit from contact with each other.

Forming opinions is a natural and useful way of interpreting the world. Remember, though, that opinions cannot prove anything; facts can.

**EXERCISE 1. Distinguishing Facts from Opinions.** Some of the following statements are facts, and some are opinions. Write *F* for each fact and *O* for each opinion. (Assume that the statements that are written as facts are true.)

1. The best time to go bicycling is at dawn.
2. Italian is one of the four official languages of Switzerland.
3. Although most people have twenty-six primary bones in the foot, some people have twenty-eight.
4. Martin Luther King, Jr., was the greatest black leader of the twentieth century.
5. Three states in the United States are named for women: Maryland, Virginia, and West Virginia.
6. Light blue is the most restful color for a bedroom.
7. A dog is a more satisfying pet than a cat.

8. Solar energy is the best form of energy.
9. The word *awful* once meant "awe-inspiring" or "full of awe."
10. Jennifer will make the best class president.

**EXERCISE 2. Writing Paragraphs Using Facts and Statistics.** For each numbered item, write an expository paragraph developed with facts and statistics.

1. **COMPLAINTS ABOUT PRO FOOTBALL**

22% Games too long

36% Too many penalties

15% Too many substitutions

33% Domed stadiums, artificial turf

60% Too many commercials

23% Too much violence

25% Teams play too much alike

Based on poll of 774 fans conducted Dec. 2–4

2.

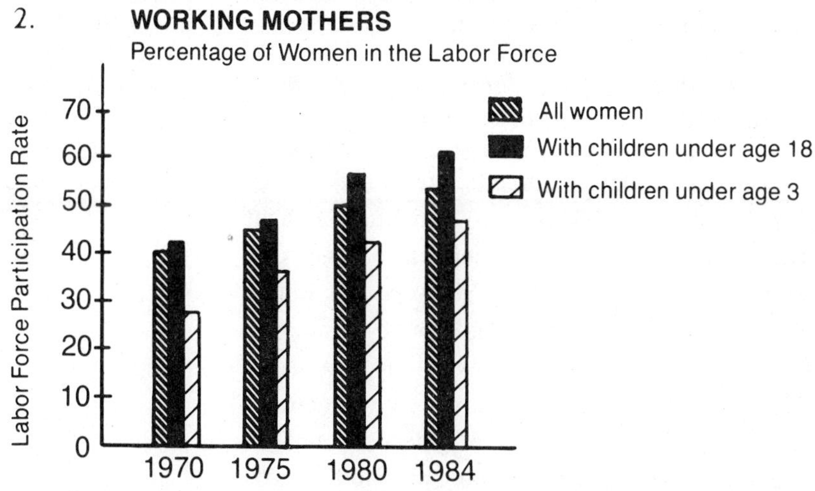

PREWRITING Both of these items provide more information than you need for a single paragraph. Considering the needs and interests of your audience, select four or five pieces of information, arrange the material in an order that will be easy for your audience to follow, and write a topic sentence that expresses your main idea. Evaluate the selected information to make sure that it effectively supports that idea.

WRITING Concentrate on expressing your ideas clearly in formal language. Be sure to define or explain any unfamiliar terms.

EVALUATING AND REVISING Ask yourself: Have I included neither too much information nor too little? Have I arranged the material in an order that will be easy for my audience to follow? You may also ask someone else to read your paragraph and tell you whether it is easy to understand. Then use the Guidelines for Evaluating Expository Paragraphs on pages 72–73 to judge your writing, and refer to the paragraph revision chart on pages 58–59 as you improve it.

PROOFREADING AND MAKING A FINAL COPY Use the Guidelines for Proofreading on page 29 as you correct your writing. Then make a final copy and proofread again.

## Developing with Examples

**3b. Develop an expository paragraph with examples.**

An *example* is an item or instance that represents others of the same kind. Examples are used to illustrate a general point concisely. In the following paragraph, the writer uses four examples to illustrate the general point in the topic sentence.

**Millions of people, despite the affection they may feel for their pets, have no compunction about discarding them when the animals become old, bothersome or inconvenient.** [topic sentence] Many people simply abandon them: [example 1] a quick look around a summer resort after Labor Day will reveal any number of dogs and cats waiting on the doorsteps of boarded-up cottages. Visit any college in June and count the [example 2] hungry, left-behind pets roaming around the campus. And most of those bodies of dogs and cats [example 3] you see along our highways are not pets that wandered out of their backyards; they are pets whose owners dumped them out of moving vehicles, making killers out of the oncoming drivers. People have even moved away and left pets locked in the vacated apartments. example 4

PATRICIA CURTIS

A writer may instead use a single example to illustrate a main idea.

> **Sometimes in houses or apartments that are open to the public we have an agreeable surprise.** It may not occur to every reader that Pavlov, the inventor of the conditioned reflex, was a man who enjoyed a joke. But the visitor to his apartment in Leningrad will find that he kept beside his desk the toy dog that had been lowered onto his lap by students in the gallery above his head when he was given an honorary degree by Cambridge. He prized the degree, but he also prized the dog, and we like him the better for it.
>
> JOHN RUSSELL

**EXERCISE 3. Writing a Paragraph Using Examples.** Write an expository paragraph developed with examples. You may use one of the following topics or one of your own.

1. Essential qualities of a successful baby sitter
2. Luxury items advertised as necessities
3. Movie stars who seem to play the same role in every picture
4. Artists whose work was not recognized until after their death
5. Important discoveries made by chance.

PREWRITING List three or more examples and any details you may need to explain the examples. Arrange the examples and supporting details in a logical order, and write a topic sentence stating the general idea that the examples illustrate. Then review your list of details, removing any that do not help clarify your main idea.

WRITING In drafting your paragraph, keep your audience and purpose in mind. Write freely, remembering to include all the details that explain one example before you go on to the next example.

EVALUATING AND REVISING Ask yourself: Have I included enough examples? Does each example clearly illustrate my main point? Use the Guidelines for Evaluating Expository Paragraphs on pages 72–73 to judge the content, organization, and style of your draft, and the paragraph revision chart on pages 58–59 to improve your writing.

**PROOFREADING AND MAKING A FINAL COPY** Use the Guidelines for Proofreading on page 29 to proofread your revised draft. Proofread again after you make a final copy.

## Developing by Means of Cause and Effect

**3c. Develop an expository paragraph by analyzing cause and effect.**

A *cause* is an event or situation that produces a result. An *effect* is anything brought about by a cause.

CAUSE The mayor and two city council members fire the city manager.
EFFECT Residents upset by the firing circulate petitions calling for removal from office of the mayor and the two council members.

To explain why something has happened, you state the effect in the topic sentence and then discuss the cause or causes.

No longer reserved for special occasions, cele- effect
brations, and vacations, eating out has become a
daily event in American life. For many it is a cause
logistical necessity since they live too far from work
to go home for lunch. For others, it is an occupa- cause
tional necessity enforced by travel obligations or
the need to conduct business over lunch or dinner.
For still others, such as students, those who live cause
alone, and those who think they can't cook, eating
out is a psychosocial necessity, the alternative to
grabbing something from a vending machine or
going hungry.

JANE E. BRODY

Another way to organize a cause-and-effect paragraph is to state a cause in the topic sentence and then to explain the effects, or results. Such a paragraph does not answer the question *Why?* Instead, it shows the consequences of a particular situation or action.

Fundamental science did not become a national cause
endeavor in this country until the time of World
War II, when it was pointed out by some influential
and sagacious advisers to the government that

whatever we needed for the technology of warfare could be achieved only after the laying of a solid foundation of basic research. During the Eisenhower administration a formal mechanism was created in the White House for the explicit purpose of furnishing scientific advice to the President, the President's Science Advisory Committee (PSAC), chaired by a new administration officer, the Science Adviser. The National Institutes of Health, which had existed before the war as a relatively small set of laboratories for research on cancer and infectious disease, expanded rapidly in the postwar period to encompass all disciplines of biomedical science. The National Science Foundation was organized specifically for the sponsorship of basic science. Each of the federal departments and agencies developed its own research capacity, relevant to its mission; the programs of largest scale were those in defense, agriculture, space, and atomic energy.

effect

effect

effect

effect

LEWIS THOMAS

**EXERCISE 4. Planning a Cause-and-Effect Paragraph.** Each of the following sentences states a cause. For each sentence, list all the possible effects (results) that you can. Write each effect as a complete sentence.

EXAMPLE *Cause:* More people are driving cars to work than ever before.
*Effects:* a. Highways are more crowded during rush hour.
b. Air pollution from exhaust fumes has increased.
c. It takes longer to drive to and from work.

1. *Cause:* Your parent gets a good job in another state.
2. *Cause:* You are chosen as the first high-school student to serve in the President's cabinet.
3. *Cause:* The legislature passes a law requiring all motorists to wear seat belts.
4. *Cause:* The high-school day is extended to last from 8:00 A.M. until 5:00 P.M.
5. *Cause:* The population of the United States doubles.

**EXERCISE 5. Planning a Cause-and-Effect Paragraph.** Each of the following sentences states an effect. For each effect, list all the possible causes that you can. Write each cause as a complete sentence.

EXAMPLE *Effect:* Mrs. Raymond has lost ten pounds in the last month.
*Causes:* a. She has been ill.
b. She has been dieting.
c. She has been too upset to eat.

1. *Effect:* The high-school basketball team has had an amazing season, winning every one of its games by a large margin.
2. *Effect:* Your hometown is chosen as the site of a national political party's nominating convention.
3. *Effect:* The average life expectancy of Americans keeps increasing.
4. *Effect:* All fish and plant life has disappeared from many of the world's lakes.
5. *Effect:* In the United States, about 30 percent of students who enter high school drop out without graduating.

**EXERCISE 6. Writing a Cause-and-Effect Paragraph.** Write an expository paragraph developed by means of cause and effect. You may use one of the topics from Exercise 4 or 5 or a topic of your own.

PREWRITING Once you have identified a cause (or an effect), list three or more related effects (or causes). If you are using a topic from Exercise 4 or 5, review the statements you wrote to make sure that they do not contradict one another and that they will produce a unified paragraph; if necessary, gather additional information. Then arrange the material in an order that will be easy for your audience to follow. Often, arranging causes from most important to least important works well, while using least-to-most important order may work better for effects. Write a topic sentence that states your main idea, and review your material to make sure that it directly supports that idea.

WRITING Write freely, trying to express your ideas clearly and concisely. Remember to link ideas within and between sentences with direct references and appropriate transitional expressions.

EVALUATING AND REVISING Ask yourself: If my supporting statements are causes, do they clearly explain why an effect came about? If they are effects, do they clearly show the consequences of a cause? Then use the Guidelines for Revising Expository Paragraphs on pages 72–73 to judge your writing, and refer to the paragraph revision chart on pages 58–59 as you improve it.

**PROOFREADING AND MAKING A FINAL COPY** Use the Guidelines for Proofreading on page 29 to correct your paragraph. Proofread again after you make a final copy.

## Developing by Definition

### 3d. Develop an expository paragraph by definition.

A *definition* is a precise explanation of the meaning of a word or a phrase. An effective definition identifies the general class to which the object or idea belongs and shows how it is different from all other members of its class. A dictionary definition of the word *robin*, for example, is "a North American songbird [general class] having a rust-red breast and gray and black upper plumage" [distinguishing characteristics]. A more extensive definition would list additional characteristics that distinguish the robin from other North American songbirds.

The following paragraph is an extended definition of *tundra.*

> The tundra is a flat, treeless area north of the coniferous forest along the Arctic Ocean. It is snow-covered eight months of the year. Since only the surface soil ever thaws, vegetation is limited to mosses, lichens, small trees and shrubs, and a few brilliant polar flowers that bloom for only a short time. The tundra is populated chiefly by birds, rodents, carnivores, and herds of reindeer. The few human inhabitants live a nomadic existence, hunting and fishing. Coal, oil, and minerals have recently been discovered beneath some parts of the tundra.

The two-stage method is also used to define an abstract term like *happiness* or *love*. In the following paragraphs quoting a psychologist's definition of *love,* for example, Dr. Sternberg begins by identifying five qualities that all types of love have in common and ends by citing examples of qualities that distinguish different kinds of love from one another.

> "There is a basic core of what love is that is the same in any loving relationship, whether with a lover or with one's child," according to Dr. Sternberg. That core includes such elements as being able to count on the loved one in times of need; having a mutual understanding and sharing oneself and one's things with the loved one; giving and getting emotional support; promoting the welfare of the person; and valuing and being happy when with the person.
>
> "These are the things that really seem to matter when it comes to love," Dr. Sternberg said in an interview. "These qualities of loving are quite general. They can apply equally to a lover or to your child."

"But there are some additional components that differ in each kind of relationship that give love its different qualities," he added. "For example, with your parents there's a sense of gratitude and devotion for all they've done for you, while with your children, there's a strong element of identification—you see yourself in them."

**EXERCISE 7. Writing an Extended Paragraph Developed by Definition.** Write a paragraph developed by definition. You may use one of the following terms or another term.

1. peace
2. alligator
3. friendship
4. ballet
5. war

***Techniques for Prewriting.*** As you prepare to write an expository paragraph:

- Determine the method of development or combination of methods you will use: facts and statistics, examples, cause and effect, or definition.
- Arrange the information you have gathered in a logical order that will be easy for your audience to follow.
- Write a topic sentence that identifies your limited topic and sets forth your main idea clearly and concisely.

## Evaluating and Revising Expository Paragraphs

You will find the following guidelines useful for evaluating the expository paragraphs you write. After determining in what areas your paragraph needs improvement, use the paragraph revision chart on pages 58–59 as you make the needed changes.

### GUIDELINES FOR EVALUATING EXPOSITORY PARAGRAPHS

| | |
|---|---|
| Topic Sentence | 1. Does the topic sentence identify a sufficiently limited topic and suggest that the purpose of the paragraph is to explain or to inform? |
| Topic Development | 2. Is the method of development (or combination of methods) appropriate for the main idea and for the audience? Are enough details given to make the main idea clear? Is the information accurate? |

| | |
|---|---|
| Unity | 3. Is each sentence directly related to the main idea as it is stated in the topic sentence? |
| Conclusion | 4. Does the clincher sentence, if any, provide a strong conclusion for the paragraph? |
| Order of Ideas | 5. Are the ideas arranged in a logical order that is easy for the audience to follow? |
| Relationships Between Ideas | 6. Do the ideas flow smoothly from one sentence to the next? Are they linked with direct references and appropriate transitional expressions (*for instance, since, consequently,* etc.)? |
| Word Choice | 7. Is the language clear, specific, and appropriate for the audience? Are technical terms and difficult words defined or explained? |

**EXERCISE 8. Evaluating and Revising an Expository Paragraph.** Use the guidelines above to evaluate the following paragraph. Then revise the paragraph, using the paragraph revision chart on pages 58–59.

Clothing fads change frequently. People like change and get bored with the same style of clothing. Manufacturers always want to sell new products and spend lots of money making them look attractive. People want to imitate fashion leaders.

**REVIEW EXERCISE A. Identifying Methods of Paragraph Development.** Indicate the method or methods used to develop each of the following paragraphs: (a) facts and statistics; (b) examples; (c) cause and effect; (d) definition.

1. So it is a warm gratification to find the new Hemingway book, *Men Without Women,* a truly magnificent work. It is composed of thirteen short stories, most of which have been published before. They are sad and terrible stories; the author's enormous appetite for life seems to have been somehow appeased. You find here little of that peaceful ecstasy that marked the camping trip in *The Sun Also Rises* and the lone fisherman's days in "Big Two-Hearted River" in *In Our Time*. The stories include "The Killers," which seems to me one of the four great American short stories. (All you have to do is drop the nearest hat, and I'll tell you what I think the others are. They are Wilbur Daniel Steele's "Blue Murder," Sherwood Anderson's "I'm a Fool," and Ring Lardner's "Some Like Them Cold," that story which seems to me as shrewd a picture of every woman at some time as is Chekhov's "The Darling." Now what do *you* like best?) The book also includes "Fifty Grand," "In Another Country," and the delicate and tragic

"Hills Like White Elephants." I do not know where a greater collection of stories can be found.

DOROTHY PARKER

2. The chronically depressed outlook of major-league batters was pushed to the edge of paranoia in the nineteen fifties by the sudden and utterly unexpected arrival of the slider, or the Pitcher's Friend. The slider is an easy pitch to throw and a hard one to hit. It is delivered with the same motion as the fastball, but with the pitcher's wrist rotated approximately ninety degrees (to the right for a right hander, to the left for a southpaw), which has the effect of placing the delivering forefinger and middle finger slightly off center on the ball. The positions of hand, wrist, and arm are almost identical with those that produce a good spiral forward pass with a football. The result is an apparent three-quarter-speed fastball that suddenly changes its mind and direction. It doesn't break much—in its early days it was slightingly known as the "nickel curve"—but a couple of inches of lateral movement at the plateward end of the ball's brief sixty-foot-six-inch journey can make for an epidemic of pop-ups, foul balls, and harmless grounders. "Epidemic" is not an exaggeration. The slider was the prime agent responsible for the sickening and decline of major-league batting averages in the two decades after the Second World War, which culminated in a combined average of .237 for the two leagues in 1968. A subsequent crash program of immunization and prevention by the authorities produced from the laboratory a smaller strike zone and a lowering of the pitcher's mound by five inches, but the hitters, while saved from extermination, have never regained their state of rosy-cheeked, pre-slider good health.

ROGER ANGELL

3. There is always a danger of wanting what you cannot have. At the beginning of my birding days, I found myself impatient to see a pileated woodpecker. Dashing and crow-sized, this bird with its dramatic black, white and red markings is usually private, almost furtive. Frequently I encountered the impressive oblong holes it hammers out of dead trees. As the months turned into a year, then more than two, I sometimes heard its powerful drumming, its ringing cry. Too often I was present but looking the other way, when others briefly glimpsed it among the trees. I became obsessed.

GRAEME GIBSON

**REVIEW EXERCISE B. Writing an Expository Paragraph.** Write an expository paragraph on one of the following topics or a topic of your own. First, plan your paragraph: Determine your specific purpose and identify your audience; gather information; choose a method of development or a combination of methods; arrange the material in a logical order; and write a topic sentence. Then draft the paragraph, and use the guidelines on pages 22–23 to evaluate your draft. Refer to the paragraph revision chart on pages 58–59 as you improve your writing and to the guidelines on page 29 as you proofread it. Then make a final copy and proofread again.

1. The computer as an aid to learning
2. How laws protect people from themselves
3. An important medical advance
4. Learning to ski (box, bowl, play an instrument, etc.)
5. What is honesty?

## THE PERSUASIVE PARAGRAPH

The purpose of persuasive writing is to convince an audience to agree with an opinion and, sometimes, to perform a specific action, such as voting for a particular candidate or signing a petition.

### Developing with Reasons

**3e. Develop a persuasive paragraph with reasons.**

The topic of a persuasive paragraph should be a serious, debatable issue that is significant and not merely a personal preference.

NOT APPROPRIATE The best kind of pizza has mushrooms and onions.
NOT APPROPRIATE Fall is a pleasanter time of year than summer.
APPROPRIATE High school students should be required to pass a two-year foreign language course in order to graduate.
APPROPRIATE The President of the United States should be limited to one six-year term in office.

The topic sentence, or *position statement,* of a persuasive paragraph should state the writer's opinion clearly and succinctly. It should not be so brief that it is uninteresting, however.

TOO BRIEF The United States should send surplus food abroad.
EFFECTIVE The federal government should develop a program for distributing this nation's surplus food to nations with food emergencies.

The position statement should be supported by at least three *reasons,* statements that explain why the writer holds the opinion. Reasons are most convincing when they are supported by evidence such as facts, statistics, or examples. The reasons and the evidence make up the writer's *argument.* Notice that each reason in the following paragraph is supported by a sentence that provides additional information.

Cellular telephones for the car, the latest gadg- *position statement*
et for people who have everything, should be
outlawed. First, they are a threat to the safety of *reason 1*
pedestrians and other motorists. A driver using a
telephone cannot possibly remain fully alert at the
wheel; talking on the phone while driving is as
distracting as watching television. Second, a car is a *reason 2*
potentially lethal weapon. Statistics show that accidents kill and maim other people more often than
they do the driver who was at fault. Third, car *reason 3*
phones are too big a temptation for most people to
resist while they drive. In some cities, such as New
York, police officers ticket drivers who talk on the
phone while driving, but people who have such
phones cannot realistically be expected to use them
only while their cars are parked. Forbidding the *clincher sentence*
installation of cellular telephones in automobiles
would save lives as well as millions of dollars in
property damage and insurance premiums.

One type of reason that you may use to support an opinion is a quotation from an *authority,* an expert in the field being discussed. In the following paragraph the writer cites (quotes) an economist to support the point that paying teen-agers less than the minimum wage would be of questionable value.

> Beyond all that, there is also the matter of creating a two-tier wage structure. Even economists who favor getting rid of the minimum wage or exempting parts of the economy question the value of this. Asks Michael Wachter, a University of Pennsylvania economist who served on the Minimum Wage Study Commission, "Do you really want to have jobs that youths can hold and adults can't?"
>
> ELLEN GOODMAN

Reasons in a persuasive paragraph are usually arranged in order from least important to most important, thus building to a forceful conclusion. If you have one very important reason and several less important ones, however, the opposite order may be more effective.

Whichever order you use, the reader should be able to distinguish more important from less important reasons.

A persuasive paragraph may end with a *clincher sentence,* a concluding statement that reemphasizes the writer's opinion, summarizes the argument, or specifies a course of action. In the paragraph on page 76, for example, the clincher sentence reemphasizes the writer's opinion. Such a sentence is not required, but it can provide an effective ending for a persuasive paragraph.

The tone of a persuasive paragraph should be serious and unemotional. This helps convey the impression that your argument is fair and reasonable. Avoid name-calling and using words with negative connotations, such as *un-American* and *silly*. Concentrate on being specific and accurate and on expressing your ideas clearly.

***Techniques for Prewriting.*** In planning a persuasive paragraph:

- Make sure that your topic is a serious, debatable issue, not just a personal preference.
- State your opinion clearly and concisely in a position statement.
- Gather at least three reasons and evidence to support each reason, and arrange the material in order of importance.

## Evaluating and Revising Persuasive Paragraphs

The following guidelines will help you evaluate the persuasive paragraphs you write. Once you have identified areas that need to be improved, you can use the strategies suggested in the paragraph revision chart on pages 58–59 to revise your writing.

### GUIDELINES FOR EVALUATING PERSUASIVE PARAGRAPHS

| | |
|---|---|
| Topic Sentence | 1. Does the position statement express an opinion on a serious, debatable issue? Is it clear, concise, interesting? |
| Topic Development | 2. Are at least three reasons given to explain the opinion? Is each reason supported by accurate details (facts, examples, etc.)? |
| Unity | 3. Is each sentence directly related to the main idea in the position statement? |

| | |
|---|---|
| Conclusion | 4. Does the clincher sentence, if there is one, provide a strong conclusion? |
| Order of Ideas | 5. Are the reasons arranged in order of importance? Does the order help the reader distinguish between more important and less important reasons? |
| Relationships Between Ideas | 6. Is the line of reasoning easy to follow? Are direct references and appropriate transitional expressions (*first, most important,* etc.) used to link ideas? |
| Word Choice | 7. Have name-calling and words with negative connotations been avoided? |
| Tone | 8. Is the tone consistently serious and unemotional? |

**EXERCISE 9. Analyzing a Persuasive Paragraph.** Find a persuasive paragraph in a newspaper or a magazine, cut it out or copy it, and bring it to class. (Newspaper editorials and letters to the editor will be your best sources for such paragraphs.) Analyze the paragraph by answering the following questions.

1. Does the paragraph have a topic sentence? If so, which sentence is it, and how effective do you think it is?
2. What is the writer's opinion? Do you agree or disagree with that opinion?
3. How many reasons does the writer give to support the opinion? Is each reason supported by additional details?
4. Can you think of any additional reasons to support the opinion? If so, what are they?
5. Does the paragraph contain a clincher sentence? If so, what specific function does it perform? If not, would adding one make the paragraph more effective?

**REVIEW EXERCISE C. Writing a Persuasive Paragraph.** Write a persuasive paragraph supporting one of the following opinions or an opinion of your own.

1. Students of all ages should (should not) be allowed to use calculators during math tests.
2. Elementary-school children's television viewing should (should not) be restricted to two hours a day.
3. The annual earnings of professional athletes should (should not) be limited to $100,000.

4. United States citizens eighteen years and older should (should not) be required to vote in every election.
5. High-school students should (should not) be required to read a local newspaper every day.

**PREWRITING** Begin by deciding which position you will take —*should* or *should not*—and listing all the reasons you can think of to support that position. Next, evaluate the reasons and select the three or four that you think your audience will find most convincing. Then gather evidence (facts, statistics, examples, or evidence from experts) to support each reason. (You may need to do some research to find the evidence you need.) Outline your argument by arranging your reasons and evidence in order of importance, and consider rewording the position statement to make it more interesting.

**WRITING** As you write, concentrate on expressing your ideas clearly and unemotionally. Consider writing a clincher sentence to provide a strong conclusion to your argument.

**EVALUATING AND REVISING** Ask yourself: Have I built a logical and convincing argument? Have I established and maintained a serious, unemotional tone? You may also have someone else read your paragraph and comment on it. Then use the Guidelines for Evaluating Persuasive Paragraphs (pages 77–78) and the paragraph revision chart (pages 58–59) to judge and improve your writing.

**PROOFREADING AND MAKING A FINAL COPY** Use the Guidelines for Proofreading (page 29) to proofread your revised draft. Proofread again after making a final copy.

## THE DESCRIPTIVE PARAGRAPH

Descriptive writing uses details that appeal to the senses—sight, hearing, taste, touch, and smell—to create images in the reader's mind. Most paragraph-length descriptions focus on one person, object, place, or event.

### Developing with Concrete and Sensory Details

**3f. Develop a descriptive paragraph with concrete and sensory details.**

In the following paragraph, the writer is searching for a grave in the forest. Through the use of many carefully selected concrete and sensory details, he re-creates for the reader the experience of being in the woods.

> But I didn't wait until morning. The smell in the pines was sweet, the spring peepers sang, and the trail over the first hill was easy. Whippoorwills ceaselessly cut sharp calls against the early dark, and a screech owl shivered the night. Then the trail disappeared in wiry brush. I began imagining flared nostrils and eyed, coiled things. Trying to step over whatever lay waiting, I took longer strides. Suddenly the woods went silent as if something had muffled it. I kept thinking about turning back, but the sense that the grave was just over the next hill drew me in deeper. Springs trickled to the lake and turned bosky coves to mud and filled the air with a rank, pungent odor. I had to walk around the water, then around the mud—three hundred yards to cross a twenty-foot inlet. Something heavy and running from me mashed off through the brush.
>
> WILLIAM LEAST HEAT MOON—
> BLUE HIGHWAYS: A JOURNEY INTO AMERICA

One way to create vivid images is to use *figures of speech* such as similes and metaphors to make comparisons. In the following paragraph, which combines exposition and narration with description, the writer uses metaphors to compare a jai-alai game to ballet or theater and the moving ball to a white comet; he uses a simile to compare the motion of the ball to a line drive in baseball. Notice how the writer uses specific words to describe the sounds of the ball and the players' shoes.

> Once under way, the game suggests, from moment to moment, a variety of sports: baseball, lacrosse, handball, polo, squash, duelling, golf. It is cool and uncluttered. (The *cesta* may be the most elegant piece of sculpture used in any game.) The action is fast and dangerous. The sweeping proportions of the court, the looming volume of the playing space, the relation of player to architecture lend a classicism, a grandeur to the sport. Sometimes it is less a game than ballet on a vast scale, or theatre: the silence as the ball soars forward, a white comet cutting across the green side wall, then a *crack!* as it hits the front, and a silent return to the players. During these tense moments, the only sound may be the abrupt squeak of a sneaker as one of the players, anticipating the angle, velocity, and spin of the ball, turns and darts into position. The ball is caught in the *cesta* with a loud smack; the player contorts himself, coiling, uncoiling, slinging the ball forward. It flies in silence to the front wall—*crack!*—rebounds, and another player leaps to meet it, executing a jet up the side wall, and, in a nearly continuous motion, sends it back again. The ball hits the front, then goes like a line drive all the way to the rear wall; a player snags it inches from the floor and throws it forward, falls to the floor, rolls over, and jumps to his feet again; a screech of sneakers . . . *crack!*
>
> JAMES STEVENSON—*The New Yorker*

The details in a descriptive paragraph are usually arranged in spatial order, so as to direct the reader's attention from left to right, near to far, top to bottom, and so on (see pages 47–48).

Often, as in the two model paragraphs here, the main idea of a descriptive paragraph is implied (suggested) rather than stated directly in a topic sentence. The accumulation of details reveals a main impression or mood. In the paragraph by William Least Heat Moon, the details create an eerie, suspenseful mood; in James Stevenson's paragraph, the details create a single main impression of constant, electrifying motion.

***Techniques for Prewriting.*** To create a mood or a main impression in a descriptive paragraph:

- Use the information-gathering techniques to list precise concrete and sensory details on your topic.
- Select from your list only those details that will reinforce the mood or main impression of the paragraph, and arrange them in spatial order.
- Decide whether you will state the mood or main impression directly in a topic sentence or imply it through the amassing of details.

## Evaluating and Revising Descriptive Paragraphs

You can use the following guidelines to evaluate any descriptive paragraph you write. The paragraph revision chart on pages 58–59 will help you revise (by cutting, adding, replacing, and reordering) those aspects of your writing that need improvement.

## GUIDELINES FOR EVALUATING DESCRIPTIVE PARAGRAPHS

| | |
|---|---|
| Purpose | 1. Does the paragraph focus on a single person, place, object, or event? Does the paragraph state or imply a single main idea? |
| Topic Development | 2. Are enough concrete and sensory details included to enable the reader to visualize or otherwise mentally experience the topic? |

| | |
|---|---|
| Unity | 3. Is every sentence directly related to the main idea? |
| Order of Ideas | 4. Are the details arranged in spatial order or in another logical order? |
| Relationships Between Ideas | 5. Do the ideas flow smoothly from one sentence to the next? Are direct references and appropriate transitional expressions (*nearby, alongside,* etc.) used to show where the details are in relation to one another? |
| Word Choice | 6. Is the language specific rather than general? If figures of speech are used, are they appropriate and effective? |

**EXERCISE 10. Evaluating and Revising a Descriptive Paragraph.** Use the guidelines above to evaluate the following paragraph. Then revise the paragraph, using the paragraph revision chart on pages 58–59. Write your revised version on a separate sheet of paper.

The stands were filled with noise. The air was cold, and the fans wore a lot of clothing. We could smell the food from the refreshment stands. The floors were covered with dirt.

**REVIEW EXERCISE D. Writing a Descriptive Paragraph.** Write a paragraph describing one of the following topics or a topic of your own.

1. A used pencil
2. A fire
3. A concert
4. A beach
5. An athlete
6. A traffic accident
7. The car I would like to own
8. An ideal boyfriend or girlfriend
9. A frightening event
10. A place that makes me feel good

PREWRITING Begin by observing or recalling the topic you have chosen, taking detailed notes on the sights, sounds, tastes, textures, and smells you experience or remember. Then review your notes carefully; determine what mood or main impression you want to create; and decide whether you will state your main idea directly or imply it. Eliminate any details that do not contribute to your main idea, and arrange the remaining details in spatial order or in another logical order. If you have decided to state your main idea directly, write a topic sentence that identifies your topic and clearly sets forth that idea.

**WRITING** With your notes in front of you, write your first draft freely, concentrating on getting your ideas down in a form that you will be able to follow when you evaluate your writing. Remember that you will have time later to improve content, organization, and style.

**EVALUATING AND REVISING** Ask yourself: Have I included enough concrete and sensory details to create a clear picture for my audience? Are all of the details directly related to my main idea? Then use the Guidelines for Evaluating Descriptive Paragraphs on pages 81–82 to judge your writing, and refer to the paragraph revision chart on pages 58–59 as you improve your description.

**PROOFREADING AND MAKING A FINAL COPY** Proofread your paragraph carefully, using the Guidelines for Proofreading on page 29. Remember to proofread again after you make a final copy.

## THE NARRATIVE PARAGRAPH

A narrative paragraph tells a story or relates a series of events. Although most narrative paragraphs appear as parts of longer works, such as novels or short stories, an experience that occurs within a short time can be the basis for a one-paragraph narrative that is complete in itself.

### Developing with an Incident

**3g. Develop a narrative paragraph with an incident or an anecdote.**

Many narrative paragraphs do not have topic sentences that directly state a main idea. Instead, an introductory or concluding sentence may summarize the action, tell how it came about, or comment on its significance. In the following paragraph from *The Red Badge of Courage,* for example, the first sentence summarizes the action of the battle.

> The men dropped here and there like bundles. The captain of the youth's company had been killed in an early part of the action. His body lay stretched out in the position of a tired man resting, but upon his face there was an astonished and sorrowful look, as if he thought some friend had done him an ill turn. The babbling man was grazed by a shot that made the blood stream widely down his face. He clapped both hands to his head. "Oh!" he said, and ran. Another grunted suddenly as if he had been struck by a club

in the stomach. He sat down and gazed ruefully. Farther up the line a man, standing behind a tree, had had his knee joint splintered by a ball. Immediately he had dropped his rifle and gripped the tree with both arms. And there he remained, clinging desperately and crying for assistance that he might withdraw his hold upon the tree.

STEPHEN CRANE

Narrative writing often includes many descriptive details, as in the following paragraph by Annie Dillard. Notice that in this paragraph the first sentence tells how the incident came about.

Yesterday I set out to catch the new season, and instead I found an old snakeskin. I was in the sunny February woods by the quarry; the snakeskin was lying in a heap of leaves right next to an aquarium someone had thrown away. I don't know why that someone hauled the aquarium deep into the woods to get rid of it; it had only one broken glass side. The snake found it handy, I imagine; snakes like to rub against something rigid to help them out of their skins, and the broken aquarium looked like the nearest likely object. Together the snakeskin and the aquarium made an interesting scene on the forest floor. It looked like an exhibit at a trial—circumstantial evidence—of a wild scene, as though a snake had burst through the broken side of the aquarium, burst through his old, ugly skin, and disappeared, perhaps straight up into the air, in a rush of freedom and beauty.

ANNIE DILLARD

Narrative paragraphs may also include the thoughts and feelings that the events evoke. In the following paragraphs, for example, Holocaust survivor Elie Wiesel not only tells what happened when he returned to Sighet, the town of his boyhood, but also expresses what the visit meant to him.

At Sighet, I visited the Jewish cemetery, where lies the grave of the grandfather whose name I bear. It was strange: I felt more at home among the graves than among the living beyond the gate. An extraordinary serenity dwelt in the graveyard, and I spoke quietly to my grandfather, and told him what I have done with his name.

Then, with a childhood friend, a fellow pilgrim, we ambled through the streets and alleys in silence, not daring to glance at one another. I recognized each window, each tree. Names and faces spring before me as if from nowhere, as if preparing to reoccupy their former homes. I stopped before my old house and with a beating heart, nearly beside myself, I waited for a youth to come out, to beckon me nearer, to demand to know what I was doing there, in his life. A nameless anguish overcame me: What if all that I had lived had only been a dream?

ELIE WIESEL

The order of ideas in a narrative paragraph is usually chronological—the order in which the events occurred. Since a paragraph is limited in length, the writer must rely to a great extent on organization to make the meaning of the events clear.

***Techniques for Prewriting.*** In developing a narrative paragraph:

- Use the *5 W-How?* questions to gather details of the incident.
- Arrange the ideas in chronological order.
- Consider writing an introductory or concluding sentence that summarizes the action, tells how it came about, or comments on its significance.

## Evaluating and Revising Narrative Paragraphs

You will find the following guidelines useful for evaluating the narrative paragraphs you write. The paragraph revision chart on pages 58–59 provides strategies (adding, cutting, reordering, and replacing) for revising those areas that need improvement.

## GUIDELINES FOR EVALUATING NARRATIVE PARAGRAPHS

| | |
|---|---|
| Purpose | 1. Does an introductory or concluding sentence summarize the action, tell how it came about, or comment on its significance? |
| Topic Development | 2. Are enough details included so that the audience can understand what happened? |
| Unity | 3. Have repetitive and unrelated details been left out? |
| Order of Ideas | 4. Are the events arranged in the order in which they occurred? |
| Relationships Between Ideas | 5. Do the ideas flow smoothly from one sentence to the next? Are direct references and appropriate transitional expressions (*then, after, meanwhile,* etc.) used to link ideas? |
| Word Choice | 6. Are precise nouns, verbs, and modifiers used to help the audience picture the action? Is the language appropriate for the audience? |

**EXERCISE 11. Evaluating and Revising a Narrative Paragraph.** Use the guidelines on page 85 to evaluate the following paragraph. Then use the paragraph revision chart on pages 58–59 to revise it. Write your revised version on a separate sheet of paper.

> Thornwell Jacobs, president of Oglethorpe College in Atlanta, Georgia, had a good idea. He decided in 1935 that a time capsule would be a good way to preserve civilization. Construction began in 1938 beneath the campus of Oglethorpe College on a time capsule that was as big as a swimming pool. It was a vault, and it was filled with thousands of items. There were seed samples, scientific instruments, writings, newsreels, a set of Lincoln logs, a pacifier, and a Donald Duck doll. They were supposed to represent American civilization of the late 1930's. The time capsule was sealed in 1940. It contains a device to teach English. It is scheduled to be opened in 8113.

**REVIEW EXERCISE E. Writing a Narrative Paragraph.** Write a narrative paragraph using an incident to illustrate one of the following ideas or an idea of your own.

1. Procrastination (delaying doing something until the last possible minute) can cause enormous problems.
2. One way to gain self-confidence is to overcome a fear.
3. In my family, just the mention of —— is enough to set off gales of laughter.
4. My earliest happy memory is —— .
5. A decision made in anger may be regretted later.

**PREWRITING** Make a list of details that the reader will need to know in order to understand the incident. For example, where does the event take place? If it is outdoors, what is the weather like? Who are the main characters? How can you describe them briefly, yet interestingly? Where will you begin the story? Make a list of the actions that are needed to understand the incident, and arrange them in chronological order. Then consider what you (or your main character) feel about the incident or what you learned from it, and write an introductory or concluding sentence that comments on the meaning of the incident.

**WRITING** As you write, concentrate on telling the story clearly and concisely. Try to vary sentence beginnings and structure, avoiding sentences that begin, "And then I. . . ."

**EVALUATING AND REVISING** Ask yourself: Have I included enough details to make the incident clear and interesting? Have I used direct references and transitional expressions to clarify the order of events?

Then use the Guidelines for Evaluating Narrative Paragraphs (page 85) to judge your writing, and refer to the paragraph revision chart (pages 58–59) as you revise it.

**PROOFREADING AND MAKING A FINAL COPY** Use the Guidelines for Proofreading on page 29 to proofread your paragraph. Then make a final copy and proofread it.

---

## CHAPTER 3 WRITING REVIEW

**Writing Paragraphs for Different Purposes.** Select a commonplace subject—a shopping mall, a school assembly, a part-time job—to use as the starting point for planning and writing four paragraphs, one for each of the types of writing you have studied in this chapter. Remember to keep your audience and purpose in mind as you limit the subject to find a topic for each paragraph. To plan your paragraphs, follow the steps of the writing process: Gather information; arrange it in a logical order; and write a topic sentence that states your main idea. (For the descriptive and narrative paragraphs, you may imply your main idea instead of stating it directly.) Then write a first draft, and use the appropriate guidelines in this chapter to evaluate your writing. Refer to the paragraph revision chart on pages 58–59 as you improve your paragraphs and to the Guidelines for Proofreading on page 29 as you correct them. Remember to proofread again after making final copies.

## CHAPTER 4

# Writing Expository Compositions

## INFORMATIVE AND EXPLANATORY COMPOSITIONS

The purpose of exposition is to inform or explain. An expository composition presents the information and explanations related to its topic through a series of paragraphs organized into an introduction, a body, and a conclusion.

Writing an expository composition is best approached in the stages that make up the writing process—prewriting, writing, evaluating, revising, proofreading, and writing the final version. For short compositions you may be able to combine two or more steps in the writing process into one. For longer compositions, however, you will find it helpful to take each step separately and in order.

## PREWRITING

### SEARCHING FOR SUBJECTS

**4a. Search for subjects for your expository composition.**

Many of your composition assignments provide a list of topics for you to choose from. At other times, however, you might be given an open-ended composition assignment; for example, "Write an expository composition in which you explain something you know about." Here, the responsibility for finding a suitable subject is yours. For assignments that are not based on extensive library research, this search need not go beyond your personal resources—your background of interests, knowledge, and experiences.

***Techniques for Prewriting.*** To find possible subjects for an open-ended assignment, ask yourself:

- What memorable, significant, or interesting **experience** have I had?
- What are my special **ambitions?** What am I doing to achieve them?
- What special **skills** do I have? What use have I made of these abilities?
- What are my personal **interests?**
- What **knowledge** do I have by participating directly in an activity or by reading about a particular subject?

**EXERCISE 1. Listing Your Personal Resources.** On a sheet of paper write each boldfaced category in the questions above. Then, in a column under each category, list at least five items that you might use as subjects for an expository composition. The subjects should be drawn from your answers to the questions. Keep your lists.

### Tapping Your Personal Resources

Three techniques will be especially helpful in tapping your personal resources for potential subjects for expository compositions: (1) keeping and using a writer's journal, (2) brainstorming, and (3) clustering.

A *writer's journal,* in which you record your thoughts, experiences, and feelings, can be a rich source of composition subjects. To use your writer's journal in the search for subjects, review your entries to discover if you have written about something that you could explain to someone else, or if your entries contain other information appropriate for an expository composition. As you react to your entries, you might think of related subjects that could lead to a possible composition subject. For example, a series of entries about your participation in a school play might suggest several subjects for expository compositions: selecting plays for high-school students to perform, how to obtain stage props, the role of a prompter, and challenges in building scenery.

You can also search for subjects by *brainstorming,* a technique in which you generate as many ideas as possible without stopping to evaluate them. To search for subjects for a composition explaining something that you know well, for example, you might brainstorm answers to the question "What do I know about?" Your brainstorming might result in a list of subjects similar to the one that follows:

| | |
|---|---|
| some kinds of seashells | tennis rules |
| lifesaving techniques | outdoor cooking |
| family history | arts and crafts festivals |
| local politicians | forming intramural teams |
| scientific careers | local sports facilities |

You might also brainstorm about "What interests me?" and "What have I experienced?" The personal resource on which you focus will be determined by your composition assignment.

Another brainstorming technique, *clustering,* enables you to search for subjects by generating ideas and seeing the connections between those ideas. Clustering consists of writing down each idea, circling it, and then drawing lines to connect it to the ideas that both precede and follow it. As with brainstorming, your aim in clustering is to generate as many ideas as possible without evaluating them. Clustering has the added advantage of letting you see the connections between your ideas—how one idea leads to and is related to a subsequent idea, and how your ideas cluster, or fall naturally into groups.

In the following example of clustering, one student starts by thinking of a personal interest—science. Clustering is then used to generate the ideas shown below. Each circled word or phrase is a possible subject for an expository composition.

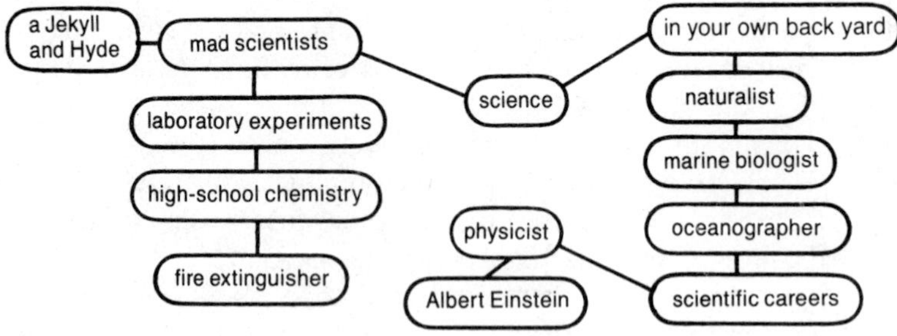

**EXERCISE 2. Using a Writer's Journal to Search for Subjects.** For several days, keep a writer's journal, one which you are willing to share with others. If you already keep a journal, you may select a series of entries for this exercise. After reviewing and reacting to your entries, list at least ten possible subjects for expository compositions. Keep your list for use in later exercises in this chapter.

**EXERCISE 3. Brainstorming to Search for Subjects.** By drawing upon your personal resources—that is, your interests, knowledge, and experiences—brainstorm at least ten possible subjects for expository compositions. Brainstorm specifically in response to the following three questions: What interests me? What do I know about? What have I experienced? Before you begin brainstorming, you may find it helpful to refer to the lists you developed in Exercise 1. Keep your brainstorming lists for use in later exercises in this chapter.

**EXERCISE 4. Clustering to Search for Subjects.** Select any one of the following three words: *interests, knowledge,* or *experiences.* Then use the clustering technique to search for subjects for an expository composition. Be sure to circle each word or phrase that occurs to you and to connect your ideas with lines so that your train of thought is clear to you. Keep the results of this exercise since you may decide to use one of the subjects in later exercises in the chapter.

**EXERCISE 5. Using Discovery Techniques to Search for Subjects.** Use either a writer's journal, brainstorming, or clustering to search for subjects for your own expository composition. Keep these subjects and be prepared to explain why you chose this particular discovery technique.

## SELECTING AND LIMITING SUBJECTS

**4b. Select and limit the subject for your expository composition.**

Having used different techniques to tap your personal resources for possible composition subjects, you are now ready to select one subject and limit it to a topic of manageable size for an expository composition. To select a subject, carefully review the possible broad subjects you discovered through using a writer's journal, brainstorming, and clustering. Allow yourself time to think about each subject and the extent of your interest in it. That interest should be deep enough to enable you to develop several paragraphs in an expository composition.

### Selecting a Subject

***Techniques for Prewriting.*** Use the following questions to select a subject for an expository composition.

- Which subject interests me the most? Does that subject interest me enough to want to explain it at length to someone else?
- Which subject do I know about? Do I know enough about that subject to explain it at length to someone else?
- For which subject do I have firsthand experience? Is that experience extensive enough to enable me to write at length about the subject?

When answering these questions, you may find that a subject you know about may not necessarily be one in which you are interested, or vice versa. In considering the brainstormed list of subjects on page 90, for example, you might determine that you are interested in arts and crafts festivals but do not understand them well enough to write several paragraphs about them. On the other hand, you might know a great deal about local sports facilities, but you may not be interested enough to want to write about them. Evaluating each subject in terms of your interest, knowledge, and experience enables you to select the best subject for your expository composition.

**EXERCISE 6. Selecting a Subject.** Using the lists of subjects you developed in previous exercises, select one subject for your expository composition. Use the questions above to help you make the best choice. The subject you select might be the one you decide to write about in later exercises in this chapter.

### Limiting a Subject

To limit the broad subject you have selected, analyze it—divide it into its smaller parts—by focusing on successively smaller aspects of the subject until you arrive at one that you can manage in an expository composition. For example, starting with the broad subject "science," the limiting process might work like this:

| | |
|---|---|
| NOT LIMITED | Science |
| SLIGHTLY LIMITED | Modern science |
| LIMITED FOR 2,000-WORD TREATMENT | The work of modern scientists |
| LIMITED FOR 1,000-WORD TREATMENT | Careers in science |
| LIMITED FOR 500-WORD TREATMENT | Preparing for a career in science |

Each limited *subject* that results from analysis, or division, is called a *topic.*

***Techniques for Prewriting.*** To limit a subject, ask yourself the following questions:

- What are some aspects, or smaller parts, of the subject?
- Which of these aspects are limited enough to cover fully in the space available?
- Which of these aspects lend themselves to the purpose of an expository composition: to inform or explain?

To select one topic to write about, ask yourself this question:

- Which topic best suits my knowledge, interests, and experiences?

**EXERCISE 7. Selecting and Limiting Subjects.** Select five of the following broad subjects. Then, referring to the questions above, analyze each broad subject and list at least five limited topics for each subject you selected. As you limit each subject, keep in mind the explanatory or informative purpose of expository writing.

1. Education
2. Health habits
3. Relatives
4. Computers
5. Astronomy
6. Medicine
7. Recreation
8. Modern Literature
9. Pollution
10. Fads
11. Neighborhoods
12. Vacations
13. Music
14. Newspapers
15. Theater

**EXERCISE 8. Analyzing to Limit a Subject for Your Expository Composition.** Limit the subject you selected for Exercise 6 by using analysis to narrow your broad subject into a topic suitable for an expository composition.

## CONSIDERING PURPOSE, AUDIENCE, AND TONE

**4c. Evaluate your topic: consider purpose, audience, and tone.**

Once you have a limited topic for your expository composition, you need to evaluate it in terms of purpose, audience, and tone.

### Considering Purpose

In an expository composition, your purpose is to inform or to explain. Consider your topic in terms of the space available. For example, the topic "dolphin behavior" is obviously too broad for a composition; whole books have been written on this topic. A more suitable topic for a composition might be "feeding behavior in newborn dolphins."

Second, ask yourself if your topic is suited to a composition that informs or explains. For example, suppose you developed the topic "why the driving age should be raised." This topic clearly has a persuasive purpose: to present reasons that will convince an audience that the driving age should be raised. A more suitable topic for an expository composition would be "the efforts in our state to raise the driving age." The second topic has the required expository purpose: *to explain* what one state is doing to raise the driving age.

As you evaluate your topic, keep in mind that purposes for writing often overlap. You can often combine narration or description with exposition. In the following excerpt, notice how the first two paragraphs make use of the narrative mode to introduce an expository article.

The night is balmy. The highway is lit by a full moon. Suddenly, as the car crests a hill, there it is, just 50 yards ahead, a terrorist roadblock: two small foreign cars parked across the pavement. With only a second to react, the driver lunges at the emergency brake to lock the rear wheels, then jams down hard on the brake pedal too. He jerks the steering wheel to the right. The rear of the car twists savagely in a 180° "bootleg" turn.

introduction

relates an incident

There is a horrible screeching and the hot stink of brake pads and burning tires. Heart pounding, the driver guns his motor, racing away from the barricade. But now another car pulls out of a dark

writing in the narrative mode

side road to cut him off. Though half blinded by its headlights, he jams on the brakes again, and just as his car is shuddering to a stop, he slams it into reverse and guns the engine. Seconds later he takes his foot off the gas and turns the steering wheel hard. Tires screaming, the car spins around once more, but is again facing the roadblock. There is no choice now but to pray, step on the gas and try to ram his way through.

He hits. But no deafening, jolting crash occurs. On impact, the two cars swing away easily, for they are on casters and covered with polyurethane foam pads. The terrorist threat was not for real, but still there is genuine sweat on the driver's palms. This is part of the final exam given at the BSR Counter-Terrorist Driving School. It is the culmination of a four-day course held at Summit Point, W. Va., about 80 miles west of Washington. Instructor Bill Scott, 42, a Yale Ph.D. in geology and an ex-champion Formula Super Vee race-car driver, started the course in 1976 after the Air Force asked him to provide driver training for some of its officers. Since then, Scott and three other instructors, backed by a team of mechanics, have trained hundreds of chauffeurs and corporation executives in how to foil attempts to kill or capture them on the road. The basic course, including films and lectures plus actual driving, costs $1,495.

indicates expository purpose of article

ROBERT C. WURMSTEDT

***Techniques for Prewriting.*** To evaluate a topic in terms of purpose, ask yourself:

- Is the topic limited enough to explain thoroughly in several paragraphs?
- Does the topic lend itself to informing or explaining?

**EXERCISE 9. Limiting Topics for an Expository Purpose.** None of the following topics has an expository purpose. Limit each so that its purpose is to explain or inform.

1. Girls are better dancers than boys
2. The most frightening dream I have ever had
3. Television commercials: airwave clutter
4. When I first felt the joy of victory
5. The sights and sounds of the school cafeteria

## Considering Audience

The purpose of expository writing clearly emphasizes conveying information *to someone.* This "someone"—your particular audience—influences how your topic should be limited; that is, what aspects of the topic should be explained in your composition.

Suppose, for example, that you plan to write a composition about participating in school athletics. For an audience composed of your classmates, an appropriately limited topic might be "how to participate in the intramural program." This topic reflects two points your classmates might be interested in: (1) how to participate and (2) the intramural program. For an audience of school-board members, on the other hand, you might limit the topic to "four ways students can participate in school athletics." This audience, because of their responsibilities, would be interested in more general information that applies to more students. The topic has therefore been limited to reflect the needs and interests of a particular audience.

***Techniques for Prewriting.*** Use the following questions to evaluate your topic in terms of a particular audience:

- For what audience am I writing?
- What aspect of the topic will be of special interest to this audience?
- What background knowledge does this audience already have about the topic?
- What does this audience want to know or need to know about the topic?
- What aspects of this topic will this audience be readily able to understand?

**EXERCISE 10. Evaluating Topics in Terms of Audience.** For each topic and its intended audience listed below, determine if the topic is appropriately limited. To do so, ask each of the five questions listed above. Write your answer to each question on a sheet of paper; then explain why each topic is or is not appropriately limited.

1. Cultivating tomatoes in backyard gardens—for a high school agricultural group
2. Writing adventure stories for fun and profit—for a seventh-grade English class
3. Recent slang expressions in American English—for foreign students studying English
4. How to prepare for academic achievement tests—for a teachers' association
5. The big wave: Hawaiian surfing adventures—for intermediate swimming students

## Considering Tone

The tone of a composition reflects the writer's attitude, or point of view, toward a particular topic. The tone may be humorous or serious, formal or informal, personal or impersonal, critical or enthusiastic. A writer may sometimes have more than one attitude toward a topic. For example, suppose that your topic is "how to pass a driver's license exam." You may decide to adopt a humorous outlook toward the topic. At the same time, however, you may also decide to be critical of the exam itself. If you write about this topic from each point of view, your tone should convey that you are being both humorous and critical.

Tone is conveyed mainly through *diction,* the writer's choice of words. For example, consider the topic "how you can support teen rock groups." The writer chooses words—such as *you, teen,* and *rock groups*—that convey an informal tone. By contrast, the topic "fund-raising efforts to subsidize the symphony orchestra" conveys a formal tone.

You should also consider whether your tone is appropriate for the purpose of exposition and for your audience. Remember that the purpose of an expository composition is to inform or explain. Because of this purpose, the tone of an expository composition is, more often than not, serious. Other tones—humorous, critical, admiring, satirical, light—may be conveyed only if they do not interfere with your efforts to explain or inform.

***Techniques for Prewriting.*** Evaluate your attitude toward your topic by asking these questions:

- What attitude do I have toward my topic?
- Is that attitude appropriate for my purpose and my audience?
- Does the language I have used to express my topic reflect the attitude I want to convey?

**EXERCISE 11. Limiting Topics According to Tone.** Limit each of the following topics to convey the tones indicated. For example, for a *humorous* tone the topic "raising children" can be limited to "how to raise children and survive." For a *serious* tone, the same topic can be limited to "responsible child-rearing practices."

1. *Topic:* Monster movies for young people
   a. *Tone:* Serious
   b. *Tone:* Humorous
2. *Topic:* How to tie your shoes
   a. *Tone:* Formal
   b. *Tone:* Informal
3. *Topic:* Household responsibilities for teen-agers
   a. *Tone:* Personal
   b. *Tone:* Impersonal
4. *Topic:* Three famous movie stars
   a. *Tone:* Enthusiastic
   b. *Tone:* Critical
5. *Topic:* Visiting relatives on holidays
   a. *Tone:* Serious
   b. *Tone:* Humorous

**REVIEW EXERCISE A. Evaluating Your Own Topic.** Evaluate a topic of your own in terms of purpose, audience, and tone. You may use a topic you have developed in previous exercises. Refer to the Techniques for Prewriting on pages 95, 96, and 98 to evaluate your topic.

## THINKING OF A TITLE

**4d. Think of a title that suggests the topic and purpose of your expository composition.**

You are now ready to think of a title for your composition. As you do so, keep in mind that—besides suggesting the topic and the purpose—a title should also attract interest.

For a formal composition exploring the basic requirements of a career in science, you might use the title "Telescopes, Beakers, and Lasers: Preparing for a Career in Science." For a less formal composition detailing the interest of scientists in extinct creatures, you might use the title "In Search of the Wild and the Weird." Note that each title clearly attracts interest and reflects both the purpose and the topic. Keep in mind that any title you write now may be subject to change at later stages in the writing process.

**EXERCISE 12. Writing Titles.** For each of the following topics, write a title that arouses interest and suggests both the purpose and topic of the expository composition.

1. Recreational activities for teen-agers during winter vacations
2. Changes in the community since my birth
3. My reading preference
4. TV commercials that are most annoying
5. How an escalator works

**EXERCISE 13. Writing Your Own Title.** Write a title for a composition on a topic of your own. You may use a topic you evaluated in a previous exercise.

## GATHERING INFORMATION

**4e. Gather information on your topic.**

Several *questioning strategies* are useful for gathering information on a topic: (1) The *5 W-How?* questions—*Who? What? When? Where? Why? How?*—enable you to collect a wide range of information on any topic. (2) *Questions about a topic* enable you to explore specific aspects of any topic. Such topic questions include What is it? What are its parts? How is it made or done? How is it put together? What is it good for? What is its value? What do I think of it? (3) *Point-of-view* questions enable you to gather information by considering your topic from three different perspectives: What is it? How does it change or vary? What are its relationships? By using any one of these questioning strategies, you will be able to gather the information you need on your topic.

The *writer's journal,* useful for discovering composition subjects, can also be used to gather information. For example, suppose that an entry in your journal explains your responsibilities as equipment manager for your school's tennis team. You might use this entry as a source of information for a composition explaining how teams depend on non-players.

*Brainstorming,* a useful strategy in searching for subjects, can also be used to gather information on your topic. Your aim in brainstorming for information is to generate a free flow of ideas about your particular topic. Suppose, for example, that you are gathering information on the topic "preparing for a career in science." To brainstorm about this topic, you should record every random idea that occurs to you without stopping to think about phrasing or the specific relevance of each idea to your topic. Your purpose is simply to draw on your personal knowledge of the topic. The following list might result from brainstorming about requirements for a scientific career:

good grades
curiosity about science
chance to help humanity
solid background and skill in mathematics
science concerns everything we do
different fields of scientific work
basic subjects
enthusiasm for a scientific field
changes in scientific training
work in pure science and applied science
high-school courses
college training
hobbies and extracurricular activities
other courses required for a scientific career
requirements for different scientific careers
personality of good science student
teaching science
rewards of a scientific career

No matter which strategy you decide to use, the information you gather will later be classified and arranged when you develop a plan for your composition.

**EXERCISE 14. Gathering Information on a Topic.** Select any three topics from the following list; then use a different strategy to gather information on each topic. Be prepared to explain why you preferred a particular information-gathering technique for a particular topic. Keep the information you gather for use in later exercises in this chapter.

1. Types of popular music
2. How our local government is organized
3. How to break bad habits
4. Difference between junk and family heirlooms
5. Creative uses for rainy days
6. Why I value privacy
7. Investigating travel opportunities in the United States
8. Why TV cartoons are (or are not) fascinating
9. Books that changed my life
10. Exercising without expensive equipment

**EXERCISE 15. Gathering Information on Your Own Topic.** Gather information on a topic of your own, using any one of the information-gathering strategies. You may use a topic you have developed in previous exercises. Keep the information you gather for use in later exercises in this chapter.

## CLASSIFYING AND ARRANGING IDEAS

**4f. Classify and arrange your ideas.**

Once you have gathered information about your topic, you should classify your ideas into related groups and arrange them in a logical order.

### Classifying Ideas and Details

Begin classifying your ideas by carefully studying the items in your lists of information about your topic. Your immediate aim is to determine which ideas are related and can therefore be classified, or grouped, together. As you review your ideas, looking for relationships among them, you may notice that some items will be readily eliminated because they do not specifically relate to your topic or to the other ideas in your list. In the brainstormed list on page 100, for example, several items have little or nothing to do with the specific topic of the composition: "requirements for a scientific career." The unrelated items are "chance to help humanity," "science concerns everything we do," "different fields of scientific work," and "rewards of a scientific career."

Other items in the brainstormed list cannot possibly be covered adequately in an expository composition; thus, "changes in scientific training" and "requirements for different scientific careers" might be eliminated. Another item, "basic subjects," duplicates points already suggested by three other items: "high-school courses," "other courses required for a scientific career," and "solid background and skill in mathematics." "Basic subjects" might therefore be eliminated.

Having eliminated the ideas that do not belong in your composition, your next task is to group similar ideas together. As you go over your list of ideas once again, certain items should begin to stand out as major points. For example, in the list on page 100, the "personality of good science student" is an important concept, under which "curiosity about science" and "enthusiasm for a scientific field" might be grouped. Other closely related items are "high-school courses," "college training," and "hobbies and extracurricular activities," which clearly belong together as parts of the academic training required of a prospective scientist. The item "work in pure science and applied science" suggests the major grouping "scientific careers." Three main headings, or groupings —personality, academic training, and scientific careers—are now available to the writer.

## Arranging Ideas and Details

After classifying your ideas, arrange your main headings, or groupings, into the order in which you will discuss them in your composition. The specific purpose of an explanation often suggests a logical order. If your purpose is to explain a process, for example, either chronological order or spatial order is effective because in such explanations one step depends on another. In a composition in which the ideas are not so dependent, you might arrange your ideas in order of importance, working from the less important to the more important or from the simple to the more complicated.

Usually, however, you will find that one of your groupings may depend upon another for its full meaning. For example, in the three main groupings developed for the composition about preparing for a scientific career, readers should know something about available careers before considering the rigorous preparation for those careers. Thus, a brief discussion of careers in science makes a logical opening for the composition. Similarly, a discussion of personality logically precedes a discussion of academic training. Within this order of groupings, the other ideas fall naturally into place:

Group 1. *Scientific careers:* pure science; applied science
Group 2. *Personality:* scholarship (general aptitude, special skills); curiosity about science; enthusiasm for a scientific field
Group 3. *Academic training:* high-school courses; college training; extracurricular activities

By classifying and arranging your ideas, you have developed an informal plan for your composition. As the writing process continues, you will find yourself rephrasing, combining, and eliminating some of the ideas and details included in this plan.

***Techniques for Prewriting.*** To classify and arrange the information you have gathered, ask yourself:

- Which ideas are related and can be grouped together?
- What main headings show how the ideas and details in each group are related?
- What arrangement of groupings does the specific purpose of my composition suggest?
- What arrangement will enable my audience to fully understand my ideas?

**EXERCISE 16. Classifying and Arranging Ideas.** In Exercise 14 you selected three topics and then gathered information on them. For each of your three lists, classify and arrange the ideas and details you gathered. Be sure to group related items together and to organize them in the most logical order for that particular topic.

**EXERCISE 17. Classifying and Arranging Your Own Ideas.** Classify and then arrange the ideas and details you gathered for a topic of your own. Keep your work for later use in this chapter.

### Developing a Topic Outline

Having classified your ideas and details into groups and arranged these groups into some kind of order, you are ready to make an outline. An outline shows at a glance the order, relationship, and relative importance of the ideas and details you will use to develop your expository composition.

There are two main kinds of outlines: a *topic outline,* in which the ideas are stated in words or brief phrases, and a *sentence outline,* in which the ideas are expressed in complete sentences. A topic outline is easier to make and sufficient for most student writing. When you prepare a topic outline for your composition, observe these rules:

1. Place the title and your statement of purpose above the outline. These items are not numbered topics.

2. Do not use the terms *introduction, body,* and *conclusion* in the outline. These are not topics to be discussed and therefore have no place in a topic outline.

3. Number main topics with Roman numerals; letter the subtopics under each main topic with capital letters. Divisions of subtopics, in descending order of importance, are given numbers and letters as follows: Arabic numerals, small letters, Arabic numerals in parentheses, small letters in parentheses.

4. Indent subtopics so that all corresponding letters or numbers are in a vertical line.

***Correct Outline Form***

I. Main topic<br>
  A.} Subtopics of I<br>
  B.}<br>
    1.} Subtopics of B<br>
    2.}<br>
      a.} Subtopics of 2<br>
      b.}<br>
        (1)} Subtopics of b<br>
        (2)}<br>
          (a)} Subtopics of (2)<br>
          (b)}<br>
II. Main topic<br>
  A. etc.

5. Never allow a subtopic to stand alone. Since subtopics are divisions of the topic above them, you must have two or more subtopics or none at all.

6. Begin each topic and subtopic with a capital letter; otherwise, capitalize only proper nouns and adjectives. In a topic outline, do not follow topics with a period.

7. Use parallel form for each main topic and for each group of subtopics. For example, if the first main topic is a noun, the other main topics must also be nouns; if the first subtopic under a main topic is an adjective, the corresponding subtopics must also be adjectives.

In the following example, the main topics and subtopics are not parallel in form.

I. There are two kinds of science. [sentence]
  A. Working in pure science [gerund phrase]
  B. Applied science [noun and modifier]
II. Personality [noun]
  A. A good scholar [noun and modifiers]
    1. General aptitude [noun and modifier]
    2. Has special skills [verb, noun, and modifier]
  B. Curiosity [noun]
  C. Enthusiastic [adjective]

Now study the first two sections in the following complete outline. Notice that main topics I and II have been rewritten as nouns with modifiers and are parallel in form with main topic III. Each group of subtopics consists either of a single noun or a noun and modifier.

***Topic Outline***

*Title:* Preparing for a Career in Science
*Purpose:* To explain the requirements for a career in science

I. Basic types of science careers
  A. Pure science
  B. Applied science
II. Personal characteristics of the science student
  A. Scholarship
    1. General aptitude
    2. Special skills
  B. Curiosity
  C. Enthusiasm
III. Academic training of the science student
  A. High-school courses
  B. College courses
  C. Extracurricular activities

**EXERCISE 18. Revising a Topic Outline.** As you revise the following outline, refer to the rules and the sample above.

*Title:* Learning to Live with Nature
*Purpose:* To explain natural disasters and how to survive them

I. Introduction: Natural forces often cause great destruction
II. Nature against people
    A. Earthquakes
    B. Volcanoes
    C. Storms
        1. The violent storms called hurricanes
        2. Tornadoes
    D. The damage caused by floods
    E. Erosion is a natural force
    F. Droughts
    G. Other natural forces
        1. Forest fires
III. What people can do and have done
    A. Taming the floods
    B. Protecting the soil
    C. Conservation
    D. Saving the forests: How people fight forest fires
    E. Preparedness: Guarding against drought
IV. Working with nature
V. Conclusion: People can learn to live with nature

**EXERCISE 19. Developing a Topic Outline.** In Exercise 16 you classified and arranged ideas and details you gathered on three topics. For each topic, develop your classified and arranged ideas and details into a topic outline. Keep your work for later use.

**EXERCISE 20. Writing Your Own Topic Outline.** In Exercise 17 you classified and arranged the ideas and details you gathered on a topic of your own. Now develop that informal plan as a topic outline. Refer to the rules for outlining on pages 104–105, and retain your topic outline for later use.

## WRITING THE THESIS STATEMENT

**4g. Write the thesis statement for your expository composition.**

Like the topic sentence in an expository paragraph (page 35), the thesis statement in an expository composition should indicate the purpose of the composition and should make clear to the audience what aspects of the topic will be discussed. To write a thesis statement, you use the critical thinking skill of synthesis.

---

## CRITICAL THINKING:
### Using Synthesis to Write a Thesis Statement

Synthesis comes from two Greek words meaning "to place together." In writing a thesis statement, you place together the understanding of your purpose and topic that you have acquired by progressing through each step in the prewriting process. The thesis statement, or synthesis, succinctly summarizes in a single sentence your understanding of your topic.

As you develop your thesis statement, keep in mind that your topic outline is an outgrowth of the previous stages in the writing process. You should therefore review and carefully consider the main topics or groupings in that outline. By referring to the topic outline on "preparing for a career in science," for example, you might write the following thesis statement: *As this composition will explain, a career in pure or applied science starts with a certain kind of personality and with academic training.*

The purpose of the thesis statement is to guide the development of your composition. Thus, you might include your thesis statement, or a revised version of it, in the introductory paragraph of your composition. It is not essential, however, that you include an *explicit* statement of your thesis in the introduction. Instead, you may strongly suggest what your composition will be about. Whether you include it or not, it is important that you develop a thesis statement because it will bring together your thinking about your topic.

***Techniques for Prewriting.*** In developing a thesis statement, keep these points in mind:

- Clearly indicate the purpose of your composition.
- Make clear to yourself and your audience what aspects of your topic you plan to discuss.

**EXERCISE 21. Writing Thesis Statements.** In Exercise 19 you developed three topic outlines. After carefully considering each outline, write a thesis statement for each topic. Exchange papers with a classmate, and discuss how the thesis statements you have each written do or do not succinctly state the purpose and topic of the composition.

**REVIEW EXERCISE B. Writing Your Own Thesis Statement.** Using the topic outline you developed in Exercise 20 for a topic of your own, write a thesis statement for your expository composition.

## WRITING

### WRITING THE FIRST DRAFT

**4h. Write a draft of your expository composition, organized into an introduction, a body, and a conclusion.**

Having developed a topic outline and a thesis statement, you are ready to begin writing a draft of your expository composition. You have settled on what you want to say; it remains to find the best way of saying it—that is, the way that expresses your ideas about the topic clearly, logically, and thoroughly.

Begin writing as soon as you have your ideas in order. Although your completed first draft will consist of an introduction, a body, and a conclusion, it is not essential that you begin at the beginning. If you cannot think of a strong opening sentence or paragraph right away, begin with the first main topic of your outline, and come back to the introduction later.

When writing your first draft, write as rapidly and freely as you can. Do not try at this stage to evaluate word choice, sentence structure, and punctuation. Improving what you have written is a slow process, requiring evaluation and attention to detail that will interrupt your flow of ideas. Later there will be time to evaluate and revise your first draft.

As you write, keep this point in mind: your writing will never be purely expository. For example, to explain a point you might write a paragraph relating an incident—writing that is clearly in the narrative mode. This overlap of modes is both natural and acceptable. You must be sure, however, that an informative or explanatory purpose is the one that you achieve in an expository composition.

## Writing the Introduction

The introduction to an expository composition may consist of a single sentence or a whole paragraph, depending on your subject and the length of the paper. The introduction should catch the interest of your audience and get the composition moving. Experienced writers introduce what they have written in many different ways. Among the most effective are (1) beginning with a general statement showing point of view and purpose; (2) beginning with a fact or example; and (3) beginning with a question. The examples below illustrate these kinds of introductions.

GENERAL STATEMENT

I read Doris Lessing's *Shikasta* immediately after finishing *The African Stories*. Although both works are written by the same author, there is an enormous difference between them, not only in their subjects but also in their styles of writing and their points of view. That the same woman's thinking had gone into the creation of each was intriguing. It was then that the notion of comparing the two works first came to mind.

IMPORTANT FACT

The atomic age began at exactly 5:30 mountain war time on the morning of July 16, 1945, on a stretch of semi-desert land about fifty air miles from Alamogordo, New Mexico, just a few minutes before the dawn of a new day on that part of the earth. At that great moment in history, ranking with the moment when man first put fire to work for him, the vast energy locked within the heart of the atoms of matter was released for the first time.

WILLIAM L. LAURENCE

QUESTION

What colors can animals see? Is the world more brightly colored or duller to animals than it is to us? To find the answers to these questions, scientists have used a method of training the animals to come to the different colors, which is similar in principle to the method used in studying the sense of hearing in animals.

H. MUNRO FOX

The introduction may, but need not, include your thesis statement. However, the purpose of your exposition—as developed in your thesis statement—should be clearly expressed in your introduction. Notice, for example, how the following introductory paragraph suggests that the writer will discuss how Stonehenge's massive stones were placed there. Although this thesis is not directly stated, the purpose and topic of the exposition are nonetheless clearly indicated.

The massive stones on England's Salisbury Plain have stood for over 4,000 years, witness to the wanderings of prehistoric nomads, to the rise and fall of tribes, to rites, mysteries, and ceremonies forever eclipsed. Well before the complexity of its design was revealed, the elegance and imposing size of Stonehenge inspired scores of theories about its ancient origins and purpose. Was it a defensive structure? A cemetery? A druidic temple of the moon? A ring of Irish petrified giants, magically carried from abroad, as one imaginative legend suggests?

CAROLINE SUTTON

***Techniques for Writing.*** When writing your introduction

- Arouse the interest of your audience.
- Clearly indicate what your composition will be about—either by including your thesis statement or by strongly suggesting your specific purpose.

**EXERCISE 22. Writing Your Own Introductory Paragraph.** Using the three model introductions as guides, write two *different* introductory paragraphs for the same expository composition on a topic of your own. You may choose to write an introduction for a topic you have developed in previous exercises.

## Writing the Body

The body, or main part, of a composition states and develops the main ideas in your outline. In shorter compositions, you may decide to devote a paragraph to each main topic in your outline. In longer compositions, however, you may need to devote a paragraph to the development of important subtopics. The amount of space you devote to an idea is an indication of the emphasis you think it deserves. In any case, each paragraph should have a clear relationship to an item on your outline.

Each paragraph should be developed according to one of the methods of paragraph development (see Chapter 2). Keep in mind that a paragraph is not merely a physical division of a page; it is also a stage in your thinking. A good paragraph develops a main idea, stated in a topic sentence and clearly related to the purpose of the composition. Also remember that a paragraph must have enough details to develop its main idea fully. In your first draft, be generous with details. It is easier to cut when you are revising than it is to gather additional information for an underdeveloped main idea.

## Achieving Coherence

As you write the body of your composition, you must decide which logical arrangement of ideas—chronological or spatial, for example —will give your composition coherence. You must also connect the ideas within and between paragraphs. In doing so, you will establish a smooth and coherent flow of ideas throughout your composition.

A new paragraph is a signal to your audience that a new idea is about to be introduced. You must tell your audience how this new idea is related to the idea that precedes it. To accomplish this, you must provide a transition from one paragraph to the next.

Two kinds of transitions—direct references and transitional expressions—will help you make clear connections between your ideas. *Direct references* refer the reader to the preceding paragraph (1) by repeating the last idea in the preceding paragraph, or (2) by repeating one or more key words from the preceding paragraph. *Transitional expressions* are words or phrases that indicate to the reader the connection between the ideas in the preceding paragraph and those in the new paragraph. These expressions include words such as *however, besides, nevertheless, therefore, first* (*second*, etc.), and *here*. For a more extensive discussion of coherence and transitions, see Chapter 2, pages 45–55.

***Techniques for Writing.*** When writing the body of your composition

- Use your thesis statement and topic outline as guides for the ideas you will develop.
- Use a separate paragraph for each main topic in your outline; as necessary, develop important subtopics in separate paragraphs.
- Include in each paragraph a topic sentence clearly related to the purpose of your composition and developed according to one of the methods of paragraph development.
- Arrange your ideas in logical order.
- Establish a coherent flow of ideas by providing transitions within paragraphs and from one paragraph to the next.
- Feel free to add new ideas that develop your thesis statement as they occur to you while you are writing.

**EXERCISE 23. Analyzing the Use of Transitions.** In a current newspaper or magazine, find five examples of transitions used to link paragraphs. Clip these out or copy the paragraph endings and beginnings. Underline the transitions. Be prepared to discuss how these transitions effectively and clearly connect ideas.

**EXERCISE 24. Writing the Body of Your Composition.** Using your topic outline and thesis statement as guides, write the body for an expository composition on a topic of your own.

## Writing the Conclusion

The conclusion of a composition has two main functions: It rounds out your treatment of your topic and tells your audience that you have finished. The conclusion may be a single sentence at the end of a longer paragraph, or it may be a separate paragraph. Since the conclusion is your last word to the audience, it is important that it reinforce the main idea of your composition. There are several ways of leaving a strong final impression with your audience: (1) by summarizing the main idea of your composition; (2) by repeating in different words the main idea stated in the introduction; and (3) by making a final statement that is an outgrowth of the points discussed in the composition.

The following example consists of two excerpts from an essay. The first is taken from the introduction, the second from the conclusion. Notice how neatly the restatement of the main idea ties the conclusion to the introduction.

FROM INTRODUCTION

> When most visitors go to the People's Republic of China, they see factories, communes, and schools. Near Peking they see the Great Wall, the Ming Tombs, and the Summer Palace. On a recent trip I saw all these, but also saw something else, something that few go to China to see: their own family.

FROM CONCLUSION

> . . . I doubt that I have realized the full implications of my visit and I don't know if I ever will. I would like to return and get to know my family in China as well as I know my family in the United States. I did find that while the roots of my ancestry were Chinese, they have been lost. My visit suggested that there once was something there, but today my life is inextricably rooted in America.

LESLIE WONG

***Techniques for Writing.*** When you write your conclusion, ask yourself:

- Does the conclusion reinforce the main idea of the composition?
- Does it do so by summarizing, by rephrasing, or by making a final statement that is an outgrowth of the ideas discussed in the composition?
- Will the conclusion leave the audience with a strong final impression?

**EXERCISE 25. Evaluating a Conclusion.** Bring to class an expository essay or article from a current magazine or newspaper. Be prepared to explain how the conclusion does or does not bring the article or essay to an effective close.

**EXERCISE 26. Writing Your Own Conclusion.** Write a conclusion for the expository composition you are writing on a topic of your own.

## STUDYING A SAMPLE COMPOSITION

Below is an expository composition on the topic "preparing for a career in science." As you read the composition, notice how the introduction arouses the interest and clearly indicates what the writer will discuss. Notice, too, how the main topics in the outline on page 105 are developed. Pay special attention to how transitions are used to connect ideas smoothly, and note how the conclusion repeats the points made in the introduction.

TELESCOPES, BEAKERS, AND LASERS:
PREPARING FOR A CAREER IN SCIENCE — *title*

*introduction*

In an Age of Science—and no period in history merits that name better than our own—trained scientists are fortunate people. Their training is a matter of national concern, for our nation badly needs more scientists than it has. Their futures are boundless; they can advance as fast and as far in science as their ambitions and talents permit. Most important, they stand at the very center of the forces which are conquering and remaking the world around us. It is small wonder that young people everywhere dream of entering one or another scientific profession. As this composition will explain, a career in pure or applied science starts with a certain kind of personality and with academic training.

thesis statement

No matter which of the many fields of science you choose, there are two main types of scientific careers. On the one hand, there is the "pure scientist," who specializes in research. On the other, there is the "applied scientist," who finds practical applications for the researcher's discoveries. To a certain extent, these two types of careers lead in different directions and appeal to different talents and dispositions. The dreamer and thinker will choose pure science, looking toward a career in a university or an industrial laboratory. The practical person, who is challenged by the excitement and activity of actual production, will choose a career as an engineer or a technologist.

topic sentence

development of main topic I

Both pure and applied science, however, have certain requirements in common. Both, for example, make stern demands on a student. Science is not a career for the average student. It demands that a student be of better-than-average aptitude, with a high-school record good enough to justify further training. Within that good record, certain grades should stand out. For example, engineering and the physical sciences (such as astronomy, physics, and chemistry) depend upon mathematics; a student who finds algebra and geometry puzzling or boring should perhaps look elsewhere for a career.

transitional sentence; also topic sentence

development of main topic II

Yet academic grades alone do not make a scientist. "Born scientists" are people of endless

transition; topic sentence

curiosity—curiosity about nature. They want to know how things are put together and how they work; they are driven to understand natural processes and their causes. To sustain this curiosity, scientists must have enthusiasm. Once their attention is focused upon a problem, they will want to know all there is to know about it as they search for answers. They must be prepared for disappointments, discouragement, and doubts. Without their enthusiasm, their training may be worthless.

development of main topic II

Scholarship, curiosity, enthusiasm—these qualities, then, distinguish even the youngest "scientists-to-be." With this foundation, students can undertake their academic training with confidence. In high school they should try to study the science of their choice, at least one related science, as much mathematics as possible, and a foreign language. They will then go on to four years of study at a college or university, leading to either a Bachelor of Science or an engineering degree. At this point the paths of the pure scientist and the applied scientist are likely to diverge. For teaching or for research, additional years of formal study and a graduate degree may very well be required; an engineer or technician, on the other hand, will probably go directly to a job in industry.

transition

topic sentence

development of main topic III

Both kinds of scientists, however, really spend a lifetime of constant learning. Even during their years at school, they participate in extracurricular projects, such as science fairs and science clubs. In later years they go on learning, in the laboratory or on the job.

transition

development of main topic III

Clearly, the road to success in science is not an easy one. Yet, as the beginning of this composition pointed out, the rewards are great. Those who love science, who have basic qualities of the scientist,

transition

and who can master college work have the ability and the opportunity to prepare themselves for a career in science. conclusion

**EXERCISE 27. Studying an Expository Composition.** Answer each of the following questions about the sample composition. Be prepared to explain your reasons for each answer you give. You may find it helpful to refer to the explanations of the parts of the composition on pages 108–13.

1. How does the introduction arouse interest in the topic while also indicating the purpose of the composition? How effective, in your opinion, is the introduction?
2. In the body of the composition, why do you think the writer devotes varying amounts of paragraph space to different main topics in the outline?
3. How effectively are transitions used within paragraphs and between paragraphs?
4. What final impression does the conclusion leave? How does this final impression relate to the thesis statement in the introduction? How effective, in your opinion, is the conclusion?
5. If you were to revise this composition, what changes would you make? For example, what information would you add or omit to improve the composition? Why?

---

## EVALUATING

---

### EVALUATING A FIRST DRAFT

**4i. Evaluate your first draft for content, organization, and style.**

Evaluation involves identifying the strong points and weak points in your draft. Although you have been asked to do some evaluating at different stages in the writing process, you will find that evaluation is easier and more effective when you have your completed first draft in front of you. Problems that might have stemmed the natural flow of writing had you tried to solve them earlier can be more readily addressed at this stage. As you evaluate, remember that every draft —even one written by an experienced writer—has its strengths and its weaknesses.

Evaluating your draft requires several readings. During those readings, you must approach your draft from the point of view of a member of your audience who is seeing your composition for the first time. When you evaluate, you must consider three aspects of your draft: content (what you have said), organization (how you have arranged your ideas), and style (how you have used words and sentences to express your ideas).

When you evaluate the first draft of your expository composition, use the following guidelines as a checklist:

## GUIDELINES FOR EVALUATING EXPOSITORY COMPOSITIONS

| | |
|---|---|
| Purpose | 1. Does the introduction clearly indicate the purpose of the composition? |
| Audience | 2. Does the introduction attract the attention of the audience by making a general statement, giving an important or unusual fact, or asking a question? |
| Paragraph Unity | 3. Does each paragraph in the body discuss a single main idea? Is each idea clearly related to the purpose of the composition? |
| Paragraph Development | 4. Are enough details included in each paragraph to develop the main idea fully? |
| Conclusion | 5. Does the conclusion leave the audience with a strong final impression? |
| Coherence | 6. Does the composition have a clear organizational plan that suits the topic? |
| | 7. Are transitions used to connect ideas within paragraphs and between paragraphs? |
| Emphasis | 8. Does the amount of space devoted to a topic help the audience identify the most important ideas in the composition? |
| Word Choice | 9. Are technical terms and unusual words defined or explained? Is the language suitable for the audience? |

For further help in evaluating your draft, refer to the general evaluating guidelines in Chapter 1, pages 22–23.

**EXERCISE 28. Applying the Guidelines for Evaluating Expository Compositions.** Below is an early draft of the second paragraph in the sample composition on pages 113–15. As you read the draft, apply the Guidelines for Evaluating Expository Compositions. Then answer each question that follows the draft. Be prepared to give reasons for your answers.

> No matter which of the many fields of science turns you on, there are two scientific careers. On the one hand, there is the "pure scientist," who likes research. There is the "applied scientist," who finds applications for the researcher's discoveries. The idle dreamer and thinker will choose pure science, looking toward a career in a lab. One wonders why Albert Einstein, of all people, chose a career as a theoretical physicist. To a certain extent, these two types of careers lead in different directions and appeal to different talents and dispositions. The practical person, who digs the excitement and activity of actual production, will pick being an engineer or a technologist.

1. What is the main idea of the paragraph?
2. Which, if any, of the details that support the main idea seem to be out of order? Which, if any, details do not support the main idea?
3. Are there any instances in which the addition of a transitional expression is needed to connect the ideas in the paragraph?
4. In which, if any, instances should the wording be changed to make the tone of the paragraph more appropriate?
5. What specific changes do you think the writer should make in this paragraph? Give a reason for each change you suggest.

**EXERCISE 29. Evaluating Your Own First Draft.** Evaluate your draft by applying each of the Guidelines for Evaluating Expository Compositions. Mark places in your draft where you should make changes, and keep the marked draft for later use. You may also want to exchange papers with a classmate to evaluate one another's work.

---

## REVISING

---

### REVISING A FIRST DRAFT

**4j. Revise your first draft, making any changes needed to improve the content, organization, and style.**

After you have evaluated your first draft, you are ready to revise it. Most of the problems that are found in compositions can be corrected with one of four techniques: cutting, adding, reordering, or replacing. The chart that follows suggests how you can use these techniques to revise your draft.

## REVISING EXPOSITORY COMPOSITIONS

| PROBLEM | TECHNIQUE | REVISION |
|---|---|---|
| The introduction is dull. | Add | Begin with a general statement, an important or unusual fact, or a question. |
| The introduction does not indicate what the composition will be about. | Add | Include your thesis statement or a sentence that strongly suggests the purpose of the composition. |
| More than one main idea is discussed in a paragraph. | Cut/Add | Remove details that are not related to one main idea. Develop a new paragraph with these details, or add them to an existing paragraph on the same idea. |
| There are not enough supporting details for the main idea of the composition. | Add | Add at least one more paragraph to support the main idea. The paragraph should include a topic sentence backed up with facts, details, statistics, examples, incidents, or reasons related to the main idea of the composition. |
| The composition does not end with a strong impression. | Add | Add details that reinforce the main idea without repeating it word for word. |
| It is not clear how ideas are connected to one another. | Add | Add transitions that help connect ideas: *these, other, first, then, thus,* etc. |
| The order of ideas is difficult to follow. | Reorder | Find the sentence or paragraph where ideas become unclear; move the sentence or paragraph so that the order of ideas is clear. |

| PROBLEM | TECHNIQUE | REVISION |
|---|---|---|
| It is not clear which idea is the most important. | Add | Emphasize the most important idea by adding a paragraph with additional details related to that idea. |
| Some of the words are not appropriate to the audience. | Add/Replace | Add definitions and explanations. Replace informal expressions with language more suitable to the topic. |

The revision below shows the changes made by the writer in the draft of the second paragraph (page 118) of the sample composition (pages 113–15). As you study the revisions, refer to the notes in the margin. They indicate the revision strategies used by the writer. The lines have been numbered for easy reference in Exercise 30.

No matter which of the many fields of science
~~turns you on~~ [you choose], there are two [main types of] scientific careers. On the — replace/add
one hand, there is the "pure scientist," who ~~likes~~ [specializes in] — replace
research. [On the other,] ~~T~~[t]here is the "applied scientist," who finds — add
[practical] applications for the researcher's discoveries. The — add
~~idle~~ dreamer and thinker will choose pure science, — cut
looking toward a career in a ~~lab~~ [university or an industrial laboratory]. ~~One wonders why~~ — add/cut
~~Albert Einstein, of all people, chose a career as a~~ — cut
~~theoretical physicist.~~ To a certain extent, these two — cut/reorder
types of careers lead in different directions and
appeal to different talents and dispositions. The
practical person, who ~~digs~~ [is challenged by] the excitement and activi- — replace

ty of actual production, will ~~pick being~~ choose a career as an engineer replace or a technologist.

**EXERCISE 30. Evaluating a Revised Paragraph.** Answer the following questions by referring to the preceding revised paragraph.

1. Why do you think the writer replaced certain words and phrases in lines 2, 3, 12, and 13? Which of these changes alter the tone?
2. Why do you think the writer added words in lines 2, 4, 5, and 7?
3. How does the addition of "On the other" in line 4 help the reader?
4. Why do you think the writer cut the sentence about Albert Einstein in lines 7–9?
5. Why do you think the writer moved the sentence in lines 9–11?
6. Does the revision correct the problems you identified in Exercise 28? If not, what other changes would you make?

**EXERCISE 31. Revising Your Expository Composition.** Use the chart on pages 119–20 to decide what techniques you should use to revise your composition. Then make the necessary changes. Exchanging papers with a classmate may also be helpful. To achieve greater sentence variety, you may find it helpful to refer to Chapter 17.

## PROOFREADING

### PROOFREADING YOUR COMPOSITION

**4k. Proofread your expository composition for errors in spelling, grammar, usage, and mechanics.**

Use the Guidelines for Proofreading on page 29 to proofread your revised draft. By avoiding and correcting errors in spelling, grammar, usage, and mechanics, you can make your expository composition clearer—and, therefore, more effective.

**EXERCISE 32. Proofreading Your Expository Composition.** Proofread the expository composition you revised in Exercise 31. You might find it helpful to exchange papers with a classmate to double-check each other's accuracy. You might also want to refer to the chapters on spelling, grammar, usage, and mechanics found throughout this book and to the Symbols for Proofreading and Revising found on page 33.

## WRITING THE FINAL VERSION

### PREPARING A FINAL COPY

**4l. Prepare the final copy of your expository composition.**

After you have proofread your revised draft, you are ready to prepare the final version of your expository composition. You should be concerned primarily with the accuracy and appearance of your manuscript. Copy your revised and proofread draft carefully, using a typewriter if one is available to you. Follow correct manuscript form (see pages 30–32) or the specific instructions of your teacher. After you recopy, proofread again to locate any accidental errors or omissions.

EXERCISE 33. **Preparing Your Composition.** Prepare a final version of your revised and proofread expository composition. Proofread again after copying the final version.

### CHAPTER 4 WRITING REVIEW 1

Select and limit a topic of your own for an expository composition. Then, referring to the guidelines below, write an expository composition on this topic. Be sure to refer to the revision chart on pages 119–20 and to the Guidelines for Proofreading on page 29.

### CHAPTER 4 WRITING REVIEW 2

Select an expository essay you have written in one of your other classes, such as history or science. Evaluate this essay, using the guidelines on page 117; then revise it by referring to the revising chart on pages 119–20. Be prepared to discuss how what you have learned about expository compositions specifically applies to the writing you do in all your school subjects.

## GUIDELINES FOR WRITING EXPOSITORY COMPOSITIONS

***Prewriting***

1. Select a topic you know about and in which you are interested.
2. Limit the topic so that you can discuss it specifically and thoroughly in the space available.
3. Gather information on your topic, asking yourself what someone unfamiliar with this topic might need or want to know about it.
4. Identify any technical terms or unusual words that need to be explained in your composition.
5. Carefully organize the information you gather. Keep in mind your expository purpose; then group and arrange related ideas and details into a topic outline. Use this outline to draft a thesis statement that indicates the specific purpose of your composition.

***Writing***

6. Write an introductory paragraph that arouses your audience's interest and clearly indicates the composition's purpose.
7. Refer to your topic outline as you draft the body of the composition. Write separate paragraphs for the main topics and important subtopics in your outline. Support the topic sentence in each paragraph with ideas or details from your outline. Use transitions to connect ideas, both within and between paragraphs.
8. As you write, pay attention to the tone of your writing. Choose words that are appropriate for your particular audience.
9. Write a concluding paragraph that leaves your audience with a strong final impression about your topic.

***Evaluating, Revising, and Proofreading***

10. After writing your first draft, determine if you have included the right kind of information and enough information to meet your purpose and the needs of your audience. Consider whether the arrangement of paragraphs in the body allows a thorough and clear explanation of the topic. Also consider how appropriate your language is for your audience and for the tone you wish to convey. Make any necessary changes in your first draft. Proofread for inaccuracies in spelling, grammar, usage, and mechanics.

CHAPTER 5

# Writing Expository Compositions

## SPECIFIC EXPOSITORY WRITING ASSIGNMENTS

In this chapter you will practice writing four kinds of expository compositions: explanations of complex processes, informal or personal essays, critical reviews, and essays of literary analysis. During the year your teacher may direct you to write any one of these types of exposition. In all cases, the principles of the writing process still apply.

### EXPLANATIONS OF COMPLEX PROCESSES

When you explain how to make or do something or how something works, you are explaining a process. A process explanation can be as simple as how to boil an egg or as complex as how to plan a nutritious meal.

#### Prewriting Hints for Process Explanations

1. ***Select and limit your subject.*** Choose as your subject a process that can be explained in an introduction, three or more paragraphs of explanation, and a conclusion. For example, a subject such as "how to play baseball" cannot be adequately explained in a few paragraphs. The subject can, however, be limited to a more manageable topic: "how to steal bases successfully."

2. ***Identify the audience for whom you are writing.*** Consider your audience when deciding on the complexity of the ideas and of the language that you will use in your explanation.

3. ***Gather sufficient information on your topic.*** Before writing, determine what someone unfamiliar with the process may need to know or may want to know about your topic. Develop lists of ideas and details about your topic, using any one of the information-gathering techniques described in Chapter 1. For a process explanation, the questions about a topic (pages 16–17) are especially useful. Then identify and list each step in the process.

4. ***Organize your information in a logical way.*** Study your list, making sure that everything essential is included and that no unrelated information is given. Review the steps in the process to determine whether they can be divided into groups for treatment in the same paragraph. Using an informal plan or topic outline (page 103), arrange your list in chronological order (page 45). A clear sequence of steps is central to a good process explanation.

5. ***Determine which terms you need to define.*** Be prepared to explain any technical vocabulary to your audience.

6. ***Determine beforehand which materials, supplies, or tools are needed.*** Be prepared to give exact amounts, measurements, etc.

## Writing Process Explanations

The following composition is a process explanation of how to jump-start a car that has a dead battery. Note that the last sentence in the first paragraph is the thesis statement and that the second paragraph describes certain safety measures implied in the thesis statement.

As you read the body of the explanation, notice how the writer has arranged the steps in the process in chronological order, sometimes treating more than one step in the same paragraph. Note also how the writer achieves coherence by using transitional words.

HOW TO JUMP-START YOUR CAR

introduction (two paragraphs)

The time-proven way to start a car with a dead battery is to get a jolt of energy from the live battery of another vehicle. Called "jump-starting," the procedure is effective but potentially dangerous. Here is how to get your car going without risking injury to you or damage to either vehicle.

*thesis statement: presents topic and purpose*

Before you begin, keep the risks in mind. All batteries—maintenance-free (sealed) or not—emit volatile hydrogen which can explode from sparks or flame. Batteries can also cause severe electrical burns, and unsealed batteries may splatter acid. To protect yourself whenever you are working with a car battery, put out cigarettes and remove watches and rings so that current won't flow into the metals and burn your skin. Work gloves and goggles will guard against acid spills. Also be sure to use quality jumper cables made of 8-gauge or heavier (the smaller the number, the heavier the gauge) copper wire at least sixteen feet long. Bargain-priced cables that are lighter gauge or shorter may burn out easily and are not long enough for all car-to-car positions.

*signals preliminary explanation*
*signals additional information*
*explanation*

The first step in jump-starting your car is to position the boosting vehicle as close as possible to the lifeless one—nose to nose or side by side—without the vehicles touching. Next, turn off the ignition switches and accessories in both vehicles, place both transmissions in park or neutral, and apply the parking brakes. Now check to see if the battery caps in both vehicles are tight and level. Then place a damp rag over both sets of caps. Sealed batteries won't have caps, but if there is a glass indicator on top that shows clear or pale yellow instead of green, do not attempt to jump-start, because volatile hydrogen is trapped inside.

*body*
*first step*
*signals transition*
*second step*
*emphasis*
*signals additional check*
*transition*
*next step*
*describes critical condition*

You are now ready to stretch out the cables, untangling the clamps on each end so that they can be connected to the vehicles without coming into contact with each other. Clamp the positive (usually red) jumper cable to the positive terminals on both batteries. Positive terminals are marked "POS" or "(+)." At this stage, be careful that the

*another step*
*next step*
*explanation*
*explanation*

clamps on the negative cable do not touch the positive clamps.

Next, connect one clamp of the ground (negative) jumper cable to the negative terminal of the live battery. This terminal is marked "NEG" or "(-)." Then connect the other negative clamp to a clean unpainted metal part of the lifeless engine. Make sure that the attaching point is separated from the lifeless battery since sparks may fly from the point of attachment.

transition
next step
explanation
another step

Make a final check of the jumper cable connections. If the cables are switched—positive to negative—even momentarily, the electrical systems of both vehicles may be damaged when the engine cranks. Also check to see that the cables won't be hit by moving parts such as fans and pulleys.

cautionary step

After making the recommended checks, start the engine of the boosting vehicle. Then start the lifeless engine. Don't keep the engine cranking for more than 30 seconds; you may burn out the starter motor. If the motor fails to turn over, reconnect the positive cables for better contact and wait a few minutes for the live battery to put some life into the dead one before trying again. Once the dead engine starts, and is idling strongly, disconnect the negative jumper cable from that car and then from the boosting battery. Disconnect the positive jumper cable from both batteries and remove the rags from the cell caps. Your car is now ready to take you wherever you want to go.

refers to preceding paragraph
signals transition
next step
additional steps
emphasis
another step
final steps
concluding sentence



## GUIDELINES FOR EVALUATING PROCESS EXPLANATIONS

Topic

1. Is the topic limited to a process that can be explained adequately in a few paragraphs?

| | |
|---|---|
| Purpose | 2. Does the introduction clearly state what process will be explained in the composition? |
| Coherence | 3. Are the steps in the process presented in chronological order? |
| | 4. Are transitional expressions included to clarify the order of the steps in the process? |
| Word Choice | 5. Are terms that might be unfamiliar to the audience explained appropriately? |
| Topic Development | 6. Is all necessary equipment mentioned and described in specific terms? |

**EXERCISE 1. Writing a Process Explanation.** Use the following suggestions to write a process explanation.

1. Choose a topic suitable for a process explanation, and develop it in an essay of no more than seven paragraphs. A topic should relate to how to make or do something (for example, "how to develop photographs" or "how to break a code") or how something works (for example, "how an electric eye works" or "how hurricanes are tracked"). As you write your first draft, refer to the Prewriting Hints for Process Explanations on pages 124–25 and to the model.
2. Using the Guidelines for Evaluating Process Explanations, (pages 127–28) and the Guidelines for Evaluating Expository Compositions (page 117), identify any problems in your first draft.
3. Referring to the revising chart on pages 26–27, use the four basic revising techniques to improve your first draft.
4. Referring to the Guidelines for Proofreading (page 29), proofread your revised draft for any errors in spelling, punctuation, grammar, and usage.
5. As you write the final draft of your process explanation, follow correct manuscript form (see pages 30–32) or your teacher's specific instructions for this assignment. Before giving your final version to your audience, proofread it once again for any copying errors.

## INFORMAL (PERSONAL) ESSAYS

The informal essay reveals its author's thoughts and feelings on a subject in a personal, informal, and entertaining way. To create interest, the writer often relies on vivid incidents and anecdotes to support the essay's central idea. Because the informal essay is so personal, its organization may be looser than more formal essays. However, the writer of a successful informal essay is careful to develop a main point about the subject and follow a distinct plan set out in the prewriting stage. Otherwise, the essay would ramble, annoying and boring the audience with a jumble of details.

## Prewriting Hints for Informal Essays

1. ***Select and limit your subject.*** Choose an event, object, person, or idea that strongly interests or affects you. Determine exactly what leads you to think or feel as you do about the subject; then limit your subject to that area. For example, if you take great pride or pleasure in owning your car, ask yourself what it is that gives you those feelings. Do you enjoy the freedom that owning a car gives you? The admiration of your friends? The pleasure and sense of accomplishment you get from fixing up the engine? You could choose one or two of these aspects to focus your topic—"the joy of driving a car you have rebuilt yourself."

2. ***Gather sufficient information on your topic.*** Jot down specific incidents, descriptions, anecdotes, and other details that illustrate or explain your feelings. For the sample topic above, you might compare how the engine ran before and after it was rebuilt, describe the security you feel knowing that your car will now run reliably, or relate an anecdote of how someone laughed at your car before but now offers compliments.

3. ***Organize your information in a logical plan.*** Order your specific reasons and details in a sequence that will catch and hold your audience's attention. Start with a humorous, surprising, or otherwise engaging event or description; then bring in your personal response(s), and show how you formed or changed your stance due to the incidents and other details that you use to present your topic.

4. ***Decide upon an appropriate tone.*** As you choose the tone for your essay, make sure that it is appropriate to your subject. The tone that you would use to tell of your clumsiness on your first date is not the same tone you would use to write about your commitment to a cause or your sorrow at the loss of a pet.

5. ***Make sure that your audience can follow your discussion and will find it interesting.*** Do not assume that your audience is as familiar with or interested in your topic as you are. Be certain that you have provided all necessary information and that you will be able to link it together in a coherent, entertaining way. Before you begin writing, ask yourself:

Would I find this essay interesting if it were expressing someone else's views and experiences? If you would not, change your plan and keep changing it until you are confident that your essay will appeal to your audience.

## Writing Informal Essays

The following informal essay is one in which the author, Russell Baker, discusses his experience with cuisine, by presenting a humorous, tongue-in-cheek discussion that pokes fun at both himself and "New York cuisine veterans." As you read the essay, note how Baker develops the subject and his opinion about it, first stated in the introductory paragraph, by recounting personal experiences. Notice how the casual tone, humorous anecdotes, and specific examples of cuisine detail his change of attitude toward his subject. Also note how Baker concludes with an absurd recipe that clinches this humorous essay.

ENJOY YOUR INNARDS

One of the many delightful things we do in New York is eat cuisine. I recommend it to everybody. *introduction*

When I first moved here I still ate food, even though people all around me were eating cuisine. In this I was trying to remain loyal to my roots back home, where my folks had eaten food for generations. *language conveys casual tone*

When I told them I was moving to New York, they took it hard. "I guess when you come back you won't be eating food any more," Aunt Phyllis said. "You'll be eating that there cuisine." *anecdote*

"Don't you believe it, Aunt Phyllis," I said. "You can take the boy out of the country, but you can't make him eat cuisine."

"Don't go up there talking like a hick," Aunt Phyllis said. "If you must spout clichés, at least get them right. That one goes, 'You can take a gentleman out of the country, but you can't take the country out of a gentleman.'"

Anyhow, I came to New York predisposed against cuisine. People would phone and say, "Will you come to dinner?" and I would say, "What are *anecdote* you going to serve?" and they'd say, "Just a little perfectly exquisite cuisine," and I'd say, "Thanks, but I've got something to do that night."

Naturally, I couldn't hold out forever. One night the people downstairs invited me in and served something I just couldn't get enough of. "What is this stuff?" I asked.

"Braised capers," came the answer. "That's what we call cuisine."

I was hooked. If that was what cuisine tasted like, the folks back home could have their food. Before long I was just as excited about new cuisine developments as the most hardened New Yorker.

When news came that Fenélon, the chef at Jeté la Plume à Nez, had finally succeeded in producing a butterfly crepe that, when pierced with a knife, emitted dozens of brilliant little butterflies to share your feast, I stood in line like everybody else to experience the ultimate in what the newspaper intestinal supplements quickly dubbed "la cuisine de la cuisine." anecdote

I didn't even complain when the butterflies ate almost all of my crepe before I could get a fork into it. Later I learned that's how this dish was supposed to work. The butterflies eat the crepe, then the diner eats the butterflies.

By the time I learned that, though, Fenélon had been arrested on a warrant obtained by the Society for the Prevention of Cruelty to Animals.

When I wrote to Aunt Cassie about this beautiful dish, she wrote back asking where the butterflies came from. It shows how out of touch people can get when they spend their lives eating food instead of cuisine, because the butterflies come from the same place almost 90 percent of all cuisine comes from: abroad.

I used to think it was silly having to eat things like *chanterelles, foie gras, chervil, tortellini, canard* specific examples *au fruits de mer, fromage mit caraway seeds* and *beige strudel mit die Tür aufgemacht, schwein*! But that was just because they were hard to pronounce, and the reason they were hard to pronounce, of course, was that they came from abroad.

They were imported, just like Japanese cars. I figured everything had to be imported or it couldn't qualify as real cuisine.

Now, of course, I know better. I can have a dozen New York cuisine veterans in to dinner and serve them rutabaga Wellington basted with ball-park mustard and every one of them will phone next day to get my recipe. This is because there also exists something called "la cuisine Americano," which requires no imports whatever.

I am not saying that cuisine will be everybody's cup of tea. Or pound of salad sprinkled liberally with ground goat cheese, if I may shift to cuisine metaphor. What I do say, though, is that if you don't eat cuisine you're going to have a hard time making conversation in New York, because New Yorkers talk about their eating the way most people talk about their tax shelters, and unless you can talk of some new trick for pampering intestines, you're not going to get much of an audience in New York.

Right now, for example, I am about to cook Immelman with pineapple slices and Moroccan oasis water, which, interestingly enough, is a dish that can be cooked successfully only over a bed of live coals on which two swamis have slept for a month of Sundays. First, however, the Immelman must be shaved with a straight razor, be stuffed with seared upholstery springs and marinated overnight in— conclusion

Well, you get the idea. It gives you a lot to talk about while the stomach juices are finishing their work.

—RUSSELL BAKER

## GUIDELINES FOR EVALUATING INFORMAL ESSAYS

| | |
|---|---|
| Purpose | 1. Does the introductory paragraph state the thesis and attract the audience's attention? |
| Tone | 2. Is the tone appropriate for the subject and audience? |
| Coherence | 3. Is the central idea developed in a logical way that also keeps the audience's interest? |
| Topic Development | 4. Do specific details, incidents, or examples support personal views and opinions? |
| Word Choice | 5. Are incidents, anecdotes, and examples described in vivid language? |

**EXERCISE 2. Writing an Informal Essay.** Use the following suggestions to write an informal essay.

1. Choose a suitable topic, and develop it in an informal essay 300–500 words long. Examples of possible topics include "daydreams," "getting up in the morning," and "my favorite time-wasters." Before you begin writing, review the Prewriting Hints for Informal Essays and the model above.
2. Using the Guidelines for Evaluating Informal Essays on this page and the Guidelines for Evaluating Expository Compositions (page 117), read your first draft to identify areas that need improving. Also, ask a friend, relative, or classmate to read your draft and indicate where changes might be made.
3. Use the revising chart on pages 26–27 and the four revision strategies to revise your first draft.
4. Consult the Guidelines for Proofreading (page 29) as you proofread your revised draft for errors in spelling, punctuation, grammar, and usage.
5. Follow correct manuscript form (see pages 30–32) or your teacher's specific instructions to prepare the final draft of your informal essay. Before submitting your final draft to your audience, proofread again to catch any copying errors.

## CRITICAL REVIEWS

Critical reviews are written about books, films, television programs, recordings, paintings, and all forms of creative work. The critical review informs its audience about a work so that they can determine if the work would appeal to them. Your critical review should include (1) a brief, objective summary of the work's subject, central theme, or story line, (2) a discussion of the work's major points or elements, and (3) your subjective judgment of how successfully the work accomplishes its main purpose. The reviewer's evaluation may be favorable or unfavorable; often it is a mixture of both, finding fault with some aspects of the work and praising others.

## Prewriting Hints for Critical Reviews

1. ***Identify and limit your subject.*** Begin your objective analysis by classifying the work according to one or more categories, such as *subject matter* (fiction, nonfiction, symphony, etc.), *medium* (novel, television series, oil painting, etc.), *genre* (mystery, situation comedy, portrait, etc.), and *audience* (children, attorneys, antique collectors, etc.). Next, briefly summarize the work's central topic or story line by noting the work's main sections or scenes. Limit the summary to not more than a third of your review.

2. ***Gather sufficient information on your topic.*** Familiarize yourself completely with the work you are reviewing. Reread all or part of a book, watch several episodes of a television series, or listen to a recording a number of times. Take note of specific quotes, incidents, and other details that express or support what you will say in your review. Identify major points and elements of the work by asking yourself: What elements of the work are repeated? What elements are given the most space or time? What elements are emphasized by the characters or by the work's creator(s)?

3. ***Organize your information in a logical plan.*** Order the summary notes you made, following the organization of the work itself. Then organize the major points or elements of the work according to their order of appearance, their order of importance, or their interrelationships. Next, evaluate the work's strengths, weaknesses, and overall effectiveness. When evaluating elements, state how they singly or as a group affect the general effectiveness or enjoyment of the work. To arrive at an overall evaluation, ask yourself: Why is the work worthwhile or of little value? Why would I recommend or not recommend this work to someone else? Remember always to give specific information from the work itself to support your evaluations and opinions.

4. ***Give your audience an accurate representation of the work.*** Include in your review all important elements of the work, and be careful to give

them proper emphasis so that you do not distort the work's content, style, or theme.

5. ***Describe any special features of the work.*** Mention any distinctive methods of presentation that would affect the audience's enjoyment or use of the work. In a film, these methods might include the use of music to heighten dramatic effect, or the mixing of color and black-and-white photography to indicate changes in time or mood. Some of the special features that a book might offer include bibliographies, footnotes, maps or diagrams, and illustrations.

6. ***Give your individual response to the work.*** Avoid simple statements of whether you liked or disliked the work. Be specific about why you found the work enjoyable or boring, worthwhile or of little value. Avoid overstatement, and use specific facts, quotes, and information from your summary and discussion of the work's main elements to support your evaluation. Give your honest appraisal of the work in a short, reasoned discussion.

## Writing Critical Reviews

Notice that each of the following critical reviews is preceded by the work's title. Book reviews also give the author's name and often include the publisher, publishing date, and the cost of the book. Reviews of television programs may include the names of the starring cast, the station that carries the program, the day and time it appears, and whether it is a series, movie, or special program.

In the review of *Smith and Other Events,* the reviewer begins by praising the book, giving specific reasons for his comments, and comparing the book's author to two highly respected short story writers. By referring to these two famous writers, the reviewer indicates not only the quality of the stories being reviewed, but also the nature of their content and style, so that the audience learns a great deal about *Smith and Other Events* in a short section of the review.

In the paragraphs that follow, the reviewer includes specific quotes and major scenes from the stories as he praises them. Notice in the fourth paragraph that the reviewer refers to a famous story, "Leiningen and the Ants," which is also highly regarded. This comparison is included to suggest the quality and content of the story being reviewed. In the concluding paragraph the reviewer discusses his personal response, informing the audience that the stories range in emotion: in them there is both humor and sadness.

SMITH AND OTHER EVENTS

By Paul St. Pierre

title

author

Not since Mark Twain or the early Bret Harte have you run into a writer of short stories this good, this evocative of a lost time and dimly recollected events, with echoes pulling at memory long after the reading's done. You become nostalgic for a place you've never seen. If those are marks of high craftmanship then Canadian author St. Pierre earns them in highest measure.

introduction

description of stories

evaluation of author

Imagine Chilcotin county in British Columbia some thirty to forty years ago, a place of pine forests, deer and moose, ranches providing the scantiest of bare necessities, and peopled by marvelously strange inhabitants. All of them are touched, sometimes lightly but always lovingly, by the magical hands of this author, may he live a hundred years.

body

subject of stories

evaluation of author

There are tales torn from the depths of human emotion and delivered up fresh and full of meaning. An Indian woman in modern Vancouver destroys a priceless ancient artifact just being bought from her for a sum that would return her husband's truck from police impound. And you cheer her all the way.

evaluation of stories

specific stories cited to support evaluation

A loner named Stettler fights a battle against hostile weather even as the much-anthologized Leiningen fought his ants—Stettler, too, wins, but having had to turn at the last to others for help, feels he's betrayed himself.

Incisive phrase and humor abound. There are "children who, like the old machinery, were repaired at home when ailing." Or Miss O'Day, a grey little political secretary: " . . . there was a rumor in the Jamieson building that at night Miss O'Day did not have a home to go to, but instead scurried up and down the dark corridors, nibbling bits of cheese left from people's lunches . . ."

specific quotes support evaluation of major element

Or a school inspector: "He didn't look like much, that was for sure: old, wrinkled as a raisin, pale as a maggot. He was crowding retirement . . . a year to go. I wouldn't have laid money on him making it. To me, he looked to be good for about one more clean shirt."

If, when at school, you were ever the victim of another child's thoughtless cruelty, the story of the little Indian girl in a white classroom will open all kinds of boxes long since sealed in the attic of your mind. About this story, and indeed about all of this superb collection, as one of St. Pierre's people might put it, I laughed a lot, and cried some. — conclusion; reviewer's response

A.B. [ARNOLD BERMAN] reviewer's initials

The subject of the next critical review is *The Cosby Show,* a situation comedy series on television. Notice how the reviewer grabs his audience's attention and leads them to continue reading by quoting a specific, shocking line of the program's dialogue. In the paragraphs that follow, the reviewer cites specific scenes from several episodes to illustrate what he feels are the program's humor, realistic themes, and circumstances. Notice also that the reviewer points out faults in the program, even though he praises it overall. The reviewer's opinions are not collected in a single paragraph or two but, instead, are spread throughout the review in paragraphs that include supporting evidence from the program.

THE COSBY SHOW — program title

Review by Robert MacKenzie — reviewer's name

"Son, your mother asked me to come up here and kill you." — specific dialogue presents theme and main character

Bill Cosby gets everything into the line: the slightly absurd business of dispensing parental authority, the balancing act of being a father and a husband, the touchy and funny relations between kids and grown-ups.

Cosby is one of the rare comedians who age well, who manage to get wiser without getting — discussion of starring actor sadder. In his stand-up act he keeps drawing fresh material from that bottomless source, his childhood; he has never forgotten what it's like to be a kid. But he also draws on parenthood, marriage, and middle age for material.

subjects of episodes

All the Cosby themes are percolating in this NBC series (currently being shown Thursdays at 8 P.M., ET), and some of the writing seems to show his touch. His deadpan acting style has reached perfection. In my view this is the best new show of the season.

station and time

reviewer's response

Cosby plays an obstetrician married to a pretty lawyer (Phylicia Ayers-Allen Rashad), with five kids. Cosby's character is a conservative type. When his teen-age daughter, Denise (Lisa Bonet), in tight pants, announced she was going out for the evening, Cosby said, "Not in those. Blood can't get up to your brain."

description of main character

specific scene supports description

There's no talk about love in this show, nor much embracing to provide cheap cues for the audience to say, "Aww." But Cosby's character is a loving guy, trying to pick his way through the intricate negotiations of family life without hurting anyone's feelings. Watch him try to explain to his littlest daughter, Rudy (Keshia Knight Pulliam), that her goldfish is dead. In one story, there was a scene every husband knows about. Cosby's wife demanded he sit down and listen to her for a change. Cosby made a noble effort to pretend he was hanging on every word, while his beeper interrupted with emergency messages.

major theme

specific scenes that illustrate theme

When teen-age son Theo (Malcolm-Jamal Warner) decided he intended to skip college, get a job and be "like regular people," Cosby pointed out that the most he could expect to earn was $1200 a month. Handing the kid $1200 in play money, he immediately took back $350 for taxes. "The Government comes for the regular people first." Then he took $400 for apartment rent, and continued extracting money for the usual expenses. "You plan to have a girlfriend?" When Theo said yes, Cosby snatched the remainder of the money.

The child actors are appealing enough, but, as is common with kids, they garble some of the dialogue. Ayers-Allen Rashad as the wife is attractive but not especially interesting. Cosby doesn't need a comedienne to play against, but there should be more snap in their scenes together.

evaluation of supporting cast

What makes the show is Cosby's feel for everyday life and his inability to fall into television clichés. In one episode Theo was doing badly in school and Cosby kept prodding him to do better. Finally the boy said poignantly, in one of those sitcom moments of truth, "Maybe you should accept and love me as I am because I'm your son." In any other show that would have been the signal for tearful hugs. Cosby just let a beat pass, then said glumly, "Theo, that's the dumbest thing I've heard in my whole life."

program evaluation

specific scenes cited to support evaluation

## GUIDELINES FOR EVALUATING CRITICAL REVIEWS

| | |
|---|---|
| Purpose | 1. Does the review accurately summarize the work's subject, main thesis, or story line? |
| Topic Development | 2. Does the review go into sufficient detail about the work so that the audience can understand what the work is about? |
| | 3. Are the work's main strengths and weaknesses analyzed? |
| | 4. Are the reviewer's evaluations and opinions supported by specific evidence taken from the work itself? |
| Purpose | 5. Does the review offer evaluations of the work that would help the audience determine its worth and appeal? |
| Emphasis | 6. Is the summary limited to not more than one third of the essay, leaving sufficient space for evaluation and supporting information? |
| Background Information | 7. Does the review give the title and other helpful background information about the work? |

**EXERCISE 3. Writing a Critical Review.** Use the following suggestions to write a critical review.

1. Choose a work and write a critical review of it 350–500 words long. You can select a work from any of the following categories: a nonfiction book, a novel or collection of short stories, a film, a television program, a recording, a painting, or a music video. Before you begin writing, review the Prewriting Hints for Critical Reviews and the models above.
2. Consult the Guidelines for Evaluating Critical Reviews on page 139 and the Guidelines for Evaluating Expository Compositions on page 117 to identify where changes are needed in your draft. Ask a friend or relative to read your draft and make suggestions for improving your essay.
3. Revise your draft, using the revising chart on pages 26–27 to improve content, organization, and style.
4. Refer to the Guidelines for Proofreading (page 29) to check your revised draft for errors in spelling, punctuation, grammar, and usage. Pay special attention to the use of quotation marks and of other marks of punctuation with them.
5. Follow correct manuscript form (see pages 30–32) or your teacher's directions to prepare your final draft. Before submitting your review to your audience, carefully proofread your final draft to check for copying errors.

## ESSAYS OF LITERARY ANALYSIS

The purpose of writing an essay of literary analysis is to broaden understanding and appreciation of the work being studied. Analyzing and writing about a literary work will lead you to discover much about its meaning and about the literary techniques that are used in it. By reading your essay, your audience shares in the knowledge you have discovered.

Before you begin a literary analysis, become familiar with major literary elements, such as theme, imagery, symbolism, and point of view. Also consider the individual elements that apply to the type of work you are analyzing. In fiction you would consider plot, character, and dialogue, while in poetry you need to know about meter, rhyme scheme, figurative language, and other poetic elements.

Remember to apply the rules that govern any well-written composition to your essay of literary analysis. Open with an introductory paragraph that states the work's author and title and a clearly defined thesis. Next, develop two or three body paragraphs that analyze the work and support your thesis. Then close with a paragraph that summarizes your analysis and suggests further implications.

## Prewriting Hints for Essays of Literary Analysis

1. ***Identify and limit your subject.*** To focus your subject into a topic, identify categories that apply to the work you are analyzing, and then ask questions within these categories. The literary elements that apply to your work is one category that always needs examining. For a short story, ask yourself: What is the main conflict faced by the protagonist? What does the dialogue reveal about the characters?

Apply categories from other fields of knowledge to your work. You could draw from history. For example, how are the characters' actions typical of a particular era? How does a historical setting affect the story's action? You could ask psychological questions. For example, are any characters mentally unbalanced, and if so, how does this condition affect the plot? Do any themes develop psychological insights about human behavior?

You can focus your topic by asking questions of it from nearly any category of human activity. Using more than one category will quickly limit and focus your topic. For example, you could explore how a story's setting (literary category) portrays a climate of fear (psychological category) that turns into anarchy (political category). Specific topics can sometimes stem from concerns or questions you may have about the author's ideas or techniques. Be alert to topics suggested by textbook exercises and study guides or by class discussions. Be certain that you can find sufficient information within the literary work to develop your topic.

2. ***Gather sufficient information on your topic.*** Reread or look back over the work, closely examining the plot, theme, imagery, rhyme scheme, and other literary elements. Search for and write down all ideas, quotations, and details that relate to specific aspects of your topic. Keep collecting information until you have enough to develop your topic thoroughly. Be sure to place quotation marks before and after all word-for-word quotations taken from the work. If you quote two successive lines of poetry, place a slash (/) where one line ends and the next begins.

3. ***Organize your information in a logical plan.*** Group your details, quotations, and other information under the defining features of your

topic. For example, if you were going to analyze how the setting of a work depicted an atmosphere of fear that grew into anarchy, you would group information under *setting, fear,* and *anarchy.* Some quotations and details may fall into more than one grouping; others will not fit in anywhere. Keep in mind those that belong to more than one group; they may provide a good place for a transition between paragraphs later when you write your essay. Set aside, but do not discard, information that does not fit in; you may need it later.

Study your groups and look for relationships between them. One common relationship that you could use to analyze the work is comparison-contrast, which is based upon similarities and differences between separate items and groups. (For further discussion of comparison-contrast, see pages 50–51.) Your groups could also be linked together by cause and effect, time sequence, or process of development.

Examine each relationship you find between your topic and information. What do these relationships reveal about the work that will increase your and your audience's knowledge and appreciation of the work? State your insight in one sentence, which will be the thesis for your essay. If your thesis or topic only summarizes, but does not analyze the work, reorganize your information.

4. ***Consider your audience's familiarity with the work.*** If your audience is familiar with the work you are analyzing, you do not need to provide any summary of it. Simply provide a reference and quote from the work at appropriate points in your discussion. If your audience is not familiar with the work, offer a brief summary of its main elements, such as its theme, figurative language, setting, and other significant components. Place the summary in a short paragraph just after the introduction. You may also need to summarize additional information at specific points within your analysis to clarify your point(s), but keep the summarizing to a minimum.

5. ***Support your analysis with specific information from the work.*** Make sure that you give specific details and quotations from the work to support each point that you make in your analysis. Whenever you use a direct quotation, copy it accurately and completely from the work and enclose it in quotation marks. Be sure all quotations fit smoothly and correctly into your text. (See pages 632–34 for more information about using direct quotations in a composition.)

## Writing Essays of Literary Analysis

Read the following poem:

THE SILKEN TENT

She is as in a field a silken tent
At midday when a sunny summer breeze
Has dried the dew and all its ropes relent,
So that in guys it gently sways at ease,
And its supporting central cedar pole,
That is its pinnacle to heavenward
And signifies the sureness of the soul,
Seems to owe naught to any single cord,
But strictly held by none, is loosely bound
By countless silken ties of love and thought
To everything on earth the compass round,
And only by one's going slightly taut
In the capriciousness of summer air
Is of the slightest bondage made aware.

ROBERT FROST

Begin analyzing this poem by reading it a number of times, both silently and aloud, to become familiar with its content and technique. Look up meanings of any unfamiliar words; for example, the word *guys* in line four means "ropes or rods attached to something to secure or steady it." As you examine this poem, you might notice that it is an extended simile, comparing a woman and a silk tent. You could decide to explicate—make a line-for-line examination of—this simile to discover its main points of comparison, the author's purpose in developing it, and its effectiveness. To organize your explication, make a chart of significant elements of the poem and your thoughts about them, perhaps in this way:

POINTS OF COMPARISON BETWEEN THE TENT AND THE WOMAN

| *The Tent* | *The Woman* |
|---|---|
| Silken tent is in a field at midday in summer. | Silk suggests beauty, softness, elegance. |
| A breeze is blowing (lines 1–2). | |
| Dew has evaporated (line 3). | |
| The ropes ("guys") that anchor tent to ground slacken (line 3). | |
| The tent sways gently in breeze (line 4). | Gentle movements suggest grace. |
| The tent is held up by a cedar pole in the center (line 5). | Cedar, a fragrant and durable wood, suggests strength and loveliness. |

| | |
|---|---|
| The pole points "to heavenward" (line 6). | The woman has strong convictions. She looks toward heaven and has "sureness of the soul" (line 7). |
| Pole doesn't depend on any individual rope but is held loosely by all (lines 8–9). | The woman has not one tie but "countless" ties of affection and concern (line 10).<br>She is bound to earth by "silken ties of love and thought" (line 10). |
| Pole responds when any of the ropes go taut (line 12). | She is pulled toward those who need her. |
| Tent appears to move freely in the breeze but is actually held by the ropes (lines 12–14). | The woman appears to be free, yet she has many bonds to those she loves. |

### *Form of the Poem*

Entire poem consists of a single sentence.
Poem is an English sonnet: *abab cdcd efef gg*—three quatrains and a couplet.
Form is well suited to subject matter. It requires adherence to a fixed pattern while it allows poet considerable freedom of phrasing.
Line 8 varies from metrical pattern—begins with a trochee.
Line 13 has four stresses only.
Sibilant sounds in opening lines emphasize softness: *she, is, as, silken, sunny, summer, breeze.*
Alliteration is used for euphony and emphasis: *signifies, sureness, soul* (line 7).
Subject in line 1 is completed by the predicate in line 14.
Poem gains intensity as it moves toward the final line.

As you review these charts, you might conclude that Frost seems to discuss freedom and personal ties to others in human relationships. You could use this insight as a tentative topic and then analyze your charts to determine if you could write a thesis statement for your essay. Your analysis might lead you to the more specific conclusion that Frost uses the comparison between the woman and the tent to show that individual strength and freedom are gained through personal ties to others. This conclusion would provide a suitable thesis under which you could organize your information into three main groups: the use of an extended simile, characteristics that the woman and tent share, and the function of the poem's form. After assigning specific details and quotations to these headings, you could go on to write your essay, such as the one that follows. Notice how the writer develops a topic sentence about each group and then uses specific details to support each point.

FREEDOM AND PERSONAL COMMITMENT
IN "THE SILKEN TENT"

title

In "The Silken Tent," Robert Frost draws an extended comparison between a tent in a summer breeze and a woman who has numerous close ties to others. Through this comparison, Frost reveals how a person is strongest and most free when bound by personal commitments.

introduction

thesis

The poem consists of an extended simile developing a comparison between a silken tent and a woman. The tent Frost asks us to visualize is circular ("the compass round") and is supported in the center by a cedar pole, which is kept in place by ropes ("guys") anchored to the ground. At midday, when the dew has evaporated, the ropes slacken. The "sunny summer breeze" causes the ropes and the silk fabric to sway gently. The central pole is not held by "any single cord." Instead, it is "loosely bound" so that it responds to the tug of any of the guy-ropes, which go "slightly taut" when the tent is stirred by the "capriciousness of summer air."

body

topic sentence

specific supporting details and quotations summarize important points of comparison

The characteristics of the tent are intended to parallel the qualities of the woman. Silk is often associated with beauty, softness, elegance, while the gentle swaying of the tent suggests feminine grace. The central pole of the tent is made of cedar, a fragrant, durable wood that is known for its strength as well as for its loveliness. Lines 6–7 add a spiritual dimension to the image as well. The woman's spiritual strength, her "sureness of soul," looks "to heavenward," just as the center pole is still "loosely bound" to the earth "By countless silken ties of love and thought/To everything on earth the compass round." In other words, she is bound to a great many people by

specific quotations given to support thesis and develop topic affection and concern. In the same way that the wind in its "capriciousness" pulls the ropes taut on the tent, so the woman is pulled toward those who need her.

topic sentence

The form of the poem is well suited to its subject matter. In the opening lines of the poem, Frost suggests feminine softness through the alliteration of sibilant sounds: *sh*e, i*s*, a*s*, *s*ilken, *s*unny, *s*ummer, bree*z*e. In line 7, this same form of alliteration links the key words *s*ignifie*s*, *s*urene*ss*, and *s*oul. The poem is an English sonnet, which follows a fixed pattern while still allowing the poet considerable freedom of expression. In this way the poem itself is like the woman and the tent that are fixed by personal ties and ropes but at the same time are "loosely bound" as well. The entire poem is a single sentence that gathers force as the subject, "silken tent," in line 1 is completed by the predicate in the last line. By making the poem a single sentence, Frost combines the ideas of freedom and restraint in one statement just as real freedom and restraint are combined in the tent and in the woman.

analysis of poem's form

interpretation suggested by analysis of form

interpretation suggested by analysis of form

Frost is able to make his unusual comparison work because he shows many symbolic points of resemblance between the lady and the silken tent. The tent provides a powerful visual image for the woman's "sureness of soul" that is held secure by "silken ties of love and thought." Through this specific image the poem offers the insight that a person gains spiritual strength and freedom from commitments to others. As this insight suggests, freedom does not result from a total absence of restraints but, instead, from those that offer "the slightest bondage."

insight revealed by analysis of poem

## GUIDELINES FOR EVALUATING ESSAYS OF LITERARY ANALYSIS

| | |
|---|---|
| Purpose | 1. Does the introduction contain the author's name, the work's title, and a thesis statement? |
| Thesis Development | 2. Does the thesis analyze, not merely summarize, some aspect of the work? |
| Topic Development | 3. Is the thesis supported by several paragraphs of convincing, thorough literary analysis in the body of the essay? |
| | 4. Is each idea in the analysis supported by specific details and quotations from the work? |
| Quotations | 5. Are all quotations enclosed in quotation marks and given as they appeared in the work? |
| Conclusion | 6. Does the conclusion present a summary of the literary analysis and also offer a further understanding or implication of the thesis? |
| Background Information | 7. Is any necessary summary or explanatory information included which the audience might need to follow the literary analysis in the essay? |

**EXERCISE 4. Writing an Essay of Literary Analysis.** Use the following suggestions to write an essay of literary analysis.

1. Write an essay of literary analysis on a novel, short story, drama, or poem of your choice. Before you begin writing, review the Prewriting Hints for Essays of Literary Analysis on pages 141–42 and the model above.
2. Evaluate your draft using the guidelines on this page and the Guidelines for Evaluating Expository Compositions discussed in Chapter 4 (page 117). Read your essay several times, looking at content, organization, and style.
3. Use the four revision strategies and the revising chart on pages 26–27 to improve your first draft.
4. Use the Guidelines for Proofreading (page 29) to check the spelling, punctuation, grammar, and usage in your draft. Pay special attention to the correct use of quotation marks.
5. Follow correct manuscript form (see pages 30–32) or your teacher's directions when you write the final draft of your essay. Proofread your essay again before submitting it to your audience to catch any recopying errors.

CHAPTER 6

# Clear Thinking

## REASONING AND LOGIC

Writing down your ideas for someone else to read is an excellent test of the clarity of your thinking. Faulty reasoning is much more noticeable in writing than in speech, because when readers are confused or unconvinced, they can go back over your words, carefully inspecting your train of thought. If your writing is to withstand this close scrutiny, you must constantly challenge your reasoning.

Clear reasoning is especially important in persuasive writing. Some kinds of writing allow you to wander freely from one idea or image to another. Persuasive writing, however, requires you to construct an argument, an orderly sequence of ideas. To do so, you must follow the rules of *logic,* the science of correct reasoning.

In this chapter you will study the two basic types of reasoning: inductive and deductive. You will also learn to identify some common *fallacies,* or errors, in logical reasoning.

### INDUCTIVE REASONING

When you think inductively, you begin by observing a number of specific, concrete pieces of evidence. Then you arrive at a conclusion that, based on your evidence, is probably true. The more evidence you have collected, the more likely it is that your conclusion is true.

## The Argument from Analogy

The most common type of inductive reasoning—one we all use every day—is the *argument from analogy*. This form of reasoning compares two things and concludes that because they are similar in many respects, it is likely that they will also be similar in an as-yet-undemonstrated respect. For example, Marty reads that a new comedy-adventure movie has the same director and the same leading actor as an earlier movie which he enjoyed. Therefore, he decides to go see the new movie.

Reasoning from analogy can never *prove* that a conclusion is true, however. Marty must make what logicians call "the inductive leap" between his evidence and his conclusion. He won't know whether he will enjoy the movie until he sees it. For an argument based on analogy to be convincing, there must be *enough* similarities between the things compared, and the similarities must be *relevant.* You cannot conclude that George probably plays chess as well as Tony based on the evidence that they both work at the burger place and both wear glasses.

## Scientific Induction

**6a. Use scientific induction to make a generalization based on a number of specific observations.**

Scientific induction is the method used by scientists to draw conclusions based on experiments and measurements. It is also the form of thinking we all use whenever we characterize a group of persons or things based on our observations. Scientific induction involves three steps:

1. Gather many specific pieces of evidence, and record your observations.
2. Look carefully at the evidence.
3. Make a generalization about the entire group from which your examples were drawn, taking into account all of your evidence.

Suppose, for example, that you were visiting the earth for the first time and that you tried to grow various kinds of plants outdoors and in a dark cave. You might gather the following facts:

EVIDENCE A patch of grass needs light in order to grow.
A marigold plant needs light in order to grow.
A daisy plant needs light in order to grow.
A patch of clover needs light in order to grow.
A willow tree needs light in order to grow.

A stalk of corn needs light in order to grow.
An oak tree needs light in order to grow.
A pine tree needs light in order to grow.

After examining these observations, you might reach the following conclusion:

GENERALIZATION All plants need light in order to grow.

To make this generalization (or to draw any conclusion by inductive reasoning), it is necessary to make the inductive leap from your evidence to your conclusion. It would be impractical, if not impossible, to prove your conclusion by testing every single plant on earth. The following guidelines will help you to decide when you have enough evidence:

**(1) A generalization must be based on sufficient evidence.**

One or two observations are not enough to support a generalization; a thousand are probably more than necessary. As a rule, though, the more supportive evidence you can gather, the more likely it is that your generalization will be sound.

**(2) The evidence must be drawn from a random sampling of the population.**

When you gather evidence, you are collecting samples (specific observations) from the population (the group) you are studying. Suppose, for example, that you want to learn what students at your school think about a certain issue. Instead of interviewing just your friends, who are likely to share similar views, you should sample the population randomly—perhaps by interviewing every tenth person entering the door of the school.

**(3) The generalization must explain all of the evidence.**

If you encounter a piece of evidence that disagrees with your conclusion, you cannot discard that evidence; instead, you must discard your conclusion, or revise it to reflect the new evidence. Sometimes, it will be sufficient to add a qualifier such as "usually," "probably," or "most of those studied." In other situations, you may have to make a major change in your generalization. Suppose, for example, that as you are testing plants, a new piece of evidence shows that mushrooms can grow in a dark cave. This disproves your generalization, but you can revise it to read:

GENERALIZATION All green plants require light to grow.

Now, try your hand at scientific induction. Look carefully at the following evidence, and see what generalization, if any, you can make from it.

EVIDENCE Whenever the weather changes, Helen gets a sinus headache.
Lee's sinuses bother him when it turns cold.
Maria has never had any sinus headaches.
David has sinus problems when the weather changes.
Mr. Washington had a headache for two days last week when it rained.
Tom has two or three sinus infections every winter.
Fran has never had any sinus problems.

On the basis of this evidence, which of the following generalizations is best?

GENERALIZATION

1. Everyone gets sinus headaches when the weather changes.
2. For people who have a history of sinus problems, changes in weather are likely to cause sinus problems.
3. Cold weather causes sinus headaches.
4. Changes in weather cause sinus infections.

Generalization 1 is not sound, because it includes "everyone," and we know that Maria and Fran never have sinus headaches. Similarly, generalizations 3 and 4 do not account for all of the evidence. Only generalization 2 explains all our evidence. It includes both headaches and infections under the broader term "sinus problems"; it restricts itself to people with a history of sinus problems; and it is careful to state only that these people "are likely to" have sinus problems, not that they will have sinus problems.

**EXERCISE 1. Drawing a Conclusion Based on an Analogy.** For each of the following situations, draw a conclusion. If no conclusion can be reached, explain why.

1. You are in the open on the beach on a pleasant August day. All of a sudden, the weather becomes ominous, and the sky, clouds, temperature and wind resemble those present on a day last August when a boy was struck by lightning on this very beach.
2. Jack's blue car has a turbocharged engine, electronic ignition, and a stereo system. I saw one for sale that is exactly like his in all these respects. Jack's car also gets good mileage, and I need a car that gets good mileage. Should I buy the car I saw, based on this evidence?

**EXERCISE 2. Making a Generalization Based on Scientific Induction.** For each of the following situations, write a sound generalization based on the evidence presented. If no sound generalization is possible, explain why. (*Hint:* For some items, many generalizations are possible.)

1. Out of a total school population of 867, 127 randomly-sampled students offered the following opinions about food served in the school cafeteria. The answers are given as percentages of those surveyed.

| | EXCELLENT | GOOD | FAIR | POOR |
|---|---|---|---|---|
| Size of Portions | 4% | 19% | 47% | 30% |
| Variety of Food | 4% | 50% | 35% | 11% |
| Appearance of Food | 8% | 14% | 46% | 32% |
| Taste of Food | 2% | 10% | 52% | 36% |

2. In a nearby shopping mall last Saturday, 225 people interviewed said that they exercise strenuously at least four times a week. Of those 225 people, 8 said that they were currently cigarette smokers, 80 had once smoked cigarettes but had stopped, and 137 had never smoked.

**EXERCISE 3. Outlining an Argument.** Each of the following generalizations is a conclusion arrived at through scientific induction. Tell what evidence you would need to support each generalization. If you disagree with the generalization, reword it to your satisfaction.

1. Men are physically stronger than women.
2. Reading is the most important skill that you can learn while in school.
3. Every home should have a smoke alarm.
4. Left-handed people are more creative than right-handed people.
5. In raising children, rewarding good behavior is more effective than punishing bad behavior.

---

## CRITICAL THINKING:
### Evaluating an Inductive Argument

The argument of a persuasive paper may be based on scientific induction. Use the following guidelines to evaluate this kind of argument.

## GUIDELINES FOR EVALUATING AN ARGUMENT BASED ON SCIENTIFIC INDUCTION

1. What is the conclusion? What evidence is it based on?
2. Is the evidence sufficient? Does it come from a reliable source?
3. Does the generalization explain or reflect all of the evidence? Is the generalization contradicted by some of the evidence?
4. Does the generalization make a universal statement or a limited statement?
5. Does the argument contain any fallacies? (See pages 158–60.)

## DEDUCTIVE REASONING

**6b. Use deductive reasoning to apply a generalization to a specific example.**

### The Syllogism

You have seen that scientific induction begins with specific evidence and moves to a generalization. Deductive thinking reverses this sequence: it begins with a generalization and then moves to a specific example. The generalization and the example form the two premises of the argument, from which a conclusion is drawn. This three-step deductive argument is called a *syllogism*.

| | |
|---|---|
| GENERALIZATION | (*Premise 1*) All planets in our solar system revolve around the sun. |
| SPECIFIC EXAMPLE | (*Premise 2*) The Earth is a planet in our solar system. |
| CONCLUSION | The Earth revolves around the sun. |
| GENERALIZATION | All reptiles are coldblooded. |
| SPECIFIC EXAMPLE | A snake is a reptile. |
| CONCLUSION | A snake is coldblooded. |

The premises in a syllogism do not always have to be scientific facts. When a deductive argument is used in persuasive writing, for example, the first premise (the generalization) is often an opinion:

| | |
|---|---|
| GENERALIZATION | Elderly people are happiest when they are active. |
| SPECIFIC EXAMPLE | Maria Loeb is eighty-three years old. |
| CONCLUSION | Maria Loeb is happiest when she is active. |

Certain rules must be strictly followed in deductive reasoning.

**(1) Both premises in a syllogism must be true.**

Look carefully at the premises in the following syllogisms, and see if you can find the errors.

| | |
|---|---|
| GENERALIZATION | All reptiles are coldblooded. |
| SPECIFIC EXAMPLE | A whale is a reptile. |
| CONCLUSION | A whale is coldblooded. |

| | |
|---|---|
| GENERALIZATION | All high-school students are irresponsible. |
| SPECIFIC EXAMPLE | You are a high-school student. |
| CONCLUSION | You are irresponsible. |

In each of these syllogisms, the conclusion is false because one of its premises is false. A whale is not a reptile; therefore, the conclusion in the first example is false. Neither are all high-school students irresponsible (the generalization in the second example), so the conclusion in the second example is untrue.

**(2) The first premise (generalization) in a syllogism must make a universal statement.**

A universal statement includes (or implies) *all* or *every.* A statement containing a limiting word, such as *some, many,* or *most*, is not universal.

| | |
|---|---|
| UNIVERSAL STATEMENTS | Insects (All insects) have six legs. |
| | Every insect has six legs. |
| LIMITED STATEMENTS | Many (Most, Some) people can swim underwater. |

When the generalization is *not* a universal statement, no logical conclusion is possible.

| | |
|---|---|
| GENERALIZATION | Some eleventh-grade students are taking a computer programming class. |
| SPECIFIC EXAMPLE | Karen Milewski is an eleventh-grade student. |
| CONCLUSION | |

You cannot tell from the information given whether Karen is one of the "some" eleventh-graders who are taking a computer class. A logical conclusion is possible only when the first premise makes a universal statement:

| | |
|---|---|
| GENERALIZATION | All eleventh-grade students are taking a computer programming class. |
| SPECIFIC EXAMPLE | Karen Milewski is an eleventh-grade student. |
| CONCLUSION | Karen Milewski is taking a computer programming class. |

**(3) The second premise (specific example) must be an example of the subject of the first premise.**

What can be concluded from the following premises?

GENERALIZATION All ducks can swim.
SPECIFIC EXAMPLE This bird is a duck.

From this information, we can logically draw a conclusion about "this bird":

CONCLUSION This bird can swim.

However, if the second premise is not a specific example of the *subject* of the first premise (in this case, a duck), we can draw no sound conclusion:

GENERALIZATION All ducks can swim.
SPECIFIC EXAMPLE This bird can swim.

Even though both premises are true, we can draw no conclusion about "this bird." For all we know, it might be a seagull or a pelican.

**EXERCISE 4. Using Deductive Reasoning.** For each of the following syllogisms, write the conclusion. Then tell whether the conclusion is true or false. (*Hint:* For some items, no logical conclusion is possible.) Be prepared to explain your answer.

1. Young children need discipline as well as love.
   Samantha is two years old.
2. All red flowers are roses.
   This hibiscus is a red flower.
3. Every violinist who gets to play at Carnegie Hall has put in years of practice.
   I have put in years of violin practice.
4. Many mothers of preschool children work outside the home.
   Mrs. Lawrence is the mother of two preschool children.
5. It is easier to swim in salt water than fresh water.
   The Atlantic Ocean is salt water; Lake Erie is fresh water.
6. People who participate in sports are much more fun to be with than those who don't participate in sports.
   Gerry is on the basketball team; Ralph does not participate in any sport.
7. Proper adjectives should begin with a capital letter.
   The word *French* is a proper adjective.
8. All eighteen-year-old U.S. citizens may register to vote.
   Lee Ann is eighteen years old and a U.S. citizen.

9. Politicians cannot be trusted.
   Senator X is a politician.
10. All mammals are warmblooded.
    The blue whale is a mammal.

**EXERCISE 5. Writing Syllogisms.** Use the rules of deductive reasoning to write three original syllogisms that reach true conclusions. Be sure that you follow the rules on pages 153–55.

---

## CRITICAL THINKING:
## Evaluating a Deductive Argument

In the preceding pages you learned three of the many rules that govern the logic of deductive reasoning. As you write persuasive compositions and as you read or listen to persuasive arguments, use the following guidelines to determine whether the rules of logic are being followed.

### GUIDELINES FOR EVALUATING A DEDUCTIVE ARGUMENT

1. What are the writer's premises? (Are they clearly stated or only assumed?)
2. Are the premises true? How can I tell if they are true?
3. Does the generalization make a universal statement?
4. What is the author's conclusion?
5. Does the conclusion follow logically from the premises? Is the conclusion true?
6. Does the argument contain any fallacies? (See pages 158–60.)

---

**REVIEW EXERCISE. Analyzing the Reasoning in a Persuasive Article.** As you read the following article, outline the writer's argument. Then answer the questions that follow the article.

SMOKING IS A CRIME AGAINST THE BODY

Suppose you suddenly found out that someone you knew well and long, and loved very much, was gradually but steadily poisoning you.

What a shock this would be, as if the whole earth were coming up to swallow you. What would you do? Call the police? Run away? Or confront the poisoner with your appalling knowledge of the plot?

No greater betrayal can be imagined than this—that [your] mate, or child, or parent, or best friend, was secretly infiltrating your system with an insidious chemical that might not make its deadly effect felt for years.

But if you are smoking cigarettes, you are doing this very same thing to yourself, to the one you know best and love best in the world.

If someone else sprinkled nicotine and other noxious chemicals onto your food and drink, it would be cause for a criminal action, for horror and disbelief.

But when you do it to yourself, it is not seen as a crime, or a betrayal—merely as a form of self-indulgence.

And, in this case, you are not simply hurting, or killing, yourself. You are injuring those nearest you, who love you and need you and want you to live longer.

You have no more "right" to do this to yourself than someone close to you has the right to inflict serious injury to your lungs, your heart, your arteries, and your bloodstream.

It is demonstrably not true that you are not hurting anyone but yourself. You are hurting everyone near you, both personally and socially, for it is also society that pays—and pays billions—for the crippling effects of your self-indulgence.

In past generations, young people were warned that smoking was a "sin" or "immoral." This only incited more of them to steal puffs, because it was excitingly illicit and daring and "grown-up." Millions of youngsters became hooked on this false sophistication.

Now we are smarter. We know that smoking cigarettes is not a moral problem, but a physical and medical one. It is not preachers we need, but health counselors and fitness advisers.

Look upon smoking as a crime against yourself, as a gross violation of your body's integrity. You may think I am writing this for your benefit, but you are wrong. I am writing it principally for myself.

SYDNEY J. HARRIS

1. Is the writer's argument basically an inductive argument or a deductive argument? Explain your answer.
2. Can you find an argument from analogy? An example of scientific induction? A syllogism?
3. Which of the following statements would you say are premises in the writer's argument? (*Hint:* More than two premises are possible.)
   a. It is wrong to harm your body purposely.
   b. Smoking cigarettes harms your body.
   c. People can control whether or not they smoke cigarettes.
   d. It is wrong to injure the people who love you.
   e. Cigarette smoking injures society.
4. Which of these premises are clearly stated in the article? Which ones are not clearly stated?
5. Evaluate each of the statements in question 3. Do you believe that

each statement is true? Explain your answer.
6. State the author's conclusion in your own words. Do you believe that this conclusion is true? Explain your answer.
7. Is the author guilty of any fallacies? (See pages 158–60.)

## ERRORS IN LOGICAL REASONING

**6c. Learn to identify fallacies and to avoid them in your writing.**

An error in reasoning is called a fallacy. An argument that seems to be reasonable may, on close examination, be found to contain an error, so that its conclusion is not supported. Learning to recognize fallacies will help you to think more clearly, to write more convincingly, and to evaluate the logic in what you hear and read. There are over a hundred kinds of fallacies. Here are some of the most common.

### Hasty Generalization

A *hasty generalization* is one that is based on too few or on atypical instances and is therefore unsound.

FAULTY I will never again eat at a Motor Gorge restaurant. Last Saturday afternoon their food was poor and their service was terrible.

FAULTY Don't go fishing at Beaver Lake. My friend went there twice last month and didn't catch a thing.

### Stereotype

The *stereotype* is the fallacy responsible for prejudice. It asserts that all members of a particular group share certain characteristics—usually negative ones.

FAULTY All Scots are quick-tempered.

FAULTY You can't trust anyone over thirty.

### False Cause

This fallacy asserts that one thing has caused another, when in fact it hasn't. One variation of the *false cause* fallacy is called, in Latin, *post hoc, ergo propter hoc* ("[it happened] after this, therefore [it happened] because of this"). Certainly a cause always precedes its effect, but the mere fact that one event happened before another doesn't prove that it caused the second event.

FAULTY Every time I wear my good sweater, it rains. If I wear it Friday night, surely the outdoor concert will be rained out.

FAULTY I didn't do well on the math test in first period because I had French toast for breakfast.

### False Analogy

A *false analogy* is an analogy comparing two things so dissimilar that the argument falls apart and the conclusion is not sound.

FAULTY Taking an honors course is like being forced to eat three full-course dinners every day. You are expected to learn so much that you lose your appetite for learning the subject.

FAULTY Schools are students' homes during the day. Since people should always feel comfortable in their homes, students should have more comfortable chairs to sit in.

**EXERCISE 6. Identifying Fallacies.** Number your paper 1–5. Evaluate the reasoning in each of the following examples. If you find a fallacy, write its name. If you think the reasoning is sound, write OK after the proper number. Be prepared to explain your answers.

1. Don't invite the Smith twins to your party. Twins are always noisy and unfriendly.
2. Students pay to attend this university; they employ it to educate them. Just as the administration gives orders to the faculty it employs, the students should have a voice in how the university conducts their education.
3. A household is like a ship. The parent is captain; the children are crew. There can be only one captain, and a captain's orders must be carried out by the crew; divided authority and crew failure always imperil a ship. Hence, if children misbehave, the family will sink.
4. The plane that crashed at the airport last night had just been completely overhauled. Obviously some mechanic had not done the job properly.
5. It is extremely dangerous to drive in Boston. The one time that I visited there I was involved in an automobile accident.

## Attacking One's Opponent

The Latin title of this fallacy, *argumentum ad hominem,* means "an argument directed to the person" rather than to the point being debated. It offers no proof that the opponent's argument is false, but merely asserts that it must be false because the opponent is a certain kind of person.

FAULTY Senator B's proposal for lower tariffs can't possibly be any good because he's too busy running for reelection to pay any attention to what's going on in the government.

FAULTY I don't see why we should pay any attention to what you have to say about the proposed reforms in student government. We all know you're only interested in power for yourself.

## Either-or Fallacy

Thinking of a situation as having only two possible causes or outcomes is the *either-or* fallacy. The writer claims that either this is true or that is true, and ignores other possible alternatives.

FAULTY Kevin's business must have failed either because he's lazy or because he's incompetent. I know he's not lazy; therefore, he must be incompetent.

FAULTY Either we will have to sell more candles to raise funds for the school band, or we will have to discontinue the band entirely.

## Begging The Question

When you *beg the question*, you assume in your "proof" that which you are supposed to be proving. In other words, anyone agreeing with your premise will necessarily agree with your conclusion.

FAULTY Cats are not as friendly as dogs because it is their nature to be more aloof.

FAULTY Excessive sugars and fats should be avoided in a heart patient's diet because too much of either of them is not good for people with cardiac problems.

## Circular Reasoning

*Circular reasoning* is simply a longer (and more exasperating) form of begging the question. It contains more steps but has the same structure: what is being proved turns out, in the end, to be its own proof.

FAULTY We should buy a computer for our firm, because all the top business consultants recommend it. Who are these top consultants? The ones with the sense to recommend that businesses purchase computers.

**EXERCISE 7. Identifying Fallacies.** Number your paper 1–10, and identify the fallacy in each item. (In some cases there may be more than one fallacy.) Be prepared to explain your answers.

1. I wondered what had gone wrong with our TV until I remembered that I had seen Jo fiddling with it earlier.
2. No one should take seriously Marcia's ideas about abolishing capital punishment. You know what a silly person she is, and she changes her mind every half hour.
3. Because freedom to express one's opinions is a basic human right, freedom of speech should not be denied to anyone under any circumstances.
4. "Theology teaches that the sun has been created in order to illuminate the earth. But one moves the torch to illuminate the house, and not the house in order to be illuminated by the torch. Hence it is the sun which revolves around the earth, and not the earth which revolves around the sun." —BESIAN ARRAY (1671)
5. Either Joyce earned the money she's been spending lately, or she inherited it. I know she hasn't had a job for months, so she must have inherited it.
6. The kids that go to Mitchell Academy are all snobs. Look at the Perez twins!
7. On his 101st birthday, Mr. Jordan attributed his long life to the fact that he has smoked five big cigars every single day since he was 21 years old.
8. I love you because you're beautiful. You're beautiful because I love you.
9. Everyone agrees that nuclear energy is a dangerous and undesirable source of electricity.
10. Either you're my friend or you're not my friend; and if you're my friend, you'll do what I want you to do.

**EXERCISE 8. Detecting Fallacies in Writing.** Read the editorials and letters to the editor in several issues of a daily newspaper. Bring to class any examples you find of fallacies in reasoning.

## CHAPTER 6 REVIEW

**Identifying Fallacies.** Find in current newspapers and magazines an example for each of the fallacies listed. The example may be only one sentence long, or it may be a paragraph. Be sure that the error in reasoning is clearly shown. Be prepared to discuss your examples in class.

1. Hasty generalization
2. Stereotype
3. False cause
4. False analogy
5. Attacking one's opponent
6. Either-or fallacy
7. Begging the question
8. Circular reasoning

CHAPTER 7

# Writing Persuasive Compositions

## LANGUAGE AND LOGIC

Of all the types of writing that you do, persuasive writing is probably the most demanding. It requires that you think clearly about an issue, decide what you believe, and support your belief convincingly. The rules of logic that you studied in Chapter 6 will help you create sound arguments in your persuasive writing.

## PREWRITING

### CONSIDERING FORM AND AUDIENCE

A *letter to the editor*, a brief essay that expresses the writer's views on a specific topic, appears on the editorial page of a newspaper or magazine. The audience for the letter depends on the publication. If you write to your school newspaper, your audience will be other students and the faculty. If you write to a sports magazine, your audience will be people interested in sports. For a local newspaper, your audience is a cross-section of your community's population.

A *persuasive composition* is longer than a letter to the editor. Usually, it has at least five paragraphs (an introduction, three or more paragraphs in the body, and a conclusion). It is often much longer. You may write a persuasive composition for your teacher and classmates, another school group, or a specific audience outside of school.

Both forms, the letter and the composition, require that you present a sound argument. However, your reasoning in the brief form of a letter must be very concise. The longer form of a composition allows you more room for supporting evidence.

Both forms also require that you respond to *audience attitude.* Some audiences may have a particular bias (an opinion for or against an idea). For example, if you are arguing for improved safety devices at railroad crossings, you may find that people who live near the crossings are opposed to any improvements that cause noise, such as bell or whistle warnings. If your audience is opposed to your view, you will have to provide additional evidence to try to convince them. For those living near railroad crossings, for instance, you would have to show that noise-making devices work best and would *not* create a great disturbance in the neighborhood. If you expect your audience to agree wholeheartedly with you, you might choose a more challenging topic —one that is likelier to stir some discussion. Keep in mind that your audience's knowledge and interests will also affect their attitude toward your topic.

***Techniques for Prewriting.*** To consider your audience, ask yourself:

- Will the readers be interested in the topic?
- How much background information do they need?
- Are they likely to hold a particular bias on the issue?

**EXERCISE 1. Identifying Audience Attitude.** Decide what attitude each of the following audiences is likely to have about the expressed opinion—violently opposed to it, moderately opposed, in favor, strongly in favor, or neutral (no particular bias). Be prepared to explain your answers.

1. *Opinion:* Students in this high school should be required to do at least three hours of homework every night.
   a. High-school students who hold part-time jobs
   b. High-school students who do not work
   c. High-school teachers

2. *Opinion:* All four-year-old children should be required to attend full-day public school prekindergarten classes.
   a. Parents of four-year-old children
   b. Teachers who would be hired for the proposed classes
   c. State legislators asked to pass the requirement law
   d. Group of four-year-old children
3. *Opinion:* Tax dollars are being wasted on ugly sculptures, murals, and paintings for public buildings.
   a. Committee that decides what works of art to buy
   b. Local artists who have sold works of art to the city
   c. Group of homeowners, who pay real estate taxes
   d. City council members, who set the budget for buying art
   e. Group of third-graders

**EXERCISE 2. Writing a Letter to the Editor.** Some letters to the editor are written not to criticize, but to praise or congratulate a person, an organization, or an institution. Read the following letter. Then write a letter to the editor in appreciation of someone or something in your school, your community, or the nation.

To the Editor:

I like the New York subway system.

I calculate that during the 18 years I have worked in this city, I have ridden the subways a minimum of 5,000 times. That ought to be enough to get a fair sample of the service.

I have never been stuck in a darkened tunnel for over five minutes. I have never been on a train that jumped the track. I have never been on a car that caught fire. I have never been mugged, nor have I witnessed anyone else being mugged. I have never had my pocket picked, nor have I ever been around when anyone else was victimized.

Sure, I know these things happen. I read about them in the newspapers and hear of them on the nightly news.

The cars are overcrowded in rush hours, naturally. I wish the cars were cleaner. It would be more pleasant if noise levels in the stations could be lowered by several hundred decibels. So what? The purpose of a transit system is to move people, and the subways do that magnificently.

Days I do not ride the New York subways are days I am out somewhere else across the country paying outrageous prices to rent a car or searching in vain for a taxi stand, since there isn't any public transit system to get me around from place to place.

I applaud Atlanta, Washington and San Francisco, with their sparkling new rapid transits. The cars are cleaner and quieter, the stations more attractive to the eye—and nose. But they carry only a fraction of the daily passenger load and don't begin to measure the 725 miles of track that bring the subterranean serpentine network within easy walking distance of every resident of this city.

We've got nothing to compare to the art-gallery stations of the Paris Metro, the rubber-cushioned ride of Toronto or the punctuality of Moscow. But our subway moves people. I'll trade that kind of dependability for the esthetics of other cities any day.

DON McEVOY—*New York Times 12/8/84 p. Y18*

## CHOOSING A TOPIC

### 7a. Choose a limited topic that is debatable and serious.

The topic for a persuasive essay must be an issue, that is, a proposition which can be argued for (pro) and against (con). The topic, therefore, must concern an opinion, not a fact, because facts are not debatable. A *fact* is a statement that can be proved to be true. An *opinion*, on the other hand, is a judgment or belief. It cannot be proved and thus may be debated.

NOT SUITABLE Astronauts can reach the moon and walk on the moon's surface. (fact)
SUITABLE The United States should establish a space colony on the moon. (opinion)

NOT SUITABLE Nineteen-year-olds can buy alcohol in this state. (fact)
SUITABLE The legal drinking age should be 21 in all states. (opinion)

A persuasive composition should be about an important or serious issue, not merely a matter of personal preference.

NOT SUITABLE Delicious apples are better than Macintosh apples. (personal preference)
NOT SUITABLE Billie Holiday is the best American blues singer of all time. (personal preference)

---

## CRITICAL THINKING:
## Distinguishing Facts from Opinions

To choose an appropriate topic for persuasion, you must be able to distinguish facts from opinions. Remember that a fact is something that actually happened or that can be proved to be true. An opinion states a judgment or belief; it cannot be proved. In the following examples, notice that the opinions contain the word *should*. Other expressions that indicate opinions include "I believe," "in my opinion," "I think," and "I feel."

FACT The President of the United States can serve two four-year terms.
OPINION The President of the United States should serve only one six-year term.

FACT Several species of whale are nearly extinct.
OPINION Commercial whaling should be strictly limited.

Statements that make (or imply) value judgments are also opinions. Words such as *best, greatest, least, most important,* and other superlatives signal that a value judgment is being made.

OPINION The single most important issue facing our government is eliminating the possibility of a nuclear war.
OPINION Lincoln's Gettysburg Address is the greatest political speech ever made.

**EXERCISE 3. Distinguishing Facts from Opinions.** Number your paper 1–5. For each of the following items, write *F* if the statement expresses a fact or *O* if the statement expresses an opinion.

1. According to the latest statistics, the unemployment rate for teenagers is higher than it is for adult workers.
2. The most serious problem facing this community today is the increase in crime.
3. The federal government must find some way of stopping acid rain, which causes great damage to plants and animals.
4. The average working woman earns less money than the average working man.
5. New medicines are tested on animals in research laboratories before the medicines are approved for use by humans.

## WRITING A POSITION STATEMENT

### 7b. Express your opinion clearly in a single sentence.

Once you have chosen an issue to discuss, you need to express your opinion clearly in a single sentence called a *position statement* (also called a *thesis statement* or the *proposition*). Your position statement should tell exactly where you stand on the issue.

EXAMPLES Television networks' news programs should not be allowed to project election results until after the polls have closed all over the country.

This community should have a noise law that prohibits all loud and unnecessary noises after 10:00 P.M.

Some issues may interest you but are so complicated that it is not easy to decide what your opinion is. Take the time to do some research, in the library and in discussions with people whose opinions you respect.

***Techniques for Prewriting.*** To decide what your position is, ask yourself:

- What different conclusions can people draw on the issue?
- Which conclusion do I favor?
- What action do I think should be taken?

---

## CRITICAL THINKING:
### Making Position Statements Specific

The position statement should be specific. Whenever possible, it should clearly state a plan for solving a problem. Consider the following position statements. Which is the most specific?

1. Something should be done about dogs barking at night.
2. The community should pass a noise law about dogs barking at night.
3. The community should pass a law prohibiting loud noises (such as dogs barking, music playing, outdoor parties) after 11:00 P.M. and before 7:00 A.M.

Of the three statements, the third is the most specific. It tells exactly what should be done and defines noises. Statements 1 and 2 leave too many questions unanswered: What should be done? When is "at night"? What should the noise law do?

**EXERCISE 4. Making Position Statements Specific.** The following statements are too vague or general to serve as position statements. Make up any information you need to rewrite each one so that it is specific enough to be a position statement. (*Hint:* Most position statements contain *should* or *should not.*)

1. I think that the requirements for high-school graduation aren't fair.
2. The toxic-waste site in this community is a problem.
3. Someone should do something about the high-school dropout rate.
4. It would be wonderful if there were some kind of program to help students find summer jobs.
5. Don't you think the salaries paid to some professional athletes are too high?

**EXERCISE 5. Writing Position Statements.** Read the following news items carefully. Decide what your opinion is on each issue, and write a clear position statement. Remember that, whenever possible, a position statement should suggest a specific course of action.

1. A historical landmark of sorts was set in the Presidential election. The United States moved from its traditional position as the next-to-worst nation of the world in voter turnout to the absolute lowest, at 52.4 percent of eligible voters. Botswana, the traditional doormat, experienced a surge of voter participation this year—a respectable 76 percent of eligible voters.

   In a recent meeting with government representatives and journalists from more than 20 nations, I was struck by the strong correlation between turnout and voters' impressions of how much their lives will be affected by an election. The most extreme was provided by an official of an underdeveloped country who said: "I will vote and a very high percentage of my people will vote. You see, if the wrong person gets elected in my country, it could mean the end of my life."

   ANDREW E. MANATOS

2. According to figures from the latest U.S. census, the median time that American elementary school and high school students spend doing homework is 5.4 hours a week. (*Median* indicates a midpoint in a collection of statistics. Half of the students are above the median and do more homework; half of the students are below the median and do less homework.) The same statistics show that girls do 5.7 hours of homework a week, while boys do 5.2 hours. Students in private schools do considerably more homework than public school students, according to this study. High school students in private schools spend 14.2 hours a week doing homework, compared to 6.5 hours spent by high school students in public schools.

   And what do the parents think of all this? According to a Gallup poll 59 percent of the parents of elementary school students believe that their children do not have enough homework, and 67 percent of the parents of high school students also think their children do not spend enough time studying.

MIAMI HERALD

3. The following results are from a telephone survey (poll) of 848 randomly selected adults.

*Survey Statement:* "A professional athlete has a bigger responsibility to set a good example for children than the average person."

| | |
|---|---|
| AGREE | 86% |
| DISAGREE | 12% |
| OTHER | 2% |

*Survey Question:* "Do you think that pro athletes today are better or worse role models for children than pro athletes were in the past?"

| | |
|---|---|
| BETTER | 26% |
| WORSE | 47% |
| ABOUT SAME | 19% |
| DON'T KNOW | 8% |

Respondents were asked to explain, in their own words, why they thought that today's athletes were better or worse role models for children.

*Reasons why today's pro athletes are better role models:*

| | |
|---|---|
| Athletes' charity-community work | 24% |
| The good publicity today's athletes get | 11% |

(No other reason received more than 5 percent of the total)

*Reasons why today's athletes are worse role models:*

| | |
|---|---|
| Drug Use | 49% |
| Athletes overpaid, greedy | 20% |
| Bad publicity | 9% |

MIAMI HERALD

**EXERCISE 6. Writing Position Statements.** On each of the following issues, express your opinion clearly in a position statement. If you need more information before making up your mind, do some research in the library or discuss the issue with others.

1. Adding another year to high school so that students graduate at the end of the thirteenth grade
2. Requiring that every driver *not* use his or her car two days a week to reduce air pollution

3. Strictly limiting the amount of money that candidates can spend during political campaigns
4. Drafting women into the armed services
5. Shortening the regular work week from five to four days

## BUILDING AN ARGUMENT

**7c. Support your position statement with reasons and evidence.**

The underlying structure of a persuasive composition is the *argument* —the position statement and its supporting reasons and evidence. To be convincing, the argument must be logical. That is, it must present believable reasons and sound evidence in a clear, orderly manner.

### Choosing Reasons

A *reason* is a statement that explains why you hold your opinion and why the reader also should hold that opinion. Reasons should be clear and evident to the reader. Words like *first, second, third,* and *finally* help to highlight reasons.

*Position statement:* Amateur and professional boxing should be stopped immediately for the following three reasons.

1. First, we have laws against pitting roosters or dogs against each other because such fighting is seen as inhumane. However, boxing, in which two humans set out to injure each other, is perfectly legal.
2. Second, boxing is a kind of legalized violence in an increasingly violent society.
3. Finally, boxing causes acute and long-term brain injury to those who participate in the sport.

---

### CRITICAL THINKING: Evaluating Reasons

The reasons given for an opinion must meet three requirements. They must be *sufficient,* they must be *distinct,* and they must be *relevant.*

To have *sufficient* reasons, you usually should state at least three. The more sound reasons you have, the more convincing your argument will be. Consider the example about abolishing boxing. If only the first of the three reasons had been mentioned, the argument would be much weaker.

Each reason also must be *distinct.* It must not simply restate the position or another reason. Each reason must say something different.

*Position statement:* The seven-period school day (to 3:30 P.M.) should be shortened to a six-period school day (to 2:30 P.M.).

FAULTY

REASON 1 Some students have after-school jobs and need to get to work earlier than 3:30 P.M.

REASON 2 The seven-period school day is too long.

REASON 3 Students should only go to school till 2:30 P.M.

Reasons 2 and 3 illustrate the fallacy of circular reasoning (see page 160) because they merely restate the main opinion. They are not distinct reasons; the argument, therefore, is weak.

IMPROVED

REASON 1 Some students have after-school jobs and need to get to work earlier than 3:30 P.M.

REASON 2 Students do not have the attention span to cover seven different subjects.

REASON 3 It is too much of a load on teachers to have six periods of classes with approximately forty students in each class.

A *relevant* reason is one that directly relates to the position statement. Information that is not directly related to the position should be eliminated. Such information is said to be irrelevant.

*Position statement:* The seven-period school day (to 3:30 P.M.) should be shortened to a six-period school day (to 2:30 P.M.).

IRRELEVANT High-school students must take four years of English and three years of math, science, and social studies. [This information is true but has nothing to do with the position statement.]

IRRELEVANT A high-school student needs twenty-one credits to graduate. [This information is true but is not directly related to the position statement.]

Adding irrelevant information to your argument will weaken it considerably and probably confuse the reader. An argument should be "streamlined" so that it contains only relevant reasons.

**EXERCISE 7. Evaluating Reasons.** Read each position statement, and carefully consider the reasons that follow. Choose the reasons that you think would best support the position. Be prepared to explain your choices.

1. *Position statement:* Everyone under the age of eighteen should have an 11:00 P.M. curfew on nights when there is school the next day.
   a. Students need a good night's sleep to function effectively in school.
   b. Some students work until midnight.
   c. Fifty-three parents have requested that the city council pass an 11:00 P.M. curfew for everyone under the age of eighteen.
   d. Eighty-five percent of students questioned said they object to the proposed curfew.
   e. Statistics show that young adults are more likely to get into trouble after 11:00 P.M.
   f. According to a well-known psychologist, parents should know where their children are and what they are doing after 11:00 P.M.

2. *Position statement:* The United States government should establish a long-term space colony on the moon.
   a. A moon colony would be good for America.
   b. We could do scientific research on the long-term psychological and physiological effects of life in space on human beings.
   c. The moon is so close to the earth that it can be reached in three days.
   d. The United States should establish a space colony on the moon before some other nation does.
   e. An American moon colony would enable the United States to claim the moon as its territory. Eventually, the moon could become a state.
   f. The United States has the technology to create a moon colony.
   g. In the event of a nuclear war, a self-sufficient colony on the moon would ensure the survival of the human race.
   h. Solving problems for an American moon colony would enable us to learn how to found colonies on other planets and in other galaxies.
   i. A moon colony would relieve the overcrowding in many American cities.

**EXERCISE 8. Choosing Reasons.** Choose one of the position statements that you wrote for Exercises 4, 5, or 6, or write another position statement. Then write as many reasons as you can think of to support your opinion. Evaluate the reasons on your list, eliminating those that are not distinct and relevant. Make sure you still have at least three sound reasons for your opinion.

## Choosing and Gathering Evidence

*Evidence* is the specific factual information that you use to back up a reason. Pieces of evidence are often facts such as statistics. You can also use examples, incidents, and quotations from experts. Whenever possible, each reason in an argument should be supported by some kind of evidence. Evidence should come from a reliable source, such as an expert in the field or an unbiased research report, or should be the result of many personal observations. Using a variety of kinds of evidence is usually more effective than using only one kind.

***Techniques for Prewriting.*** To gather evidence:

- Use observation, interviews, and surveys for familiar topics.
- Use library sources such as magazines for less familiar topics.

---

## CRITICAL THINKING:
### Evaluating Evidence

Any piece of evidence that is given to support a reason must be relevant to that reason—that is, it must directly relate to the reason. All irrelevant evidence should be eliminated. Which of the following pieces of evidence are relevant to the given reason?

*Reason:* Some students have after-school jobs and need to get to work earlier than 3:30 P.M.

*Evidence:* a. Mrs. Nan Wampler, a speech teacher, says that after-school jobs really prevent students from functioning effectively as students.

b. More than 70 percent of the students who work say they are paid the minimum wage.

c. Twenty-eight percent of 150 eleventh-grade students surveyed said they work after school.

d. Of the eleven twelfth-grade students surveyed, almost a third said they had tried to get after-school jobs but were refused because they could not come to work until 3:45 P.M., the end of the school day.

The first two items of evidence are irrelevant. They have nothing to do with students' need to get to work earlier than 3:30 P.M. The last two items of evidence would strongly support the reason.

**EXERCISE 9. Selecting Relevant Evidence.** Choose the items of evidence that are relevant to the reason given.

*Reason:* Students need a good night's sleep to function effectively in school.

*Possible Evidence:*

a. Results of a three-year study by doctors on the relationship between sleep and the ability to learn and think clearly
b. Quotation from a teacher who has taught math for twenty-two years on her experiences with students who have had too little sleep
c. Results of a survey of high-school seniors on the amount of sleep they get
d. Statement by a doctor that some people require little sleep throughout their lives
e. Results of a study made by psychologists in which students were taught a new concept and tested after having had eight hours of sleep and after having had five hours of sleep
f. Results of a study made by safety experts on how driving reflexes are affected by lack of sleep

**EXERCISE 10. Choosing and Gathering Evidence.** Using the position statement and reasons that you listed for Exercise 8, think of the kinds of evidence you would look for to support each reason. Write as many kinds of relevant evidence as you can think of. (*Note:* If you cannot think of any evidence to support a reason, change the reason to one you can support.) Once you have decided on the kinds of evidence that work for your argument, gather the information.

## OUTLINING THE ARGUMENT

### 7d. Outline your argument.

The outline for an argument consists of the position statement and the supporting reasons and evidence. If you plan to ask readers to do something, such as write a letter or attend a meeting, add that statement at the end as a *call to action.* Your outline should follow this format:

Position statement
  Reason 1
    Evidence
    Evidence
  Reason 2 *etc.*
Call to action

Of course, the number of reasons and the amount of evidence that supports each reason will vary. In general, a persuasive composition should have at least three reasons, and, whenever possible, each reason should be supported by evidence. The more specific, factual evidence you can offer to support each reason, the more convincing your argument will be.

Also, think about the order in which you list your reasons. For persuasion, writers almost always use the order of importance, usually moving from least important to most important. Decide which reason is your strongest. Save it for last, so that your argument builds up to it.

---

## CRITICAL THINKING:
### Evaluating an Argument

The basis for all persuasive writing is an argument: an opinion supported by reasons which are, in turn, supported by evidence. To write convincingly, you must be able to judge how effective your argument is. Before you begin writing the first draft, you should evaluate the argument as a whole, using the following guidelines.

### GUIDELINES FOR EVALUATING A PERSUASIVE ARGUMENT

1. Is a specific position clearly stated?
2. Do at least three reasons support the position?
3. Is each reason relevant to the position?
4. Is each reason distinct from other reasons and the position statement?
5. Is each reason backed up by relevant, reliable evidence?

**EXERCISE 11. Evaluating Persuasive Arguments.** The following chart gives a position statement and outlines two opposing arguments. In the Pro (*for*) column reasons are listed to support the position statement. In the Con (*against*) column, reasons are given to argue that the United States *should not* adopt the amendment. Study both arguments carefully, and then answer the questions that follow the chart.

*Position statement:* The United States should adopt a Constitutional amendment limiting Presidents to a single six-year term of office.

| PRO | CON |
|---|---|
| a. During the last year of a President's first term, too much of the President's time is spent running the reelection instead of governing the nation. | a. The President does not spend too much time campaigning for a second term. Usually the President decides whether or not to run for reelection during the last year of the first term. |
| b. In an election year a President may refuse to make difficult decisions or deal with controversial problems for fear of alienating voters and not getting reelected. | b. In the past, Presidents have made difficult decisions and dealt with controversial problems whenever they had to. |
| c. In a one-term, six-year presidency, the President will remain sensitive to public opinion on all of the important issues. | c. Running for reelection makes the President more accountable to the voters. During an election campaign the President has direct contact with many ordinary Americans and listens to their problems and views. |
| d. To win support for reelection, a President may cater to the demands of special-interest groups. | d. A one-term presidency will not give a President more honesty or integrity. The President either has it or doesn't. |
| e. The presidency is such a stressful job that six years is as much as any one person can stand. | e. The requirements for the presidency have been working well for many years. There is no need to tamper with a system that works. |

1. Which position do you favor—pro or con? Why?
2. For the position that you favor, which reason do you think is the strongest? The weakest? Why?
3. Looking at the reasons for both sides, which ones would you say are facts? Which are opinions?
4. What evidence can you think of to support each reason for the position that you favor? How could you find such evidence?
5. Are the pro and con reasons distinct from each other? Is the same reason, written in different words, used in both arguments?

6. What are some additional reasons for either side?
7. If you were writing an essay based on these reasons, which three reasons would you choose to support your position? In what order would you arrange these reasons?

**EXERCISE 12. Outlining and Evaluating an Argument.** Use the topic you worked with in Exercise 10, or develop another debatable topic. Outline your argument in detail, listing your position statement, each reason, and the supporting evidence. Then evaluate your argument, using the guidelines on page 176, and revise the outline as needed.

## CONSIDERING EMOTIONAL APPEALS

### 7e. Recognize emotional appeals.

As you have seen so far, convincing arguments require appeals to logic. Also, as you saw with a persuasive paragraph, the *tone* of written persuasion should be formal and unemotional. You will find, however, that certain emotional appeals are used often in persuasion because they can be quite effective, especially with readers and listeners who do not recognize them. Always be alert to emotional appeals. In your own writing, you may find some of them occasionally helpful—for example, in making an interesting introduction or a forceful conclusion to your argument. Use these emotional appeals sparingly and in addition to sound argument.

### Loaded Words

*Loaded words* carry either positive or negative connotations (see pages 301–304) that reveal the writer's attitude and influence the reader's attitude toward the topic. Words such as *honesty, integrity, justice, family,* and *patriotism* have positive connotations and influence a reader to have positive feelings about the ideas being discussed. Examples of loaded words with negative connotations are *cheating, untrustworthy, filthy, destroy,* and *murderous.* What are the loaded words in the following paragraphs?

STOP THE KILLER AIR BAGS

There is a movement afoot to require installation of auto air bags in all new cars.

The consequences of this campaign could endanger your life. Your only protection against bad drivers is careful defensive driving, and the hope that the bad drivers will collide with another object, preferably inanimate, before they hit you.

If a vehicle is struck from any angle other than the front, the air bags are useless. Many frontal collisions are the driver's fault. With air bags, bad drivers survive to kill or maim additional people. Some have already done so. If additional protection is required, it should protect from rear or side collisions.

Write your congressman about this problem. The life you save could be your own.

BOB KUNNECKE

Words used here with positive connotations include *protection* and *careful defensive driving.* Words with negative connotations, intended to influence the reader's attitude toward air bags, are *killer, endanger your life, bad drivers, useless,* and *kill or maim.*

## Bandwagon Appeal

The *bandwagon appeal* urges the reader to "jump on the bandwagon" before it is too late. To not feel left out, the reader is supposed to perform a specific action that "everybody else" has already done.

EXAMPLE Today is the last day to register to vote. More than 96 percent of the senior class has already registered. Don't be one of the very few seniors who won't be able to choose their elected officials.

## Name-Calling

In the heat of a political campaign, a candidate may call an opponent *radical, liberal,* or *conservative*—names that may have negative connotations to particular audiences. Without knowing anything about the opponent, a reader may be prejudiced by the negative connotations of the label. Avoid such *name-calling* in your writing; it is not an acceptable persuasive technique.

EXAMPLE Candidate X's radical proposals threaten the American way of life.

## Glittering Generalities

*Glittering generalities* use words with such strong positive connotations that they make a reader feel good without understanding precisely why. Expressions such as *the American Dream, equal opportunity,* and *justice for all* are examples of the powerful emotional appeal of glittering generalities. Although glittering generalities sometimes lack substance, they can be meaningful if defined or supported in an argument.

EXAMPLE Every human being should have the opportunity to reach his or her fullest potential in order to achieve the American Dream of peace, prosperity, freedom, and justice for all.

### Testimonial

When an expert or authority on the subject being discussed is quoted, such a quotation is an acceptable logical appeal. However, when a famous person who is *not* an expert in the field endorses a product or a candidate, such a *testimonial* is an unacceptable emotional appeal. The glamour or glory surrounding the famous person is not a reason for believing everything the person says.

EXAMPLE Vote for candidate X, the favorite of gorgeous movie star Lorelei Mason and the rugged athlete Super Sam.

### Plain Folks Appeal

The *plain folks appeal* shows or describes average-looking, middle- and working-class people involved in an activity and having a wonderful time. The unstated message is that the reader, too, should take some action, such as buy a product, because "people just like you" are doing it. The plain folks appeal, like glittering generalities, is a powerful persuasive technique.

EXAMPLE People everywhere are discovering that the decent, hard-working way of life they grew up with is somehow disappearing.

### Snob Appeal

The *snob appeal* technique tries to make a reader feel one of a special, privileged few. For example, when advertisers show or describe glamorous, well-dressed people using their products, they imply that the reader's life will also be glamorous and exciting if he or she buys the products. Snob appeal is not used very frequently in persuasive essays.

EXAMPLE You are one of the outstanding young adult leaders in this community who have been invited to this meeting.

**EXERCISE 13. Identifying Emotional Appeals.** Read the following paragraphs carefully. Be prepared to identify loaded words and other emotional appeals.

It would be much better to make the seven-period day mandatory for school districts to offer but optional for their pupils. With such flexibility, some pupils might take seven courses in grades 9 and 10, then a lighter load so that they can work after school in grades 11 or 12. Likewise, other pupils with different needs or interests could tailor their schedules to suit them. Supervised, non-credit study periods also could be made available for pupils who need them.

Such a flexible system takes into account the individualism that is fundamental to the American system of education. Each pupil is unique. None deserves to be put on an educational assembly line.

It matters not at all that the Soviets or the Japanese inflict such drudgery or worse on their schoolchildren. The American system is supposed to be different. Its aim is to prepare young people to live in a democracy, not a beehive or a gulag. American schools may need the academic enrichment and added rigor that a longer school day can provide, but they need not betray their principles to get it.

ROBERT F. SANCHEZ

**REVIEW EXERCISE. Analyzing a Persuasive Essay.** Read the following essay carefully, noting the remarks in the margin. Then answer the questions that follow the essay.

"ALI'S BRAIN AND CRUELEST SPORT"

Should planes stop flying because people die in a crash? Should they stop all cars because 10 people die in them every 24 hours? Because a boxer gets hurt, should they stop boxing?

*introductory paragraph: catches reader's attention; opens argument by analogy posed as questions*

"That would be crazy," Muhammad Ali answered his own questions. "More people die in bathtubs," he said, from the New York City hospital where he was having neurological tests.

*body*

As of this writing, Ali's condition is reported to have improved with adjustments in medications he has been taking for what is tentatively diagnosed as "Parkinson's syndrome." The three-time world champion has been suffering from chronic fatigue. He no longer floats like a butterfly, but shuffles. His speech has been slurred and stumbling. "I'm

*background information on specific case of injured boxer*

still the greatest of all time," he reassured reporters and a TV audience. But the words lacked the old sparkling, punning wit that endeared him even to fans of other sports.

authorities cited

So far, Ali's physicians have said only that blows to the boxer's head "very possibly" could be responsible for his neurologic problems, although there could be other causes, and a diagnosis may not be final without an autopsy. No one is using words like "punch drunk" except to deny that is Ali's problem. Ali himself told reporters, "I've taken all the punches, so there's a great possibility of brain damage."

statement of issue to be debated; writer's position implied but not directly stated

But the possibility that head injury may have caused Ali's deterioration should be reason enough to start public discussion about banning boxing as a public sport. Unlike cars or planes or bathtubs, boxing has no purpose except to inflict enough brain damage on an opponent to make him unconscious. Unlike other sports where head injury can occur accidentally, head injury—a knockout—is the point of boxing.

reason 1, with reference to introduction

Coincident with Ali's hospitalization, *Science* magazine has published a full issue of articles and studies on the brain and the rapidly growing neurosciences. Specialists in neuroanatomy, neurobiology, neurochemistry, neuropharmacology, molecular biology, and genetics are integrating their research and generating an exciting mass of new information about how the brain grows, works, thinks, and directs its owner's life.

authorities referred to but not quoted

Much of science is too complex for nonscientists. But these reports and others are beginning to give us a better understanding of that fantastically complicated, incredible organ that directs the rest of the body's systems and makes us capable of creating music, art, books, civil rights, skyscrapers, planes, computers, dreams—and concern for each other.

background information

The old simplistic comparisons of the brain to a telephone switchboard relaying messages to and from muscles and nerves, or a computer with input and output functions, have given way to much more complicated understandings. Some scientists are reporting that the brain may have as many as 50 billion nerve cells, most of them different. Already, about 50 chemical neurotransmitters that help neurons "talk" to each other and "think" have been identified. No one knows how many more there may be.

background information

Scientists are also learning more about what can go wrong in the brain, about chemical imbalances that can cause mental illness, about structural defects and changes that may result in tragedies such as Alzheimer's disease, about the role of slow-acting viruses, drugs, aging—and injury. Much of what hurts the brain is now unavoidable, given how much still remains to be discovered.

background information

reason 2

But much brain injury is preventable. Surely given what we already know about the brain and getting at least a glimpse of its awesome complexities, we should not be making sport out of deliberately trying to do damage.

It is sometimes argued that, if nothing else, boxing should be encouraged because it provides a ladder up out of poverty for young fighters. What could be more cynical and cruel? Does TV really need revenue so much that it must show young men trying to damage each other's brains? Are we so desperate for entertainment, or an excuse for gambling, that we consider it good sport to inflict head injury?

opposing view

reason 3: refutes opposing view

What does it say about us if we make it clear to poor, ambitious, courageous, young men that their best hope of improving themselves lies not in using their brains but in risking them to provide us sport?

Some of them, less quick and skilled in dodging

punches than Ali, have paid a higher price for taking that risk than Ali has so far.

Surely a Muhammad Ali, with his wit, courage, and charisma would have found a better way to be somebody, if millions of people had not been willing to pay—directly or indirectly—to watch him and his opponents try to punch each other's brains out. The alternatives wouldn't have paid so much. But then, at age 42, he would not have been telling reporters asking about his prognosis, that the "terrible truth is I don't know."

The terrible truth is that boxing is not a sport —and it's time to stop pretending it is. concluding statement

JOAN BECK

1. Do you agree or disagree with the writer's opinion? Tell why.
2. What is the writer's argument? Outline the position and reasons in your own words.
3. What additional reasons and evidence can you think of to support the writer's opinion?
4. Are paragraphs 7 and 8 (from "Much of science . . ." to ". . . more there may be") relevant? Explain your answer.

## WRITING A FIRST DRAFT

### WRITING THE ARGUMENT

#### 7f. Write a first draft based on your outline.

Use your argument outline as a working plan for the composition. Begin with an *introductory paragraph* that sets the topic and includes your position statement. This paragraph should also arouse your audience's interest and may provide background information.

Everything between the introductory and concluding paragraphs is called the *body*. Each reason and its supporting evidence should take up one paragraph. You may also decide to discuss the opposing viewpoint. Refuting an opposing argument shows the reader that you have researched your topic, thus making your own argument more believable.

The *concluding paragraph* should summarize the argument, usually by restating the position and main supporting reasons. In this paragraph you may also ask the reader to perform a specific action, such as writing a letter or appearing at a meeting. Such a *call to action* can make an effective and forceful ending.

***Techniques for Writing.*** Remember to

- Consider audience attitudes
- Keep your tone serious and formal

**EXERCISE 14. Writing a First Draft.** Use the argument you outlined in Exercise 12 to write the first draft of a persuasive composition. Include a position statement in your introductory paragraph. If you have a call to action, add it to your conclusion. If you wish, you may develop a different debatable topic. Make sure that you outline your argument in detail before you write the first draft.

## EVALUATING AND REVISING

**7g. Evaluate the content, organization, and style of your draft.**

Read your draft carefully three times, concentrating on one aspect at a time. Improve your draft, using the following guidelines.

### GUIDELINES FOR EVALUATING PERSUASIVE COMPOSITIONS

| | |
|---|---|
| Position Statement | 1. Does a position statement clearly express a specific opinion on a debatable, serious topic? |
| Introduction | 2. Does the introduction catch the reader's interest? Is the position statement in the introductory paragraph? |
| Reasons | 3. Is the opinion supported by at least three relevant and distinct reasons? Is each reason the main idea of a separate paragraph? |
| Evidence | 4. Is each reason supported by relevant, reliable evidence? |
| Audience | 5. Is audience background and attitude considered? |
| Conclusion | 6. Does the concluding paragraph summarize the argument? |

| | |
|---|---|
| Coherence | 7. Are the reasons arranged in an effective order? |
| | 8. Do transitional expressions make the argument easy to follow? |
| Tone | 9. Is a serious, formal tone used throughout the draft? |

**EXERCISE 15. Evaluating a First Draft.** Using the guidelines above, evaluate the draft you wrote for Exercise 14.

**7h. Revise your draft to improve its content, organization, and style.**

Remember the four revising techniques you can use: *cut* words, phrases, or sentences; *add* words or ideas; *reorder* words, sentences, or paragraphs; and *replace* words or ideas. The following chart suggests how you can use these techniques based on your evaluation of a first draft.

## REVISING PERSUASIVE COMPOSITIONS

| PROBLEM | TECHNIQUE | REVISION |
|---|---|---|
| The main opinion is not clear. | Replace/Add | Make sure you have said whether you are pro or con. Add a suggested action to your opinion. |
| A reason supports or repeats another reason, or repeats the main opinion. | Replace/ Reorder | Replace the weak reason with a distinct reason. Consider using the weak reason as evidence, or discard it. |
| A reason or some evidence does not fit the argument. | Cut/Replace | Remove irrelevant ideas. Make sure you still have sufficient reasons and evidence. Do more research if needed. |
| The argument does not build forcefully. | Add | Add ideas that clearly refute opposing views. Take into account audience attitude and knowledge. |

| PROBLEM | TECHNIQUE | REVISION |
|---|---|---|
| The argument does not respond to known audience bias or opposing argument. | Reorder/Add | Move the strongest reasons and evidence toward the end. Add or reorder ideas in the last paragraph to emphasize the logic of the argument. |
| The introduction is dull. | Add | Begin with an incident or example that makes the issue more personal for the reader. |
| The argument is hard to follow. | Add/Replace | Add transitional words, such as *first* and *also.* Add background information to help connect ideas. Replace long expressions with more concise wording. |
| The tone is informal or too emotional. | Replace/Cut | Replace slang, contractions, and other informal words with formal wording. Remove unacceptable emotional wording, or replace it with serious, reasonable language. |

Look carefully at the revisions a writer has made in the following first draft of a paragraph. It comes from the body of a composition and gives the writer's second reason for supporting an 11:00 P.M. curfew on school nights for everyone under the age of eighteen.

| | |
|---|---|
| Second, ~~S~~students need a good night's sleep in order to | add |
| function effectively in ~~perform up to their capacity during~~ school~~hours. If not,~~ | replace/cut |
| ~~they're not doing much more than occupying a seat~~. Dr. | cut |
| Janice Hullman, ~~is~~ a psychologist and director of ~~at~~ the State University | add/replace |
| Sleep Research Center, ~~She~~ has just completed ~~done~~ a three-year | replace |

study of [how] ~~the relationship between~~ sleep [affects] ~~and~~ the ability to — replace
learn and to think clearly. [According to Dr. Hullman,] ~~She says that~~ "every person — replace
needs a certain amount of sleep, including a certain
number of hours of deep sleep, to refresh the brain and
make it ready to absorb new material." The number of
hours [required] varies from person to person. ~~I need at least eight~~ — add/cut
~~or nine~~. Dr. Hullman's ~~study~~ reports that people who — cut
[do not] ~~don't~~ get enough [sleep] ~~shuteye~~ for a long period of time — replace
become irritable, ~~and angry at other people. They~~ have — cut
less control of motor skill functions, and ~~they generally~~ — cut
do not learn well.

**EXERCISE 16. Revising a Draft.** Carefully revise the draft that you evaluated for Exercise 15. Refer to the techniques in the revising chart on pages 186–87.

## PROOFREADING AND WRITING A FINAL VERSION

### PROOFREADING AND WRITING A FINAL VERSION

**7i. Proofread your revised composition and make a final copy.**

Do not underestimate the value of proofreading in presenting a convincing argument on paper. Your readers may question your careful thinking or simply find the argument difficult to follow if they are distracted by errors in grammar, usage, and mechanics. Read your revised version several times, focusing on one aspect each time. Using the Guidelines for Proofreading on page 29, check your spelling, punctuation, capitalization, grammar, and word use. Use your dictionary to check doubtful spellings. Refer to the Index of this book to find a point of grammar or usage that you want to review.

When you have finished proofreading, write the final version on a separate paper, following an appropriate manuscript form. Proofread this version once more to check for copying errors.

**EXERCISE 17. Proofreading and Making a Final Copy.** Proofread the composition that you revised in Exercise 16. On a separate paper, write the finished version of your composition, proofreading again to check for copying errors.

## CHAPTER 7 WRITING REVIEW

**Writing to Persuade.** Choose one of the topics given below and write a persuasive essay as suggested. You may also select a topic of your own, for either a letter to the editor or a composition. Follow each step in the writing process, as described in this chapter.

1. Select a school issue that interests you. Gather details by talking with teachers, administrators, and other students. Take a stand and write a letter to the editor of your school paper. Some possibilities to investigate include cafeteria regulations, the honor system, library procedures, new courses, homework policies, school publications, censorship, the powers of student government, appropriate dress, the marking system.
2. Investigate a controversial community issue. Review published research, talk to influential citizens, and consult with local officials. Write a letter to the editor of your local paper. Some possibilities include vandalism, zoning laws, parks and playgrounds, local taxes, pollution, the school budget.
3. Investigate the qualifications of candidates for a local, state, or national office; choose the one for whom you would vote. Write a campaign article in which you try to convince your audience to vote for your candidate.

## CHAPTER 8

# Expressive and Imaginative Writing

## PERSONAL NARRATIVES, STORIES, PLAYS, POETRY

Writing is a form of sharing. Writers may write from *experience,* events they have observed or participated in; or they may write from *imagination,* images, characters, and scenes they have created. Whether you write from experience, imagination, or a combination of the two, you share part of yourself with others. In this chapter you will explore four forms of writing: (1) the personal narrative, a first-person narrative or description based on the writer's experience; (2) the short story, an imaginative narration; (3) the play, a story told through dialogue and actions on a stage; and (4) the poem, a word picture, developed with images and rhythms.

### WRITING A PERSONAL NARRATIVE

In a personal narrative, you share a story about something you have experienced. In some ways this is no different from the everyday stories you relate about funny, exciting, or unusual incidents. Before you write a personal narrative, think about an experience that stands out for some reason. In this excerpt from *The Big Sea,* for example, Langston Hughes shares an experience that taught him something.

It had never occurred to me to be a poet before, or indeed a writer of any kind. But my mother had often read papers at the Inter-State Literary Society, founded by my grandfather in Kansas. And occasionally she wrote original poems, too, that she gave at the Inter-State. But more often, she recited long recitations like "Lasca" and "The Mother of the Gracchi," in costume. As Lasca she dressed as a cowgirl. And as Cornelia, the mother of the Gracchi, she wore a sheet like a Roman matron.

On one such occasion, she had me and another little boy dressed in half-sheets as her sons—jewels, about to be torn away from her by a cruel Spartan fate. My mother was the star of the program and the church in Lawrence was crowded. The audience hung on her words; but I did not like the poem at all, so in the very middle of it I began to roll my eyes from side to side, round and round in my head, as though in great distress. The audience tittered. My mother intensified her efforts, I, my mock agony. Wilder and wilder I mugged, as the poem mounted, batted and rolled my eyes, until the entire assemblage burst into uncontrollable laughter.

My mother, poor soul, couldn't imagine what was wrong. More fervently than ever, she poured forth her lines, grasped us to her breast, and begged heaven for mercy. But the audience by then couldn't stop giggling, and with the applause at the end, she was greeted by a mighty roar of laughter. When the program was over and my mother found out what happened, I got the worst whipping I ever had in my life. Then and there I learned to respect other people's art.

LANGSTON HUGHES

In a personal narrative, you may also share an experience that made a lasting impression or evoked a strong emotional response. For example, in *One Writer's Beginnings,* Eudora Welty shares an experience that made a lasting impression on her.

Thursday was Miss Eyrich and Miss Eyrich was Thursday. She came to give us physical training. She wasted no time on nonsense. Without greeting, we were marched straight outside and summarily divided into teams (no choosing sides), put on the mark, and ordered to get set for a relay race. Miss Eyrich cracked out "Go!" Dread rose in my throat. My head swam. Here was my turn, nearly upon me. (Wait, have I been touched—was that slap the touch? Go on! Do I go on without our passing a word? What word? Now am I racing too fast to turn around? Now I'm nearly home, but where is the hand waiting for mine to touch? Am I too late? Have I lost the whole race for our side?) I lost the relay race for our side before I started, through living ahead of myself, dreading to make my start, feeling too late prematurely, and standing transfixed by emergency, trying to think of a password. Thursdays still can make me hear Miss Eyrich's voice. "On your mark—get set—GO!"

EUDORA WELTY

In the examples on page 191, Hughes and Welty share interesting and unusual events of great personal significance. Both use the first-person point of view and informal, natural language that invites the reader to share the writers' experiences.

## PREWRITING

### CHOOSING A PERSONAL EXPERIENCE

**8a. Choose a personal experience that is significant or unusual.**

For writing a personal narrative, choose a personal experience that stands out or that has affected your behavior or ideas. Search for such an experience by reading through your journal or by interviewing family members and friends.

***Techniques for Prewriting.*** To identify significant or unusual experiences, ask yourself:

- What event was a turning point in my life—one that sparked my interest or revealed an unknown talent?
- What was an important "first" (the first time I drove a car, went to a dance, or gave a speech)?
- What experience was the best or worst (funniest or saddest, etc.)?
- What experience taught me something about myself, other people, or life in general (such as learning the meaning of loyalty in a friend)?
- What vivid memory brings back the emotions and details I experienced when it happened?

### CRITICAL THINKING: Evaluating

Evaluation is the critical thinking skill you use when you judge something's value. This skill helps you judge whether a personal experience has significance that extends beyond itself.

***Techniques for Prewriting.*** To evaluate the significance of personal experiences, ask yourself:

- Did I learn anything about myself, other people, or life in general from this experience? Did it influence my thoughts, actions, or feelings?
- Is this experience interesting to anyone other than me and my family or close friends? Could others share my feelings or learn something valuable about life by reading this?
- Would it be an invasion of anyone's privacy to share this experience?
- Does this experience seem more important or less important with each passing year? What are the most memorable details about it?
- Could this experience be explained adequately in a brief personal narrative?

**EXERCISE 1. Evaluating the Significance of Personal Experiences.** Using your journal or interviews with friends and relatives, choose three personal experiences that stand out in some way. Using the questions above, evaluate each experience to determine which one would be most suitable for a personal narrative.

## IDENTIFYING AUDIENCE AND TONE

**8b. Identify your audience and choose an appropriate tone.**

The purpose of a personal narrative is to share an event from your own experience. How you write about that event will depend in part upon the people, or audience, with whom you will share it. You may have a specific audience (devotees of science fiction) or a general audience (people of varying ages, interests, and backgrounds). Your audience may be people you know well or unknown readers of your school newspaper. Whoever your readers may be, you should consider how much you want to share with them. You may be willing to reveal more (or less) about yourself to an audience you know well than to a more general audience.

After identifying your audience, determine the tone of your narrative, the attitude you wish to convey toward your audience and topic.

With a first-person point of view, the tone is personal, creating a close relationship with the audience. The tone is less personal when you focus on the event instead of on your feelings about the event. For example, Hughes focuses on the event itself (page 191) while Welty reveals her feelings (page 191). Hughes' attitude toward his audience is therefore less personal. Hughes' attitude is one of amusement, as conveyed in his retelling of an onstage experience with his mother. Welty's attitude is one of embarrassment or discomfort, as conveyed in her experience with Miss Eyrich. Each writer uses details and language that convey either amusement ("uncontrollable laughter," "giggling," "roar of laughter") or discomfort ("marched . . . outside," "cracked out," "Dread rose"). Your attitude toward your topic will also affect the language and details you use in your narrative.

***Techniques for Prewriting.*** To identify audience and tone, ask yourself:

- Will my audience be specific or general?
- How much of myself do I want to reveal?
- Do I want my attitude toward my audience to be as personal as possible or somewhat less personal?
- What is my attitude toward the experience—one of amusement, embarrassment, disillusionment, hope?
- How does my attitude toward audience and topic affect the language and details that I will use?

**EXERCISE 2. Analyzing Audience and Tone.** Using the questions above, analyze the audience and tone for a personal narrative about the experience you selected in Exercise 1. Write your answers.

## GATHERING INFORMATION AND PLANNING YOUR PERSONAL NARRATIVE

**8c. Gather information and plan your personal narrative.**

### Gathering Information

Now that you have selected an experience and have identified your audience and tone, you are ready to gather information. Since the memory of an event may be unreliable, you should assist your memory by using such techniques as brainstorming, questioning, interviewing, or clustering (see pages 12–17).

The following writer refreshed her memory of the details related to a journal entry by applying the *5 W-How?* questions.

JOURNAL ENTRY

Today I did it. I rode a horse and lived to tell about it. I feel proud of myself, but I also feel sweaty, dusty, and sore.

*Questions:*

1. Who participated in the event? [Myself, my riding instructor, and the horse, Cerise—a gentle mare with a glossy brown coat]
2. What happened? [I groomed and rode a horse for the first time in my life.] What were my personal reactions to the experience? [An overwhelming sense of pride in overcoming my fear of horses; a feeling of affection toward Cerise and other horses] What did I learn from the experience? [That fears can be overcome; that once I made a decision, there was no thought of backing down]
3. Where did the event happen? [At the Forest Park Riding Stables]
4. When did it happen? [One bright autumn day two years ago]
5. Why did it happen? [Because a friend who worked at the stables encouraged me to watch other people ride] Why was it significant? [Because I decided to learn how to ride despite my fears]
6. How did it happen? [Arriving at the stables, I walked through the stalls with the instructor, inhaling the smell of horses, straw, liniment. I met Cerise, who nuzzled my unsteady hand. The businesslike instructor showed me how to groom and saddle my mount. Then she boosted me into the saddle, giving me instructions in position, posture, and how to move *with* the horse. In the riding ring, Cerise walked; then she trotted. My fears gradually faded.]

Using the *5 W-How?* questions, the writer has recalled sensory details (bright autumn day, stable smells) as well as actions (the details of the riding instruction). As you gather information, use a technique that will help you keep both sensory details and actions in mind.

The actions in any narrative must involve a conflict, a situation, or a problem that must be resolved in some way. The conflict may be between two persons, between a person and a natural force, or within a person. In the journal entry above, the writer hints at a conflict. With the *5 W-How?* questions, she recalls in detail the conflict between her fear of riding and her desire to ride.

**EXERCISE 3. Gathering Information for Your Personal Narrative.** Use the *5 W-How?* questions and one other information-gathering technique to gather information about the experience you selected in Exercise 1. As you gather information, keep in mind the need for sensory details and actions related to the experience. Use questions to determine the conflict involved and to recall your personal reactions to the experience. Be prepared to share this information with your classmates.

## Planning the Personal Narrative

When you think you have gathered enough information, *plan* your narrative. Like all narratives, the personal narrative must have a beginning, a middle, and an end. Most personal narratives use chronological order (the order in which actions occurred). Notice that Hughes' narrative proceeds chronologically from his appearance onstage through the end of his mother's performance. Welty's narrative proceeds chronologically from the moment the teams are selected through the end of the race. In both narratives, the actions that create the most interest are in the middle.

To plan your personal narrative, arrange the information you have gathered in chronological order. Decide how you will begin and end the narrative. Include only the information that is central to the significance of the personal experience. To complete your plan, determine the final points or comments you will make in the conclusion. Notice that both Hughes and Welty conclude with comments on the significance of the personal experience.

***Techniques for Prewriting.*** To plan your personal narrative, ask yourself:

- What background information will the audience need to understand the experience? [Introduction]
- What is the first action that occurred during the experience? [Beginning]
- In chronological order, what are subsequent actions that occurred? [Middle]
- What is the final significant action? [End]
- What final comments can I make on the significance or importance of the experience? [Conclusion]

**EXERCISE 4. Planning Your Personal Narrative.** Using the information you gathered for Exercise 3, plan your personal narrative. Follow the questions above to develop your plan.

## WRITING

### WRITING THE FIRST DRAFT

**8d. Write a first draft of your personal narrative.**

By now you have a fairly clear idea of what you are going to include in your personal narrative. Even so, you should review each step of your plan prior to beginning your first draft. Write the first draft as freely as possible; you can evaluate and revise it later.

***Techniques for Writing.*** To write the first draft of your personal narrative, keep in mind:

- Your purpose for writing (to share a significant event or experience)
- Your audience
- The tone you want to convey
- The point of view (Maintain a first-person point of view throughout.)

**EXERCISE 5. Writing the First Draft of a Personal Narrative.** After reviewing the information you gathered and the plan you developed in Exercise 4, write the first draft of your personal narrative.

## EVALUATING, REVISING, AND PROOFREADING

### EVALUATING, REVISING, AND PROOFREADING YOUR PERSONAL NARRATIVE

**8e. Evaluate, revise, and proofread your personal narrative.**

After you have written one or more drafts of your personal narrative, you will be ready to evaluate and revise it. Try to set your narrative aside for a few days so that you can come back to it with a clear mind and an objective eye.

The processes of evaluating and revising require that you reread your narrative several times, each time looking for something different. First, judge its *content*. Have you included enough supporting details? Have you included any irrelevant information? Then examine its *organization*. Have you clearly and logically arranged the actions? Finally, judge its *style*. How does the narrative sound? Study the words and sentences you have used to determine whether they seem appropriate for your intended audience and tone. If possible, read the narrative aloud. You and your listeners can catch words that sound unnatural, stiff, or unsuitable. Use the following guidelines to evaluate your first draft.

## GUIDELINES FOR EVALUATING PERSONAL NARRATIVES

| | |
|---|---|
| Topic | 1. Is the experience appropriate for the audience? Is it interesting or unusual? |
| Introduction | 2. Does the introduction provide any background information that the audience may need to understand the narrative? |
| Topic Development | 3. Are enough supporting details included to develop the experience accurately? |
| Conclusion | 4. Does the conclusion make the significance of the experience apparent? |
| Tone | 5. Is the tone (attitude toward the experience and audience) consistent throughout the narrative? |
| Coherence | 6. Are the actions in the narrative arranged in chronological order? |
| Point of View | 7. Is the first-person point of view used throughout the narrative? |

You can revise your draft in four ways: you can *cut*, or omit, material; you can *add* ideas or events; you can *reorder* words, phrases, sentences, and paragraphs; and you can *replace* one thing with another. The chart below suggests how you can use these techniques to revise your personal narrative. When you have revised your draft, you should proofread it, referring to the Guidelines for Proofreading on page 29.

## REVISING PERSONAL NARRATIVES

| PROBLEM | TECHNIQUE | REVISION |
| --- | --- | --- |
| The experience is not appropriate for the audience. | Cut/Replace | Cut any words or ideas that are not suitable. Replace with material that is more suitable. |
| The experience does not seem interesting or unusual in any way. | Add | Add details and lively descriptions that will appeal to your audience. |
| The introduction fails to give necessary background information. | Add | Add details the audience needs to understand and appreciate your narrative. |
| More details are needed to develop the experience. | Add | Add sensory details and actions that a reader might need to understand this experience. |
| The significance of the experience is not apparent. | Add | Add a comment about significance to your last paragraph. |
| The tone is not consistent throughout. | Cut/Replace | Cut terms that are either too formal or too informal for your topic and audience. Replace formal words with informal ones, or vice versa. |
| The actions are not clearly organized. | Reorder | Rearrange any actions that are not in chronological order. |
| The point of view shifts. | Replace | Substitute first-person pronouns (I, me, myself, etc.) for second- and third-person pronouns. |

**EXERCISE 6. Analyzing a Writer's Revisions.** Read the following excerpt from an evaluated and revised draft of a personal narrative. Study the writer's changes; then answer the questions that follow the model.

|  | |
|---|---|
| The instructor lifted my foot into the stirrup and ~~shoved~~ boosted | replace |
| ~~my trembling body up~~ me onto the saddle. Trembling with fear, I led Cerise into | replace/add |
| the ~~arena~~ ring. ~~He told~~ The instructor showed me ~~the proper position for the~~ how to hold my legs | replace |
| and arms and ~~the correct posture.~~ how to sit in the saddle. First ~~we~~ Cerise walked slowly | replace |
| in a circle. Then ~~we trotted~~ I cautiously urged her into a trot. I bounced up and down and | replace |
| ~~hung on to~~ clutched the saddle. After an hour of ~~riding~~ excitement and terror, the | replace |
| instructor finally told me ~~I could~~ to stop and ~~climb down~~ dismount. | replace |
| ~~from the horse.~~ The lesson was finished. | replace |
| As I led Cerise around the ~~arena~~ ring to cool her down, my legs wobbl~~ing~~ed | replace |
| and my muscles ~~starting to complain, I thought, "I~~ twinged, but my mind did | replace |
| ~~actually did it! I rode a horse and lived to tell about it!"~~ cartwheels. | replace |
| ~~Then~~ I felt a tired, warm sense of pride. I had made a decision to | cut/add |
| learn something new, something that I ~~was~~ had been afraid to do, | replace |
| and I didn't back down—or fall off! | add |

1. Why do you think the writer changed *shoved* to *boosted*, and *hung on to* to *clutched?* How do these changes improve the draft?
2. Why do you think the writer added the sentence, *The lesson was finished?*
3. Why do you think the writer added the words *Trembling with fear, excitement and terror,* and *or fall off?*
4. What revision technique did the writer use most? Give two examples that show how these changes improve the draft.
5. In your opinion, what additional changes would improve the draft further? Explain your answers.

**EXERCISE 7. Evaluating, Revising, and Proofreading Your Personal Narrative.** Evaluate, revise, and proofread the personal narrative you drafted for Exercise 5. Read your narrative critically several times. If possible, exchange papers with another student to evaluate each other's work. Use the Guidelines for Evaluating and the Guidelines for Proofreading on pages 22–23 and 29, as well as the Guidelines for Evaluating Personal Narratives in this chapter. Prepare a neat, carefully proofread final paper.

## WRITING SHORT STORIES AND ONE-ACT PLAYS

Both the short story and the one-act play narrate an experience—real or imagined—that occurs within a short period of time and involves relatively few characters and settings. The short story's audience relies on the writer's descriptions and, to some extent, on dialogue to understand plot and character. The play's audience relies almost entirely on dialogue and, to a lesser extent, on action. Plot, character, setting, dialogue, conflict, and action are elements of both the short story and the play.

The writer of a short story or play combines imagination with a strong sense of how people (characters) think and act (action) in a particular set of circumstances (plot). This sense comes from personal experience and observation—both of which are available even to the inexperienced writer.

---

## PREWRITING

---

### CHOOSING A SITUATION

**8f. Choose a situation suitable for a short story or a one-act play.**

For the subject of a short story or a play, find a situation that leads to a conflict (a struggle or a problem). The conflict, which must be resolved by the end of the story or the play, is not necessarily a violent struggle. A character may be in conflict with another character (possibly someone in authority); a character may be in conflict with a force of nature (a wild animal or a raging storm); the conflict may be within a character (a struggle between believing one thing and doing another).

The idea for a story or play does not have to come solely from your imagination. You can also find story ideas by recalling personal experiences, by reading magazines and newspapers, by watching and listening to newscasts, and by observing the people around you. Once you have found an idea, you can create a fictional story or a play by making up your own characters and changing the details. Suppose a news story about a homeless family catches your attention. Imagine yourself then as part of a family with similar problems. Having identified a suitable situation, you can use your imagination to create a story or play.

**EXERCISE 8. Choosing a Situation for a Story or a Play.** Identify five situations suitable for a short story or a play. Narrow your choice to two, and develop two or more conflicts for each. Identify your source, and be ready to discuss your choices.

EXAMPLE *Source:* Story on evening news.
*Situation:* The monorail at the amusement park breaks down: several people are stranded thirty feet above the ground.
*Possible Conflict:* One of the people involved has a fear of heights but agreed to ride to hide his fear from his companion.
*Possible Conflict:* The operator of the monorail reported that the monorail needed repairs, but the park manager insisted that nothing was wrong.

## CONSIDERING AUDIENCE, PURPOSE, AND TONE

**8g. Consider the audience, purpose, and tone of your story or play.**

Consider the effect the background of your audience will have on what you include in your story or play. For example, perhaps your school is located in a small town and your audience is a group of students who read the school magazine. Consider how you would describe being caught in a subway fire to this audience, whose only means of public transportation is the local bus. Your readers may need additional background information to appreciate what you have written.

The general purpose of a short story or a play is to entertain your audience. The specific purpose, however, may be to move your audience to feel a particular way or come to a different understanding of a social problem. The tone should be appropriate to your purpose and your audience. For example, if you want your audience to laugh, you must convey an attitude of humor toward the conflict. If your purpose is to make your audience think seriously about a conflict, a humorous tone would be inconsistent. The details and language you use should reflect the tone accurately. (Note: *irony* is a device whereby experienced writers intentionally choose details and language that are opposite from what they wish to convey.)

***Techniques for Prewriting.*** To consider your audience, purpose, and tone, ask yourself:

- Who is my audience? What background information will this audience need to understand this conflict?
- What is my specific purpose? (to move the audience to laughter or tears? to make the audience feel terror, nostalgia, compassion, indignation?)
- What tone should I choose to achieve my specific purpose? (humorous, angry, concerned, mysterious?)

**EXERCISE 9. Considering Audience, Purpose, and Tone.** Select one situation and conflict from Exercise 8. Then answer the preceding questions about audience, purpose, and tone.

## ESTABLISHING A POINT OF VIEW

**8h. Establish a point of view that is appropriate for your story.**

In a play, your characters will speak. In a short story, however, you must decide whose voice will speak for you—(1) a participant in the story or an observer speaking from the first-person point of view or (2) you as the writer speaking from the third-person point of view. Most fiction writers use the third-person point of view because it gives them greater flexibility.

***Techniques for Prewriting.*** To establish a point of view for your story, ask yourself:

- Do I want the audience to feel close to the action? (If so, use a first-person narrator.)
- Do I want the narrator to know what the other characters are thinking and feeling? (If so, use a third-person, omniscient narrator.)

**EXERCISE 10. Determining Point of View.** In an anthology, find examples of these points of view: (1) first person, directly involved in the story; (2) first-person, an observer of the conflict; and (3) third-person, omniscient. Be prepared to discuss your examples.

## OUTLINING THE PLOT FOR A SHORT STORY OR A PLAY

**8i. Develop a plot outline for your story or play.**

Plotting your short story or play means planning the action from beginning to end. Usually a plot begins by introducing the characters, setting, and conflict; continues chronologically through a sequence of rising actions that leads to the climax (the point at which the conflict is most intense); and ends with the outcome of the conflict (resolution).

Note how the plot is developed in the excerpt from "The Last Bullet" by MacKinlay Kantor.

Jameson thought he saw something stirring on the burnt sullenness of the desert's face. He thought he saw a quiver among the furious slopes of brown and red.

beginning: characters (Jameson, the horse Poco, and—eventually—a posse) introduced, setting (a desert) established, conflict (survival) established

He opened his dry, cracked mouth; his mouth had been open for a long time, but he opened it wider. He tried to say, weakly, "Posse."

It wasn't a posse. Jameson never thought he'd see the day when he'd be glad to have a posse come smoking up to him; but he reckoned that if a man lived long enough he saw different days from those he had expected to see.

No quiver in the blue, no twisting and dividing in the brown . . . Jameson turned his head and felt the vast, round, hot flame of sky searing his eyeballs. He managed to lift his hand, and in the scant shade granted by the swollen fingers, he tried to find some buzzards. He couldn't find any buzzards. Nothing lived on this dry pan of desertion —nothing lived here but Jameson and Poco.

The man twisted the upper part of his body,

and sighed. Poco's head lay against the burning shale a few feet away; when Jameson stirred, the little horse moved his neck with the agony of a movement five hundred times repeated.

"How you doing?" Jameson wanted to ask his horse.

[Several paragraphs in which Jameson dreams of his past and awakens briefly have been omitted.]

middle:
incidents and actions leading to climax

The sky changed from white back into yellow and orange. The shadow of the steep stone ridge grew longer; it went past the two suffering shapes —the swollen mass of living horseflesh—the dry-skinned, crippled man who lay beside it.

"Not another night," said Jameson. "I can't stand it. Pity there ain't two shells."

Again the muzzle found his temple, but the horse still looked at him.

Jameson breathed softly. "Okay," he croaked. He remembered something about the Bible and a merciful man being merciful to his beast, but Jameson would never call Poco a beast.

climax:
point at which conflict is most intense

He inched forward, suffering horrors until he felt the metal barrel sinking against Poco's ear cavity, soft and warm and silky despite all endurances.

"Be seeing you," he said, and pulled the trigger.

The gun jumped loose from his hand, after it was over . . .

He did not know how many dreams possessed him, but not many; the night came closer every second. And then his ears picked out a faint scrambling, a sound of sliding gravel. Hoof rims scraped the burnished gray rocks.

outcome:
resolution of conflict

They rode up; they were angels in leather and flannel; they wore guns. They would carry Jimmy Jameson behind the bars. But still they were angels.

The sheriff was on his knees beside him.

"Can't understand it," Jameson whispered. "So late. Nobody comes . . . Llano Diablo."

The sheriff looked at the dead horse. He shook his head, even while his hands moved to his water bottle.

"One shell," Jameson said. "It was him or me. Poco needed a break."

The brown, lined face of the sheriff bent closer, and there were other faces behind. Water touched Jameson's lips.

"I guess you got a break yourself, this time," the sheriff said. "We hadn't come across your trail, and we agreed to ride back to Dundee. We were just turning our horses, behind that hill, when we heard you shoot."

a touch of irony in the closing sentence

MACKINLAY KANTOR

***Techniques for Writing.*** To develop a plot outline, use this framework:

- Who are the characters? What is the setting? What is the conflict? [Beginning]
- What sequence of incidents makes up the rising action? Where is the conflict most intense (climax)? [Middle]
- How is the conflict or problem resolved? Is this outcome the likely result of actions and events? [Outcome]

**EXERCISE 11. Developing a Plot Outline.** Using the framework above, create a plot outline for a story or a play. Use the conflict you chose in Exercise 9 on page 203, or develop a conflict from one of the following situations.

1. The class practical joker plans a joke on a new student.
2. A student musician needs to study for final exams but is offered the chance to be the opening act for a popular rock group.
3. Several people are marooned in a stalled tour bus during a blizzard.
4. An engineer who has worked in a space station for twenty years finally returns to Earth.

## WRITING

### DEVELOPING CHARACTERS IN A SHORT STORY OR PLAY

**8j. Develop characters that are believable.**

The main character involved in the conflict of a story or a play is called the *protagonist.* Sometimes another character, called the *antagonist,* opposes the wishes or plans of the protagonist. Your choice of other, secondary characters will depend upon the requirements of your plot.

***Techniques for Writing.*** To create believable characters, remember that:

- The characters' behavior should be consistent. Give the audience a logical reason for dramatic changes in behavior (for example, *happy* to *miserable*).
- The characters' motivation—why they speak and behave as they do—should be clear to the audience.
- The characters should have real qualities. Few people are all good or all bad: heroes may have weaknesses, and villains may have redeeming qualities.

**8k. Develop characters through description.**

One way to present your characters is through description. In a play, description consists of notes—usually set apart from the dialogue—that specify any physical, personality, or behavioral traits that are part of the characterization. The actors and the director must use these notes to determine how the actors look and act onstage. In a short story, the description is built into the narrative, where it is intended to be read by the audience.

In the following excerpt from the short story "The Moustache," the main character, Mike, visits his grandmother in a nursing home. Since the story is written from a first-person point of view, the author uses Mike's voice to describe the grandmother. Notice how the writer uses vivid, specific language to create a dominant impression of a frail, bedridden grandmother.

> I finally found the room and saw my grandmother in bed. My grandmother looks like Ethel Barrymore. I never knew who Ethel Barrymore was until I saw a terrific movie, *None But the Lonely Heart,* on TV, starring Ethel Barrymore and Cary Grant. Both my grandmother and Ethel Barrymore have these great craggy faces like the side of a mountain and wonderful voices like syrup being poured. Slowly. She was propped up in bed, pillows puffed behind her. Her hair had been combed out and fell upon her shoulders. For some reason, this flowing hair gave her an almost girlish appearance, despite its whiteness.
>
> She saw me and smiled. Her eyes lit up and her eyebrows arched and she reached out her hands to me in greeting. "Mike, Mike," she said. And I breathed a sigh of relief. This was one of her good days. My mother had warned me that she might not know who I was at first.
>
> I took her hands in mine. They were fragile. I could actually feel her bones, and it seemed as if they would break if I pressed too hard. Her skin was smooth, almost slippery, as if the years had worn away all the roughness the way the wind wears away the surfaces of stones.
>
> ROBERT CORMIER

Although character descriptions in a play are not usually read by the audience, they must nevertheless be complete and accurate. Here are excerpts from William Gibson's notes for two characters in *The Miracle Worker:*

> [1] The chair contains a girl of 20, ANNIE SULLIVAN, with a face which in repose is grave and rather obstinate, and when active is impudent, combative, twinkling with all the life that is lacking in HELEN'S, and handsome; there is a crude vitality to her.
>
> [2] HELEN, six and a half years old, quite unkempt, in body a vivacious little person with a fine head, attractive, but noticeably blind, one eye larger and protruding; her gestures are abrupt, insistent, lacking in human restraint, and her face never smiles.
>
> WILLIAM GIBSON

Gibson's physical descriptions of the two principal characters in his play are part of the stage directions just before the characters appear onstage for the first time. In subsequent stage directions, the writer provides additional descriptions of each character's personality and behavior.

***Techniques for Writing.*** To write effective character descriptions,

- decide how you want your audience to respond to the character, and choose an appropriate tone. (This will help you select details that contribute to this dominant impression.)
- avoid stereotypes—trite, one-sided, predictable characters.
- imagine how your character looks and sounds, what the character's habits and dreams are.
- reveal physical appearance through vivid, specific language that helps the reader visualize details of features, clothing, etc. (Only include details essential to the plot; for example, if height and weight are not relevant, omit them.)
- let personality traits emerge through the character's actions, behavior, and words. (Rather than saying someone is shy, let behavior or words reveal this.)
- select actions that reveal character. (Tapping a pencil could suggest nervousness or impatience, for example.)

**EXERCISE 12. Writing a Description of a Character for a Short Story.** Write a one- or two-paragraph description of a character for a short story. Use one of the conflicts you have developed, or select one of the following characters: a child who is used to getting his or her own way, a librarian who plays the drums in her spare time, a bus driver who has driven the same route for ten years. Refer to the preceding hints about writing descriptions.

### 8l. Develop characters through dialogue.

A character's words and how they are spoken can reveal personality, background, and motivation. Dialogue can also reveal the attitudes and interactions between characters. In a short story or a play, therefore, the effective use of dialogue will help bring your characters to life.

Dialogue should be the natural expression of a character's personality and background. If a character has an outgoing personality, free-flowing dialogue will reveal that trait; if a character is uneducated, substandard language will reflect that lack.

In the second act of *Death of a Salesman,* a play by Arthur Miller, Willy Loman talks to his boss, Howard, about his job. What does the dialogue reveal about Willy's background and about Howard's attitude toward him?

**Howard.** Say, aren't you supposed to be in Boston?
**Willy.** That's what I want to talk to you about, Howard. You got a minute? (*He draws a chair in from the wing.*)
**Howard.** What happened? What're you doing here?
**Willy.** Well . . .
**Howard.** You didn't crack up again, did you?
**Willy.** Oh, no. No . . .
**Howard.** Geez, you had me worried there for a minute. What's the trouble?
**Willy.** Well, tell you the truth, Howard. I've come to the decision that I'd rather not travel any more.
**Howard.** Not travel! Well, what'll you do?
**Willy.** Remember, Christmas time, when you had the party here? You said you'd try to think of some spot for me here in town.
**Howard.** With us?
**Willy.** Well, sure.
**Howard.** Oh, yeah, yeah. I remember. Well, I couldn't think of anything for you, Willy.
**Willy.** I tell ya, Howard, the kids are all grown up, y'know. I don't need much any more. If I could take home—well, sixty-five dollars a week, I could swing it.
**Howard.** Yeah, but Willy, see I—
**Willy.** I tell ya why, Howard. Speaking frankly and between the two of us, y'know—I'm just a little tired.
**Howard.** Oh, I could understand that, Willy. But you're a road man, Willy, and we do a road business. We've only got a half-dozen salesmen on the floor here.
**Willy.** God knows, Howard, I never asked a favor of any man. But I was with the firm when your father used to carry you in here in his arms.
**Howard.** I know that, Willy, but—
**Willy.** Your father came to me the day you were born and asked me what I thought of the name of Howard, may he rest in peace.
**Howard.** I appreciate that, Willy, but there just is no spot here for you. If I had a spot I'd slam you right in, but I just don't have a single solitary spot. *[He looks for his lighter.* **Willy** *has picked it up and gives it to him. Pause.]*
**Willy.** *[with increasing anger.]* Howard, all I need to set my table is fifty dollars a week.
**Howard.** But where am I going to put you, kid?
**Willy.** Look, it isn't a question of whether I can sell merchandise, is it?
**Howard.** No, but it's a business, kid, and everybody's gotta pull his own weight.

ARTHUR MILLER

Through dialogue, Willy is portrayed as a desperate man. Which lines reveal that Willy feels that the company should pay him back with a job because of his loyalty? What lines reveal Willy's increasing desperation? What does Willy's use of a phrase such as *I could swing it* tell about him? Which lines most clearly reveal that Howard thinks business is more important than people? What does Howard's use of the word *kid* tell us about his feelings toward Willy?

When writing dialogue for a short story, you will need to include explanatory details that let your audience know which character is speaking, to whom, and how he or she is speaking. This information is obvious in a play. For example, in short story form the first few lines of the Miller excerpt might read this way:

> Howard looked at Willy, who was walking toward him. "Say, aren't you supposed to be in Boston?"
>
> Concerned about how to approach Howard, Willy hesitated momentarily. "Well . . ."
>
> "You didn't crack up again, did you?"

***Techniques for Writing.*** To plan dialogue, ask yourself:

- Under what circumstances would the main character and the other character be likely to speak to one another?
- How do these two characters feel about each other? Are they friends? Strangers? Enemies?
- Are these characters likely to use standard or substandard language in this situation?
- How do the characters feel? Are they nervous? Angry? Relaxed?
- How might the characters show their feelings in words?

**EXERCISE 13. Developing Characters Through Dialogue.** Write a brief dialogue between the character you described in Exercise 12 and another character. Use the format of a short story or a play.

## CREATING A SETTING

**8m. Create a setting for a short story or a play.**

### Using Stage Directions in a Play

Stage directions are the playwright's detailed notes on setting (the time and location of the actions), props, and, sometimes, characters. Note how Susan Glaspell describes the setting and the characters at the beginning of her one-act play, *Trifles:*

> The scene is the kitchen in the farmhouse of JOHN WRIGHT, a gloomy kitchen, abandoned without having been put in order—the walls covered with a faded wallpaper. A door leads to the parlor at right. On the wall near this door is a built-in kitchen cupboard with shelves in the upper portion and drawers below. In the rear wall, up two steps, is a door opening onto stairs leading to the second floor. In the rear wall there is another door which leads to the shed and from there to the outside. Between these two doors is an old-fashioned black iron stove. Running along the wall at left from the shed door is an old iron sink and sink shelf, in which is set a hand pump, and an uncurtained window. Near the window is an old wooden rocker. In the center of the room is an unpainted wooden kitchen table with straight chairs on either side. There is a small chair near the parlor door. Unwashed pans under the sink, a loaf of bread outside the breadbox, a dish towel on the table—other signs of incomplete work. At the rear, the shed door opens and the SHERIFF comes in, followed by the COUNTY ATTORNEY and HALE, a neighboring farmer. The SHERIFF and HALE are men in middle life, the COUNTY ATTORNEY is a young man; all are much bundled up and go at once to the stove. They are followed by two women—the SHERIFF'S wife, MRS. PETERS, first; she is a slight, wiry woman, a thin, nervous face. MRS. HALE is larger and would ordinarily be called more comfortable looking, but she is disturbed now and looks fearfully about as she enters. The women have come in slowly, and stand close together near the door.
>
> SUSAN GLASPELL

The writer creates a particular mood with the details she uses. What are some of those details and what mood do they create? Notice how the directions indicate the movement of the characters before any words are spoken. What do these stage directions reveal about the time of year and how the characters feel about the situation?

Stage directions are also written to move the characters around the stage. In the dialogue on page 210, for example, the directions in parentheses tell Howard to look for his lighter.

☞ **NOTE** Directions for *right* and *left* are from the standpoint of someone on the stage, looking toward the audience. The back of the stage is called *upstage;* the front of the stage is *downstage;* the middle of the stage is *center.*

***Techniques for Writing.*** To gather information for stage directions, ask yourself:

- When does the dialogue take place (time of day, year, season)?
- Where does it take place (inside: living room, kitchen; outside: beach, forest, street corner)?
- What details of setting are appropriate for the tone of the play?
- Which items, or props, should be included?
- How will the characters enter and leave the stage?
- What details of the characters' appearances and actions are important to the setting (clothing, attitude, sitting)?

**EXERCISE 14. Writing Stage Directions.** Using the same situation for which you developed dialogue in Exercise 13, gather information for the setting of a play. Then write the stage directions for the play.

### Describing the Setting in a Short Story

Descriptive details in a short story are combined with action and dialogue to create a setting. The setting provides background, represents the surroundings with which the characters interact and contributes to the mood or tone of the story. It can also be part of the conflict.

In "The Last Bullet" (pages 204–206), for example, the desert is part of the conflict. Without this harsh environment, Jameson would not have had to decide between ending his own suffering or that of the horse. In the following paragraph from this story, note how setting and character interact:

> The blue sky came down and struck him across the face. It was a red sky—now it was yellow—now white. "Old sky," he wanted to say, "do you see any posses? I sure would like to see one."
>
> MACKINLAY KANTOR

In few words, the writer conveys the changeability of the desert sky; the specific, detailed language he uses evokes the image of the sky and reveals the character's feelings.

***Techniques for Writing.*** To describe the setting for a short story, include

- details that contribute significantly to the tone.
- sensory details (sounds, smells, colors).
- language that is precise and vivid, but brief.
- characters that interact with the setting.

**EXERCISE 15. Writing a Description of Setting in a Short Story.** Use the same setting you created for Exercise 14 or select a new one. Write a description of setting appropriate for a short story.

## WRITING A FIRST DRAFT OF YOUR SHORT STORY OR PLAY

**8n. Write a first draft of your short story or play.**

Now that you have your conflict, plot outline, characters, and setting, you are ready to write the first draft of your story or play. This is your opportunity to put ideas on paper that will interest and entertain your audience.

***Techniques for Writing.*** To write a first draft,

- create an interesting beginning that will make the audience want to go on reading.
- include complications to give the audience a chance to share in the tensions and problems the protagonist is experiencing.
- build suspense into the actions leading to the climax and resolution: make the audience wonder what happens next.

**EXERCISE 16. Writing a First Draft of Your Short Story or Play.** Write a first draft of your short story or one-act play. You may use the conflict, plot outline, characters, and setting from earlier exercises; or you may develop a new plan for a different conflict.

# EVALUATING, REVISING, AND PROOFREADING

## EVALUATING, REVISING, AND PROOFREADING YOUR STORY OR PLAY

**8o. Evaluate, revise, and proofread your story or play.**

A first draft is rarely a final product. Professional writers evaluate their stories and plays carefully and revise their writing many times.

## CRITICAL THINKING:
### Evaluating a First Draft

When you evaluate your first draft, read it critically to determine whether it meets the needs of audience and purpose and whether the tone is appropriate. Evaluation means judging how well the first draft succeeds, as well as noting ways in which it does not.

## GUIDELINES FOR EVALUATING SHORT STORIES AND PLAYS

| | |
|---|---|
| Setting | 1. Do the details of setting contribute to the audience's understanding of the characters and the conflict? For a play, do the stage directions adequately describe the setting? |
| Conflict | 2. Does the beginning establish the conflict and arouse the reader's interest? |
| Plot | 3. Are the actions in the story clearly organized and told in chronological order? Do they lead to the climax and resolution and develop a feeling of suspense? Does this resolution grow naturally out of the story's actions and characterization? |
| Point of View | 4. Is the point of view (in a short story) consistent throughout? |
| Characters | 5. Are the characters consistent, motivated, and believable? Have the important characters been fully developed through description, dialogue, action, or a combination of these? |
| Dialogue | 6. Is the dialogue natural and appropriate for the characters? |
| Tone | 7. Is the tone of the draft appropriate for the purpose and the audience? Does the language indicate how the writer feels about the characters and the conflict? |

**EXERCISE 17. Evaluating the First Draft of a Short Story or Play.** Using the guidelines above, evaluate your draft. Then exchange drafts with another member of the class, and offer each other suggestions using these same questions as a guide. Remember to evaluate the positive, as well as the negative. Jot notes indicating where the draft is strong and where it should be improved.

## Revising Your Short Story or Play

As you revise your short story or play, think about the various elements of character, setting, and plot. The chart below will help you correct specific problems that you discovered in evaluating your draft. Once again you will use the four revision strategies: adding, cutting, reordering, and replacing. Proofread your revised draft, using the guidelines on page 29.

### REVISING SHORT STORIES AND PLAYS

| PROBLEM | TECHNIQUE | REVISION |
|---|---|---|
| The stage directions do not give enough information. | Add | Add more information about the stage, props, details of characters, etc. (See *Techniques for Prewriting,* page 203.) |
| The setting does not seem "right" for the characters and the conflict. | Cut/Replace | Review the main characters and the conflict. Cut descriptions of setting that are unrelated to them. Replace with descriptive details that are more appropriate. |
| The actions are not clearly organized. | Reorder | Reorder any events that are confusing. |
| A feeling of suspense is missing. | Add | Find places in the story or play, especially as the action *rises,* where you can add details that contribute to the suspense. Appeal to your audience's curiosity and interests. |
| The point of view is inconsistent. | Cut/Replace | Cut places where the narrator knows too much, and replace with material that is consistent with the point of view. |

| PROBLEM | TECHNIQUE | REVISION |
|---|---|---|
| The characters are not fully developed. | Add | Add details that make flat characters more consistent, motivated, and believable, using dialogue and actions to reflect character. |
| The dialogue is not natural. | Cut/Replace | Cut dialogue that sounds unnatural. Replace inappropriate language with language suited to the characters. |
| The tone is not appropriate for the audience. | Cut/Replace | Cut words or ideas that are inappropriate. Replace them with ones suited to your audience's knowledge, interests, age, and biases. |
| The writer's feelings about the conflict are not indicated by the language. | Replace/Add | Replace dialogue, descriptions, and stage directions with ones that reflect how you feel. Add material to let your audience know your feelings, but reveal them through word choice, details, etc. (Don't just bluntly state how you feel.) |

EXERCISE 18. **Revising and Proofreading Your Story or Play.** Using the chart above, revise the first draft of your short story or play. When you are ready to make a clean, final copy, proofread your revision. You may find it helpful to review punctuation rules for dialogue (page 634) and the Guidelines for Proofreading on page 29.

## WRITING POETRY

Poetry, the most musical form of imaginative writing, may tell a story or simply create an impression. You experience poetry, like music, through the senses—whether reading it or writing it. Some forms of poetry follow definite patterns of meter and rhyme, but others do not. All, however, express meanings that touch responsive feelings in readers. There are as many ways to write poetry as there are poets, but you may find some of the following techniques helpful as you write your own poems.

## PREWRITING

### CHOOSING A SUBJECT AND GATHERING IDEAS FOR POETRY

**8p. Choose an appropriate subject and gather ideas for poetry.**

When you plan to write a poem, begin with a memory that has special meaning for you. Once you have discovered a moment or an image that stands out in your mind, use techniques such as brainstorming and clustering to stimulate your thought process. For example, if your memory is of a sunset on the beach, you might think of words and phrases such as *silver-edged clouds; heels and toes in cool damp sand; screeching sea gulls; waves surging to the shore; a bright orange ball slowly swallowed by the ocean.*

Some poems are meant to be shared with others and some are very private and personal. Since you may share your poem in class, choose an image or experience you feel comfortable sharing with others.

***Techniques for Prewriting.*** To find a subject for a poem,

- search your memory for one special person or event that made a strong impression on you.
- sit quietly, allowing your mind freedom to wander through moments and places from your past.
- concentrate on sensory experiences—sights, sounds, feelings, scents, and tastes.
- brainstorm (or just talk about ideas) with a small group of family members, friends, or other students.
- review your journal, looking for places where you felt deeply about some person or situation.

**EXERCISE 19. Choosing a Subject for Poetry.** Using the ideas on page 218, select one of the categories listed below to discover a subject for a poem. Write the words and images that come to mind. Then circle the ones that have a significant meaning for you. You may also select other categories to find personally meaningful subjects.

| | |
|---|---|
| Nature | Sports |
| People | Music |
| Emotions | Objects |
| Holidays | Wishes and Dreams |
| Hobbies | Sounds |

**EXERCISE 20. Gathering Ideas for Poetry.** Select a subject from your list in Exercise 19; then use a technique such as clustering or brainstorming to gather additional ideas and details. Allow your mind to flow freely from one image or impression to the next, stopping momentarily to jot down sights, sounds, scents, feelings, or tastes that come to mind.

## ORGANIZING YOUR IDEAS FOR A POEM

**8q. Organize your ideas to form an impression or to convey meaning.**

Once you have gathered a list of images and sensory details, you can begin to think about how all these images relate to one another. What impression do they form for you? What meaning does this impression have?

After you have determined a dominant impression, look for logical relationships among ideas. There is no one way to arrange the ideas in a poem. If your poem is going to tell a story, as in a ballad, consider chronological order. Even if you are not telling a story, your poem might be organized in a time sequence. For example, if your poem is about a special birthday when you were a small child, you might want to think about which images came first, next, and so forth. If your poem is about the sunset on the beach, you might begin with sounds, then feelings, then sights.)

In organizing your ideas and images, continue to bring into focus your poem's meaning. Experiment with the order of the details as you clarify and refine this meaning. Your poem will take its final form when you write it; sound patterns, combined with meaning, will affect the final organization of details.

***Techniques for Prewriting.*** To organize ideas for a poem, ask yourself:

- What ideas, images, and details do I have to work with?
- Which of these ideas, images, or details makes the strongest impression on me?
- What meaning do I associate with this detail? (for example, the peace, beauty, and harmony of nature)
- What other details can I use that will contribute to the meaning? Which ones should I discard?
- How can I best organize these ideas to capture the main impression and to convey meaning? (chronologically, spatially, details of one sense and then another, etc.)

**EXERCISE 21. Organizing Ideas for a Poem.** Read through your list of images and sensory details from Exercise 20. Using the questions above, write these images and details in order. Be prepared to discuss how you arrived at this order.

## WRITING

## USING RHYTHM AND REPEATED SOUNDS IN POETRY

**8r. Use rhythm and repeated sounds to develop the meaning of your poem.**

Poetry is special partly because of its musical sounds. These sounds, which enhance meaning, are created through rhythm and repeating sounds.

### Rhythm

The rhythmic pattern of a poem, *meter,* is created by using a pattern of accented and unaccented syllables in each line. The poet combines words so that their natural accents contribute to the rhythm of the poem. For example, the most frequently used regular meter is the *iamb,* which is an unstressed syllable followed by a stressed syllable: nŏw

/ ˇ / ˇ /
that / the win / ter's gone. The poet selects words and uses meter to stress the words that most effectively convey meaning. Notice how the stressed syllables contribute to the meaning of these lines from a sonnet by William Shakespeare.

ˇ / ˇ / ˇ / ˇ / ˇ /
All days are nights to see till I see thee,
ˇ / ˇ / ˇ / ˇ / ˇ /
And nights bright days when dreams do show thee me.

WILLIAM SHAKESPEARE

In formal poetry, a regular pattern of rhythm is used. The patterns vary greatly, but within each pattern there is a regular, systematic combination of stressed and unstressed syllables to create a beat like the beat in music. The beat may be varied from line to line (five beats in the first line, three beats in the second, five in the third, and so on), but a regular pattern exists within the whole poem. As you read the following stanzas from "The Raven" by Edgar Allan Poe, notice how the rhythm changes in some lines but is repeated from one stanza to the next. Which syllables are accented, and which are unaccented? How does the rhythm relate to the meaning?

Once upon a midnight dreary, while I pondered, weak and weary,
Over many a quaint and curious volume of forgotten lore,
While I nodded, nearly napping, suddenly there came a tapping,
As of some one gently rapping, rapping at my chamber door.
"'Tis some visitor," I muttered, "tapping at my chamber door—
Only this and nothing more."

Ah, distinctly I remember it was in the bleak December,
And each separate dying ember wrought its ghost upon the floor.
Eagerly I wished the morrow;—vainly I had sought to borrow
From my books surcease of sorrow—sorrow for the lost Lenore—
For the rare and radiant maiden whom the angels name Lenore—
Nameless here for evermore.

EDGAR ALLAN POE

Poetry with a regular rhythm and rhyme is sometimes called traditional poetry because it was the established way of writing until the nineteenth century. At that time, poets such as Walt Whitman, Amy Lowell, and Emily Dickinson began writing free verse.

Poetry that does not have a regular rhythm or rhyme is called *free verse.* In free verse rhythm exists, but the pattern is less regular, "freer" than it is in formal poetry. Much modern poetry uses free verse; the poets try to create rhythms that imitate the sounds of speech. (Natural speech does not use a regular rhythmic pattern.) Read the following poem by Theodore Roethke, and then compare the *natural* rhythms in this poem to the *regular* rhythms in the excerpt of the Poe poem.

CHILD ON TOP OF A GREENHOUSE

The wind billowing out the seat of my britches,
My feet crackling splinters of glass and dried putty,
The half-grown chrysanthemums staring up like accusers,
Up through the streaked glass, flashing with sunlight,
A few white clouds all rushing eastward,
A line of elms plunging and tossing like horses,
And everyone, everyone pointing up and shouting!

THEODORE ROETHKE

After you have read Roethke's poem, think about how it works. How do you respond to the poem? How does its language help you understand the significance of the speaker's experience? Would regular meter have been suitable for the subject? Why or why not?

## Repeated Sounds

Poets use repeated sounds, in addition to rhythm, to stress words and ideas and to convey meaning. Repeated sounds may be regular or random, exact or inexact. A regularly repeated sound may occur at the end of each line, at the end of every other line, in the middle of every line, and so forth. An exact sound is a perfect *rhyme,* as in *bright/light,* or *sensation/elation.* Repeated sounds that are inexact include *assonance, consonance,* and *alliteration.* The repetition of vowel sounds (*buzz/hum* and *say/weight*) is *assonance; consonance* is the repetition of consonant sounds (*tick/clock* and *fling/strong*); and *alliteration* is repeated identical sounds at the beginnings of words (*spritely, springy steps* and *battered, broken boards*).

Formal poetry contains regular rhyme as well as regular rhythm. Look at the lines from Shakespeare and Poe on page 221. The lines by Shakespeare have identical sounds at the ends of the lines (*thee/me*). The pattern of rhyme in the stanzas from "The Raven" is also regular, but it is more complex. The first line in each stanza has internal rhyme (*dreary/weary* and *remember/December*). Each stanza also has end rhyme (*lore/door/door/more* and *floor/Lenore/Lenore/more*). Rhyme, like the accented syllable in rhythm, creates emphasis, and so rhymed words should be important to the poem's meaning.

The repeated sounds in free verse are much more likely to be irregular and inexact. The following poem by Marianne Moore describes the adaptable reindeer and its contributions to the Eskimo. Notice how the irregular use of alliteration contributes to the meaning of the poem by stressing significant images and ideas.

RIGORISTS[1]

"We saw reindeer
browsing," a friend who'd been in Lapland, said:
"finding their own food; they are adapted
to scant *reino*[2]
or pasture, yet they can run eleven
miles in fifty minutes; the feet spread when
the snow is soft,
and act as snow-shoes. They are rigorists,
however handsomely cutwork artists
of Lapland and
Siberia elaborate the trace
or saddle-girth with saw-tooth leather lace.
One looked at us
with its firm face part brown, part white,—a queen
of alpine flowers. Santa Claus' reindeer, seen
at last, had grey-
brown fur, with a neck like edelweiss or
lion's foot,—*leontopodium* more
exactly." And
this candelabrum-headed ornament
for a place where ornaments are scarce, sent
to Alaska,
was a gift preventing the extinction
of the Esquimo. The battle was won
by a quiet man,
Sheldon Jackson,[3] evangel to that race
whose reprieve he read in the reindeer's face.

MARIANNE MOORE

What are some examples of alliteration in this poem? How does it contribute to the poet's meaning?

[1] *rigorist:* one who adheres to strict rules or leads an austere life.
[2] *reino:* pasture.
[3] *Sheldon Jackson:* Former U.S. Agent for Education for Alaska.

***Techniques for Writing.*** As you write a poem with regular rhyme and rhythm,

- decide what impression you want to convey.
- select a beat or rhythm that helps to convey this impression. (brisk and lively, heavy and threatening, quiet and somber)
- search for words that rhyme with the important words and that contribute to the poem's meaning.

**EXERCISE 22. Writing a Poem with Regular Rhyme and Rhythm.** Using the images and ideas you organized in Exercise 21 or another group of images and ideas, write a poem of at least four lines. Follow the suggestions above as you write.

***Techniques for Writing.*** To write a free-verse poem,

- read aloud and listen carefully to the natural sound patterns of the phrases and words you have gathered.
- write two or three lines of your poem, allowing the natural speech patterns to shape the rhythm.
- decide which words are the most important to your poem's meaning. From these, you may select beginning sounds to repeat or vowel and consonant sounds to stress. (Use alliteration, consonance, and assonance so they contribute to the poem's overall effectiveness.)

**EXERCISE 23. Writing a Free-Verse Poem.** Using the images and ideas you organized in Exercise 21 or another group of images and ideas, write a free-verse poem of at least eight lines. As you write, follow the suggestions listed above.

## USING FIGURATIVE LANGUAGE

### 8s. Use figurative language in your poetry.

Figurative language combines words in new ways to form fresh images in the reader's mind. Three of the most commonly used types of figurative language are simile, metaphor, and personification.

The simile and the metaphor are similar in that they both make comparisons between two seemingly unlike things. They are different in that the simile makes a direct comparison while the metaphor makes an implied comparison.

In a *simile,* words such as *like, than, as,* or *appears* are used to introduce the comparison. Review the poem by Roethke on page 222. He uses a simile to compare the chrysanthemums to accusers. What other simile does he use in this poem?

A *metaphor,* like a simile, compares two different things. A comparison is suggested that cannot literally be true. However, in contrast to the simile, the metaphor does not use words such as *like, than,* or *appears* in the comparison. While the comparison "My thoughts are skittish butterflies" is a metaphor, the comparison "My thoughts are like skittish butterflies" is a simile. In the poem on page 223, Marianne Moore uses a metaphor to compare a reindeer to a "candelabrum-headed ornament."

Your daily language is filled with similies and metaphors that have been used so often that they have become cliches. Avoid such overused comparisons as "He's as neat as a pin," "She's a bump on a log," and "My love is like a rose."

Another type of figurative language is *personification,* in which human characteristics are attributed to things, animals, or ideas. For example, "The pencil sharpener devoured the lead" attributes the human characteristic of eating, "devouring," to an object. In the following poem, "Cry Silent," Donna Whitewing personifies a tree. What human characteristics are given to the tree?

CRY SILENT

I touched a tree
    whereon a Sparrow sat
    and felt him fly away.
The tree followed,
    raising many leaf-feathered branches to
    rustling air.
Then, trembling on my hand
    the tree stood solid
    where we stood—together.
Walking away,
    "I might come again
    to touch
    that tear-streaked bark,"
        I thought.

DONNA WHITEWING

***Techniques for Writing.*** To write a poem using figurative language,

- decide where you can use figurative language. Select important words you want to startle or delight your audience.
- in writing similes and metaphors, make sure your comparisons are new and fresh. Old comparisons are often trite (for example, *as quiet as a mouse*).
- make certain that the two things you compare in similes and metaphors are basically *unlike.* (To say that one kind of flower is like another kind of flower is not a simile.)
- in using personification, search for vivid, precise verbs. (The wave *swallowed* the ball; the pencil sharpener *devoured* the lead.)

**EXERCISE 24. Using Figurative Language in Poetry.** Write a poem of at least eight lines in which you use two examples of figurative language. You may use formal rhyme and rhythm or free verse. If you do not wish to use ideas and images from Exercises 19 and 20, search for new ones.

## EVALUATING

### EVALUATING YOUR POEM

**8t. Evaluate your poetry for content and form.**

Because you must express a thought, image, or experience in a limited form, careful evaluation of a poem is essential. As with other kinds of writing, you can evaluate a poem more objectively if you set it aside for a while. Then, read your poem several times. In your final reading, focus on punctuation and capitalization. Punctuation in poetry indicates pauses in rhythm and marks the end of a complete thought or image. Commas indicate a brief pause and dashes a longer pause. A line of poetry does not have to end with a punctuation mark unless a complete thought is expressed.

In many poems (usually those with regular rhyme and meter), each line begins with a capital letter. As you evaluate your poem, decide what punctuation and capitalization will be appropriate. Use the following guidelines to evaluate your poems.

## GUIDELINES FOR EVALUATING POETRY

| | |
|---|---|
| Content | 1. Does the poem express a complete thought or image? |
| Rhyme and Meter | 2. If the poem has regular rhyme and meter, do they enhance the meaning? If the poem has an irregular rhythm, does it seem natural and appropriate for the meaning of the poem? |
| Language | 3. Are the descriptions and sensory details written in vivid, precise language? Does the figurative language evoke fresh, interesting images? |
| Mechanics | 4. Does the punctuation clarify the meaning and also enhance the rhythm? Is capitalization used in accordance with poetic form, or is it used effectively to enhance meaning? |

**EXERCISE 25. Evaluating Your Poem.** Select any poem you have written in this chapter, and evaluate it for form and content. Use the Guidelines for Evaluating Poetry as you mark those places that need revision. If possible, read it aloud to a small group of students, asking for their reactions and suggestions before you revise.

## REVISING

### REVISING YOUR POEM

**8u. Revise your poetry for content and form.**

In evaluating your poem, you discovered areas that require revision. Now you are ready to cut, add, reorder, or replace as you seek to make your poem as effective as possible. The following chart presents techniques for revising poetry. After you revise your poem, proofread it and prepare a final copy.

## REVISING POETRY

| PROBLEM | TECHNIQUE | REVISION |
|---|---|---|
| The poem does not express a complete thought or image. | Add | Add details, images, or ideas to produce a complete thought. |
| The rhyme and meter do not help convey the meaning. | Replace/ Reorder | Review the overall tone of your poem. Is it sad, joyous, angry? Replace and reorder words until the rhyme and meter enhance the tone and meaning. |
| The irregular rhythm seems unnatural or inconsistent with the meaning. | Replace/ Reorder | Detect where the rhythm does not fit the meaning; then replace and reorder words until the rhythm sounds natural. |
| The language lacks sensory details. | Replace | Replace the language you have used with words that appeal to the senses. |
| The figurative language is trite. | Cut/Replace | Cut any figures of speech that are worn out or that do not evoke a new, fresh image. Replace trite figures of speech with creative ones. |
| Punctuation is confusing. | Cut/Add | Cut unneeded punctuation at the end of lines. Add punctuation that would add to the clarity and effectiveness of the poem. |

**EXERCISE 26. Revising Your Poem.** Use the chart above to revise the poem you evaluated in Exercise 25. Then proofread, using the guidelines on page 29, and prepare a final copy.

## CHAPTER 8 WRITING REVIEW 1

**Writing A Short Story.** Write a short story about a character whose internal conflict involves making a difficult decision. (Ideas: meeting a responsibility or having fun; being loyal to a friend or following the crowd; trying to overcome a fear or giving in to it)

PREWRITING As you focus on a conflict and gather information, review your journal; check newspapers, magazines, and television programs; brainstorm; or interview relatives and friends. Identify how you want readers to respond to your story; state a purpose; then choose an appropriate tone. Think of all the possible events and problems your character might encounter.

Plan the beginning, the events that build suspense and lead to a climax in the middle, and the outcome or resolution of the conflict. Consider which details contribute to the character's qualities, and decide how you will reveal these qualities through description, action, and dialogue. Consider the sensory details of the setting and how they contribute to events. Organize this information for each stage of the plot.

WRITING Write a first draft of your story. Focus on details, description, and action that build suspense. Decide how to make the climax the most critical point of the conflict. Also consider the believability of your characters' actions, responses, and dialogue.

EVALUATING AND REVISING When you are ready to evaluate, identify what you need to improve in the plot (more suspense, a different outcome), in character development (dialogue that is truer to life, important information about the character, a reason for an action), and in the setting (sensory details that make the setting more real). Check your story against the guidelines on page 215. Then revise, consulting the chart on pages 216–17. Then proofread the story, following the guidelines on page 29. Pay close attention to punctuation of dialogue. Prepare a neat final copy.

## CHAPTER 8 WRITING REVIEW 2

**Writing A Play.** Choose a conflict that involves a struggle between two characters. The struggle need not be violent, but it should involve an adversary situation.

PREWRITING Identify your conflict and main characters. Gather ideas about possible conflicts and interesting characters by reviewing your journal, by reading news features and human interest stories, or by interviewing people. Select the most interesting and likely events to include in your play.

Summarize the plot, outlining what will occur in the beginning, middle, and end. Develop the main characters and decide how dialogue can reveal their personalities, values, and beliefs. Visualize your characters on stage and note how they will move in relation to the setting. Note items the characters will use or wear. Also consider how to make the setting reveal tone and mood.

WRITING Write your first draft in a play format. As you write dialogue, think about your goals for character and plot development. Also decide what you want each character to do and include specific stage directions. Put yourself in the place of each character, writing what you think the character would say. Ask yourself if the dialogue, actions, scenes, and outcome are believable.

EVALUATING AND REVISING Read your play silently and then read it aloud. Refer to the guidelines on page 215 to evaluate your play. Concentrate on character development through dialogue and actions. Focus also on moving the plot smoothly from the first scene to the last. Make the necessary revisions, using the chart on pages 216–17.

Before making a final copy, proofread your play, referring to the guidelines on page 29.

## CHAPTER 8 WRITING REVIEW 3

**Writing Free Verse.** Write a poem about a scene that makes you feel especially happy, peaceful, sad, or angry. Use the free-verse form, which has no regular rhyme or meter. Your purpose will be to share the scene and your feelings about the scene with your audience.

**PREWRITING** Review your journal to find memorable descriptions. Also use brainstorming and close observation of life around you. After selecting a subject, concentrate on the details of the scene, including sensory impressions and imaginative comparisons. Note words that describe the scene through their literal meanings as well as their sound patterns.

**WRITING** As you write, picture the scene in your mind and recall the rhythms that evoke a strong feeling. Use sensory details and vivid language. Decide whether a detail can be compared to something else with a simile or metaphor.

**EVALUATING AND REVISING** Read your poem both silently and aloud, using the Guidelines for Evaluating Poetry on page 227. Then use the revising chart on page 228 to improve your poem. Proofread your poem carefully and make a final copy.

# CHAPTER 9

# Writing a Research Paper

## RESEARCH, WRITING, DOCUMENTATION

A research paper is an extended expository composition that uses information gathered from a number of sources that is shaped by the thinking and judgment of the writer. In this chapter you will learn how to use the stages of the writing process to write a research paper. You will also learn some special procedures relating to papers based on library sources.

## PREWRITING

### SELECTING A SUBJECT

**9a. Select a subject suitable for research, one in which you have a genuine interest.**

Finding the right subject for your paper is crucial. A poor choice of subject makes it difficult to write a good paper. Choose a subject that interests you—perhaps a subject you studied briefly in one of your courses and would like to investigate in depth.

***Techniques for Prewriting.*** To choose a subject for a research paper, follow these suggestions:

- To gather subject ideas, thumb through the subject cards in the library card catalog, skim articles in current magazines and newspapers, or look at articles and pamphlets in the library's vertical file.
- Avoid straight biography. Although it is sometimes possible to write a successful research paper on a person's life, this kind of subject presents problems that you will do well to avoid. If the subject is already famous, your report will simply be a summary of other biographies; if the subject is not well known, information may be scarce.
- Before you make a final decision, check your library to make sure that ample, up-to-date sources about the subject will be readily available to you. In general, it is a good idea to avoid subjects that are too technical in nature or too recent in development.

**EXERCISE 1. Selecting a Subject.** List five possible subjects for a research paper. Then, using the suggestions above, select one for the subject of your research paper.

## GETTING AN OVERVIEW

**9b. Begin your research with some preliminary reading to get an overview, or general understanding, of your subject.**

Smart tourists use maps and other guides to identify the best route to their destination and to decide how to use their time. In a similar way, good researchers begin their work by reading general articles in encyclopedias and scanning books to develop an overview, or mental map, of the territory covered by their subject. This overview gives them ideas about how to limit the subject and helps them determine what basic questions they will try to answer in their research. It also helps later on when they begin the time-consuming process of reading and taking notes. Because they have a general understanding of the topic, they do not waste their energy taking notes on information they won't use.

***Techniques for Prewriting.*** To get an overview of your subject,

- find two or more general articles about your subject in encyclopedias or specialized reference books (see pages 681–88). Note headings and subheadings in each article as possible ways to limit the subject. After your reading, begin a list of possible limited topics and basic questions about your subject.
- look up your subject in the *Readers' Guide to Periodical Literature* (see pages 677–78) and review any relevant articles listed there.
- use the subject cards in the library card catalog to locate two or more books on your subject. After examining the table of contents and the major headings in the index, add to your list of possible topics and basic questions.
- look for your subject in the library's vertical file. Skim any available articles or pamphlets, and add any new ideas to your list of possible topics and basic questions.

**EXERCISE 2. Getting an Overview.** Begin researching the subject you chose in Exercise 1 by following the suggestions above.

## LIMITING YOUR SUBJECT

**9c. Limit your subject so that it can be handled within the assigned length of your paper.**

Students who try to write a research paper on too broad a subject may either spend hours producing a paper that is too long, or they may do a superficial job. It is essential to limit the scope of the subject. Suppose you are interested in the works of Willa Cather and think that you would like to do a research paper on her writing. Successive limitations of the topic may go something like this:

1. Willa Cather
   2. The works of Cather (specific aspect of Willa Cather)
      3. The novels of Cather (specific type of work)
         4. *O Pioneers!, The Song of the Lark, My Ántonia* (specific novels)
            5. Heroines in *O Pioneers!, The Song of the Lark, My Ántonia* (specific aspect of the novels)

The last item is a manageable topic, one that is sufficiently limited for a research paper.

***Techniques for Prewriting.*** As you limit your subject, keep the following suggestions in mind:

- To think of specific ways to limit your subject, review the information on pages 8–11 of Chapter 1, "Writing and Thinking."
- Consider the number of available sources on the subject. If many sources can be found, choose a narrower topic. Usually, the more limited the topic, the fewer the available sources.
- Consider the length of your report and how much detail you can include.

**EXERCISE 3. Recognizing Suitable Topics.** Some of the following topics are suitable for a research paper; others are not. For each faulty topic, indicate the nature of the weakness, and suggest how the topic might be improved.

1. The works of Doris Lessing
2. Water-skiing
3. The changing role of women
4. New safety procedures for the space shuttle program
5. Careers in science
6. Chemical composition of the atmosphere on Mars
7. The life of Ernest Hemingway
8. The Pulitzer Prize
9. The contributions of Asian-Americans
10. The concept of evil in modern American literature

**EXERCISE 4. Limiting Your Subject.** Limit the subject you selected in Exercise 1 to three topics suitable for a research paper.

## CONSIDERING PURPOSE, AUDIENCE, AND TONE

**9d. Evaluate your topic in terms of purpose, audience, and tone.**

Your purpose in writing a research paper, as with other types of exposition, is to explain or to inform. Evaluate your topic by asking yourself, "Will this topic result in a paper that explains or informs rather than one that narrates, describes, or persuades?" If not, you will need to select another basis on which to limit your original subject. The topic "the childhood of Willa Cather," for example, would most likely result in a chronological narrative, because it is developed on the basis of time periods.

Unless your teacher specifies otherwise, you can assume that the audience for your research paper is a general audience: educated readers, with a wide variety of backgrounds, who are interested in practically any topic that has significance or lasting importance and that is developed with fresh and specific information. A general audience would, for example, be interested in a nontechnical explanation of the effects of acid rain on plant life in the United States. This topic would not be suitable for an audience of botanists, however, because it would not offer them any information they do not already know.

Since a research paper is a serious undertaking, your tone should convey an objective and impartial attitude. You should adopt a formal, impersonal tone, one that avoids the use of informal language and first-person pronouns. Check the wording of your topic carefully to make sure that it reflects a formal, serious, impersonal tone.

**EXERCISE 5. Evaluating Topics.** Evaluate the following topics in terms of purpose, audience, and tone. Be prepared to explain why each topic is or is not suitable for a research paper.

1. Thomas Wolfe's childhood home in Asheville, North Carolina
2. Why the voting age should be raised to twenty-one
3. The 1986 appearance of Halley's Comet: what scientists learned
4. My opinion of Alice Walker's poetry
5. Heart abnormalities in beef cattle lacking biotin

**REVIEW EXERCISE A. Evaluating and Selecting Your Topic.** Evaluate the topics you developed in Exercise 4 in terms of the purpose, audience, and tone. If you determine that any topic is inappropriate or faulty, revise it. Then select one topic for your research paper.

## PREPARING A WORKING BIBLIOGRAPHY

**9e. Prepare a working bibliography.**

Once you have settled on a topic, your next step is to prepare a working bibliography, a compilation of potential source materials. Your search for specific sources will involve the research aids explained in Chapters 32 and 33. Unless you can tell at a glance that you know the information in those chapters, now would be a good time to study these chapters carefully.

***Techniques for Prewriting.*** To locate specific sources with information about your topic,

- record the titles listed at the end of articles in encyclopedias or in specialized reference books, and look for these sources.
- check all possible subject headings in the card catalog and the *Readers' Guide*. Sources with information on Willa Cather, for example, might be found under "American Literature," "Twentieth Century Literature," or "Literary Criticism." Remember, too, that past volumes of the *Readers' Guide* as well as current ones will be useful.
- check the bibliography (a list of books and articles the author used) in one of the sources you have located in order to identify other possible sources.
- check the index and table of contents in books to find out how much information they have about your topic.

## CRITICAL THINKING:
### Evaluating Potential Sources

Your objective at this point is to locate as many books and articles as possible that may prove to be useful. You will not always be able to tell whether a book or an article will be helpful from the information given in the library catalog, in the *Readers' Guide*, or in a bibliography. In general, however, it is wise to include in your working bibliography even items about which you are doubtful. If such items turn out to be of little use later on, you can simply drop them when you prepare your final bibliography.

To evaluate potential sources, use the following questions:

1. *Is the author an authority on the topic?* As you begin your research, you may not be able to answer this question. However, an author who has written several books or articles on a topic may turn out to be an authority—particularly if the author's work is often referred to

in other books on your topic. As you read, be on the watch for writers whose views are quoted or otherwise mentioned. You will probably want to consult the works from which such views are drawn.

2. *Is the book or article listed in any of the bibliographies you have consulted?* The first bibliographies you will look at are those in reference books. However, many of the books in your working bibliography are likely to contain bibliographies of their own. When you find one of these, check your own list of possible sources against it. Books and authors that appear again and again on such bibliographies are worth investigating.

3. *If a magazine article, what kind of magazine did it appear in?* In general, articles appearing in popular general-interest magazines, such as those you see on the newsstand, are not suitable sources for research papers because they do not go deeply into subjects. You can usually afford to ignore such articles unless they turn up in one of the bibliographies you encounter.

4. *If a book, for what audience is it intended?* Many interesting books on a variety of subjects are intended for younger readers. Such books are usually too simple. Other books contain technical information intended for experts, making them too complex to be suitable source material.

**EXERCISE 6. Evaluating Potential Sources.** Suppose you are doing a research paper on the heroines in three of Willa Cather's novels. Read the following list of books and consider what the titles suggest about the contents of the books. On your paper, indicate which of the following books sound as if they would be quite helpful, which you would be doubtful about, and which you could probably ignore safely.

Arnold, Marilyn. *Willa Cather's Short Fiction*
Bennett, Mildred R. *The World of Willa Cather*
Cather, Willa. *April Twilights, and Other Poems*
Crane, Joan. *Willa Cather: A Bibliography*
Daiches, David. *Willa Cather: A Critical Introduction*
Hartwick, Harry. *The Foreground of American Fiction*
Lewis, Edith. *Willa Cather Living: A Personal Record*
Rapin, René. *Willa Cather*
Van Doren, Carl. *The American Novel*
Woodress, James. *Willa Cather, Her Life and Art*

## Bibliography Cards

Use a separate 3 x 5-inch card or slip for each bibliographical reference. This system makes it easy to alphabetize the items and to add or delete items without recopying all of them. As you find materials that look promising, you may be tempted merely to jot down title and author in a rough list. However, the care you take now will eventually save you a great deal of time. Your bibliography cards should contain the following information:

BOOKS

1. Call number, in upper right-hand corner
2. Full name of author or editor, last name first for alphabetizing later (Indicate editor by placing *ed.* after the name.)
   If a book has two or more authors, only the name of the first author is given last name first; the names of the others are given first name first.
3. Title and subtitle, underlined (and edition, if second or later; and number of volumes, if more than one)
   Pamphlets only: series and number, if any
4. Place of publication (city)
5. Publisher (shortened, if clear)
6. Most recent copyright year (or date, for some pamphlets)

MAGAZINE, SCHOLARLY JOURNAL, NEWSPAPER, AND ENCYCLOPEDIA ARTICLES

1. Full name of author (unless article is unsigned)
2. Title of article, enclosed in quotation marks
3. Name of magazine, journal, newspaper, or encyclopedia, underlined
4. For magazines: date and page numbers. For scholarly journals: volume, year of publication (in parentheses), page numbers. For newspapers: date, edition, section, page numbers. For encyclopedias arranged alphabetically: edition (if given) and year of publication.

As you proceed, the importance of recording full bibliographical data for each source will become clear. For the present, note the importance of giving each card a number (the circled number at the upper left-hand corner of the following samples). As you complete your paper, your card numbers will spare you from having to copy source details to identify every note and quotation. Also note the punctuation on the sample cards, which follows the form recommended by the Modern Language Association (MLA). (*UP* is an abbreviation for University Press.) You may also want to note where the source can be found (city library, school library) at the bottom of the card. Your teacher may instruct you to use a different form.

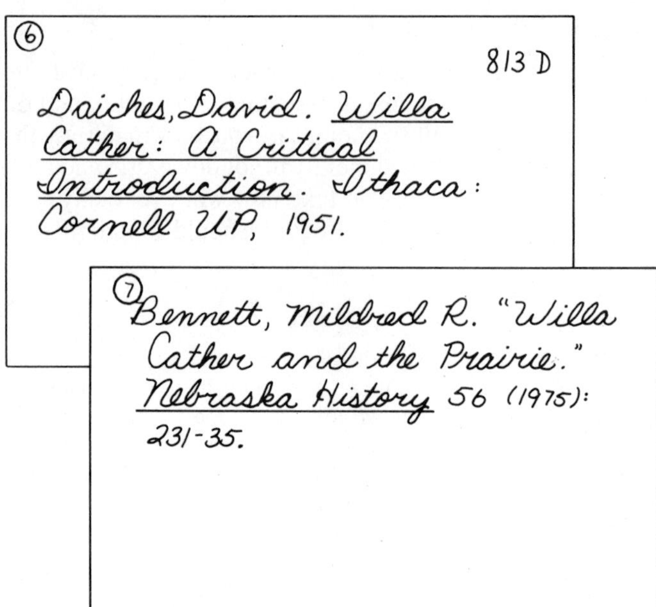


Sample Working-Bibliography Cards

**EXERCISE 7. Preparing Bibliography Cards.** Prepare bibliography cards for the following five items. You may want to look at the examples on this page for additional help. Underline titles and place quotation marks as necessary.

1. A book entitled Florida Wild Flowers and Roadside Plants, written by C. Ritchie Bell and Bryan J. Taylor and published by Laurel Hill Press in Chapel Hill in 1982
2. A book entitled Why We Can't Wait, written by Martin Luther King, Jr., and published by Harper & Row, Publishers, in New York in 1964
3. A book entitled Hanta Yo, written by Ruth Beebe Hill and published by Doubleday and Company, Inc., in Garden City in 1979
4. A journal article entitled Grammar, Grammars, and the Teaching of Grammar, by Patrick Hartwell in the February 1985 issue of College English, volume 47, pages 105 through 127
5. A book entitled The Story of Story Magazine: A Memoir, written by Martha Foley and published by W. W. Norton and Company in New York in 1980

**EXERCISE 8. Preparing Your Working Bibliography.** Prepare a working bibliography for the topic you selected in Review Exercise A. Your teacher may specify how many bibliography cards you should prepare.

## WRITING A PRELIMINARY THESIS STATEMENT

**9f. Bring your topic into focus by stating your thesis.**

A thesis statement for a research paper is like the thesis statement for an expository composition—it limits the scope of your topic, revealing both your purpose and attitude. (See pages 106–108.) It also controls the direction of your research by stating what you intend to show in the paper. In a more formal sense, the thesis is a proposition you will prove or support with the rest of your paper. A thesis statement should be a declarative sentence. The limited topic for the Willa Cather paper discussed on page 234 is "heroines in the novels *O Pioneers!, The Song of the Lark,* and *My Ántonia.*" Restated as a declarative sentence—the thesis statement—the topic might read as follows:

> The heroines in *O Pioneers!, The Song of the Lark,* and *My Ántonia* embody Willa Cather's heroic ideal.

Since your thesis statement should reflect the formal, objective tone appropriate to a research paper, choose your words carefully. Avoid slang and words that suggest an informal, personal tone (*I think, why I like, in my opinion,* etc.). Remember that you may revise your thesis statement as you work on your research paper.

**EXERCISE 9. Writing a Preliminary Thesis Statement.** Write a preliminary thesis statement for your research paper, keeping in mind your purpose and audience and the attitude you want to convey. Remember that the thesis statement should be a declarative sentence.

## PREPARING A PRELIMINARY OUTLINE

**9g. Prepare a preliminary outline as a guide for reading and taking notes.**

You now have a stack of cards—your working bibliography—and a preliminary thesis statement. Your next step is to prepare a rough outline that will suggest the general headings under which you will be taking notes.

Begin by thinking through your topic and asking *questions about the topic* (see pages 16–17) to see what major divisions and subdivisions appear. Using your answers to these questions as headings and subheadings, make your preliminary outline. Do not worry about matters of style or about the final organization of the headings. As your reading progresses, you will find some points irrelevant or inadequately covered in the sources available to you; these can be eliminated. On the other hand, your reading will suggest new points that you will want to include. Revise your preliminary outline as you take notes, after you complete your research, and again before you prepare the final version of your paper.

When you are ready to draw up your preliminary outline, follow these suggestions:

1. Put the title of your paper at the top.
2. Immediately below the title, write the word *Thesis* followed by your thesis statement.
3. Do not include too much detail in your preliminary outline. You will add more detail as you go along.

The following preliminary outline shows how the writer of the Cather paper expanded the topic and thesis into a plan of action for a research paper. (You may want to compare this preliminary outline with the final outline on page 265.)

*Title:* A Study of the Heroines in Three Novels by Willa Cather
*Thesis:* The heroines in *O Pioneers!, The Song of the Lark,* and *My Ántonia* embody Willa Cather's heroic ideal.

1. Cather's novels about the West
   —American pioneer life
   —symbolism of her heroines
2. Cather's heroines
   —characteristics
   —union of European and American traditions
3. The heroine of *O Pioneers*!
4. The heroine of *The Song of the Lark*
5. The heroine of *My Ántonia*
   —victory over hardship and sacrifice
   —feeling for tradition
6. Change in emphasis in Cather's later work

**EXERCISE 10. Preparing a Preliminary Outline.** Using your preliminary thesis statement and your working bibliography, develop questions about your topic. Then draw up a preliminary outline to use as a guide for gathering information.

## GATHERING INFORMATION ON YOUR TOPIC

**9h. Take notes on your research, using cards classified according to the points in your preliminary outline.**

With your working bibliography, preliminary thesis statement, and outline before you, you are ready to continue your research. Now you have a clear idea of what you are looking for. *Never read sources for a research paper without taking notes on your reading.* Even for the main points in a paper, your memory is an unreliable guide. When it comes to specific facts and quotations, you *must* have a full and accurate record of the material you have accumulated.

Take all notes on 4 x 6-inch index cards. Using the larger size will help you prevent your note cards from getting mixed up with your bibliography cards. Follow the form and style of the sample note card on this page. Explanations of the various entries on the card appear below. (For a list of abbreviations, see page 261.)

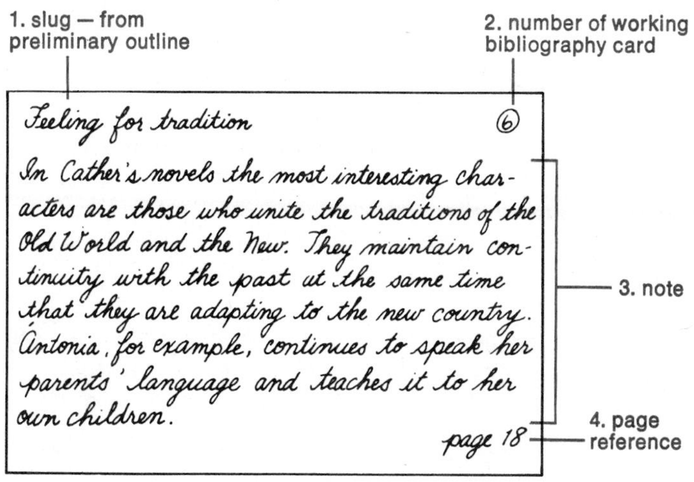


**Sample Note Card—Paraphrase**

1. **The "slug."** The line at the upper left, called a "slug," is simply a heading or subheading from your preliminary outline. Include on a card only notes pertaining to one slug; use a different card for each source.

You may delete part of the outline if your sources clearly do not contain usable material on a heading. If you decide during your reading that two headings should be combined, remember to change both the outline and the slugs on the appropriate cards.

Victory over hardship and sacrifice ②

"She [Ántonia] is the person whose inner strength enables her to live the enviable life.... [when she makes her last appearance, her hair is grizzled and most of her teeth have gone; but she 'was still there in the full vigor of her personality.' Looking at her, one feels that is how one should have lived - if one could."

pages 206-07

**Sample Note Card—Quotation**

2. **Bibliographical reference.** At the upper right-hand corner of each note card, enter the number you assigned to the source on the working bibliography card. For example, the number on the annotated sample note card on page 243 is the number of the working bibliography card for a book entitled *Willa Cather: A Critical Introduction,* by David Daiches. By referring to the card in the working bibliography, you can check source information whenever you need to.

3. **The note.** The notes you take should generally be in your own words. Read a passage carefully and then *paraphrase* it; that is, restate the ideas in your own words. This will save you unnecessary copying. It will also prevent you from committing unintentional *plagiarism*—the use of another person's words or ideas without acknowledging the source. Occasionally, you will want to copy down an author's exact words. Do so when the author expresses a point so well that he or she

clearly supports your own ideas, or when paraphrasing might distort the meaning of the passage. Keep in mind, however, that a research paper is not just a collection of quotations from various authors on one subject. Sometimes you might want to combine paraphrase and quotation on the same card. The sample note cards on pages 243–44 are examples of paraphrase and quotation; the sample note card below is an example of a combined paraphrase and quotation.

Change in emphasis in Cather's later work ⑧

After My Antonia Cather experienced a crisis in her art. The heroism and romance she had found in pioneer life were disappearing. The contemporary life she saw filled her with despair. "Once she had created symbols of triumph in Alexandra, Thea, and Antonia, but now she concerned herself with symbols of defeat."

page 706

**Sample Note Card—Combined Paraphrase and Quotation**

There are some special points of punctuation to note on the card on page 244. First, the double quotation marks are used to indicate a verbatim (word-for-word) quotation. Next, observe that the note-taker has added the word *Ántonia* to the quoted material in order to clarify the reference for the pronoun *she*. Brackets are placed around this word to indicate that it did not appear in the original. Third, the ellipsis ( . . . ) is used to indicate that some words have been omitted from the original. Fourth, a slash (/) indicates the point at which page 206 in the source ends and page 207 begins. Finally, single quotation marks are used to indicate a quotation from the novel used by the author of the source.

4. **Page reference.** Beneath the note, jot down the page or pages on which you found the material. This page reference serves two important purposes. First, you may want to return to a page later to clarify a point; and second, you will need exact page references when you write your paper.

***Techniques for Prewriting.*** To take notes from a source, follow these suggestions:

- To avoid taking notes you won't use, begin with a source that provides a thorough, detailed treatment of your topic. If the same information appears later in other sources, you will not need to record it again.
- Think carefully about the kind of note you want to make from this source: *summarize* to present the author's main ideas, *paraphrase* to record specific facts or details, and *quote* to record the author's exact words (when the author's language is as important as the idea).
- Do not put notes about different slugs on the same card.
- Do not put notes from different sources on the same card.
- Be sure you have recorded the source number, the slug, and the page number of the information.

**EXERCISE 11. Gathering Information on Your Topic.** Using the preliminary outline you prepared in Exercise 10 as a guide, gather information on your topic. Follow the preceding guidelines for taking notes, too.

## CLASSIFYING AND ORGANIZING INFORMATION

### 9i. Classify and organize your note cards and prepare a formal outline.

When you prepared your preliminary outline, you had only a general understanding of your topic. As a result of your research, your knowledge of the topic has changed. You have probably discovered important new information that should be included in your paper; you may also have found that a point you planned to develop in detail is not as significant as you first thought. As a result of your research, you will need to organize your notes and revise your original outline.

Essentially, you will be preparing a formal topic outline, as described on pages 103–106. However, do not let your outline get out of hand. Usually your material, however rich and varied, can be organized under no more than six main headings. If you find that you have more than six, recheck your organization to make sure that you have not mistaken subtopics for main ideas or tried to include too much information. Your teacher may ask you to submit your revised outline with your completed research paper.

***Techniques for Prewriting.*** To prepare a formal outline, follow these guidelines:

- Put all cards with the same slug (heading) in one stack.
- Review each stack separately. Do your notes adequately explain that point, or will you need to gather additional information? Do any cards contain unrelated information? If so, take them out. Does each group of cards relate to your thesis? Should any be omitted?
- Compare each group of cards with the headings in your preliminary outline. What new headings or subheadings should be added? What headings or subheadings should be taken out or changed?
- Think carefully about organization. Are headings and subheadings arranged in a logical order that will be easy for readers to follow? Is each subheading a logical division of that particular heading? (For help in organizing ideas, see pages 101–103.)
- Prepare a topic outline, using Roman numerals, capital letters, and Arabic numerals correctly to indicate smaller and smaller divisions of the topic. (See pages 103–106 about outline form.)

**REVIEW EXERCISE B. Preparing a Revised Outline.** Classify and organize your note cards, revise your thesis statement, and prepare a revised outline. Your teacher may ask you to submit your note cards, thesis, and outline for approval before you begin to write your paper.

## WRITING

### WRITING THE FIRST DRAFT

**9j. Write the first draft from your revised outline.**

With your outline as complete as possible and your note cards sorted and arranged to conform to the outline, you are ready to put your information and ideas down on paper. Above all, remember that this is a first draft. Simply set your ideas and information down freely, in a form you will be able to follow when you revise the paper.

Keep your note cards in front of you as you write, and take advantage of the information they contain. Also make constant use of the information on your bibliography cards. A research paper is not the place for speculation or unsupported opinions, but for solid information drawn from your research and carefully credited to its source. As you write, maintain the objective, serious tone appropriate to a research paper. Also be sure to apply your knowledge of the paragraph and of the expository composition.

---

## CRITICAL THINKING:
### Synthesizing

Like the first draft of any composition, the first draft of a research paper is a synthesis, or putting together, of separate elements to form a new whole. The greater complexity of the synthesis involved in writing a research paper is evident from the number of different parts you must mesh into a unified, coherent presentation.

As you write your first draft, you will need to reconsider all the decisions you made during the prewriting stage, keeping in mind your audience, purpose, and tone. You will also need to incorporate the information gathered from your research in such a way that it clearly and forcefully supports your thesis. In addition, you must document, or credit, your sources, using one of the methods explained in the following pages, and provide transitions that will enable your readers to follow your line of reasoning. As you can see, the critical thinking skill of synthesis involves other critical thinking skills such as analysis and evaluation. If you have worked carefully through the prewriting stage, you should be able to concentrate on interweaving the various elements to produce a well-written paper. If not, you will have to retrace your steps in the writing process.

## Documentation

The three methods of documenting sources used for research papers are footnotes, endnotes, and parenthetical citations. Your teacher will indicate which method you should use in your research paper.

Whichever method you use, keeping in mind that your audience is a general one will help you decide which ideas and facts to document.

Facts likely to be known to a general audience, such as the fact that Willa Cather was a famous American writer, need not be documented. Be careful not to assume too much knowledge on the part of your audience, however. If you are not sure whether a specific fact is general or specialized knowledge, you should give its source.

***Techniques for Writing.*** To decide whether a source should be documented in your research paper, use the following guidelines:

- Always document the source of a direct quotation.
- Document the source of specific surveys, scientific experiments, polls, and research studies.
- Document a new or unusual theory or opinion, or one held by a particular author, even if you present the author's ideas in your own words.
- Document rare, unusual, or questionable facts and statistics, especially if they appear in only one source.
- Usually it is not necessary to document facts or ideas that appear in several sources. Also, do not document facts widely available in reference books (the Civil War began at Fort Sumter; the UN was organized on November 4, 1946) or commonly accepted theories and opinions (labor unions affect the American economy; nuclear warfare would result in vast destruction).

## Footnotes

To indicate the addition of a footnote to your text, write or type a number slightly above and to the right of the punctuation mark at the end of the sentence, phrase, or clause that contains a quotation or an idea from a source. There are two common ways of numbering footnotes; be sure that you know which method your teacher wants you to follow. One way is to begin the numbering over again on each page—that is, two footnotes on page one would be numbered 1 and 2, and the first footnote on page two would be numbered 1. The second way is to number the footnotes consecutively throughout the paper; in a paper with a total of twenty footnotes, for example, the last one would be numbered 20. The MLA prefers the second method.

The footnotes themselves are added at the bottom of the page. As you write each page, plan ahead so that there will be enough space for all the necessary footnotes.

Be sure first to number your footnotes correctly, so that each footnote reference in the text has an identically numbered footnote at the bottom of the page. Within the footnotes themselves, be sure that you include all necessary items in their correct order. The correct items and order for the *first* mention of a source are given below and on the next page. (A footnote for an anonymous work begins with the title.) Each footnote should end with a period. Months of the year—except May, June, and July—are abbreviated.

BOOK OR PAMPHLET

1. Author's name (first name first), followed by a comma
2. Book or pamphlet title (underlined)
3. City followed by a colon, publisher followed by a comma, and date, all within parentheses
4. Page number(s) followed by a period

MAGAZINE OR SCHOLARLY JOURNAL

1. Author's name (first name first), followed by a comma
2. Title of article (in quotation marks), followed by a comma
3. Name of magazine or scholarly journal (underlined)
4. Volume number (if any) of scholarly journal
5. Year (in parentheses), followed by a colon, for a scholarly journal; month and year, followed by a colon, for a magazine
6. Page number(s) followed by a period

EXAMPLES

[1]Katherine Anne Porter, The Collected Essays and Occasional Writings (New York: Delacorte, 1970) 47. [book by one author]

[2]William Strunk, Jr., and E. B. White, The Elements of Style, 3rd ed. (New York: Macmillan, 1978) 33. [book by two authors; also the third edition]

[3]Anaïs Nin, The Diary of Anaïs Nin, 7 vols. (New York: Harcourt Brace Jovanovich, 1979) 7: 120. [one volume in a multivolume work in which all have the same title]

[4]Winston S. Churchill, The Age of Revolution, vol. 3 of A History of the English-Speaking Peoples (New York: Dodd, 1957) 123. [one volume in a multivolume work with different titles]

[5]Homer, Odyssey, trans. Richmond Lattimore (New York: Harper, 1967) 153. [translation]

[6]Martin Eban, "A History of Parapsychology," Psychic Exploration: A Challenge for Science, ed. John White (New York: Putnam's, 1974) 133–34. [one article in a collection by different authors]

[7]James M. Cox, "Learning Through Ignorance: *The Education of Henry Adams*," *The Sewanee Review* 88 (1980): 227. [article in a scholarly journal that numbers its pages continuously throughout each volume year]

[8]"Rabies," *Sciquest* Mar. 1980: 28. [unsigned article in a magazine that numbers its pages issue-by-issue]

[9]Hans Jurgen Eysenck, "Theories of Parapsychological Phenomena," *Encyclopaedia Britannica: Macropaedia*, 1979 ed. [article in an encyclopedia arranged alphabetically]

[10]Dr. Melanie Smith, personal interview, 14 May 1980. [interview]

[11]"Caffeine," *The MacNeil/Lehrer Report*, PBS, WQED, Pittsburgh, 4 Sept. 1980. [television program]

[12]*Logic*, computer software, Fathom Software, 1985. [computer software]

Once you have given complete documentation for a source in one footnote, you can use a shortened form in later references to the same source. Usually, the author's last name and the page number are sufficient.

EXAMPLES

[1]Katherine Anne Porter, *The Collected Stories of Katherine Anne Porter* (New York: Harcourt Brace Jovanovich, 1985) 113.
[2]Porter, 122.

If you are using two or more sources by the same author, include a shortened form of the specific title each time you cite either source.

EXAMPLES

[4]Porter, *Collected Stories* 204.
[5]Porter, *Collected Essays* 312.

If you mention the title of the work in the text, you do not need to repeat the title in the footnote. Similarly, if you mention the author's name in the text, you need not include the name in the footnote.

EXAMPLES

[8]Porter, *Collected Stories* 142. [neither name nor title mentioned in text]
[8]Porter, 142. [title mentioned in text]
[8]*Collected Stories* 142. [name mentioned in text]

**EXERCISE 12. Preparing Footnotes.** The following items contain all the information needed to write a group of footnotes. Assign footnote numbers, and write the five footnotes in the order given. Assume that neither the authors' names nor the titles are mentioned in the text, and that the last footnote on page 6 was numbered 8.

*Footnotes on page 7 of manuscript:*

1. A book entitled Mark Twain and Southwestern Humor, written by Kenneth S. Lynn and published in 1959 in Boston by Little, Brown and Co. Reference to page 112.
2. An article entitled Mark Twain: The Writer as Pilot, by Edgar J. Burde, published in PMLA, volume 93, October 1978. Reference to page 878.
3. A book entitled Sam Clemens of Hannibal, by Dixon Wecter, published in 1952 in Boston by Houghton Mifflin Co. Reference to page 27.

*Footnotes on page 8 of manuscript:*

4. A second reference to Wecter's book. Reference to page 44.
5. An article entitled Mark Twain, by Dixon Wecter, collected in the fourth edition of Literary History of the United States, published in New York in 1974 by Macmillan Publishing Co., Inc. Reference to page 931.

## Endnotes

Endnotes contain the same information as footnotes and follow the same format. Instead of appearing at the bottoms of the pages, however, they are collected on a separate page headed "Notes," immediately before the bibliography. Endnotes are always numbered consecutively within the text of the paper.

## Parenthetical Citations

Parenthetical citations supply information about sources within parentheses positioned close to the author's ideas or exact words. This method is recommended by the Modern Language Association (MLA), a highly respected organization of language and literature scholars. With this method, numbered notes are used only for extensive explanatory comments that would interrupt a paper if included. Such notes may be treated as footnotes (see pages 249–51) or endnotes.

A parenthetical citation is placed before the punctuation mark at the end of the sentence, phrase, or clause containing a quotation or idea from a source. The exception is the extended quotation (more than four lines), which is set off from the text by indentation; in this case, the citation follows the last punctuation mark. (See page 268 for an example.)

While it may seem that information within the parentheses is sometimes scanty, remember that the main purpose of the citation is to refer the reader to complete source information in the bibliography. Documenting sources in this manner frees the writer for the real work of research—pulling together and interpreting information about a topic.

To use parenthetical citations, follow these MLA guidelines:

1. In most instances, the only necessary information is the author's last name and the page number or numbers from which the idea or quotation is taken. There is no punctuation between the author's last name and the page number or numbers, and the words *page* and *pages* and their abbreviations *p.* and *pp.* are not used. If there are works by authors with the same last name in the bibliography, both authors' first and last names are used.

EXAMPLE Cather's heroines are all superior women of epic stature, protagonists with "tenacious wills and an extraordinary capacity for struggle" (Edel 8).

By referring to the bibliography of the sample research paper (see page 272), you know that the source of this information is a book by Leon Edel entitled *Willa Cather: The Paradox of Success,* published by the Library of Congress in 1960. If there had been another work by an author named Edel in the bibliography, the citation would have read (Leon Edel 8).

2. If a work in the bibliography has two or more authors, either use all last names, followed by the page number or numbers, or use just the first author's last name, followed by *et al.* (Latin, meaning "and others") and the page number or numbers. For example, if the Leon Edel book mentioned above had also been written by two other authors, such as Samuel Johnson and Eleanor Smith, the citation could have been written as either (Edel, Johnson, and Smith 8) or (Edel et al. 8).

3. If there is more than one title by the same author in the bibliography, use the author's last name and the title or a shortened form of it in your citation. In this case, a comma comes between the author's last name and the title, but not between the title and the page number or numbers.

EXAMPLE Throughout her life Alexandra maintains a spiritual bond with the land. Her youngest and favorite brother, Emil, observes that when she looks at the land her face is radiant. She is overwhelmed by her own feelings of joy: "It seemed beautiful to her, rich and strong and glorious. Her eyes drank in the breadth of it, until her eyes blinded her" (Cather, *O Pioneers!* 65).

In the example above, the reference to the title is necessary because three different books by Willa Cather are listed in the bibliography.

4. If a work in a bibliography has no author, use the title or a shortened form of it in your citation. Do not place a comma between the title and the page number or numbers: (*MLA Handbook* 34)

5. In any instance in which the author's name or the title of the work is mentioned nearby in your paper, it is not necessary to repeat either the author or the title in your citation. In that instance, you might have a citation such as the following one:

EXAMPLE As Alfred Kazin has noted, "The tenacious ownership of the land, the endless search of its possibilities, become the very poetry of her character" (252).

The following items show other types of parenthetical citations you might use in preparing your research paper:

(Johnson 2: 21, 142) [the source is a multivolume work]
(Costello) [the entire work, rather than a specific page is cited]
(Smith 93; Scheftner and Andreasen 81) [two sources are cited for the same information]
(qtd. in Wong 83) [original source not available; material quoted from an indirect source]
(3.1. 57–58) [quoted from Act 3, Scene 1, lines 57–58 of a play]

## The Bibliography

All the information you need to prepare the bibliography, sometimes titled "Works Cited," is already on your working-bibliography cards. Your tasks in writing the first draft include selecting entries and writing them in the correct style. The bibliography should include only the sources that you actually cite in your paper.

In arranging bibliographical entries, observe the following guidelines:

1. Alphabetize items according to the last names of authors or, for anonymous articles, the first important word in titles. (You can do this simply by arranging the cards from your working bibliography in alphabetical order.) Do *not* number the entries.

2. When a bibliography includes more than one work by an author, do not repeat the author's name after its first appearance. Instead, substitute three hyphens for the author's name in the second and subsequent entries, and alphabetize the works by title.

3. When an entry takes more than one line, indent five spaces all lines after the first line.

4. Use a period at the end of each entry.

EXAMPLES [The following entries are examples of different bibliographic forms. They are not in alphabetical order because they are from different bibliographies. For a complete bibliography in alphabetical order, see page 272.]

Porter, Katherine Anne. The Collected Essays and Occasional Writings. New York: Delacorte, 1970. [book with one author]

---. The Collected Stories of Katherine Anne Porter. New York: Harcourt Brace Jovanovich, 1965. [book by the author of the previous entry]

Strunk, William, Jr., and E. B. White. The Elements of Style. 3rd ed. New York: Macmillan, 1978. [book with two authors]

Nin, Anaïs. The Diary of Anaïs Nin. 7 vols. New York: Harcourt Brace Jovanovich, 1979. [one volume of a multivolume work used; specific references to volume numbers appear in the text]

Homer. Odyssey. Trans. Richmond Lattimore. New York: Harper, 1967. [translation]

Eban, Martin. "A History of Parapsychology." Psychic Exploration: A Challenge for Science. Ed. John White. New York: Putnam's, 1974. 172–75. [one article in a collection of articles]

Cox, James M. "Learning Through Ignorance: The Education of Henry Adams." The Sewanee Review 88 (1980): 198–227. [article, continuous-pagination scholarly journal]

"Rabies." Sciquest Mar. 1980: 28. [unsigned article, separate-pagination magazine]

Eysenck, Hans Jurgen. "Theories of Parapsychological Phenomena." Encyclopaedia Britannica: Macropaedia 1979 ed. [article in alphabetized encyclopedia]

Molotsky, Irvin. "Advertised Baldness Drugs Useless, U.S. Says." New York Times 15 Jan. 1985, natl. ed.: 1. [newspaper article]

Smith, Dr. Melanie. Personal interview. 14 May 1980. [interview]

"Caffeine." The MacNeil/Lehrer Report. PBS. WQED, Pittsburgh. 4 Sept. 1980. [television program]

**EXERCISE 13. Preparing a Bibliography.** The following items contain information for a bibliography to accompany a research paper on Willa Cather. Arrange the items correctly and use the proper form in each.

1. A book by James Woodress entitled *Willa Cather, Her Life and Art,* published in New York by Pegasus in 1970.
2. An article by Quentin Anderson entitled "Willa Cather: Her Masquerade," published in *New Republic,* pages 28–31, on November 27, 1965.
3. An anonymous article entitled "Willa Catherland: Memorial at Red Cloud," published in *Nebraska Holiday,* page 70, in January 1974.
4. An article by Willa Cather entitled "Nebraska: The End of the First Cycle," published in *The Nation,* pages 236–38, on September 5, 1923.
5. An article by James E. Miller, Jr., entitled "Willa Cather and the Art of Fiction." It appears in a book of articles entitled *The Art of Willa Cather,* edited by Bernice Slote and Virginia Faulkner, published in 1974 by the University of Nebraska Press in Lincoln.

### Charts, Diagrams, and Illustrations

Include such material whenever you believe it will help your paper, being careful to indicate the source. It is usually best to copy or trace these items. *Never* cut apart library sources to use in this way.

**REVIEW EXERCISE C. Writing the First Draft.** Using your note cards, thesis statement, revised outline, and bibliography cards, write the first draft of your research paper. Express your ideas clearly, incorporate your research, document your sources carefully, and remember your purpose, audience, and tone.

## EVALUATING AND REVISING

Although evaluation and revision are two different processes, they are closely related. When you evaluate your writing, you examine it carefully and judge its strengths and weaknesses. When you revise, you make specific changes in your writing to correct the weaknesses you have identified. Because a research paper is a longer, more complicated expository composition, you may want to evaluate, then revise, one aspect of your writing at a time.

## EVALUATING YOUR FIRST DRAFT

**9k. Evaluate the content, organization, style, and format of your research paper.**

Since any changes you make in the content of your paper may affect organization and style, evaluate this aspect of your paper first. When you are satisfied with the content of your paper, look closely at your organization. Then, evaluate matters of style and format (especially documenting sources and incorporating quotations). Use the following guidelines to evaluate your research paper. You may also find it helpful to refer to the Guidelines for Evaluating Expository Compositions on page 117.

### GUIDELINES FOR EVALUATING RESEARCH PAPERS

| | |
|---|---|
| Introduction | 1. Does the introduction include a thesis statement that clearly states the purpose of the paper? Does it catch the audience's attention? |
| Topic Development | 2. Does each paragraph in the body develop one idea about the topic? Does each paragraph include specific details and examples from the writer's research? |
| Topic Development | 3. Is there enough information for readers to follow the line of reasoning? Is there any unrelated or irrelevant information? Are quotations and ideas from sources incorporated into the text to achieve the paper's purpose? |
| Conclusion | 4. Does the end of the paper obviously conclude the presentation? Does it reinforce the thesis statement? |
| Coherence | 5. Are ideas about the topic presented in a logical order, both in paragraphs and in sentences within each paragraph? Are there clear and logical transitions, or connections, between paragraphs and between major sections in the paper? |

| | |
|---|---|
| Emphasis | 6. Is the emphasis on various ideas made clear by means of the wording, placement, or amount of text devoted to them? |
| Word Choice | 7. Is the language appropriate for a general audience? Are technical terms and unusual vocabulary defined or explained? Does the language reveal the serious tone appropriate for a research paper? Does the title clearly indicate the paper's topic? |
| Format | 8. Are sources documented in the text, using the MLA format (parenthetical notes) or some other acceptable format? Are short quotations incorporated into the text? Are longer quotations set off from the text? Are correct form and alphabetical order used in the bibliography? |

**EXERCISE 14. Evaluating Your First Draft.** Evaluate the first draft of your research paper, using the guidelines above and the Guidelines for Evaluating Expository Compositions on page 117. Keep notes on your draft about items you need to improve. You may also want to exchange papers with a classmate to evaluate each other's papers.

## REVISING YOUR FIRST DRAFT

**9l. Based on your evaluation, revise the content, organization, style, and format of your first draft.**

Revision, the process of making changes to improve your writing, involves analyzing, or carefully examining, a weakness in your writing and determining how to eliminate or correct the problem. To revise your research paper, you will use the same basic techniques (adding, removing, reordering, and replacing) you use to revise other forms of expository composition. Use the revising chart on pages 26–27 to revise your research paper. However, as you make changes in the text of your paper, remember that you may also need to revise the outline, citations, and the bibliography.

As you work on your first draft, pay special attention to improving the unity and coherence of the entire paper and of each paragraph. Irrelevant material or illogical organization that makes your paper difficult to understand will detract from the time and effort you have spent on careful research. (For more information on revision techniques, see pages 24–27 in the chapter "Writing and Thinking.")

**EXERCISE 15. Revising Your Research Paper.** Using the revision chart on pages 26–27 and the techniques you learned in Chapter 1, revise your research paper. You may need to revise the paper more than once before you are satisfied with it.

## PROOFREADING

### PROOFREADING YOUR RESEARCH PAPER

**9m. Proofread for grammar, usage, and mechanics.**

Once you are satisfied with your research paper's content, organization, style, and format, proofread it carefully to correct errors in grammar, usage, and mechanics. You may want to review the section on proofreading in Chapter 1 before you begin.

**EXERCISE 16. Proofreading Your Revised Draft.** Using the correction symbols on page 33, proofread your paper carefully for errors in grammar, usage, and mechanics. You should also refer to the Guidelines for Proofreading on page 29.

## PREPARING A FINAL VERSION

### PREPARING THE FINAL VERSION OF YOUR RESEARCH PAPER

**9n. Prepare a final version of your research paper, following correct manuscript form.**

As a final step, prepare a clean copy of your revised and proofread draft. You will need to proofread this final version as well, to make sure that you have not made any errors in recopying. As you prepare this clean copy, use the following MLA guidelines:

1. Type or write your paper neatly and legibly on one side of acceptable paper.
2. Leave one-inch margins at the top, bottom, and sides of each page.
3. Double-space throughout, including title, quotations, and bibliography.

You will also need to assemble the parts of the paper in the following order or in the order your teacher requires.

1. *The cover.* Using staples, metal clasps, or other fasteners, bind your paper in a stiff cover. Give the title of the paper on the outside; make the cover simple but attractive.

2. *The title page.* Use a separate page as a title page. Following your teacher's directions, place your name, information about your class (name and number of the course), and the date one inch from the top of the first page, even with the left margin. Double-space between these lines. Center the title with double-spacing between the information described above and the title. Double-space twice between the title and the first line of your paper. Do not put quotation marks around your title.

3. *The final outline.* Insert your final revised topic outline directly after the title page. In this position, the outline serves as a kind of table of contents.

4. *The paper itself.* Begin the page numbering with the first page. Number consecutively all the pages of the paper, including the bibliography and those containing only charts or diagrams. Place page numbers in the upper right-hand corner of each page, one-half inch below the top of the page and fairly close to the right margin. Use a number without *page, pages,* or their abbreviations.

5. *The bibliography.* Use as many pages as you need for the bibliography, allowing the same margins as those on the pages of the paper itself.

**REVIEW EXERCISE D. Preparing the Final Version of Your Research Paper.** Prepare the final version of your research paper. Proofread it carefully, and assemble the parts of the paper according to your teacher's instructions.

## CHAPTER 9 WRITING REVIEW

**Writing a Research Paper.** Select a research paper you have written in one of your other classes, such as history or science. Evaluate this paper by applying the Guidelines for Evaluating Research Papers on page 257. Then revise the paper by referring to the revision chart on pages 26–27. Be prepared to discuss how knowledge of the writing process and of the research paper can be applied to improve your work in your other classes.

### *Abbreviations Used in Sources*

In reading for a research paper, you will encounter a number of scholarly abbreviations established by long usage. A short list of the most common abbreviations follows. Avoid using these abbreviations in your own work, except those such as *ed.* and *trans.*

c *or* © *copyright*; used before a date to indicate the year in which copyright was obtained: ©1978. If a date appears on the *title page* of a publication, use that date in your bibliographical references; otherwise, use the copyright date on the *back* of the title page.

*c., ca.* *about* (from the Latin *circa, circum*); used with dates: c 100 B.C.; ca. A.D. 500

*cf.* *compare* (from the Latin *confer*): cf. Declaration of Independence ["Compare (this statement, etc.) with the Declaration of Independence."]

ed. *editor, edited, edition*

*e.g.* *for example* (from the Latin *exempli gratia*)

*et al.* *and others* (from the Latin *et alii*); also, *and elsewhere* (from the Latin *et alibi*)

f., ff. *following page, pages:* p. 51f. ("page 51 and the following page"); p. 51ff. ("page 51 and the following pages)"

*ibid.* *in the same place* (from the Latin *ibidem*); no longer recommended by the MLA

*id.* *the same* (from the Latin *idem*)

*i.e.* *that is* (from the Latin *id est*)

l., ll. *line, lines*

*loc. cit.* *in the place* (source) *previously cited* (from the Latin *loco citato*) ms., mss. *manuscript, manuscripts*

*N.B.* *note well* (from the Latin *nota bene*)

n.d. *no date*; used in bibliographies when a source contains no indication of a publication or copyright date

*op. cit.* *in the work previously cited* (from the Latin *opere citato*); no longer recommended by the MLA

*q.v.* *which see, whom see* (from the Latin *quod vide* or *quem vide*)

*sic* *thus* (from the Latin); always italicized or underlined. This abbreviation is used (in brackets) in direct quotations from a source, particularly when the quotation contains an error, to indicate that a specific fact or statistic is correctly copied.

*vide* *see* (from the Latin)

## HELPFUL HINTS FOR RESEARCH PAPERS

1. Do not return any of the sources you may have read for your paper until your final draft is complete, including any additional revision your teacher may ask you to do. As you write, you may find information on your note cards that is incomplete or that needs additional checking.

2. As you prepare working-bibliography cards, double-check the spelling of such items as authors' names, titles of books and magazines, and names of publishing companies against your original sources. When you transfer the information to your final bibliography, you will need only to check the same information against your bibliography cards.

3. As you insert names of authors and page numbers into your rough draft, check page numbers and the spelling of authors' names against the original sources.

4. In preparing note cards, use special symbols, such as a star (★), to indicate notes you especially want to use. These may include particularly interesting quotations or important definitions.

5. Keep a good dictionary nearby, and use it for more than checking the spelling or definitions of words. For example, the writer of the sample research paper on pages 264–72 needed to understand what the word *epic* means when applied to character. In a good dictionary, this information is concisely explained under the entry for *epic*.

6. Be especially careful in checking the spelling of foreign words and the meaning and spelling of technical terms. Remember that it is extremely easy to miscopy such items as numbers and dates. Check this carefully in your original sources.

7. Before you begin work on your paper, make a chart for yourself that outlines the steps involved (for example, choosing and limiting the subject, developing an overview of the topic, locating sources and gathering information, filling out bibliography cards). If your teacher has given you a deadline for each step, note that date. Then check off each step as you complete it.

8. If possible, make a copy of your paper for yourself before handing it in. In this way you will not only protect yourself against loss of your paper, but you will also have a model to study for your next paper.

Leslie Griffin

English 5

May 4

A Study of the Heroines in Three Novels

by Willa Cather

[Following are sample pages from a research paper. Use them as a model in preparing your own paper.]

OUTLINE

Thesis: An examination of the protagonists in O Pioneers!, The Song of the Lark, and My Ántonia reveals the development of Cather's heroic ideal.

I. Cather's novels about the West
   A. Her concern with American pioneer life
   B. The symbolic importance of her heroines
II. Characteristics of Cather's heroines
   A. Strength of will and purpose
   B. Independence from family and society
   C. Success in uniting European and American traditions
III. The heroine of O Pioneers!
   A. Her sense of mission
   B. Fulfillment in devotion to the land
   C. Appreciation of Old World culture
   D. Sacrifice of personal relationships
IV. The heroine of The Song of the Lark
   A. Her dedication to purpose
   B. Inspiration of culture and environment
   C. Fulfillment through mastery of art
V. The heroine of My Ántonia
   A. Fulfillment in motherhood
   B. Victory over hardship and sacrifice
   C. Feeling for tradition
VI. Importance for Cather's development
   A. Change in emphasis in Cather's later work
   B. Assessment of early novels

# A Study of the Heroines in Three Novels by Willa Cather

Willa Cather's early novels about the West--O Pioneers! (1913), The Song of the Lark (1915), and My Ántonia (1918)--celebrate the American pioneer experience and the human qualities that were most admirable in it. Cather found her most memorable symbols of the heroic and creative spirit of the frontier in women who were immigrants or daughters of immigrants. An examination of the women protagonists in these novels--Alexandra Bergson in O Pioneers!, Thea Kronborg in The Song of the Lark, and Ántonia Shimerda in My Ántonia--reveals the development of Cather's heroic ideal. [thesis]

Cather's heroines are all superior women of epic stature, protagonists with "tenacious wills and an extraordinary capacity for struggle" (Edel 8). They refuse to accept conventional roles or bend to meanness and pettiness. Their aspirations--whether mastery of the land or of art--inevitably bring them into conflict with family and society. In their struggle to fulfill themselves, they assert their independence from their families and also from men.

Although they are rebels in one sense, they do not reject their European backgrounds; on the contrary, each one has a love of tradition and order, and of the language and art of the Old World. But unlike those immigrants who are unable to adapt to the American environment and who are defeated by the struggle, Cather's heroines succeed in meeting the challenge of the new country by blending the traditions of the Old World and the New.

Alexandra Bergson, the first of Cather's epic characters, has been described as a "heroine of the Sagas" (Whipple 153); that is, a character of legendary dimensions. When the reader first meets her, she is still a girl but already determined and resolute, and austere in her habits. She has a sense of mission--to finish the job her father had not completed, that of conquering the land.[1] After her father's death Alexandra

---

[1]Edel draws a parallel between the heroine of O Pioneers! and Alexander the Great by noting that "the name Alexandra itself reminds us of one of history's greatest conquerors . . ." (8)

holds the family and the farm together through her strength of will and intelligence. By contrast, her brothers Lou and Oscar are not made of pioneer stuff. They lack imagination and a sense of purpose. During a time of drought and crop failure, they wish to give up the struggle. Alexandra convinces her brothers to mortgage the homestead and to invest in more land, a shrewd maneuver that eventually brings all of them prosperity. As Alfred Kazin has noted, "The tenacious ownership of the land, the endless search of its possibilities, become the very poetry of her character" (252). [direct quotation: author's name in text]

Throughout her life Alexandra maintains a spiritual bond with the land. Her youngest and favorite brother, Emil, observes that when she looks at the land her face is radiant. She is overwhelmed by her own feelings of joy: "It seemed beautiful to her, rich and strong and glorious. Her eyes drank in the breadth of it, until her eyes blinded her" (Cather, _O Pioneers!_ 65). [direct quotation: more than one work by an author] Years later, when Alexandra has one of the richest farms on the Divide, her big house is "curiously unfinished and uneven in comfort." She has no talent for the indoors, but all over the great farm there is a sense of order and arrangement: "Alexandra's house is the big out-of-doors, . . . [ellipsis] it is in the soil that she expresses herself best" (Cather, <u>O Pioneers!</u> 83–84).

While she is the most visionary of the figures in the book, Alexandra never relinquishes her ties to the past. In her home she keeps the furniture from the family's first log house, the family portraits, and keepsakes from Sweden. Her household becomes a haven for "old-time people," those who like to do "all the old things in the old way" (Cather, <u>O Pioneers!</u> 95).

Alexandra fulfills her destiny, but her single-mindedness exacts a price. In subordinating herself to her life's work, she sacrifices the opportunity for profound human relationships:

> Her personal life, her own realization of herself, was almost a subconscious existence. . . . She had never been in love, she had never indulged in sentimental reveries. Even as a girl she had looked upon men as work-fellows. She had grown up in

5

serious times. (Cather, O Pioneers! 203–205) [extended quotation]

After Emil's tragic death Alexandra turns to the companion of her childhood, Carl Linstrum, for comfort. Their marriage is based on friendship and affection, but not on passion.

The renunciation of personal relationships is more pronounced in The Song of the Lark. In this novel Cather traces the development of an artist from her childhood in a Colorado town to her triumphant fulfillment as an operatic singer at the Metropolitan Opera House in New York City. Thea Kronborg's fierce dedication to her art is like Alexandra Bergson's devotion to the land--it is an all-consuming drive that leaves no room for other passions. [transitional paragraph]

*[The next two pages of the paper go on to discuss Thea Kronborg and the way she manifests the heroic character of the artist. The part of the paper that follows shows a transition to the next major section of the paper.]*

8

For many readers Ántonia Shimerda is the richest, warmest, and most sympathetic of Cather's creations. Although she has none of Alexandra Bergson's austerity or Thea Kronborg's ambition, she is perhaps Cather's most successful embodiment of the pioneer spirit, the woman who finds fulfillment in motherhood. Cather describes her as "a rich mine of life, like the founders of early races" (My Ántonia 398).

*[The paper goes on to discuss the characteristics of Ántonia Shimerda. The paper concludes as follows.]*

10

Granville Hicks has noted that after My Ántonia, Cather experienced a crisis in her art and became concerned with "symbols of defeat" rather than "symbols of triumph." [paraphrase and direct quotation] The heroism and romance she had found in pioneer life were disappearing. The contemporary life she saw filled her with despair (Hicks 706). In the impressive body of Cather's works, her early novels may be viewed as a brief but glorious tribute to human endeavors. In her unforgettable portraits of Alexandra Bergson, Thea Kronborg, and Ántonia Shimerda, Willa Cather gave expression to the exuberant creative and heroic spirit that triumphs over tragedy and adversity.

*[The bibliography follows on a separate page.]*

# BIBLIOGRAPHY

Bennett, Mildred R. "Willa Cather and the Prairie." Nebraska History 56 (1975): 231–35.

Brown, Edward K., and Leon Edel. Willa Cather: A Critical Biography. New York: Knopf, 1953.

Cather, Willa. My Ántonia. Boston: Houghton Mifflin, 1918.

---. O Pioneers! Boston: Houghton Mifflin, 1913.

---. The Song of the Lark. Boston: Houghton Mifflin, 1915. References are to the new edition, which includes revisions made in 1937.

Daiches, David. Willa Cather: A Critical Introduction. Ithaca: Cornell UP, 1951.

Edel, Leon. Willa Cather: The Paradox of Success. Washington: Library of Congress, 1960.

Hicks, Granville. "The Case Against Willa Cather." English Journal 22 (1933): 703–10.

Kazin, Alfred. On Native Grounds: An Interpretation of Modern American Prose Literature. New York: Harcourt Brace Jovanovich, 1942.

Robinson, Phyllis C. Willa: The Life of Willa Cather. Garden City: Doubleday, 1983.

Welty, Eudora. "The House of Willa Cather." The Eye of the Story: Selected Essays and Reviews. New York: Random House, 1978. 128–37.

Whipple, T.K. Spokesmen: Modern Writers and American Life. New York: Appleton, 1928.

Woodress, James Leslie. Willa Cather, Her Life and Art. New York: Pegasus, 1970.

## CHAPTER 10

# Writing Business Letters and Completing Forms

## STANDARD PRACTICE IN BUSINESS CORRESPONDENCE

During the next few years you will have occasion to write many business letters and to complete many forms: to apply to a college or for a job, to order merchandise or tickets by mail, to write to a newspaper editor or senator about an issue, or to obtain a car title. In each case, you must follow standard practices to supply complete and accurate information.

## PREWRITING

### APPEARANCE AND FORM

Unlike friendly letters and social notes, business letters follow strict conventions for form and for the placement of parts.

**10a. Observe standard practice in writing business letters.**

**(1) Use appropriate stationery.**

Business stationery is cut in two standard sizes: $8\frac{1}{2}$ x 11 inches and $5\frac{1}{2}$ x $8\frac{1}{2}$ inches.

**(2) Make an attractive "letter picture."**

Before a single word of a letter is read, the person who receives it forms an impression of the writer based upon the overall "picture" presented by the letter. Business letters should be typed neatly. You can make your letters attractive by checking each one for the following items.

1. ***Regular margins.*** Think of the margins as a well-balanced frame enclosing the letter picture. The left margin should be about as wide as the right one and the top margin about as deep as the bottom one.

2. ***Placement.*** Begin the inside address at a point that will produce balanced, nearly identical top and bottom margins. Retype a letter that is not centered on the page.

3. ***Indentation.*** Adopt a single indentation style (see below), and follow it consistently in each letter.

4. ***Paragraphing.*** Do not use too many short paragraphs, but do not make your paragraphs too lengthy: avoid writing a single paragraph more than half a page long. A short letter, however, may well consist of a single paragraph.

5. ***Correct spacing.*** Space the letter parts carefully and consistently, following the directions given on pages 276–80.

6. ***Typing standards.*** Type carefully, and avoid uneven typing, strikeovers, messy erasures, and heavily struck punctuation marks.

**(3) Follow a standard form of indentation.**

Standard forms for business letters differ in certain respects from the style of the personal letter. The models shown on the next page illustrate three styles, any of which is acceptable.

1. ***Block style.*** This style eliminates paragraph indentations, and places the heading, complimentary close, and signature flush with the right-hand margin.

2. ***Semiblock, or indented block style.*** Similar to block style, this style indents each paragraph five to seven spaces.

3. ***Full block style.*** Every line—for both paragraphs and letter parts—begins at the left-hand margin, thus eliminating all indentations.

BLOCK

FULL BLOCK

**Model Business-Letter Forms**

**(4) Follow standard practice when a second page is needed.**

A business letter should be completed on one side of a single page, but if this cannot be done without crowding (with a one-inch margin following the last line), go to a second page. The second page should be the same size as the first, but plain paper, without a letterhead.

The second page of a letter also has distinctive characteristics. One inch (about six typewriter lines) from the top of the page, prepare a one-line heading, with the name of the addressee at the left, the page number at the center, and the date of the letter at the right.

Mr. R. H. Dodd          2          April 4, 1988

Continue the letter four spaces below this heading. Never carry over fewer than three lines of the body onto a second page or begin a second page with the last line of a paragraph; such a continuation will end up looking "lost on the page." Use the same margins as those on the first page.

### (5) Learn the six parts of a business letter.

The model letter below illustrates the six parts of the business letter. Study this model carefully, and refer to it as you read.

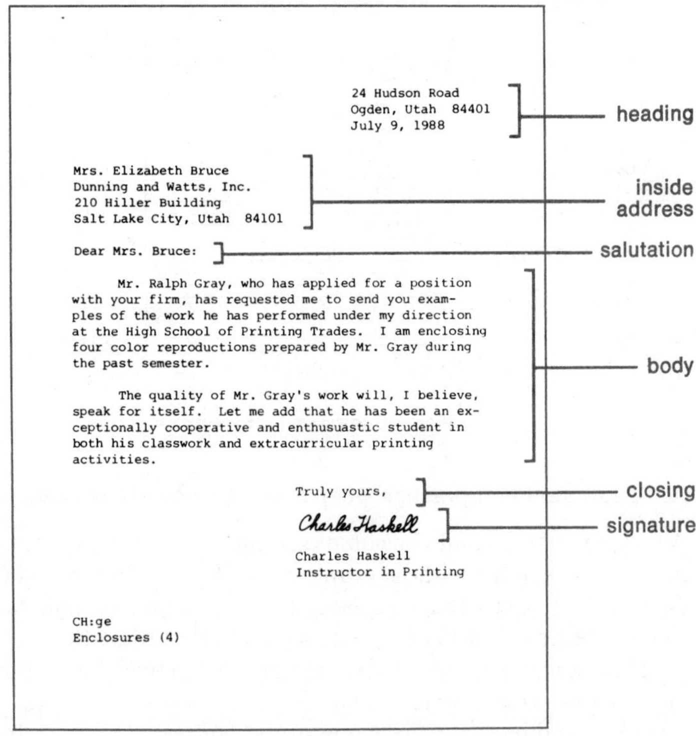

24 Hudson Road
Ogden, Utah 84401
July 9, 1988

Mrs. Elizabeth Bruce
Dunning and Watts, Inc.
210 Hiller Building
Salt Lake City, Utah 84101

Dear Mrs. Bruce:

Mr. Ralph Gray, who has applied for a position with your firm, has requested me to send you examples of the work he has performed under my direction at the High School of Printing Trades. I am enclosing four color reproductions prepared by Mr. Gray during the past semester.

The quality of Mr. Gray's work will, I believe, speak for itself. Let me add that he has been an exceptionally cooperative and enthusuastic student in both his classwork and extracurricular printing activities.

Truly yours,

Charles Haskell

Charles Haskell
Instructor in Printing

CH:ge
Enclosures (4)



**Model Business Letter (Semiblock Style)**

## The Heading

When using stationery imprinted with a business letterhead, you add only the date to complete the heading. Depending on the letter style you choose, the date may be centered or typed flush with the left-hand margin; it should always be at least four spaces below the bottom of the letterhead.

A business letter typed on plain stationery begins with a full three-line heading: your street address on the first line; the city and state (separated by a comma) and the ZIP code on the second line; and the date (with a comma between the day and year) on the third line.

## The Inside Address

The inside address, essential to a business letter, is typed flush with the left-hand margin. It generally begins four spaces below the date. It consists of the addressee's name (the name of a firm, an individual, or both) and full address. The style of abbreviation and punctuation should be identical to that of the heading.

## The Salutation

Type the salutation flush with the left-hand margin, two spaces below the last line of the inside address. The salutation of a business letter is always followed by a colon; in all other respects, its form depends upon the first line of the inside address. The following examples show a variety of inside addresses, with the salutation appropriate to each address. Study these examples and compare the first line of each address with the corresponding salutation.

1. ***Inside address to a firm or group.*** The first line of the address is the name of the firm or group; the traditional salutation is *Gentlemen* followed by a colon. Here it is understood that you may be writing to both men and women. You may use an impersonal salutation instead (*Editor, Personnel Department*).

EXAMPLE Western Electric Company
195 Broadway
New York, New York 10007
Gentlemen:

2. ***Inside address to an individual by title rather than name.*** When you are writing to a specific official but do not know his or her name, use the official title as the first line of the inside address; the traditional salutation is *Dear Sir:* or *Dear Madam:* (do *not* use *Dear Miss:*). The impersonal salutation *(Sales Manager:)* is also used.

EXAMPLES Sales Manager
Corning Silver Company
1790 Shattuck Avenue
Berkeley, California 94704

Dear Madam:

Design Consultant
Bon Marché Shops
292 Rose Boulevard
Chicago, Illinois 60607

Design Consultant:

3. ***Inside address to an individual whose name is used.*** The first line of the address is the individual's name, preceded by a title and possibly followed by an official position; the correct salutation is *Dear Mr.* —— *:*. The abbreviations *Mr., Mrs., Ms.,* and *Dr.* may be used for these titles; all other titles, such as *Professor, Captain,* or *Reverend,* should be spelled out. If you do not know a woman's marital status, address her as *Ms.* The official title following a name in the inside address should not be abbreviated; if it is a long title, type it in full on a second line.

EXAMPLES Mrs. Elinor S. Clark, President
Clark Electronic Corporation
26 Bowdoin Street
Boston, Massachusetts 02109

Dear Mrs. Clark:

Ms. Dorothy Adams
Mutual Fidelity Company
710 Roanoke Building
Milwaukee, Wisconsin 53202

Dear Ms. Adams:

Professor Bruce Cunningham
Department of Mathematics
University of New Hampshire
Durham, New Hampshire 03824

Dear Professor Cunningham:

Dr. Irene Sosa
Dean, School of Education
Doremus University
Orlando, Florida 32802

Dear Dr. Sosa:

4. ***Special forms of address and salutation.*** Occasionally, you may write a letter to a high government official or a religious dignitary. The addresses and salutations of such letters follow standard forms established by custom.

EXAMPLES

PRESIDENT OF THE UNITED STATES
The President
The White House
Washington, DC 20013

Dear Mr. President:
*or*
Dear President _______:

UNITED STATES SENATOR
The Honorable Robert Dole
Senate Office Building
Washington, DC 20013

Dear Senator Dole:

UNITED STATES REPRESENTATIVE
The Honorable Patricia Saiki
House Office Building
Washington, DC 20013

Dear Ms. Saiki:

GOVERNOR OF A STATE
The Honorable William O'Neill
Governor of Connecticut
Hartford, Connecticut 06115

Dear Sir:
*or*
Dear Governor O'Neill:

MAYOR OF A CITY
The Honorable Edward Koch
Mayor, City of New York
New York, New York 10007

Dear Sir:
*or*
Dear Mayor Koch:

PRIEST OF A ROMAN CATHOLIC CHURCH
Reverend Joseph R. Murphy
St. Patrick's Church
Lancaster, Pennsylvania 17601

Dear Father Murphy:

RABBI
Rabbi David S. Josephson
Temple Israel
Lancaster, Pennsylvania 17601

Dear Rabbi Josephson:

MINISTER OF A PROTESTANT CHURCH
The Reverend John R. Jones
Lancaster Community Church
Lancaster, Pennsylvania 17061

Dear Mr. Jones:
*or*
Dear Dr. Jones: (if applicable)

## The Body

Begin the body of a business letter two lines below the salutation. In most letters, the body is single-spaced, with a double space between paragraphs.

Business, as the word suggests, is conducted by busy people. Your business letters should be as short and clear as you can make them. Decide in advance just what you want to say, preparing notes or a first draft if necessary. Decide upon the order of the points to be covered, and never try to develop two topics at once. Devote a single paragraph to each important point.

Because of the brevity and clarity of a business letter, good manners—courtesy, tact, and friendliness—are especially important. Writers of good business letters convey their ideas by simplicity and directness of language, without curtness or rudeness.

Study and restudy the phrasing of every business letter you write. Have you used wordy phrases for simple words—*at an early date,* when you mean *soon;* or *at the present time,* when you mean *now*—in a mistaken attempt to give an effect of dignity? Even worse, have you used trite and meaningless expressions because you hoped they sounded businesslike? A student of English usage once called the business letter "the great warehouse of clichés." Do not muddy your language with stilted, old-fashioned phrases such as *as per your inquiry, yours of the 15th received, we beg to reply, contents carefully noted, enclosed please find, wish to state, please be advised, thanking you in advance.*

## The Closing

Type the closing two spaces below the last line of the body of the letter, beginning at a point just to the right of the middle of the page. Capitalize the first word only, and follow the entire closing with a comma.

The closing *Yours truly* and its variations—*Very truly yours, Yours very truly, Truly yours*—are acceptable in any business letter. When the writer and receiver of a letter have a close personal or business relationship, a more informal closing, such as *Sincerely yours* or *Cordially yours,* may be used. For extremely formal letters, the closing *Respectfully yours* is appropriate.

## The Signature

Type your name at least four spaces below the closing; place your written signature in the space between the closing and the typed signature. The typed signature may be followed by an official title.

EXAMPLES

Very truly yours,<br>*Donald Kennedy*<br>Donald Kennedy

Very truly yours,<br>*Joanne Spencer*<br>Joanne Spencer<br>Manager, Track Team

**(6) Follow standard practice when addressing the envelope.**

Always be sure that the name and address on the envelope are identical in form to the inside address on the letter itself.

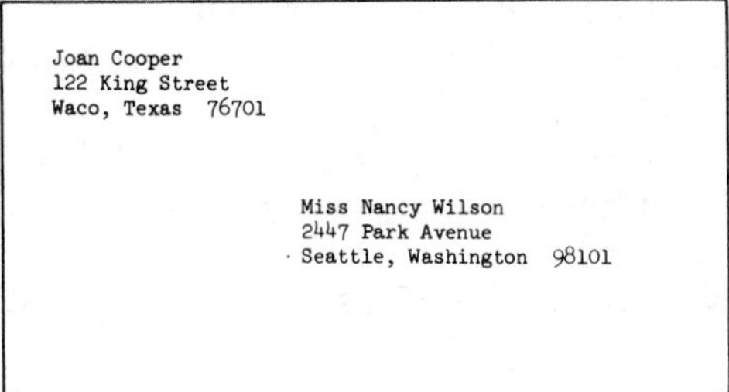


**A Model Envelope**

**(7) Learn how to fold a letter according to the procedure described.**

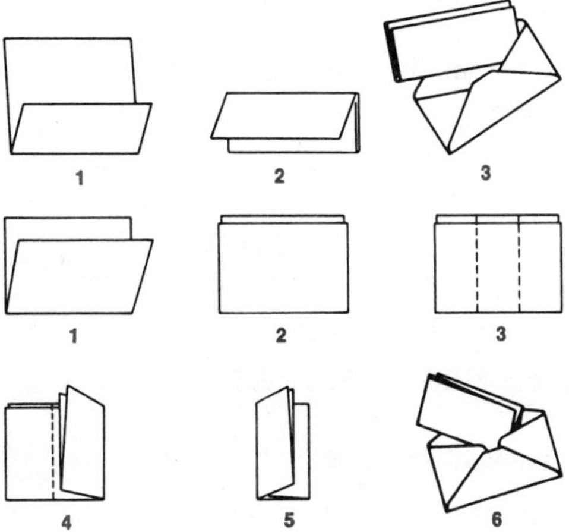


If the sheet is the same width as the envelope, fold up the sheet one third from the bottom, then down from the top about one third. If the sheet is wider than the envelope, fold it up from the bottom to within a quarter of an inch of the top; then fold the right side over a third of the way, and fold the left side over that. Always insert the letter along its folded edge.

**EXERCISE 1. Writing the Inside Address and Salutation.** Each example below contains the information for an inside address and salutation. Write or type each inside address in block form; beneath it, in the correct position, add the appropriate salutation.

1. The Director of Personnel, Erica Wilson, at the Alting Aircraft Corporation, located in ZIP code area 92104 in San Diego, California, at 4297 Lake Road.
2. N.O.M.A., or the National Office Management Association, located at Number 12 on East Chelten Avenue, in Philadelphia, Pennsylvania, ZIP code area 19144.
3. One of the two United States senators from your state. Address the senator by name.

**EXERCISE 2. Writing the Closing and Signature.** Write an appropriate closing and signature for each letter described below. Type or print the lines that would be typed in a business letter; write out any line that would be written.

1. A letter of application responding to an advertisement in your local newspaper
2. A formal letter from George Maclaren, a physician, to his representative in Congress

---

## WRITING

---

## TYPES OF BUSINESS LETTERS

**10b. Learn to write various types of business letters.**

You can write an effective business letter merely by using the proper form and applying what you already know about good writing. However, some letters of the kind you will write most often pose special problems of content, arrangement, and emphasis, although each follows standard business letter form.

### The Letter of Inquiry or Request

Most people occasionally write letters asking for information: college applicants request catalogs or interviews, travelers write for maps and information about regions they plan to visit, and business people request samples, price quotations, or terms of payment.

Be aware that authors and public figures often object to letters that ask, "Please tell me all about yourself, as I am doing a term paper on you," or "Please tell me all you know about New Mexico." First check to be sure that the information you seek has not been published. If you feel you must write, be courteous, check the letter's form and appearance, make a specific request, and enclose a self-addressed, stamped envelope.

Letters of inquiry should be clear and short. To ask a question, phrase it specifically to avoid misunderstanding and receiving less information than you need. To ask for printed matter, make clear what you want; then stop. If the recipient of your letter makes a special effort for you, you should write a letter of appreciation afterward.

Students planning to attend college will write two request letters: one asking for a catalog and application forms and the other requesting an interview. Models for both follow.

22 Roosevelt Avenue
Hightstown, New Jersey 08520
January 3, 1988

Director of Admissions
Douglass College
Rutgers University
New Brunswick, New Jersey 08901

Dear Sir:

Please send me your catalog of courses and an application form for admission to Douglass College. Although I shall not complete my high school courses at North High School until June of next year, I am already attempting to choose the college and program most suitable for me. In particular, I would like to know the admission requirements for liberal arts students and for students seeking a teaching certificate.

Very truly yours,

June L. Proctor

June L. Proctor

**Model Letter Requesting College Information**

22 Roosevelt Avenue
Hightstown, New Jersey 08520
March 16, 1988

Director of Admissions
Douglass College
Rutgers University
New Brunswick, New Jersey 08901

Dear Sir:

Since I have had the chance to examine the catalog which you so kindly sent me and have had the opportunity to talk with my counselor, I have become even more interested in applying for admission to Douglass College. In order to gain some first-hand knowledge of your campus and facilities and to talk personally with someone from the admissions office, I would like very much to arrange for a visit and an interview.

North High School, which I attend, will be on vacation from April 10 to April 17; and I understand that classes at Douglass will be in session then. That week, then, would be an ideal time for me to visit, and I would be very happy to come on any day and at any time you would suggest.

Will you please let me know when such an interview could be arranged? I look forward very much to this opportunity of visiting your college.

Very truly yours,

June L. Proctor

June L. Proctor

**Model Letter Requesting College Interview**

## The Letter of Adjustment or Complaint

Errors often occur in business transactions; the letter of adjustment or complaint calls attention to them. Consider the following points to write this type of letter.

1. ***What exactly is wrong?*** Go as far into the history of the transaction as necessary to explain the error.

2. ***What do you want the company to do about it?*** Always indicate clearly how you would like the error corrected. If you do not know the best way, say so, and tell the addressee that you will wait for suggestions.

3. ***Courtesy.*** A courteous, restrained tone, which implies that the firm is honest, will get the best results.

278 Ellsworth Road
Springfield, Illinois 62714
October 26, 1988

The Hiller Store, Inc.
1905 Grant Avenue
Springfield, Illinois 62702

Gentlemen:

On October 18 I bought a green wool skirt at your Sport and Travel Shop for $19.95 and had it charged to the account of my mother, Mrs. Henry R. Benson. When the skirt was delivered to my home on October 25, I found that the package had burst open and that the skirt itself was badly torn. I cannot judge whether the skirt was poorly packed or whether the damage was the fault of your parcel delivery service. Whatever the cause, I am returning the skirt and would like to have its cost credited to my mother's account. You will receive the package containing the skirt by parcel post.

Very truly yours,

Shirley Benson

Shirley Benson

**Model Letter of Adjustment or Complaint**

## The Letter of Application

Of all the types of business letters, the letter of application requires the most care in preparation. A prospective employer frequently makes a decision about an applicant on the basis of neatness, spelling, and wording. A good position attracts many applicants, so many letters must be discarded after a single hasty reading. If your application includes spelling errors or is messy, it may be tossed aside without serious consideration.

Include the following items in a letter of application:

1. ***Opening.*** Name the position for which you are applying and explain how you heard of the vacancy.

2. ***Personal information.*** State your age, and briefly state any other personal details relevant to the position you seek.

3. ***Education.*** Name your school, list any courses which qualify you for the position, and mention any special training which may interest your prospective employer.

4. ***Experience and qualifications.*** Describe the experience you have, if any; then go on to give your reasons for feeling qualified to do the job well. Your interest, familiarity with the position's requirements, and confidence in your ability will help you sell yourself in your letter.

588 Beverly Drive
Reading, Pennsylvania 19606
June 2, 1988

Mr. Morton Miller
Baker and Miller, Inc.
710 Raleigh Building
Reading, Pennsylvania 19601

Dear Mr. Miller:

I have learned from Mrs. Grace Thomas, your associate, that a vacancy exists in your stenographic staff for the summer months. Please consider me as an applicant for this position.

I am seventeen years old and a student in the junior class at West Falls High School in this city. My course of study has been a commercial one; during the past two years I have had classes in shorthand, typing, bookkeeping, business English, and office practice. I can take dictation at the rate of ninety words a minute and can type either from shorthand notes or from recordings at a rate of about fifty words a minute. For over a year, I have spent part of my weekends assisting my father, Mr. Frank Stacy, president of the Imperial Welding Company, 28 Field Boulevard, as a stenographer and typist. In addition, I have been employed at various times since last December as a part-time typist at the Reading office of the Hartford Fidelity Company. My interest in this work and the fact that I shall return to school for my senior year in September make me especially suited, I feel, for the full-time summer position with your company.

**Model Letter of Application**

5. ***References.*** Three is the usual number of references in a letter of application. Your references should be qualified to discuss both your ability and your general character. Be sure to secure permission from the persons involved.

6. ***Closing.*** End with a request for an interview at the employer's convenience. Explain where and when you may be reached.

Mr. Morton Miller 2 June 2, 1988

My father can, of course, give you information about the work I have done under his supervision. I also have permission to refer you to the following people:

Mr. Frederick Tuttle, Office Manager, Hartford Fidelity Company, 211 Hilton Building, Reading, Pennsylvania.

Mrs. Jane Hess, principal of West Falls High School, Reading, Pennsylvania.

Reverend Francis McGinnis, rector of St. Ann's Church, 400 Manchester Drive, Reading, Pennsylvania.

May I have a personal interview at your convenience? My telephone number is 489-1645.

Very truly yours,

Helen Stacy

Helen Stacy

## The Personal Résumé

Sometimes it is appropriate to submit information about your qualifications and background in the form of a personal résumé, rather than in an application letter. The personal résumé is a summary of your education, experience, and relevant personal characteristics. It has several advantages: it is easier to read than a lengthy letter; copies can be made and used for many purposes; it has a businesslike appearance.

One model for a résumé is shown below. If possible, keep your résumé to a single page; later on, when you have had more experience and more education, an additional page or pages might be necessary.

John R. Jones

Address: 1632 Esther Drive Telephone: 235–1760
Glenside, Pennsylvania 17109
Personal: Date of birth: April 3, 1968
Place of birth: Glenside, Pennsylvania
Marital status: Single
Height: 5′8″ Weight: 150
Health: Excellent
Social Security Number: 194–12–2818
Education:
High school: Abington Senior High School, Abington, Pennsylvania, June, 1986: business course.
Skill achievements: Shorthand: 120 words a minute
Typing: 70 words a minute
Business Machines: dictating, calculating, and duplicating machines.
Extracurricular activities: Vice President, Future Business Leaders of America; member, National Honor Society.
Experience:
Abington Memorial Hospital, 1200 York Road, Abington, Pennsylvania--volunteer secretarial work after school, 1985.
Camp Holiday, Beaver Lake, Pennsylvania--camp counselor, summers of 1984 and 1985.
References:
Dr. Walter A. Smith, Principal, Abington Senior High School, Abington, Pennsylvania.
Mrs. Esther A. Jones, Supervisor of Volunteers, Abington Memorial Hospital, Abington, Pennsylvania.
Mr. Walter A. Bruce, Director, Camp Holiday, Beaver Lake, Pennsylvania.

**Model Personal Résumé**

As you prepare your résumé, keep in mind its essential function: to interest an employer in interviewing you by briefly presenting the highlights of your qualifications. Do not feel obliged to include every minor detail about your background. Include only information that gives the employer a reason for hiring you. What you want most is to create a favorable impression; be sure that both form and content create the effect you want.

If you include a résumé with your letter of application, do not repeat any résumé information in your letter. Your letter, or "cover letter," will be briefer than the model on pages 286–87. Like the model, it will indicate which position you are applying for and how you learned of the vacancy. Do not discuss your qualifications. Instead, simply refer to the résumé: "I am enclosing with this letter a résumé of my experience and education." The letter can then close with a request for an interview.

**EXERCISE 3. Writing Business Letters.** Write any two of the following business letters, observing standard practice.

1. Write a letter of adjustment or complaint. Inform a store's credit department that items (name them) you ordered but returned to the store have not been credited to your account; ask that your account balance be adjusted.
2. Write a letter ordering two tickets (at $8.00 apiece) for a performance of *Candide,* to be given at the Watermill Summer Theater, Saugus, Massachusetts 09106, July 10 (current year).
3. Write a letter of application answering a help-wanted advertisement in your local newspaper. Cut the advertisement out of the paper and hand it in to the teacher with your letter.
4. Write a letter to a local television station expressing your opinion about a show you have seen recently.

## COMPLETING FORMS

Forms and applications require you to supply a great deal of information, some of it very specific. Always read the entire form to make sure that you have supplied the necessary information and placed it on the correct line. Complete each line except those that are clearly labeled "Do not write in this space." Write *none* or *not applicable* (NA) rather than leaving a space empty. Observe these procedures when completing forms:

1. Print legibly and press down firmly, since you may be making additional copies.
2. Use blue or black ink, or type the form.

3. Do not make up information instead of verifying it.
4. Keep the form neat, clean, and unfolded unless you are instructed to fold it.

## The Automobile Title Application

If you own a car, you must register a title with your state government. The title is proof that you do in fact own and are responsible for the vehicle listed. The form on page 291 asks for information in three general areas: your personal identification, specific information about the car, and verification of complete and accurate information. Title applications will vary somewhat from state to state.

To complete the application, you would write your social security number, name, address, and vehicle information (odometer reading, make, identification number, year, type, and model number). You may also have to provide information about a bank loan to purchase the car, indicated by references to "lien." You will not necessarily complete all spaces on the form. For example, in the model title application, the entire center section, the dealer number in line 4 and the new license number and the Form S block in line 8 would be completed by a government clerk. The form may also have sections that must be completed by a police officer.

Be sure to read any small print that may require you to provide additional information about previous liens, or loans, for the car and an application for transfer of license plates. You may also be required to pay an application fee. Your signature might be notarized by the clerk. This verifies that you signed the application yourself.

## The Automobile Insurance Application

Most states require you to have insurance coverage to drive an automobile. The information you give on an insurance application determines whether you will be covered and how much you will pay for the coverage. Insurance applications will vary somewhat.

In the model below, notice the categories of information required. Some spaces you would complete, while others would probably be completed by an insurance agent ("Coverages" and "Underwriting Information"). In either case, you should, of course, supply the correct information about your personal identification, your vehicle, and your driving violations. You may also be required to sign the application, indicating that you stand behind the accuracy and truthfulness of the information you have supplied.

**STATE OF INDIANA • APPLICATION FOR CERTIFICATE OF TITLE • BUREAU OF MOTOR VEHICLES**

TITLE NUMBER: 302-40-5557 | BRANCH NO.: 28 | BRANCH INVOICE NO.: 231870

1★ SOCIAL SECURITY OR FEDERAL I.D. NUMBER: 431-25-6958 ★ APPLICANT'S NAME OR FEDERAL I.D. ABBREVIATION: Mary Alice Keene ★ ODOMETER: 236 #

2★ STREET ADDRESS: 927 Fall Creek Pkwy ★ CITY: Indianapolis ★ STATE: IN ★ ZIP CODE: 46268 #

3★ VEH. MAKE: Buick ★ VEHICLE I.D. NUMBER: IG4AS9853BG331523 ★ VEH. YEAR: 1986 ★ VEH. TYPE: 2drht ★ VEH. MODEL NO.: GM8628 #

4★ FORMER TITLE NUMBER: 103-20-2234 ★ PURCHASE DATE: 2/8/86 ★ LIEN: Yes ★ WFRS: 607 ★ DEALER NO.: 11528 #

5★ FIRST LIEN'S NAME OR FEDERAL I.D. ABBREVIATION: GMAC ★ STREET ADDRESS OR FEDERAL I.D. NUMBER: 9211 North Meridian #

6★ CITY: Indianapolis ★ STATE: IN ★ ZIP CODE: 46240 #

7★ SECOND LIEN'S NAME OR FEDERAL I.D. ABBREVIATION: ★ STREET ADDRESS OR FEDERAL I.D. NUMBER: #

8★ CITY: ★ STATE: LICENSE YEAR: 19 86 | LICENSE NUMBER: 49S4472 | FORM S SIGNED: yes

The law requires that you apply for Certificate of Title within 21 days from the date of purchase of a motor vehicle. There is a **delinquency penalty** of **$10.00** for failure to do so. Attach Certificate of Title assigned by seller (or other legal evidence that Title should be issued). On endorsed Titles, liens must be released on release form on reverse side of title. Supporting documents surrendered with this application cannot be returned to the applicant. There must also be an application for license plates or transfer of license plates, or Form S signed. State fee for applying for Title is **$5.00**.

DO NOT TYPE IN THIS AREA

TITLE NUMBER | BRANCH NO. | BRANCH INVOICE NO.

SOCIAL SECURITY OR FEDERAL I.D. NUMBER | APPLICANT'S NAME OR FEDERAL I.D. ABBREVIATION | ODOMETER

STREET ADDRESS | CITY | STATE | ZIP CODE

VEH. MAKE | VEHICLE I.D. NUMBER | VEH. YEAR | VEH. TYPE | VEH. MODEL NO.

FORMER TITLE NUMBER | PURCHASE DATE | LIEN | WFRS | DEALER NO.

NOTE - IF ADDITIONAL LIENS ARE EVIDENCED IN THIS OWNERSHIP, PLEASE STATE SUCH ON AN ADDITIONAL ATTACHMENT BEFORE SIGNING THIS APPLICATION.

FIRST LIEN'S NAME OR FEDERAL I.D. ABBREVIATION | STREET ADDRESS OR FEDERAL I.D. NUMBER

CITY | STATE | ZIP CODE

SECOND LIEN'S NAME OR FEDERAL I.D. ABBREVIATION | STREET ADDRESS OR FEDERAL I.D. NUMBER

CITY | STATE | LICENSE YEAR 19 | LICENSE NUMBER | FORM S SIGNED

DO NOT TYPE IN THIS AREA

SAMPLE

**GROSS RETAIL & USE TAX AFFIDAVIT - I (WE) HEREBY CERTIFY THAT SALES OR USE TAX ON THIS VEHICLE WAS PAID AS INDICATED BELOW.**

| SELLING PRICE | LESS TRADE-IN* | AMOUNT SUBJECT TO TAX | AMOUNT OF TAX | DEALER | BRANCH | EXEMPT | IF EXEMPT PLACE PARAGRAPH # |
|---|---|---|---|---|---|---|---|
| $12,650.00 | $5,000.00 | $7,650.00 | $459.00 | 11528 | 2 | | |

| SELLER'S NAME | *IF TRADE-IN VEHICLE TRADED YEAR | MAKE | ADDRESS | CITY | STATE | ZIP CODE |
|---|---|---|---|---|---|---|
| O. Tucker | 81 | Buick | 7106 N. Keystone | Indianapolis | IN | 46240 |

TO BE FILLED OUT BY A POLICE OFFICER FOR OUT OF STATE TITLES. I HEREBY CERTIFY THAT I PERSONALLY EXAMINED THE FOLLOWING VEHICLE AND FIND THE IDENTIFICATION NUMBER TO BE AS FOLLOWS:

VEHICLE IDENTIFICATION NUMBER | TYPE | MAKE | YR.

OFFICER'S TITLE | CITY

OFFICER'S SIGNATURE X | BADGE NO. | DATE

STATE OF INDIANA COUNTY OF } SS:

I/WE THE UNDERSIGNED, HEREBY SWEAR THAT THE ABOVE STATED FACTS ARE TRUE, COMPLETE AND CORRECT. FURTHERMORE, I/WE AGREE TO IDEMNIFY AND HOLD HARMLESS THE INDIANA BMV FROM ANY LIABILITY ARISING FROM THIS TRANSACTION.

X Mary Alice Keene

X

SUBSCRIBED AND SWORN BEFORE ME THIS DAY OF

APPLICANT(S) SIGNATURE (IF SIGNING FOR A COMPANY, ALSO GIVE POSITION)

NOTARY'S SIGNATURE X | COUNTY OF RESIDENCE | COMM EXPIRES MO. YR. 19

**STATE OF INDIANA • APPLICATION FOR CERTIFICATE OF TITLE • BUREAU OF MOTOR VEHICLES**

COMPUTER COPY — TO BE MAILED WITH T&T REPORT

**Model Automobile Title Application**

## AUTOMOBILE INSURANCE APPLICATION

### I. APPLICANT INFORMATION

Name Mary Alice Keene Home Phone (317)631-7107 Office Phone (317) 898-2760
Street Address 927 Fall Creek Parkway
City Indianapolis County Marion State Indiana ZIP Code 46268
Employer Name General Telephone
Employer Address 11161 North Meridian, Indianapolis, IN 46032
Job Description/Title sales Years Employed 2
Vehicle Owner, if not applicant ______ Relationship ______
Use of Vehicle: Pleasure Only ______ Work ______ Miles one way 15
Business Use ______ Pleasure/Work ✓

### II. VEHICLE INFORMATION

| Vehicle | Year | Make/Model | Serial or ID Number | Date Purchased | New N Used U | Purchase Price |
|---|---|---|---|---|---|---|
| 1 | 1986 | Buick Regal | 1G4A5475BH-118529 | 2/8/86 | N | $12,650.00 |
| 2 | | | | | | |

Lien [loan] holder's Name and Address None

### III. COVERAGES

| Coverage | Limits of Liability | | Premium | |
|---|---|---|---|---|
| Single Limit Liability | EACH PERSON | EACH ACCIDENT | VEHICLE 1 | VEHICLE 2 |
| Bodily Injury | 100,000 | 3000,000 | 28.50 | |
| Property Damage | | 50,000 | 29.50 | |
| Medical Payments | 5,000 | | 4.10 | |
| Uninsured Motorist | 25,000 | 50,000 | 3.20 | |
| Comprehensive | **Ded. 1** | **Ded. 2** | 42.90 | |
| Collision | **Ded. 1** | **Ded. 2** | 54.50 | |
| Towing and Labor? Y ✓ N ______ | | | 162.70 | |

### IV. UNDERWRITING INFORMATION

| Drivers | Occupation | Sex | Date of Birth | Driver's License No. | Date Issued | State |
|---|---|---|---|---|---|---|
| 1 Insured | Sales | F | 9-21-36 | 5325304243 | 1954 | IN |
| 2 | | | | | | |
| 3 | | | | | | |

In the past three years, have any drivers listed on this application:

1. Had a driver's license suspended or revoked? Y ______ N ✓
2. Been convicted of a moving traffic violation? Y ______ N ✓
3. Been involved in an accident? Y ______ N ✓

Describe all accidents and/or violations. ______

The statements made in this application are true and correct, to the best of my knowledge and belief.

Signature *Mary Alice Keene* Date 2/8/86

**Model Automobile Insurance Application**

**EXERCISE 4. Completing Forms.** Choose one of the following activities:

1. Obtain an application for a driver's license or a learner's permit and complete it correctly.
2. Complete an auto insurance application (perhaps one provided by your teacher), using information for your own car or a car owned by your family.
3. Complete an application for license plates for your state (provided by your teacher).

## EVALUATING

### EVALUATING LETTERS AND FORMS

**10c. Evaluate the content, organization, style, and format of your business letter or form.**

You should evaluate, or judge, the business letters you write and the forms you complete just as you do with other kinds of writing. The following guidelines provide standards to help you to evaluate your business letters and forms.

#### GUIDELINES FOR EVALUATING LETTERS AND FORMS

| | |
|---|---|
| Appearance | 1. Is the letter or form attractive and neat? |
| Letter Parts | 2. Are all the parts of the business letter included, and is each correctly placed? Is the inside address accurate and complete? Is the salutation appropriate and followed by a colon? Is the closing appropriate and followed by a comma? Does only its first word begin with a capital letter? Is the signature typed as well as handwritten? |
| Development of the Body | 3. Are enough of the right kinds of details included to explain the information, service, or adjustment needed? Are they arranged in a clear, logical order? |
| Style | 4. Is there consistent use of block or semiblock style? Is block style used on the envelope? |

| | |
|---|---|
| Tone | 5. Is the tone of the letter courteous? |
| Envelope | 6. Is the address on the envelope accurate, complete, and attractively placed? Is the return address on the envelope? Has the letter been folded appropriately to fit the envelope? |
| Forms | 7. Is all required information supplied? Is the form legibly completed? |

**EXERCISE 5. Evaluating a Business Letter.** Use the preceding Guidelines for Evaluating Letters and Forms to evaluate any business letter you wrote for Exercise 3. Jot notes on the letter to indicate where you would make changes to improve it. You may also want to exchange letters with a classmate.

## REVISING, PROOFREADING, AND MAKING A FINAL COPY

### REVISING AND PROOFREADING LETTERS AND FORMS

**10d. Revise and proofread your letter or form; then prepare a final copy.**

By evaluating your draft, you locate places where you should make changes to improve your writing. You can use four revision techniques —adding, cutting, reordering, and replacing—to correct the problems you have discovered. The Revising Business Letters and Forms chart on page 295 suggests how to use the revision techniques to improve your letters and forms.

After revising your writing, you should proofread it to locate and correct any errors in grammar, usage, spelling, capitalization, and punctuation. Your letter or form represents you, so take care that errors will not distract your reader from the information you are presenting or requesting. When you have proofread your work, you should prepare a final copy. Then proofread once again to catch any accidental errors or omissions made in copying.

## REVISING BUSINESS LETTERS AND FORMS

| PROBLEM | TECHNIQUE | REVISION |
|---|---|---|
| The letter or form is messy. | Replace | Retype or rewrite the letter or form to make a neat, attractive appearance. |
| The letter parts are incomplete, incorrect, or improperly placed. | Add/Reorder/ Replace | Add missing details. Reorder parts so that they are in the proper position. Replace incorrect details with accurate information. |
| There is not enough information. Some of the information is irrelevant. | Add/Cut | Add details which explain what you want your letter to achieve. Add information to blank spaces on a form. Cut details that do not explain your purpose. |
| The ideas are not clear. | Reorder | Rearrange details so that they clearly convey what you want to say. |
| The letter uses more than one style. | Reorder | Use either block or semiblock style throughout. |
| The letter sounds rude. | Replace | Substitute polite terms and expressions for those that sound impolite. |

**EXERCISE 6. Revising, Proofreading, and Making a Final Copy.** Revise, proofread, and make a final copy of the letter you evaluated in Exercise 5. Refer to the preceding chart as you revise, and use the Guidelines for Proofreading on page 29 to check your work. Proofread again after you prepare a final copy. Send your letter only if your teacher indicates that it is acceptable to do so.

NOTE The United States Postal Service recommends the use of two-letter codes for states, the District of Columbia, and Puerto Rico. The service also recommends the use of nine-digit ZIP codes. When you use these codes, the address on business correspondence should look like this:

EXAMPLE Ms. Terry McGovern
602 Vera Park Boulevard
San Diego, CA 92128-4224

The two-letter code is in capital letters and is never followed by a period. A list of two-letter codes follows.

Alabama AL
Alaska AK
Arizona AZ
Arkansas AR
California CA
Colorado CO
Connecticut CT
Delaware DE
District of Columbia DC
Florida FL
Georgia GA
Hawaii HI
Idaho ID
Illinois IL
Indiana IN
Iowa IA
Kansas KS
Kentucky KY
Louisiana LA
Maine ME
Maryland MD
Massachusetts MA
Michigan MI
Minnesota MN
Mississippi MS
Missouri MO
Montana MT
Nebraska NE
Nevada NV
New Hampshire NH
New Jersey NJ
New Mexico NM
New York NY
North Carolina NC
North Dakota ND
Ohio OH
Oklahoma OK
Oregon OR
Pennsylvania PA
Puerto Rico PR
Rhode Island RI
South Carolina SC
South Dakota SD
Tennessee TN
Texas TX
Utah UT
Vermont VT
Virginia VA
Washington WA
West Virginia WV
Wisconsin WI
Wyoming WY

# CHAPTER 11

# Effective Diction

## THE MEANINGS AND USES OF WORDS

*Diction* means the use of words in speaking or writing. Some writers use *formal diction,* which we find in scholarly books and formal speeches. Some use *informal diction,* or the kinds of words and expressions we hear in casual spoken language. A few writers are fond of *inflated diction*. As the term suggests, they use long, cumbersome words, to produce the sort of writing that is like a balloon—full of gas or hot air and not very substantial.

To see at a glance how important diction is, read these two versions of the opening of the story of Red Riding Hood. They differ only in word choice.

1

> Once upon a time, a little girl named Red Riding Hood packed a picnic basket full of food to take to her grandmother who lived in the woods.

2

> Once upon a point in time, a small person named Little Red Riding Hood initiated plans for the preparation, delivery and transportation of foodstuffs to her grandmother, a senior citizen residing at a place of residence in a wooded area of indeterminate dimension.
>
> RUSSELL BAKER

Baker's spoof makes us laugh at inflated diction, but it also has a sobering effect: It reminds us that improperly used words actually can make sentences harder to understand.

## SEMANTICS: THE MEANINGS OF WORDS

In this scene from Lewis Carroll's *Through the Looking-Glass,* Humpty Dumpty offers some famous (and arrogant) remarks about words:

> "When *I* use a word," Humpty Dumpty said, in rather a scornful tone, "it means just what I choose it to mean—neither more nor less."
>
> "The question is," said Alice, "whether you *can* make words mean so many different things."
>
> "The question is," said Humpty Dumpty, "which is to be master—that's all."

Of course, words cannot mean what one person wants them to mean. Language "works" because words have meanings that their users agree on. As you study words—their meanings and the ways they are used—you are studying *semantics.* You will need to use a dictionary for all the exercises in this chapter.

### Distinguishing Word Meanings

The dictionary can help you choose the "right" words—the ones that express your meaning precisely. And it will help you avoid pitfalls. For example, some words, such as *effect* and *affect,* are spelled so similarly that people often confuse them.

Other words are not look-alikes but have such subtle distinctions in meaning that people often become confused and use one word when they really mean the other. They may say *imply*, for instance, when they really mean *infer.*

Which of the following sentences is correct?

> The perfect anecdote for a broken heart is a new romance.
> The perfect antidote for a broken heart is a new romance.

The second sentence uses the correct word. An *antidote* is a remedy for some unwanted condition. The word usually refers to a medicine that counteracts poison or relieves pain. An *anecdote* is something else entirely—a very brief story.

**EXERCISE 1. Defining Words.** Look up the following words and write a brief definition of each to show that you can distinguish between the meanings in each pair.

1. simulate—stimulate
2. simultaneous—spontaneous
3. different—diffident
4. proscribe—prescribe
5. uninterested—disinterested
6. volatile—versatile
7. appraise—apprise
8. emancipated—emaciated
9. allude—elude
10. allusion—illusion

**EXERCISE 2. Identifying Misused Words.** Here are some sentences taken from student papers. Identify the misused word in each sentence and supply the word the writer meant to use.

1. The three kinds of blood vessels are arteries, veins, and caterpillars.
2. The dodo is a bird that is totally distinct now.
3. A liter is a nest of young baby animals.
4. A magnet is a worm you find in a bad apple.
5. The earth makes a resolution every twenty-four hours.
6. Geometry teaches us to bisect angels.
7. Many young women are now joining the Marine Corpse.
8. When you haven't got enough iodine in your blood, you get a garter.
9. It is well known that a deceased body can affect the mind.
10. To collect the gases, hold a baker over the flame.

## Using Specific Words

A writer's diction may be correct but still be weak and imprecise. We see this when writers overuse such bland adjectives as *nice* and *great* and such verbs as *do, say,* and *go*. Good writers try to find specific adjectives and verbs to express themselves more exactly.

| *Vague* | *Specific* |
|---|---|
| The day was nice. | The day was mild and breezy. |
| Julie is a great dancer. | Julie seems to glide when she dances. |
| I did the grass. | I mowed and edged the lawn. |
| Bridget said good night. | Bridget whispered good night. |
| Jack went through the leaves. | Jack shuffled through the leaves. |

**EXERCISE 3. Replacing Vague Words with Specific Ones.** Rewrite the following sentences, replacing the vague words in italics with specific words or phrases.

1. Harold is wearing a *nice* shirt.
2. It is a *nice* beach.
3. The movie was *nice.*
4. The house is *great.*
5. Nelson has to *do* a report tomorrow.
6. "Get out of here," May *said* to the thief.
7. Arthur *says* that he never has any luck.
8. The train *goes* through Peoria.
9. The car *went* past.
10. Six people *came* down the mountain.

Suppose you want to describe Harriet's dress: "Harriet wore a red dress." You might want to be more specific about the color: Was it fire-engine red, brick red, or strawberry red? You might want to be more specific about the material: Was it silk, polyester, wool?

Suppose you write: "Marion lived in a small house on Second Street." You can make the house more specific: a Cape Cod cottage, a split-level, a row house.

Suppose you write that you made a sandwich. Be specific: cheese and steak with onions, peanut butter and bananas, processed cheese that tasted like cardboard.

Here is a general statement about a journey home:

> I saw more and more familiar sights as the train brought me closer to my home in Ames, Iowa.

This is the way in which a professional writer added excitement to that same incident:

> Soon we were passing through towns whose basketball teams I had booed, whose cheerleaders I might recognize, whose Presbyterian youth fellowships had attended our synod conferences. I even welcomed the swinging signposts at the tiny stations we whipped past, because they bore names I recognized: Mechanicsville, Belle Plaine, Tama, State Center. As our train meandered through the center of larger towns, I saw people on the streets who looked like people in Ames, doing their shopping, driving their cars, or standing at corners. Most of them didn't notice us, and I was aware how removed they were from the excitement I felt. Of course, they couldn't know I was going home. I was glad to see the store signs, Sears, Super Valu,

Our Own Hardware; I liked the new developments with their tract ramblers dotting the edges of town; I wanted to wave at an old brick school that looked just like Louis Crawford Elementary, back in Ames.

IVY DAYS: *Making My Way Out East* by SUSAN ALLEN TOTH

**EXERCISE 4. Using Specific Words.** The following sentences are general. Rewrite each one, making it more specific and vivid. Use more than one sentence in each revision, if you wish.

1. The unfavorable weather began on July 4.
2. The person by the door made a point.
3. She took a vacation.
4. Fred has bad manners.
5. The dog made a mess of the room.
6. Florence has nice eyes.
7. The TV set was on.
8. The car is well kept.
9. Louie left the house.
10. The kitchen was full of stuff.

### Understanding Connotations

The strict dictionary definition of a word is called its *denotation.* Many words also carry associations and emotional overtones, called *connotations*—from a Latin word meaning "to make in addition." A few connotations are personal. Their meanings vary from one person to the next. Most connotations are common to most speakers of the language, since they come from shared experience and usage.

For an obvious example, the denotation or strict dictionary definition of the word *pig* is "a domesticated animal (*Sus scrofa*) with a long, broad snout, and thick, fat body covered with coarse bristles." However, most speakers make certain associations with the word *pig* and have emotional responses to the word. We might think "barnyard, mud, dirt, overeating, garbage, fat, snort." We might feel disgust. That is why it is such an insult to call a person a pig.

**EXERCISE 5. Identifying Connotations.** The animal in each of the following sentences has a favorable or unfavorable connotation. Describe the feelings or associations each triggers for you.

1. Maurice has proved he is a rat.
2. The senator is really an old bear.

3. Everyone in that family is a snake in the grass.
4. Who is that viper on the planning commission?
5. Felice has always been a lamb.

Many synonyms—words that have similar denotative meanings—have very distinct connotations. The following sentences say more or less the same thing, but they offer different images of Dorothy by changing one word.

EXAMPLE Dorothy is the slender lifeguard.
Dorothy is the skinny lifeguard.

*Slender* and *skinny* both denote "thin," but their connotative meanings are different. *Skinny* suggests extreme thinness that is unattractive, perhaps bony. We react negatively to it.

*Slender,* on the other hand, carries positive connotations. It is a word we might associate with the tender, supple shoot of a willow tree. *Slender* makes us believe Dorothy is attractive.

Here is the *Webster's New World Dictionary* discussion of the synonyms for the word *fault.* Which synonym has the most negative connotations for you?

> *SYN.—fault,* in this comparison, refers to a definite, although not strongly condemnatory, imperfection in character [her only *fault* is stubbornness]; *failing* implies an even less serious shortcoming, usually one of those common to mankind [tardiness was one of his *failings*]; *weakness* applies to a minor shortcoming that results from a lack of perfect self-control [fattening foods are her *weakness*]; *foible* refers to a slight weakness that is regarded more as an amusing idiosyncrasy than an actual defect in character [eating desserts first is one of his *foibles*]; *vice,* although stronger in its implication of moral failure than any of the preceding terms, does not in this connection suggest actual depravity or wickedness [gambling is his only *vice*]—*ANT. virtue*

**EXERCISE 6. Distinguishing the Connotations of Words.** Suppose each of the following words was used to describe or name a person or a thing. Which word in each pair has the more favorable connotation? List the impressions and associations each word calls forth.

1. statesman, politician
2. arrogant, self-confident
3. female, woman
4. manly, macho
5. resolute, stubborn
6. fickle, changeable
7. rigid, firm
8. deserter, defector
9. blunt, frank
10. rarity, oddity

Some words have no connotations at all; they mean to most people just what their dictionary entries indicate. *Amino acid, table, shoe, see, specific gravity, and*—none of these words has connotative meanings to most speakers of English. Some words, however, have different connotative meanings for different people. The associations and emotions that come to you when you hear the words *liberal Democrat,* for instance, will depend on your own political persuasion.

**EXERCISE 7. Defining Connotations.** Is your response to each of the following words positive or negative? List the associations each word calls up for you. Compare your responses with those of your classmates.

1. taxes
2. Democrat
3. Republican
4. Hollywood
5. New York

## THE USES OF WORDS

### Loaded Words

Writers can use words to manipulate our feelings. Suppose you want to describe someone who is extraordinarily careful about saving money. If you decide to call that person a *miser,* you are controlling your reader's feelings. *Miser* means a greedy, stingy character who selfishly hoards money. We entertain harsh feelings about a miser. If, on the other hand, you call the person *thrifty*, you do not force the reader to make a negative judgment. Thrift is generally an admirable characteristic.

**EXERCISE 8. Identifying Loaded Words.** The sentences in each of the pairs that follow have more or less the same denotative meaning. Yet they differ greatly in connotative meanings. Which words are loaded positively? Which negatively?

1. The first witness was a showgirl.
   The first witness was an actress.
2. Aunt Jane's manners are antiquated.
   Aunt Jane's manners are old-fashioned.
3. The steak was rare.
   The steak was bloody.

4. A handful of people showed up for the speech.
   A loyal group of supporters heard the speech.
5. The Prime Minister is pigheaded.
   The Prime Minister is firm.

**EXERCISE 9. Using Loaded Words.** The words in the pairs that follow carry different connotative overtones. Use each word in a sentence to show how it can change the way the reader feels about the person being described.

1. mediocre, average
2. lonely, solitary
3. foolhardy, daring
4. subtle, vague
5. realistic, shocking
6. cheap, reasonable
7. childish, childlike
8. dreamer, escapist
9. fastidious, fussy
10. ideals, illusions

**EXERCISE 10. Recognizing Loaded Words.** Advertisers are particularly conscious of the way words can manipulate and direct our feelings. Select at least five advertisements from magazines and television. Make a list of the words and phrases that appeal to particular emotions or that associate the product with positive or glamourous experiences. In addition, select five brand names that carry certain connotations: What are the names supposed to make you think of?

## Idioms

When diction is described as "idiomatic," it means that the writer uses many *idioms*—expressions, peculiar to his or her own language, that mean something beyond the definitions of the individual words. The phrase *dropped in,* as in "Who dropped in to see you today?" is an idiom. It cannot be accepted literally.

Idioms cannot be transferred from one language to another. Idioms in English will not make sense in other languages. Idioms in Spanish, French, German, and other languages are meaningless when translated into English.

Some idioms are metaphors: "It makes my blood boil" is an example. Dictionaries label some idioms as informal, colloquial, nonstandard, or even slang. Others are in standard usage. Some have become clichés and should be avoided in all writing (see pages 307–308).

When you use idioms, you must be sure you do so correctly. If you try to be idiomatic and say, "Jake pitched off and helped make the cookies," you will confuse your audience. The idiom is "pitched in."

**EXERCISE 11. Using Idiomatic English Correctly.** Write a sentence using each of the following idiomatic expressions.

1. undercut
2. dress up
3. dress down
4. give up
5. give in
6. carry out
7. carry over
8. carry on
9. carry forward
10. carry off

If you have a question about the phrasing of an idiom or about its precise meaning, you will find the information you need in a dictionary. Idiomatic phrases are often defined at the end of an entry, where they are printed in boldface type and listed alphabetically. *Webster's New World Dictionary* lists several idioms for the word *business.* Note that this particular dictionary labels one of the idioms slang and another colloquial. The asterisk indicates that one idiom originated in American English.

> *business is business* sentiment, friendship, etc. cannot be allowed to interfere with profit making—*do business with 1.* to engage in commerce with *2.* to have dealings with—**give* (or *get*) *the business* [Slang] to subject (or be subjected) to rough treatment, practical joking, etc.—*mean business* [Colloq.] to be in earnest

## Colloquialisms

*Colloquial* comes from the Latin word *colloquium,* meaning "conversation." A colloquialism is a word or an expression used in informal conversation but not accepted as good usage in formal written English. Some colloquialisms have acquired enough permanence to be used in informal writing, however. Colloquial language is, of course, often reproduced in literature to create convincing dialogue as a reflection of character.

If you declared in conversation that there was something "weird" about the testimony in a murder case, you would be using a colloquialism. If you were writing about the case in a formal report, you would assert there was something *inconsistent* or *doubtful* about the testimony. (Notice that *inconsistent* and *doubtful* are much more precise than the colloquialism.)

If you told someone a baseball "got" someone else in the eye, you would be using a colloquialism. In a formal report of the accident, you would write that the ball *hit* him or *struck* him in the eye.

If you announced you finally "got it" after struggling to understand a subject, you would be using a colloquialism. If you were writing about your experience in a formal report, you would relate that you finally *understood* or *comprehended* the material.

**EXERCISE 12. Replacing Colloquialisms.** Write one or two sentences of dialogue using each of the following expressions colloquially. Then rewrite the sentences, replacing the colloquialism with the more precise words or phrases you would use in a formal report.

1. pretty much
2. kind of
3. a lot of
4. run out on
5. get out from under
6. sorehead
7. in a fix
8. fizzle
9. get a handle on
10. needle (someone)

## Slang

*Slang* is nonstandard language usually marked by three characteristics: its liveliness and inventiveness, its quick popularity, and its almost equally rapid disappearance from the language, as a rule. Slang is formed in several ways:

1. Old words are given new slang meanings. *Flaky* in standard English means "tending to form thin, crisp fragments." It is standard English when it is used to describe a pie crust. But when *flaky* is used to describe a person who is unconventional or odd or unstable, it is slang. Other examples of old words given new slang meanings are *cool, cough up,* and *jerk.*

2. New words are coined and become part of an "in" group's slang: *Boob tube* and *goof* are examples.

3. Words are clipped. *Psych* is a clip of *psychoanalyze.* To say "we psyched him out" is to use slang.

4. Existing words are combined to form new compound words. *Rubberneck* is an old example. *Up-tight* is a new one.

Slang should not be used in informal or formal written English because (1) it is imprecise, (2) not everyone knows what it means, (3) it is often vulgar, and (4) most of it goes out of fashion so quickly that it dates your composition. "Goo-goo eyes," "flappers," and "greasers" have all gone out of style. A few slang words are so useful that they do eventually enter standard English. A few others survive for centuries but never rise above slang status. For instance *duds,* meaning clothing, has been with us since the sixteenth century and still hasn't been accepted as standard English.

In any case, slang is used with great zest in informal spoken English, and it is used with skill—even genius—in imaginative literature to reproduce dialects and reflect character.

**EXERCISE 13. Identifying Slang and Replacing It with Standard English.** Identify the slang words or expressions in each of the following sentences, and replace each with a precise word or expression that is acceptable in informal or formal English.

1. The director goofed when he decided to cast that guy as the hero.
2. Soap operas have cornball plots.
3. Segal's novel *Love Story* is a tear-jerker, but I went ape over it.
4. Jack Lemmon plays an up-tight office worker.
5. The family in *The Pearl* is in a lousy situation.
6. Kino decides they had better scram before the killers find them.
7. If they make a movie of "Contents of the Dead Man's Pockets," they should beef up the part where the guy is stuck on the window ledge.
8. Jan breezed through the course on computer literacy.
9. I really dug the character of Brutus.
10. First-year Latin was a piece of cake for me.

## Clichés

A *cliché* is an expression that has been used so often it has lost its original effectiveness. Clichés are often called "tired and worn-out expressions"—a description that itself has become a cliché! Some clichés are comparisons:

light as a feather
tough as nails
as old as the hills

Clichés can also be other kinds of expressions:

Have a nice day.
last but not least
all that jazz

Even an imaginative expression becomes a cliché when it is overused. To label someone "a wet blanket" was once an imaginative way of asserting that the person was so dull or pessimistic that he or she snuffed out the enthusiasm of others, just as a wet blanket thrown over a fire extinguishes its light and warmth. Today the expression "a wet blanket" has been so overused that it has lost its original force.

Writers who express themselves in clichés reveal they haven't made the effort to think very carefully or originally. Almost everything you write can be improved if you examine your diction to be sure you have not, unawares, picked up one of these ready-made expressions. For each cliché you notice, think of a fresh replacement in simple, straightforward English. You will discover that it is harder to express your ideas in original language than it is to use clichés, but it is worth the effort.

**EXERCISE 14. Replacing Clichés with Fresh Comparisons.** Replace each cliché in the sentences that follow with a fresh comparison of your own.

1. The investigator turned as white as a sheet.
2. Ernestine is as fresh as a daisy every morning.
3. The producer's hand was as cold as ice.
4. Alma's teeth are like pearls.
5. Her eyes sparkle like diamonds.
6. She sings like a bird.
7. Eduardo drives like the wind.
8. Mary Alice is just as cute as a button.
9. In August the weather is hot as Hades.
10. The baby was as quiet as a mouse.

**EXERCISE 15. Replacing Clichés.** Rephrase each of the sentences so that you omit the cliché and express the idea in precise language of your own.

1. Katherine has been a brick.
2. The escapee went from the frying pan into the fire.
3. The President is urging us to tighten our belts again.
4. Isabel is singing the blues about her term paper.
5. The patient did well at first, but now it's a yo-yo situation.
6. The soccer team is going down the drain.
7. The sisters thought they had it made.
8. Our candidate says she's still in the horse race.

9. Congress has given the green light to tax reform.
10. Scott has a crush on the new girl.

## Jargon

*Jargon* has more than one meaning. It can refer to the specialized vocabulary of a particular group of people who do the same work or who share the same interests, such as computer users, social workers, actors, short-order cooks, lawyers, doctors, government bureaucrats, and sportswriters. Jargon also can refer to language that is almost incoherent, especially language that is full of unnecessarily long or obscure words and cumbersome, roundabout sentences. This kind of jargon also uses a large number of clichés. It usually says much less than it first appears to.

Jargon in the first sense is perfectly acceptable, especially when the person using it is addressing a member of his or her own group. When a doctor writes a medical report and says a patient has a "circumorbital hematoma," he or she is using medical jargon in a perfectly acceptable way. In fact, the doctor is using extremely precise language. But if the doctor writes about that patient for a magazine of general interest, he might use the simpler term "black eye."

A computer expert who talks with her colleagues about glitches and menus and bytes is using computer jargon in a perfectly acceptable way. But she would be misusing the jargon of her trade if, in an article about politics, she used "glitch" instead of "problem."

A sportswriter who writes the headline "Islanders Snap Sabers' Winning Streak" is using sports jargon in an acceptable, even vivid, way. On the other hand, if he said in an essay on Edgar Allan Poe that Poe "had a short winning streak and then struck out," he would be misusing the jargon of his trade.

Writers must chiefly be aware of the second kind of jargon—the kind of language that obscures rather than clarifies meaning. The paragraph about Little Red Riding Hood on page 297 is a mockery of the kind of inflated language that obscures meaning.

Edwin Newman, in a book called *Strictly Speaking: Will America Be the Death of English?* strikes out against the jargon of the social scientists:

> To know oneself is to have self-awareness, communities being studied are target areas, thinking is conceptualization, patterns are configurations, and people do not speak but articulate or verbalize; nor are they injured: they are traumatized.

The jargon may, on rare occasions, take on a vigorous flavor, so that you hear of imperatives and of dynamic hypotheses. Usually, however, the words are leaden—archetypal, misspecification, disaggregates.

Once you've caught on to the technique, it's easy. For example, in the social sciences as in business language, inputs and outputs are everywhere. You do it this way: In a school textbooks and students and faculty-student ratios are inputs; so are chalk and basketballs. Good citizenship and reading scores are outputs.

You can move on quickly to more complex constructions. Siblings are conflicted in their interpersonal relationships means that children of the same parent or parents don't like each other. Exogenous variables form the causal linkage that explains the poverty impact, the behavior modification, and the intergroup dissonance in the target area means that outside factors cause the poverty and the changes in people that lead to trouble in the neighborhood. A recommendation by a medical ethicist that a physician obtain an input from the patient's own value system means that the patient should be asked whether he wants the treatment.

**EXERCISE 16. Replacing Jargon with Plain English.** The sentences that follow contain jargon that obliterates meaning. Rewrite each of them in plain, precise English.

1. The pilot experienced some apprehension as the plane fell toward the ground.
2. I am speaking in reference to your comment of yesterday.
3. I have deemed it advantageous to terminate our association.
4. The computer has been rendered inoperative and cannot be utilized.
5. Her uncle passed away during the armed conflict in Korea.

**EXERCISE 17. Identifying Jargon, Clichés, and Slang.** Here is Russell Baker's full parody of Little Red Riding Hood (see page 297). Make a list of at least twenty words and expressions in this story that are examples of jargon. Beside each example, write its equivalent in plain, precise English. Then make a list of at least ten examples of clichés and slang you find.

LITTLE RED RIDING HOOD REVISITED

In an effort to make the classics accessible to contemporary readers, I am translating them into the modern American language. Here is the translation of *Little Red Riding Hood.*

Once upon a point in time, a small person named Little Red Riding Hood initiated plans for the preparation, delivery and transportation of foodstuffs to her grandmother, a senior citizen residing at a place of residence in a wooded area of indeterminate dimension.

In the process of implementing this program, her incursion into the area was in mid-transportation process when it attained interface with an alleged perpetrator. This individual, a wolf, made inquiry as to the whereabouts of Little Red Riding Hood's goal, as well as inferring that he was desirous of ascertaining the contents of Little Red Riding Hood's foodstuffs basket, and all that.

"It would be inappropriate to lie to me," the wolf said, displaying his huge jaw capability. Sensing that he was a mass of repressed hostility intertwined with acute alienation, she indicated.

"I see you indicating," the wolf said, "but what I don't see is whatever it is you're indicating at, you dig?"Little Red Riding Hood indicated more fully, making one thing perfectly clear—to wit, that it was to her grandmother's residence and with a consignment of foodstuffs that her mission consisted of taking her to and with.

At this point in time the wolf moderated his rhetoric and proceeded to grandmother's residence. The elderly person was then subjected to the disadvantages of total consumption and transferred to residence in the perpetrator's stomach.

"That will raise the old woman's consciousness," the wolf said to himself. He was not a bad wolf, but only a victim of an oppressive society, a society that not only denied wolves' rights, but actually boasted of its capacity for keeping the wolf from the door. An interior malaise made itself manifest inside the wolf.

"Is that the national malaise I sense within my digestive tract?" wondered the wolf. "Or is it the old person seeking to retaliate for her consumption by telling wolf jokes to my duodenum?" It was time to make a judgment. The time was now, the hour had struck, the body lupine cried for decision. The wolf was up to the challenge. He took two stomach powders right away and got into bed.

The wolf had adopted the abdominal distress recovery posture when Little Red Riding Hood achieved his presence.

"Grandmother," she said, "your ocular implements are of an extraordinary order of magnitude."

"The purpose of this enlarged viewing capability," said the wolf, "is to enable your image to register a more precise impression upon my sight system."

"In reference to your ears," said Little Red Riding Hood, "it is noted with the deepest respect that far from being underprivileged, their elongation and enlargement appear to qualify you for unparalleled distinction."

"I hear you loud and clear, kid," said the wolf, "but what about these new choppers?"

"If it is not inappropriate," said Little Red Riding Hood, "it might be observed that with your new miracle masticating products you may even be able to chew taffy again."

This observation was followed by the adoption of an aggressive posture on the part of the wolf and the assertion that it was also possible for him, due to the high efficiency ratio of his jaw, to consume little persons, plus, as he stated, his firm determination to do so at once without delay and with all due process and propriety, not withstanding the fact that the ingestion of one entire grandmother had already provided twice his daily recommended cholesterol intake.

There ensued flight by Little Red Riding Hood accompanied by pursuit in respect to the wolf and a subsequent intervention on the part of a third party, heretofore unnoted in the record.

Due to the firmness of the intervention, the wolf's stomach underwent ax-assisted aperture with the result that Little Red Riding Hood's grandmother was enabled to be removed with only minor discomfort.

The wolf's indigestion was immediately alleviated with such effectiveness that he signed a contract with the intervening third party to perform with grandmother in a television commercial demonstrating the swiftness of this dramatic relief for stomach discontent.

"I'm going to be on television," cried grandmother. And they all joined her happily in crying, "What a phenomena!"

## APPROPRIATE DICTION

You know that, as you prepare to write, you must first find a subject and limit it to manageable size; you must next gather details that will illustrate your topic or support your opinion. Before you start writing, you should also consider your diction.

The kind of diction you will use depends on three factors:

1. Your audience
2. Your purpose in writing
3. The tone or attitude you want to convey to your subject or the mood you wish to create

### Audience

In your lifetime, you will write for many different audiences. In high school, you write chiefly for your teachers, but you also write letters to personal friends, and perhaps you write for the school newspaper. You might someday have to write a personal statement for the college you wish to attend. In your adult life, you will address many other kinds of audiences. You will have to consider the appropriate diction for each audience.

The definitions that follow were prepared for two distinct audiences, and the diction is adjusted accordingly. The first definition is from a dictionary for children; the second is from a dictionary for adults.

> 1. *gene:* one of the protein molecules in the chromosomes of all plants and animals that govern the passing on of hereditary traits
>
> 2. *gene:* any of the units occurring at specific points on the chromosomes by which hereditary characters are transmitted and determined; each is regarded as a particular state of organization of the chromatin in the chromosome, consisting primarily of DNA and protein

Notice that the definition for the children's dictionary uses far fewer words and details. It also replaces the verb *transmit* with its simpler synonym *pass on.*

If you were discussing a novel with your friends, you might use colloquial diction or even slang and exclaim, "The book was great! But I could have brained Marjorie when she wouldn't marry Ned." In a report to your teacher, however, you would use more formal language because you would want to make your meaning clearer—something on this order:

> The plot was suspenseful enough to hold my interest. I thought the writer did a particularly effective job in creating believable characters, because I cared intensely about whether Marjorie would marry Ned.

**EXERCISE 18. Adapting Diction to Your Audience.** Complete one of the following assignments.

1. Explain a game you have just seen to a foreigner who is visiting the United States for the first time and who has never heard of the sport. You will have to avoid using too many American idioms and the jargon of the sport.
2. In a letter, describe the same game to a friend. Now you are free to use idioms and the jargon of the sport.
3. Take some issue that is controversial in your school right now. Write one letter to the principal of the school expressing your opinions on the controversy. Write a second letter on the subject to your best friend, who has moved to another state.

## Purpose

Writing, like any kind of communication, can have many purposes. The first and perhaps the most common is to give information. That would be your purpose in answering essay questions or in writing a report on

Dutch elm disease for a biology class. Another purpose might be to share an emotion—to capture an experience in words, perhaps in poetry or fiction. Still another might be to convince someone to think as you do, perhaps to agree with you that *The Pearl* has a happy ending. Most difficult of all, your purpose might be to persuade someone to act in a certain way, such as to vote for new zoning legislation or donate to the Latin Club.

You will choose your diction with your purpose in mind. Informative writing must use words that are precise and unambiguous.

> There are three main arenas for nuclear negotiations between the United States and the Soviet Union: medium-range nuclear forces stationed in and around Europe; strategic or intercontinental-range missiles and bombers; and space-based weapons, including antisatellite weapons.
>
> *NEW YORK TIMES*

Descriptive writing must use words that evoke emotions and appeal to the senses, particularly the sense of sight.

> . . . I am a large, big-boned woman with rough, man-working hands. In the winter I wear flannel nightgowns to bed and overalls during the day.
>
> ALICE WALKER

Writing that argues a point or presents a persuasive case often uses words with strong connotative associations in order to influence an audience's opinions.

> The resignation of Michael K. Deaver from the White House and his prospective entry into the lush, well-cultivated fields of Washington public relations threatens to create a fierce private-sector competition that could make current differences between George P. Shultz and Caspar W. Weinberger look like a duel with cream puffs.
>
> *NEW YORK TIMES*

**EXERCISE 19. Choosing Diction to Suit Your Purpose.** Complete one of the following assignments.

1. Write a paragraph in which your purpose is to convince a reader to accept your point of view about a topic in the news today. Use at least three words with connotations that will "load" your composition in favor of your opinion.
2. Write a paragraph in which your purpose is to describe as precisely as possible a scene, an animal, an object, or a person. You could choose the window you see, the clothes you are wearing, the book you are holding, the food that is cooking on the stove. Use at least three

words that will help bring the subject to life for your reader, calling upon whatever senses are appropriate—sight, sound, smell, taste, feeling.

3. Write a paragraph in which your purpose is to explain as accurately as possible the layout of some room—a bedroom, a kitchen, a coffee shop, a garage. Remember, your purpose is *not* to make your reader *experience* the room; your purpose is to make your reader understand the layout of the room so that he or she could enter the room blindfolded and know exactly where everything is.

## Tone

Tone refers to your attitude toward your subject or your audience. Tone can always be described by an adjective: formal, informal, lighthearted, serious, critical, bitter, condescending, mocking, sympathetic, admiring, romantic, ironic, emotional, disgusted, loving. When you read, you detect tone from the diction the writer chooses. In the same way, your own tone in writing will be controlled by your diction.

If you want to convey an informal tone, you will use informal diction, possibly some colloquialisms.

> English majors are encouraged, I know, to hate chemistry and physics, and to be proud because they are not dull and creepy and humorless and war-oriented like the engineers across the quad.
>
> KURT VONNEGUT

If you want to convey a formal, serious tone, you will avoid any diction that suggests a casual conversation.

> By a strange paradox, most of the earth's abundant water is not useable for agriculture, industry, or human consumption because of its heavy load of sea salts, and so most of the world's population is either experiencing or is threatened with critical shortages.
>
> RACHEL CARSON

If you want to express a tone of admiration, you must find positive words that reveal your feeling.

> Serene was a word you could put to Brooklyn, New York. Especially in the summer of 1912.
>
> BETTY SMITH

If you want to express a tone of apprehension, you must find words that suggest fear or uneasiness.

> Daylight began to forsake the red room; it was past four o'clock, and the beclouded afternoon was tending to drear twilight. I heard the rain still beating continuously on the staircase window, and the wind howling in the grove behind the hall; I grew by degrees cold as a stone, and then my courage sank.
>
> CHARLOTTE BRONTË

If you want to express a critical or mocking tone, you must use words that ridicule.

> I would like to put all professional cheerleaders on a permanent taxi squad. Autumn Sunday afternoons have become one big pompon shaking in the face of America. There are exceptions to everything, of course; but, basically, when you have seen one shaking pompon, you have seen them all.
>
> LEWIS GRIZZARD

One or two words alone can reveal tone. If you see rain on the window and describe it as looking like a string of diamonds, your tone is positive, even romantic. If you see rain on the window and describe it as looking like tears streaking a face, your tone is sad and mournful.

At times, you will state your attitude directly, and your tone will be immediately clear. If you say you admire a character, you reveal an approving tone. If you say that a plot is contrived, you are directly revealing a critical tone.

Almost all writing reveals some tone. Textbooks and scientific articles often have a neutral tone, because this suits the writers' purposes. In the case of high-school history textbooks, for example, the writers would want the students to evaluate the issues for themselves. In the case of a biology book, the writer would be interested solely in imparting scientific information, not in revealing an attitude toward it.

But in fiction, drama, essays, editorials, sports articles, biographies, and autobiographies, you will detect a tone, an attitude that the writer is revealing. This tone is communicated largely through diction.

**EXERCISE 20. Distinguishing Tone.** Here are three accounts of a coyote. Which account has a neutral tone? What is the tone of each of the other accounts? Which words contribute to the tone of each?

1

> *coyote:* a small wolf *(Canis latrans)* of the western prairies of North America.

2

> "Next to God, the coyote is the smartest person on earth," an old Mexican saying goes. Then may come a tale making a fool of this

"sagacious" personage. Well, it's no fun to make a fool of a fool. To Indians of coyote land, he is the supreme trickster. To everybody who knows him, even a sheep owner, he is a character.

J. FRANK DOBIE

3

The coyote is a long, slim, sick, and sorry-looking skeleton, with a gray wolf-skin stretched over it, a tolerably bushy tail that forever sags down with a despairing expression of forsakenness and misery, a furtive and evil eye, and a long, sharp face, with slightly lifted lip and exposed teeth. He has a general slinking expression all over. The coyote is a living, breathing allegory of Want. He is *always* hungry. He is always poor, out of luck, and friendless. The meanest creatures despise him, and even the fleas would desert him for a velocipede. He is so spiritless and cowardly that even while his exposed teeth are pretending a threat, the rest of his face is apologizing for it.

MARK TWAIN

**EXERCISE 21. Creating Tone.** Write two accounts of some ordinary subject with which you are familiar. In the first account, define and describe your subject as if you were preparing an entry for an encyclopedia. Your tone should be neutral. In the second account, use diction that reveals your attitude toward the subject, whether it be admiration, disgust, hatred, love, fear, awe, or something else. You might choose a subject as ordinary as an insect, a piece of furniture, a dance, or a type of haircut.

# PICTURE THE POSSIBILITIES:

## IDEAS FOR WRITING

Pictures have the power to prompt the memory, stir the emotions, and spark the imagination. In this section you will learn how to use pictures as a powerful source of ideas for writing.

## Probing the Picture

One way to use this picture would be as a source of topics for an **expository** composition. You could then use the *point-of-view questions* to gather information. For example, suppose you decide to write on the topic "spending time alone in the wilderness." You might develop questions such as *What are the rewards of spending time alone in the wilderness? What are the drawbacks? What hobbies can a solitary person pursue in the wilderness? How is being alone in the wilderness different from being alone elsewhere?* For the topic "nature photography" you might ask, *What training is needed to become a nature photographer? What equipment does a nature photographer need? How did some of America's best-known nature photographers launch their careers?*

You could instead use the picture as a starting point for a **narrative.** Using the *5 W-How?* questions would help you develop the elements of your story. For example, *Who* is the woman? *Why* is she taking pictures? *When* and *where* does the action take place? *How* does the situation in the picture lead to a conflict? *How* is the conflict resolved? *Who* is the narrator of the story—the woman in the picture, another character in the story, or an unspecified observer?

## Writing Activities

Using the steps of the writing process, complete one of the following activities.

- Write an expository composition on a topic the picture suggests to you.
- Use the picture to write a short story in which the woman is the protagonist.

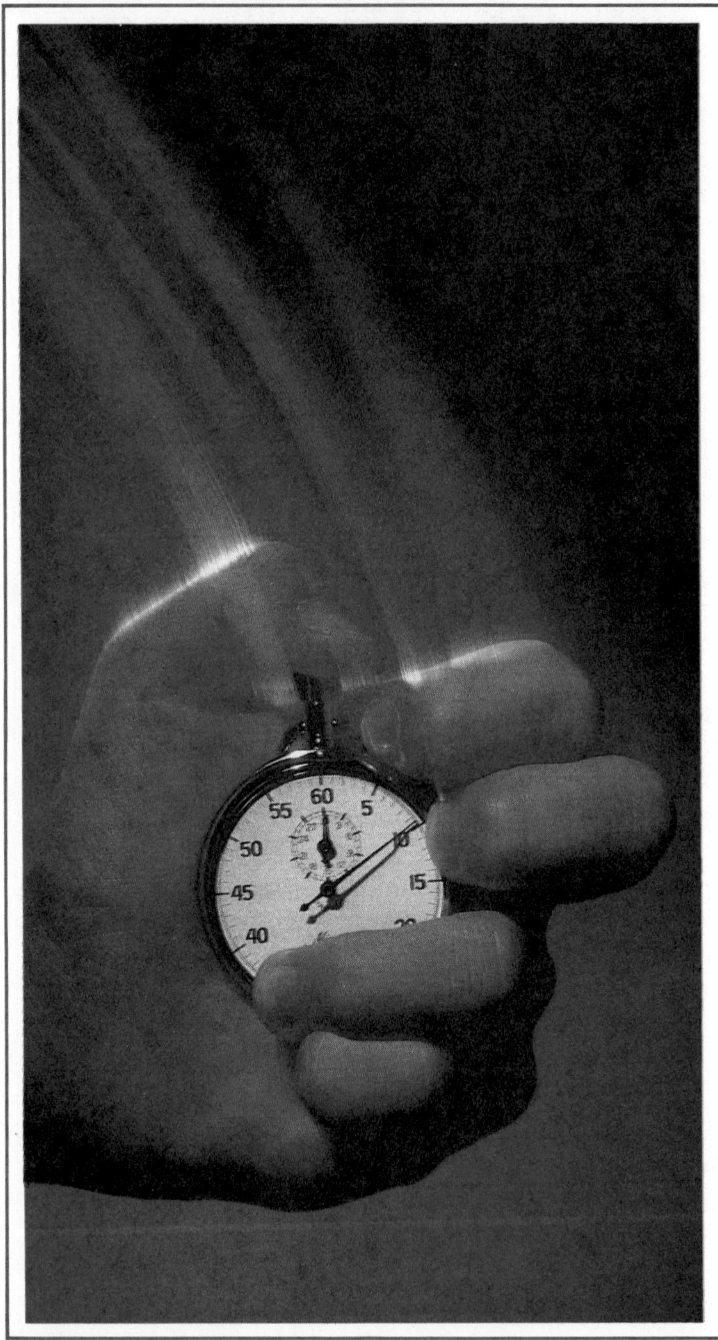

GRIDLOCK BUSTERS
DON'T BLOCK
THE BOX
FINE+2 POINTS
ON LICENSE
E 58 ST
NO
STANDING
ANY
TIME
ONE WAY
WALK

## Probing the Picture

You could use this picture to generate ideas for **persuasive** writing. To find possible debatable issues, you could focus on the principal elements of the picture: the signs directing pedestrians and those directing vehicles. Thinking about the relationship between pedestrians and vehicles in your own town, you could brainstorm to develop a list of debatable issues such as *Should trucks be banned from the downtown area during rush hour? Should certain lanes be set aside for buses and other vehicles with two or more passengers? Should more streets be made one-way? Should a limited-access highway be built around the town?*

A second approach would be to use the picture to write a **description.** For example, you could imagine yourself standing at the intersection shown in the picture and gather concrete and sensory details by asking questions such as *What sounds do I hear from the vehicles? From the drivers? From the other pedestrians? How does the air feel on my skin? What colors stand out in the scene? How are the people around me moving? What odors can I distinguish?* The description you write could either stand on its own or be incorporated into a narrative set in a large city.

## Writing Activities

Using the steps of the writing process, complete one of the following activities.

- Write a persuasive composition on one of the issues mentioned above or on another issue the picture suggests.
- Use the picture to write either a descriptive paragraph or the stage directions for the opening scene of a one-act play.

3)那个公园
很容易找

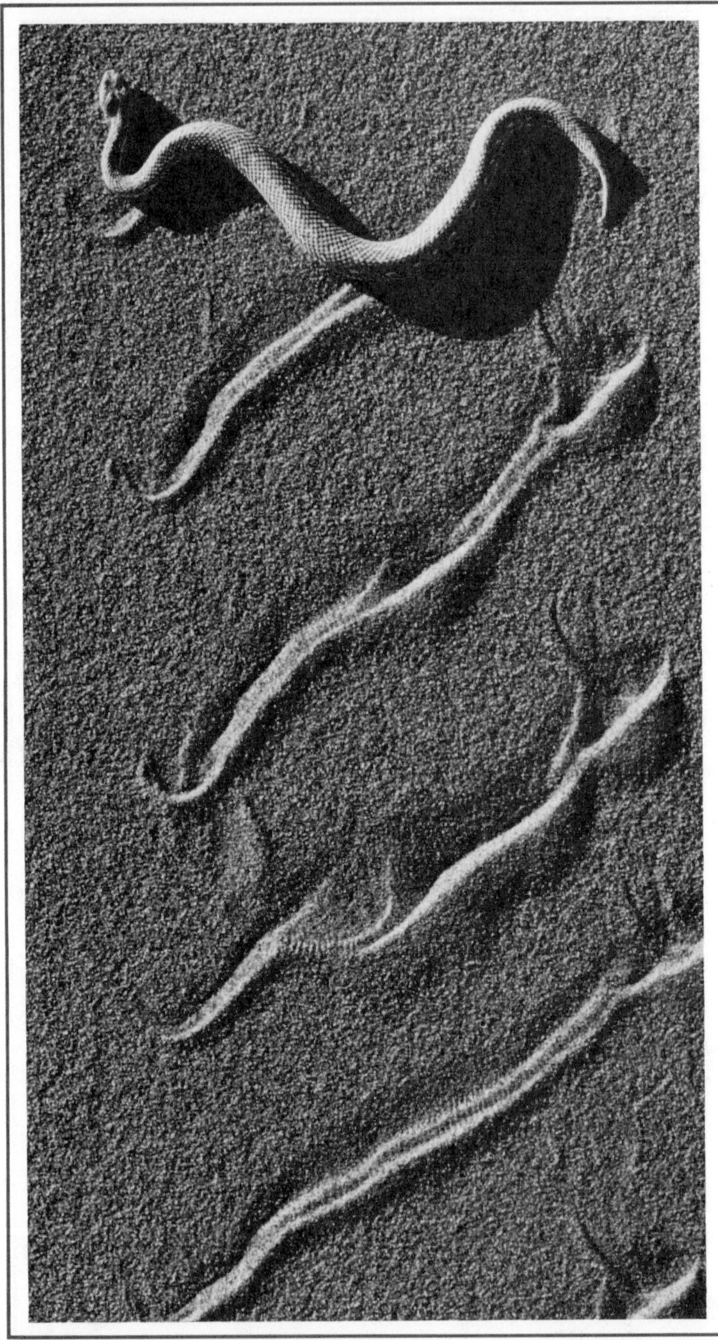

## Probing the Picture

Your first reaction to this picture might be to wonder how—and why—the snake is moving sideways. You could use that idea as the topic of an **expository** paper. By observing the picture carefully, you could gather details that would answer such questions as *What characteristics of sand prevent the snake from moving straight ahead? How does the snake position its body in relation to the direction in which it is moving? How does that angle affect the amount of sand that comes into contact with the snake's body? Which part of its body does the snake move first? How are the snake's movements related to those of a skier who uses poles to climb a snow-covered slope?*

Another possibility would be to write an objective **description** of the picture, one without reference to your emotional response to the snake. Instead of imagining yourself in the scene, as you did with the picture on page IW 7, you could focus on the composition of the picture, asking questions such as *What do I notice first about the picture? In what direction do my eyes then move? What shapes, textures, and patterns do I observe? How does the shadow cast by the snake help create the impression of motion?*

## Writing Activities

Using the steps of the writing process, complete one of the following activities.

- Write an expository composition on a process you find by limiting the subject "snakes"—anything from "how biologists classify snakes" to "how snakeskin shoes are made."
- Write an objective description of the picture.

LINES
DOUGLAS
DC 3
MOBILITY
FOR MANKIND
THEATER

## Probing Pictures to Discover Writing Ideas

The following questions will help you use any picture to discover ideas for writing.

1. What about this picture most interests me? What specific idea does it suggest?
2. For what purpose could I use this idea?
3. What are the strongest elements of the picture? How could I combine those elements to achieve my purpose?
4. Would using the *5 W-How?* questions help me gather information to use?
5. What might have happened just before or just after the picture was taken? What might the person(s) have said?
6. What main impression do I get from this picture?
7. What concrete and sensory details do I observe as I examine the picture? What details do I imagine when I think of myself as being in the scene?
8. Could I explain how to make or do what the picture shows?
9. Could I give information about what the picture shows by telling who or what the subject is, what its history is, or how it is related to others of its kind?
10. What debatable issues does the combination of elements in the picture suggest to me?

## On Your Own

Using any picture you have not written about, write a paper for your classmates. You may choose the form (paragraph, composition, letter to the editor, short story, etc.) and the purpose (to narrate, to describe, to explain or to give information, or to persuade). Follow the steps of the writing process.

# PART TWO

# COMPOSITION: Writing and Revising Sentences

## CHAPTER 12

# Complete Sentences

## FRAGMENTS AND RUN-ON SENTENCES

*A sentence is a group of words containing a subject and a verb and expressing a complete thought.* As you do more writing, you will develop a "feeling for sentences" or a "sentence sense," through which you will recognize almost at once whether a group of words is or is not a complete sentence. To a great extent, this sense can be developed consciously by studying each of your sentences after you have written it and by guarding against the carelessness that causes most sentence errors. You must learn to watch for the two basic sentence errors, the *sentence fragment* and the *run-on sentence*.

A sentence fragment is a *part* of a sentence used as though it were a *whole* sentence. The fragment may be written with a capital letter at the beginning and an end mark (a period, question mark, or exclamation point) at the end; nevertheless, it is not a sentence because it does not express a complete thought. A run-on sentence consists of two or more sentences that may be separated by a comma instead of a period or some other end mark.

### DIAGNOSTIC TEST

**Identifying Sentences, Fragments, and Run-ons.** Some of the following groups of words are sentences; a few are fragments; others are run-on sentences. Number your paper 1–10. Write *S* after the number corresponding to each complete sentence, *F* for each sentence fragment, and *R* for each run-on sentence.

1. Hoping that she will remember the assignment.
2. We were certain that the referee did not see the foul.
3. Although I realize that your other teachers have assigned homework to be done over the holidays.
4. The President addressed the nation last night, his tone was very serious.
5. Did you know that three-dimensional images can be projected by laser beams?
6. Exciting news about a Hollywood screen test.
7. The first time she saw that horror movie she was scared, the second time she couldn't stop laughing.
8. There are many advantages to studying classical Latin, for example, Latin uses fewer words than modern languages do.
9. English is a Germanic language, its structure is similar to that of many Scandinavian languages.
10. Gaining insights into other cultures by traveling.

---

## SENTENCE FRAGMENTS

**12a. A *sentence fragment* is a group of words that does not express a complete thought. Because it is part of a sentence, it must not be allowed to stand by itself; it should be kept in the sentence of which it is a part.**

Compare the following sentence and sentence fragment.

SENTENCE High in the sky a silver plane swooped toward the horizon.
FRAGMENT High in the sky a silver plane swooping toward the horizon

Because it lacks a verb, the sentence fragment does not express a complete thought. The word *swooping* may deceive you momentarily, but it is not a verb. Words ending in *-ing*, like *swooping,* are not verbs unless *helping verbs* are added to them to make a verb phrase. If you are uncertain about what a helping verb is and how it is used, turn to the discussion of verb phrases on pages 389–90. Notice how *-ing* words are used in verb phrases in the following examples.

| | |
|---|---|
| NO VERB | A blue haze settling over the rooftops |
| VERB PHRASE | A blue haze **was settling** over the rooftops. |
| NO VERB | Playing football on Saturday |
| VERB PHRASE | He **was playing** football on Saturday when he hurt his knee. |
| NO VERB | Writing novels for ten years |
| VERB PHRASE | She **had been writing** novels for ten years before she was recognized as a great author. |

In these examples, the helping verbs round out the verb phrase to express a thought completely. Without a verb or verb phrase, we have only a part of a sentence, a fragment.

**EXERCISE 1. Identifying Sentences and Fragments; Correcting Fragments.** Some of the items in this exercise consist of one or more complete sentences; others contain sentence fragments. If an item contains *only* complete sentences, write *C* after its number. If an item contains a sentence fragment, revise it to eliminate the fragment.

1. Many great Americans had little or no formal education. Among these are political leaders, writers, artists, scientists, and business executives.
2. When Abraham Lincoln was a young man, he worked in a general store. And at the same time studied books on law.
3. Carl Sandburg is another example. Leaving school when he was thirteen years old but later going on to Lombard College after serving in the army during the Spanish-American War.
4. Our first President, George Washington, was a slow reader and a poor speller. Who struggled in later life to overcome his educational deficiencies.
5. Andrew Carnegie, who gave away many millions to charity, started to work at the age of thirteen. He attended school in Scotland but did not go to high school.
6. Eleanor Roosevelt had little formal education. Susan B. Anthony the equivalent of high school.
7. Gordon Parks attended high school. And later was named photographer of the year by a major magazine.
8. Booker T. Washington walked five hundred miles to attend school at Hampton Institute. And later founded Tuskegee Institute.
9. One of the great letter writers of all time, Abigail Adams, had no formal schooling. It was something she regretted.

10. On the other hand, many famous Americans had excellent educations. As a child, Willa Cather, for instance, was taught Greek and Latin by a Nebraska shopkeeper.

## The Phrase Fragment

A phrase is a group of words that is used as a single part of speech but does not contain a verb and its subject. In Chapter 20, many different kinds of phrases are explained—prepositional, participial, gerund, infinitive, appositive. All phrases, however, have one important characteristic in common: They are *parts* of a sentence. A phrase should never stand alone; it must never be separated from the sentence in which it belongs. In the following examples, the italicized words are phrase fragments. Notice how the fragments are eliminated by attaching them to the sentences in which the phrases belong.

FRAGMENT The blustery wind made an eerie noise. *Like a screech owl's cry.* [The prepositional phrase in italic type acts as an adjective modifying the noun *noise.* Like any other adjective, the phrase belongs in the sentence that contains the word it modifies.]

FRAGMENT CORRECTED The blustery wind made an eerie noise like a screech owl's cry.

FRAGMENT The haughty Estella denounced Pip. *Calling him a clumsy laboring boy.* [This participial phrase fragment modifies *Estella.* The fragment is corrected by joining it to the sentence in which it belongs.]

FRAGMENT CORRECTED The haughty Estella denounced Pip, calling him a clumsy laboring boy.

FRAGMENT Immediate aid was given to the stricken town. *Not only to feed the hungry but also to help the sick.* [Here two infinitive phrases have been separated from the verb phrase *was given*, which they explain. Both phrases must be joined with the verb they modify in order to complete the sentence.]

FRAGMENT CORRECTED Immediate aid was given to the stricken town not only to feed the hungry but also to help the sick.

## The Appositive Fragment

An appositive is a word or group of words that closely follows a noun or pronoun and identifies or explains it. Such a word is "in apposition with" the word it explains. It cannot stand alone as a sentence; it is always part of the sentence containing the word it explains.

SENTENCE FRAGMENT At nightfall the caravan wound into the fabled city of Kabaka. *A cluster of ruins.* [The italicized words stand in apposition with the noun *city*. Within the appositive we find a main noun, *cluster*, modified by a prepositional phrase. The entire appositive must be included in the sentence of which it is a part.]

SENTENCE COMPLETED At nightfall the caravan wound into the fabled city of Kabaka, a cluster of ruins.

## The Subordinate Clause Fragment

A clause is a group of words that contains a subject and a predicate and is used as a part of a sentence. A subordinate clause does not express a complete thought and cannot stand alone. Separated from the main clause, the subordinate clause becomes a sentence fragment.

If you are not sure of the distinction between main clauses and subordinate clauses, refer to Chapter 21. You must understand the difference if you are to write complete sentences.

In the following examples, the subordinate clauses are printed in italics.

FRAGMENT Everyone liked the poem "Childhood." *Which was written by Margaret Walker.*

FRAGMENT CORRECTED Everyone liked the poem "Childhood," *which was written by Margaret Walker.*

FRAGMENT American students still enjoy Lady Gregory's plays. *Although they were written in Ireland in the early 1900's.*

FRAGMENT CORRECTED American students still enjoy Lady Gregory's plays, *although they were written in Ireland in the early 1900's.*

**12b. Do not separate a phrase, an appositive, or a subordinate clause from the sentence of which it is a part.**

You can avoid the use of sentence fragments by being certain that all your sentences contain complete thoughts. Reading your first draft aloud helps a great deal.

While checking over your work, you may find that two other constructions cause you trouble. They are items in a series and compound verbs.

FRAGMENT Many reading lists for high-school students include translations from Scandinavian writers. *Such as Lagerlöf, Undset, and Ibsen.* [Items in a series should never be separated from the sentence of which they are a part.]

FRAGMENT CORRECTED Many reading lists for high-school students include translations from Scandinavian writers such as Lagerlöf, Undset, and Ibsen.

FRAGMENT When Pip moved to London, he lived with Herbert Pocket. *And was tutored by Matthew Pocket.* [The two verbs *lived* and *was tutored* have the same subject. They should be included in the same sentence.]

FRAGMENT CORRECTED When Pip moved to London, he lived with Herbert Pocket and was tutored by Matthew Pocket.

**EXERCISE 2. Revising to Eliminate Sentence Fragments.** Some of the items in this exercise consist of one or two complete sentences; others contain sentence fragments. If an item contains *only* complete sentences, write *C* after its number. If an item contains a sentence fragment, revise the entire item with the fragment included in a complete sentence.

1. After I began running long distances, I realized that runners must wear specially designed running shoes. These shoes protect the feet from injury.
2. I could not go to his aid. Because, as luck would have it, we had not taken the precaution of bringing a spare paddle with us. I could only sit and look at him.
3. As far as competition is concerned, the team has done well. Though they were generally smaller than their opponents, the boys have turned in a good record.
4. Few of those who left the Discussion Club had ever been members of our debating team. Frank Neilson, our former secretary, is the most important exception to the rule.
5. Beyond the high buildings, over the opposite bank of the river, the sun hung low. Its glow smothered by a haze.
6. Listen! It is midnight. Standing on this cliff over the town, you can hear the great bell in the church tower.
7. The ship in which Theseus returned from his victory over the Minotaur was preserved by the Athenians. Who removed the old, decayed planks, putting new and stronger timbers in their place.

8. Whenever she went to the country, she went for long hikes. Then she would take a long bike ride into town. Realizing how healthy the fresh air and exercise made her feel.
9. During the nineteenth century, England was the center of a vast world trade. Ships going to England brought raw materials. On the outbound voyage the ships carried finished products for resale.
10. The book tells the story of how a magazine publisher rose to power. Aided by a group of editors whom he alternately indulged and disciplined.

## RUN-ON SENTENCES

When two complete sentences are separated by a comma or are not separated at all, the result is called a "run-on sentence." The first sentence "runs on" into the second. Of all sentence errors, the run-on sentence is probably the most common in high-school writing.

**12c. Avoid run-on sentences. Do not use a comma between sentences. Do not omit punctuation at the end of a sentence.**

The ordinary run-on sentence, in which a comma is misused to separate sentences or main clauses, is sometimes said to contain a "comma fault" or "comma splice." The run-on sentence in which punctuation is completely omitted between main clauses is less common, probably because even the most casual inspection will show that something is wrong with such a sentence. Both errors are usually caused not by a lack of understanding but by carelessness—carelessness in punctuation, in writing, and in checking written material.

RUN-ON SENTENCE The meeting seemed to last for hours, nothing was accomplished.

This run-on sentence consists of two independent clauses, each capable of standing alone as a complete sentence. We can eliminate the error by *separating* the two sentences completely, using a period as punctuation.

The meeting seemed to last for hours. Nothing was accomplished.

We can correct the sentence by using a semicolon.

The meeting seemed to last for hours; nothing was accomplished.

We can link the two main clauses by using a comma and a *coordinating conjunction.*

The meeting seemed to last for hours**, and** nothing was accomplished.

We can change one of the clauses to a subordinate clause, using a *subordinating conjunction.*

The meeting seemed to last for hours **because** nothing was accomplished.

The last correction showed one possible relationship between the ideas of the two clauses: The second clause explained *why* the meeting seemed long. Using a semicolon and a conjunctive adverb, we can bring out a different relationship between the two ideas.

The meeting seemed to last for hours**; however,** nothing was accomplished.

So far we have found five different ways in which a single run-on sentence can be corrected. Essentially, the reason for all of these corrections is simple: Two complete sentences cannot be run together. The sentences should be either completely separated by a full stop or joined by a semicolon or by a comma and a conjunction.

**EXERCISE 3. Revising Run-on Sentences.** All items in this exercise are run-on sentences. Number your paper 1–10. After each number, write the last word in any complete sentence of the corresponding item, and write the first word of the following sentence. As you write these words, indicate how you would correct the comma fault. You may use a period and a capital letter, a comma and a conjunction, a subordinating conjunction, or a semicolon, with or without an additional word. Do *not* be satisfied with using a period and a capital letter in every item; to make clear the relationship of ideas, some of the items should be revised in other ways.

EXAMPLE 1. Jane's schedule allowed her only two days in Washington, she can hardly be said to know the city well.
1. *Washington; consequently, she*

1. In the past a college education in America was a privilege for a few people, today, higher education has become widely available.
2. In the year 1295, Edward I of England gave the Dutch permission to fish in English waters later the English regretted this generosity when the Dutch became a wealthy and powerful competitive nation as a result of the prosperity of their fishing industry.

3. Artifacts from the sixth century have been found at Cadbury Castle in England, this might be the site of King Arthur's Camelot.
4. Proper names, spelled with a capital letter, sometimes become common nouns, spelled with a small letter and used to name one of a class of things, an example of this kind of language evolution is the word *maverick*.
5. About three of every four Americans graduate from high school, many millions of young people every year have difficulty finding work in a society that places value on a high-school diploma.
6. According to some, the mind of a newborn child is like a tablet upon which nothing has been written, then learning and experience write upon the tablet until life is done.
7. Under ordinary circumstances the meetings of the Student Disciplinary Committee are rather routine affairs, on Wednesday the problem facing the committee was not an ordinary one.
8. Honey is formed from the nectar that bees gather from flowers, enzymes in the bees' bodies change the nectar to honey, which is then stored as a food supply in cells in the beehive.
9. In spoken English the voice usually drops at the end of a sentence and always pauses, in written English this full stop is indicated by punctuation.
10. The very room in which the Dramatic Society held its meetings always excited Nancy, it might look to a visitor like an ordinary classroom, smelling faintly of chalk and ink, to her it was a theater, with a theater's magic and mystery.

**REVIEW EXERCISE. Revising to Eliminate Fragments and Run-ons.** Each item in this exercise contains one or more sentence errors. Revise the items to eliminate fragments and run-ons.

1. Some imaginative thinkers have proposed that Antarctica be used as a huge, germ-free "refrigerator." Where all nations' surpluses of food can be stored against lean years. There is no doubt about the refrigeration, many an Antarctic traveler has used food left behind years before by a predecessor.
2. Since its beginning, the United Nations has faced one crisis after another. Not a year has passed without moments of drama and decision. But the organization has always found measures that preserved the peace. Often in the nick of time.

3. Anyone who knows the early history of the United States can understand the spirit of the new nations born since World War II. Nations that have freed themselves from the domination of another country. Led by patriots who have devoted their lives to bringing independence and self-government to their native lands.
4. The brakes of an automobile generate heat. Far more heat than most of us realize, for example, bringing a car to a full stop from seventy miles per hour generates enough heat to melt a pound of iron.
5. Lightning reaches our eyes at 186,000 miles per second through the air. While thunder, which occurs almost simultaneously, creeps along to our ears at 1,087 feet per second. So that we sense the same event twice, in different ways, at different times.
6. Bearing small white or pink flowers, and also thorns. The hawthorn is the state flower of Missouri.
7. Stravinsky was most widely praised for his energetic rhythmic effects, he seemed to have a special genius for creating a highly charged, restless, driving movement; but I like his harmonies, which he always worked out at the piano keyboard.
8. In 1969 the Pulitzer Prize for fiction was awarded to N. Scott Momaday. Who is of Kiowa and Cherokee descent. For his novel *House Made of Dawn.*
9. Many people feel that the expression of a newspaper's opinions should be confined to its editorial page. So that readers can judge the news for themselves. "Slanted" news can be much more misleading than no news at all.
10. The neutron does not carry a positive electric charge, the proton does. And is slightly lighter in weight. Despite their differences, at very high energies these particles act similarly.

CHAPTER 13

# Coordination and Subordination

## EMPHASIS AND RELATIONSHIP OF IDEAS

### COORDINATE IDEAS

A single sentence frequently contains one or more ideas which may be equal or unequal in importance. Those that are equal are called *coordinate* ideas.

COORDINATE IDEAS Mr. Jones teaches French. Mrs. Yi teaches math.

These sentences may be joined into a *compound* sentence that shows the relationship between the two ideas. When this is done so that the equality of the ideas is maintained, we call the clauses in the new sentences *coordinate* clauses.

EXAMPLES Mr. Jones teaches French, and Mrs. Yi teaches math. [ideas added together]
Mr. Jones teaches French, but Mrs. Yi teaches math. [ideas contrasted]

In these examples, it is the connecting words *and* and *but* that make the sentences different in meaning. Conjunctions that connect ideas of equal importance are *coordinating conjunctions.*

Connectives may show other kinds of relationships between coordinate clauses.

EXAMPLES Mr. Jones may teach French, or he may teach Spanish. [alternative ideas expressed]
Mr. Jones speaks French fluently; accordingly, he has been appointed faculty adviser to the French Club. [result expressed]

Other connectives that may be used to link coordinate ideas are *yet, however, likewise, therefore, still, either . . . or,* and *furthermore.*[1]

## SUBORDINATE IDEAS

To include two unequal ideas in a single sentence, we introduce the secondary statement with a *subordinating conjunction.* Note, for example, the following sentences.

Maria and I often disagree.
I always respect her opinions.

If we wish to make the second sentence secondary to the first, or less important, we may place a subordinating conjunction in front of it and join the two sentences.

Maria and I often disagree, **although** I always respect her opinions.

The position of the clauses may be changed without changing the relationship of the ideas.

**Although** I always respect her opinions, Maria and I often disagree.

Both these sentences focus attention on the fact that Maria and I often disagree, and "play down" or subordinate the fact that I always respect her opinions. If we wish to focus attention on my respect for Maria's opinions, that can be done in the same way. The same process is used. The statement to be made secondary or subordinate is introduced with the subordinating conjunction.

**Although** Maria and I often disagree, I always respect her opinions.
I always respect Maria's opinions, **although** she and I often disagree.

In the sentences that follow, note how one idea is subordinated to the other.

Marie, who has a bad cold, may have to cancel her party.
When the cattle were stranded on the mountain, a helicopter dropped fodder to them.

[1] For sentence-combining exercises in coordination, see page 365. For more information on the proper use of connectives, see Chapter 2.

Because no women were permitted on the Elizabethan stage, female roles were played by boys.
When the coach finally announced tryouts for the varsity team, candidates crowded into the gym.

In your writing you should learn how to subordinate ideas by putting them into adverb or adjective clauses.[1]

## Adverb Clauses

Subordinate adverb clauses may tell *time, cause* or *reason, purpose* or *result,* or *condition* (see pages 367–68). These meanings are expressed by the subordinating conjunctions that introduce the clauses.

TIME **Before** we could leave for the trip, we had to obtain permission from our parents.
CAUSE Many new nations have economic difficulties **because** they are not prepared for self-government.
PURPOSE We had to take a shortcut **so that** we could get to the station in time.
CONDITION **Although** wages are generally higher than they were ten years ago, the cost of living has also gone up considerably.

**13a. Make clear the relationship between subordinate adverb clauses and independent clauses by selecting subordinating conjunctions that express the relationship exactly.**

You will find it easy to use subordinate adverb clauses effectively if you learn the following subordinating conjunctions that introduce them:

1. Subordinating conjunctions used to express *time:*

after until
as when
before whenever
since while

2. Subordinating conjunctions used to express *cause or reason:*

as because since whereas

3. Subordinating conjunctions used to expressed *purpose or result:*

that in order that so that

[1] For sentence-combining exercises in adjective and adverb clauses, refer to pages 366–69.

4. Subordinating conjunctions used to express *condition:*

| although | even though | unless |
|---|---|---|
| if | provided that | while |

**EXERCISE 1. Selecting Appropriate Subordinating Conjunctions.** Number your paper 1–10. From the lists on pages 333 and 334, choose an appropriate subordinating conjunction to fill the blank in each sentence, and write the conjunction after the proper number on your paper. Notice that when an adverb clause begins a sentence, it is followed by a comma.

1. —— it is called a lake, Moraine is really a three-acre pond located beneath a high, majestic ridge on Grapetree Mountain.
2. —— we visited Lake Moraine, we heard wild geese and saw beavers building dams.
3. —— we were sitting by the tent one summer evening, a snowshoe hare crept from behind the pine trees three times to eat lettuce from our hands.
4. Lake Moraine, a wonderful, peaceful place, is now threatened —— bitter rains, called acid rains, are destroying the brook trout that swim in its waters.
5. Acid pollutants from factory fumes are carried by atmospheric winds —— the pollutants, mostly sulfates and nitrates, fall to the earth in rain and snow.
6. High-altitude ponds such as Lake Moraine get a heavy dose of acid rains —— the mountains trap moisture-bearing air masses.
7. —— the acid pollutants end up in the mountain ponds, fish, especially trout, suffer and die in great numbers.
8. Many remote trout ponds are encased in granite —— little soil or organic matter exists to trap or buffer the acid rain.
9. —— it is possible to develop acid-tolerant strains of trout, such a program will likely take many years.
10. More and more isolated ponds such as Lake Moraine will become trout graveyards —— a way to combat the effects of acid rain is found.

**EXERCISE 2. Revising Sentences by Adding Subordinate Clauses.** Revise each of the following sentences by adding a subordinate clause at the beginning or at the end of the sentence. Vary your choice of subordinating conjunctions.

EXAMPLE 1. Television crews rushed to the scene.
1. *Television crews rushed to the scene after the volcano erupted.*

1. The eruption of the volcano caused little damage to nearby communities.
2. Rescue teams were able to find stranded campers quickly.
3. No one expected the volcano to erupt so suddenly.
4. A black cloud of volcanic dust darkened the sky for days.
5. The next explosion may be more lethal.
6. We decided to take a closer look at the smoldering volcano.
7. We rented a small plane for a day.
8. We wanted to take photographs of the inside of the crater.
9. Ash and wind made visibility poor.
10. We returned to the airport without any photographs.

## Adjective Clauses

**13b. Make clear the relative emphasis of ideas in an independent clause and a subordinate adjective clause by placing the idea you wish to emphasize in the independent clause and subordinate ideas in subordinate clauses.**

So far you have learned how to subordinate ideas in a sentence by means of an *adverb* clause. Another way in which a writer may indicate the relative importance of ideas is using a subordinate *adjective* clause, which modifies a noun or a pronoun. Suppose you wish to combine in one sentence these ideas: *The Taj Mahal is located in India. It was built as a mausoleum for a maharani.*

If you wish to emphasize the location in India, you will put the information in the first sentence in the main clause and the information in the second sentence in the subordinate clause.

**The Taj Mahal**, which was built as a mausoleum for a maharani, **is located in India**.

On the other hand, if you wish to emphasize the purpose for which the Taj Mahal was built, you will put that information in your main clause and place the location in the subordinate clause.

**The Taj Mahal**, which is located in India, **was built as a mausoleum for a maharani.**

Adjective clauses usually begin with *who, whom, whose, which, that, when,* or *where.*

In the following sentences, notice how the subordinate ideas are stated in the subordinate clauses.

The parade, **which began at noon,** ended at two.
Everyone **who marched in it** went over to the rally.
They raced toward the library, **where the noise came from.**

**EXERCISE 3. Subordinating Ideas by Using Adjective Clauses.** Change the emphasis in each of the following sentences by placing in the independent clause the idea that is now in the subordinate clause and by placing in the subordinate clause the idea that is now in the independent clause. You may have to delete unnecessary words and change word order. Be prepared to discuss which sentence, the original or the revised version, you prefer.

EXAMPLE 1. American government, of which democracy is the underlying principle, is as strong today as ever before.
1. *Democracy is the underlying principle of American government, which is as strong today as ever before.*

1. Antibodies, which are the body's first line of defense against disease, are the subject of intense medical research.
2. Dr. Lewis Thomas, who is one of the country's foremost specialists on cancer, writes a column in the *New England Journal of Medicine*.
3. Alaska, which is the largest state in the Union, contains vast reserves of forests, minerals, and wildlife.
4. The recipe, which includes many complicated steps, is a challenge for even the boldest cook.
5. Evelyn, whom you met yesterday, is a cousin of Jan, the youngest member of our class.
6. In this chapter, which describes the advent of the Industrial Revolution, we learned of the invention of the steam engine.
7. The Grand Canyon, which is usually one of the most popular tourist areas in the West, has temperatures of over 100°F during the summer.
8. Zora Neale Hurston, who was the most prolific black woman writer in America between 1920 and 1950, is the subject of this biography.

9. The article on engineering, which everyone seemed to enjoy, discussed job opportunities.
10. This unabridged dictionary, which probably contains more than 400,000 entries, weighs about twenty pounds.

## Correcting Faulty Coordination

**13c. Correct faulty coordination by placing ideas of lesser emphasis in a subordinate position. Any idea may be given less emphasis by being expressed in a subordinate clause, a modifying phrase, or an appositive.**

Faulty coordination occurs when two ideas of unequal importance are connected by a coordinate conjunction.

FAULTY COORDINATION The white gulls almost hid the sun from view, and they circled over the water in a great cloud.

Correct faulty coordination by subordinating one idea in a subordinate clause, a modifying phrase, or an appositive. In the faulty sentence just presented, we may subordinate the second idea by revising the sentence in one of these ways:

SUBORDINATE CLAUSE **As they circled over the water in a great cloud,** the white gulls almost hid the sun from view.

MODIFYING PHRASE **Circling over the water in a great cloud,** the white gulls almost hid the sun from view.

Here is another example of faulty coordination, corrected by the use of an appositive.

FAULTY COORDINATION The minister was a woman from Kentucky, and she administered a stinging rebuke to the city council.

APPOSITIVE The minister, **a woman from Kentucky,** administered a stinging rebuke to the city council.

**EXERCISE 4. Revising Sentences by Correcting Faulty Coordination.** Correct the faulty coordination in the following sentences by placing the idea to which you wish to give less emphasis in a subordinate adverb or adjective clause. Choose appropriate subordinating conjunctions to introduce the adverb clauses.

1. Wanda Landowska was a famous harpsichordist, and she came to the United States after 1941.

2. *The Night Watch* is in a museum in Amsterdam and is one of Rembrandt's greatest paintings.
3. The math teacher explained the new proposition, and she made it look quite simple.
4. Many new drugs are tested each year, and not all of them are successful.
5. Paperbacks are now selling at the rate of hundreds of millions a year, and they can be bought practically everywhere.
6. The film won many awards, and the producers were pleased.
7. Bob won the speaking contest, and he is very shy.
8. My aunt is an actress, and she gave me the tickets.
9. Air conditioners have become common appliances, and they require a great deal of electricity.
10. A temple was discovered in Yucatán, and it is considered to be about a thousand years old.

**EXERCISE 5. Revising Sentences by Correcting Faulty Coordination.** Correct the faulty coordination in the following sentences by placing the less important idea in an appositive.

1. The opera *Aïda* is by Giuseppe Verdi, and he was an Italian composer.
2. The pirate scanned the sea for a Spanish ship, and he was an Englishman.
3. My aunt is a pianist, and she invited me to her concert.
4. Coleridge was a famous poet, and he had once wanted to establish a utopian community near Pittsburgh.
5. The rocket was the product of a long series of experiments, and it set a speed record.
6. Visit the Franklin Institute and you will find it one of the most remarkable scientific museums in America.
7. Shep Morrison was a newcomer on the team, and the fans roared with delight when he scored.
8. Georgia O'Keeffe was a well-known and highly respected American painter, and she was influenced by the Southwest.
9. Joan Crawford was a member of the board of directors of a large company, and she projected a new image of women in films.
10. When we were in Spain, we visited the Prado, and it was one of the most interesting museums we had seen.

## SUMMARY

1. Make clear the relationship between ideas in a sentence by using connectives that express the relationship exactly.
2. Correct faulty coordination by placing subordinate or secondary ideas in an adverb or adjective clause, a modifying phrase, or an appositive.

---

**REVIEW EXERCISE. Revising Sentences by Correcting Faulty Coordination.** The relationship between ideas in the following sentences is not clear, either because the conjunctions used are not exact or because the sentences contain faulty coordination. Improve the sentences by revising them. Some can be improved in more than one way.

1. Wedgwood china is beautiful, and it is made in England.
2. The 1980 Winter Olympics were over, and skater Beth Heiden won a bronze medal.
3. Vincent van Gogh left his home, and he wanted to preach to the miners in southern Belgium.
4. Lindbergh was the first to fly alone across the Atlantic, and he was acclaimed by all.
5. Cyrano thought no one could love him, and he had a very big nose.
6. Odysseus was a very clever man, and it took him ten years to reach home after the fall of Troy.
7. Franklin D. Roosevelt contracted polio as a mature man and later became President of the United States.
8. In *The Caine Mutiny* the captain is put on trial, and he is a bitter character.
9. Grandma Moses became a world-famous artist, and she didn't begin to paint until she was seventy-six.
10. We had a severe drought, and it had begun in June.

## CHAPTER 14

# Clear Reference

## PRONOUNS AND ANTECEDENTS

One cause of ambiguity in writing is the use of pronouns without clear antecedents. A pronoun has no definite meaning in itself; its meaning is clear only when the reader knows what word it stands for. This word is called the *antecedent* of the pronoun. For instance, the pronoun *she* has no clear meaning in the sentence *The gym teacher told Mary that she needed to exercise on a regular basis.* Although the context suggests that it is Mary who needs the exercise, we cannot be sure. When we know that *she* stands for *Mary,* the pronoun has a definite meaning. We could revise the sentence to read *The gym teacher said, "Mary, you need to exercise on a regular basis"* or *The gym teacher said that Mary needed to exercise on a regular basis.*

In the following sentences arrows point from the pronouns to their antecedents.

The Pope asked Michelangelo to do the sculpture, but he refused.

The math teacher gave the students a problem that they couldn't solve.

After trying on the long blue dress, Mary said, "This fits perfectly."

**14a. A pronoun must refer clearly to the right antecedent. Avoid *ambiguous reference, general reference,* and *weak reference.***

## AMBIGUOUS REFERENCE

**(1) Avoid *ambiguous reference.* Such reference occurs when a pronoun refers to two antecedents so that the reader does not know at once which antecedent is meant.**

AMBIGUOUS Mr. Smith smiled at Mr. Jones when he was awarded the trophy.

In this sentence we do not know whether Mr. Smith or Mr. Jones was awarded the trophy. We can clarify the sentence by rearranging it.

CLEAR When Mr. Smith was awarded the trophy, he smiled at Mr. Jones.

AMBIGUOUS The purser explained to the passenger the meaning of the regulation he had just read. [Who read it?]
CLEAR After reading the regulation, the purser explained its meaning to the passenger.

AMBIGUOUS After the children carefully wrapped the packages, Mrs. Graham sent them off. [the packages or the children?]
CLEAR Mrs. Graham sent off the packages that the children had carefully wrapped.

As you can see, ambiguous references may be corrected in several ways. The object is always to make your meaning clear.

**EXERCISE 1. Revising Sentences by Correcting Ambiguous References.** Find the ambiguous meanings in each of the following sentences. Make the sentence clear by revising it.

EXAMPLE 1. When the airplane struck the hangar, it burst into flames. [airplane or hanger?]
1. *When it struck the hangar, the airplane burst into flames.*

1. The loyal forces fought the guerrillas until they were almost entirely destroyed.
2. The police officer told the sergeant that he had a button missing on his uniform.
3. The guide explained to the tourist the value of the stone she had found.
4. Marc informed Darryl that his tooth would stop hurting if he were to visit the dentist.
5. When Anna brought Lena to the conference, we asked her for her credentials.

6. Since the show was scheduled for the same night as the election, it had to be postponed.
7. The manager told the waiter that he would have to replace all broken dishes.
8. When the ambassador said goodbye to the foreign minister, reporters thought he looked confident.
9. When the large truck hit the wall in front of the building, it was hardly damaged.
10. Before the gate could fit the opening of the fence, it had to be made smaller.

## GENERAL REFERENCE

**(2) Avoid *general reference.* General reference occurs when a pronoun refers confusingly to an idea that is vaguely expressed. The antecedent is expressed in terms that are too general to be clear. Pronouns commonly used in this way are *which, this, that,* and *it.***

GENERAL More than 20 percent of those who enter college fail to graduate, *which* is a shame.

In this sentence the pronoun *which* refers to the fact that *more than 20 percent of those who enter college fail to graduate,* but because the pronoun *which* has no clear antecedent, the reader is confused. The sentence needs correction:

CLEAR It is a shame that more than 20 percent of those who enter college fail to graduate.

In the following example, the pronoun *this* does not have a clear antecedent.

GENERAL In the fall our school specializes in football, in the winter in basketball, and in the spring in baseball, tennis, and crew. *This* makes for a balanced athletic program.

CLEAR Emphasizing all these sports makes for a balanced athletic program.

In the next example, the pronoun *it* does not have a clear antecedent. A definite noun makes the meaning clearer.

GENERAL The ancient Romans conquered more of the world than they could reach readily with their troops. The troops themselves were frequently hired from a foreign power. Meanwhile, at home, the existence of slavery made honest labor no longer respectable. Eventually, *it* caused the great Roman Empire to collapse.

CLEAR All these conditions eventually caused the great Roman Empire to collapse.

Sometimes general reference can best be corrected by revising the whole sentence.

GENERAL The wind rose, the trees showed the pale undersides of their leaves, dark clouds appeared, and an ominous silver curtain moved in from the distant hills. *This* caused us to finish bringing in the hay as quickly as possible.

CLEAR We brought in the hay as quickly as possible when we noticed how the wind rose, the trees showed the pale undersides of their leaves, dark clouds appeared, and an ominous silver curtain moved in from the distant hills.

**EXERCISE 2. Revising Sentences by Correcting General References.** The following sentences contain examples of the general reference of pronouns. Revise the sentences or replace the unclear pronouns with nouns to make the meaning clear.

1. The sale included household furniture, men's and women's clothing, automobile accessories, and sporting goods. This was sure to bring in many customers.
2. Our star basketball player stole the ball and passed it to her teammate, who made the winning basket. It had us on our feet, cheering the whole time.
3. The guidance counselor asked me whether I wanted German, French, or Spanish, which was difficult to decide.
4. My parents bought a new rug and new curtains, and we hired someone to paint the walls and ceiling. That certainly improved the appearance of the room.
5. After the storm, the trail to the top of the mountain was washed out in some spots and was littered in many places with fallen branches. It made the ascent nerve-racking.
6. The first part of the test was on chemistry, the second on mathematics, the third on physics. This made it very difficult.
7. Some of the eyewitnesses described the man as short, others said he was tall, and yet others said he was "about average." It confused the police investigators.

8. The principal said that the play would have to be given in the old auditorium unless by some miracle the new auditorium were to be completed ahead of schedule, which will be a blow to the Maude Adams Drama Club.
9. We walked up a long, dreary road, cut through a thicket of unpruned trees, and cautiously approached the lonely old house, which made us all tired and depressed.
10. I received a notice that two of my library books were overdue, which was a complete surprise.

## WEAK REFERENCE

**(3) Avoid *weak reference*. Weak reference occurs when the antecedent has not been expressed but exists only in the writer's mind.**

WEAK Every time a circus came to town, Alice wanted to join *them.*

In this sentence there is no antecedent for the pronoun *them. Them* refers to the people with the circuses, but these people are not specifically mentioned in the sentence.

CLEAR Every time a circus came to town, Alice wanted to ***become one of the troupe.***

In the following sentence, you will see that there is no clear antecedent for the pronoun *these*.

WEAK He was a very superstitious person, and one of *these* was that walking under a ladder would bring bad luck.

In this sentence the antecedent for the pronoun *these* should be the noun *superstitions,* but the noun is only implied by the adjective *superstitious*. The error may be corrected by substituting a noun for the pronoun or rewriting the first part of the sentence.

CLEAR He was a very superstitious person; ***one of his superstitions*** was that walking under a ladder would bring bad luck.

BETTER He had many ***superstitions, one of which*** was that walking under a ladder would bring bad luck.

WEAK Mother is very much interested in psychiatry, but she doesn't believe *they* know all the answers.

CLEAR Mother is very much interested in psychiatry, but she doesn't believe that ***psychiatrists*** know all the answers.

Weak reference may be corrected by replacing the weak pronoun with a noun or by giving the pronoun a clear and sensible antecedent.

**EXERCISE 3. Revising Sentences by Correcting Weak References.** Correct the weak reference in each of the following sentences.

1. Arthur Conan Doyle began his career as a doctor, and it explains his interest in careful observation.
2. She is a careful gardener, watering them whenever the soil gets dry.
3. They planned to eat dinner outdoors by candlelight, but a strong wind blew them out.
4. For years after Mark Twain saw the steamboat in Hannibal, Missouri, he wanted to become one of them.
5. Even though it rained on the night of the concert, Ed went because his favorite ones were being played.
6. He visited the clothing store but did not try any on.
7. Although he is fond of poetry, he has never written one.
8. Tia's uncle has a huge vegetable garden, and he keeps them supplied with fresh vegetables all summer long.
9. In Central City, Colorado, opera is performed in the summer at the Teller Theater, but we did not see any of them.
10. Trout fishing is not much sport unless you catch one.

## INDEFINITE USE OF PRONOUNS

**14b. In formal writing, avoid indefinite use of the pronouns *it, they,* and *you.***

Although the indefinite use of these pronouns in sentences like the following may occur in ordinary conversation, such use is not acceptable in most writing.

INDEFINITE In the paper *it* said that a volcano erupted in the Indian Ocean.
BETTER The newspaper reported that a volcano erupted in the Indian Ocean.

INDEFINITE In this history book *they* refer to the Civil War as the War Between the States.
BETTER This history book refers to the Civil War as the War Between the States.

INDEFINITE In some nineteenth-century novels *you* are always meeting difficult words.
BETTER In some nineteenth-century novels, the vocabulary is quite difficult.

In the first of each of these pairs of sentences, the pronouns *it, they,* and *you* have no clear antecedents.

> ☞ **NOTE** Expressions such as *it is snowing, it is too early,* and *it seems* are, of course, entirely correct.

**EXERCISE 4. Revising Sentences by Correcting Indefinite Pronouns.** The sentences in this exercise contain examples of the indefinite use of *it, they,* and *you.* Strengthen the sentences either by replacing the faulty pronoun with a noun or by revising the entire sentence. Make the meaning unmistakably clear.

1. In *The Diary of Anne Frank* it shows a young girl's courage during two years of hiding.
2. Everyone is excited about graduation because you have worked so hard for it.
3. In southern Africa they mine diamonds and sell them to jewelers to be cut.
4. In the sports sections of the daily newspapers, it tells all about the day's events in sports.
5. When Grandfather was a child, you were supposed to be absolutely silent at the table.
6. Because modern artists have an idiom of their own, it leads to much misunderstanding.
7. On the book jacket they say that the author herself experienced these thrilling adventures.
8. They had whirled so fast it made them dizzy.
9. Among the attractions of the tour, they listed free admissions to all places of interest.
10. When Katharine Hepburn's play came to town, they sold out all the tickets far in advance.

**REVIEW EXERCISE. Revising Sentences by Correcting Faulty References.** The sentences in this exercise contain examples of ambiguous, general, weak, and indefinite reference. Correct the errors by using a noun instead of the faulty pronoun or by revising the entire sentence.

1. I heard the owl hoot from a tree nearby, but I couldn't see it.
2. In small print on the insurance policy, it said that they were not responsible for damage caused by floods.
3. We hiked almost twelve miles to the campsite, erected our tents, arranged our sleeping bags, and then made our supper. This so exhausted us that we immediately went to sleep.
4. Many of our Presidents began their political careers as minor public officials, which is a good thing.
5. Jane Austen was one of the greatest English novelists of the nineteenth century, and I like them very much.
6. In *Mama's Bank Account,* it tells how a Norwegian-American family lives in San Francisco.
7. When we saw the flock of geese, they told us that they had flown all the way from northern Canada.
8. After the barbers had cut the children's hair, some of them looked like billiard balls.
9. The shipwrecked men paddled their raft with their hands day after day, but this brought them no closer to land.
10. Out in the country, far away from city lights, they say you can frequently see the aurora borealis.

# CHAPTER 15

# Placement of Modifiers

## MISPLACED AND DANGLING MODIFIERS

Many young writers unintentionally become humorists through the careless use of modifiers. In the sentence *The tense hunter watched the raging lion come charging at him while readying a bow and arrow*, the lion is made to appear the owner of the bow and arrow. Successful writers make their meaning clear at first reading. If your readers are puzzled by what you write and have to read the sentence several times, they waste time, become confused, and may lose interest in what you have written. A misplaced modifier, like the one just mentioned, is an obstacle to understanding.

### MISPLACED MODIFIERS

**15a. Place phrase and clause modifiers as near as possible to the words they modify.**

Sentences like the following may be clear at first glance; yet, because of a misplaced word or group of words, they may mislead the reader or force a second look.

CONFUSING We listened breathlessly to the stories told by Scheherazade in *The Arabian Nights,* munching peanuts and crackers.

As the sentence reads, the storyteller, Scheherazade, is munching peanuts and crackers. That impression was obviously not intended, and it makes us either laugh or stop and reread. It would be better to place the participial phrase closer to the word it modifies, which is *we.*

CLEAR Munching peanuts and crackers, we listened breathlessly to the stories told by Scheherazade in *The Arabian Nights.*

CONFUSING Lenny spied a dog gnawing a bone on his way to school.

According to this sentence, the dog was on his way to school.

CLEAR On his way to school, Lenny spied a dog gnawing a bone.

CONFUSING They were delighted to see a field of daffodils climbing up the hill.
CLEAR Climbing up the hill, they were delighted to see a field of daffodils.

In all the examples, the meaning was made clearer when the modifier was placed near the word it modifies.

**EXERCISE 1. Revising Sentences by Correcting Misplaced Modifiers.** The following sentences are not entirely clear because they contain misplaced modifiers. Place the modifiers near the words they modify.

1. Louise projected the photographs on a large screen that she had taken at the zoo.
2. The judge sentenced the man to twenty years in solemn tones.
3. I pointed to the fish tank and showed my friends my new puffer, swelling with pride.
4. My mother asked me whether I would like a kitten with a sly grin.
5. I offered the guests some cheese, fruit, and crackers, not knowing how to cook.
6. My aunt finally taught me how to make stuffed cabbage, filled with a sense of accomplishment.
7. I like to walk along the beach at low tide, digging for clams without a care in the world.
8. Mrs. Jennings sang some folk songs about working on the railroad in the Lincoln School auditorium.
9. There is an Egyptian bracelet in the museum that is four thousand years old.
10. I found a book about Virginia Woolf written by her husband at a garage sale.

## DANGLING MODIFIERS

**15b. A modifying phrase or clause must clearly and sensibly modify a word in the sentence. When there is no word that the phrase or clause can modify, the modifier is said to dangle.**

EXAMPLE Eating my dinner quietly, the explosion made me jump up.

The *explosion* could not be eating my dinner, but that is what the sentence seems to say. Here is one way in which the sentence may be corrected:

Eating my dinner quietly, I jumped up when I heard the explosion.

In this instance a word (**I**), which is modified by the participial phrase, has been added. You may also correct the dangling modifier this way:

While I was eating my dinner quietly, the explosion made me jump up.

Here the participial phrase has been changed to an adverb clause.

Study the following examples of dangling modifiers and the ways in which they have been corrected. You will note that usually there is more than one way to eliminate such an error.

DANGLING MODIFIER While correcting papers, the message came from the principal.
CORRECTED While correcting papers, we received the message from the principal.
CORRECTED While we were correcting papers, the message came from the principal.

DANGLING MODIFIER To finish her paper on time, Mary's weekend was spent in the library.
CORRECTED So that Mary could finish her paper on time, her weekend was spent in the library.
CORRECTED To finish her paper on time, Mary spent her weekend in the library.

A few dangling modifiers have become accepted in idiomatic expressions.

**Generally speaking,** Americans are living longer.
**To be honest,** the party was rather boring.

However, you should avoid making your sentences sound absurd or impossible because of dangling modifiers.

**EXERCISE 2. Revising Sentences by Correcting Dangling Modifiers.** Each of the following sentences is confusing because of a dangling modifier. Remove the danglers by revising the sentences.

1. Frightened by our presence, the rabbit's ears perked up.
2. To interpret this poem intelligently, a knowledge of mythology is needed.
3. All bundled up in a blanket, the baby's first outing was a brief one.
4. When performing onstage, the microphone should not be placed too near the speaker cones.
5. To be a good singer, clear enunciation and correct breathing are extremely important.
6. Tying the kerchief tightly over the head, the wind blew violently.
7. Before living in Sacramento, Pittsburgh was their home.
8. While reaching into his pocket for change, the car accidentally rolled into the side of the tollbooth.
9. To work efficiently without sticking, be sure to clean and oil your typewriter periodically.
10. Before being painted, you should first put a coating of primer on the surface.

## TWO-WAY MODIFIERS

When a modifier may refer to more than one person or thing, it is difficult to understand what the writer means.

The Prime Minister said in the press interview her opponent spoke honestly.

This sentence may be interpreted in two ways. Did the Prime Minister hold the press interview? Or did her opponent? The two-way modifier fails to clarify the question.

Study the following examples of modifiers that modify two words.[1]

NOT CLEAR Joan of Arc declared after considerable pressure she would maintain her convictions.

CLEAR After considerable pressure, Joan of Arc declared she would maintain her convictions.

NOT CLEAR The mayor said when the city council met she would discuss the proposed budget.

[1] Some grammar books call these "squinting modifiers."

CLEAR When the city council met, the mayor said she would discuss the proposed budget.

CLEAR The mayor said that when the city council met, she would discuss the proposed budget.

NOT CLEAR The manager told the rookie after the game had begun to report to the dugout.

CLEAR After the game had begun, the manager told the rookie to report to the dugout.

CLEAR The manager told the rookie to report to the dugout after the game had begun.

**REVIEW EXERCISE. Revising Sentences by Correcting Faulty Modifiers.** The following sentences contain errors in the use of modifiers. Revise each sentence so that on first reading there will be no doubt about the meaning.

1. Having eaten the remains of the zebra, we watched the lion lick its chops.
2. After making many discoveries, the scientific acumen of the chemist was appreciated.
3. The girls counted twelve shooting stars sitting on the porch last night.
4. To do well on examinations, good study habits should be developed.
5. He regarded Helen Hayes after twenty years of playgoing with respectful admiration.
6. The leader of the safari promised in the morning we would see a herd of eland.
7. While running for the bus, my wallet must have dropped out of my pocket.
8. Catching the pop fly with her usual accuracy, the inning was completed.
9. She came to Paris especially to see the *Venus de Milo* in her new car.
10. After crumbling for a hundred years, we found the castle quite dilapidated.

# CHAPTER 16

# Parallel Structure

## MATCHING IDEA TO FORM

Good writing is not only clear to the reader but also correct in form. The careful writer or speaker expresses ideas of equal importance in parallel form.

### 16a. Express parallel ideas in the same grammatical form.

You should be able to use three kinds of parallel structure: *coordinate, compared or contrasted,* and *correlative.*

Coordinated ideas are of equal rank and are connected by *and, but, or,* or *nor,* which are called coordinate conjunctions (or coordinate connectives). For proper coordination, a noun is paired with another noun, a phrase with a phrase, a clause with a clause, an infinitive with an infinitive, a word ending in *-ing* with another word ending in *-ing*. In parallel constructions, observe this principle of pairing one part of speech with another or one kind of construction with another.

POOR In the winter I usually like skiing and to skate. [gerund paired with an infinitive]

BETTER In the winter I usually like **skiing** and **skating.** [gerund paired with a gerund]

BETTER In the winter I usually like **to ski** and **to skate.** [infinitive paired with an infinitive]

POOR The company guaranteed increases of salary and that the working day would be shortened. [noun paired with a noun clause]

BETTER The company guaranteed **that salaries would be increased** and **that the working day would be shortened**. [noun clause paired with a noun clause]

Ideas that are compared or contrasted are parallel.

POOR Einstein liked mathematical research more than to supervise a large laboratory. [noun contrasted with an infinitive]

BETTER Einstein liked mathematical **research** more than **supervision** of a large laboratory. [noun contrasted with a noun]

POOR To think logically is as important to me as calculating accurately. [infinitive contrasted with a gerund]

BETTER **Thinking** logically is as important to me as **calculating** accurately. [gerund contrasted with a gerund]

Correlative constructions are formed with the correlative conjunctions *both . . . and, either . . . or, neither . . . nor, not only . . . but* (*also*). They should be expressed in parallel form.

POOR With *Ship of Fools,* Katherine Anne Porter proved she was talented not only as a short-story writer but also in writing novels.

BETTER With *Ship of Fools,* Katherine Anne Porter proved she was talented **not only** as a short-story writer **but also** as a novelist.

### 16b. Place correlative conjunctions immediately before the parallel terms.

POOR A President of the United States must not only represent his own political party but also the entire American people. [*Not only . . . but also* should directly precede the parallel terms *his own political party* and *the entire American people.*]

BETTER A President of the United States must represent **not only** his own political party **but also** the entire American people.

POOR Washington both experienced the gloom of Valley Forge and the joy of Yorktown.

BETTER Washington experienced **both** the gloom of Valley Forge **and** the joy of Yorktown.

**EXERCISE 1. Revising Sentences by Using Parallel Structures.** Revise the following sentences by putting parallel ideas into the same grammatical form. Correct any errors in the placement of correlatives.

1. Dentists advise brushing the teeth after each meal and to avoid too much sugar in the diet.

2. Coretta King spoke warmly and with feeling to the people in the hall.
3. Eudora Welty's short stories have good plots, good characterization, and their style is interesting.
4. In John Steinbeck's "The Leader of the People," the old grandfather delighted in telling his grandson how he had led the wagon train across hostile territory and his final success in reaching the ocean.
5. Swimming in a lake is more fun for my family than to swim at the seashore.
6. Margaret Bourke-White not only photographed men in frontline trenches but also notable figures such as Gandhi.
7. My grandmother neither enjoyed modern music nor modern art.
8. A modern physician in a small town must not only be proficient in general medicine but surgery as well.
9. Mathematics has opened many avenues of research in improving communications and in how to live better.
10. Unfortunately, Aristotle not only relied on his own firsthand investigations but also on hearsay reports.

**EXERCISE 2. Revising Sentences by Using Parallel Structures.** Revise the following sentences by putting parallel ideas into the same grammatical form. Correct any errors in the placement of correlatives.

1. Many poets at some time in their careers began painting and then to write.
2. Mary Renault is both a novelist and does amateur archaeology.
3. Listen to Judith Anderson's recording of Lady Macbeth not only to get the meaning but also the speech patterns.
4. When Mark Twain went to Oxford for his honorary degree, he was cheered wildly by admirers, wined and dined by prominent people, and gave many coveted interviews to the press.
5. To absorb what a lecturer says, to have a clear mind and taking good notes are necessary.
6. Francis Bacon, the first great inductive thinker, neither had scientific equipment nor knowledge of experimentation.
7. Iris Murdoch is both a philosophy don at Oxford and she writes best-selling novels.

8. In her commencement address the famous author spoke sincerely and in a simple manner about the role of the educated woman in modern American society.
9. The great writer Ruskin used to say that he could tell a person's character by observing the things that made him laugh and what he cried about.
10. King Ferdinand and Queen Isabella clearly indicated to Columbus not only that they had faith in him but also would supply funds for the trip.

**16c. In parallel constructions repeat an article, a preposition, or a pronoun whenever necessary to make the meaning clear.**

AMBIGUOUS After the celebration we were introduced to the president and master of ceremonies. [Does this mean that the same person held both jobs?]

CLEAR After the celebration we were introduced to the president and **to the** master of ceremonies. [These are two individuals.]

AMBIGUOUS Winning the Westinghouse Scholarship was as great a pleasure to the teacher as the student. [This means that the student was as great a pleasure as winning the scholarship.]

CLEAR Winning the Westinghouse Scholarship was as great a pleasure to the teacher as **to the** student.

AMBIGUOUS The mansion of the Duke of Suffolk was as magnificent as the Duke of Bedford.

CLEAR The mansion of the Duke of Suffolk was as magnificent as **that of** the Duke of Bedford.

**EXERCISE 3. Revising Sentences by Correcting Faulty Parallelism.** Correct the parallelism in each of the following sentences by supplying the omitted words.

1. The paintings in the Kansas City Museum of Art are probably as famous as the Buffalo Museum.
2. Mahalia Jackson's style was different from Billie Holiday.
3. In the Folger Library in Washington are more first folios of Shakespeare than the Bodleian Library in Oxford.
4. The award she received for the painting was much smaller than the collection of prints.
5. You will discover that the facts in the latest edition of an encyclopedia are more up-to-date than an old edition.

6. The Nancy Drew books are similar to the Hardy boys.
7. The reaction of the amoeba to the stimulus was similar to the paramecium.
8. Seats in the balcony are always cheaper than the orchestra.
9. The howling of the dogs was louder than the wolves.
10. While traveling in England, my friend preferred the food in the little wayside inns to the cafeterias at home.

**REVIEW EXERCISE. Revising Sentences by Correcting Faulty Parallelism.** The following sentences are weak because of faulty parallelism. Correct each so that the meaning is clear.

1. Riding on the roller coaster and to spin the Wheel of Luck were her two greatest pleasures at the carnival.
2. In college you will be both required to study on your own and to take good notes.
3. Many immigrants came to America to seek their fortune or because they desired freedom of worship.
4. The new baby sitter was very strict about having children get to bed early and brushing their teeth themselves.
5. The budget discussion centered on the large appropriations for defense and paying the bills promptly.
6. The frightened private did not know whether he had been ordered to stand trial for disorderly conduct or because he had disobeyed.
7. The writing of a research paper is a much greater challenge than an ordinary essay.
8. Recent historians attribute events to the acts of leaders of nations as well as wishes of the people.
9. Virginia Woolf's success as a novelist was as great a tribute to her style as her plots.
10. To milk a goat is more difficult than a cow.
11. Advertising executives place great emphasis on creating a need for a product, making the product attractive, and that the product be fairly inexpensive.
12. In Elizabethan days many playgoers preferred the plays of Ben Jonson to Shakespeare.
13. Dentists advise us to cut down on sweets and brushing our teeth after each meal.

14. If you listen intently enough you will be able to distinguish the singing of Leontyne Price from Marilyn Horne.
15. Playing lacrosse can sometimes be more dangerous than to play football.
16. The lecturer lacked appeal because of her difficult topics and the fact that she spoke poorly.
17. Soil conservation should not only be studied by rural students but by urbanites as well.
18. Tchaikovsky's *1812 Overture* makes you imagine the thunder of cannon, the marching of soldiers, and how they celebrated the victory.
19. Dorothy Sayers' short stories have suspense, style, and they are well constructed.
20. The murals in Santa Fe depict the past glory of the Aztec ancestors of the artists and how the artists hope for the future.

## CHAPTER 17

# Sentence Combining and Revising

## EMPHASIS AND VARIETY

Good writing means more than putting down the first words that come to mind. It means careful revising and rewriting until you have expressed yourself in the best possible way. One of the great writers of the nineteenth century, Robert Louis Stevenson, never stopped learning. Read the statement that follows. Notice particularly not only *what* he says, but *how* he says it. Although his choice of words sounds old-fashioned to a twentieth-century audience, Stevenson's writing style is an excellent example of sentence variety.

> All through my boyhood and youth I was known and pointed out for the pattern of an idler; and yet I was always busy on my own private end, which was to learn to write. I kept always two books in my pocket, one to read, one to write in. As I walked, my mind was busy fitting what I saw with appropriate words. When I sat by the roadside, I would either read, or a pencil and a penny-version book would be in my hand, to note down the features of the scene or commemorate some halting stanzas. Thus I lived with words. And what I thus wrote was for no ulterior use, it was written consciously for practice. It was not so much that I wished to be an author (although I wished that too) as that I had vowed that I would learn to write.[1]

[1] Robert Louis Stevenson, *Memories and Portraits.*

## SENTENCE COMBINING

Sentence-combining exercises encourage you to make choices with regard to sentence structure and emphasis. They provide useful practice that can help you achieve a fluent writing style, rich in variety and interest.

**17a. Combine short, related sentences by inserting adjectives, adverbs, and prepositional phrases.**

Note how the following three sentences are combined.

THREE SENTENCES Anne Bradstreet was an author.
She was an American author.
She was an author during colonial times.

ONE SENTENCE Anne Bradstreet was an American author during colonial times.

To combine these sentences, repetitious words have been deleted. An adjective, *American,* has been taken from the second sentence and inserted into the first sentence. A prepositional phrase, *during colonial times,* has been taken from the third sentence and inserted into the first sentence.

Often there may be more than one correct way to combine short, related sentences.

THREE SENTENCES The minutes ticked away.
They ticked away slowly.
They ticked away on the clock.
ONE SENTENCE The minutes ticked slowly away on the clock.

*or*

On the clock, the minutes ticked away slowly.

Can you think of any other ways to combine these three short sentences?

Although you often have some degree of choice in combining short, related sentences, you may find that some combinations do not read smoothly, such as *On the clock, slowly, the minutes ticked away.* You should avoid these combinations, as well as those that change the meaning of the original short sentences.

**EXERCISE 1. Combining Sentences by Inserting Adjectives, Adverbs, or Prepositional Phrases.** Combine each group of short, related sentences by inserting adjectives, adverbs, or prepositional phrases into the first sentence and by deleting repetitious words. Add commas where they are necessary.

EXAMPLE 1. Iroquois Indians moved to the Northeast.
They moved during the thirteenth century.
They moved from the Mississippi region.
1. *During the thirteenth century, Iroquois Indians moved from the Mississippi region to the Northeast.*

1. The Iroquois formed a confederation of tribes.
   The confederation was powerful.
   The Iroquois formed it within two hundred years.
2. A central council of the confederation made decisions.
   The council made decisions unanimously.
3. Women nominated delegates.
   They were women among the tribes.
   They nominated delegates to the central council.
4. The Iroquois confederation subdued other tribes.
   The other tribes were nearby.
   The confederation subdued them systematically.
5. Tribes exchanged belts to ratify treaties.
   Their belts were of wampum.
   The exchanged belts ratified treaties permanently.
6. The Iroquois developed trade routes.
   The trade routes were extensive.
   The trade routes were along waterways and trails.
7. Hunting was an important element.
   It was an element in the Iroquois economy.
   It was always an important element.
8. The Iroquois also depended on farming.
   They depended heavily on farming.
   They depended on farming for their food.
9. Entire villages moved in search of soil.
   They moved in search of richer soil.
   The soil was for farming.
10. The structure of Iroquoian life changed.
    The structure was complex.
    It changed considerably.
    It changed during the late seventeenth century.

**17b. Combine closely related sentences by using participial phrases.**

Like adjectives, participial phrases help you add concrete details to nouns and pronouns in sentences. In the following example, the participial phrases are printed in boldfaced type. Notice how they describe the subject of the sentence, the Olympic athletes.

> **Dressed in bright blue costumes** and **holding small American flags in their hands,** the Olympic athletes marched into the sports arena.

Participial phrases are often a useful way to combine sentences and to express ideas concisely, as in the following example.

TWO SENTENCES The hikers rested at the summit.
The hikers were exhausted by the climb.
ONE SENTENCE The hikers, exhausted by the climb, rested at the summit.

The second sentence has been turned into a participial phrase, *exhausted by the climb,* and attached to the first sentence. Unnecessary words have been deleted.

A participle or participial phrase (see pages 421–25) must always be placed close to the noun or pronoun it modifies; otherwise the sentence may confuse the reader.

MISPLACED Hidden under a bench, we found the kitten.
IMPROVED We found the kitten **hidden under a bench.**

**EXERCISE 2. Combining Sentences by Using Participial Phrases.** Combine each of the following pairs of sentences into one sentence by turning the second sentence of each pair into a participial phrase and inserting it into the first sentence. Punctuate the combined sentence correctly.

EXAMPLE 1. The Brooklyn Bridge spans the East River.
The Brooklyn Bridge was built in 1883.
1. *Built in 1883, the Brooklyn Bridge spans the East River.*

1. Hoover Dam is one of the largest dams in the world.
   Hoover Dam measures 221 meters high and 379 meters wide.
2. Lake Mead extends for 184 kilometers.
   Lake Mead was formed by Hoover Dam.
3. The massive wall of a dam is an impressive sight.
   The wall is made from millions of tons of concrete.
4. The Alaskan Pipeline runs over vast regions of frozen tundra.
   The tundra is populated by caribou and other creatures.

5. Engineers of the Alaskan Pipeline sought to preserve the ecology of the tundra.
   The engineers were working together with environmentalists.
6. The Delaware Aqueduct carries fresh water.
   The water is drawn from reservoirs.
7. People depend on water from these reservoirs.
   These people live in or near New York City.
8. The Golden Gate Bridge spans Golden Gate Strait.
   The bridge is known to tourists from around the world.
9. The Mackinac Bridge is over eight kilometers long.
   The bridge was once considered impossible to build.
10. The Chesapeake Bay Bridge-Tunnel is an engineering marvel.
    It consists of two tunnels, two fixed steel bridges, and over sixteen kilometers of trestles.

**17c. Combine short, related sentences by using appositives or appositive phrases.**

Appositives and appositive phrases add definitive detail to nouns or pronouns in sentences by helping to identify or explain them. Note how the appositive phrase in the following sentence helps identify the noun, *calligraphy.*

Calligraphy, **an elegant form of handwriting,** requires a special pen.

Two sentences can often be combined in a variety of ways by using an appositive or appositive phrase.

TWO SENTENCES Arna Bontemps wrote for the magazine *Opportunity.* Arna Bontemps was a major figure in the Harlem Renaissance.

ONE SENTENCE Arna Bontemps, a major figure in the Harlem Renaissance, wrote for the magazine *Opportunity.*

*or*

A major figure in the Harlem Renaissance, Arna Bontemps wrote for the magazine *Opportunity.*

*or*

Arna Bontemps, a writer for the magazine *Opportunity,* was a major figure in the Harlem Renaissance.

The last combination emphasizes Bontemps' stature, whereas the first two combinations emphasize Bontemps' work for *Opportunity.* All the combinations are correct; the context of the sentence should determine which choice is preferable.

**EXERCISE 3. Combining Sentences by Using Appositives or Appositive Phrases.** Combine the following pairs of sentences by turning one of the sentences into an appositive phrase. Punctuate the combined sentence correctly.

EXAMPLE 1. Harlem is a large section of New York City.
Harlem is the birthplace of many American artists and writers.
1. *Harlem, a large section of New York City, is the birthplace of many American artists and writers.*

1. The Harlem Renaissance was a period of intense creativity among black Americans.
   The Harlem Renaissance was a literary movement during the 1920's.
2. Claude McKay was the oldest of the Harlem Renaissance writers.
   Claude McKay was an emigrant from Jamaica.
3. *Cane* is an interesting collection of sketches, stories, poems, and a one-act play.
   *Cane* is a work by Jean Toomer.
4. The Imagist movement began with Ezra Pound.
   Ezra Pound was an American poet.
5. Ezra Pound's followers included two college friends.
   William Carlos Williams and Hilda Doolittle were the two friends.
6. Amy Lowell was a Pulitzer Prize winner.
   Amy Lowell was a member of the Imagist movement.
7. Edna St. Vincent Millay's poetry includes many examples of the sonnet.
   Sonnets are a traditional form of verse.
8. Gwendolyn Brooks writes superbly crafted poetry.
   Gwendolyn Brooks has been a resident of Chicago for many years.
9. The poet Marianne Moore spent most of her life in Brooklyn.
   She was an avid baseball fan.
10. Free verse is the poetic form Walt Whitman used.
    Margaret Walker often writes free verse.

**17d. Combine short, related sentences by using compound subjects or verbs or by writing a compound sentence.**

Joining two subjects or two verbs by the conjunctions *and, but,* or *or* is common in most writing, as is the joining of two independent clauses to make a compound sentence.

EXAMPLES Richard **and** Marie will attend the dance. [compound subject]
Marie will go to the dance **but** will join us later. [compound verb]

Two subjects or two verbs may also be joined by correlative conjunctions such as *either . . . or, neither . . . nor,* and *both . . . and.*

EXAMPLES **Neither** Richard **nor** Marie will attend the dance.
We will **either** attend the dance **or** go to the movies.

Independent clauses are joined into a compound sentence by conjunctions such as *and, but, for,* and *or* and by other connectives such as *furthermore, yet, for example, however, either . . . or,* and *neither . . . nor.* The relationship of the independent clauses determines which connective works best.

EXAMPLES The baseball player argued vehemently, **but** the umpire refused to listen.
The invading army has blocked off our supply routes; **furthermore**, it has begun guerrilla raids on our outposts. [Notice the use of the semicolon.]

Ideas in separate sentences can be combined by using the appropriate connecting words.

TWO SENTENCES The judge showed early signs of genius.
She began law school when she was only nineteen.
ONE SENTENCE The judge showed early signs of genius; for example, she began law school when she was only nineteen.

**EXERCISE 4. Combining Simple Sentences into Compound Sentences.** Combine each group of sentences into one sentence by choosing one of the connectives listed in parentheses. Punctuate your sentences correctly.

1. Totalitarian governments suppress free speech.
   They mislead their people intentionally. (yet, furthermore)
2. Shakespeare is famous the world over.
   We know very little of his life. (yet, and)
3. Dress may not indicate character.
   Many people do judge by appearances. (and, but)

4. Our team won the final game.
   Our season record was still poor. (however, either . . . or)
5. The short-necked tortoise is an endangered reptile.
   We must take steps to protect it. (or, therefore)
6. Much evidence favors this position.
   We must not decide hastily. (nevertheless, and)
7. The anglers fished all day.
   The fish refused to bite. (therefore, but)
8. Clothes are expensive.
   I had to pay a fortune for this shirt. (for example, and)
9. The weather will clear tomorrow.
   We shall have to cancel the picnic. (either . . . or, and)
10. Congress must pass this bill.
    The President must sign it. (however, and)
    The welfare of the nation is at stake. (however, for)

**17e. Combine short, related sentences into a complex sentence by putting one idea into a subordinate clause.**

Subordination allows you to express the relationship between two unequal ideas within a single sentence. Methods for subordinating ideas include the use of the adjective clause, the adverb clause, and the noun clause. Mastering these methods of subordination will improve the variety and clarity of your writing.

**(1) Use an adjective clause to combine sentences.**

Adjective clauses, like adjectives, modify nouns or pronouns. In the following sentence, the adjective clause is printed in boldfaced type.

> The National Air and Space Museum, **which contains many exhibits on the history of aeronautics,** is in Washington, D.C.

To combine sentences by using an adjective clause, you must first decide which idea to emphasize (see page 335). Then you must choose the correct relative pronoun to join the sentences.

RELATIVE PRONOUNS who, whom, whose, which, that, where

The adjective clause must always be placed next to the word or words it modifies.

TWO SENTENCES I read the life of Matthew Henson.
He traveled to the North Pole with Robert Peary.

ONE SENTENCE I read the life of Matthew Henson, who traveled to the North Pole with Robert Peary.

TWO SENTENCES The heat wave may end in a few days.
It has caused a drought in the Midwest.

ONE SENTENCE The heat wave, which has caused a drought in the Midwest, may end in a few days.

**EXERCISE 5. Combining Sentences by Using Adjective Clauses.** Combine the following pairs of sentences by subordinating one idea in an adjective clause. Punctuate your sentences correctly.

EXAMPLE 1. The general greeted his former mess sergeant.
He had not seen him in many years.
1. *The general greeted his former mess sergeant, whom he had not seen in many years.*

1. Emma Lazarus' sonnet is inscribed on the Statue of Liberty.
It is called "The New Colossus."
2. Mary Cassatt was an American artist.
She participated in the movement called Impressionism.
3. The poem "Renascence" was written by Edna St. Vincent Millay.
It was assigned yesterday.
4. He was an American artist. James McNeil Whistler was renowned throughout the world for his wit.
5. Many secrets were known to the ancient world.
These secrets are unknown to us.
6. James Earl Jones is a famous Shakespearean actor.
He appeared in the televised version of *Roots*.
7. In Paris we visited the Louvre Museum.
Many famous paintings are hung there.
8. Next week we are going to read about Lorraine Hansberry.
She wrote *A Raisin in the Sun*.
9. Frances Perkins was Franklin Roosevelt's Secretary of Labor.
She was the first woman Cabinet member.
10. Marie Curie discovered polonium.
She named Polonium for her native Poland.

**(2) Use an adverb clause to combine sentences.**

Adverb clauses can express a relationship of time, cause, purpose, or condition between two ideas in a single sentence.

EXAMPLE Arthur and Carol both receive high grades **because they work hard.** [*Because they work hard* gives the cause of Arthur's and Carol's receiving high grades.]

To combine sentences by using an adverb clause, you must first decide which idea should become subordinate. You must then decide which subordinating conjunction best expresses the relationship between the two ideas.[1]

TWO SENTENCES General Burgoyne attacked a second time.
The Americans won a decisive victory.

ONE SENTENCE When General Burgoyne attacked a second time, the Americans won a decisive victory.

TWO SENTENCES You should buy that suit.
It looks well on you.

ONE SENTENCE You should buy that suit because it looks well on you.

**EXERCISE 6. Combining Sentences by Using Adverb Clauses.** Combine each pair of sentences by placing one idea into an adverb clause. Use the list of subordinating conjuctions on pages 333–34, if necessary. Punctuate the combined sentences correctly.

EXAMPLE 1. Hand in your paper.
You should revise it carefully.
1. *Before you hand in your paper, you should revise it carefully.*

1. Robert F. Kennedy died in 1968.
   He was at a high point in his political career.
2. Emily Dickinson wrote many poems.
   Not all of them are equally famous.
3. The soldiers waited to make their attack.
   The full moon rose.
4. We had supper early.
   We would get to the theater on time.
5. S. I. Hayakawa wrote *Language in Thought and Action.*
   He wanted to explain the importance of semantics.
6. Beethoven wrote several symphonies in his later years.
   He was almost totally deaf.

[1] See pages 333–34 for a list of common subordinating conjunctions.

7. Alvin Ailey starred as a high-school athlete.
   He won international fame as a dancer and choreographer.
8. The Incas had a highly developed civilization.
   It crumbled under Spanish attacks.
9. I will go to the concert.
   You will come along too.
10. Poet Gwendolyn Brooks was born in Topeka, Kansas.
    Many of her poems are about Bronzeville, in Chicago.

**(3) Use a noun clause to combine sentences.**

A noun clause is a subordinate clause used as a noun. Note the following examples of noun clauses and how they are used.

> **Whoever visits Hannibal, Missouri,** should visit the home of Mark Twain. [noun clause used as subject]
> In class we discussed **what Twain wrote** while he worked as a journalist. [noun clause used as direct object]
> Twain often invested his money in **whatever struck his fancy.** [noun clause used as object of preposition]

A noun clause can also be used as a predicate nominative and as an indirect object. Noun clauses are usually introduced by *that, what, whatever, why, who, whom, whoever,* or *whomever.*

The introductory word *that* is sometimes omitted before a noun clause.

EXAMPLE The doctor said the patient could leave.

**EXERCISE 7. Combining Sentences by Using Noun Clauses.** Combine each of the following pairs of sentences by turning the second sentence in each pair into a noun clause. Use one of the introductory words *that, what, whatever, why, who, whom, whoever, whomever.*

EXAMPLE 1. Ramon is going to the carnival tonight.
Eliza told me.
1. *Eliza told me that Ramon is going to the carnival tonight.*

1. Juanita mentioned the idea to someone.
   She mentioned it to whoever would listen.
2. You should eat balanced meals.
   Do you know why?

3. A recording gives sports information.
   It gives information to whoever dials that number.
4. Someone borrowed my newspaper.
   Do you know who?
5. This is an interesting statistic.
   Everyone under twenty-five years of age pays more for auto insurance.

**REVIEW EXERCISE A. Using Sentence-Combining Methods.** Using the sentence-combining methods you have practiced thus far, combine each group of sentences into one smooth, well-written sentence. You may omit unnecessary words and change the word order, but you may not change the meaning of the original sentences. Punctuate your combined sentences correctly.

1. Red Grange played for the University of Illinois.
   He was one of the greatest football players.
   He was called "the Galloping Ghost."
2. Countee Cullen was a lyric poet.
   He was American.
   He was a member of Phi Beta Kappa.
   He received a master's degree from Harvard University.
3. Reading improvement is now taught in many colleges.
   Students take the course.
   The course speeds up their reading.
   It also improves their comprehension.
4. There are streets named after Lafayette, Pulaski, Kosciusko, De Kalb, and Von Steuben.
   These were all foreign generals who aided America in the Revolutionary War.
   The streets are in the borough of Brooklyn, New York.
5. The Statue of Liberty was presented to us by the French government.
   Frédéric Bartholdi designed it.
   It is one of the first sights to greet newcomers to America.
6. There are now many kinds of dictionaries.
   One such is a dictionary of synonyms and antonyms.
   Another is a biographical dictionary.
   A third is a geographical dictionary with pronunciations given.

7. A symphony orchestra has many sections.
   One consists of the strings.
   Another consists of the woodwinds.
   The third is the brass.
   Then there is the percussion section.
8. Neon lighting works on a unique principle.
   A glass tube is filled with a rare gas called neon.
   Neon becomes fluorescent when activated by electricity.
9. *Roget's Thesaurus* was written over a hundred years ago.
   The author was Peter Mark Roget.
   He was a physician by profession.
   He lived in England.
10. You can review your mythology by reading about spacecraft.
   There is one called *Jupiter.*
   Another is called *Gemini.*
   A third is called *Atlas.*

**REVIEW EXERCISE B. Using Sentence-Combining Methods.** Combine the short, choppy sentences in the following paragraph into longer, smoother sentences. Be sure that the sentences you write add variety to the paragraph but do not change the original meaning. Punctuate the paragraph correctly.

Mildred "Babe" Didrikson Zaharias was born in Beaumont, Texas, in 1914. She was one of the finest track-and-field performers of all time. Babe gained national attention in 1930. She gained national attention at a track-and-field meet in Dallas. She won two events. In a third event, the long jump, she broke the world record. Babe competed in the Olympic Games in 1932. She entered the high jump, the long jump, and the hurdles. She set world records in all three events. Only two of the records were made official. Babe's high jump was nullified. It was nullified over a technicality. Babe was a world champion in women's track and field for over a decade. Babe later became a world-champion golfer.

## VARYING SENTENCE OPENINGS

**17f. Give variety to your sentence structure by varying the beginnings. Begin some of your sentences with a transposed appositive or with a modifier.**

### *Appositives*

| | |
|---|---|
| SUBJECT FIRST | Easter Island, the outpost of Polynesia, has always been a land of mystery. |
| TRANSPOSED APPOSITIVE FIRST | **The outpost of Polynesia,** Easter Island has always been a land of mystery. |

### *Single-word Modifiers*

| | |
|---|---|
| SUBJECT FIRST | Emily Dickinson was shy and retiring and did not enjoy social activities. |
| SINGLE-WORD MODIFIERS FIRST | **Shy and retiring,** Emily Dickinson did not enjoy social activities. |
| SUBJECT FIRST | Many of the committee's suggestions have been rejected lately. |
| SINGLE-WORD MODIFIERS FIRST | **Lately**, many of the committee's suggestions have been rejected. |

### *Phrase Modifiers*

| | |
|---|---|
| SUBJECT FIRST | Alicia de Larrocha was incomparable on the concert platform. |
| PREPOSITIONAL PHRASE FIRST | **On the concert platform,** Alicia de Larrocha was incomparable. |
| SUBJECT FIRST | The examiners worked around the clock to finish correcting all the papers in one week. |
| INFINITIVE PHRASE FIRST | **To finish correcting all the papers in one week,** the examiners worked around the clock. |
| SUBJECT FIRST | The engineer examined the blueprint carefully and then said that the bridge could never be constructed that way. |
| PARTICIPIAL PHRASE FIRST | **Examining the blueprint carefully,** the engineer said that the bridge could never be constructed that way. |

### *Clause Modifiers*

| | |
|---|---|
| SUBJECT FIRST | The chemists analyzed the sodium compounds after they had analyzed the potassium. |
| CLAUSE FIRST | **After they had analyzed the potassium,** the chemists analyzed the sodium compounds. |
| SUBJECT FIRST | Edna St. Vincent Millay moved to New York City and soon became a leading literary figure. |
| CLAUSE FIRST | **Soon after she moved to New York City,** Edna St. Vincent Millay became a leading literary figure. |

**EXERCISE 8. Revising Sentences by Varying Sentence Beginnings.** Revise each sentence as instructed in the brackets.

1. Madame Curie, after completing the experiments, decided to publish an account of them. [Begin with a prepositional phrase containing a gerund phrase.]
2. Dr. Jonas Salk was convinced that his vaccine would prevent polio and asked the American Medical Association to test it. [Begin with an adverb clause.]
3. Narcissa Whitman traveled across the Continental Divide in 1836 along with Eliza Spaulding. [Begin with a prepositional phrase.]
4. The English poet Keats was weak and consumptive and died at the age of twenty-six. [Begin with single-word modifiers.]
5. School will open right after Labor Day, as usual, unless circumstances compel a postponement. [Begin with an adverb clause.]
6. Bolivar, an idol among his contemporaries, has been the inspiration for many modern revolutions. [Begin with an appositive.]
7. The old soldier, thin and haggard, could barely drag along with the rest. [Begin with single-word modifiers.]
8. Lila Acheson Wallace, a cofounder of the *Reader's Digest,* was also a patron of the arts. [Begin with an appositive.]
9. Amy Lowell, by working tirelessly on behalf of the Imagist poets, developed a reputation for eccentricity. [Begin with a prepositional phrase containing a gerund phrase.]
10. Constant research has brought color television to a high level of efficiency, and more people are buying color sets. [Begin with an adverb clause.]

**EXERCISE 9. Revising Sentences by Varying Sentence Beginnings.** Revise each of the following sentences so that it will begin with an appositive or a modifier. You may have to change the wording slightly in some sentences.

1. Football players frequently take on strenuous jobs in the summer to get into good physical condition.
2. The Prime Minister, harassed and weary, closed the session of the Cabinet.
3. The audience sang along with the chorus while the conductor tapped out the rhythm.

4. The Portuguese sailors, expert navigators, often went out to sea in threatening weather.
5. Cervantes wrote his great comedy, *Don Quixote,* while he was in prison.
6. Shinichi Suzuki is seen as one of the world's great violin teachers as a result of his method for early music education.
7. The Pulitzer Prize for drama, awarded each year, is coveted by every professional playwright.
8. This statue of solid marble should endure for centuries.
9. Pelé scored an incredible 1,220 goals in 1,253 games in his eighteen years of professional soccer in Brazil.
10. Homer, in his description of the Aegean, calls it the "wine-dark sea."

## AVOIDING STRINGY STYLE

**17g. Give variety to your writing by avoiding the "stringy" style that results from the overuse of *and* and *so*.**

In your daily conversation you may have noticed how many people use *and* and *so* over and over again when they are telling a story. Such a practice soon makes conversation and writing monotonous. Here are some ways of overcoming this tendency.

### (1) Correct a stringy sentence by subordination of ideas.

STRINGY Jane went to Cornell University to study hotel management and she liked it very much and urged her friends to study it also.

IMPROVED At Cornell University, Jane studied hotel management, which she liked so much that she urged her friends to study it also.

STRINGY The small cars are inexpensive and they are more maneuverable in parking and travel more miles on a gallon of gasoline.

IMPROVED The small cars, which are inexpensive and more maneuverable in parking, travel more miles on a gallon of gasoline.

STRINGY The mayor was an astute politician, so she refused to discuss the issue until after the election.

IMPROVED Because the mayor was an astute politician, she refused to discuss the issue until after the election.

STRINGY Vermeer used a special kind of blue paint and was the only one to use it, so it has become known as "Vermeer blue."

IMPROVED A special kind of blue paint, which Vermeer was the only one to use, has become known as "Vermeer blue."

**(2) Correct a stringy sentence by dividing it into two sentences.**

STRINGY The representatives visited several locations for a permanent site of the United Nations and they were turned down by the communities so they decided to come to New York.

IMPROVED The representatives who were visiting several locations for a permanent site of the United Nations were turned down by several communities. They then decided to come to New York. [stringiness corrected by subordination and division into two sentences]

STRINGY Dr. Fleming was studying a colony of bacteria and noticed that a substance in the dish was impeding the growth of bacteria, so he continued his investigations and discovered penicillin.

IMPROVED While Dr. Fleming was studying a colony of bacteria, he noticed a substance impeding its growth. After further study he discovered penicillin. [stringiness corrected by subordination and by division into two sentences]

**(3) Correct a stringy sentence by reducing coordinate clauses to a compound predicate.**

STRINGY Henry David Thoreau built a hut on Walden Pond, and he furnished it simply and settled down for a life of contemplation and writing.

IMPROVED Henry David Thoreau built a hut on Walden Pond, furnished it simply, and settled down for a life of contemplation and writing.

**EXERCISE 10. Revising Stringy Sentences.** Revise the following stringy sentences by one or more of these methods: subordination, division into more than one sentence, reduction of coordinate clauses to a compound predicate. Avoid excessive use of *and* and *so*.

1. Isabella Stewart Gardner built a palace on a Boston dump, and she filled it with rare treasures, and then in her will she said that each item must stay forever where she placed it.
2. It is easy to complain of our petty discomforts and forget that people all over the world may be so much worse off and so perhaps we should really be grateful.
3. Jessica Mitford wrote *The American Way of Death,* and this best-selling book led eventually to an official investigation of the funeral industry.
4. In studying an assignment it is wise to read it over quickly at first and then to see the major points and finally to outline the material.
5. Until the mid-1970's America had been importing large quantities

of oil from the Middle East, and the American dollar was weakened as a result.

6. In *Silas Marner* Eppie is discovered by Silas asleep on the hearth, and he takes care of the little girl and becomes very fond of her.
7. Suburban life has made many commuters into clockwatchers and trainwatchers, and this development has not helped either their peace of mind or their digestion.
8. Many museums offer special services to schools and these include lectures and guided tours.
9. Willa Cather was a high-school teacher, and it is believed that her short story "Paul's Case" was based on an experience in her school, and it is a very moving story.
10. A great tragedy in Beethoven's life is that he became deaf, and he could not hear his *Ninth Symphony* and when he conducted it, he did not even hear the applause.

# PART THREE

# TOOLS FOR WRITING AND REVISING:

## Grammar ▪ Usage ▪ Mechanics

GRAMMAR

CHAPTER 18

# The Parts of Speech

## IDENTIFICATION AND FUNCTION

Noah Webster, the American lexicographer who gave his name to many dictionaries, was concerned with more than definitions and pronunciations. In his *Rudiments of English Grammar,* published in 1790, he wrote:

> What is English grammar? The art of speaking and writing the English language correctly, according to the rules and general practice.
>
> Where are the rules of the language to be found? In the language itself.

In order to speak and write "according to the rules," you have to learn what those rules are. Furthermore, in order to discuss the rules or the workings of language in general, you have to learn to use certain standard terms such as *noun* or *predicate*—very much as a mechanic uses certain standard terms to refer to the workings of a car.

### DIAGNOSTIC TEST

**Identifying the Parts of Speech of Words.** List the italicized words in the following sentences, numbering them as they are numbered in the test. Study the way each word is used in its sentence; then write after it what part of speech it is.[1]

[1] The word *his,* which is the possessive form of the pronoun *he,* is called a pronoun throughout this book. Some teachers, however, prefer to think of *his* and other possessive pronouns (*your, their, her, its, our,* etc.) as adjectives. Follow your teacher's direction in labeling these words.

Thursday, April 4, 1974, (1) *was* a day that will (2) *always* be remembered in the history of (3) *baseball.* At 2:40 P.M. in Riverfront Stadium in Cincinnati, Henry Aaron (4) *of* the Atlanta Braves tied Babe Ruth's (5) *unbroken* record of 714 home runs during a major league baseball career. Aaron, forty years old, was at bat for the first time in the (6) *baseball* season. It was the first inning. He hit a 3–1 pitch (7) *that* sailed (8) *solidly* out to left center field and traveled four hundred feet, zooming neatly over the twelve-foot fence and driving in the first runs of the 1974 baseball season. Braves rooters cried (9) *"Bravo!"* from the packed stands as the spectators rose to their feet. The (10) *horsehide* ball was caught on the first bounce by Clarence Williams, a twenty-two-year-old Cincinnati (11) *police officer,* while he was covering the area (12) *behind* the fence. "I couldn't see what was going on," said Williams, (13) *one* of Aaron's fans, (14) *"but* I knew he was up when I saw 44 on the scoreboard under the 'at bat' sign." After the game, while being interviewed by the press, Aaron smiled in his usual gracious (15) *fashion* (16) *and* said he was (17) *simply* delighted to have tied the Babe's (18) *longstanding* record. "It's a load off my back," he said. Such great events seldom (19) *occur,* and there will always be (20) *someone* eager to tell the story of that day.

---

## THE NOUN

**18a. A *noun* is a word used to name a person, place, thing, or idea.**

Nouns may be classified as *proper* or *common* and as *abstract* or *concrete.* A further classification for some nouns is *collective.*

A *proper noun* is the name of a particular person, place, or thing. Proper nouns are always capitalized: *Sylvia Bryan, F. Scott Fitzgerald, Scotland, Indianapolis, Ohio River, Brooklyn Bridge, U.S. Senate.*

A *common noun* is a noun that does not name a particular person, place, or thing. Common nouns are not capitalized except at the beginning of a sentence: *woman, designer, author, nation, city, river, bridge.*

An *abstract noun* names a quality, a characteristic, or an idea: *courage, illness, strength, charm, ability.*

A *concrete noun* names an object that can be perceived by the senses: *cat, flower, house, church.*

A *collective noun* names a group: *swarm* (of bees), *pack* (of wolves), *faculty, team.*

With reference to all these classifications, the noun *orchestra* is a common, concrete, collective noun.

Sometimes two or more words will be joined to form a *compound noun*. They may be written as one word (*sidewalk*), as two words (*attorney general*), or as a hyphenated word (*father-in-law*).

**EXERCISE 1. Classifying Nouns as Concrete or Abstract.** Classify each of the following nouns as concrete or abstract.

1. tradition
2. flower
3. courage
4. cafeteria
5. dancers
6. honor
7. security
8. lake
9. happiness
10. bench

**WRITING APPLICATION A:**
**Using Precise Nouns in Your Writing**

When you write, you should select each noun carefully so that it conveys the meaning or creates the picture you wish. Complete the following sentence with each of the nouns in parentheses, and notice how each noun helps to create a different picture.

> The ________ stood behind the tall oak tree. (house, cottage, bungalow, shack)

**Writing Assignment**

Write a narrative about an outing; for example, a picnic, a ski weekend, or your high-school football game. Make a point of using precise nouns; and when you revise your narrative, check to make sure that you have done so.

## THE PRONOUN

**18b. A *pronoun* is a word used in place of a noun or of more than one noun.**

EXAMPLE Jim delivered the winning speech. **He** had worked three days to prepare **it.** [The pronoun *he* takes the place of the noun *Jim.* The pronoun *it* takes the place of the noun *speech.*]

The word to which a pronoun refers (whose place it takes) is the *antecedent*[1] of the pronoun. In the preceding example, *Jim* is the antecedent of *he,* and *speech* is the antecedent of *it.*

> ☞ **NOTE** A pronoun may also take the place of another pronoun.

EXAMPLE **Several** of the students entered the essay contest. **They** typed their entries on standard-size paper. [The pronoun *they* takes the place of the pronoun *several.*]

There are several kinds of pronouns: *personal* (including the *possessive* and *reflexive* forms), *relative, interrogative, demonstrative,* and *indefinite.*

### *Personal Pronouns*

*Personal pronouns* are so called because they refer to first person (*I*), second person (*you*), and third person (*it, she, he*). (See pages 497–98.)

| | | | |
|---|---|---|---|
| I, me | he, him | it | they, them |
| you | she, her | we, us | |

### *Possessive Forms*

| | | | |
|---|---|---|---|
| my, mine | his | its | their, theirs |
| your, yours | her, hers | our, ours | |

Personal pronouns combined with *-self, -selves* may be used in two ways.

(1) They may be used *reflexively.*

EXAMPLE Jenny hurt **herself** on the car door.

(2) They may be used *intensively* for emphasis.

EXAMPLE Leonora **herself** gave the information to reporters.

### *Reflexive and Intensive Forms*

| | | | |
|---|---|---|---|
| myself | himself, herself | ourselves | themselves |
| yourself | itself | yourselves | |

[1] Not all pronouns have antecedents. For example, in the sentence "*Nobody* was in the room," the pronoun *nobody* does not stand for a specific noun. However, it is used "in place of" a noun in the sense that it is used in a sentence in the place where a noun would ordinarily occur, as in the sentence "A *person* was in the room."

### *Relative Pronouns*

*Relative pronouns* are used to introduce subordinate clauses (see pages 440–41).

who whom whose which that

EXAMPLES The house **that** you saw is a historical landmark.
The woman **whose** name is on the program is running for mayor.

### *Interrogative Pronouns*

*Interrogative pronouns* are used in questions.

who whom which what whose

EXAMPLES **What** is the answer to the puzzle?
**Whose** name was submitted?

### *Demonstrative Pronouns*

*Demonstrative pronouns* point out a particular person or thing. When they are used before nouns, they are considered adjectives (*these houses, that flag, those books*).

this these that those

EXAMPLES **This** is the best answer.
**Those** are the flowers I picked.

### *Commonly Used Indefinite Pronouns*

*Indefinite pronouns* refer generally, not specifically, to persons, places, or things.

| | | |
|---|---|---|
| all | everyone | none |
| another | everything | no one |
| any | few | one |
| anybody | many | several |
| anyone | more | some |
| both | most | somebody |
| each | much | someone |
| either | neither | such |
| everybody | nobody | |

EXAMPLES **Everything** was in disorder.
**Anybody** could have taken the camera.

**EXERCISE 2. Identifying Pronouns in Sentences.** Number your paper 1–5. After the proper number, write the pronoun or pronouns in the sentence in the order in which they appear.

1. Harry himself knew everyone who either had a ticket or could get one for him at a low price.
2. Nobody has bought more than one of the records on sale at the discount store.
3. Someone once said that humorists are people who laugh at one or more of the world's foibles.
4. Some of the most famous contemporary figures who engage in politics are women.
5. Nearly everybody is familiar with P.L. Travers' stories about Mary Poppins, an ever-popular character with young people.

**WRITING APPLICATION B:**
**Using Pronouns in Place of Nouns**

Using pronouns in your writing enables you to avoid repeating nouns. Notice in the following example how the writer has avoided repeating the proper noun *Itzhak Perlman.*

> Itzhak Perlman is a renowned violinist. **He** performed at Bob Carr Auditorium in Orlando, Florida, on February 4, 1985.

**Writing Assignment**

Write a summary about a current news event. Use pronouns, where appropriate, to avoid repeating nouns. When you revise your summary, check that you have used pronouns where necessary.

## THE ADJECTIVE

**18c. An *adjective* is a word used to modify a noun or a pronoun.**

*To modify* means "to describe or make more definite" the meaning of a word. Adjectives may modify nouns or pronouns in one of three different ways.

1. By telling *what kind:*

> **brown** shoes, **large** animals, **uncertain** plans

2. By pointing out *which one*:

   **those** bricks, **this** street

3. By telling *how many:*

   **ten** boxes, **several** stacks of books

Usually an adjective precedes the noun it modifies. Sometimes, for emphasis, a writer may place it after the noun.

EXAMPLE The deer, **wild** and **graceful,** ran through the forest.

A *predicate adjective* (see page 411) is separated from the word it modifies by a linking verb.

EXAMPLES Katie is **young.**

The beans were **delicious.**

Athens is **dry** in the summer.

Louie appeared **ill.**

## Articles

The most frequently used adjective are *a, an,* and *the*. These little words are usually called *articles.*

*A* and *an* are indefinite articles; they refer to one of a general group.

EXAMPLES **A** saleswoman knocked on the door.
George took **an** orange.
Martha read for **an** hour.

*A* is used before words beginning with a consonant sound; *an* is used before words beginning with a vowel sound. Notice in the third example above that *an* is used before a noun beginning with the consonant *h,* because the *h* in *hour* is not pronounced. *Hour* is pronounced as if it began with a vowel (like *our*). Remember that the *sound* of the noun, not the spelling, determines which indefinite article will be used.

*The* is a definite article. It indicates that the noun refers to someone or something in particular.

EXAMPLES **The** saleswoman knocked on the door.
George took **the** orange.
**The** hour had gone by quickly.
We searched everywhere for **the** keys.

## The Same Word as Adjective and as Pronoun

A word may be used as one part of speech in one context and as a different part of speech in another context. This is especially true of the following words, all of which may be used as either *pronouns* or *adjectives:*

| | | |
|---|---|---|
| all | more | that |
| another | most | these |
| any | much | this |
| both | neither | those |
| each | one | what |
| either | other | which |
| few | several | |
| many | some | |

ADJECTIVE **Which** museum did you visit? [*Which* modifies the noun *museum.*]
PRONOUN **Which** did you visit? [*Which* takes the place of the noun *museum.*]

ADJECTIVE Leslie Silko wrote **these** stories. [*These* modifies *stories.*]
PRONOUN Leslie Silko wrote **these.** [*These* takes the place of the noun *stories.*]

## Nouns Used as Adjectives

Sometimes nouns are used as adjectives.

| | |
|---|---|
| **stone** wall | **blood** bank |
| **hospital** room | **business** letter |

When you are identifying parts of speech in any of the exercises in this book and find a noun used as an adjective, call it an adjective.

**EXERCISE 3. Identifying Adjectives in Sentences.** Number your paper 1–10. Find the adjectives in each of the following sentences and write them in order after the proper number. In some sentences there may be only one adjective. For this exercise, do not include articles (*a, an,* and *the*).

1. John lives on this street.
2. You need four cups of flour for this recipe.
3. Your apartment, so spacious and sunny, is ideal for you.
4. Thomas is loyal to his friends.
5. Which bookstore did you go to today?
6. These books are by Mark Twain.
7. Neither film was enjoyable.

8. The local stores open at 9:00 A.M.
9. The book has a happy ending.
10. Tom bought a new tie for the dance.



**REVIEW EXERCISE A. Identifying Nouns, Pronouns and Adjectives.** List the italicized words in order in a column, numbering as in the example. After each word, tell whether it is a noun, a pronoun, or an adjective. If it is an adjective, write the word it modifies after it.

EXAMPLE 1. *Most* people do not realize the *tremendous* number of books the library has available for *them.*
1. *Most, adj., people*
*tremendous, adj., number*
*them, pron.*

1. Many *shop* owners decided to close *their* shops on Halloween night.
2. *What* are the *other* choices on the menu?
3. A *social* gathering is usually a *pleasant* occasion.
4. Most of Gerard Manley Hopkins' *poems* were first published twenty-nine years after *he* had died.
5. As people encounter different *ways* of life, *they* gradually alter their *speech* patterns.
6. Thanks to the development of *digital* recording, symphony *performances* can now be played back with even higher fidelity.
7. *Oboe* players carry *extra* reeds with *them* because of the *possibility* that a reed might split during a performance.
8. He had never bought *that* brand before.
9. *Most* of the players felt nervous and excited about the *athletic* contests.
10. *They* were penalized *fifteen* yards for holding.

## THE VERB

**18d. A *verb* is a word that expresses action or otherwise helps to make a statement.**

Some verbs make a statement by expressing action. The action may be physical, as in *push, crush, throw,* and *send,* or mental, as in *remember* and *believe.*

GRAMMAR

## Action Verbs

Action verbs may or may not take an object. An object is a noun or pronoun that completes the action by telling who or what is affected by the action. Action verbs that take objects are called *transitive* verbs. The verbs in the following examples are transitive.

EXAMPLES The student **wrote** two reports. [*Reports* is the object of *wrote.*]
Emily **understood** the complex problem. [*Problem* is the object of *understood.*]
Everyone in the school **cheered** the football team. [*Team* is the object of *cheered.*]

*Intransitive verbs* can express action without an object.

EXAMPLES Jane **stood.**
The accountant **resigned.**
The child **screamed.**

Although some action verbs are transitive only (*avoid*) and some intransitive only (*fall*), most action verbs can be either.

EXAMPLES We **ate** our lunch quickly.
We **ate** quickly.
The woman **sawed** the boards skillfully.
The woman **sawed** skillfully.

## Linking Verbs

Some intransitive verbs that do not express action are called *linking verbs.* They connect, or link, to the subject a noun, pronoun, or adjective that identifies or describes it. The word that is linked to the subject is called the *subject complement.*

EXAMPLES Patience **is** the best remedy for every trouble. [*Remedy* is the *subject complement* that refers to the subject *patience.*]
He **remained** the leader. [*Leader* refers to *he.*]
The apple **looked** delicious. [*Delicious* refers to *apple.*]

The subject complement may identify the subject, as in the first two examples, or describe it, as in the third.

Linking verbs are sometimes called state-of-being verbs because they help describe the condition or state of being of a person or thing. The most common linking verb is the verb *be:*[1] *am, is, are, was, were, be, being, been,* and all verb phrases ending in *be, being,* or *been;* for example, *have been, could have been, can be, should be,* etc. Other common linking verbs are listed here.

| | | |
|---|---|---|
| appear | look | sound |
| become | remain | stay |
| feel | seem | taste |
| grow | smell | |

EXAMPLES Rebecca **is** the president of the council.
Edmonia Lewis **became** a highly respected sculptor in America.
The building **looked** drab in the winter.

In these sentences the verb does not express action; it acts as a link between the subject and the words following the verb.

Some verbs may be used either as action verbs or as linking verbs.

ACTION We **tasted** the soup.
LINKING The soup **tasted** spicy.

ACTION The explorers **felt** rain on their faces.
LINKING She **felt** good about her presentation.

In general, a verb is a linking verb if you can substitute *is* or *was* for it. For instance, in the sentence *The milk tasted sour,* you can substitute *was* for *tasted:* The milk **was** sour. You cannot make the substitution, however, in a sentence with an action verb.

EXAMPLE Martha first **tasted** snails in a French restaurant.

## The Helping Verb and the Verb Phrase

A *verb phrase* is a verb of more than one word. It is made up of a main verb and one or more *helping verbs.* Helping verbs are so called because they help the main verb express action or make a statement. The helping verbs in the following verb phrases[2] are printed in boldfaced type:

| | |
|---|---|
| **has** spoken | **may have** known |
| **could be** arriving | **should have been** announced |

[1] The verb *be,* and some other linking verbs, can also be followed by certain adverbs of place: He was *there.* She stayed *home.* In these instances the verbs are not linking verbs.

[2] A word ending in *-ing* may be used as part of a verb phrase or as an adjective: The spectators *were encouraging* the athletes with screams and shouts. [*Encouraging* is part of a verb phrase.] The news was *encouraging.* [*Encouraging* is an adjective modifying *news.*]

GRAMMAR

*Common Helping Verbs*

| | | |
|---|---|---|
| do | has | can (may) have |
| did | had | could (would, should) be |
| does | can | could (would, should) have |
| am | may | will (shall) have been |
| are | will (shall) be | might have |
| is | will (shall) have | might have been |
| was | has (had) been | must have |
| were | can (may) be | must have been |
| have | | |

The parts of a verb phrase may be separated from one another by other words; that is, the helping verb may frequently be separated from the main verb.

EXAMPLES **Should** we **leave** immediately?
He **had** never **heard** of the famous explorer.
She **might** not **have heard** the story.

**EXERCISE 4. Identifying Verbs; Classifying Verbs as Transitive, Intransitive, or Linking.** List in order the verbs and verb phrases in the following sentences, placing before each the number of the sentence in which it appears. After each verb, tell whether it is a *transitive (v.t.)* or an *intransitive (v.i.)* verb. If intransitive, tell whether it is a *linking verb (l.v.)*. Be sure to list all parts of a verb phrase.

1. Over the centuries, English has borrowed many words from other languages.
2. Because a newly borrowed word sounds unfamiliar, people sometimes do not hear it correctly.
3. They will pronounce the word and will spell it as if it had come from other, more familiar English words.
4. The wrong spelling hides the true origin of the word and gives the false impression that its source is contemporary English.
5. The word *woodchuck,* for example, might have come from two English words, *wood* and *chuck.*
6. Actually, *woodchuck* came from the Cree *otchek.*
7. Another word of Algonquian origin is the word *musquash.*
8. When English-speaking settlers adopted the word, it became *muskrat.*

9. In a similar way the Dutch word for cabbage salad, *koolsla,* became the English word *coleslaw,* and the French word for a kind of cart, *cariole,* is now the English word *carryall.*
10. Linguists usually call this kind of word history "folk etymology."

**WRITING APPLICATION C:**
**Using Precise Verbs in Your Writing**

Sometimes the verbs you select for your writing do not express your ideas precisely. By brainstorming or using a thesaurus or dictionary, you can find the verb that expresses the meaning or creates the picture you wish. Notice the difference in meaning between the two verbs in the following pair of sentences.

EXAMPLE The rider *rode* across the plain.
The rider *galloped* across the plain.

**Writing Assignment**

Write a paragraph narrating a lively sports event. Select your verbs carefully to convey the meanings you wish to express. When you revise your paragraph, check for precise verbs.

## THE ADVERB

**18e. An *adverb* is a word used to modify a verb, an adjective, or another adverb.**

The adverb is most commonly used as the modifier of a verb. It may tell *how, when, where,* or *to what extent* (*how often* or *how much*) the action of the verb is done.

EXAMPLES Marian Anderson sang **magnificently.** [*Magnificently* tells *how* Marian Anderson sang.]
Marian Anderson sang **earlier.** [*Earlier* tells *when* Marian Anderson sang.]
Marian Anderson sang **there.** [*There* tells *where* Marian Anderson sang.]
Marian Anderson sang **frequently.** [*Frequently* tells *how often* Marian Anderson sang.]

An adverb may modify an adjective.

EXAMPLE The players are **exceptionally** competent. [*Exceptionally* modifies the adjective *competent,* telling *how* competent the players are.]

An adverb may modify another adverb.

EXAMPLE Tim ran **very** rapidly. [*Very* modifies the adverb *rapidly,* telling *to what extent* Tim ran rapidly or *how* rapidly he ran.]

Adverbs like *really, truly, actually, indeed,* etc., which are used primarily for emphasis, should be classified as adverbs of extent.

EXAMPLES She had **truly** tried her best. [*Truly* emphasizes the extent to which she had tried.]
It was **indeed** fortunate that we arrived in time. [*Indeed* emphasizes the extent to which our arrival was fortunate.]

## Nouns Used as Adverbs

Some nouns may be used adverbially.

They were happy to come **home.**
The teacher reviewed what had been covered **yesterday.**

In identifying parts of speech, label nouns used in this way as adverbs.

> NOTE *Not* is classified as an adverb; it tells *to what extent.*

**EXERCISE 5. Identifying Adverbs and the Words They Modify.** List the adverbs in the following sentences in order, placing before each the number of the sentence in which it appears. After each *adverb,* write the word or words it modifies, and be prepared to state whether the adverb tells *how, when, where,* or *to what extent.*

1. Her calm, friendly manner always inspired confidence.
2. I understand now what he was saying.
3. The index lists all the book's topics alphabetically.
4. The guests have already left.
5. They thought that the decorations would be too expensive.
6. The pupils in the first row noisily moved their desks.
7. He feared he had accidentally dropped his notes somewhere.

8. The messenger felt rather uncertain about the quickest route.
9. "Are you quite sure this is the person?" the detective asked.
10. The teacher told the students, "Take your essays home for revision and hand them to me tomorrow."



**REVIEW EXERCISE B. Identifying the Parts of Speech of Words.** On a piece of paper, list in a column the italicized words in the following sentences, placing before each word the number of the sentence in which it appears. After each word, tell what part of speech it is; after each adjective or adverb, tell what word or words it modifies.

1. He *recognized everybody* who had contributed *time* or money.
2. Jesse Owens *won* four gold medals in the 1936 *Olympics.*
3. In *ancient* Rome the new year began on March 1, and September *was* the *seventh* month of the year.
4. In 6000 B.C. the *usual* transportation for long distance was the *camel* caravan, *which* averaged *eight* miles per hour.
5. The *play* received *generally* excellent reviews, but *several* critics were disappointed with the *rather dull* costumes.
6. When *we* approached Santorini, I saw sparkling *white* houses along the *steep* hillsides.
7. The teacher *posted* a list of students *who* would give *reports* about Sacajawea.
8. *Many* readers complained *angrily* about the editorial *that* appeared in yesterday's newspaper, but *others* found *it* amusing.
9. *Silently,* the drifting *snow blanketed* the *narrow* road.
10. *I* recall *vividly* that small town in the *southern part* of Texas.

## THE PREPOSITION

**18f. A *preposition* is a word used to show the relationship of a noun or pronoun to some other word in the sentence.**

In the following sentences, the prepositions are shown in boldfaced type. The words related by the preposition are in italics. Note that the sentences are alike in wording except for the prepositions *across, inside,* and *around.* The change in relationship between *ran* and *yard* is due to the change of preposition.

EXAMPLES The dog *ran* **across** the *yard*.
The dog *ran* **inside** the *yard*.
The dog *ran* **around** the *yard*.

A preposition always introduces a phrase (see page 418). The noun or pronoun that ends a prepositional phrase is the *object* of the preposition.

***Commonly Used Prepositions***

| | | | |
|---|---|---|---|
| about | below | for | throughout |
| above | beneath | from | to |
| across | beside | in | toward |
| after | besides | into | under |
| against | between | like | underneath |
| along | beyond | of | until |
| amid | but (meaning "except") | off | unto |
| among | by | on | up |
| around | concerning | over | upon |
| at | down | past | with |
| before | during | since | within |
| behind | except | through | without |

Sometimes a group of words may act as a preposition: *on account of, in spite of, along with, together with.*

## THE CONJUNCTION

**18g. A *conjunction* is a word that joins words or groups of words.**

In the following sentences, the conjunctions are printed in boldfaced type; the words or groups of words that the conjunctions join are italicized.

*Cinderella left the ball* **when** *the clock struck midnight.*
*Pearl Buck* **and** *Selma Lagerlöf* won the Nobel Prize.
*The crowd cheered* **because** *our team had won.*
She **neither** *moved* **nor** *spoke.*

There are three kinds of conjunctions: *coordinating, correlative,* and *subordinating.*

***Coordinating Conjunctions***

and    but    or    not    for    yet    so

### *Correlative Conjunctions*

| | | |
|---|---|---|
| either . . . or | both . . . and | whether . . . or |
| neither . . . nor | not only . . . but (also) | |

Correlative conjunctions are always used in pairs.

**Both** athletes **and** singers must train for long hours.
**Either** your fuel line is clogged **or** your carburetor needs adjusting.

### *Commonly Used Subordinating Conjunctions*[1]

| | | | | |
|---|---|---|---|---|
| after | before | provided | though | whenever |
| although | how | since | till | where |
| as | if | so that | unless | wherever |
| as much as | inasmuch as | than | until | while |
| because | in order that | that | when | |

Subordinating conjunctions are used to begin subordinate clauses (see pages 445–46), usually adverb clauses.

In the following sentences, the subordinating conjunctions are printed in boldfaced type, and the subordinate clauses that the conjunctions begin are italicized.

She didn't know the real reason **until** *she left the valley.*
We arrived late **because** *our train was delayed.*

A subordinating conjunction need not come between the sentence parts it joins. It may come at the beginning of a sentence.

**While** *Dr. Watson explained his theory,* Sherlock listened quietly.

**EXERCISE 6. Identifying Prepositions and Conjunctions; Classifying Conjunctions.** Number your paper 1–5. For each of the following sentences, write the word or words that are the part of speech indicated in parentheses. Next to each conjunction, write whether it is a coordinating (*coord.*), correlative (*correl.*), or subordinating (*subord.*) conjunction.

EXAMPLE 1. Since Sue excels in mathematics, she will enjoy calculus. (*conjunction*)
1. *Since, subord.*

[1] Some of these words may also be used as prepositions: *after, before, since, until;* others may also be used as adverbs: *how, when, where. That* is often used as a pronoun or an adjective.

1. Eli Whitney invented not only the cotton gin but also the interchangeable part. (*conjunction*)
2. Nowadays we take the idea of interchangeable parts for granted, but it was a revolutionary concept at that time. (*conjunction*)
3. For example, when a rifle is constructed with interchangeable parts, a defective part can be replaced quickly and easily with another identically made piece. (*preposition*)
4. Before Eli Whitney introduced the idea of interchangeable parts, manufacturers had to employ many skilled workers. (*preposition*)
5. Although this was good for the manufacturers, it put many workers out of work, and this has been the case with most technological advances. (*conjunction*)

**WRITING APPLICATION D:**
**Using Subordinating Conjunctions to Indicate Levels of Importance**

In the following sentence by N. Scott Momaday, the subordinating conjunction comes at the beginning of the sentence because the more important thought is at the end.

> Although my grandmother lived out her long life in the shadow of Rainy Mountain, the immense landscape of the continental interior lay like memory in her blood.

**Writing Assignment**

Think back to a time when you revisited a relative, an old friend, or a place that meant something special to you. Describe the person or place visited; emphasize your reactions to the visit. Use at least four subordinating conjunctions. Underline those conjunctions.

## THE INTERJECTION

**18h. An *interjection* is a word that expresses emotion and has no grammatical relation to other words in the sentence.**

EXAMPLES Oh! Alas! Ha! Behold!

## THE SAME WORD AS DIFFERENT PARTS OF SPEECH

You have already learned that a word may be used as more than one part of speech. For instance, you learned in your study of pronouns and adjectives that a word like *those* may be an adjective (*those* books) or a pronoun (She asked for *those*); *home* may be a noun (Our *home* is comfortable) or an adverb (We decided to stay *home*); *green* may be a noun (*Green* is my favorite color) or an adjective (a *green* umbrella). Many words cannot be classified by part of speech until you see them in a sentence.

EXAMPLES The coach decided that they needed more **practice.** [*Practice* is the name of something; it is a noun.]
The women **practice** on Saturday afternoon. [*Practice* expresses action; it is a verb.]
She had a **practice** session after school on Wednesday. [*Practice* modifies the noun *session;* it is an adjective.]

A **well** person needs no medicine. [*Well* is an adjective.]
He pitches **well.** [*Well* is an adverb.]
They dug a **well.** [*Well* is a noun.]
**Well**, I'm going to go see a movie. [*Well* is an interjection.]

**REVIEW EXERCISE C. Identifying the Parts of Speech of Words.** Number your paper 1–25. After the proper number, write the italicized words in the following passage. Consider carefully the way each word or phrase is used in its sentence; then write after each word what part of speech it is.

The radio announcer broke in on the (1) *musical* selection. "A (2) *funnel* cloud (3) *has been sighted.* (4) *All* people should take immediate (5) *precautions!*" (6) *Those* were the (7) *last* words Denise Moore heard (8) *before* the electricity went off and the (9) *terrible* roar came closer. (10) *She* and her two children (11) *ran* to the basement (12) *quickly.*

When they (13) *emerged* forty-five minutes later, (14) *they* weren't sure what they might see. (15) *Oh,* the terrible wind had (16) *truly* performed freakish tricks! It had driven a fork (17) *into* a brick up to the handle. It had sucked the (18) *wallpaper* from a living room (19) *but* had left the picture hanging (20) *there* intact. It (21) *had driven* a blade of grass into the (22) *back* of Denise Moore's neighbor. But the citizens of the (23) *town* considered (24) *themselves* lucky because (25) *no one* had been killed.



## CHAPTER 18 REVIEW: POSTTEST 1

**Identifying the Parts of Speech of Words.** Each of the following items contains at least one example of the part of speech specified for that sentence. Find these words, and write them on your paper. Base your answers on the way each word is used in the sentence.

EXAMPLE 1. The Declaration of Independence is not only a list of grievances but also a statement of values. (*conjunction*)
1. *not only, but also*

1. What do you buy as a birthday present for someone who has everything? (*pronoun*)
2. Because they lacked pleasant speaking voices, many of the silent screen stars could not adapt to the "talkies." (*preposition*)
3. In ancient mythology the sirens were beautiful sea-maidens who enticed sailors to the shores of islands and to their deaths. (*adjective*)
4. We practiced and practiced until we had every line and gesture in the play down perfectly. (*conjunction*)
5. When Diana gets one of her "absolutely brilliant ideas," she speaks rapidly and almost breathlessly. (*adverb*)
6. If you are a science fiction enthusiast, you should read *The Other Side of the Sky* or *Tales of Ten Worlds* by Arthur C. Clarke. (*verb*)
7. "Did you know that Mary Lou Retton was the first American woman to win a gold medal in Olympic gymnastic competition? Wow!" (*interjection*)
8. If you want to improve your ability to think clearly and logically, join the Debating Club. (*noun*)
9. Elizabeth Cady Stanton, an avowed feminist, stated that "all men *and women* are created equal." (*verb*)
10. *Blind Ambition* by John Dean, counsel to President Richard M. Nixon, presents the Watergate scandal that ultimately led to the President's resignation. (*adverb*)

## CHAPTER 18 REVIEW: POSTTEST 2

**Writing Sentences with Words Used as Specific Parts of Speech.** Write twenty sentences according to the following guidelines. Use the dictionary for help.

1. Use *ride* as a verb.
2. Use *hammer* as a noun.
3. Use *sink* as a verb.
4. Use *whose* as an adjective.
5. Use *some* as a pronoun.
6. Use *fast* as an adverb.
7. Use *paper* as an adjective.
8. Use *inside* as a preposition.
9. Use *well* as an interjection.
10. Use *but* as a conjunction.
11. Use *country* as an adjective.
12. Use *power* as a verb.
13. Use *which* as a pronoun.
14. Use *play* as a noun.
15. Use *smell* as a noun.
16. Use *have* as a helping verb.
17. Use *tomorrow* as a noun.
18. Use *down* as an adverb.
19. Use *before* as a subordinating conjunction.
20. Use *as* as a subordinating conjunction.

GRAMMAR

## SUMMARY OF PARTS OF SPEECH

| *Rule* | *Part of Speech* | *Use* | *Examples* |
|---|---|---|---|
| 18a | noun | names | child, Matthew, humanity |
| 18b | pronoun | takes the place of a noun | I, her, theirs, who, it |
| 18c | adjective | modifies a noun or pronoun | popular, lovely, significant |

GRAMMAR

| *Rule* | *Part of Speech* | *Use* | *Examples* |
|---|---|---|---|
| 18d | verb | shows action or otherwise helps to make a statement | write, might, see, is |
| 18e | adverb | modifies a verb, an adjective, or another adverb | frantically, easily, rather, often |
| 18f | preposition | relates a noun or a pronoun to another word | at, near, with |
| 18g | conjunction | joins words or groups of words | and, either . . . or, because |
| 18h | interjection | shows emotion | Ah! |

# CHAPTER 19



# The Parts of a Sentence

## SUBJECTS, PREDICATES, COMPLEMENTS

Much of Winston Churchill's success in leading England during World War II was due to the impact his speeches had on the minds and hearts of his compatriots. In his school days, Churchill says, he was considered a dull pupil, unable to cope with the complexities of Latin. He was made to repeat his English courses instead. He described the effect of this in his own words:

> I gained an immense advantage over the cleverer boys . . . I got into my bones the essential structure of the ordinary British sentence—which is a noble thing.

Since your elementary-school days you too have been "getting into your bones" the structure of the ordinary sentence. You began by dividing the sentence into two parts, *subject* and *predicate*. Later you learned the terms *object, predicate nominative,* and *predicate adjective* to fill out the description of the predicate. These elements form the essential structure of all the English sentences you will ever speak, read, or hear, no matter how varied or complex they may be.

## DIAGNOSTIC TEST

**A. Identifying Subjects, Verbs, and Complements.** Number your paper 1–10. After the proper number, identify the italicized word or words, using these abbreviations: *s.* (subject), *v.* (verb), *d.o.* (direct object), *i.o.* (indirect object), *p.n.* (predicate nominative), or *p.a.* (predicate adjective).

EXAMPLE 1. Computers *have provided* work and play in today's world.
1. *v.*, *decl.*

1. Frances Perkins, the first woman in the history of the United States to hold a Cabinet post, was *Secretary of Labor* during Franklin Roosevelt's administration.
2. Thanks to my "green thumb," these squash *plants* are spreading vines and fruits all over the garden!
3. Did Kimi write *you* a letter about her trip to Norway?
4. Since the ballots have not yet been counted, the names of next year's class representatives are not *available* at this time.
5. After World War I, the United States signed separate peace *treaties* with Germany, Austria, and Hungary.
6. Bring *me* the hacksaw and two pipe wrenches from the garage.
7. If I never again have to repair a kitchen sink or solve any other plumbing problem, it *will be* too soon!
8. Martin Luther King, Jr., a nonviolent activist and civil rights leader, was a *recipient* of the Nobel Peace Prize.
9. Do *you* know that the difference between wasps and bees is that wasps have long, narrow bodies and slim waists?
10. How beautifully *Beverly Sills* sings!

**B. Classifying Sentences.** Classify each sentence in part A according to purpose, using these abbreviations: *decl.* (declarative), *int.* (interrogative), *imp.* (imperative), and *excl.* (exclamatory).

---

## THE SENTENCE

**19a. A *sentence* is a group of words that expresses a complete thought.**

Consider the following group of words:

The weary travelers

A sentence must always express a *complete* thought. The words *The weary travelers* create a mental image, but in terms of communicating a thought to the reader, something is lacking. To complete the thought, you must tell what the travelers *did,* or what *happened to* the travelers, or who or what the travelers *are.*

| INCOMPLETE THOUGHT | COMPLETE THOUGHT |
|---|---|
| The weary travelers | found rooms. |
| | were greeted warmly. |
| | are from another city. |
| | left their bags on the train. |
| | became very frightened. |
| | crossed the last mountain range. |

NOT A SENTENCE Many athletes entering the Olympics . . . [thought not complete]

SENTENCE Many athletes were entering the Olympics. [complete thought]

NOT A SENTENCE The offices designed for high efficiency . . . [not a complete thought]

SENTENCE The offices have been designed for high efficiency. [complete thought]

NOT A SENTENCE Plans every month for future growth . . . [thought not complete]

SENTENCE The board of directors plans every month for future growth. [complete thought]

## SUBJECT AND PREDICATE

**19b. A sentence consists of two parts, the *subject* and the *predicate*. The subject is the part about which something is being said. The predicate is the part that says something about the subject.**

| *Subject* | *Predicate* |
|---|---|
| Lightning | strikes. |
| *Predicate* | *Subject* |
| Into the silent sea sailed | the ancient mariner. |

### The Simple Predicate, or Verb

**19c. The principal word or group of words in the predicate is called the *simple predicate,* or the *verb*.**

EXAMPLES Ana **ran** swiftly and gracefully. [The complete predicate is *ran swiftly and gracefully*. The simple predicate, or verb, is *ran*.]

The dog **chased** its tail frantically. [The complete predicate is *chased its tail frantically*. The verb is *chased*.]



## The Simple Subject

**19d. The *simple subject* is the main word or combination of words that names the person, place, thing, or idea about which something is being said.**

EXAMPLES The **scenes** in these tapestries show the beauty of Pennsylvania in the late 1700's. [The complete subject is *The scenes in these tapestries*. The simple subject is *scenes*.]

**Athletes** on various teams received awards. [The complete subject is *Athletes on various teams*. The simple subject is *Athletes*.]

> ☞ NOTE Throughout the rest of this book, the term *subject,* when used in connection with the sentence, refers to the simple subject; the term *verb* refers to the simple predicate.

## Compound Subjects and Compound Verbs

**19e. A *compound subject* consists of two or more subjects that are joined by a conjunction and have the same verb. The usual connecting words are *and* and *or*.**

EXAMPLES The **ship** and all the **cargo** had been lost. [compound subject: *ship* and *cargo*]

**Athens, Delphi,** and **Nauplia** are on the mainland of Greece. [compound subject: *Athens, Delphi,* and *Nauplia.*]

**19f. A *compound verb* consists of two or more verbs that are joined by a conjunction and have the same subject.**

EXAMPLES The small man **chose** a seat near the door and carefully **sat** down. [compound verb: *chose* and *sat*]

Truth **enlightens** the mind, **frees** the spirit, and **strengthens** the soul. [compound verb: *enlightens, frees,* and *strengthens*]

### How to Find the Subject of a Sentence

Most often we expect to find the subject at the beginning of the sentence and the verb following the subject. But this word order is not always maintained. For example, in the sentence *Out of the stillness came the sound of laughter,* the verb precedes the subject. A simple way to identify the subject is as follows:

1. First find the verb (the simple predicate).
2. Then ask yourself the question, "Who or what . . . ?

EXAMPLE Supported by grants, scientists constantly search for a cure for cancer. [The verb is *search.* Who or what searches? The answer is *scientists,* the subject.]

This procedure will aid you in selecting the subject from the most complicated and involved sentences. There are several additional ways to help you locate the subject in certain special cases.

1. In sentences expressing a command or request, the subject is always understood to be *you,* even though the word *you* may not appear in the sentence.

EXAMPLES You tell me the story now. [*You* is expressed.]
Go two blocks farther. [*You* is understood.]

2. The subject of a sentence is never in a prepositional phrase.

EXAMPLES A group of students gathered near the library. [Verb: *gathered.* Who gathered? *A group. Group* is the subject. *Students* cannot be the subject because it is the object of the preposition *of.*]

Either of the books will provide that information. [Verb: *will provide.* What will provide? *Either. Either* is the subject. *Books* is the object of the preposition *of.*]

3. To find the subject in a question, turn the question into statement form.

QUESTION Have you read Shakespeare's early plays?
STATEMENT You have read Shakespeare's early plays. [Verb: *have read;* subject: *you*]

4. The word *there* (or *here*) is never the subject of a sentence.

EXAMPLES **There** is the famous *Mona Lisa.* [Verb: *is;* subject: *Mona Lisa.* In this sentence the word *There* is an adverb indicating location.]

**There** is a game after school every Friday. [Verb: *is;* subject: *game. There* in this sentence is called an *expletive.* It indicates that a subject will follow the verb. Sometimes the word *it* may be used as an expletive: *It is profitable to budget one's time.*]

**EXERCISE 1. Identifying Subjects and Verbs.** Number your paper 1–10. After the proper number, write the simple subject and verb of each sentence. Be certain to include all parts of compound forms and all words in a verb phrase.

1. There are many unverified legends and conjectures about the life of William Shakespeare.
2. Actual facts concerning his life remain few.
3. He was born in 1564 in Stratford-on-Avon, a market town about eighty miles from London.
4. Records establish the dates of the baptisms of his children as 1583 for Susanna and 1585 for the twins, Hamnet and Judith.
5. Another known fact is the date of his death, April 23, 1616.
6. None of Shakespeare's contemporaries set down a record of the playwright's life.
7. The life and works of a mere dramatist were not thought important enough to merit a biography.
8. In the eighteenth century James Boswell wrote *The Life of Samuel Johnson,* an entertaining account of the life and times of the great English writer and wit.
9. This classic has been read with enjoyment for nearly two hundred years.
10. Boswell's book, unlike many of the full-length biographies of the next century, was an accurate and faithful record.

## COMPLEMENTS

By definition a sentence expresses a complete thought. Some sentences express a complete thought by means of a subject and verb only. *(We won!* or *He graduated.)* Sometimes even briefer sentences are possible (such as *Stop!* or *Run!*) in which the subject *you* is understood. Most sentences, however, have one or more words in the predicate that complete the meaning of the subject and verb. These completing words are called *complements.*

EXAMPLES The author wrote a **book.**
The publisher sent **him** a **check.**
Sidney Poitier is a black **actor.**
The air seemed **heavy** with moisture.
The judges named **Consuelo** the **winner.**

## Direct and Indirect Objects

Transitive verbs require a direct object to complete their meaning. They may also be followed by an indirect object.

**19g. The *direct object* of the verb receives the action of the verb or shows the result of the action. It answers the question *What?* or *Whom?* after an action verb.**

Except when it ends in *-self* (*myself, himself*), the object of a verb never refers to the same person or thing as the subject.

EXAMPLES Drought destroyed the **crops.** [Drought destroyed *what?*]

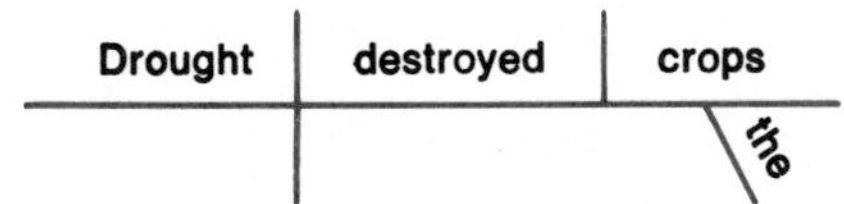


> ☞ NOTE The diagrams are given to help students who have already studied diagraming. For review purposes, the following principles should be remembered. On the main horizontal line the subject is followed by a vertical line that crosses the main line and separates the subject from the verb. Another vertical line, which does not cross the main line, follows the verb and separates it from the direct object. A single-word modifier slants downward from the word it modifies. An indirect object (page 408) is represented on a horizontal line attached to the verb by a slanting line.

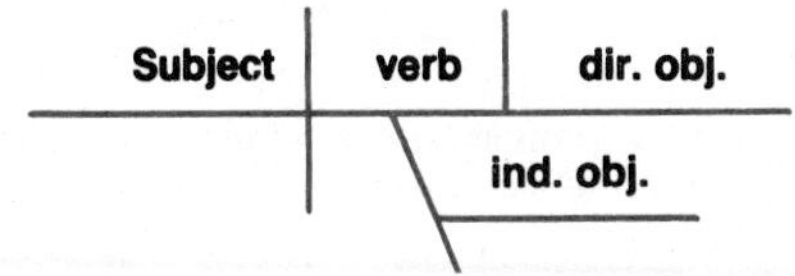

GRAMMAR

A predicate nominative or predicate adjective (pages 410–12) is separated from the verb by a slanting line.

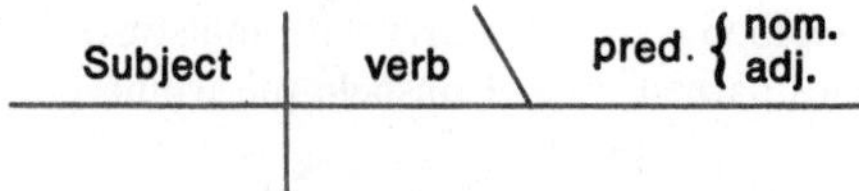


Sometimes there may be a compound direct object.

Beethoven composed sonatas and symphonies.

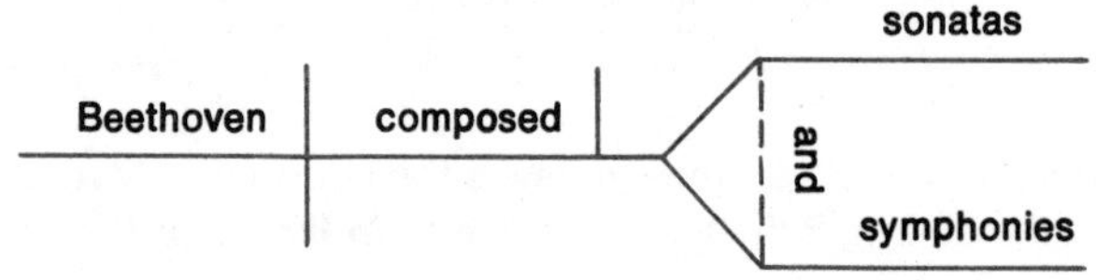


**19h. The *indirect object* of the verb precedes the direct object and usually tells to whom or for whom the action of the verb is done.**[1]

The principal gave **her** the award. [*Her* is the indirect object.]
The principal gave the award **to her.** [*Her* is part of a prepositional phrase.]

The indirect objects in these sentences are in boldfaced type.

EXAMPLES His artistic skill won **him** many honors.

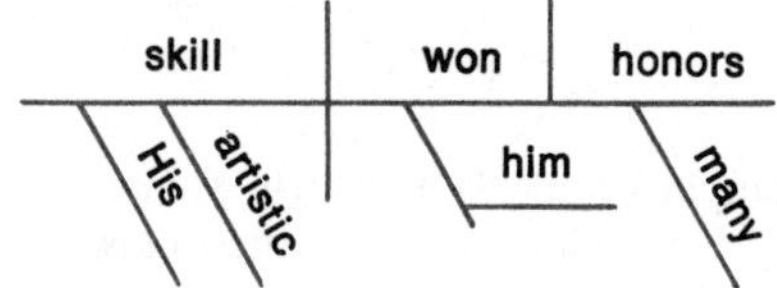


The senator gave **Jaime** and **me** a copy of her speech.

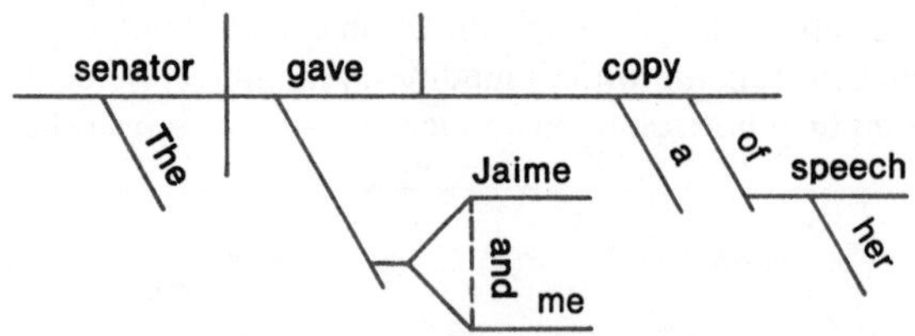


[1] If the word *to* or *for* is used, the pronoun or noun following it is part of a prepositional phrase and is thus not an indirect object. Like subjects, objects of verbs are never part of a prepositional phrase.

### The Objective Complement

To complete their meaning, some action verbs require an additional complement following their objects. This additional complement is called an *objective complement* because it refers to the object; it may be a noun or an adjective.

> They named Mary **secretary.** [The noun *secretary* refers to the direct object *Mary* and helps to complete the meaning of the verb *named.* It is an objective complement.]

They | named | Mary \ secretary

> Everyone considered him **foolish.** [The adjective *foolish* modifies the direct object *him* and helps to complete the meaning of the verb *considered.* It is an objective complement.]

Everyone | considered | him \ foolish

Only a few verbs take an objective complement. They usually mean "make" or "consider": *make, consider, elect, appoint, name, choose, render,* etc.

> The flood had swept the valley **clean.** [*made* the valley clean]
> They deemed Jim the **star** of the show. [*considered* Jim the star]

**EXERCISE 2. Identifying Direct Objects and Indirect Objects.** Number your paper 1–10. After the proper number, write the object of the verb in each sentence (do not include modifiers). After each object, write *d.o.* for a direct object or *i.o.* for an indirect object. Some sentences contain more than one object.

1. Candles have tremendous appeal as decorative, religious, and utilitarian objects.
2. The United States has been consuming annually many tons of paraffin for candle making.
3. Tutankhamen's tomb contained a candleholder.
4. Ancient customs gave candles emphasis in funeral rituals.
5. Early people paid the church a tithe of beeswax.
6. A true candle must contain a wick of some material.

7. Candle making offers the interested person a relaxing hobby.
8. With practice you can make friends and relatives various sizes of tapers from bayberries.
9. The color of a candle can give an occasion a special mood.
10. Learn this wonderful pastime!



**WRITING APPLICATION**
**Writing Periodic Sentences**

In plays, the action is supposed to build up to a climax. This creates suspense, which is usually exciting for an audience. Sometimes it is similarly exciting to use an occasional "periodic sentence" in writing—one which changes the usual word order to place the main idea or climax last.

EXAMPLE "In all my life—though surrounded by many people—I had not had a single satisfying, sustained relationship with another human being and, not having had any, I did not miss it."
RICHARD WRIGHT

**Writing Assignment**

Write four periodic sentences, placing the main idea or climax near the end of each sentence. Use the following sentence beginnings, or create your own.

1. Sitting alone in the corner of the school gym . . .
2. Although my friends mean well . . .
3. Creeping down the stairs . . .
4. As long as my parents . . .

## Subject Complements

A complement that follows a linking verb (see pages 388–89) is either a *predicate nominative* or a *predicate adjective.* These complements refer to (describe or explain) the subject.

**19i. A *predicate nominative* is a noun or pronoun complement that refers to the same person or thing as the subject of the verb. It follows a linking verb.**

EXAMPLES Adela Rogers St. Johns was a famous **journalist.** [*Journalist* refers to the subject *Adela Rogers St. Johns.*]

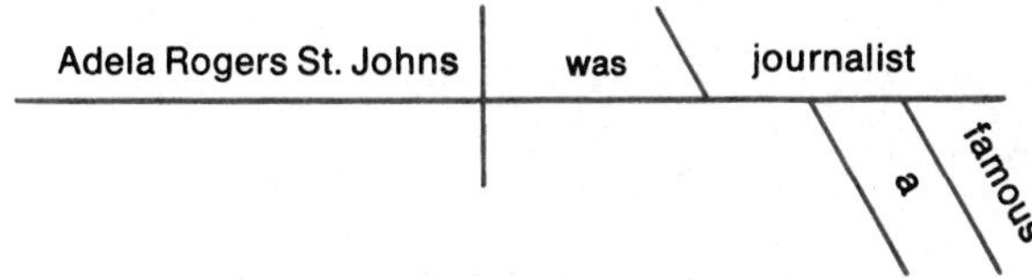


The Twin Cities are **St. Paul** and **Minneapolis.** [compound predicate nominative]

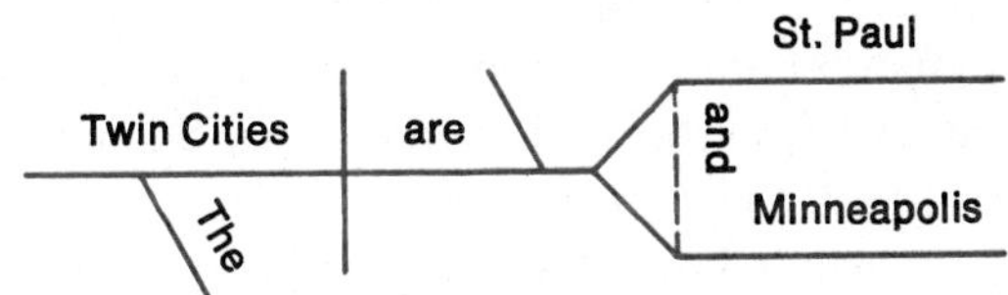


**19j. A *predicate adjective* is an adjective complement that modifies the subject of the verb. It follows a linking verb.**

EXAMPLES The sea is **calm.** [The predicate adjective *calm* modifies the subject *sea.*]

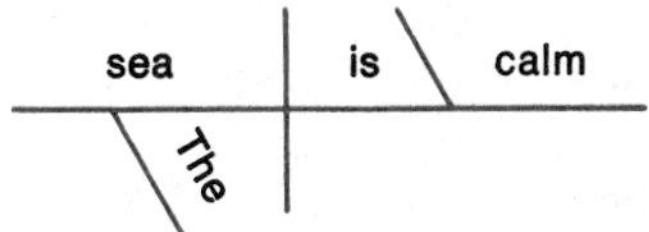


Illuminated manuscripts are **rare** and **valuable.** [compound predicate adjective]

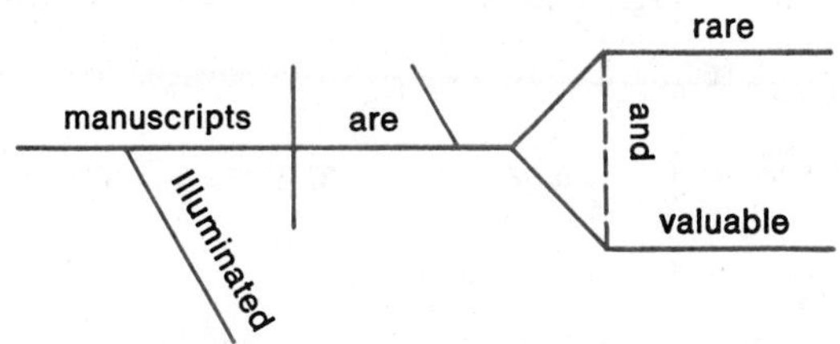


Normally, complements follow the verb; but occasionally, they may precede the verb for the purpose of emphasis.

**Deep** is the well of the past. [*Deep* is a predicate adjective modifying the noun *well.* Normal order: The well of the past is deep.]

**EXERCISE 3. Identifying Predicate Nominatives and Predicate Adjectives.** Number your paper 1–10. After the proper number, write the predicate nominatives or predicate adjectives in the sentence; identify each answer with the abbreviation *p.n.* or *p.a.*



1. The most common deer in India is a species of axis deer.
2. Icy is the stare of the glacier.
3. Was Jane Austen the author of *Pride and Prejudice*?
4. Wilhelm Roentgen was the discoverer of the X-ray.
5. The violin solo sounded mournful but beautiful.
6. The animals grew restless at the sound of the crackling flames.
7. Harriet Tubman became active in the Underground Railroad.
8. A massive work of carved stone is the Great Sphinx.
9. Does the spaghetti sauce taste spicy?
10. He felt increasingly unhappy with the actions of his friends.

## CLASSIFICATION OF SENTENCES

**19k. Sentences may be classified according to their purpose.**

Sentences may have four purposes: (1) to make a statement, (2) to ask a question, (3) to command or request, or (4) to exclaim.

**(1) A *declarative sentence* is a sentence that makes a statement.**

EXAMPLE Geriatrics deals with the diseases of old age.

**(2) An *interrogative sentence* is a sentence that asks a question.**

EXAMPLE Have you seen a sculpture by Augusta Savage?

**(3) An *imperative sentence* is a sentence that gives a command or makes a request.**

EXAMPLES Head your paper in the usual way.
Please give me the dates for the class meetings.

**(4) An *exclamatory sentence* is a sentence that expresses strong feeling or emotion.**

EXAMPLE Ah, you have discovered the secret!

One advantage of speech over writing is that by a change of tone or emphasis you can convey different meanings with the same words.

> Shakespeare is the greatest writer the world has ever known. [Declarative]
>
> Shakespeare is the greatest writer the world has ever known? [Interrogative; the speaker is questioning the statement.]
>
> Shakespeare is the greatest writer the world has ever known! [Exclamatory; you can almost hear the speaker's voice rise for emphasis.]

Without the inflection of the speaker's voice, the different meanings of this sentence are communicated by punctuation.

**REVIEW EXERCISE. Identifying Subjects, Verbs, and Complements; Classifying Complements.** On your paper, identify the subject, the verb, and the complements in each sentence. After each complement, write what kind it is, using abbreviations as follows: *d.o.* (direct object), *i.o.* (indirect object), *p.n.* (predicate nominative), *p.a.* (predicate adjective).

1. Mozart was a musical genius.
2. His accomplishments seem both breathtaking and unbelievable.
3. By the age of eight, he had written minuets, sonatas, and a symphony.
4. His father offered him the opportunity of a European tour of musical capitals.
5. Great musicians tested him.
6. They would play a melody just once, and Mozart would listen and reproduce it exactly.
7. His sensitive ear could detect even the smallest change.
8. Blindfolded, he could identify all the elements of a chord.
9. His feeling for balance and sound was phenomenal.
10. At the age of thirty-five, he became very ill, and death claimed the life of this great genius.

---

## CHAPTER 19 REVIEW: POSTTEST 1

**Identifying Subjects, Verbs, and Complements; Classifying Sentences.** Number your paper 1–20. After the proper number, identify the italicized word or words using these abbreviations: *s.*

(subject), *v.* (verb), *d.o.* (direct object), *i.o.* (indirect object), *p.n.* (predicate nominative), and *p.a.* (predicate adjective). Classify each sentence according to purpose, using these abbreviations: *decl.* (declarative), *int.* (interrogative), *imp.* (imperative), and *excl.* (exclamatory).

EXAMPLE 1. The *school* is five blocks from here.
2. *s., decl.*

1. The umpire called a *strike.*
2. Please mail these *letters* for me.
3. By whom *is* the mail *sent?*
4. The *rosebush* and the *pear tree* grew well in our back yard.
5. The cab driver *accepted* our money and *handed* us our change.
6. *Two* of the giraffes were eating the leaves from the trees.
7. The rain *nourished* our plants.
8. His hard work earned *him* a promotion.
9. The day was *sunny* and *warm.*
10. Anita ran *errands* during most of the day.
11. Why did *Earl* leave the party so early?
12. Martha Graham is a *choreographer.*
13. The water in the ocean was *cold.*
14. Please meet *me* at 5:00 P.M.
15. What a wonderful day we *had* yesterday!
16. Please hold my *umbrella* and *coat* for a minute.
17. Where did *you* park the car?
18. *Leave* your classrooms quickly and quietly!
19. Two of the books *had been torn.*
20. *We* often went to the shops and the restaurants in the hotel.

---

## CHAPTER 19 REVIEW: POSTTEST 2

**Writing Sentences.** Write your own sentences according to the following guidelines:

1. A declarative sentence with a compound subject
2. An interrogative sentence with a compound verb
3. An exclamatory sentence
4. An imperative sentence with a compound direct object
5. A declarative sentence with an indirect object

6. A declarative sentence with a predicate nominative
7. An interrogative sentence with a compound predicate adjective
8. A declarative sentence with a direct object and an object complement
9. A declarative sentence with a direct object and an indirect object
10. A declarative sentence with a predicate adjective



## SUMMARY OF SENTENCE PATTERNS

Every sentence has two basic parts, subject and predicate. Within the subject there is a simple subject, usually just called the subject; within each predicate there is a simple predicate, usually called the verb. Some sentences consist of subject and verb only.

| S | V |
|---|---|
| Birds | fly. |

Modifiers may be added to the subject and verb without changing the basic pattern of such a sentence.

The lovely birds (S) of the forest fly (V) gracefully through the branches of the trees.

Complements, which are additions to the predicate, create other sentence patterns. Because there are different kinds of complements, each produces a different sentence pattern. The seven common sentence patterns are shown in the following list:

| | | | |
|---|---|---|---|
| S<br>Children | V<br>play. | | |
| S<br>Children | V<br>play | D.O.<br>games. | |
| S<br>Children | V<br>give | I.O.<br>pets | D.O.<br>love. |
| S<br>Children | V<br>consider | D.O.<br>adults | OBJ. COMP. (ADJ.)<br>strong. |
| S<br>Children | V<br>fancy | D.O.<br>themselves | OBJ. COMP. (N.)<br>stars. |
| S<br>Children | V<br>are | P.N.<br>dreamers. | |
| S<br>Children | V<br>appear | P.A.<br>healthy. | |

GRAMMAR

# CHAPTER 20

# The Phrase

## KINDS OF PHRASES AND THEIR FUNCTIONS

A phrase is a group of related words not containing a subject and predicate. A phrase may function as a subject, a verb, an object, a predicate nominative, or a modifier. You have already learned the *verb phrase* (a verb of more than one word: *am writing, could have gone*). In this chapter you will review the other types of phrases and how they function in a sentence.

### DIAGNOSTIC TEST

**Identifying Phrases.** Number your paper 1–20. Each of the following sentences contains an italicized phrase. After the proper number, identify each phrase, using the following abbreviations: *prep. adj.* (prepositional phrase used as an adjective), *prep. adv.* (prepositional phrase used as an adverb), *ger.* (gerund phrase), *part.* (participial phrase), *inf.* (infinitive phrase), and *app.* (appositive phrase).

EXAMPLE 1. *Smiling warmly,* they greeted us on our arrival.
1. *part.*

1. Thomas Nast, *a nineteenth-century illustrator and political cartoonist,* is famous for his many drawings of Santa Claus.

2. In Israel farmers meet the difficulties of *growing food in a desert country with innovative agricultural methods.*
3. To conserve rainwater, the farmers water only the roots of plants through a series *of underground irrigation pipes.*
4. *Capturing the attention of the English-speaking world,* Edward VIII, King of England, abdicated his throne in 1936.
5. Harriet Beecher Stowe wrote *to awaken the country's consciousness to the evils of slavery.*
6. Woodrow Wilson, *President during World War I,* tried to prevent another world war with his Fourteen Points.
7. By *building the railroads across the continental United States,* Chinese and Irish immigrants contributed to America's growth.
8. Are you ready *to stack this cord of wood*?
9. On our vacation in Hawaii, we saw Mauna Loa, a volcano *rising six miles from the floor of the ocean.*
10. *Being the eleventh of twelve children* was an education in survival for my Uncle Jesse.
11. Withdrawing from the race, the candidate cited personal reasons for her unexpected decision *to return to private life.*
12. After *capturing the gold in the 1984 Olympics,* marathon runner Joan Benoit returned home to her simple life style in Maine.
13. To improve your photography skills, register *for the senior elective course, Optical Images.*
14. Governor Parker has refused *to debate Lucia Delano,* his opponent in the upcoming election.
15. *In the Roaring Twenties* the Teapot Dome scandal contributed to American dissatisfaction with the presidency of Warren Harding.
16. Although Harding was not personally corrupt, the "Ohio Gang," friends Harding had named to government positions, profited illegally from the sale *of government oil.*
17. Though we shall never be certain of the exact cause *of Harding's death,* some historians cite a "broken heart."
18. *Scheduled for launch in 1986,* the space telescope will give the United States new visions of our complex universe.
19. In a speech *delivered to the graduating class,* the principal encouraged the graduates to improve the quality of life in our world.
20. The governor has done everything possible *to retain the present tax structure.*

**20a. A *phrase* is a group of related words used as a single part of speech and not containing a verb and its subject.**

Five types of phrases are explained in the following pages: *prepositional phrases,* (as adjectives and as adverbs), *participial phrases, gerund phrases, infinitive phrases,* and *appositive phrases.*

## THE PREPOSITIONAL PHRASE

**20b. A *prepositional phrase* is a group of words beginning with a preposition and ending with a noun or a pronoun.**

EXAMPLES in the room — before the party
under the sea — along the path

The noun or pronoun that ends the phrase is the object of the preposition that begins the phrase.

### The Adjective Phrase

**20c. An *adjective phrase* is a prepositional phrase that modifies a noun or a pronoun.**

EXAMPLE That tall building **with the red tower** is our new library. [The prepositional phrase *with the red tower* modifies—describes or limits the meaning of—the noun *building* and is therefore an adjective phrase.]

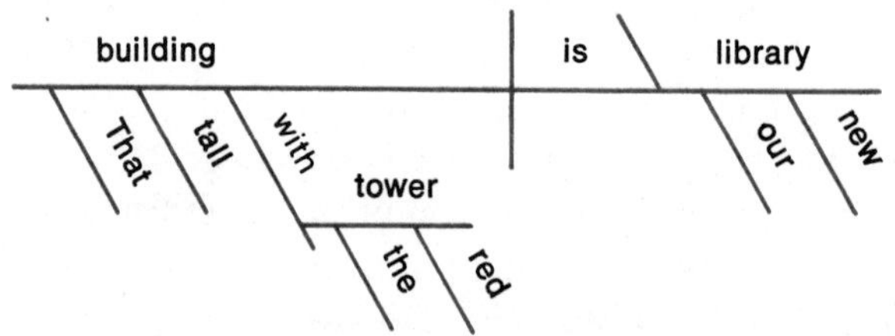


In diagraming a prepositional phrase, the preposition that begins the phrase is placed on a line slanting downward from the word the phrase modifies. The object of the preposition is placed on a horizontal line extending to the right from the line with the preposition. Single-word modifiers in the phrase are diagramed in the usual way.

**EXERCISE 1. Identifying Adjective Phrases and the Words They Modify.** Write in a column the adjective phrases from the following sentences. Before each phrase, place the number of the sentence in which it appears. After each phrase, write the noun or pronoun the phrase modifies. There are ten phrases in all.

1. The instinct of self-preservation is perhaps the most basic drive in living things.
2. Yet lemmings, small animals in Scandinavia, occasionally follow a pattern of self-destruction.
3. Ordinarily, the lemmings peacefully eat a diet of moss and roots.
4. But every few years the population of lemmings exceeds their food supply, and abandoning their burrows, they ford streams and lakes, devouring everything in their path and leaving no trace of vegetation.
5. When they reach the shore along the sea, they swim until they drown.
6. Explanations of their actions are only guesses, and the lemming remains a mystery to scientists.

## The Adverb Phrase

**20d. An *adverb phrase* is a prepositional phrase that modifies a verb, an adjective, or another adverb.**

Notice in the following sentences the different ways in which an adverb phrase can modify a verb.

Louisa May Alcott wrote **with great care.** [how she wrote]
Louisa May Alcott wrote **in the nineteenth century.** [when she wrote]
Louisa May Alcott wrote **for thirty years.** [how long she wrote]
Louisa May Alcott wrote **in America.** [where she wrote]
Louisa May Alcott wrote **for her own pleasure.** [why she wrote]

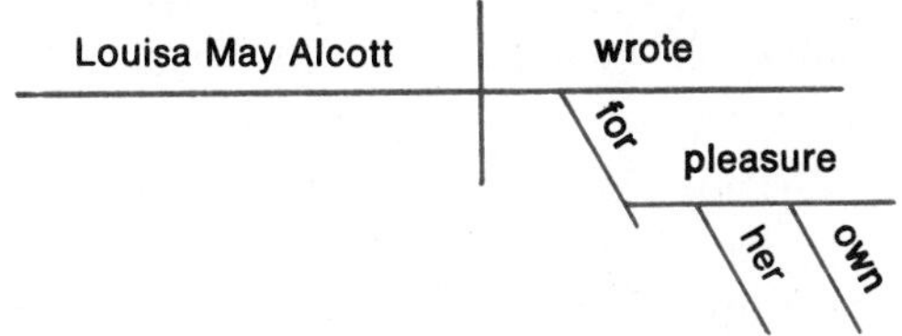

In the following sentence, the adverb phrase modifies an adjective.

The old manor was rich **in traditions.**

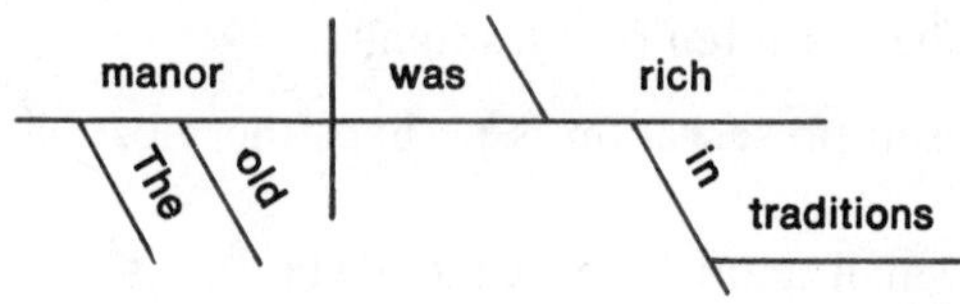


In the next sentence, an adverb phrase modifies an adverb.

Thomas Hardy wrote poetry late **in life**.

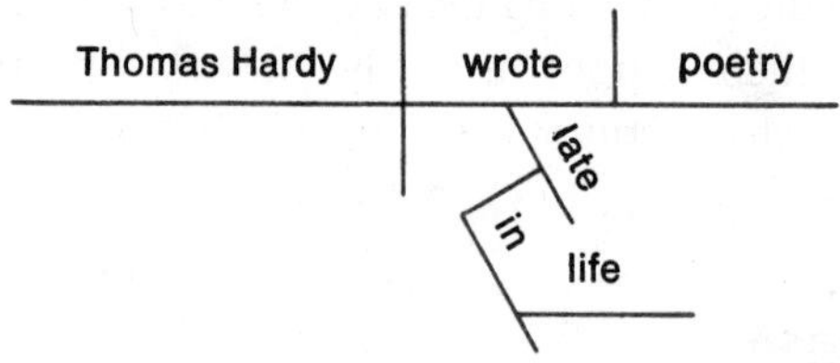


**EXERCISE 2. Identifying Adverb Phrases and the Words They Modify.** Write in a column the adverb phrases in the following sentences. Before each phrase, place the number of the sentence in which it appears. After each phrase, write the word or words it modifies.

1. Duncan is sitting in his chair, eating a bowl of oatmeal and spilling it all over the place.
2. A great part of our life is spent in sleep.
3. The children ran out into the street and screamed for help.
4. Every rumor in the world must be started by somebody.
5. They were assembled on benches for the presentation.
6. "Silently in the infinite meadows of heaven blossomed the stars," recited the poet.
7. She wore a costume similar to the queen's.
8. Fear sometimes springs from ignorance.
9. In winter we wear warm clothes.
10. I haven't seen a winter like that in seventeen years!

**WRITING APPLICATION A:**
**Using Prepositional Phrases to Make Comparisons**

Speakers and writers use comparison to make an idea clear. The heart of some comparisons is a prepositional phrase.

EXAMPLE The fullback looked *like a tank.*

**Writing Assignment**

Use one of the following ideas or one of your own to describe a person, place, or situation by developing a comparison. When you review your description, check for effective use of prepositional phrases.

1. my room—a battleground
2. preparing for a test—preparing to play in an athletic event
3. a car, bicycle, or other vehicle—an old friend

## VERBALS AND VERBAL PHRASES

Verbals are formed from verbs. They act like verbs in some ways—showing action, having modifiers, taking complements—but they are not used as verbs in a sentence. Instead they are used as nouns, adjectives, or adverbs.

The three verbals are *participles* (verbal adjectives), *gerunds* (verbal nouns), and *infinitives* (which can serve as verbal adjectives, verbal nouns, or verbal adverbs). A *verbal phrase* is a phrase consisting of a verbal and its complements or modifiers.

### The Participle

**20e. A *participle* is a verb form that can be used as an adjective.**

EXAMPLES The **waving** campers boarded the bus.

**Waving,** the campers boarded the bus. [In these sentences, *waving,* like the verb *wave,* expresses action; like an adjective, it modifies the noun *campers.*]

We could hear the wind **howling.** [Here *howling* expresses action, like a verb; it also modifies the noun *wind.*]

There are two forms of participles: *present participles* and *past participles.* The perfect tense of a participle is formed with the helping verb *having.*

having seen having been seen

Present participles end in *-ing.* Past participles end in *-ed, -d, -t, -en, -n:* talk*ed,* sav*ed,* crep*t,* bitt*en,* see*n.*

PRESENT PARTICIPLE They heard Lena Horne **singing.**
PAST PARTICIPLE The audience, **pleased,** applauded enthusiastically.

The words *singing* and *pleased* modify nouns and hence are used as adjectives. They show action but do not serve as verbs in the sentences. The verbs are *heard* and *applauded.* A participle may, however, be part of a verb phrase when it is used with a helping verb.

The **skidding** car stopped just in time. [*Skidding* modifies *car.*]
The car was **skidding** on the ice. [The verb phrase *was skidding* consists of the helping verb *was* and the present participle *skidding.*]

Think of the participle in a verb phrase as part of the verb, not as an adjective modifying the subject.

Like verbs, participles may be modified by adverbs.

EXAMPLE **Speaking dramatically,** she enthralled the audience. [The participle *speaking* is modified by the adverb *dramatically.*]

A participle, again like a verb, may take an object.

EXAMPLE **Writing the request for a second time,** she insisted on an answer. [The object of the participle *writing* is *request.* It answers the question *Writing what?* Notice that *for a second time* is an adverb phrase modifying *writing.*]

## The Participial Phrase

**20f. A *participial phrase* is a phrase containing a participle and any complements or modifiers it may have.**

The participle[1] introduces the phrase, and the entire phrase acts as an adjective to modify a noun or a pronoun.

[1] For work on the participial phrase as a sentence fragment, see page 324. For exercises on the dangling participle, see pages 350–51.

EXAMPLES **Nodding his head,** the defendant acknowledged his guilt. [The participial phrase is made up of the participle *nodding* and the complement *head,* which is the direct object of *nodding.*]

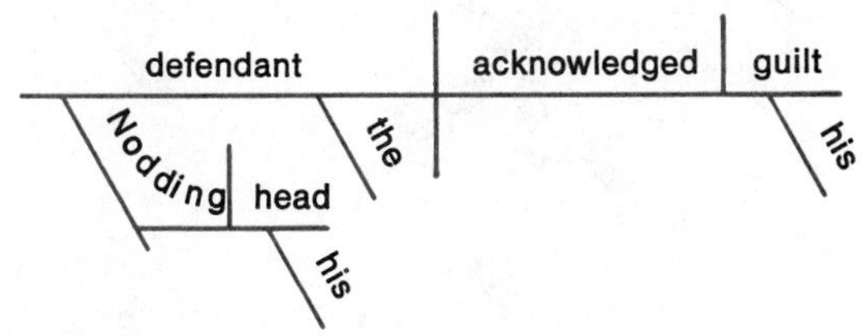


**Convinced by his family,** he submitted his book for publication. [The participial phrase is made up of the participle *convinced* and its modifier *by his family,* which is an adverb phrase modifying *convinced.*]

**EXERCISE 3. Identifying Participial Phrases and the Words They Modify.** List the participial phrases in the following sentences. Before each phrase, write the number of the sentence. After each phrase, write the word or words it modifies.

1. Known as Johnny Appleseed, John Chapman distributed apple seeds and saplings to families bound for the West.
2. Needing a sustained wind for flight, the albatross rarely crosses the Equator.
3. As many as forty adders coiling together can prevent heat loss.
4. The salmon, deriving its pink color from its diet, feeds on shrimp-like crustaceans.
5. Having been aided by warm weather and clear skies, the sailors rejoiced as they arrived on time.
6. Smiling broadly, our champion entered the hall.
7. Searching for old clothes in a trunk, John found directions for finding a treasure buried on the shore.
8. Sparta and Athens, putting aside their own rivalry, fought off the Persians.
9. Trained on an overhead trellis, a white rose bush in Tombstone, Arizona, covers some 8,000 square feet of aerial space.
10. I would love to see it bursting into bloom in the spring; it must be quite a sight!

**WRITING APPLICATION B:**
**Using Participial Phrases in a Biographical Sketch**

Learning about the lives of famous people from the past can be both inspiring and informative. For example, despite the loss of both sight and hearing, Helen Keller lived a noble and useful life.

**Writing Assignment**

Do some research on the life of an American whom you find interesting. Write a biographical sketch of that person's life. As you tell about his or her life, use at least four participial phrases. Underline these phrases.

EXAMPLE *Deeply concerned about poor Kentucky children,* Jesse Stuart taught in small and often primitive classrooms.

**REVIEW EXERCISE A. Identifying Prepositional and Participial Phrases and the Words They Modify.** After the proper number, write each italicized phrase and the word it modifies. Then indicate whether the phrase is prepositional or participial. Consider each italicized group as one phrase.

EXAMPLE 1. *Delighted by the new symphony,* the critic applauded *with great enthusiasm.*
1. *Delighted by the new symphony, critic, participial*
*with great enthusiasm, applauded, prepositional*

1. Mahalia Jackson, *called the greatest potential blues singer since Bessie Smith,* would sing only religious songs.
2. Her version of "Silent Night" was one *of the all-time best-selling records* in Denmark.
3. *Setting out in a thirty-one-foot ketch,* Sharon Sites Adams, a housewife *from California,* sailed *across the Pacific* alone.
4. *Having been rejected by six publishers,* the story *of Peter Rabbit* was finally published privately *by Beatrix Potter.*
5. *Known for his imaginative style,* architect Minoru Yamasaki designed the World Trade Center *located in New York City.*
6. *In 1932* Amelia Earhart, *trying for a new record,* began her solo flight *over the Atlantic.*

7. Maria Tallchief, an Osage Indian, was the prima ballerina *of the New York Ballet Company.*
8. *Dancing to unanimous acclaim in the United States and Europe,* she was known *for her interpretation* of Stravinsky's *Firebird.*
9. *Continuing research on radium after her husband's death,* Marie Curie received the Nobel Prize *in chemistry.*
10. *Elected to the House of Representatives in 1958,* Shirley Chisholm became the first black female member *of Congress.*

## The Gerund

**20g. A *gerund* is a word ending in *-ing* that is formed from a verb and used as a noun.**

Although the gerund and the participle are both formed from verbs, the gerund differs from the participle in that it is used as a noun, while the participle is used as an adjective.

EXAMPLE **Reading** is a great pleasure. [*Reading* is formed from the verb *read* and, as the subject of the sentence, is used as a noun.]

A gerund is a verbal noun. Like any other noun, it may be used as a subject, as the direct or indirect object of a verb, as a predicate nominative, or as the object of a preposition.

**Swimming** is excellent exercise. [gerund as subject]
She has always loved **dancing.** [gerund as direct object]
He gave **studying** all his attention. [gerund as indirect object]
Janetta's hobby is **knitting.** [gerund as predicate nominative]
In **cooking,** use salt sparingly. [gerund as object of preposition]

**EXERCISE 4. Identifying Gerunds and Their Functions.** Identify the gerund in each of the following sentences; then state whether the gerund is used as a subject, a direct object, an indirect object, a predicate nominative, or the object of a preposition.

EXAMPLE 1. By reading the newspaper daily, you will become an informed citizen.
1. *reading, object of a preposition*

1. Judging is an exercise in objectivity.
2. Do you enjoy skiing?
3. I sometimes dream about flying.

4. This year my favorite activity has been skating.
5. I have given camping a fair try, but I still do not like it.
6. Some of my friends earn extra money by baby-sitting.
7. My exercise schedule includes jogging.
8. Snorkeling gives me hours of pleasure.
9. Typing is a useful skill.
10. Have you ever wished for a career in acting?



**EXERCISE 5. Distinguishing Between Participles and Gerunds.** Number your paper 1–10. Select the participles and gerunds from each of the following sentences, and write them after the proper number. Indicate by writing *p.* or *g.* whether the words are participles or gerunds.

1. Mary Shelley wrote *Frankenstein* after entering a ghost-story contest with friends.
2. Marguerite Henry has charmed readers for thirty years by writing sensitive stories about horses.
3. Beginning with *Pippi Longstocking,* Astrid Lindgren has written a whole series of stories for children.
4. Marian Anderson, the first black employed as a member of the Metropolitan Opera, was born February 17, 1902.
5. Carrie Chapman Catt dedicated her life to fighting for women's suffrage.
6. Appointed principal of the Mason City Iowa High School in 1881, Catt became the city's first female superintendent.
7. The Nineteenth Amendment of the Constitution, adopted in 1920, was largely the result of Catt's efforts.
8. Mildred "Babe" Zaharias, entering the 1932 Olympics as a relatively obscure athlete, won gold and silver medals.
9. Margaret Bourke-White, working for *Life* throughout her long career, was the first woman war photographer.
10. Phyllis McGinley, who gained fame as a writer of light verse, began publishing while still in college.

## The Gerund Phrase

**20h. A *gerund phrase* is a phrase consisting of a gerund and any modifiers or complements it may have.**

EXAMPLE **Boiling an egg properly** is not easy for me. [The gerund *boiling* has *egg* as its direct object and is modified by the adverb *properly*.]

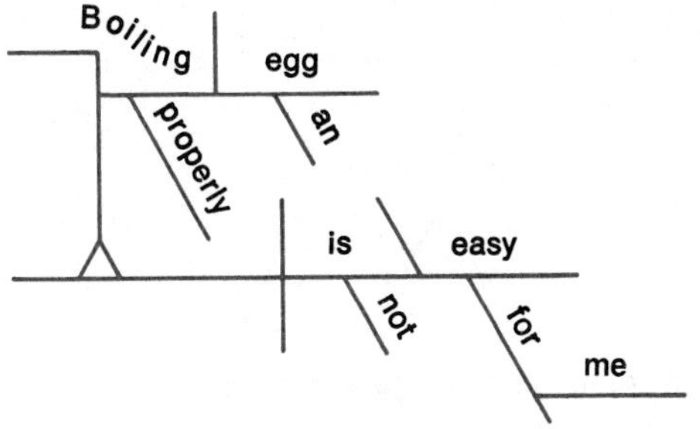


Like a gerund alone, a gerund phrase may be used in any place that a noun would fit.

EXAMPLES **Playing the piano** was his greatest talent. [gerund phrase as subject]

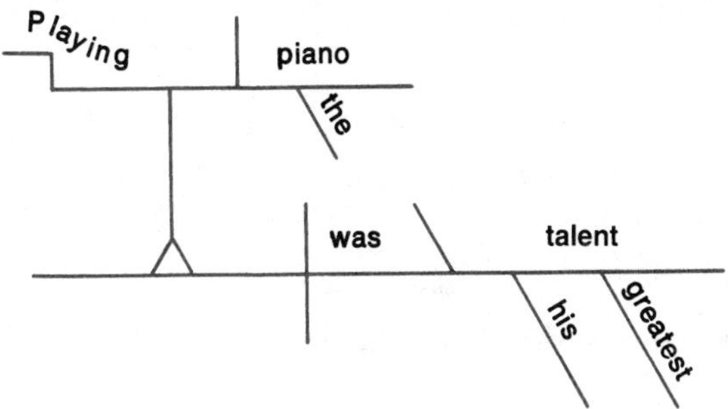


The general admitted **sending the order.** [gerund phrase as object of the verb *admitted; order* is the object of the gerund *sending*]

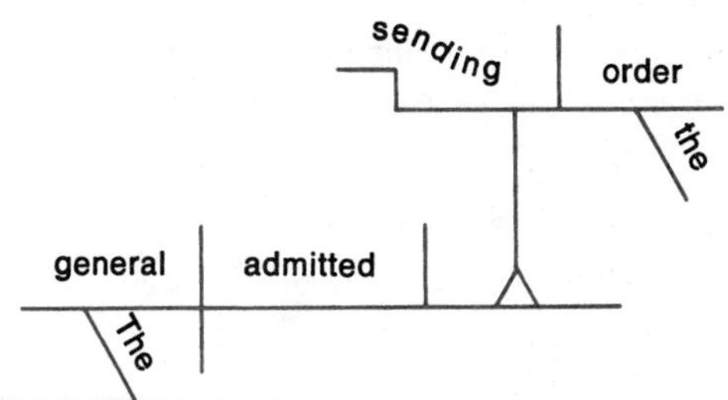

GRAMMAR

The judge warned him about **telling lies.** [gerund phrase as object of the preposition *about*]

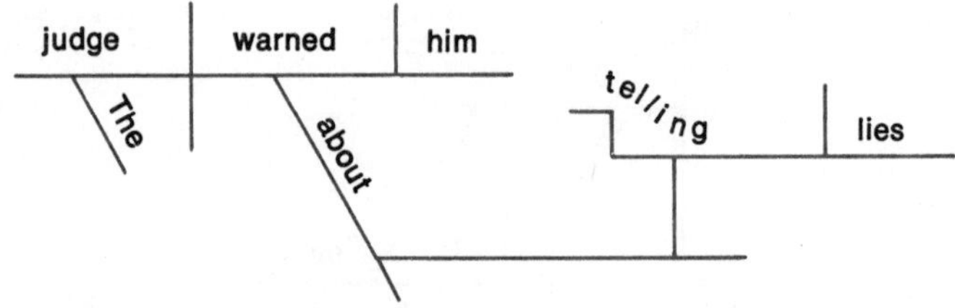


**Reading good books** is **using time well.** [gerund phrases as subject and predicate nominative]

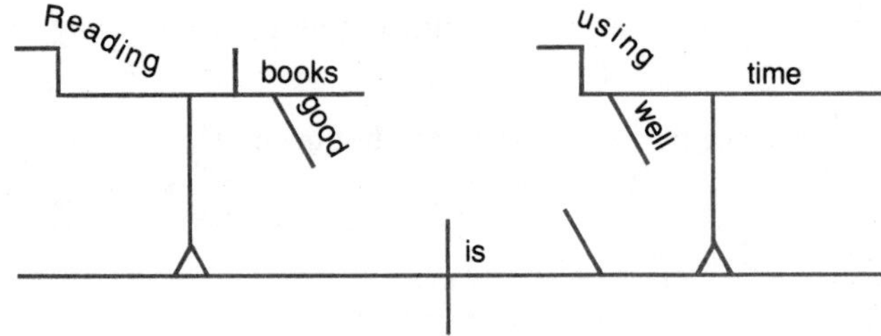


## The Infinitive

**20i. An *infinitive* is a verb form, usually preceded by *to,* that can be used as a noun or a modifier.**

to explore    to worry    to live

An infinitive is generally used as a noun, but it may also be used as an adjective or as an adverb.

THE INFINITIVE USED AS A NOUN

**To give** is praiseworthy. [infinitive as subject]
Samuel Johnson liked **to argue.** [infinitive as direct object]
Darius Green's ambition was **to fly.** [infinitive as predicate nominative]

THE INFINITIVE USED AS AN ADJECTIVE

Darius Green's attempt **to fly** was a failure. [The infinitive modifies the noun *attempt.*]

THE INFINITIVE USED AS AN ADVERB

It was too raw **to eat.** [The infinitive modifies the adjective *raw.*]

> ☞ **NOTE** Do not confuse the infinitive, which is a verbal beginning with *to,* and the prepositional phrase beginning with *to,* which consists of *to* plus a noun or pronoun.

| INFINITIVES | PREPOSITIONAL PHRASES |
| --- | --- |
| to go | to the game |
| to know | to thousands |
| to understand | to Ecuador |

The word *to,* the sign of the infinitive, is sometimes omitted.

Let us [to] **sit** down.
Please make him [to] **stop** that noise.
We wouldn't dare [to] **disobey**.
Will you help me [to] **finish?**

**EXERCISE 6. Identifying Infinitives and Their Functions.** Each of the following sentences contains an infinitive. Identify the infinitive and state whether it is used as a noun, an adjective, or an adverb. If it is a noun, state whether it is used as a subject, direct object, or predicate nominative.

EXAMPLE 1. Swans and geese are fascinating to watch.
1. *to watch, adverb*

1. To land on the moon became our national goal during the sixties.
2. For me, one of the worst chores is to clean my room.
3. We discovered an antique shop with unusual objects to sell.
4. Since I have taken up track in addition to my other extracurricular activities, it seems I haven't a moment to spare.
5. Did you find that book difficult to understand?
6. According to our judicial system, the state makes the decision to prosecute the defendant in criminal cases.
7. Infinitives are usually easy to recognize.
8. Anita's job was to interview all qualified applicants.
9. I did not have the time to watch the football game on television.
10. In my spare time I like to read historical fiction.

**REVIEW EXERCISE B. Identifying Participles, Gerunds, and Infinitives.** Number your paper 1–10. List the participles, gerunds, and infinitives in order after the proper number. Identify each word. For each participle, state the word it modifies. For each gerund, state what part of a sentence it is used as. For each infinitive, indicate what part of speech it is used as.

EXAMPLE 1. Determined to help Romeo, Benvolio suggests going to the ball.
1. *Determined, participle, Benvolio*
*to help, infinitive, adverb*
*going, gerund, direct object*

1. In writing *Hamlet,* Shakespeare achieved one of his greatest triumphs.
2. Playing Hamlet is the province of great actors.
3. Watching *Hamlet* is a moving experience.
4. In this play, Shakespeare tried to show us the complexity of the human mind.
5. A specter claiming to be the ghost of Hamlet's father appears to Hamlet.
6. Upon learning that his uncle Claudius is his father's murderer, Hamlet is torn by grief and rage.
7. He decides to seek revenge.
8. His attempts to avenge his father's murder lead to the deaths of many others.
9. Hamlet's last act is to kill his uncle.
10. Hamlet's loyal friend Horatio wishes to die by his own hand but consents to stay alive so that he may tell Hamlet's story.

## The Infinitive Phrase

**20j. An *infinitive phrase* consists of an infinitive and any complements or modifiers it may have.**

She wanted **to visit her aunt.** [*Aunt* is the object of the infinitive *to visit.*]
He must try **to eat properly.** [*Properly* is an adverb modifying *to eat.*]

Like an infinitive alone, an infinitive phrase may serve as the subject of a verb or as the direct object of a verb. It may also be used as an adjective or an adverb.

EXAMPLES **To write a good term paper** is a difficult task. [infinitive phrase as subject]

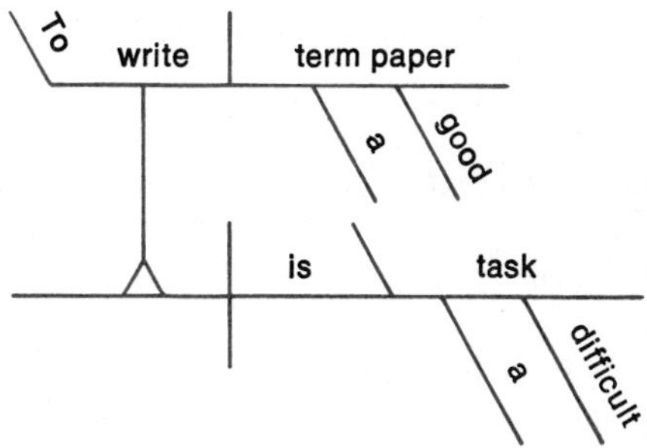


Chico wanted **to open his own business.** [infinitive phrase as object of verb]

Napoleon's plan **to conquer the whole world** failed. [infinitive phrase used as adjective, modifying the noun *plan*]

She hurried **to find the information.** [infinitive phrase as adverb, modifying the verb *hurried*]

### The Infinitive Clause

Unlike other verbals, an infinitive may have a subject as well as complements and modifiers.

EXAMPLES The director asked **Rebecca to star in the play.** [*Rebecca* is the subject of the infinitive *to star.* The entire group of words *Rebecca to star in the play* is the object of the verb *asked.*]

The sergeant commanded **them to march faster.** [*Them* is the subject of the infinitive *to march.*]

When an infinitive has a subject, as in the examples just given, the construction is called an *infinitive clause.* Notice that the subject of the infinitive in the second example (*them*) is in the objective case.[1]

**REVIEW EXERCISE C. Identifying Prepositional, Participial, Gerund, and Infinitive Phrases.** Number your paper 1–10. In the

[1] For rules concerning the use of the objective case, see pages 501–504.

following sentences, most of the phrases have been numbered and italicized. After the proper number, write the kind of phrase: prepositional, participial, gerund, or infinitive.

EXAMPLE (1) *Winning a scholarship* is the result (2) *of hard work.*
1. *gerund*
2. *prepositional*

a. (1) *Parking her car at the depot,* Mrs. Romano decided (2) *to take the bus* (3) *to town.*
b. (4) *To finish her term paper on time,* Angela spent Saturday (5) *in the library,* (6) *doing her research.*
c. (7) *Having joined a volunteer program,* Mark helps by (8) *reading stories to patients* (9) *in the children's ward.*
d. (10) *Washing dishes* is the task I dread.

**WRITING APPLICATION C:**
**Using Infinitive Phrases**

It is not a bad idea to think occasionally about the future. Have you thought about what you want to be or do after your high-school years? If so, how do you plan to realize these goals?

**Writing Assignment**

Write a paragraph in which you explain what and where you would like to be ten years from now. Include at least four infinitive phrases in your paragraph. Underline these phrases.

EXAMPLE Ten years from now I hope *to be in medical school.*

## THE APPOSITIVE[1]

**20k. An *appositive* is a noun or pronoun that follows another noun or pronoun to identify or explain it. An *appositive phrase* is made up of an appositive and its modifiers.**

In the following sentences, the appositives and appositive phrases are in boldfaced type.

[1] For rules on the punctuation of appositives, see page 616. For the use of appositives in the subordination of ideas, see pages 363–64.

Her brother **Bill** called for her.
We visited Boston harbor, **the site of the Boston Tea Party.**
George Washington, **our first President**, was a great military leader.

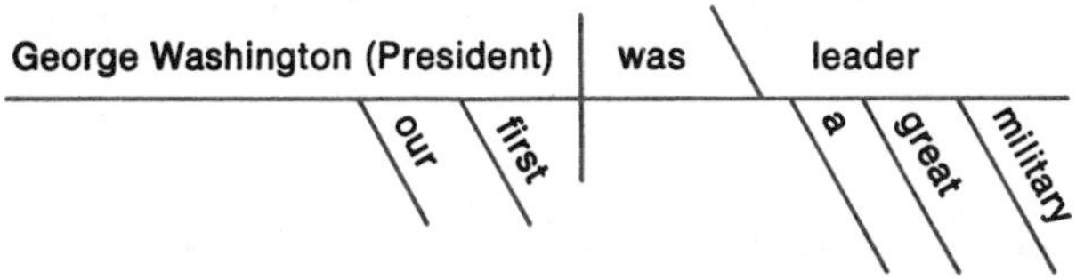

George Washington (President) | was \ leader
our, first; a, great, military



**WRITING APPLICATION D:**
**Using Appositives and Appositive Phrases in Your Writing**

Appositives and appositive phrases are useful in your writing because they identify or explain the noun or pronoun they follow. As you read the following sentences, notice that the appositives and appositive phrases add important information for the readers.

EXAMPLES My brother **Stu** is three years younger than I.
Mr. English, **the superintendent of schools in our district,** spoke at the PTA meeting yesterday evening.

**Writing Assignment**

Think of a current event in which heads of state met. Write a summary of their meeting. Use at least three appositive phrases.

**REVIEW EXERCISE D. Identifying Prepositional, Participial, Gerund, Infinitive, and Appositive Phrases.** Number your paper 1–10. Each sentence contains at least one italicized phrase. After the proper number, identify the phrase or phrases as prepositional, participial, gerund, infinitive, or appositive.

Thousands of Americans travel (1) *to all points of the globe* annually. The eager packer, (2) *anticipating glamour and excitement,* often takes too much clothing and equipment. The most effective way to pack is (3) *to set out clothes for the trip* and then put half back (4) *into the closet.* Travelers should give careful thought to footwear, (5) *the most crucial item of apparel* at times. Comfortable walking shoes are essential (6) *for any kind* of sightseeing expedition. Travelers can find tours (7) *for a wide range* of prices. Comfort and charm can be found (8) *in spite of low budgets.* Perhaps the most important thing to remember is (9) *to accept new customs,* putting aside expectations of (10) *finding things exactly like home.*

## CHAPTER 20 REVIEW: POSTTEST 1

**Identifying Phrases.** Each of the following sentences contains an italicized phrase. Identify each phrase, using the following abbreviations: *prep. adj.* (prepositional phrase used as an adjective), *prep. adv.* (prepositional phrase used as an adverb), *part.* (participial phrase), *ger.* (gerund phrase), *inf.* (infinitive phrase), and *app.* (appositive phrase).

EXAMPLE 1. *Talking after the bell rings* is strictly forbidden.
1. *ger.*

1. *Bubbling with excitement and energy,* the children described their day on the rides at the theme park.
2. Do you understand all the talk nowadays *about modems, semiconductors, and microchips?*
3. *Working on the school newspaper* has taught me responsibility.
4. If you are interested in *attending the concert tonight,* give me a call after school and let me know.
5. *Delayed by the snowstorm,* the flight from Chicago to Seattle was finally cleared for takeoff.
6. Please wrap that delicate bone china *with extreme care!*
7. Today's crossword puzzle is difficult *to complete correctly.*
8. The emu, *a flightless bird from Australia,* is similar to the ostrich.
9. *Practicing the piano,* she completely ignores the rest of the world.
10. At the beginning of language class, we sang "La Marseillaise," *the French national anthem.*
11. *Preserving rare and valuable books* is one of the challenges facing the Library of Congress.
12. There is a new method for *preventing the decay of books.*
13. The method, *a complex process,* works by extracting moisture and neutralizing any acid in the paper.

14. *In history class* we read about Booker T. Washington, founder of Tuskegee Institute.
15. *In the last few decades* people have become concerned about proper eating habits.
16. Thomas Jefferson, President, philosopher, and scientist, is also famous for his decision *to purchase the Louisiana Territory.*
17. In the summer our local community college schedules special two-week courses *for gifted elementary- and high-school students.*
18. In 1936 Adolf Hitler refused to congratulate the great Jesse Owens, *winner of four gold medals in the Berlin Olympics.*
19. Invigorated by the cool breeze, I sat down *to resume my work on my science project.*
20. The United States, a true "melting pot," has been enriched *by many diverse cultures.*



## CHAPTER 20 REVIEW: POSTTEST 2

**Writing Sentences with Phrases.** Write ten sentences according to the following guidelines:

1. Use *whistling softly* as a participial phrase.
2. Use *by the lake* as an adverb phrase modifying a verb.
3. Use *with the green shirt* as an adjective phrase.
4. Use *with kindness* as an adverb phrase modifying an adjective.
5. Use *for me* as an adverb phrase modifying a verb.
6. Use *of fruits and vegetables* as an adjective phrase.
7. Use *buying a gift for Jane* as a participial phrase.
8. Use *diving into the pool* as a gerund phrase.
9. Use *to be happy* as an infinitive phrase.
10. Use *a city in Mexico* as an appositive phrase.

# CHAPTER 21

# The Clause

## ADJECTIVE, NOUN, ADVERB CLAUSES

When you first begin to write, you use simple sentences. However, as you grow older and more mature in your thinking, you write more complicated sentences, in order to express your thoughts more effectively. One sign of maturity in writing is the use of subordination. Studying the different kinds of subordinate clauses—the adjective, the adverb, and the noun clause—will help you write sentences that have greater clarity, smoothness, and force.

### DIAGNOSTIC TEST

**A. Identifying Independent and Subordinate Clauses; Classifying Subordinate Clauses.** Number your paper 1–10. After the proper number, identify each italicized group of words as an independent or a subordinate clause. If it is a subordinate clause, identify it as an adjective clause, an adverb clause, or a noun clause.

EXAMPLE 1. This novel, *which is the latest best seller,* will be the perfect birthday gift for my mother.
1. *subordinate, adjective*

1. *The Civil War, often called the War Between the States, resulted in the deaths of over 600,000 Americans;* it devastated the nation socially, politically, and economically.

2. *In the early thirties many Americans believed in and voted for the political philosophy of Franklin D. Roosevelt, the New Deal.*
3. *When you travel abroad,* you gain greater perspective on being American.
4. She thought *that it was an easy course,* but she learned more than she expected.
5. *Since both of Len's parents are short,* people do not expect Len to be tall.
6. *When he addresses the legislature,* the governor will have to answer several questions about the budget.
7. Please turn down that stereo *so I can think!*
8. Sandra Day O'Connor, *who was an Arizona judge,* became the first female Supreme Court Justice in 1981.
9. *Scientists are carefully monitoring the amount of carbon dioxide present in the universe.*
10. *If there is an increase in the amount of carbon dioxide present in the atmosphere,* plant growth will also increase.

**B. Identifying Simple, Compound, Complex, and Compound-Complex Sentences.** Number your paper 11–20. Identify each of the following sentences as simple, compound, complex, or compound-complex.

11. In laboratory studies, scientists have determined that various plants respond differently to increases in carbon dioxide levels; some plants grow at a faster pace.
12. People depend on plants for food.
13. If you enjoy mysteries, look for books by Ngaio Marsh.
14. My study of genealogy has taken up much of my spare time, and it has afforded me a great deal of enjoyment.
15. Galileo was not the first person to assert that the planets revolve around the sun and not around the earth.
16. According to some modern scientists, Galileo's observations, which were made possible by the invention of the telescope, were long overdue.
17. Be careful when you are driving on that street; there are always many little children playing in it.
18. Military historians have written extensive reports on the battles of World War II.

19. The shots fired at Lexington and Concord were "heard 'round the world," and a revolutionary democracy emerged.
20. Jazz is my favorite style of music; I can listen to it for hours!

---

GRAMMAR

**21a. A *clause* is a group of words containing a subject and a predicate and used as part of a sentence.**

An *independent clause*[1] expresses a complete thought and can stand alone as a sentence. A *subordinate clause* does not express a complete thought and cannot stand alone.

## INDEPENDENT CLAUSES

When an independent clause stands alone, it is called a simple sentence.

Ms. Craig taught us the binary number system.

It is called an independent clause only when it is combined with one or more additional clauses in a sentence.

Ms. Craig taught us the binary number system, but we have not really mastered it yet. [The conjunction *but* joins two independent clauses.]

It is an important number system to know because it is used by computers. [In this sentence the independent clause *It is an important number system to know* is combined with a subordinate clause.]

## SUBORDINATE CLAUSES

Subordinate clauses[2] cannot stand alone as sentences. They are always joined in some way to an independent clause.

that you brought
who the culprit had been
when we arrived

Combined with an independent clause, each of these subordinate clauses plays a part in completing the meaning of the sentence.

[1] *Independent* clauses are sometimes called *main* clauses.
[2] *Subordinate* clauses are sometimes called *dependent* clauses.

The favorite dessert was the cake **that you brought.**
The principal knew **who the culprit had been.**
**When we arrived,** they greeted us warmly.
**After she finished her homework,** she went to the ball game.



**EXERCISE 1. Identifying Independent and Subordinate Clauses.** Number your paper 1–10. If the italicized clause is an independent clause, write *I* after the proper number; if it is a subordinate clause, write *S*.

1. Do you know *how chickens' eggs are automatically processed?*
2. When an egg is laid, *it gently rolls along the slanted floor of the cage to a narrow conveyor belt.*
3. These narrow conveyor belts eventually converge into one wide belt *that runs directly into the processing plant.*
4. *As soon as the eggs reach the processing plant,* they are automatically sprayed with detergent and water.
5. The eggs then pass through a specially lit inspection area, *where defective eggs can be detected and removed.*
6. After the eggs are weighed, *they are separated by weight into five groups.*
7. Each group of eggs goes onto a separate conveyor belt, *which leads to a forklike lifting device.*
8. *This device lifts six eggs at a time* while the empty egg cartons wait two feet below it.
9. *The eggs are gently lowered into the cartons,* which are then shipped to grocery stores and supermarkets.
10. *What is truly amazing* is that no human hands ever touch these eggs during the entire process.

## The Adjective Clause

**21b. An *adjective clause* is a subordinate clause that, like an adjective, modifies a noun or pronoun.**

EXAMPLES The novel **that you are reading** is a great work of literature.

The room **where the treasure is kept** is well guarded.

GRAMMAR

The first man **who circumnavigated the globe** was Magellan. [The subordinate clause *who circumnavigated the globe* modifies the noun *man.*][1]

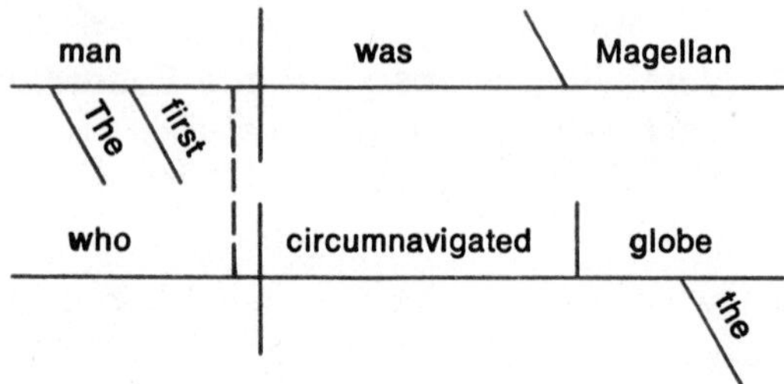


## Relative Pronouns

Adjective clauses often begin with the pronouns *who, whom, whose, which, that.* When used in this way these *relative* pronouns refer to, or are *related to,* some word or idea that has preceded them.[2]

**21c. A *relative pronoun* is a pronoun that begins a subordinate clause and is related to another word or idea.**

A relative pronoun may be the subject of the clause it begins.

The President decorated the astronaut **who had orbited the earth.** [The relative pronoun *who* is the subject of the verb *had orbited.*]

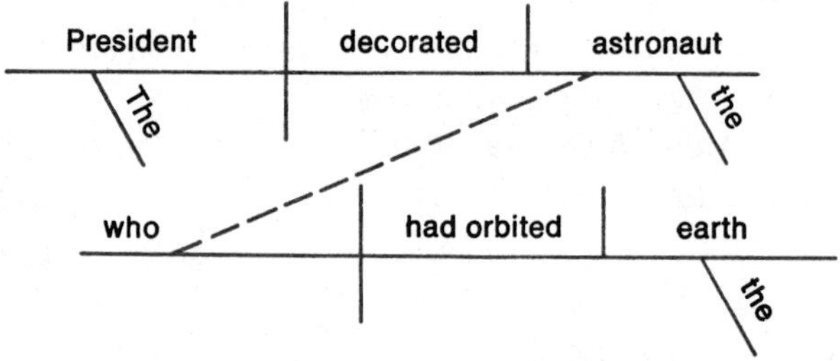


[1] Since a subordinate clause has a verb and a subject and may contain complements and modifiers, it is diagramed very much like a sentence. Adjective and adverb clauses are placed on a horizontal line below the main line. An adjective clause introduced by a relative pronoun is joined to the word it modifies by a broken line drawn from the modified word to the relative pronoun.

[2] The compound relative pronouns *whoever, whomever, whichever, whatever* may also begin clauses. Occasionally, an adjective clause may begin with a relative adverb—for example, *This is the place* where *they found the treasure.*

A relative pronoun may be the object of the verb in the clause it begins.

The bouquet was presented to the singer, **whom everyone was applauding wildly.**

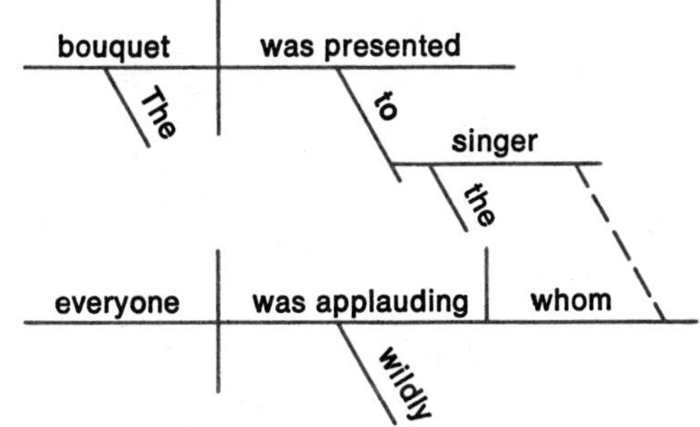


A relative pronoun may be the object of a preposition in the clause.

She is the doctor **for whom you called.**

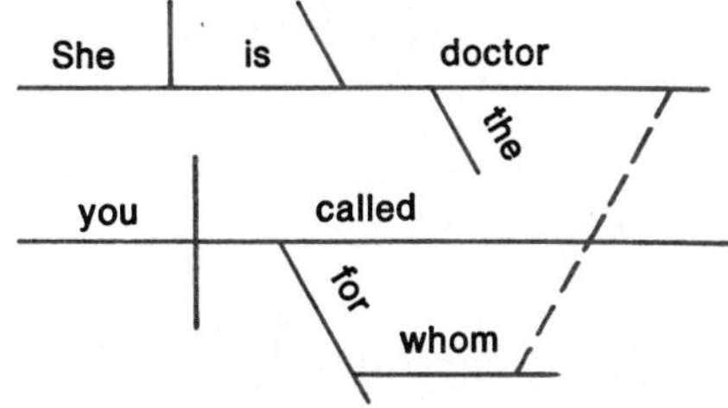


**EXERCISE 2. Identifying Adjective Clauses and the Words They Modify.** Number your paper 1–10. After the proper number, write each adjective clause in the following sentences. After each clause, write the noun or pronoun that the clause modifies. Be prepared to say whether the relative pronoun is used as the subject, object of the verb, or object of the preposition within its clause.

1. Some of us have read *Native Son,* which was written by Richard Wright.
2. The book to which he referred was ordered yesterday.
3. Many countries have festivals in March that can be traced back to ancient celebrations of spring.
4. The fish that I caught yesterday weighed three pounds.
5. The nominee was a statesman whom everyone admired.

6. It's not easy to pay attention to a speaker who mumbles.
7. The children found my briefcase, which had been missing for weeks.
8. Please list the names of all the people to whom we should go for help.
9. They permitted only people who had membership cards to enter.
10. Everyone cheered for the player that had the better serve.

GRAMMAR

## The Noun Clause

**21d. A *noun clause* is a subordinate clause used as a noun.**

EXAMPLE We appreciated **what the violinist played.**[1]

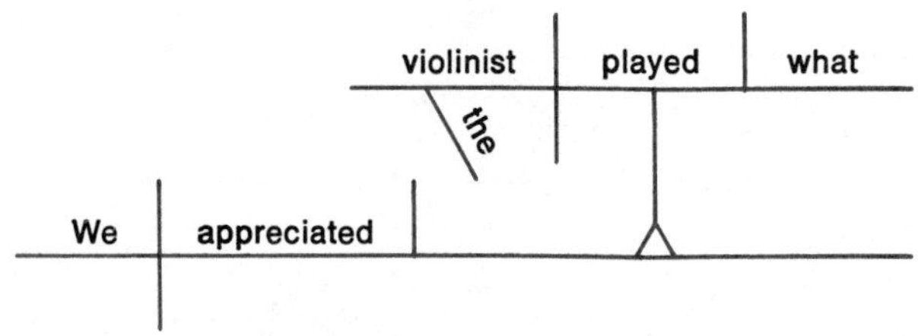


The entire clause *what the violinist played* is the direct object of the verb *appreciated.* Study the following pairs of sentences to see how a noun clause may be the subject of a verb, a predicate nominative, a direct object, an indirect object, or the object of a preposition.

His **anger** was evident. [*Anger* is a noun used as the subject of the verb *was.*] **That he was angry** was evident. [*That he was angry* is a noun clause used as the subject of the verb *was.*]

This is his **statement.** [*Statement* is a noun used as a predicate nominative.] This is **what he said.** [*What he said* is a noun clause used as a predicate nominative.]

[1] In diagraming, a noun clause is pictured as a unit by being placed at the top of a vertical line, like a pedestal, rising from the part of the diagram (subject, object, predicate nominative) to which the clause belongs.

She believes your **statement.** [*Statement* is a noun used as a direct object.]
She believes **that you told the truth.** [*That you told the truth* is a noun clause used as a direct object.]

The choreographer will give the best **dancer** the part. [*Dancer* is a noun used as an indirect object.]
The choreographer will give **whoever dances the best** the part. [*Whoever dances the best* is a noun clause used as an indirect object.]

The knowledge of his **actions** helped us all. [*Actions* is a noun used as the object of the preposition *of*.]
The knowledge of **what he had done** helped us all. [*What he had done* is a noun clause used as the object of the preposition *of*.]

Adjective and noun clauses are frequently used without an introductory relative pronoun or other joining word. Note that the introductory word is omitted in the second sentence in each of the following pairs.

George Washington said **that he did not want a third term.**
George Washington said **he did not want a third term.**

We interviewed the poet **whom everybody admired.**[1]
We interviewed the poet **everybody admired.**

**EXERCISE 3. Identifying Noun Clauses.** There is a noun clause in each of the following sentences. Write each noun clause on your paper, and label its subject and verb. After each clause, tell whether it is the subject of the sentence (*s.*), the direct object (*d.o.*), the indirect object (*i.o.*), the predicate nominative (*p.n.*), or the object of a preposition (*o.p.*).

EXAMPLES 1. Please address your letter to whoever manages the store.
S V
1. *Whoever manages the store, o.p.*

2. Do you know where the new municipal center is?
S V
2. *where the new municipal center is, d.o.*

1. Tell me what the past tense of the verb *swing* is.
2. Do you know why Jason is absent?
3. Whatever you decide will be acceptable to me.
4. Give whoever wants it the book.

[1] For exercises on *who* and *whom* in standard usage, see pages 505–507.

5. That Jill was worried seemed obvious to everyone at the party last night.
6. I will listen carefully to whatever you say.
7. The teacher said we could leave now.
8. In biology class Mrs. Carter explained how hornets build their nests.
9. The president can appoint whomever she wants to the committee.
10. All I ask is that you write legibly.



**REVIEW EXERCISE A. Distinguishing Between Adjective and Noun Clauses.** List in order on your paper the subordinate clauses in the following sentences. Before each clause, place the number of the sentence in which it appears. After each clause, tell what kind it is—adjective or noun. Be prepared to tell what word each adjective clause modifies and how each noun clause is used in the sentence—as a subject, as the object of a verb or of a preposition, or as a predicate nominative.

1. Until recently, scientists believed that the giant sequoias of California were the oldest living trees on earth.
2. Now, however, that honor is given to the bristlecone pine, a tree that few people have ever heard of.
3. Everyone who respects hardiness and pluck respects the bristlecone pine.
4. Its leaves or needles last on the branches for twelve to fifteen years, a length of time that is considered extraordinary.
5. Botanists know that the bristlecone is a member of the foxtail family.
6. What its needle clusters resemble gives the foxtail pine its interesting name.
7. The pine is a tree that is central to the economy of most northern nations.
8. Species that are native to North America are divided into two types, hard pines and soft pines.
9. Bristlecone is a species of soft pine that is highly valued for its resin.
10. The southern Rockies are where the bristlecone pine thrives naturally.

## The Adverb Clause

**21e. The *adverb clause* is a subordinate clause that, like an adverb, modifies a verb, an adjective, or an adverb.**

In the following examples, the adverb clauses modify the verb by telling *how, when, where, why, to what extent,* or *under what conditions.*

The nervous young pitcher felt **as though all eyes were on him.** [*how* he felt]
**Before she left,** she counted us. [*when* she counted us]
The students sat down **wherever they could find seats.** [*where* they sat down]
**Since no one was there,** we left. [*why* we left]
She understands mathematics better **than I do.** [*how much* or *to what extent* she understands mathematics]
Will you go to the party **if the weather is nice?**[1] [*under what conditions* you will go]

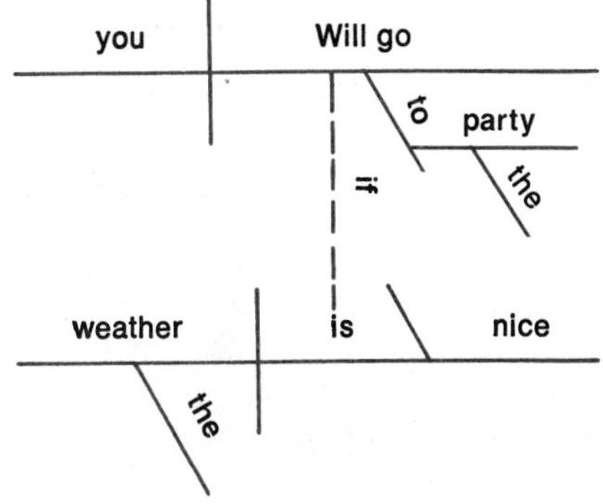


ADVERB CLAUSE MODIFYING AN ADJECTIVE

Alexander the Great was sure **that he would conquer the world.** [The adverb clause *that he would conquer the world* modifies the adjective *sure.*]

ADVERB CLAUSE MODIFYING AN ADVERB

He will arrive earlier **than I will.** [The adverb clause *than I will* modifies the adverb *earlier.*]

[1] In diagraming, an adverb clause is written on a horizontal line below the main line of the diagram. The conjunction beginning the clause is written on a broken line that links the verb of the clause to the word the clause modifies.

GRAMMAR

## The Subordinating Conjunction

**21f. A conjunction that begins an adverb clause is called a *subordinating conjunction.* It joins the clause to the rest of the sentence.**

*Common Subordinating Conjunctions*[1]

| | | | |
|---|---|---|---|
| after | as though | since | when |
| although | because | so that | whenever |
| as | before | than | where |
| as if | if | though | wherever |
| as long as | in order that | unless | while |
| as soon as | provided that | until | |

## The Elliptical (Incomplete) Clause

Sometimes in their writing and speaking, people do not complete the adverb clauses they use.

EXAMPLES Roger was more familiar with the rules than Elgin [was].
While [he was] painting, Rembrandt could concentrate completely.

In these adverb clauses, the part of the clause given in brackets has been omitted. The complete clause, however, is in the writer's and the reader's mind. Such incomplete clauses are said to be *elliptical.* (For the correct use of pronouns in elliptical clauses see pages 508–509.)

An elliptical clause is diagramed as if the missing element or elements were present.

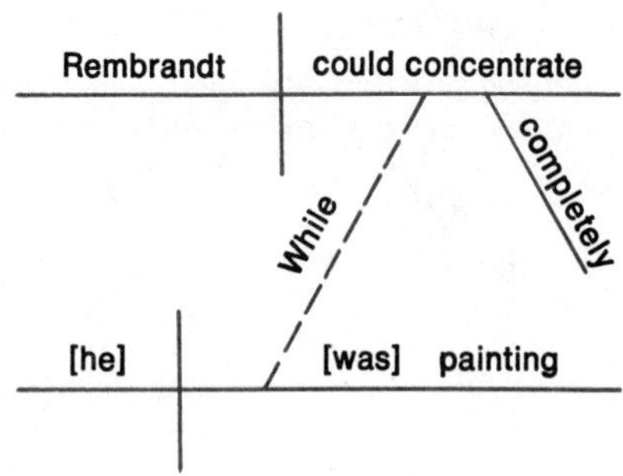


[1] Many of these words may also be used as other parts of speech.

**EXERCISE 4. Identifying Adverb Clauses and the Words They Modify.** After the proper number, write the adverb clauses in the following sentences. Draw a line under the subordinating conjunction that introduces the clause. After each clause, write the word or expression that the clause modifies. Be prepared to state whether the clause describes *how, when, where, why, to what extent,* or *under what conditions.* (Since interpretations of the meaning may differ, more than one correct answer may be possible.)

EXAMPLE 1. If we stop by the mall, then we might be late for the movie.
1. *If we stop by the mall; might be; under what conditions.*

1. When our school has a fire drill, everyone must quickly leave the building.
2. Do not raise your hand in this class unless you know the answer to the question.
3. She walked until she was too tired to take another step.
4. Because Mr. Jimeney had many papers to carry, he bought a briefcase.
5. Gazelles require speed so that they can outrun their enemies.
6. Return this radio for a full refund if you are not completely satisfied.
7. When you go to Washington, visit the Folger Library.
8. You can help by setting the table while I prepare the salad.
9. The beavers are astounding builders because they use only their powerful front teeth and broad, flat tails.
10. You understood the situation much better than I did.

**REVIEW EXERCISE B. Identifying Independent and Subordinate Clauses; Classifying Subordinate Clauses.** Identify each of the following italicized clauses as independent or subordinate. If the clause is subordinate, identify it as an adverb, an adjective, or a noun clause. State the function of each noun clause within its sentence.

EXAMPLE 1. *Whoever wins the next match* must play the state champion.
1. *subordinate, noun clause, subject*

1. *If you buy your ticket in advance,* you will not have to worry.
2. My grandparents, *who came to the United States fifty years ago,* can captivate me for hours with their stories.
3. *Unless you are looking for an argument,* don't discuss politics with Uncle Frank.

4. According to some experts on nutrition, you are *what you eat.*
5. We had a heated discussion about altering the electoral college, but *we could not resolve our differences of opinion.*
6. The assignment *that we were given* was to write a short essay.
7. In a speech today, Governor Lee announced *she would do everything possible to limit the proposed sales-tax increase.*
8. *When it was first built in 1825,* the Erie Canal, connecting the Atlantic seaboard to the West, charged tolls.
9. The newscaster announced *that the cornerstone for the new city library would be set in place in a ceremony later today.*
10. Franklin Roosevelt, *who was the only man elected to the Presidency four times,* died early in his fourth term.

### WRITING APPLICATION A:
### Using Subordination in Your Writing

Subordination allows you to express the relationship between two unequal ideas within a single sentence. You, as the writer, determine which of the two ideas to subordinate, or give less importance to. As you read the following sentences, notice which ideas the writer has subordinated.

(adverb clause)
**When we were in Washington, D.C., last September,** we went to the National Air and Space Museum.

(adjective clause)
Mrs. Borden, **who was my eighth-grade social studies teacher,** moved to Florida.

### Writing Assignment

Write a fictional narrative, using subordination wherever appropriate. When you revise, check to see that you have used subordination effectively.

## SENTENCES CLASSIFIED ACCORDING TO STRUCTURE

**21g. Classified according to their structure, there are four kinds of sentences:** ***simple, compound, complex,*** **and** ***compound-complex.***

**(1) A *simple sentence* is a sentence with one independent clause and no subordinate clauses.**

EXAMPLE The defeat of Napoleon at Waterloo was a victory for England.

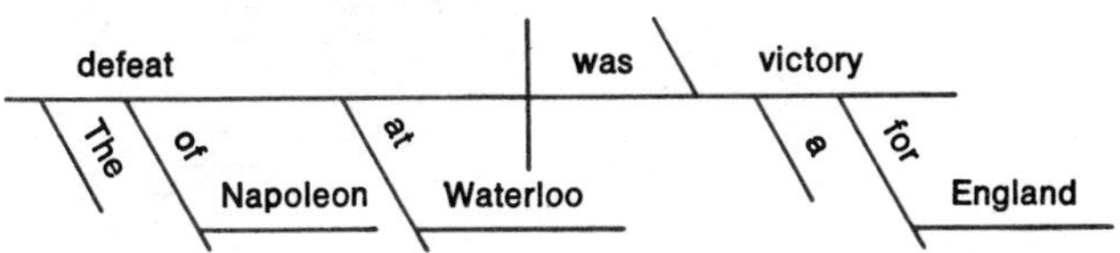


**(2) A *compound sentence* is a sentence that is composed of two or more independent clauses but no subordinate clauses.**

EXAMPLE The defeat of Napoleon was a victory for England, but it meant the end of an era of French grandeur.

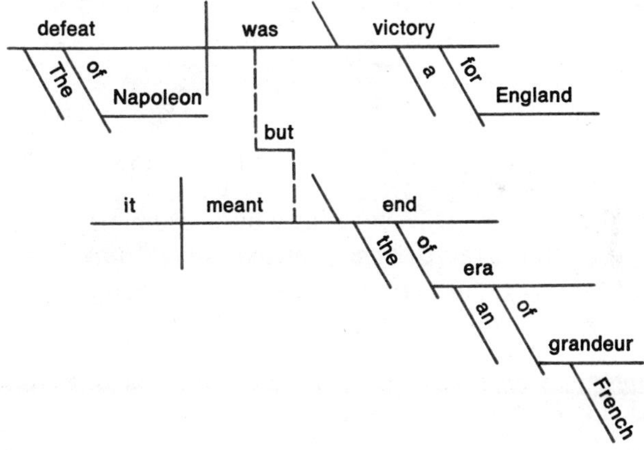


> NOTE Be careful not to confuse the compound subject or predicate of a simple sentence with the clauses of a compound sentence.

The archaeological discovery was made in the spring and was widely acclaimed in the fall. [simple sentence with compound predicate]

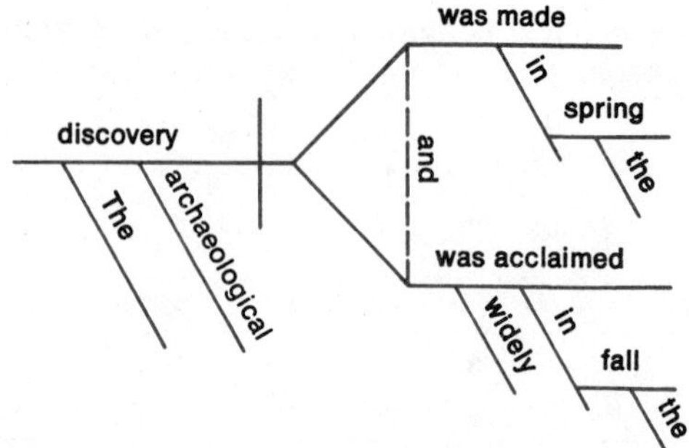


The archaeological discovery was made in the spring, and it was widely acclaimed in the fall. [compound sentence with two subjects and two verbs]

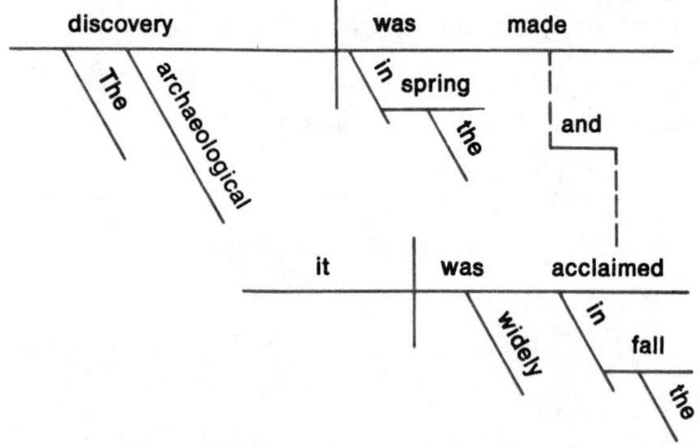


Independent clauses may be joined by coordinating conjunctions (*and, but, for, nor, or, yet*) or by conjunctive adverbs (*accordingly, also, besides, consequently, furthermore, hence, however, moreover, nevertheless, still, then, therefore, thus*).

**(3) A *complex sentence* is a sentence that contains one independent clause and at least one subordinate clause.**

The man who looks for trouble often finds it. [The independent clause is *The man often finds it.* The subordinate clause is *who looks for trouble.*]

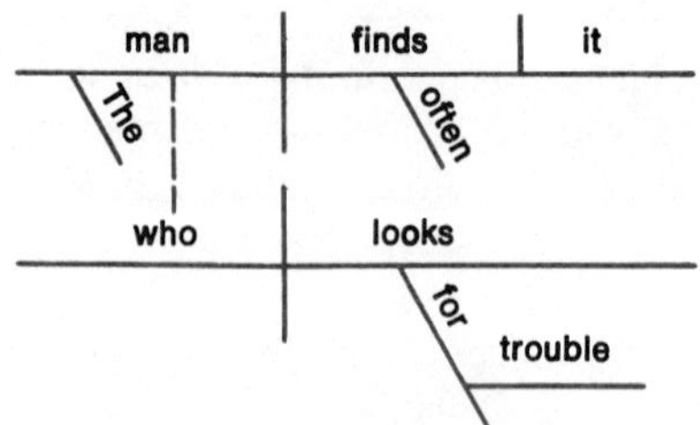

**(4) A *compound-complex sentence* is a sentence that contains two or more independent clauses and at least one subordinate clause.**

The man who looks for trouble often finds it, but then he does not want it.

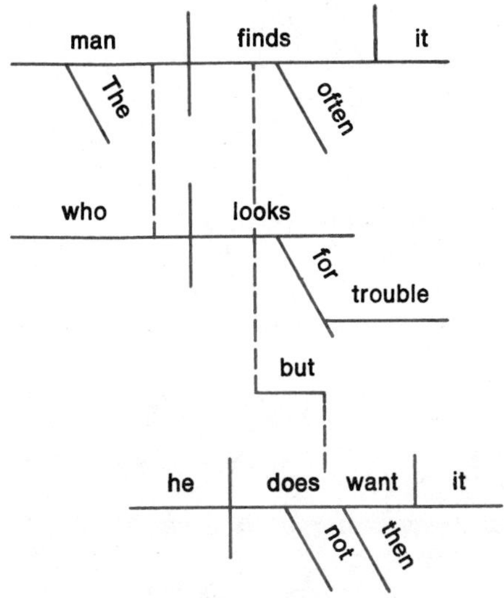


**EXERCISE 5. Identifying Sentences as Simple, Compound, Complex, or Compound-Complex.** Number your paper 1–10. After the proper number, tell which kind each sentence is: simple, compound, complex, or compound-complex.

1. Charles Drew did research on blood plasma and helped develop blood banks.
2. The month of March supposedly comes in like a lion and goes out like a lamb.
3. The Malayans believe that sickness will follow the eating of stolen foods.
4. When World War I ended in 1918, almost everybody thought that there would be no more wars; but twenty-one years later, World War II began.
5. In his letter to Mrs. Bixby, Abraham Lincoln consoled her for the loss of several sons and hoped that time would ease her sorrow.
6. After the announcement had been made, students cheered the team and clapped enthusiastically.

7. In England and Wales, where salmon was once king, few salmon rivers remain.
8. The great English philosopher Thomas Hobbes once aspired to be a mathematician, but he never fulfilled this career ambition.
9. As an older woman, Queen Elizabeth I always wore a dark-red wig, so no one knew whether her own hair had grayed or not.
10. Lee Trevino is considered by many to be one of the best golf players in America.

**EXERCISE 6. Writing a Variety of Sentences.** Write in the following order: two simple sentences, two compound sentences, four complex sentences, and two compound-complex sentences. In the complex and compound-complex sentences, draw a line under each subordinate clause.

### WRITING APPLICATION B: Using a Variety of Sentence Structures to Enliven Your Writing

Notice in the following paragraph that the writer has used a variety of sentence structures to add vitality to his writing.

> George Willard, the Ohio village boy, was fast growing into manhood and new thoughts had been coming into his mind. (CD) All that day, amid the jam of people at the Fair, he had gone about feeling lonely. (S) He was about to leave Winesburg to go away to some city where he hoped to get work on a city newspaper and he felt grown-up. (CD-CX) The mood that had taken possession of him was a thing known to men and unknown to boys. (CX) He felt old and a little tired. (S) Memories awoke in him. (S) To his mind his new sense of maturity set him apart, made of him a half-tragic figure. (S) He wanted someone to understand the feeling that had taken possession of him after his mother's death. (CX)
>
> SHERWOOD ANDERSON

#### Writing Assignment

Write a narrative about an important experience in your life. Use a variety of sentence structures to enliven your writing. When you revise, check to see that you have used a variety of sentence structures.

## CHAPTER 21 REVIEW: POSTTEST 1



**A. Identifying Independent and Subordinate Clauses; Classifying Subordinate Clauses.** Identify each italicized group of words as an independent clause or a subordinate clause. If it is a subordinate clause, identify it as an adverb, an adjective, or a noun clause.

EXAMPLE 1. Mike and Betty, *who were visiting us over the weekend,* left and returned to Rhode Island.
1. *subordinate, adjective clause*

1. *Whenever Jim practices the clarinet,* his neighbor's dog howls.
2. Advertisements encourage people to want products, and *many people cannot distinguish between their wants and their needs.*
3. In science class we learned *that chalk is made up mostly of calcium carbonate.*
4. Liliuokalani, *who was the last Queen of Hawaii,* was an accomplished songwriter.
5. Do you know *how you can protect yourself* if a tornado strikes?
6. *If there is a tornado warning,* go quickly to the lowest level in your house, cover your head with your hands, and lie flat or crouch low until the danger is past.
7. The Indians *who inhabited the area of Connecticut around the Naugatuck River* were called the Pequots.
8. *When you enter the school,* the principal's office is the second room on your right.
9. *That the girls' volleyball team was well coached* was demonstrated last night when the team won the state championship.
10. *American music has been enriched by Ella Fitzgerald, Lena Horne, and Leslie Uggams,* who are all contemporary black vocalists.

**B. Identifying Sentences According to Structure.** Identify each of the following sentences as simple, compound, complex, or compound-complex.

11. People frequently consider politicians dishonest, yet these same people continually reelect the same politicians.
12. Before the Pilgrims disembarked, they had agreed on a specific form of government; this decision on self-government and democracy is called the Mayflower Compact.

13. Although women and servants did not sign, forty-one adult males did sign the Mayflower Compact.
14. If you take a computer course, you will learn that the computer will respond only to specific commands.
15. John Hay, who was a writer, a historian, and Secretary of State under President McKinley, urged the nations of the world to respect Chinese rights; this idea is called the Open Door policy.
16. The proposed city hall, our city council's "architectural masterpiece," has drawn more negative than positive comments.
17. As community residents, several officials, and members of the media looked on, the mayor broke ground for the new city hall.
18. Dr. Helen Clarke, the city's health director, spoke to our biology class about the need for childhood immunizations.
19. That the class was well prepared for the test was obvious.
20. The warm weather will break once this afternoon's anticipated storm arrives.

---

## CHAPTER 21 REVIEW: POSTTEST 2

**Writing a Variety of Sentence Structures.** Write ten sentences according to the following guidelines:

1. Write a simple sentence with a compound subject.
2. Write a compound sentence with the conjunction *but.*
3. Write a complex sentence with an adverb clause modifying an adverb.
4. Write a complex sentence with an adverb clause modifying an adjective.
5. Write a complex sentence with an adjective clause introduced by the relative pronoun *who.*
6. Write a complex sentence with an adjective clause introduced by the relative pronoun *that.*
7. Write a complex sentence with a noun clause used as the subject of the sentence.
8. Write a complex sentence with a noun clause used as the direct object of the sentence.
9. Write a complex sentence with an elliptical adverb clause.
10. Write a compound-complex sentence.

# CHAPTER 22

# American English

## THE VARIETIES OF ENGLISH

USAGE

One of the first things anyone notices about language is that different groups of people speak the same language differently. English people speak differently from Americans, and New Yorkers speak differently from Texans. Special groups such as fishers, miners, or railroad workers have a special vocabulary that they use among themselves. Different social classes often use different varieties of language.

This phenomenon is the result of a historical process. Factors of distance, occupation and class isolate groups from one another. Since language is constantly changing, over time each group develops its own *dialect* of the language it shares with other groups.

In this chapter, you will study how American English has developed through the historical movements of the various groups who speak it. You will also study the levels of usage as they apply to your own listening, speaking, and writing.

### AMERICAN ENGLISH DIALECTS

The history of American English begins with the physical separation of two groups: those who remained in England and those who came to America. We must realize that the colonists, coming from many different parts of Britain, spoke as many dialects of British English. They settled in separate communities that had very little contact with each other. Thus none of the settlements was quite like any other language group anywhere. It was from these differing communities that most of the rest of the United States was ultimately settled, and it was from their dialects that modern American English dialects developed.

## Eastern New England and Southern

Eastern New England, the coastal Southeast, South Midland, North Midland, and Northern are the five most clearly definable dialect regions of the United States. They can be traced to four early centers of population—Boston, Charleston/Richmond, Pennsylvania, and northern New York/western New England. The first two regions—eastern New England and the coastal, or tidewater, region of the Southeast—shared certain circumstances of linguistic development. First, the people of each were content to stay where they were. Neither region lost many settlers to the streams of migration that populated the rest of the country. Boston prospered as a major commercial center. Other coastal cities thrived as fishing, whaling and sailing ports. The same well-being and prosperity characterized Charleston and Richmond and the plantation economy of the Southeast. As a result, the dialects of the two regions remained relatively confined geographically.



Second, the economic and cultural importance of the East and South gave their dialects a social importance not shared by the other regions. At least until recently, the tidewater dialect in the South and the eastern New England dialect in the North were the prestige dialects of American English. In the older schoolbooks and dictionaries, for example, the concept of standard English was often influenced by the writer's New England pronunciation. Even today there is a widespread notion that there is something superior about the New England way of saying *aunt* with a "broad *a*" as in *father.*

## Midland: South and North

Between the New England and the Southern coastal areas lie two other population centers through which flowed most of the migration that settled the rest of the country. In the first half of the eighteenth century, a large wave of Scotch-Irish left Northern Ireland and came to Pennsylvania. Most of them did not stay there long. They moved southward along the mountains into the valleys of West Virginia, the Shenandoah of Virginia, and the southern piedmonts of the Carolinas and Georgia.

American English Dialect Regions

Some of them crossed westward through West Virginia to the vicinity of the Ohio River. Still others traveled southwest across the mountains into Tennessee.

Because all these people came from the same part of the British Isles, they spread approximately the same dialect across the entire upland region of the middle and south Atlantic states. And they kept moving west, to the Mississippi and beyond, carrying their South Midland dialect through Tennessee and Kentucky, the northern fringe of Georgia, Alabama, and Mississippi, southern Indiana and Illinois, to Arkansas, Oklahoma, and southern Missouri.

Later, another group of people from Pennsylvania went westward to central Ohio, Indiana, and Illinois. This area, which starts in Pennsylvania, forms a distinct but related dialect region called North Midland.



### Northern

The second large group of people who moved west came from central and northern New York and western New England. This group went by way of the Erie Canal, the Great Lakes, and overland through northern Pennsylvania, Ohio, Indiana, and Illinois to Michigan, Wisconsin, and beyond. This area makes up the modern American dialect region called Northern.

### The Mississippi and Beyond

The dialects of the regions west of the Mississippi are more difficult to trace with certainty. In general, the Southern dialect has extended along the Gulf of Mexico as far west as Texas. The Northern and Midland dialects—with much mixing and crossing—have reached in parallel bands west to the Pacific. However, as a result of northward movements of South Midland settlers and southwestward movements of Northern settlers, the areas have become so mixed that any definite statement about them is open to question and is probably of no great value.

**EXERCISE 1. Understanding the Development of American English Dialects.** To test your knowledge of what you have just read, write short answers to the following questions.

1. List at least two things that lead to the growth of differences between dialects.

2. Why is it difficult to relate a particular American English dialect to a particular British English dialect?
3. List the five main dialect regions of American English, and write one or two short sentences about the source and extent of each.

## CHARACTERISTICS OF AMERICAN ENGLISH DIALECTS

The dialects of American English are becoming less distinct from one another as time passes. Many distinguishing features of our local dialects are being removed by education, television, radio, and movies, which present a relatively uniform language model. Language researchers now must turn to older residents of a dialect area to study its vocabulary, sounds, and grammar. Much of this language research can be found in the various linguistic atlases of the United States and Canada. The most complete survey of American dialect variation is Frederick G. Cassidy's *Dictionary of American Regional English.*

USAGE

### Vocabulary

Dialect differences in vocabulary are most often found among words that are handed down orally. The following list compares words as they are used in various sections of the country.

| ENE[1] | N | NM | SM | S |
|---|---|---|---|---|
| brook | creek | creek, run | branch, run | branch |
| night crawler | angleworm | fishworm | red worm, fishworm | fishing worm |
| darning needle (i.e., the dragonfly) | darning needle | snake feeder | snake doctor, snake feeder | snake doctor |
| bonnyclabber | clobbered milk | clabber (milk) | clabber (milk) | clabber |
| spider (i.e., frying pan) | spider | skillet | skillet | spider |
| carry | carry | pack | pack | tote |
| (corn) husks | husks | husks | shucks | shucks |

Most of these words are household terms, names of foods, common animals, children's games, and so forth. Occasionally, however, terms

[1] The abbreviations used here and throughout this chapter are ENE (Eastern New England), N (North), NM (North Midland), SM (South Midland), S (South).

for new things are developed independently in different regions, and these differences are preserved for a considerable time. Examples are the terms *picture show* and *central,* now generally replaced by *movie* and (*telephone*) *operator,* and words associated with the modern superhighway. The highway itself is, in different areas, *thruway, parkway, freeway,* and *turnpike;* the area at the edge of the paved strip may be the *verge, berm,* or *shoulder;* and an intersection with another road may be an *exit* or *interchange.*

## Pronunciation

Probably the first time you noticed another way of speaking, or dialect, it was brought to your attention by a different pronunciation. This is the most obvious area of dialect difference and one that persists when vocabulary and grammar have become uniform. The following list of characteristic sound features in our five dialects can be used as a test for yourself and your class to see how closely you conform to the dialect in your area. If there are differences, they can probably be traced to your parents' dialect or to the influence of education and mass media.



1. The absence of noticeable *r* sounds at the end of a word like *far* or *father* and before consonants in such words as *card, heard, fort,* etc. [S and ENE]

2. An *oo* sound, like the vowel of *food,* in words like *Tuesday, duty, new.* [ENE, NM, and N]

3. The vowels of *morning* and *mourning* are, respectively, "aw" and "oh," as "mawrning-mohrning." [N, S, and SM]

4. The vowel of *path, half, dance* is similar to the vowel of *father.* The same vowel is regularly heard also (long and without the *r*) in words like *barn* and *yard.* [ENE]

5. The vowel of *on, off, fog, frog,* and *wash* is "aw." [M and S. A shorter, but similar, sound is found in ENE.]

The vowel of *on, off,* etc., is like the vowel of *father.* [N]

6. The sound represented by the *s* in *greasy* and in the verb *grease* is the "ss" sound in *hiss.* [ENE, N, and NM]

The *s* in *greasy* and *grease* has a "z" sound. [SM and S]

7. The *ou* of *house* is made up of an "ah" plus an "oo." [ENE, N, NM]

The *ou* of *house* is made up of the short *a* in *cat* plus an "oo." [SM, S]

8. The title *Mrs.* is pronounced as one syllable with a "z"—"Mizz." [This is a notable characteristic of S and parts of SM. Other areas pronounce this as "mississ" or "mizziz."]

## Grammar

Grammar in American dialects is much less varied than are pronunciation and vocabulary. Furthermore, many grammatical differences are limited to nonstandard speech idioms. The following expressions are characteristic of the five dialect regions.

1. The past-tense form *waked up* and the phrase *all to once* are features especially characteristic of ENE. Elsewhere *woke up* and *all at once* are more common.

2. Common to ENE and the whole of the Northern region are *sick to* (one's) *stomach,* (he's not) *to home,* (you) *hadn't ought* (to do it), *begin* and *see* as past-tense forms.

3. The past-tense form *seen* is found most often in the Midland area but is spreading into the North. Also typical of Midland speech are the second-person plural pronoun *you-uns,* (this is) *all the farther* (I go), *wait on you* (i.e., "wait for you"), *want off* (i.e. "want to get off"), *a quarter till* (twelve).

4. Forms typical of SM are the *sun raised*, the past-tense form *shrinkt,* the pronouns *ourn, yourn, hisn,* etc. (for *ours, yours, his,* etc.).

5. Common to S and SM are the second-person plural pronoun *y'all, might could* (i.e., "might be able to"), the use of *done* in (she) *done* (told you), (he) *used to didn't* (like tomatoes), the ending *-es* (pronounced *-iz*) after *-st, -sp, -sk* in *postes, fistes,waspes, taskes.*

USAGE

**EXERCISE 2. Understanding the Characteristics of American English Dialects.** Make a brief dialect survey of your classmates or of members of your community. If you find differences in their speech, try to explain how they came about. These items will help you.

1. How are the following groups of words pronounced? (See the text, page 460, for the pronunciation of some of these.)
   a. dew, new, Tuesday
   b. loud, mountain, house (noun), house (verb)
   c. horse, hoarse; forty, fourteen
   d. poor, your [An "oh" vowel is common in S and SM]
   e. on, hog, fog
   f. Mary, merry, marry [These are said, respectively, with the vowels of *late, wet,* and *hat* in some areas, like the S; in other areas, for example, Midland, these are all said with the same vowel sound, that of *wet.*]

2. What is the usual term for the following? Are other terms known? (The terms supplied as answers suggest how varied the responses can be; they are not the only terms known.) In asking questions of this kind, try to avoid suggesting the possible answer.
   a. a container for liquid having a bail or movable handle: *pail, bucket.*
   b. the area of the house between the front steps and the front door: *porch, stoop, piazza.*
   c. the fresh cheese made from strained milk curd: *cottage cheese, Dutch cheese, smearcase.*
   d. a small round, tubular cake made by frying in deep fat: *doughnut, fried cake, raised doughnut, cake doughnut.*
   e. the window curtain that rolls down from the top: *roller shades, blinds, shades.*



## WRITING APPLICATION: Reflecting Varieties of English in Writing Dialogue

The varieties of language are called dialects. When people are speaking casually, their language usually shows some differences in pronunciation, idioms, vocabulary, grammar, and usage. If you are writing dialogue, you may want to reflect the speakers' dialects to make the conversation seem realistic.

EXAMPLE "How old are you," asked Jem, "four-and-a-half?"

"Goin' on seven."

"Shoot no wonder, then," said Jem, jerking his thumb at me.

"Scout yonder's been readin' ever since she was born, and she ain't even started to school yet. You look right puny for goin' on seven."

"I'm little but I'm old," he said.

HARPER LEE

### Writing Assignment

Write a dialogue between two people engaged in casual conversation. Try to experiment with dialect differences. Use nonstandard English if you like. The conversation should make some point. Remember to indent for each speaker and to use quotation marks correctly.

## LOAN WORDS

Even an emerging "standard" American English will retain a good many differences, especially of pronunciation. One thing that distinguishes American English from forms spoken elsewhere, however, is the presence of features common to the nation as a whole. For example, we have adopted a variety of *loan words* through our contacts over the generations with speakers of other languages.

### American Indian Loan Words

The first group of these loan words is borrowed from the American Indian languages of North America. Like all word borrowings, these loan words reflect the extent of the contact between two peoples. On the simplest level, they name or identify places, animals and plants, foods, and things from Indian culture. The largest group includes names given to places and to bodies of water—rivers, lakes, creeks, mountains and hills, streets, parks, towns, counties, and states. As an indication of how many words we have borrowed from the native Americans, the names of at least twenty-six of the fifty states are Indian in origin.

Our treatment of Indian words shows considerable variety. We usually shortened the words and adapted them to English sound patterns in direct borrowings. We took *Mackinac* from *michilimackinac,* for example, and altered *shahiyena* to get *Cheyenne.* Probably the majority of Indian place-names are tribal or personal or descriptive names chosen by whites who had some knowledge of Indian names or languages. Personal names of well-known Indians are preserved in the names of cities such as *Pontiac* and *Osceola,* tribal names in *Miami, Huron,* and *Mandan.* Descriptive names either were left in an approximation of their original form, as with *Chicago,* "place of wild onions," or were translated into an English equivalent, as with the *Big Horn* or *Yellowstone* rivers. Yellowstone is in fact a double translation, deriving from the French *roche jaune,* which is in turn a rendering of an Indian name *mitsiadazi.*

After the country was completely settled, contact between Indians and newcomers was drastically curtailed. Our word borrowings went into decline, until now the Indian words we use other than placenames are relatively few. Even so, the list reflects the nature of the settlers' relations with the people they joined on the new continent. The settlers learned and borrowed the names of new plants and animals (*hickory, squash, chipmunk, skunk*) and new foods (*hominy, pone, succotash*).

Usually, they kept some form of an Indian word for things associated with the Indian culture (*papoose, moccasin, tomahawk*). Many of these terms have undergone interesting changes since their adoption into English. In one such change, the original forms were altered to bring them closer to forms familiar to speakers of English. Two examples are the Algonquian words *otchek* and *musquash,* which became *woodchuck* and *muskrat.* The woodchuck does live in or near the woods and the muskrat is a rodent that gives off a musky odor.

Another type of change is semantic; that is, it affects the meaning of a word. *Powwow* and *mugwump* are interesting examples. *Powwow* was originally a term for "medicine man." Soon, however, it came to mean a ceremony at which magic or "medicine" was practiced. Later it was generalized to mean any council of Indians or conference with them. Finally it was extended to its present sense of almost any conference or gathering for discussions. The second term, *mugwump,* originally meant "great chief," but, perhaps as a result of its sound, it came to have comic or playful overtones. In 1884 it was applied to the "rump" Republicans who left the party to support the Democratic candidate, Grover Cleveland. Following this, it acquired the generally favorable sense of an independent in politics. Recently, however, it has again become a somewhat unflattering term for a political opportunist who hopes to benefit by giving support to both sides. The term in this sense is imaginatively derived from the name of a supposed bird who "sits on the fence with its 'mug' on one side and its 'wump' on the other."



## Loan Words from Other Languages

Hundreds of words in American English come from foreign languages. The words were adopted either from immigrants or from foreign-speaking areas absorbed into the United States. Waves of immigrants came first from Germany, then from Scandinavia in the nineteenth century. In the 1890's and succeeding decades they came mostly from the South European and Slavic countries. Among the foreign-language areas that became parts of the United States were Spanish settlements in the Southwest and California and French communities in Maine and Louisiana.

### French

The earliest of our foreign-language contacts were with the French. Our French borrowings, of course, have continued virtually ever since. Many of our first borrowings from French (*bayou, toboggan, caribou*) had been taken by the French from the Indians. Most of the remaining words are, like these, terms for things peculiar enough to America that the newcomers had to invent words for them. Among them were plants and animals (*pumpkin, gopher*), foods (*chowder, jambalaya*), features of the land (*butte, coulee, levee, prairie*). Others include *bureau* (furniture), *depot* (railway station), *portage, charivari, lacrosse, parlay, picayune.*

### Spanish

The majority of loan words from Spanish are of later date, deriving from relatively late nineteenth-century contacts with the ranching culture of the Southwest and Mexico. A few can be traced to South American or Central American Spanish. Borrowings include words for specific types of clothing (*chaps, poncho, sombrero*), architectural features (*adobe, patio, plaza, pueblo*), ranching terms (*cinch, corral, lariat, lasso, ranch, rodeo, stampede*), plants and animals (*alfalfa, mesquite, bronco, burro, coyote, mustang*), foods (*chile con carne, tamale, tortilla*), and a variety of other things (*canyon, filibuster, savvy, stevedore, tornado*).

Like Indian words, Spanish loan words were often changed to make them sound more like familiar English syllables or words. The *j* in the Mexican Spanish word *juzgado* ("minor court") would have sounded to English ears rather like an *h,* and the *d* in some Mexican dialects would have been entirely lost. With the stress shifted in English fashion to the first syllable, it became in American English, quite reasonably, *hoosegow.* Similarly, Spanish *vamos* or *vámonos* ("let's go") was altered at two separate times into different Anglicized forms and acquired in the process two different senses in English: *vamoose* ("leave hurriedly") and *mosey* ("move along or stroll"). The first syllable of *vaquero,* "cowboy," pronounced "bac" in Spanish, was changed to the familiar English *buck* by the natural association of cowboys with *bucking* horses. The result was the American English word *buckaroo.* The Spanish word *galón,* meaning "braid," originally applied to sombreros decorated with numerous braids at the base of the crown. It was mistakenly associated with the English word *gallon,* producing in English *ten-* (or *five-*) *gallon hat.* Thus the word is often mistakenly thought to derive from the amount of water the hat can hold.

### German

In the seventeenth and eighteenth centuries, there was extensive German immigration into areas of Pennsylvania. The communities these

Germans established remained almost completely separated in language and culture from their neighbors. The language of these communities, now known as Pennsylvania Dutch (derived from the German word *Deutsch*, meaning "German"), has been greatly affected by linguistic change, especially through the introduction of English vocabulary. In spite of this, these people have been so close-knit that even now, after nearly 200 years, about a fourth of them still speak this variety of German.

In the second quarter of the 1800's and again in the 1880's, additional very large waves of German immigrants settled principally in the cities of the Northeast and Midwest. Here, until quite recent times, large communities of German-speaking Americans maintained their own schools, churches, and even newspapers. The influence of the Pennsylvania and later German settlements on the English language appears to have been primarily in the areas of food, drink, and social activities. Some of our loan words in this area are *delicatessen, frankfurter, hamburger, noodle, pretzel,* and *sauerkraut.* A number of other borrowings testify to the English-speaking American's ability to recognize and adopt a useful and picturesque term: *bum, fresh* ("impudent"), *loafer, nix, ouch, phooey, spiel.*



### Other Languages

The variety of borrowings from other languages is nearly as great as the variety of national origins. Italian, for example, contributes the names of many foods—*spaghetti, ravioli, pizza.* From the Swedish we have *smorgasbord,* and from Dutch, *cookie, waffle, boss, dumb* ("stupid"), *spook.* Finally, from the several African languages we have a variety of words, several of which are fairly well known outside local areas of the South—*gumbo, goober, voodoo, juke* (as in "jukebox").

## AMERICANISMS

Another distinctive feature of American English is the presence of considerable numbers of expressions not found in other varieties of English—or at least not until introduced by American movies and television programs. The very large number of these Americanisms, or new coinages from native English materials, can be seen by looking at the *Dictionary of Americanisms,* published by the University of Chicago Press. This dictionary consists of 1,911 pages of definitions and includes tens of thousands of items, each of which is a word, a compound, or a special sense or meaning that appeared for the first time in American English.

This peculiarly American vocabulary is a subject that has aroused a remarkable amount of comment, much of it prejudiced, ill-informed, and even foolish. Comparative judgments are always dangerous, but it appears that American, as contrasted with British English, has been much more active in the creation of new words and senses. Many of these creations are perfectly sober terms that excite little attention and pass pretty much unnoticed. Examples are *caption* (words beneath a picture or cartoon), *schedule* (a plan of working or action, a timetable), *pocketbook* (a purse), *excelsior* (fine wood shavings used as packing material), *headlight* (light on the front of a vehicle), *chicken wire* (wire mesh used to form an enclosure for chickens), *belittle* (to disparage). But many, too, are picturesque coinages of slang or the uninhibited creations of the street and the world of commerce, all of which, in our society, move quickly into the pages of the popular newspapers and magazines, and from there into general usage. It is this kind of Americanism that is noticed by the casual critic, who at once concludes that the American vocabulary is composed chiefly of words like *rip-off, photostat, hocus-pocus,* and *brunch.* True, this is an interesting, vigorous, and distinctive element in American English; we should not conclude, however, that it is the only one.



## Generalization and Specialization

Many Americanisms are special developments of words that already existed in British English. In some of these, American English broadened, or *generalized,* the earlier sense. In British English, for example, *laundry* referred only to the place where the washing is done; in American English the term has been generalized to include the articles to be washed, as in "take the laundry to the laundry." In British English *pie* originally referred only to a type of pastry filled with meat. In American English it more often refers to one filled with fruit or some flavored sweet.

The opposite process may also have taken place, and the usual meaning of some words may be more restricted, or *specialized,* in American English. *Corn* in Britain refers to grain in general, whereas in the United States the word is applied specifically to maize. A somewhat different kind of restriction is seen in *mean.* Its British English definitions range in meaning from "low in social rank" through "petty or ignoble" to "stingy." In American English it almost always means "ill-natured" or "vicious." This is, of course, not merely a reduction in the breadth of meaning. It is a loss (or near loss) of some senses and the addition of a new one. Similarly, in England *lumber* referred to a collection of more or less useless articles, as in the term *lumber room* for what Americans would call a *storeroom.* In America *lumber* came to be applied also to cut timber, a sense which soon entirely replaced the earlier one.

## Technical Words

Another rich source of Americanisms is in the more or less technical areas where new terms have developed independently for things invented since the separation of America from Britain. In railroading we have in the United States *railroad* (British English *railway*), *conductor* (*guard*), *engineer* (*engine driver*), *freight train* (*goods train*), *cowcatcher* (*plough*), *switch* (*points*). In automobile terms we have *windshield* (*windscreen*), *fender* (*wing*), *hood* (*bonnet*), *house trailer* (*caravan*). In other areas we have *streetcar* (*tram*), *flashlight* (*torch*), *long-distance call* (*trunk call*), *wrench* (*spanner*), *thumbtack* (*drawing pin*), *installment plan* (*hirepurchase*), *hardware store* (*ironmongers*), and *five- and ten-cent store* (*bazaar*).



## Compound Words

Many American creations are compound words, which make up the largest category of new formations. Some of these were created to name things met for the first time by Americans in their new country; others derive from special developments of a new civilization; and many are metaphorical expressions of attitudes taken by Americans toward features of their environment. All these types are found in the following: *catbird, cottonwood, log cabin, hired hand, lame duck, doubleheader, rain check, stopover, soap opera, ghost town, rat race, sweatshop, double talk.*

## Other Ways of Adding Words

American English also includes many new words formed by adding suffixes, by shortening, and by combining elements in different ways. The old verb-forming suffix *-ize* and the suffixes *-ist* and *-ician,* indicating one who performs or specializes, are three of our numerous active word-forming suffixes. They give us words such as *itemize, slenderize, hospitalize, receptionist, cornetist, beautician, mortician.* Shortening, or *clipping,* of long words is an old practice in English that continues to be active in America: *coed* (from *coeducational*), *prefab* (from *prefabricated*), *gym* (from *gymnasium*), *gas* (from *gasoline*), *pop* (from *soda pop*), *phone* (from *telephone*). *Blending,* or the combining of elements of two words into one, is especially popular in recent American English. Examples are *motel* (from *motor hotel*), *paratrooper* (from *parachute trooper*), *travelogue* (from *travel monologue*), *newscast* (from *news broadcast*), *telecast* (from *television broadcast*).

The following list contains the titles of new-word dictionaries that you may find helpful in mastering new American words: *American Speech, Barnhart Dictionary Companion, Barnhart Dictionary of New English,* and *6,000 Words*, a supplement to *Webster's Third New International Dictionary*.

**EXERCISE 3. Understanding the Origins of American English Words.** It would be helpful for you, and interesting for the class, to make a notebook to record the material you gather for these questions.

1. Make a list of twenty words or terms that you think might be Americanisms. The best places to look for such terms will be in areas, occupations, or activities that have developed in the last two centuries. If you have Mitford Matthew's *Dictionary of Americanisms* in your library, check your list to see if your terms were, in fact, coined in America.

2. The following terms are all current in some part of the English-speaking world. Some are peculiar to a particular dialect of American English; some are Americanisms borrowed in America from one of the non-English languages spoken here; some have been created here out of English or foreign elements; some are not American English at all. Look up each one in a good dictionary and determine to which of these categories it belongs. *Webster's Third New International Dictionary* will have the necessary information on all of them.

| | | |
|---|---|---|
| chesterfield | cruller (doughnut) | smearcase |
| hoarding (billboard) | prairie | croker sack |
| kibitzer | ringer (cowboy) | litterbug |
| groundnuts | yam | spa (soda fountain) |
| banjo | snoop | mustang |
| cafeteria | country town | groceteria |
| cheeseburger | courthouse (county seat) | hamburger |
| | | tonic (soda pop) |

USAGE

## LEVELS OF USAGE

Dialects are not in themselves bad or incorrect English. They are simply natural, healthy varieties of English reflecting differences in the environment in which the language was learned. It is just as natural for a person to say, for example, "You hadn't ought to do that" as it is for another person to say, "You shouldn't do that." The construction in the former is considered acceptable English in the place where it was learned.

Nevertheless, everyone is familiar with the expression "good English." For example, an employer may ask about an applicant, "Does she speak good English?" Sometimes we hear it said of a person, "His English isn't very good." What is meant by such remarks is that his or her English is, in some important ways, a departure from what we call standard English.



### Standard English

In school, students are encouraged to learn "good English"—standard English, or the standard dialect. Standard English is the language form most used in mass communication. It is the language of newspapers and magazines, of most books and journals. It usually is used professionally by newscasters, disc jockeys, actors, and television personalities. Standard English is the spoken and written language of the business world, the medical and technological fields, and politics.

The language you use conveys to a listener more than just the ideas you are expressing. It often implies, sometimes inaccurately, the extent of your general education and your general sophistication. Authorities on the modern problems of urban renewal, for example, may be familiar with and even occasionally use nonstandard dialects. So may television reporters who interview them. But neither the authorities nor the reporters are likely to use nonstandard English "on the air." If they did, their competence and educational backgrounds would be questioned by the viewers.

One aim of this book, and of all English teaching, is to develop your ability to use standard English with ease. The chapters on usage will increase your understanding of the conventions of standard English. But standard English is not one set of words or expressions or pronunciations. It can be scaled on a language ruler from *formal* to *informal*. The boundaries of the ruler are often indefinite, and most standard English tends to fall somewhere in between them.

## Formal Standard English

Think of formal standard English as what you read or hear in serious essays, formal reports, research papers, some literary criticism, and speeches on serious or solemn occasions. It is written much more than spoken. Many of its words are outside the vocabulary of everyday speech. Sentences are often long and elaborately constructed. Contractions are rarely used and slang almost never.

In the following example of formal English, note the length of sentences, the repetition of structures, and the use of certain expressions—*tempered by war,* for example—not usually found in ordinary conversation.

> . . . Let the word go forth from this time and place, to friend and foe alike, that the torch has been passed to a new generation of Americans —born in this century, tempered by war, disciplined by a hard and bitter peace, proud of our ancient heritage, and unwilling to witness or permit the slow undoing of those human rights to which we are committed today at home and around the world.
>
> Let every nation know, whether it wishes us well or ill, that we shall pay any price, bear any burden, meet any hardship, support any friend, oppose any foe, to assure the survival and success of liberty. . . . And so my fellow Americans: ask not what your country can do for you; ask what you can do for your country.
>
> . . . Finally, whether you are citizens of America or citizens of the world, ask of us here the same high standards of strength and sacrifice which we ask of you. With a good conscience our only sure reward, with history the final judge of our deeds, let us go forth to lead the land we love, asking His blessing and His help, but knowing that here on earth God's work must truly be our own.[1]

## Informal Standard English

Informal standard English is the language knowledgeable people use most of the time. It is the language of newspapers, magazines, books, and talks for a general audience. It is also the language of most contemporary novels, short stories, and plays.

The conventions of informal English are not as rigid as those of formal English. Sentences may be long or short and often imitate the rhythms of everyday conversation, in contrast to the stately and regular rhythms of formal prose. Contractions often appear, and slang is sometimes used.

[1] "Inaugural Address," January 20, 1961, by John F. Kennedy.

The following example of informal standard English is from Dorothy Sarnoff's *Speech Can Change Your Life.* Notice that the speech patterns are the familiar, everyday ones; the words are simple; and the sentences, on the average, are shorter and less varied than formal sentences.

> If you enjoy shaking hands, take the initiative. Formerly the man was supposed to wait for the woman to offer her hand, but that rule went out with the one-horse shay.
>
> But know when to stop. I have seen two people shaking hands on and on, neither knowing how to let go. Their problem was like that of the two pedestrians, approaching each other, who keep sidestepping in the same direction until they finally bump into each other.
>
> Don't be a knuckle crusher, and don't go to the other extreme, extending your hand like a limp mackerel. Instead, give the other hand a light pressure or squeeze, a sort of hand-hug. Let your hand, as well as your eyes and your voice, register, "I'm glad to meet you."



## Nonstandard English

The term nonstandard English describes usage limited to a particular region, group, or circumstance. Because it includes ways of talking or writing that are not widely accepted, you will not find it in well-edited magazines, newspapers, and books. People who routinely use nonstandard English can, and often do, rise to positions of importance in business, government, and elsewhere, but they generally master standard English along the way.

Nonstandard English can be found in many novels, short stories, and stage and television plays. It is used to provide a realistic portrayal of people from various social and economic groups. In John Steinbeck's compelling novel *The Grapes of Wrath,* the author records in the speech, thoughts, and actions of the Joad family the hopes and frustrations of the thousands of poor migrant farmers who were victims of the drought that blighted southwestern farmlands in the 1930's.

> Tom slowly made a cigarette, and inspected it and lighted it. He took off his ruined cap and wiped his forehead. "I got an idear," he said. "Maybe nobody gonna like it, but here she is: The nearer to California our folks get, the quicker they's gonna be money rollin' in. Now this here car'll go twicet as fast as that truck. Now here's my idea. You take out some a that stuff in the truck, an' then all you folks but me an' the preacher get in an' move on. Me an' Casy'll stop here an' fix this here car an' then we drive on, day an'

[1] Excerpt from *Speech Can Change Your Life* by Dorothy Sarnoff. Copyright © 1970 by Dorothy Sarnoff. Reprinted by permission of Doubleday & Company, Inc.

night, an' we'll catch up, or if we don't meet on the road, you'll be a-workin' anyways. An' if you break down, why, jus' camp 'longside the road till we come. You can't be no worse off, an' if you get through, why, you'll be a-workin', an' stuff'll be easy. Casy can give me a lif' with this here car, an' we'll come a-sailin'."[1]

## Sources of Information on Usage

To find out whether a particular expression is standard usage, consult a usage reference book or a dictionary. *The American Heritage Dictionary of the English Language* is especially rich in current information on usage.

One or more of the following reference books may be available in your school or public library.

Bernstein, Theodore M., *The Careful Writer: A Modern Guide to English Usage*
Bryant, Margaret, *Current American Usage*
Copperud, Roy, *The Consensus: American Usage and Style*
Evans, Bergen and Cornelia, *A Dictionary of Contemporary American Usage*

USAGE

**EXERCISE 4. Identifying Formal Standard and Informal Standard Writing.** Bring to class two examples of formal standard writing and two examples of informal standard writing from books, magazines, and newspapers. Be prepared to give your reasons for labeling each as you have done.

**EXERCISE 5. Understanding Common Usage Problems.** The following words and expressions present usage problems that trouble many people. Choose three of them to look up in this and at least one other textbook or reference book that is available to you. Then compare the different comments.

1. double negative
2. *It's me.* [pronoun usage]
3. *like, as*
4. *good, well*
5. (*the*) *reason is because* . . .
6. *could of*

[1] From *The Grapes of Wrath* by John Steinbeck. Copyright 1939, copyright © renewed 1967 by John Steinbeck. Reprinted by permission of Viking Penguin, Inc.

USAGE

# Chapter 23

# Agreement

## SUBJECT AND VERB, PRONOUN AND ANTECEDENT

Certain words that are closely related in sentences have matching forms. When the forms match, they are said to agree. A subject and verb agree if both are singular or both are plural. Pronouns and their antecedents (the words the pronouns stand for) agree in the same way.

### DIAGNOSTIC TEST

**A. Selecting Verbs That Agree with Their Subjects.** Number your paper 1–15. After the proper number, write the subject of the corresponding sentence or clause. After each subject, write the one of the two verbs that agrees in number with the subject.

EXAMPLE 1. These plaid trousers (does, do) not match this sports jacket.
1. *trousers do*

1. More Americans (was, were) killed in the Civil War than in World War I and World War II combined.
2. Basketball, like many other games, (offers, offer) enjoyment and exercise to all who participate.
3. Smoking cigarettes in bed (is, are) the cause of many tragic fires.

4. When I begin cutting out this skirt pattern, I know I'll discover that my scissors (needs, need) sharpening.
5. Every one of the cookies I baked for the Thanksgiving bazaar (was, were) eaten by the "mystery cookie lover" in our house.
6. Everyone in our neighborhood (participates, participate) in the local crime-watch prevention program.
7. This spring the high pollen count and unseasonal weather (has, have) caused my worst allergy attacks ever.
8. Scurvy, one of the diseases modern science has conquered, (results, result) from a lack of vitamin C.
9. In earlier times, many sailors (was, were) stricken with scurvy.
10. The British navy, members of which are called "limeys" (was, were) responsible for first using limes to prevent scurvy during long sea voyages.
11. For me neither Paris nor Rome (has, have) the grandeur of Vienna.
12. The Boston Pops Orchestra (has, have) greatly increased the enjoyment and appreciation of music for millions of people.
13. Many who give their time to help the disabled (works, work) as volunteers at the Special Olympics.
14. The Special Olympics, competitive games for the handicapped, (is, are) an idea started by the famous Kennedy family.
15. Bob Beamon's record long jump in the 1968 Olympics (stands, stand) as an achievement some people believe will never be matched.

**B. Selecting Pronouns That Agree with Their Antecedents.** Number your paper 16–20. After the proper number, write the one of the two pronouns that agrees with its antecedent. Use formal standard English.

EXAMPLE 1. Each girl won (her, their) heat at the swim meet.
1. *her*

16. George has (his, their) notebook with him.
17. The students took (his, their) belongings with them.
18. Every boy must bring (his, their) own lunch to the picnic.
19. When Sue and Anita arrive, would you please show (her, them) in?
20. Neither of my sisters owns (her, their) own pair of ice skates.

## AGREEMENT OF SUBJECT AND VERB

**23a. A word that refers to one person or thing is *singular* in number. A word that refers to more than one thing is *plural* in number.**

SINGULAR computer, woman, that, he, she, it

PLURAL computers, women, those, they

**23b. A verb agrees with its subject in number.**

**(1) Singular subjects take singular verbs.**

The **course was** easy.
The **dictionary lists** names of cities.

**(2) Plural subjects take plural verbs.**

The **courses were** easy.
Both **dictionaries list** names of cities.



It is not difficult to distinguish between the singular and plural forms of nouns and pronouns. Almost without thinking, you can tell which of the words in the following list refer to one thing or person and which refer to more than one.[1]

| | |
|---|---|
| candidate | candidates |
| ox | oxen |
| T-shirt | T-shirts |
| truck | trucks |
| he | they |

Similarly, you can easily tell the difference between the singular and plural forms of a verb.

| | |
|---|---|
| demands | demand |
| votes | vote |
| has | have |
| is | are |
| was | were |

From these examples, you will note that most nouns form their plural by adding the letter *s*, as in *candidates, T-shirts, trucks*. With nouns, then, the final *s* is a clue to the *plural* form.

With many verbs, however, the opposite is true. An *s* ending on a verb is associated with the *singular* form, not the plural, as in *demands,*

[1] Detailed rules for the formation of the plural forms of nouns are given on pages 650–53.

*votes, is, was. Are, were, have,* and most other verbs not ending in single *s* are plural: they *are,* they *demand,* they *investigate.* The exceptions, which are not difficult to remember, are verbs used with *I* and singular *you: I demand, you investigate.*

All the verbs that have been used as examples so far are in the present tense. All past-tense verbs have the same form in the singular and the plural with the exception of *be,* which has the special form *was* (with the *s* sign for the singular) that is used with *he, she, I,* and *it,* and all singular nouns.

| SINGULAR | PLURAL |
|---|---|
| I demanded. | They demanded. |
| He investigated. | We investigated. |
| You were. | You were. |
| She was. | They were. |



## Intervening Phrases and Clauses

In many sentences a phrase intervenes between the subject and the verb. When the noun in this phrase does not agree in number with the subject, you may become confused about the number of the verb.

A clause can also come between the subject and the verb. Just as with the phrase, the intervening clause tends to make it more difficult for you to choose the correct form of the verb. Remember the basic principle of agreement: The verb must agree with its *subject,* not with any modifiers the subject may have.

**23c.** **The number of the subject is not changed by a phrase or clause following the subject.**

EXAMPLES This **tape is** by the Boston Pops Orchestra.
This **tape** of songs from Broadway musicals **is** by the Boston Pops Orchestra. [*Tape* is still the subject.]

The **author was** born in Texas.
The **author** who wrote *Flowering Judas* and other works **was** born in Texas. [**Author was,** not *works were.*]

In formal writing, the number of the subject is not changed when it is followed by such explanatory or parenthetical phrases as *along with, as well as, accompanied by, in addition to,* or *together with.*

EXAMPLES The humanities **class,** along with the English class, **plans** to attend the performance of *Death of a Salesman.*

The world history **classes,** as well as the humanities class, **plan** to display models of ancient Greek architecture.

**EXERCISE 1. Selecting Verbs That Agree with Their Subjects.** Number your paper 1–10. After the proper number, write the subject of the sentence. After the subject, write the one of the two verbs that agrees in number with the subject.

1. The author of the stories (is, are) Leslie Silko.
2. Tsetse flies, which carry the dreaded disease called sleeping sickness, (attacks, attack) both humans and cattle.
3. Electronic options, as well as performance, (is, are) important to buyers of new cars.
4. A single milk pail, in addition to a rotting log and bird tracks, (appears, appear) in a painting by Andrew Wyeth.
5. The Supreme Court's decision, along with discussions of the Justices' opinions, (is, are) printed in today's newspaper.
6. Clean air, as well as clean lakes and rivers, (concerns, concern) all the citizens of the United States.
7. The beauty of trees in their fall colors (attracts, attract) many tourists to New England.
8. Sufficient amounts of potassium required by the human body (is, are) found in bananas.
9. Other animals besides the elephant (is, are) classified as pachyderms.
10. Susan B. Anthony, along with Lucy Stone and Elizabeth C. Stanton, (was, were) part of the suffragist movement.

USAGE

## Indefinite Pronouns

The indefinite pronouns, such as *some, any, someone, many,* and *everything,* can present usage problems. Some of these words are always singular, some always plural, and some can be either, depending on the meaning of the sentence. In addition, many of these words are often followed by phrases. Remember to determine the number of the subject pronoun alone, without considering the intervening phrase, before you choose your verb.

**23d. The following common words are singular:** ***each, either, neither, one, everyone, no one, nobody, anyone, anybody, someone, somebody, everybody, much.***

**Neither** of the books **is** [not *are*] in the library.

Such a construction is easier to analyze if *neither* is treated as an adjective or made to stand alone as a pronoun.

**Neither** book **is** in the library.
**Neither is** in the library.

Not **one** of the pears **looks** [not *look*] ripe.
Not **one** pear **looks** ripe.
Not **one looks** ripe.

**Everyone** in the bleachers **is** [not *are*] wearing our school colors.
**Everyone is** wearing our school colors.

**23e. The following common words are plural: *several, few, both, many, others.***

EXAMPLES **Both** of the poems **are** by Walt Whitman.
**Few** of the juniors **were** finished with the test.
**Many** of our words **are** derived from Latin.
**Others** besides Janet **enjoy** Ernest Hemingway's stories.
**Several** of the paragraphs **need** to be revised.



**23f. The words *some, any, none, all,* and *most* may be either singular or plural, depending on the meaning of the sentence.**

When the words *some, any, all,* and *most* refer to a singular word, they are singular. When they refer to a plural word, they are plural.

**Some** of the money **was** invested. [*Some* refers to *money,* which is singular.]
**Some** of the paintings **were** sold. [*Some* refers to *paintings*, which is plural.]
**Most** of the sandwich **was** left uneaten. [*Most* refers to *sandwich,* which is singular.]
**Most** of the sandwiches **were** left uneaten. [*Most* refers to *sandwiches,* which is plural.]
**All** of the traffic **is** slowing down. [*All* refers to *traffic,* which is singular.]
**All** of the cars **are** moving slowly. [*All* refers to *cars,* which is plural.]

Even when it refers to a plural, the word *none* may be considered singular, meaning *not one,* or it may be considered plural, meaning *not any.*

**None** of the track records **was** broken. [*Not one* was]
**None** of the track records **were** broken. [*Not any* were]

**EXERCISE 2. Selecting Verbs That Agree with Their Subjects.** Number your paper 1–10. After the proper number, write the one of the two verbs in parentheses that agrees in number with the subject. Be prepared to explain your decision.

1. Many of the recipes (is, are) adaptable to microwave cooking.
2. Neither of my parents (is, are) comfortable using the metric system.
3. I know that all the workers (is, are) proud to help restore the Statue of Liberty.
4. Most of the English classes (stresses, stress) composition skills.
5. Few of the students (was, were) able to spell *esophagus* correctly.
6. (Do, Does) each of you know the location of Mount Everest?
7. Nobody, not even my parents, (realizes, realize) how I have to discipline myself to study instead of watching TV.
8. Some of the software for our computer (is, are) arriving late.
9. Both of the paintings (shows, show) the influence of the work of Emilio Sanchez.
10. Others besides you and me (advocates, advocate) a town cleanup day.



## Compound Subjects

Two words or groups of words may be connected to form the *compound subject* of a verb. These words are usually joined by *and* or *or* and may take singular or plural verbs, depending on what the connecting word is and on whether the words joined are singular or plural.

**23g. Subjects joined by *and* take a plural verb.**

EXAMPLES **Lettuce and tomato seem** to belong together.
**Mood, character, and plot are** elements of the short story.

*Exception:* When a compound subject is considered as a unit, not as two or more distinct things, it takes a singular verb.

**Broadway and Forty-second Street** [one place] **is** where Times Square begins.
**Bacon and eggs** [one dish] **is** a favorite American breakfast.

**23h. Singular subjects joined by *or* or *nor* take a singular verb.**

EXAMPLES **Has** your **mother or** your **father** signed the permission slip?
**Neither Juan nor Jeff has** ever heard of "Bat" Masterson.
**Either Felita or Terry plans** to report on Leonardo da Vinci.

**23i. When a singular subject and a plural subject are joined by *or* or *nor*, the verb agrees with the nearer subject.**

ACCEPTABLE Neither the **students nor** their **teacher wants** to miss the documentary film on mountain climbing.

Whenever possible, this awkward construction should be avoided.

BETTER The **students do** not want to miss the documentary film on World War II, and **neither does** their **teacher**.

Another reason for avoiding this construction is that the subjects may be different in person as well as in number. When that occurs, the verb must agree with the nearer subject. In the following example, the verb must not only be singular to agree with *I*; it must also have the form that matches *I* as a subject:

ACCEPTABLE Neither my **friends** nor **I am** planning to stay late.
BETTER My **friends are** not planning to **stay late,** and neither **am I.**



**EXERCISE 3. Making Verbs Agree with Their Subjects.** Number your paper 1–20. Read each of the following sentences. If the verb agrees with the subject, write *C* (for correct). If the verb does not agree, write the correct form on your paper.

1. Emily Dickinson's imagery and verse structure have been covered in English class.
2. The view from Edinburgh Castle's walls are unforgettable.
3. One or both of the Shakespearean plays about Henry IV are likely to be performed this summer.
4. Signs of decay that should be recognized by every citizen includes oil spills along the shoreline as well as the absence of wildlife.
5. The effective date of the new regulations for nuclear power plants have not yet been determined.
6. Not one of the participants in the debate on Central America was eager to suggest a solution to the problem.
7. Until now every one of the attempts to restore *The Last Supper* have ended in failure.
8. Neither the statement of the problems nor the solution suggested for them is clear until you have done research.
9. The terms *simile* and *metaphor* are used in the study of poetry.
10. The City Council and the Board of Governors together constitutes the Committee.

11. The idea that they do not wear out or have to be flipped over make compact discs attractive.
12. The marketing representative, with the help of her assistant, is making plans to open a new coffeehouse.
13. Combustion of oily or gasoline-soaked rags have been known to occur if they are not stored properly.
14. James Baldwin, alongside Richard Wright and Ralph Ellison, ranks as one of the major black writers of the twentieth century.
15. Besides having a financial interest in the bay, investors and the local community uses it for sports and other recreational purposes.
16. Neither the proposals of the air traffic controllers nor the recommendation of the FAA's committee have been put into effect.
17. Hot dogs with sauerkraut is a specialty of the local deli.
18. Each of the region's environmental groups have presented its recommendations to the governor.
19. Many of the member schools of the state athletic association refuse to abide by the new academic standards.
20. The debate over the rule changes have apparently thrown the meeting into a deadlock.



## Other Problems in Subject-Verb Agreement

**23j. When the subject follows the verb, as in questions and in sentences beginning with *there* and *here,* determine the subject carefully, and make sure that the verb agrees with it.**

| | |
|---|---|
| NONSTANDARD | Here's your keys. |
| STANDARD | Here **are** your keys. |
| NONSTANDARD | Where is the bat and ball? |
| STANDARD | Where **are** the bat and ball? |

**23k. Collective nouns may be either singular or plural.**

A collective noun is singular in form but names a group of persons, animals, or things: *crowd, flock, chorus, jury, family.* By its very nature, any collective noun may have either a singular or a plural meaning. When the speaker or writer is thinking of the group as a *single unit,* it takes a singular verb; when the speaker or writer is thinking of the *individual parts* or *members* of the group, it takes a plural verb.

The **band practices** every day. [The speaker is thinking of the band as a unit, as though it were a single person.]
The **band buy** their own uniforms. [The speaker is thinking of the individual members of the band, each of whom buys a uniform.]

A **group** of tourists **has** just arrived in a large, grey bus. [The group is a unit.]
A **group** of tourists **are** noisily disagreeing about what to see next. [The members of the group are acting individually and not as a group.]

A **flock** of birds **is** flying over in a triangular formation. [The flock is traveling as a unit.]
The **flock are** scattered by the sudden electrical storm. [The flock is no longer functioning as a unit.]

**23l. Expressions stating amount (time, money, measurement, weight, volume, fractions) are usually singular.**

EXAMPLES **Four and seven-tenths inches is** the diameter of a compact disc. [a single measurement]
**Seventy-four minutes of music is** provided by the one usable side. [one length of time]
**Twenty-one dollars seems** a reasonable price. [a single sum of money]

However, when an amount is considered to be individual parts rather than a single unit, a plural verb is used.

EXAMPLES **Two silver dollars were** lying on the counter. [The dollars are thought of separately.]
**Twelve thousand bricks** is a lot to carry in a pickup. [The twelve thousand bricks are thought of as a unit.]
**Twelve thousand bricks** were used to build the garden pathways. [The twelve thousand bricks are thought of separately.]

Fractions followed by phrases can sometimes cause problems. In the examples immediately following, the form of the verb seems to be determined by the number of the noun in the phrase.

One third of the **student body is** employed after school.
Two thirds of the **students are** not employed after school.

This, like rule 23f on page 479, is an exception to rule 23c on page 477, which says the number of the subject is not changed by the phrase following it. A fraction is singular when it refers to a singular word or word group—*student body* in the first example above. It is plural when it refers to a plural word—*students* in the second example.

**EXERCISE 4. Selecting Verbs That Agree with Their Subjects.** Number your paper 1–10. After the proper number, write the verb in parentheses that agrees in number with the subject. Be prepared to defend your choices.

1. The public education system for boys and girls in the United States (is, are) intended to stress basic skills.
2. The stage crew (has, have) just made a rapid scene change for Rita Moreno's entrance.
3. Alertness, as well as stamina and strength, (is, are) important to rescue workers.
4. Perhaps the best thing about calculators (is, are) their speed in arriving at accurate answers.
5. There (is, are) more than 45,000 people over the age of sixty taking college courses.
6. On our block alone, ninety-five dollars (was, were) collected for the American Cancer Society.
7. Of the world's petroleum, about one third (is, are) produced by the United States.
8. Frustration, failure, and lack of motivation (indicates, indicate) the need to talk with a guidance counselor.
9. Either brisk walks or jogging (serves, serve) as a healthful way to get daily exercise.
10. One sixth of the budget (is, are) allocated to health care.



**23m. The title of a work of art or the name of an organization or a country, even when plural in form, takes a singular verb.**

EXAMPLES Chaucer's *Canterbury Tales* **includes** many humorous characterizations.
"Tales from the Vienna Woods" **is** one of Strauss's most popular waltzes.
The United States **calls** its flag "Old Glory."

*Exception:* Some organizations (Campfire Girls, Atlanta Braves, Optimists, etc.) customarily take a plural verb.

The Knights of Columbus **are** giving this benefit.

**23n. A few nouns, although plural in form, take a singular verb.**

1. *Words that are plural in form but singular in usage*:

| EXAMPLES | aeronautics | genetics | mumps |
|---|---|---|---|
| | civics | mathematics | news |
| | economics | measles | physics |

Keep in mind that these examples do not make a rule that can be consistently followed. For example, the following similar words are more often plural than singular: *acoustics, athletics, statistics, tactics.* The word *politics* may be either singular or plural.

2. *Words that have no singular forms*:

EXAMPLES pliers
scissors
shears
trousers

Notice that these plural nouns refer to *pairs* of things. If they are preceded by the word *pair,* use a singular verb.

EXAMPLE The **pliers are** on the workbench.
The **pair of pliers is** on the workbench.

3. *Plural forms of foreign nouns*:

Certain English nouns of foreign origin retain their foreign plural forms, especially in scientific and technical writing.

| SINGULAR | PLURAL |
|---|---|
| analysis | analyses |
| nucleus | nuclei |
| parenthesis | parentheses |
| phenomenon | phenomena |
| radius | radii |

*Always* consult your dictionary when you do not know whether a specific form is singular or plural or when you do not know how to write the plural form of any word.

**23o. When the subject and the predicate nominative are different in number, the verb agrees with the subject, not with the predicate nominative.**

EXAMPLES Sore muscles **are** one of the symptoms of flu.
One of the symptoms of flu **is** sore muscles.

Quite often this construction, though correct, is somewhat awkward.

AWKWARD A great **contribution** to successful surgery **was** Joseph Lister's **discoveries** concerning antiseptics.
Joseph Lister's **discoveries** concerning antiseptics **were** a great **contribution** to successful surgery.

BETTER Joseph Lister made a great contribution to successful surgery through his discoveries concerning antiseptics.

**23p. *Every* or *many a* before a subject is followed by a singular verb.**

EXAMPLES **Every** sophomore and junior **was taking** a course in computers.
**Many a** person **chooses** television over reading, sometimes a regrettable decision.

**23q. *Doesn't* and *don't* must agree with their subjects.**

Speakers and writers sometimes forget that *don't* is a contraction for *do not,* and *doesn't* is a contraction for *does not.* With the subjects *I* and *you,* use *don't.* With other subjects, use *doesn't* when the subject is singular and *don't* when the subject is plural.

EXAMPLES **She doesn't** know where Beirut is.
**This doesn't** seem like an interesting research topic.
**It doesn't** help to cram for exams.
**They don't** always proofread carefully.

By always using *doesn't* after *he, she, it, this,* and *that,* you can eliminate most of the common errors in the use of *don't* and *doesn't.*

USAGE

**EXERCISE 5. Selecting the Correct Verb.** Number your paper 1–20. After the proper number, write the correct one of the two verbs in parentheses in each sentence.

1. *The Oxford Book of English Verse,* one of the best-known anthologies, (contains, contain) some of the most famous poems in English literature.
2. (Does, Do) every boy and girl in the city schools vote in the student council elections?
3. Physics (is, are) taken by the best science students.
4. Ships and sailors, as well as soldiers and armies, (appears, appear) in many of Shakespeare's plays.
5. Neither Robert Frost nor E. A. Robinson (has, have) written many poems about city life.

6. "Seventeen Syllables" (recounts, recount) the story of a Japanese-American family.
7. This (doesn't, don't) make sense.
8. Neither of last year's leading rushers (has, have) scored a touchdown so far this year.
9. Measles (is, are) less prevalent now that children can be inoculated against the disease.
10. In Roman mythology, the goddess of invention, who was admired for her wisdom by many, (was, were) Minerva.
11. True sonnets, whether Italian or Shakespearean, (has, have) fourteen lines.
12. One of the most important electives recommended by many colleges (is, are) advanced composition.
13. Neither of my paragraphs (is, are) ready to be typed.
14. Students who are not finished taking the exam (doesn't, don't) appreciate loud noises in the corridors.
15. (Doesn't, Don't) it seem encouraging that the life span of Americans is increasing?
16. Two teaspoonfuls of cornstarch combined with a small amount of cold water (makes, make) an ideal thickener for many sauces.
17. The people with whom I worked last summer (attends, attend) a nearby high school.
18. The unusual phenomena (was, were) explained by astronomers as being caused by sunspots.
19. The majority of high-school juniors (is, are) familiar with computers.
20. It is difficult to make a choice because there (is, are) so many styles of tennis shoes.



**EXERCISE 6. *Oral Drill.* Stressing Subjects and Their Verbs.** To fix the agreement habit in your speech, read each of the following sentences aloud several times, stressing the italicized words. State the reason for each construction.

1. *Has either* of the essays been graded?
2. *Both* green beans and broccoli *are* nourishing vegetables.
3. Here *are* the *minutes* I took at the meeting.
4. The *salary is* the minimum wage.

5. Not *one* of the driver's education students *forgets* to fasten the seat belt.
6. Where *are* her *mother and father?*
7. The *coach doesn't* want us to eat sweets.
8. *Several* of the research papers *were* read aloud.
9. *Neither Mr. Smith nor Mrs. Perez assigns* oral reports.
10. *Each* of the contestants *gets* a chance to win the grand prize.

**REVIEW EXERCISE A. Selecting Verbs That Agree with Their Subjects.** Number your paper 1–10. After the proper number, write the subject of the sentence or clause. After each subject, write the one of the two verbs that agrees in number with the subject.

EXAMPLE 1. Neither of the twins (plans, plan) on attending the Junior Prom this spring.
1. *Neither, plans*

1. If you are driving to the Hitchcock Chair factory in Riverton, neither the Litchfield nor the Torrington exit (is, are) the one you should take.
2. The President, after meeting with several of his advisers, (has, have) promised to veto the proposed tax bill.
3. According to a recent government news release, a medical study of World War II veterans (has, have) concluded that the veterans have the same health prospects as nonveterans.
4. The list of the best ballplayers of all time (is, are) dominated by outfielders.
5. Babe Ruth, Hank Aaron, Willie Mays, and Joe DiMaggio (is, are) all outfielders on the list.
6. The Mariana Trench, located in the Pacific Ocean near the Mariana Islands, (is, are) the deepest ocean area in the world; it is nearly seven miles deep.
7. Styles in clothing (seems, seem) to change as often as the weather.
8. The New York City Triborough Bridge and Tunnel Authority, whose job it is to control the collecting of bridge tolls, (has, have) a major problem with a small Mexican coin.
9. The Mexican peso, worth approximately one-half cent, (is, are) easily accepted by the present toll machines.
10. These vegetables (doesn't, don't) look fresh.

**WRITING APPLICATION:**
**Writing Sentences with Subject-Verb Agreement**

Writers make "agreement errors" when they do not see the *true* subjects of their sentences. You should always analyze your sentences for the *true* subjects so that the verbs agree with their subjects.

INCORRECT Neither of the books are in the library.
CORRECT **Neither** of the books **is** in the library.
(The subject of the sentence is *neither,* not *books.*)

**Writing Assignment**

Write ten sentences, each beginning with one of the following expressions. When you proofread your sentences, make sure that the verbs agree with the subjects of the sentences.

1. Many a writer
2. The tray with food
3. Neither of the offices
4. Ten dollars
5. Together the class
6. The doctors' diagnoses
7. Everyone on the teams
8. Some of the canoes
9. All of the food
10. Either the *New York Times* or the *Wall Street Journal*



## AGREEMENT OF PRONOUN AND ANTECEDENT

**23r. A pronoun agrees with its antecedent in number and gender.**

Pronouns also agree in person (see page 497): *I* should have proofread the assignment *myself.* Jane wants *her* car keys back.

The word to which a pronoun refers or for which it stands is called its antecedent. In the phrase *Tracy and her schedule,* the pronoun *her* has the proper noun *Tracy* as its antecedent.

In the examples that follow, both pronouns and antecedents are printed in boldfaced type. Like subjects and verbs, antecedents and pronouns agree in *number*. If its antecedent is singular, the pronoun is singular; if its antecedent is plural, the pronoun is plural. Notice, too, that a pronoun is masculine (*he, him, his*) when its antecedent is masculine; feminine (*she, her, hers*) when its antecedent is feminine, and neuter (*it, its*) when its antecedent is neuter. This second kind of agreement is agreement in *gender* (see page 497).

**Shay** has more credits than **he** needs.
The **joggers** took **their** canteens with **them.**
**Neither** of the houses has **its** furnishings yet.
The **others** can take the crafts class if **they** pay for **themselves.**

**(1) The words *each, either, neither, one, everyone, everybody, no one, nobody, anyone, anybody, someone,* and *somebody* are referred to by singular pronouns: *he, him, his, she, her, hers, it, its.* A phrase after the antecedent does not change the number of the antecedent.**

EXAMPLES **Everyone** may bring **his** lunch.
**One** of my friends has organized **her** own yard sale.

USAGE

> ☞ **USAGE NOTE** Sometimes the antecedent may be either masculine or feminine; sometimes it may be both. Some writers use the masculine form of the personal pronoun to refer to such antecedents. Other writers prefer to use both the masculine and feminine forms in such cases.

EXAMPLES Any **interested person** may submit **his** application.
Any **interested person** may submit **his or her** application.

**Everyone** carefully proofread **his** own composition.
**Everyone** carefully proofread **his or her** own composition.

You can often avoid the awkward *his or her* construction by substituting an article for the pronoun or by rephrasing the sentence in the plural.

EXAMPLES **Any interested person** may submit **an** application.
**All interested persons** may submit [**their**] applications.
**All** the students carefully proofread **their** own compositions.

In conversation, you may find it more convenient to use a plural personal pronoun when referring to singular antecedents that can be either masculine or feminine. This form is becoming increasingly popular in writing as well and may someday become acceptable as standard written English.

EXAMPLES Every new **employee** received **their** ID cards.
**Each** writer must keep **their** audience in mind.

**(2) Two or more singular antecedents joined by *and* should be referred to by a plural pronoun.**

EXAMPLES If **Jerry and Francesca** call, tell **them** that I am at the mall.
**Maria, Kay, and Laura** have donated **their** time to the hospital.

**(3) Two or more singular antecedents joined by *or* or *nor* should be referred to by a singular pronoun.**

EXAMPLES **Either Rinaldo or Philip** always finishes **his** trigonometry homework in class.
**Neither Cindy nor Carla** thinks **she** is ready to write the final draft.

**(4) The number of a relative pronoun is determined by the number of its antecedent.**

EXAMPLES A school handbook is given to **everyone who** enrolls in our school. [*Who* refers to the singular word *everyone;* therefore, it takes the singular verb *enrolls.*]
A school handbook is given to **all who** enroll in our school. [*Who* refers to the plural word *all*; therefore, it takes the plural verb *enroll.*]

USAGE

> **NOTE** Strict agreement between pronoun and antecedent is sometimes abandoned to prevent an unnatural construction.

The rules of agreement may sometimes lead to absurd constructions. This occurs when a singular pronoun is used to agree with a singular antecedent even though the meaning of the antecedent is clearly plural. When the meaning of the antecedent is plural, a plural pronoun must be used.

ABSURD Nobody left the prom early, because he was enjoying himself. [In this sentence, *nobody* is clearly plural in meaning, and the singular pronouns *he* and *himself*, though grammatically correct, are confusing and unnatural.]

BETTER **Nobody** left the prom early, because **they** were enjoying **themselves**.

ABSURD Everyone in the audience was so moved by the performance that he did not applaud immediately.

BETTER **Everyone** in the audience was so moved by the performance that **they** did not applaud immediately.

**EXERCISE 7. Writing Pronouns That Agree with Their Antecedents.** Number your paper 1–10. After the proper number, write a pronoun to fill the blank in the corresponding sentence, making sure that it agrees with its antecedent. Be sure to use standard formal English.

1. Each student prepares —— own outline.
2. One of the birds built —— nest in our chimney.
3. Both Jane and Ruth wrote —— essays about ecology.
4. If anyone else decides to drive, tell —— to notify Mrs. Marino.
5. Many of the students have revised —— compositions.
6. Not one of the students typed —— research paper.
7. Neither Angela nor Carrie has given —— dues to me.
8. Either Mark or David must hand in a slip to take —— car on the field trip.
9. Each of the boys brought —— own tennis racket.
10. Everyone in the class has paid —— lab fees.

USAGE

**REVIEW EXERCISE B. Making Verbs Agree with Their Subjects; Making Pronouns Agree with Their Antecedents.** This exercise covers agreement of both verb and subject, and pronoun and antecedent. Number your paper 1–10. If a sentence is correct, write a +; if it is incorrect, rewrite the sentence correctly.

1. My brother and I like using compact discs instead of regular records.
2. Do you know what the differences between regular records and compact discs is?
3. One of the differences are that compact discs are recorded by a computer.
4. Another difference is that the sound is played back with a laser beam.
5. You may ask: "Don't records and compact discs have the same sound?"
6. Yes, but the amounts of compression and distortion is not really the same.

7. Some people say that compact discs offers a brighter treble and truer bass than conventional records.
8. There is still other advantages in that compact discs never wear out, and they play over seventy minutes of music on one side.
9. The answer that people who like them gives is that they never wear out because needles never touch them.
10. Do you know that compact discs requires higher quality amplifiers than regular records do?

## CHAPTER 23 REVIEW: POSTTEST

**Making Verbs Agree with Their Subjects; Making Pronouns Agree with Their Antecedents.** This exercise covers agreement of verb and subject, and pronoun and antecedent. Number your paper 1–20. If a sentence is correct, write a + after the proper number; if it is incorrect, rewrite the sentence correctly.

EXAMPLE 1. Each of the members of the school board are hoping to be reelected this fall.

1. Each of the members of the school board is hoping to be reelected this fall.

1. Half the members of my history class this year is in the National Honor Society.
2. Over one thousand miles of tunnels travels through El Tieniente, the largest copper mine in the world.
3. After a tree has been cut down, the number of rings in the cross section is significant.
4. The sum of the rings divided by two tell you the age of the tree.
5. My English teacher announced a short-story contest; some of the students in my homeroom plans to enter it.
6. Every one of the English Department teachers have volunteered to judge the contest.
7. Advances in medical research has nearly eradicated many childhood diseases.
8. Lightning, which is a form of electricity, usually strikes the highest or tallest object around.

9. Everybody who are caught out in the open during a lightning storm should lie down on the ground.
10. If he already has a pair of pliers, he can exchange them for something else at the hardware store.
11. Each Fourth of July my entire family gather to watch the fireworks display at the municipal stadium.
12. For as long as I can remember, the fireworks display have always started with the arrival of three airborne parachutists.
13. When the six o'clock news comes on, be sure to listen to the weather forecast.
14. Either drizzle or heavy rain is supposed to be headed this way.
15. If you see either Veronica or Sabrena in the cafeteria, tell them that I can't meet them after school today.
16. Neither Adrianne nor Lillian expect to make the varsity softball team this year, but both girls are trying out for it.
17. To learn more about our city government, our civics class plan to invite various guest speakers to school.
18. Included on our list is the mayor, a lawyer, a probation officer, a police officer, and a local or state representative.
19. Unfortunately, neither Mayor Ella Hanson nor Mrs. Ann Powell, her top aide, have answered our invitations.
20. Listening to guest speakers explain and discuss their jobs make the class period pass quickly.

CHAPTER 24

# Correct Pronoun Usage

## CASE FORMS OF PRONOUNS

USAGE

### DIAGNOSTIC TEST

**Correcting Sentences by Using Pronouns in the Correct Case.** Number your paper 1-20. After the proper number, write the correct one of the two pronouns in the parentheses in the sentence. Be prepared to explain your choices.

EXAMPLE 1. Since (he, him) and I now have our licenses, Aunt Sally allowed us to drive her car to the lake.
1. *he*

1. Please write and tell my mother and (I, me) about your vacation.
2. Today the talent committee will audition Tina and (myself, me).
3. When I arrived home from school today, my mother asked me to help my brother and (she, her) with washing the windows.
4. I asked my mother whether she would mind (me, my) postponing this chore until later.
5. Yesterday in science class, my teacher encouraged Joanne and (I, me) to enter our project in the state competition.
6. Although (we, us) girls were hesitant to enter our amateur ideas in the state competition, our teacher assured us that our project was innovative and well done.
7. I thought that the best tennis players in my school were my cousin Adele and (he, him).

8. Adele and (he, him) agreed that I had judged their ability accurately.
9. As I waited for the elevator, I heard someone say, "(Who, Whom) shall I say is calling?"
10. My math teacher objects to (me, my) yelling out answers before I have been called on.
11. After three hours of work, the mechanic could not explain to (I, me) why the car engine was making that odd noise.
12. Jill and (I, me) think it sounds like a popcorn machine; we fear that the engine will spray apart like pieces of flying popcorn.
13. (Who, Whom) did you talk to at the information desk?
14. Because Dan and (they, them) have taken dancing lessons, the director of the play has chosen them to be in the chorus line.
15. My great-grandmother told Lois and (I, me) the story of Rudolph Valentino's death and the national mourning that followed.
16. My great-grandmother was special to me; I respected no one else as much as (she, her).
17. My great-grandmother, my grandfather, and (I, myself) have had some good talks together.
18. I learned about the Roaring Twenties from my great-grandmother and (he, him).
19. Between you and (I, me), I'm glad we aren't living back then.
20. Ellie always got into more trouble than (I, me).



---

The correct use of pronouns can be learned in various ways. One method is to depend on your ear: "Which *sounds* right—I or *me?*" Another way is to learn the case forms of pronouns and to know when to use each form.

Study the following sentences:

**I** lent **her my** pocket dictionary.
**He** lent **me his** thesaurus.
**She** and **I** lent **him our** American history notes.
**They** lent the cassette tapes to **him** and **her.**

The boldfaced words in these sentences are pronouns. Notice the number of different forms these pronouns take. These forms are called *case forms.* A pronoun that acts as the subject of a verb is in the *nominative* (sometimes called the *subjective*) *case,* a pronoun that acts as the object of a verb or preposition is in the *objective case,* and a pronoun that shows possession is in the *possessive case.*

| | |
|---|---|
| PRONOUN AS SUBJECT | **I** set the alarm. |
| PRONOUN AS OBJECT | The alarm woke **me.** |
| POSSESSIVE PRONOUN | **My** awakening was sudden. |

Notice that the pronoun has a different form in each case.

**24a. Learn the case forms of pronouns and the uses of each form.**

Of all the words in modern English, personal pronouns have the most varied and complex forms.

Pronouns have number. Like nouns, personal pronouns take different forms for singular and plural numbers (*he, they*).

Pronouns have person. Pronouns change form in three different persons—first, second, and third (*I, you, he*). The meaning of the three persons is as follows:

> **I (We)** will wait. [First person is the person speaking.]
> **You** will wait. [Second person is the person spoken to.]
> **He (She, It, They)** will wait. [Third person is a person or thing other than the speaker or the one spoken to.]

Pronouns have gender. In the third person singular, personal pronouns have three genders: masculine (*he*), feminine (*she*), and neuter (*it*).

Pronouns have case. Many personal pronouns take different forms for the nominative, objective, and possessive cases.

***Case Forms of Personal Pronouns***

| ***Singular*** | NOMINATIVE CASE | OBJECTIVE CASE | POSSESSIVE CASE |
|---|---|---|---|
| FIRST PERSON | I | me | my, mine |
| SECOND PERSON | you | you | your, yours |
| THIRD PERSON | he (masculine) | him | his |
| | she (feminine) | her | her, hers |
| | it (neuter) | it | its |
| ***Plural*** | NOMINATIVE CASE | OBJECTIVE CASE | POSSESSIVE CASE |
| FIRST PERSON | we | us | our, ours |
| SECOND PERSON | you | you | your, yours |
| THIRD PERSON | they | them | their, theirs |

In this chapter we will concentrate on the nominative and objective case forms of the personal pronouns. Memorize the following lists of nominative and objective forms.

| NOMINATIVE CASE | OBJECTIVE CASE |
|---|---|
| I | me |
| he | him |
| she | her |
| we | us |
| they | them |

Two other pronouns—*who* and *whoever*—have different forms in the nominative and objective cases. *Who* and *whoever* are not personal pronouns. They may be used either as *interrogative* pronouns, to ask a question, or as *relative* pronouns, to introduce a subordinate clause.

| NOMINATIVE CASE | OBJECTIVE CASE |
|---|---|
| who, whoever | whom, whomever |

The uses of *who* and *whom* are discussed on pages 505–507.



## NOMINATIVE FORMS

**24b. The subject of a verb is in the nominative case.**

When the subject is a single pronoun, you follow this rule without thinking about it. Few people would ever say or write "Us [objective case] ordered the tickets" instead of the correct "We ordered the tickets." When a verb has a compound subject, however, people often become confused about the form to use. We have all heard sentences like "Sally and us have seen that play," or "You and me saw it first."

Fortunately, there is a simple method for determining the correct forms of pronouns that appear in combinations.

**(1) To determine the correct pronoun form in a compound subject, try each subject separately with the verb, adapting the form as necessary. Your ear will tell you which form is correct.**

NONSTANDARD Sally and me will be going. [*Me* will be going?]
STANDARD **Sally and I** will be going. [*I* will be going.]

NONSTANDARD She and him will be going. [*Him* will be going?]
STANDARD **She and he** will be going. [*She* will be. *He* will be.]

**(2) When a pronoun is used with a noun (as in *we girls*), say the sentence without the noun. Your ear will tell you the correct pronoun form.**

NONSTANDARD Us girls took Spanish last semester. [*Us* took?]
STANDARD **We girls** took Spanish last semester. [*We* took.]

**EXERCISE 1. *Oral Drill.* Stressing Pronouns in the Nominative Case.** Read each of the following sentences aloud several times, stressing the italicized words. This is an ear-training exercise, designed to fix habits of correct usage of the nominative forms of personal pronouns.

1. You and *I* will go to the library on the corner of Orange Avenue and Central this afternoon.
2. *We* and *they* have some research to do.
3. Either John or *he* will probably select a topic about the natural environment.
4. Neither *they* nor *we* should use periodicals that are older than three months.
5. Both the seniors and *we* juniors will write research papers.
6. Sally, Irene, and *I* might write about modern art.
7. Which playwright did Kay and *she* select?
8. Suzanne said that you and *they* decided on a contemporary novelist for your reports.
9. Why are *he* and Mark waiting so long to begin working?
10. *We* three are going to the library downtown.



**24c. A predicate nominative is in the nominative case.**

A predicate nominative is a noun or pronoun in the predicate that refers to the same thing as the subject of the sentence. As its name implies, a predicate nominative is in the nominative case.

Several verbs may be followed by predicate nominatives, but the verb *be* is by far the most important. Thus, in the table below, a verb in the first column may be followed by one of the pronoun forms in the second column. Such a verb form should *not* be followed by a personal pronoun in the objective case—*me, him, her, us, them.*

| COMMON FORMS OF *BE* | | NOMINATIVE PRONOUNS |
|---|---|---|
| am<br>is, are<br>was, were<br>has been, have been, had been<br>will be, may be, can be, etc.<br>should be, would be, could be<br>must be, might be | are followed by | I<br>he<br>she<br>we<br>they<br>who |

EXAMPLES Was it **she** who was nominated for the office?
If it had been **she,** I might not have talked to her.
The ones you are thinking about might have been **they.**

> ☞ **NOTE** It is now acceptable to use the form *It's me* in informal usage. The plural form (*It's us*) is also generally accepted, but using the objective case for the third person form of the pronoun (*It's him, It's them*) is widely considered to be unacceptable in writing. When you see any of these forms in exercises, use the nominative case of the pronoun.

USAGE

**EXERCISE 2. Using Pronouns in the Nominative Case.** Number your paper 1–10. After the proper number, write the correct form of a personal pronoun to complete the sentence meaningfully. After each pronoun, write *s.* for the subject or *p.n.* for predicate nominative. Use as many different pronouns as you can, but do not use *you* or *it*. When your sentences have been corrected, read each sentence aloud several times.

1. It was —— who carried the groceries to the car.
2. —— and —— will be taking the PSAT on Saturday.
3. Neither —— nor —— will be available after school.
4. The date that —— (we, us) girls have chosen is in late April.
5. Did you know that —— and —— are holding a section rehearsal after school?
6. Either Guy or —— will be collecting funds for charity.
7. Was it —— whom you saw walking in the mall near the fountain?
8. It was —— who won the most valuable player award.
9. Either Phil or —— will collect the money for the class dues.
10. Among those selected to take part in the forum were Pia and —— .

## OBJECTIVE FORMS

**24d. The object of a verb is in the objective case.**

The object of a verb answers the question *What?* or *Whom?* after an action verb.

EXAMPLES They coached **him**. [Coached *whom?* Answer: *him*—the direct object.]
They awarded **him** a letter [Awarded *whom* a letter? Answer: *him*—the indirect object.]

As their name suggests, the objective forms (*me, him, her, us, them*) are used as objects.

EXAMPLES The class selected **her** as president.
They picked **me** as treasurer.
They preferred **us** as leaders.
Can we provide **them** with firm leadership?

Single objects, like single subjects, are usually handled correctly; few of us would ever say "I like they" or "The coach picked he for a winner." Like subjects, however, objects are often compound, with a pronoun appearing in combination with a noun or another pronoun. You can trust your ear to tell you the correct case form when you let each pronoun stand alone as an object.

NONSTANDARD They consulted my brother and **I**. [They consulted *I?*]
STANDARD They consulted my brother and **me**. [They consulted *me.*]

NONSTANDARD Naomi gave he and she the assignment. [Naomi gave *he* the assignment? Gave *she* the assignment?]
STANDARD Naomi gave **him** and **her** the assignment. [Naomi gave *him* the assignment. Naomi gave *her* the assignment.]

**EXERCISE 3. *Oral Drill.* Stressing Pronouns in the Objective Case.** Read each of the following sentences aloud several times, stressing the italicized words.

1. The teachers *asked* Carmen and *me* to explain the problem.
2. Do you *want us* boys to set up the chairs for the meeting?
3. *Call* either *her* or Ruth about the yearbook deadline.
4. *Him* I *like* but don't *ask me* to *invite them*.
5. The teachers *confuse* my brother and *me*.

6. *Give* the other girls and *her* the chemistry assignment.
7. *Were* they *accusing them* or *us*?
8. The success of the car wash *surprised* Mr. Kahn and *him*.
9. The company will *hire* Debbie and *her* for the summer.
10. Please *urge him* and Jack to study for the vocabulary test.

**EXERCISE 4. Using Pronouns in the Objective Case.** Number your paper 1–10. After the proper number, write a personal pronoun in the correct form to complete the sentence. Use a variety of pronouns, but do not use *you* or *it*.

1. Did you give Frank and —— the outside reading list?
2. He gave you and —— a demonstration of the long jump.
3. Mrs. Martin asked Lena, Chris, and —— for their notebooks.
4. Please tell —— (we, us) juniors about the plans for the prom.
5. I liked —— and —— as class officers from the first meeting.
6. Please show —— and her how to operate the copying machine.
7. The coach asked Rosa and —— to demonstrate the inward dive.
8. The play gave (we, us) students some ideas for a skit.
9. My mother is picking up both you and —— .
10. The governor is supporting both the commissioner of education and —— on their testing program.

USAGE

**24e. The object of a preposition is in the objective case.**

A preposition takes an object—the noun or pronoun in prepositional phrases. As we would expect from the name, these objects are in the objective case. Thus, if the object of a preposition is a pronoun, the objective case form must be used.[1]

| | |
|---|---|
| beside **him** | with **me** |
| after **her** | for **them** |

When a preposition has a single object, most writers use the correct forms; however, pronouns in combinations often cause trouble. The method used for finding the correct pronoun form as the subject or the object of a verb will work here as well. Whenever pronouns are used in the compound object of a preposition, make each stand alone with the preposition. Your ear will tell you the correct form.

[1] A list of commonly used prepositions will be found on page 394. Reminder: *But* is a preposition when it means "except"; *like* is a preposition meaning "similar to."

NONSTANDARD Esteban will write the speech with you and **I.**
STANDARD Esteban will write the speech **with you and me.** [with *me*]

NONSTANDARD Will you organize the VCR tapes for Mrs. Chang and **he**?
STANDARD Will you organize the VCR tapes **for Mrs. Chang and him?** [for *him*]

**EXERCISE 5. Selecting Pronouns in the Objective Case to Complete Sentences.** Number your paper 1–10. In each sentence, find the preposition, and write it after the corresponding number on your paper. After each preposition, write the correct one of the two pronouns in parentheses. When your paper has been corrected, use these sentences for oral drill.

1. Would you like to play baseball with Eugenio and (I, me)?
2. These photographs were taken by Dwight and (she, her).
3. We can rely on Theresa and (he, him) for their help.
4. Would you like to sit next to Elaine and (I, me)?
5. There should be more cooperation between the senior class and (we, us).
6. Teammates like Dave and (he, him) can almost read each other's minds on the basketball court.
7. The closing lines of the play are spoken by you and (she, her).
8. We have been studying the Elizabethans and have learned much about (they, them).
9. Most of the credit belongs to (we, us) juniors.
10. The captain tried to steer the ship between the lighthouse and (they, them).

USAGE

**REVIEW EXERCISE A. Selecting Pronouns in the Nominative or Objective Case to Complete Sentences.** Number your paper 1–10. After the proper number, write the correct one of the two pronoun forms in parentheses in the corresponding sentence.

1. I was certain that it was (she, her) and Sylvester who left.
2. In recognition of their science projects, Mrs. Hill recommended Sally and (she, her) for the state science fair.
3. She gave the sports assignment for the school newspaper to Dave and (I, me).
4. Neither the band nor (they, them) took a trip this year.
5. Just between you and (I, me), I'd rather go to Sea World.

6. The author of the story never tells us whether it was (she, her) or her sister who won the contest.
7. Our English teacher assigned Margaret and (I, me) roles for our reading of *Our Town.*
8. The speakers at the assembly will be you and (he, him).
9. I drove to the dance with (she, her) and her sister.
10. When will you learn that (we, us) drivers must stay within the speed limit?

## WRITING APPLICATION A:
## Using First-Person, Singular Pronouns in Writing

Pronouns are said to have *number* because they can be singular or plural. Pronouns also have *person.* First person uses *I* or *we.* Second person uses *you*, and third person uses *he*, *she*, *it*, or *they.* When you begin to write, you must make a decision about what person you are using, either *first*, *second*, or *third.* Then, it is usually best to use that person consistently throughout the entire paragraph or essay.

EXAMPLES *I* studied hard to raise my scores. (first person)
*You* should begin to prepare for standardized tests in an organized way. (second person)
*He* carefully set aside an hour each night to prepare for the test. (third person)

### Writing Assignment

The most obvious use of the first-person singular pronoun is in autobiographical writing. You can use it in another way, however. It is possible to pretend you are someone else. This might be an effective way to get an idea, character, or mood across to your reader. Using first person singular, write a paragraph in which you are pretending to be someone else. You may use one of the following suggestions or think of your own.

1. A poor, hungry child from another country
2. A creature from another planet
3. An outstanding sports personality
4. A modern Rip Van Winkle who has just awakened
5. A time traveler from the year 3636

## *WHO AND WHOM*

The pronouns *who* and *whom* are used in two ways in English sentences: as *interrogative* pronouns, which ask a question, or as *relative* pronouns, which introduce a subordinate clause.

The rules governing the case forms of the personal pronouns (pages 496–503) also apply to *who* and *whom. Who* is nominative; *whom* is objective. The pronoun *who* is correct whenever *he, she, we* or *they* can be substituted for it. The pronoun *whom* is correct whenever *him, her, us,* or *them* can be substituted for it.

NOMINATIVE **Who** played this role? [*Who* is the subject of the verb *played.* She played this role.]
**Who** should it be? [*Who* is a predicate nominative. It should be who.]

OBJECTIVE **Whom** did you meet today? [*Whom* is the object of the verb *did meet.* You did meet whom (him) today.]
With **whom** did you write the script? [*Whom* is the object of the preposition *with.* Did you write the script with him?]



> ☞ **USAGE NOTE** In informal English, the pronoun *whom* is gradually dropping out of use. Consequently, a sentence in which *who* is used in place of *whom* is acceptable in informal speech and writing. However, in formal English, the distinction in the nominative and objective forms should be observed.

INFORMAL **Who** did he *consult*?
FORMAL **Whom** did he *consult*? [*Whom* is the object of the verb *did consult.* Did he consult him?]

INFORMAL **Who** were you referring to?
FORMAL To **whom** were you referring? [*Whom* is the object of the preposition *to.* Were you referring to him?]

**24f. The use of *who* or *whom* in a subordinate clause is determined by the pronoun's function in the clause. The case is not affected by any word outside the clause.**

To solve a *who—whom* problem, ask yourself the following three questions:

1. What words make up the subordinate clause?
2. How is the pronoun used in the clause—as subject, predicate nominative, object of the verb, object of the preposition?
3. What is the correct case form for this use of the pronoun?

PROBLEM They were relatives (who, whom) I had not seen in years.
Step 1 The subordinate clause is *(who, whom) I had not seen in years.*
Step 2 In this clause the relative pronoun is used as the object of the verb *had seen.*
Step 3 The object of the verb is in the objective case, and the objective form of the pronoun is *whom.*
SOLUTION They were relatives **whom** I had not seen in years.

Now see if you can solve the *who—whom* problem in the following sentence.

PROBLEM Do you know (who, whom) he is?
Step 1 The subordinate clause is —— .
Step 2 In this clause —— is the subject; —— is the verb; the pronoun *(who, whom)* is used as —— .
Step 3 A predicate nominative is in the —— case; therefore —— is the correct form.
SOLUTION ——

USAGE

In the example above, the pronoun looks like the object of the verb *do know* in the main clause *you do know.* Remember, however, that the case of a pronoun in a subordinate clause is not affected by any word outside the subordinate clause. The real object of the verb *do know* is the entire subordinate clause:

**☞ USAGE NOTE** In determining whether to use *who* or *whom,* do not be misled by a parenthetical expression in the subordinate clause.

EXAMPLES This is the woman **who,** *we believe,* will be our next vice-president.
There is the teacher **who** *I think* can explain the geometry proof to you.

**EXERCISE 6. Selecting *Who* or *Whom* to Complete Sentences Correctly.** Number your paper 1–10. After the proper number, write the correct one of the two pronoun forms in parentheses in the corresponding sentence. Use the three-step method above for determining the case form.

1. Betty Smith, the author of *A Tree Grows in Brooklyn,* was an obscure writer (who, whom) became a celebrity overnight.
2. Her novel is an American classic about a young girl (who, whom) she called Francie Nolan.
3. Francie, (who, whom) we follow through girlhood to adulthood, had only one tree in her city back yard.
4. Carson McCullers, (who, whom) critics describe as a major American writer, wrote a novel about a young girl's coming of age.
5. (Who, Whom) could not be moved by *The Member of the Wedding*?
6. Do you know (who, whom) it was that played Frankie in the Broadway production of *The Member of the Wedding*?
7. Pearl Buck is a novelist (who, whom) most Americans are familiar with.
8. The Pulitzer Prize is awarded annually to (whoever, whomever) is selected by the panel of judges.
9. Gwendolyn Brooks, (who, whom) you told me won the Pulitzer Prize for poetry, also wrote a book called *Maud Martha.*
10. Guess (who, whom) Maud Martha really is.

USAGE

## WRITING APPLICATION B: Using *Who* and *Whom* Correctly in Your Writing

Most of your writing is intended for audiences that expect you to use standard formal English. When you follow the rules governing the correct uses for *who* and *whom* for standard formal English, you show consideration for your audience.

### Writing Assignment

Write five sentences according to the following guidelines:

EXAMPLE 1. Use *whom* as the direct object in a question.
1. *Whom did you see?*

1. Use *who* as a predicate nominative in a question.
2. Use *whom* as the object of a preposition in a question.
3. Use *who* as the subject of a subordinate clause.
4. Use *who* as the subject in a question.
5. Use *whom* as the direct object in a question.

## PRONOUNS IN INCOMPLETE CONSTRUCTIONS

An incomplete, or elliptical, construction is a phrase or clause from which one or more words have been omitted.[1] In English such constructions occur most commonly after the words *than* and *as*.

**24g. After *than* and *as* introducing an incomplete construction, use the pronoun case form that you would use if the construction were completed.**

In the sentence *She reads faster than you or I,* the verb *read* is omitted from the clause: *She reads better than you or I (read).* The pronoun *I* is in the nominative case because it is the subject of the unexpressed verb *read.* By supplying missing words, we can determine a correct pronoun form. Similarly, by studying the pronoun forms in incomplete constructions, we can determine what the missing words must be.

EXAMPLES We blame Fred as much as **them.** [The complete clause must be *as we blame them.*]
We blame Fred as much as **they.** [The complete clause must be *as they blame Fred.*]

USAGE

**EXERCISE 7. Selecting Pronouns for Incomplete Constructions.** Number your paper 1–10. After the proper number, write the incomplete construction in the corresponding sentence, supplying the missing word or words, and choose the correct pronoun form from the pair of pronouns in parentheses. In several of the sentences either pronoun form may be correct; the form you use must be correct in the completed construction.

EXAMPLE 1. Jo works longer hours than (I, me).
1. *than I work*

1. No one else in my class is as boastful as (I, me).
2. Judges presented Angela with a larger trophy than (I, me).
3. Can you whistle as loudly as (he, him)?
4. If you want to sell more raffle tickets than Mark, you should call on more people than (he, him).
5. The editors of our newspaper write as much as (they, them).
6. We were all more eager than (he, him).

[1] For a review of elliptical clauses, see page 446.

7. I admire Diana Ross more than (she, her).
8. My coach told me that I had more agility than (he, him).
9. They sent Lois as many get-well cards as (I, me).
10. No one gave as much time to good causes as (she, her).

**REVIEW EXERCISE B. Selecting Pronouns in the Correct Case to Complete Sentences.** Number your paper 1–10. After the proper number, write the correct one of the two choices in parentheses in the corresponding sentence. Be prepared to explain your choices.

EXAMPLE 1. You will enjoy this story about Joan and (I, me).
1. *me*

1. Yesterday my friend Joan and (I, me) were discussing what careers we might choose after graduation.
2. One of our teachers, (who, whom) we both like, suggested that we look at the classified advertisements in a newspaper.
3. I let Joan have today's classified section first because I read faster than (she, her).
4. Under one of the headings, "Careers in Education," (she and I, her and me) saw openings for school counselors and teachers.
5. Fascinated by the classifieds, we decided to read on and see what other careers might interest (we, us) seniors.
6. Most of the ads in the section dealing with health care did not appeal to Joan or (I, me).
7. Science had always given Joan and (I, me) trouble.
8. However, the best computer operators in our class were Joan and (I, me).
9. (We, Us) two job seekers found a number of ads for computer operators.
10. We reported our findings to our teacher, (who, whom) we knew would be interested in what we had discovered.

USAGE

## OTHER PROBLEMS IN THE USE OF PRONOUNS

**24h. In standard formal English the pronouns ending in -*self* and -*selves* should be used only (1) to refer to another word in the sentence or (2) to emphasize another word in the sentence.**

EXAMPLES **I** hurt **myself**. [The reflexive pronoun *myself* refers to the subject *I*.]
My **aunt** and **uncle** bought tickets for **themselves** and me. [The reflexive pronoun *themselves* refers to *aunt* and *uncle*.]
**She herself** will entertain us. [The intensive pronoun *herself* emphasizes *she*.]
**Juan** will do it **himself**. [The intensive pronoun *himself* emphasizes *Juan*.]

Do not use a reflexive or intensive pronoun in place of a simple personal pronoun.

Donna, Phil and **I** [not *myself*] did well in chemistry.
Did Ruth make macramé belts for herself and **you?** [not *yourself*]

**24i. An appositive is in the same case as the word with which it is in apposition.**



An appositive explains or identifies (but does not modify) the word with which it is in apposition. It is logical, therefore, that both the word and its appositive should be in the same case.

PROBLEM The new cheerleaders—Fay, Karen, and (I, me)—will meet during activities period. [The phrase *Fay, Karen, and (I, me)* is in apposition with *cheerleaders,* the subject of the verb *will meet.* The subject of a verb is in the nominative case; therefore, the pronoun in the phrase must also be in the nominative case.]

SOLUTION The new cheerleaders—**Fay, Karen, and I**—will meet during activities period.

PROBLEM My grandfather paid the two boys, Hal and (he, him), for raking leaves. [The phrase *Hal and (he, him)* is in apposition with *boys,* the object of the verb *paid.* Therefore, the pronoun should be in the objective case.]

SOLUTION My grandfather paid the two boys, **Hal and him**, for raking leaves.

**24j. Use the possessive case of a noun or a pronoun before a gerund.**

A gerund is a verb form ending in *-ing* that functions as a noun. Since the gerund functions as a noun, using the possessive case before it is reasonable.

I was surprised at the **computer's** [not *computer*] operating so easily.
Everyone was thrilled by **their** [not *them*] scoring in the top five percent.

Do not confuse the gerund with the present participle, which also ends in *-ing*. A gerund acts as a *noun*; a participle acts as an *adjective*. Like an ordinary adjective, a participle modifies a noun or a pronoun. It can never be used as the subject or object of a verb or as the object of a preposition.

Study the following examples carefully:

PARTICIPLE Did you notice **him waiting** outside? [The pronoun *him* is the object of the verb *did notice;* the participle *waiting* acts as an adjective modifying *him.* In this sentence the writer is emphasizing the person who is waiting rather than the act of waiting.]

GERUND His parents objected to **his waiting** outside. [In this sentence the gerund *waiting* is the object of the preposition; the possessive pronoun *his* modifies the gerund. Here the writer is emphasizing the act of waiting, not the person who performs the act.]

Distinguish the differences in meaning between the two sentences in each of the following pairs:

Can you imagine **me** driving in the desert?
Can you imagine **my** driving in the desert?

Think of **their** having to camp in the woods.
Think of **them** having to camp in the woods.

The **Glee Club** singing "Hail, Columbia!" got the most applause.
The **Glee Club's** singing of "Hail, Columbia!" got the most applause.



**EXERCISE 8. Correcting Sentences by Using Pronouns in the Correct Case.** Number your paper 1–10. After the proper number, write a + if the pronouns in the corresponding sentence are correct; write a *0* if the pronouns are incorrect. After each *0*, write the correct pronoun or pronouns.

1. My friends and me spent Saturday in the park.
2. Many of the students were happy about his being here.
3. The speech had a different effect on each of us, Mary, Dawn, and I.
4. Elected to the student council were two juniors, Frank and she.
5. Both his father and himself had musical talent.
6. I cannot understand his dropping out of the band just before his senior year.
7. The new exchange students, Michel and her, already speak some English.
8. I have no objection to him trying to get a job after school.
9. The test scores were high for both juniors, Aretha and she.
10. When I watch TV instead of studying, the person I hurt most is myself.

**REVIEW EXERCISE C. Selecting Pronouns in the Correct Case to Complete Sentences.** Number your paper 1–10. After the proper number, write the correct one of the two pronouns in the parentheses in the corresponding sentence. Be prepared to explain your choices.

1. To (who, whom) was the locker assigned?
2. Among those who had not taken Algebra II were Bobby and (I, me).
3. I thought that Beth and (he, him) would make the best officers.
4. Please use the electric typewriter between Lee and (I, me).
5. Was it (she, her) (who, whom) the guidance counselor called to her office?
6. They have many more cassette tapes than (we, us), but we have newer ones than (they, them).
7. (Who, Whom) do you think Thomas Paine was?
8. Besides Sharon and (I, me) there were no other volunteers to serve on the committee.
9. (Him, His) winning the tennis match was a surprise to all of us.
10. The title of salutatorian goes to (whoever, whomever) has the second highest academic average.



---

## CHAPTER 24 REVIEW: POSTTEST

**Correcting Sentences by Using Pronouns in the Correct Case.** Number your paper 1–20. After the proper number, write a + if the pronouns in the corresponding sentence are correct; write a *0* if the pronouns are incorrect. After each *0*, write the correct pronoun or pronouns.

EXAMPLE 1. Manuel and him are on the soccer team.
1. *0, he*

1. Don thinks that Debbie is planning a surprise party for Melissa and I.
2. Two of the best party-givers are Don and she.
3. Luis and them once held a surprise party for Donna and him.
4. Whom do you think should send out the invitations?
5. You and I should probably ask Margo, since no one else writes better than her.

6. Please send Ann and me a copy of the rough draft that you and she wrote.
7. Ann and myself will revise the letter, correcting any errors made by the typist or him.
8. The student council appointed two new members, Bob and she.
9. After our problems with a flat tire during our vacation trip, us two decided to take a course in auto repair.
10. During our first class Andrea and me learned the main parts of a car's engine.
11. Our instructor was a successful mechanic who all of us came to appreciate.
12. The instructor said to Jack, "I can't believe you not knowing what a spark plug is."
13. The ones who were having the most difficulty were Ed and him.
14. Between you and I, taking this car-repair course was the smartest thing I had ever done.
15. All of us students, including myself, feel much more confident about our handling auto repairs.
16. Who did you give the keys to the garage to?
17. Either Terry or I will leave the car keys for you or them.
18. Do you have time to show Larry and we how to change the oil?
19. Jan can change a tire faster than him.
20. Adjusting the brakes is no problem for Carlos and me.

USAGE

# CHAPTER 25

# Correct Verb Usage

## PRINCIPAL PARTS; TENSE, VOICE, MOOD

Many errors in the use of verbs occur when students do not know the principal parts of verbs or misuse the tense forms of verbs. This chapter explains verb forms and provides practice in correct verb usage.

### DIAGNOSTIC TEST

**A. Using the Correct Tense or Form.** Number your paper 1–15. After the proper number, write the correct one of the two choices in parentheses in the corresponding sentence. Be prepared to explain your choices.

EXAMPLE 1. (Sit, Set) this pitcher of juice on the table, please.
1. *Set*

1. A beautiful oak banister (rises, raises) along the staircase.
2. If you (would have, had) looked out the plane window, you could have seen the Grand Canyon.
3. Tammie says that yesterday she should have (went, gone) to the beach.
4. Edward said that he too wanted (to go, to have gone) to the beach yesterday.
5. One of the statues has (fell, fallen) off its base.

6. How long did it (lie, lay) on the floor?
7. Since last September I (missed, have missed) only one day of school.
8. By April, our new civic center (will open, will have opened).
9. Fortunately, I have never been (stinged, stung) by a bee.
10. The unusual pattern in this wool material was (weaved, woven) by Seamus MacMhuiris, an artist who uses geometric designs.
11. The house became very quiet after everyone (left, had left).
12. I (began, begun) this homework assignment an hour ago.
13. My parents' old car has (broke, broken) down again.
14. Everyone who (saw, seen) Greg Louganis dive in the 1984 Olympics recognized his superior talent.
15. He likes to (sit, set) on the porch in his rocking chair.

**B. Revising Verb Voice or Mood.** Number your paper 16–20. Revise the following sentences by correcting verbs that use an awkward passive voice or verbs that are not in the appropriate mood.

16. If I was you, I would not skate on that lake; the ice is too thin.
17. The ball that was thrown by me was caught by the dog.
18. He now wishes that he was on the field trip.
19. The quilt that was made by me won second prize at the county fair.
20. The halftime show was enjoyed by the crowd.



---

## KINDS OF VERBS

A verb is a word that expresses an action or otherwise helps to make a statement.

EXAMPLES George Foster **hit** the ball for a base hit.
The student **thought** carefully before starting his composition.

A verb that tells *what is* rather than *what is done* is called a *linking verb.* Such verbs act as a link or connection between the subject and one or more words in the predicate.

EXAMPLES The basement **was** damp and chilly. [*Was* links *basement* to *damp* and *chilly.*]
These vegetables **taste** too salty. [*Taste* links *vegetables* to *salty.*]

Some verbs can be used as either action or linking verbs.

ACTION The sculptor Noguchi **felt** the smooth marble. [*Felt* expresses action.]
LINKING The artist **felt** happy that day. [*Felt* links the subject, *artist*, with *happy*, a word that describes the subject.]

You will find a list of the most common linking verbs on page 389. The verb used most often as a linking verb is the verb *be*, whose forms are *am, is, are, was, were,* and all verb phrases ending in *be, being, been; may be, could be, will be, has been, was being,* etc.

Besides being a linking verb, *be* can also be followed by an adverb or an adverb phrase.

She **will be there** right after school.
My notebook **is on the desk.**

In this use, *be* is not generally classified as a linking verb. It does not link a word in the predicate to the subject.

USAGE

## PRINCIPAL PARTS OF VERBS

Every verb has four basic forms called the four principal parts: the *infinitive,* the *present participle,* the *past,* and the *past participle.* All other forms of a verb are derived from these principal parts.

***Principle Parts of the Verb* Rush**

| INFINITIVE | PRESENT PARTICIPLE | PAST | PAST PARTICIPLE |
|---|---|---|---|
| rush | (is) rushing | rushed | (have) rushed |

Notice the words *is* and *have* before present and past participles.These words have been inserted to show that the participial forms are used with helping verbs: *have, has, had, is, are, am, has been, have been,* etc.

### Regular Verbs

All verbs are described as either *regular* or *irregular,* according to the manner in which their principal parts are formed.

A regular verb is one that forms its past and past participle by adding *-d* or *-ed* to the infinitive form.[1]

[1] A very few regular verbs have an alternative past form ending in *-t; burn, burned,* or *burnt,* (have) *burned* or *burnt*. Other such verbs are *lean* and *leap.*

| INFINITIVE | PAST | PAST PARTICIPLE |
|---|---|---|
| outline | outline**d** | (have) outline**d** |
| revise | revise**d** | (have) revise**d** |
| talk | talk**ed** | (have) talk**ed** |
| laugh | laugh**ed** | (have) laugh**ed** |

## Irregular Verbs

An irregular verb is one that forms its past and its past participle in some other way than does a regular verb, usually, but not always, by a vowel change within the verb.

| INFINITIVE | PAST | PAST PARTICIPLE |
|---|---|---|
| sw**i**m | sw**a**m | (have) sw**u**m [vowel change] |
| ben**d** | ben**t** | (have) ben**t** [consonant change] |
| **teach** | **taught** | (have) **taught** [vowel and consonant changes] |
| **let** | **let** | (have) **let** [no change] |

USAGE

Irregular verbs cause the greatest single problem in standard verb usage because there is no single rule that applies to them. Students of our language must know the principal parts of every irregular verb that they use, and the only possible way to know them is to memorize them.

The following alphabetical list contains three principal parts of many common irregular verbs. Use this list for reference. Remember, however, that the list does not include every irregular verb. When in doubt about the principal parts of a verb, consult a dictionary, in which you will find any irregular forms listed.

### *Principal Parts of Common Irregular Verbs*

| INFINITIVE | PAST | PAST PARTICIPLE |
|---|---|---|
| bear | bore | (have) borne |
| beat | beat | (have) beaten *or* beat |
| become | became | (have) become |
| begin | began | (have) begun |
| bite | bit | (have) bitten |
| blow | blew | (have) blown |
| break | broke | (have) broken |
| bring | brought | (have) brought |

| INFINITIVE | PAST | PAST PARTICIPLE |
|---|---|---|
| burst | burst | (have) burst |
| catch | caught | (have) caught |
| choose | chose | (have) chosen |
| come | came | (have) come |
| creep | crept | (have) crept |
| dive | dived *or* dove | (have) dived |
| do | did | (have) done |
| draw | drew | (have) drawn |
| drink | drank | (have) drunk |
| drive | drove | (have) driven |
| eat | ate | (have) eaten |
| fall | fell | (have) fallen |
| fight | fought | (have) fought |
| fling | flung | (have) flung |
| fly | flew | (have) flown |
| forget | forgot | (have) forgotten *or* forgot |
| freeze | froze | (have) frozen |
| get | got | (have) got *or* gotten |
| give | gave | (have) given |
| go | went | (have) gone |
| grow | grew | (have) grown |
| hang | hung | (have) hung |
| know | knew | (have) known |
| lay | laid | (have) laid |
| lead | led | (have) led |
| lend | lent | (have) lent |
| lie | lay | (have) lain |
| ride | rode | (have) ridden |
| ring | rang | (have) rung |
| rise | rose | (have) risen |
| run | ran | (have) run |
| see | saw | (have) seen |
| seek | sought | (have) sought |
| set | set | (have) set |
| shake | shook | (have) shaken |
| shine | shone *or* shined | (have) shone *or* shined |
| shrink | shrank *or* shrunk | (have) shrunk *or* shrunken |
| sing | sang | (have) sung |
| sink | sank *or* sunk | (have) sunk |
| slay | slew | (have) slain |
| speak | spoke | (have) spoken |
| spin | spun | (have) spun |
| spring | sprang *or* sprung | (have) sprung |
| steal | stole | (have) stolen |

| INFINITIVE | PAST | PAST PARTICIPLE |
|---|---|---|
| swing | swung | (have) swung |
| sting | stung | (have) stung |
| strive | strove *or* strived | (have) striven *or* strived |
| swear | swore | (have) sworn |
| swim | swam | (have) swum |
| take | took | (have) taken |
| tear | tore | (have) torn |
| throw | threw | (have) thrown |
| wear | wore | (have) worn |
| weave | wove | (have) woven |
| write | wrote | (have) written |

**25a. Learn the principal parts of common irregular verbs.**

On the following pages, the irregular verbs that are most frequently misused are presented in four groups. Memorize the principals of the verbs in each group; next, do the exercises. Concentrate on any verb that you have not used correctly; review its principal parts, repeating them over and over until the correct forms are fixed in your mind and the incorrect forms "hurt" your ears. In doing the exercises, remember that the past participle is always used with one or more helping, or auxiliary verbs: *is, are, was, have, have been, could have, might have,* etc. To remind yourself of this fact, always use *have* before the past participle when you repeat the principal parts of a verb; thus, *bring, brought, have brought.*

### *Group I*

| INFINITIVE | PAST | PAST PARTICIPLE |
|---|---|---|
| beat | beat | (have) beaten *or* beat |
| begin | began | (have) begun |
| blow | blew | (have) blown |
| break | broke | (have) broken |
| burst | burst | (have) burst |
| choose | chose | (have) chosen |
| come | came | (have) come |
| do | did | (have) done |

**EXERCISE 1. Using the Past and the Past Participle Forms Correctly.** Number your paper 1–10. After each number, write either the past or the past participle of the italicized verb, whichever correctly fills the blank in the corresponding sentence.

1. *come* Your friends have —— to see you.
2. *do* He —— his best on the PSAT Saturday.
3. *begin* She has —— to understand the value of proofreading.
4. *choose* The poem I submitted to the contest was —— to receive a prize.
5. *come* His grandparents had —— from Portugal.
6. *blow* The winds —— the Dutch galleon off its course.
7. *break* The silence was —— by a sudden clap of thunder.
8. *beat* The doubles team easily —— its opponents.
9. *blow* Odysseus' ship was —— off course.
10. *burst* The audience occasionally —— into laughter.

### *Group II*

| INFINITIVE | PAST | PAST PARTICIPLE |
|---|---|---|
| draw | drew | (have) drawn |
| drink | drank | (have) drunk |
| drive | drove | (have) driven |
| fall | fell | (have) fallen |
| freeze | froze | (have) frozen |
| give | gave | (have) given |
| go | went | (have) gone |

USAGE

**EXERCISE 2. Using the Past and Past Participle Forms Correctly.** Number your paper 1–10. After each number, write either the past or the past participle of the italicized verb, whichever correctly fills the blank in the corresponding sentence.

1. *give* No one has ever —— me as much encouragement as my science teacher.
2. *draw* Slowly our scoutmaster —— the winning raffle ticket out of the huge fishbowl.
3. *drink* My sister —— all of the fruit juice before we even got near the picnic grounds.
4. *drive* Gale-force winds have —— many a small boat off its course.
5. *drink* We —— in the cool breeze that told us the heat wave was over.
6. *freeze* Has the lake —— over yet?
7. *go* Mrs. Garcia told us that Inez had —— to the library.

8. *go* Is it really true that if one apple has —— bad, all the others with it will also go bad?
9. *freeze* Once food has been thawed, it should not be —— again.
10. *fall* The baby has finally —— asleep.

**EXERCISE 3. Using the Past and Past Participle Forms Correctly.** This exercise covers the verbs in Groups I and II. Number your paper 1–20. After the proper number, write *C* if the italicized verb in a sentence is correct; if it is incorrect, write the correct form.

1. *Has* the bank *froze* the company's assets?
2. Our football team's undefeated record *was broke* last week.
3. The crowded roots of the plant *bursted* the flowerpot.
4. The fan *blowed* his composition off the desk.
5. Kim *was chosen* sports editor of the yearbook.
6. In April the dogwood trees *burst* into blossom.
7. We *drunk* a lot of water after jogging.
8. King Lear *was driven* to despair by his daughters.
9. When the pond *had froze,* we went ice-skating.
10. *Has* Mrs. Leong *given* out the hall passes?
11. Terry and Paul *have went* to pick up our tickets.
12. Everyone in the class *done* his best on the exam.
13. The plaster on the ceiling *has fallen.*
14. The lettuce *was frozen.*
15. They *have drove* all day to get to Miami.
16. I think that sketch *was drawn* near our house.
17. Which soprano *was chosen* to sing at graduation?
18. The cassette tape deck *must have broke* this morning.
19. Our chorus' rehearsal *began* at three o'clock.
20. The junior entrant *was beat* in the spelling bee.

USAGE

### *Group III*

| INFINITIVE | PAST | PAST PARTICIPLE |
|---|---|---|
| grow | grew | (have) grown |
| know | knew | (have) known |
| ride | rode | (have) ridden |
| ring | rang | (have) rung |

| INFINITIVE | PAST | PAST PARTICIPLE |
|---|---|---|
| run | ran | (have) run |
| see | saw | (have) seen |
| sing | sang | (have) sung |
| speak | spoke | (have) spoken |

**EXERCISE 4. Using the Past and Past Participle Forms Correctly.** Number your paper 1–20. After each number, write either the past or past participle of the italicized verb, whichever correctly fills the blank in the corresponding sentence.

1. *ride* I have never —— on a motorcycle.
2. *know* Fortunately, we —— the answer.
3. *grow* The paper mill has —— trees on that land.
4. *ring* Although the bell had —— , I was still writing.
5. *speak* Has Ramón —— to you about the poetry contest?
6. *run* Our team members have never —— faster.
7. *sing* Our choir has —— on television.
8. *see* Have you ever —— a Shakespearean play?
9. *ride* Have you ever —— on a moped?
10. *run* In *The Red Badge of Courage*, Henry Fleming —— from battle.
11. *sing* The applause was deafening after the group had —— their new hit.
12. *run* She —— for student council representative last year and again this year.
13. *see* We —— a film of "The Fall of the House of Usher."
14. *ride* They said they had —— in the rumble seat of an antique automobile.
15. *know* For as long as we have —— him, Ed has never been sick.
16. *ring* Have they —— down the curtain on *Hamlet*?
17. *grow* Your skill in writing compositions has —— considerably since the beginning of the course.
18. *speak* Had anyone —— about Spirit Week or the dance in yesterday's assembly?
19. *ring* They have —— the bell in front of the school twelve consecutive times.
20. *speak* He has always —— to the conventions on environmental concerns.

USAGE

### *Group IV*

| INFINITIVE | PAST | PAST PARTICIPLE |
|---|---|---|
| spring | sprang *or* sprung | (have) sprung |
| steal | stole | (have) stolen |
| swim | swam | (have) swum |
| swing | swung | (have) swung |
| take | took | (have) taken |
| tear | tore | (have) torn |
| throw | threw | (have) thrown |
| write | wrote | (have) written |

**EXERCISE 5. Using the Past and Past Participle Forms Correctly.** Number your paper 1–10. After each number, write either the past or past participle of the italicized verb, whichever correctly fills the blank in the corresponding sentence.

1. *take* "I'm sorry," said a voice in the dark theater, "but this seat is —— ."
2. *throw* The poet Theodore Roethke once wrote an elegy for one of his students who was —— by a horse.
3. *swim* We each —— twenty laps yesterday.
4. *write* Have you —— the outline for your composition yet?
5. *swing* I —— my chair around to get a better look.
6. *spring* Our rowboat has —— a leak.
7. *steal* My dog Rags must have —— my slipper again.
8. *swim* Diana Nyad has —— many marathons.
9. *tear* In New York City, buildings that are officially designated landmarks cannot be —— down.
10. *take* Should these clothes be —— to the dry cleaner?

**EXERCISE 6. Using the Past and Past Participle Forms Correctly.** This exercise covers the verbs in Groups III and IV. Number your paper 1–20. After the proper number, write *C* if the italicized verb in a sentence is correct; if it is incorrect, write the correct form.

1. I *have* never *known* very much about the poet Wallace Stevens.
2. She *has ridden* a float in the parade every year.
3. The telephone *has rang* six times.
4. The industrial waste *has ran* into our river.
5. It was the most exciting documentary I *have* ever *seen*.

USAGE

6. Our chorus *has* always *sung* at the mall.
7. After Sue *had spoke,* she introduced the administrators.
8. A lot of vacation homes *have sprang* up along the beach.
9. After I found my watch at home, I knew nobody *had stole* it.
10. He *had swum* in dozens of meets by the time he won his first medal.
11. The movie monster *swang* around and lunged into the woods.
12. It would *have took* a lot less time to use a calculator.
13. Our quarterback *has tore* a ligament in his knee.
14. He *had thrown* the winning touchdown pass before he was injured.
15. *Was* the tape deck *stole* out of her car?
16. His investment *grew* rapidly.
17. They *have stole* their ideas from an old TV series.
18. For exercise, she *swum* laps at the YWCA pool every afternoon.
19. If any of the pages *have been tore,* please inform the librarian.
20. As relief pitcher, Roberto *had thrown* nine straight strikes.



**REVIEW EXERCISE A. Using the Past and Past Participle Forms Correctly.** This exercise covers all the verbs in Groups I to IV. Number your paper 1–50. After each number, write either the past or past participle of the italicized verb, whichever correctly fills the blank in the corresponding sentence.

1. *come* They had —— to buy their yearbooks.
2. *freeze* Can milk be —— ?
3. *run* Rob de Castella —— for Australia in the Olympics.
4. *swim* Rick Carey —— at the University of Texas.
5. *drink* We —— tomato juice with last night's dinner.
6. *grow* We have —— accustomed to commercials on TV.
7. *see* How many of you —— Fernando Valenzuela pitch?
8. *choose* How many were —— to compete in the decathlon?
9. *grow* The microcomputer industry has really —— .
10. *ring* The bell was —— when rebuttal time was up.
11. *steal* Sometimes great art treasures are —— and later found.
12. *write* He had —— a play that was entirely a flashback.
13. *begin* The band has —— to practice for the half-time show.
14. *sing* He —— in the barbershop quartet.
15. *blow* The fierce winds —— our garbage cans over.
16. *burst* She —— into the room to greet her friends.
17. *fall* He —— when he went in for the layup.

18. *ride* Alana said she had never —— on a roller coaster.
19. *go* I've —— as far as I can with this chemistry problem.
20. *throw* Many people had —— trash on the ground.
21. *choose* Mrs. Ramirez —— Lynn's essay to be read aloud.
22. *do* Janet —— a good job discussing Martina Arroyo.
23. *drive* Herman Melville wrote about people who were —— mad.
24. *blow* The potted plant was —— over by a gust of wind.
25. *go* The government class has —— to observe the legislature.
26. *know* I would have passed if I had —— more about the stars.
27. *speak* She had —— to us about a career in journalism.
28. *tear* Can you mend the hole that was —— in the screen?
29. *swim* I have never —— in salt water before.
30. *ring* I did not know the phone had —— .
31. *break* Bring two sharpened pencils in case one gets —— .
32. *fall* A foot of snow has —— in the past five hours.
33. *drink* The mineral water he —— was refreshing.
34. *grow* The ugly duckling had —— into a beautiful swan.
35. *sing* Who —— the lead in *Carmen?*
36. *take* She had —— a rest before the tennis match.
37. *run* He has never —— a four-minute mile.
38. *spring* Mrs. Carter has —— two short quizzes on her class.
39. *give* Marcia has —— two reports this term.
40. *begin* When it —— to rain, they rolled out the tarpaulin.
41. *draw* New lines have been —— for legislative districts.
42. *go* Have you ever —— to visit a foreign country?
43. *see* Amy has —— the Statue of Liberty.
44. *swing* The typist —— around to answer the telephone.
45. *come* The time has —— to learn to write clearly.
46. *throw* Who has —— that wet towel on the floor?
47. *begin* As I learned to revise, my writing —— to improve.
48. *choose* Each of us had —— a different American writer.
49. *do* I —— an illustrated presentation on Rembrandt.
50. *give* The computer operator —— us a printout of our grades.

## SIX TROUBLESOME VERBS

The verb problems in the preceding exercises were solved by the correct choice of a verb *form.* The *meanings* of the verbs were obvious. Other verb problems arise, however, when questions about both form and meaning must be answered. Such problems occur with verbs that are similar in sound but different in their meanings and principal parts. You must first choose the correct verb. Only then will you be able to choose the proper verb form. Six verbs of this kind have been selected for detailed study and drill. Taken in pairs, they are *lie* and *lay, sit* and *set,* and *rise* and *raise*.

### *Lie and Lay*

The verb *lie* means "to rest" or "to stay, to recline, or to remain in a certain state or position." Its principal parts are *lie,* (is) *lying, lay,* (have) *lain.*[1]

The verb *lay* means "to put" or "to place (something)." Its principal parts are *lay,* (is) *laying, laid,* (have) *laid.*

Notice that the verb *lay* is transitive. It takes an object, indicated by the word *something* in parentheses after its definition. A person lays something down; a chicken lays an egg. A person lays something in a specified place: Miguel laid the newspaper on the porch. On the other hand, the verb *lie* is intransitive. It takes no object. A person simply lies down (no object), or a thing lies there (no object): The eggs lie in the nest.

Memorize the principal parts of these two verbs:

| INFINITIVE | PRESENT PARTICIPLE | PAST | PAST PARTICIPLE |
|---|---|---|---|
| lie (*to rest*) | (is) lying | lay | (have) lain |
| lay (*to put*) | (is) laying | laid | (have) laid |

With the meanings and the principal parts clearly established in your mind, you can solve any *lie-lay* problem. Work slowly and carefully, treating each of the two elements separately. A good way to attack the problem is to ask yourself two questions, one to find the correct *verb,* the other to find the correct *form of the verb.*

*Question 1* What is the meaning that I have in mind? Is it "to recline or rest," or is it "to put (something)"?

When you have answered this question, you will know whether to use a form of the verb *lie* or a form of the verb *lay*. Now you are ready to ask yourself the next question.

*Question 2* What principal part expresses the time that I have in mind?

[1] Do not confuse *lie* (to rest) with *lie* (to tell a falsehood), a regular verb whose principal parts are *lie,* (is) *lying, lied,* (have) *lied.* Because the meanings of the two verbs are so different, this error is rare, but students occasionally confuse the two sets of principal parts.

USAGE

The answer to this question will tell you which verb form to use.

Now let us apply these two questions to some typical *lie-lay* problems.

PROBLEM Yesterday afternoon I (laid, lay) down for an hour on the cot in the study.

*Question 1* Meaning? The meaning here is "to recline"; the verb meaning "to recline" is *lie.*

*Question 2* Principal part? Since the time is past, the verb must be in the past form; the past form of *lie* is *lay.* [*lie, lay,* (*have*) *lain*]

SOLUTION Yesterday afternoon I **lay** down for an hour on the cot in the study.

PROBLEM She (laid, lay) her test on the teacher's desk before the bell rang.

*Question 1* Meaning? The meaning here is "to put"; the verb meaning "to put" is *lay.*

*Question 2* Principal part? The time is past, and the verb must be in the past form; the past form of *lay* is *laid.* [*lay, laid,* (*have*) *laid*]

SOLUTION She **laid** her test on the teacher's desk before the bell rang.

PROBLEM Those books have (laid, lain) on that shelf for years.

*Question 1* The meaning here is "to remain in a certain position" or "to rest." The verb meaning "to remain or rest" is *lie.*

*Question 2* Principal part? The principal part required with the helping verb *have* is the past participle. The past participle of *lie* is *lain.* [*lie, lay,* (*have*) *lain*]

SOLUTION Those books **have lain** on that shelf for years.

PROBLEM Her rough draft is still (laying, lying) on the desk.

*Question 1* Meaning? Again the meaning is "to remain in a certain position." The verb meaning "to remain" is *lie.*

*Question 2* Principal part? Here the helping verb *is* requires the present participle. The present participle of *lie* is *lying.*

SOLUTION Her rough draft **is** still **lying** on the desk.

This two-question method may seem slow at first, but it will pay you to use it. After a few trials the process will speed up, and you will be able to select both the correct verb and the proper verb form quickly. Eventually, when the meanings and the principal parts of *lie* and *lay* have become part of your mental "furniture," you should be able to discard the method entirely.

In addition to the two-question method, the following three hints should help you to use *lie* and *lay* correctly.

1. Most errors in the use of these verbs are made when the speaker should use a form of *lie,* meaning "to rest or recline," or "to remain in a certain state or position." When this is the meaning you have in mind, be especially cautious.

2. Make use of the fact that *lay* usually takes an object, whereas *lie* does not. Thus, if a sentence contains an object, always use a form of *lay*.

3. As a final check, substitute the verb *put* for the problem verb in a sentence. If the sentence makes sense after the substitution, use a form of *lay;* if it "sounds wrong," use a form of *lie*.

EXAMPLES The tape was (lying, laying) on the car seat. [*The tape was putting* sounds wrong; therefore:]
The tape was **lying** on the car seat. [a form of *lie*]
She (lay, laid) the hair dryer on the shelf. [*She put the hair dryer* makes sense; therefore:]
She **laid** the hair dryer on the shelf. [a form of *lay*]

**EXERCISE 7. *Oral Drill.* Using *Lie* and *Lay* Correctly.** Read each of the following sentences aloud several times, stressing the italicized verbs. This is an ear-training exercise that is designed to fix the habit of using *lie* and *lay* correctly.

USAGE

1. *Lay* your composition on my desk.
2. Let the composition *lie* on my desk.
3. The ocean liner *lay* at anchor.
4. She *has lain* around the den all afternoon.
5. They *laid* out their plans for the prom.
6. How long *have* you *been lying* in the sun?
7. They *laid* the bricks for the new gym.
8. I decided to *lie* down for a few minutes.
9. The cat *has been lying* on my bed all morning.
10. The challenge *lies* in using the new vocabulary words.

**EXERCISE 8. Using *Lie* and *Lay* Correctly.** Number your paper 1–10. After each number, write the form of *lie* or *lay* that correctly fills the blank in the corresponding sentence. Use the two-question method for finding the proper verb and verb form.

1. The package has been —— outside her door.
2. The trouble arose when both parties —— claim to the same piece of property.
3. The wet towel was —— in the sun to dry.
4. Please —— your pencils down and close your test booklets.
5. The field —— fallow last year.

6. Have your fears been —— to rest?
7. We —— at the edge of the pool yesterday, too tired to move.
8. Three dictionaries were —— open on the desk.
9. Sherlock Holmes —— great emphasis on the absence of footprints in the garden.
10. He left his boots —— on the floor.

**EXERCISE 9. Using *Lie* and *Lay* Correctly.** Number your paper 1–20. After each number, write the correct one of the two verb forms in the parentheses. Use the two-question method in making your choices.

1. The old stereoscope has (lain, laid) in the attic at Grandmother's for years.
2. The interstate (lays, lies) north of town.
3. The rake is (laying, lying) in a pile of leaves.
4. When was that tile in the foyer (laid, lain)?
5. Judy and Adrian (lay, laid) their books on the table.
6. She read the paper as she (laid, lay) in the recliner.
7. The key to success (lays, lies) in determination.
8. (Lie, Lay) here and relax before going on.
9. Ms. Collins (laid, lay) the study guides on the table.
10. Jack stole the hen that (lay, laid) golden eggs.
11. The sports page is (lying, laying) on the floor.
12. (Lie, Lay) the package on the back counter.
13. A dense fog has been (lying, laying) over the bay.
14. Tower Bridge (lays, lies) over the river Thames.
15. I think I'll (lie, lay) down before dinner.
16. The new high school is (laid, lain) out like a mall.
17. That tennis racket has (laid, lain) unused all summer.
18. Each club has (lain, laid) plans for homecoming.
19. Earthquakes may occur wherever the fault (lays, lies).
20. The directions for the ceiling fan (lay, laid) in the box.

USAGE

### *Sit* and *Set*

The verb *sit* usually means "to assume or be in an upright seated position." The principal parts of *sit* are *sit,* (is) *sitting, sat,* (have) *sat.*

The verb *set* usually means "to place or to put (something)." The principal parts of *set* are *set,* (is) *setting, set,* (have) *set.*

*Exceptions:* The word *usually* in the definitions indicates that these are the most common meanings and uses. On rare occasions *sit* may be used with the meaning of *set* ("*Sit* the baby here"); in other rare uses, *sit* may take an object ("He *sits* a horse well"). The verb *set* has a few specialized meanings in which it does not take an object:

They set out for the World's Fair.
As the sun sets over the water, the sky is fiery.
Gelatin with fruit in it takes a little longer to set.

Memorize the principal parts of these verbs:

| INFINITIVE | PRESENT PARTICIPLE | PAST | PAST PARTICIPLE |
|---|---|---|---|
| sit *(to rest)* | (is) sitting | sat | (have) sat |
| set *(to put)* | (is) setting | set | (have) set |

In deciding which verb form to use, you may find it helpful at first to use the two-question method outlined in the discussion of *lie* and *lay*. In addition to the two-question method, these two hints should help you to use *sit* and *set* correctly.

1. Make use of the fact that *set* normally takes an object whereas *sit* does not. People simply *sit;* people *set* something. Thus, if the verb has an object to match *lie-lay,* use a form of *set.*

2. As a final check, substitute the verb *place* for the problem verb in a sentence. If the sentence "sounds right" with the substitution, use a form of *set;* if it "sounds wrong," use a form of *sit.*

**EXERCISE 10. Using *Sit* and *Set* Correctly.** Number your paper 1–10. After each number, write the form of *sit* or *set* that correctly fills the blank in the corresponding sentence. Use the two-question method for finding the verb and verb form.

1. I —— in the doctor's waiting room for an hour this morning.
2. Should we —— here in the sun, or do you prefer the shade?
3. —— the carton down near the door.
4. We were —— so high up in the theater that the stage looked no bigger than a postage stamp.
5. If we had —— any longer, we would have been late for class.
6. Can you —— the timer so that the lights will go on automatically?
7. Paula just —— and stares and doesn't say a word.
8. You shouldn't —— on the damp ground.
9. Will everyone please —— down?
10. We all —— around the campfire last night.

USAGE

### *Rise* and *Raise*

The verb *rise* means "to ascend" or "go up." The principal parts of *rise* are *rise,* (is) *rising, rose,* (have) *risen.*

The verb *raise* means "to cause (something) to move upward, to lift (something)." The principal parts of *raise* are *raise,* (is) *raising, raised,* (have) *raised.*

It is easy to apply the two-question method to a *rise–raise* problem. In meaning the two verbs are quite different. One *raises* something or somebody; like *lay* and *set, raise* may take an object (that is, it is transitive). Like *lie* and *sit, rise* does not take an object (it is intransitive). In answering question 1, then, remember that (1) one always *raises something* or *somebody;* (2) one cannot *"rise"* anything. Answering question 2 is simplified by the fact that *raise* is a regular verb. Be sure that you know the principal parts of both verbs.

| INFINITIVE | PRESENT PARTICIPLE | PAST | PAST PARTICIPLE |
|---|---|---|---|
| rise *(to go up)* | (is) rising | rose | (have) risen |
| raise *(to force up)* | (is) raising | raised | (have) raised |

When the meaning that you have in mind is "to lift (something)," use *raise, raised,* or *raising* (regular principal parts). For other meanings, use *rise, rising, rose,* or *risen* (irregular principal parts).

USAGE

**EXERCISE 11. Using *Rise* and *Raise* Correctly.** Number your paper 1–10. After each number, write a + if the italicized verb in the corresponding sentence is correct. If it is incorrect, rewrite the sentence, using the correct form of the verb.

1. The cost of a traffic ticket *has raised.*
2. The student council *will raise* the flag.
3. The Bunsen burner flame *has raised* too high.
4. In "The Secret Sharer," Leggatt slowly began to *raise* from the water.
5. The curling smoke *rose* from the pile of leaves.
6. The sun *was rising* behind Pikes Peak.
7. The woman who *is rising* in the audience has been nominated for vice-president.
8. The price of gasoline *was risen* by that station.
9. The price of eggs *has been raised,* but you can use this coupon.
10. *Has* the popularity of video games *risen?*

**EXERCISE 12. Using *Lie-Lay, Sit-Set,* and *Rise-Raise* Correctly.** This exercise covers the six special verbs discussed in this section. Number your paper 1–20. After each number, write the correct one of the two verb forms in parentheses. Work slowly and carefully; use the two-question method whenever you are in doubt about a choice.

1. Hours of driving (lay, laid) ahead of us.
2. Indiana and Ohio (lie, lay) directly east of us.
3. The class (set, sat) quietly while Adolfo read the sonnet.
4. The thermostat will keep the temperature from (rising, raising).
5. After the wedding, confetti was (lying, laying) all over the ground.
6. The helium-filled balloon (rose, raised) into the air.
7. The engineers (laid, lay) the wire along the edge of the highway.
8. We (set, sat) and watched her mold the soft clay.
9. Is the number of traffic fatalities still (raising, rising)?
10. San Francisco (lays, lies) southwest of Sacramento.
11. Those watermelons had (laid, lain) in the field a week, ready to be put onto the trucks.
12. Let's (set, sit) down and talk about the problem.
13. The price of citrus fruit (rises, raises) after a freeze.
14. The package is (laying, lying) inside the storm door.
15. They (sit, set) the yearbooks in Mr. Cohen's office.
16. When the sun (raises, rises), we can find the trail again.
17. He has (lain, laid) his racquetball glove on the bench.
18. A replica of *The Thinker* is (setting, sitting) there.
19. She (lay, laid) there until the paramedics arrived.
20. Where was Emily (sitting, setting) at the end of *Our Town?*

**REVIEW EXERCISE B. Using Verb Forms Correctly.** Number your paper 1–10. Each of the following sentences contains an error in verb usage. After the proper number, write the correct form of the incorrect verb.

EXAMPLE 1. When we begun shoveling the snow from the driveway, it looked like an easy job.
1. *began*

1. Early yesterday morning, Hurricane Dora torn through the city.
2. This summer our squash vines have grown so profusely that they have took over almost the entire garden.

USAGE

3. I am so tired that I wish I could just lay down and take a nap!
4. Because I forgetted where I put the keys to the storeroom, I had to call a locksmith to open the door.
5. After my younger brother had gave his teacher his excuse, she laughed and said it was the first time she had heard of a cat's eating homework papers.
6. After a swim of over eleven hours, two American women come ashore on the coast of France; they had successfully crossed the twenty-one-mile English Channel from Dover.
7. The sun rised at 6:18 this morning; I know because I had insomnia all night.
8. Please sit the bucket near the wheelbarrow.
9. My favorite scene in the movie was the one in which the comic hero bited the dog.
10. Costumed as night creatures and monsters, we crept around the side of the Smiths' house and laid in wait for them.



## TENSE

**25b. Learn the names of the six tenses and the way the tenses are formed.**

Verbs indicate the *time* of an action or a statement by changes in their form. Every form of a verb tells us something about the time of an action or statement; that is, it "places" the action or statement in the past, the present, or the future. These verb forms are called *tenses,* from the Latin word meaning "time." English verbs appear in six different tenses to indicate past, present, or future time. All six tenses are based on the principal parts of a verb: the infinitive, the present participle, the past, and the past participle.

To learn the verb forms used in each of the six tenses, study the following *conjugations* of the verbs *see* and *be.*

### *Conjugation of the Verb* See

Present infinitive: *to see* Perfect infinitive: *to have seen*

*Principal Parts*

| INFINITIVE | PRESENT PARTICIPLE | PAST | PAST PARTICIPLE |
|---|---|---|---|
| see | seeing | saw | seen |

### *Present Tense*

| *Singular* | *Plural* |
|---|---|
| I see | we see |
| you see | you see |
| he, she, it sees | they see |

Present progressive: *I am seeing,* etc.

### *Past Tense*

| *Singular* | *Plural* |
|---|---|
| I saw | we say |
| you saw | you saw |
| he, she, it saw | they saw |

Past progressive: *I was seeing,* etc.

### *Future Tense*

(*will* or *shall* + infinitive)

| *Singular* | *Plural* |
|---|---|
| I will (shall) see | we will (shall) see |
| you will see | you will see |
| he, she, it will see | they will see |

Future progressive: *I will (shall) be seeing,* etc.

### *Present Perfect Tense*

(*have* or *has* + past participle)

| *Singular* | *Plural* |
|---|---|
| I have seen | we have seen |
| you have seen | you have seen |
| he, she, it has seen | they have seen |

Present perfect progressive: *I have been seeing,* etc.

### *Past Perfect Tense*

(*had* + past participle)

| *Singular* | *Plural* |
|---|---|
| I had seen | we had seen |
| you had seen | you had seen |
| he, she, it had seen | they had seen |

Past perfect progressive: *I had been seeing,* etc.

### *Future Perfect Tense*

(*will have* or *shall have* + past participle)

| *Singular* | *Plural* |
|---|---|
| I will (shall) have seen | we will (shall) have seen |
| you will have seen | you will have seen |
| he, she, it will have seen | they will have seen |

Future perfect progressive: *I will have (shall have) been seeing,* etc.

## *Conjugation of the Verb* Be

Present infinitive: *to be* Perfect infinitive: *to have been*

### *Principal Parts*

| INFINITIVE | PRESENT PARTICIPLE | PAST | PAST PARTICIPLE |
|---|---|---|---|
| be | being | was | been |

### *Present Tense*

| *Singular* | *Plural* |
|---|---|
| I am | we are |
| you are | you are |
| he, she, it is | they are |

Present progressive: *I am being,* etc.

### *Past Tense*

| *Singular* | *Plural* |
|---|---|
| I was | we were |
| you were | you were |
| he, she, it was | they were |

Past progressive: *I was being,* etc.

### *Future Tense*

(*will* or *shall* + infinitive)

| *Singular* | *Plural* |
|---|---|
| I will (shall) be | we will (shall) be |
| you will be | you will be |
| he, she, it will be | they will be |

### *Present Perfect Tense*

(*have* or *has* + past participle)

| *Singular* | *Plural* |
| --- | --- |
| I have been | we have been |
| you have been | you have been |
| he, she, it has been | they have been |

### *Past Perfect Tense*

(*had* + past participle)

| *Singular* | *Plural* |
| --- | --- |
| I had been | we had been |
| you had been | you had been |
| he, she, it had been | they had been |

### *Future Perfect Tense*

(*will have* or *shall have* + past participle)

| *Singular* | *Plural* |
| --- | --- |
| I will (shall) have been | we will (shall) have been |
| you will have been | you will have been |
| he, she, it will have been | they will have been |

☞ **NOTE** The progressive forms of the verb are not a separate tense. Progressive forms are made up of the various tenses of the verb *be* plus the present participle. Progressive forms are used to show continuing action.



**25c. Learn the uses of each of the six tenses.**

Each of the tenses has its own special uses. The names of the tenses do not in themselves explain the uses, nor does a conjugation alone tell us more than the forms taken by a verb in different tenses. Study the following detailed explanations of each of the six tenses. As you read, review the name of each tense and the correct verb forms by referring to the conjugations of *see* and *be*. Learn the rules for the uses of each tense. Use these pages for reference whenever you meet a problem in tense that you cannot solve.

**(1) The *present tense* is used mainly to express an action (or to help make a statement about something) that is occurring now, at the present time.**

EXAMPLES Martina **raises** her hand.
Martina **looks** puzzled.
Martina **does raise** her hand. Martina **does look** puzzled. [Emphatic form; the verb with *do* or *did* is called the emphatic form.]

Use the progressive form to express a continuing action, an action in progress.

Martina **is raising** her hand. [progressive form]

The present tense has several minor uses in addition to its main one. Be sure that you understand all of the following uses.

In an idiomatic construction, the present tense may be used to express future time.

EXAMPLES The new schedule **starts** next Monday.
The schedule **changes** on Monday.

The present tense may be used to express a customary or habitual action or state of being.

EXAMPLE I **eat** cereal for breakfast.

The present tense is used to express a general truth, something that is true at all times.

EXAMPLES The earth **revolves** around the sun.
A rectangle **is** a four-sided figure having four right angles.

The present tense is used to tell of things that happened in the past when the writer wants to make the past events seem alive and vivid. This use is called the *historical present.*

EXAMPLE In a surprise move, the Greeks **construct** a huge wooden horse and **leave** it outside the walls of Troy.

**(2) The *past tense* is used to express an action (or to help make a statement about something) that occurred in the past and did not continue into the present.**

EXAMPLES She **had** dinner.
She **was having** dinner in the cafeteria.

> NOTE Past action may be shown in other ways.

I **used to hate** spicy food.
I **did hate** spicy food. [emphatic form]

**(3) The *future tense* is used to express an action (or to help make a statement about something) that will occur in the future. The future tense is formed with *will* or *shall*.**

EXAMPLES I **will jog** this afternoon.
I **will be jogging** this afternoon.

> NOTE Future time may also be indicated in other ways.

She **defends** her title tomorrow.
She is **going to defend** her title tomorrow.



**(4) The *present perfect tense* is used mainly to express an action (or to help make a statement about something) that has been completed at some indefinite time in the past. It is formed with *have* or *has* and the past participle.**

They **have bought** a computer.

Note the word *indefinite* in rule 4. The present perfect should not be used to express a *specific* time in the past.

NONSTANDARD They have bought a computer last week.
STANDARD They have bought a computer recently.
STANDARD They bought a computer last week. [past tense]

The present perfect tense may also be used to express an action (or to help make a statement about something) that began in the past and is still going on.

EXAMPLES We **have sat** here for hours.
We **have been sitting** here for hours.

**(5) The *past perfect tense* is used to express an action (or to help make a statement about something) that was completed in the past and preceded some other past action or event. It is formed with *had* and the past participle.**

EXAMPLES We suddenly realized that we **had gone** past our stop. [The going past preceded our realizing it.]
I **had packed** my bags two hours before I left for the bus station. [First I packed my bags; then I left.]

**(6) The *future perfect tense* is used to express an action (or to help make a statement about something) that will be completed in the future before some other future action or event. It is formed with *will have* or *shall have* and the past participle.**

EXAMPLES The holidays **will have begun** by the time we arrive in Tampa.
By the middle of May, she **will have been playing** in the band for three years. [Three years of playing in the band will be completed by the future date.]

**EXERCISE 13. Understanding the Uses of the Six Tenses.** Number your paper 1–10. After each number, write the names of the tenses of the verbs in the corresponding pair of sentences. All the sentences are grammatically correct; they differ only in the tenses used. Be prepared to explain how these differences in tense alter the meanings of the sentences.

1. Channel 5 News has given the latest update.
   Channel 5 News had given the latest update.
2. I took piano lessons for three years.
   I have taken piano lessons for three years.
3. We will do our research on Friday.
   We will have done our research on Friday.
4. Jane has reported on recent fossil discoveries.
   Jane had reported on recent fossil discoveries.
5. Do you know what Roy told us?
   Did you know what Roy had told us?
6. We have sent out invitations.
   We had sent out invitations.
7. I will make a time line of the Middle Ages this weekend.
   I will have made a time line of the Middle Ages by this weekend.
8. I think that I have seen her somewhere before.
   I thought that I had seen her somewhere before.
9. Did the jury reach a verdict?
   Has the jury reached a verdict?

10. Ms. Wong was the club sponsor for the past five years.
    Ms. Wong has been the club sponsor for the past five years.

**EXERCISE 14. Writing Sentences in the Present Perfect, Past Perfect, and Future Perfect.** This exercise will help you use the perfect tenses. Write ten original sentences as directed.

1. Write three sentences in the present perfect about literature.
2. Write three in the past perfect about movies and television.
3. Write four in the future perfect about animals.

## SPECIAL PROBLEMS IN THE USE OF TENSES



Now that you have learned the six tenses and their uses, you are well on the way to avoiding errors in using verbs in your speaking and writing. However, knowing about tenses will not enable you to avoid all errors. There are still some special problems that every writer needs to solve. A few of these problems are discussed in this section.

### Sequence of Tenses

Normally the verbs in a compound or complex sentence follow the principle of sequence of tense. The sentence "The gun *sounded,* and the swimmers *dive* into the water" is incorrect. The writer has needlessly switched from the past tense in the first clause to the present tense in the second clause. The entire sentence should have been written in either the present or the past tense: "The gun *sounded,* and the swimmers *dived* into the water" or "The gun *sounds,* and the swimmers *dive* into the water."

Somewhat more difficult to handle are sentences in which tense is deliberately and correctly changed to indicate a change in time. Study the following examples, in which meanings in tense are used to convey different meanings.

> I **think** that I **have** a high average. [The two present tenses agree.]
> I **think** that I **had** a high average. [The change in the second verb to the past tense implies that I no longer have a high average.]

> Lia **said** that she **lived** near the park. [The two past tenses agree.]
> Lia **said** that she **would live** near the park. [The change to *would live* implies that Lia did not live near the park at the time she made the statement.]

The relation between the tenses in these examples is simple and clear. Other constructions and combinations, however, require special attention. Study the examples that follow.

NONSTANDARD Since the new band director took over, our band won all of its contests. [The new director took over at a definite, specific time; thus the past tense is correct. The winning took place over a period of time, and the speaker has no specific contest in mind. Here the past tense is incorrect; the present perfect tense should be used.]

STANDARD Since the new band director took over, our band **has won** all of its contests.

NONSTANDARD He was now working for the *New York Times,* but he was working for the *Wall Street Journal* earlier in the year. [The second action preceded the first; therefore, the second verb should be in the past perfect form.]

STANDARD He was now working for the *New York Times,* but he **had been working** for the *Wall Street Journal* earlier in the year.



### WRITING APPLICATION A: Avoiding Unnecessary Shifts in Tense

The purpose of most writing is to communicate—an idea, a feeling, a mood—to your audience. One important way to achieve clarity in your writing is to select a tense and avoid shifting from this tense unnecessarily.

#### Writing Assignment

Write a brief account of a short story or a TV episode that you remember clearly. Use the present tense and avoid shifting from this tense unnecessarily. When you revise your account, check to see that you have not shifted from your tense unnecessarily.

**25d. Avoid the use of *would have* in "if clauses" expressing the earlier of two past actions. Use the past perfect tense.**

NONSTANDARD If she would have handed in her application, she would have gotten the job.

STANDARD If she **had handed** in her application, she would have gotten the job.

NONSTANDARD I would not have attended if I would have known it was going to snow.

STANDARD I would not have attended if I **had known** it was going to snow.

NONSTANDARD If Felita would have asked her parents, she probably could have gone with us.

STANDARD If Felita **had asked** her parents, she probably could have gone with us.

**EXERCISE 15. Using Tenses Correctly.** Number your paper 1–20. Each of the following sentences contains an error in the use of tenses. Decide how to correct each sentence; then write the corrected verb after the proper number on your paper.

1. Frances promised to bring the basket that she bought in Arizona.
2. We studied *Macbeth* after we learned about the Globe Theatre.
3. By the time we get to the picnic area, the rain will stop.
4. In August my parents will be married for twenty-five years.
5. As an eyewitness to the accident, Pam told what happened.
6. I would have agreed if you would have asked me sooner.
7. Val claims that cats made the best pets.
8. My grandmother always said that haste made waste.
9. The graduation valedictory will be delivered by then.
10. If the books have been cataloged last week, why haven't they been placed on the shelves?
11. I would have lent you my notes if you would have asked me.
12. If he would have read "The White Birds," he might have liked William Butler Yeats's poetry.
13. Who has not heard that there were a thousand meters in a kilometer?
14. I'd have tutored you if you would have asked me.
15. The book is on works of art that have been created centuries ago.
16. By next month Ms. Deloney will be mayor for two years.
17. If I would have listened more carefully, I might have taken better notes.
18. Did they know that Labor Day always came on the first Monday in September?
19. The lobbyists were waiting an hour before the governor arrived.
20. If he would have revised his first draft, he would have received a better grade.

## The Present Infinitive and the Perfect Infinitive

**25e. Use the present infinitive (*to push, to go,* etc.) to express an action that follows another action.**

CONFUSING Pam said that she had hoped to have seen the Super Bowl on television. [What did Pam hope—*to see* the Super Bowl or *to have seen* the Super Bowl? She hoped *to see* the Super Bowl, since the action expressed by *see* follows the action expressed by *had hoped.*]

CLEAR Pam said that she had hoped **to see** the Super Bowl on television.

**25f. Use the perfect infinitive (*to have pushed, to have gone,* etc.) to express an action that took place before another action.**

EXAMPLE The divers claimed **to have located** an ancient sailing vessel. [The perfect infinitive is correct because the action it expresses came before the time of the first verb, *claimed.]*



**REVIEW EXERCISE C. Using Tenses Correctly.** Number your paper 1–10. Each of the following sentences contains an error in the use of verbs (including infinitives). After the proper number, write the phrase in which the error occurs, using the correct form of the verb.

EXAMPLE 1. I would have worked harder in my geometry class if I would have known how important it was.

1. *if I had known*

1. When you charge the battery in the car, be sure to have protected your eyes and hands from the sulfuric acid in the battery.
2. After all of us decided to attend the concert at Boyer Hall, we purchased four tickets for Saturday night.
3. Before next Saturday is over, we will hear some exciting music at the concert.
4. If I would have known about the free offer, I would have sent in a coupon.
5. My old skates lay in my closet for the past two years.
6. I would have liked to have gone swimming yesterday.
7. I'll just set here for a while until Dr. Lopez returns.
8. If I had the address, I would have delivered the package myself.
9. Dave should have went to the dentist three months ago.
10. After giving me his advice, my math teacher always used to say, "A word to the wise was sufficient."

## ACTIVE AND PASSIVE VOICE

When a verb expresses an action performed *by* its subject, the verb is said to be in the *active* voice. A verb is in the *passive* voice when it expresses an action performed *upon* its subject or when the subject is the result of the action.

ACTIVE VOICE Carol **changed** the tire. [subject acting]

PASSIVE VOICE The tire **was changed** by Carol. [subject acted upon]

Nearly all verbs that take objects (transitive verbs) can be used in the passive voice.

ACTIVE VOICE Ann (S) **bathed** (V) the puppy (O).

PASSIVE VOICE The puppy (S) **was bathed** (V) by Ann.

The puppy (S) **was bathed** (V).

From these examples, you can see the formation of the passive construction and its relationship to the active. The object of the active sentence moves ahead of the verb to become the subject of the passive sentence, and the subject of the active sentence is either expressed in a prepositional phrase beginning with *by* or dropped completely.

Notice also that the verb from the active sentence becomes a past participle preceded by the form of the verb *be* that indicates the proper tense.

ACTIVE American citizens **honor** the war dead on Memorial Day.
PASSIVE The war dead **are honored** by American citizens on Memorial Day.

ACTIVE The optometrist **adjusted** the glasses carefully.
PASSIVE The glasses **were adjusted** carefully by the optometrist.

### The Retained Object

Transitive verbs in the active voice often have indirect as well as direct objects. When they do, either object can become the subject of the passive sentence.

ACTIVE She (S) gave (V) the class (IO) three writing assignments (DO).
PASSIVE The class was given three writing assignments (by her).
PASSIVE Three writing assignments were given the class (by her).

USAGE

In the two passive sentences, one of the objects becomes the subject and the other remains as a complement of the verb. In the first sentence, the indirect object, *class,* becomes the subject, and the direct object, *assignments,* is kept as a complement. In the second, it is the indirect object that is retained. An object that continues to function as a complement in a passive construction is called a *retained object.*

## Use of the Passive Voice

Choosing between the active and the passive voice in writing is a matter of style, not correctness. However, in most circumstances the passive voice is less forceful than the active voice, and a string of passive verbs often produces an awkward paragraph.

AWKWARD PASSIVE Last night, the floor was scrubbed by my dad, and the faucet was fixed by my mom.

ACTIVE Last night, my dad scrubbed the floor, and my mom fixed the faucet.

AWKWARD PASSIVE The first wristwatch was created by a court jeweler when a watch in a bracelet was requested by Empress Josephine.

ACTIVE When Empress Josephine requested a watch in a bracelet, a court jeweler created the first wristwatch.

SUCCESSION OF PASSIVES When my mother *was asked* by the local camera club to give a guest lecture on photography, we *were* all *amazed* by the request. Neither of my parents *had* ever *been chosen* to do anything like this before. Since I *was considered* the most imaginative member of my family, I *was given* by my mother the task of choosing the topics that *would be presented.* Father *was elected* by us to choose the slides that *would be shown* to the amateur photographers. Extra invitations *were sent* to us by the camera club and these, in turn, *were mailed* by us to all of our friends. When the night of the lecture finally arrived, my father, my two brothers, and I *were seated* by the usher in the first row. The lecture *was introduced* by a discussion of how modern photography *was influenced* by portrait painting and still-life painting. After the lecture *had been completed*, I *was impressed* by Mother's knowledge and command of her subject.

This paragraph is not effective because of the overuse of passive verbs.

**25g. Use the passive voice sparingly. Avoid weak and awkward passives. In the interest of variety, avoid long passages in which all the verbs are passive. Although this rule is generally true, there are a few situations where the passive voice is particularly useful.**

**(1) Use the passive voice to express an action in which the actor is unknown.**

An anonymous letter **was sent** to the police chief.

**(2) Use the passive voice to express an action in which it is desirable not to disclose the actor.**

The missing painting **has been returned** to the museum.

Sometimes the passive voice is more convenient, and just as appropriate, as the active voice. In the following sentences, the passive voice is completely acceptable and probably more natural.

Penicillin, a modern wonder drug, **was discovered** accidentally.
The person who was standing near the entrance **was asked** to close the door.
The top player **was eliminated** in the first round.



**EXERCISE 16. Revising Sentences in the Passive Voice.** Revise the following sentences by changing the passive verbs to active verbs wherever you think the change is desirable. If you think that the passive is preferable, write *no change* after the number of the corresponding sentence.

1. Roots, nuts, and berries were gathered and eaten by early human beings.
2. The discovery may have been made by them accidentally that some food is improved by cooking.
3. Slaughtered animals may have been left near the fire by these primitive people.
4. When the meat was heated and browned, it probably tasted better.
5. The first ovens were formed from pits lined with stones and hot coals.
6. It wasn't long before ovens were built above the ground with some kind of chimney constructed to diffuse smoke.
7. Primitive kettles were made by early humans by smearing clay over reed baskets and allowing it to harden.
8. The earliest cooking tools were fashioned by primitive people from wood, stones, and parts of animal bones.
9. After metal had been discovered, these earlier implements were used by later people as models.
10. Many improvements in cooking have been made by modern chefs, but the first ideas were put into practice by prehistoric people.

**WRITING APPLICATION B:**
**Using the Active Voice**

Whenever possible, you should write in the active voice. The active voice is usually more direct, more vigorous, and more concise than the passive voice.

EXAMPLE The students made a contribution. [direct and concise]
A contribution was made by the students. [indirect and awkward]

However, the passive voice is useful in situations in which the performer of the action is unknown or unimportant.

EXAMPLE On November 22, 1963, John F. Kennedy **was assassinated.**

**Writing Assignment**

Write a concise account of an important current event. Use the active voice whenever possible. When you revise your account, correct any unnecessary use of the passive voice.



## THE SUBJUNCTIVE MOOD

Verbs may be in one of three moods: *indicative, imperative,* or *subjunctive.* Almost all the verbs you use in writing and speaking are in the *indicative mood,* which is used to make statements of fact. The *imperative mood* is used to express a request or command.

IMPERATIVE Proofread your own compositions.
Please check the timer on the microwave.

The only common uses of the *subjunctive* mood in modern English are to express a condition contrary to fact and to express a wish. These usages occur principally in written English and usually apply to only one verb form—*were.* The following partial conjugation of *be* will show how the subjunctive mood differs from the indicative.

| PRESENT INDICATIVE | | PRESENT SUBJUNCTIVE | |
|---|---|---|---|
| *Singular* | *Plural* | *Singular* | *Plural* |
| I am | we are | (if) I be | (if) we be |
| you are | you are | (if) you be | (if) you be |
| he is | they are | (if) he be | (if) they be |

The present subjunctive is used only in certain rather formal situations.

EXAMPLES The moderator at the convention requested that the state delegates **be** seated.
I move that the meeting **be** adjourned.

| PAST INDICATIVE | | PAST SUBJUNCTIVE | |
|---|---|---|---|
| *Singular* | *Plural* | *Singular* | *Plural* |
| I was | we were | (if) I were | (if) we were |
| you were | you were | (if) you were | (if) you were |
| he was | they were | (if) he were | (if) they were |

**25h. The subjunctive *were* is used in contrary-to-fact statements (after *if* or *as though*) and in statements expressing a wish.**

CONTRARY TO FACT If I **were** you, I'd have those tires checked. [I am not you.]
If he **were** to proofread his papers, he would make fewer errors. [He does not proofread his papers.]

On a bad telephone connection, it sometimes sounds as though the caller **were** ten thousand miles away. [The caller is not ten thousand miles away.]

WISH I wish my aunt **were** here for the holidays.
I wish he **were** not driving so fast.

USAGE

**REVIEW EXERCISE D. Using Verbs Correctly.** Some of the following sentences contain errors in the use of verbs (including infinitives). Others are correct. Number your paper 1–20. If the verbs in the sentence are correct, write *C* after the corresponding number on your paper. If you find a verb error, write the correct verb form after the proper number.

EXAMPLE 1. After he had passed the jewelry store, he wished he went into it.
1. *had gone*

1. I wish I read the chapter before I tried to answer the questions.
2. If it was not so cloudy, we would have the party outside.
3. Nathanael West said that he'd never have written his satirical novels if he had not visited Hollywood.
4. The rock group had finished the concert, but the audience called for another set.
5. Do you think that she would have volunteered to help if she weren't highly qualified?

6. If Sherrie would not have missed the deadline, the yearbook delivery would have been on time.
7. In his haste to hand in his test paper, he failed to put his name on it.
8. Although I thought I planned my trip down to the last detail, there was one thing I had forgotten.
9. If you would have remembered to bring something to read, you would not have been so bored.
10. He would have scored the winning basket if he would have kept his eye on the clock.
11. The smell from the paper mill laid over the town like a blanket.
12. When they returned from picking berries, they sat their full bowls on the table.
13. After the scout had seen the wide receiver in action, he wished he offered the player a scholarship.
14. Several books for the research paper laid on the desk while he watched TV.
15. I wish that I kept in mind that "a stitch in time saves nine."
16. Any mention of last year's final game raises the coach's ire.
17. If Jonathan Edwards wrote shorter sentences, we would be even more fascinated by his messages.
18. By the time we had smelled the smoke, the flames had already begun to spread.
19. I am glad to have the opportunity to revise my essay for a higher grade.
20. Even though her standards would be high, she was considered the most popular teacher in the school.



## CHAPTER 25 REVIEW: POSTTEST

**Revising Verb Tense or Voice.** Revise the following sentences by correcting verbs that are in the wrong tense or use an awkward voice. If the sentence is correct, write + after the proper number on your paper.

EXAMPLE 1. If I would have seen the accident, I would have reported it to the police.

1. *If I had seen the accident*

1. From our studies we had concluded that women had played many critical roles in the history of our nation.
2. Jane Addams had founded Hull House in Chicago to educate the neighborhood poor and immigrants and to familiarize them with American ways; for her efforts she had received the Nobel Peace Prize in 1931.
3. In 1932, after a flight of almost fifteen hours, Amelia Earhart became the first woman to have flown solo across the Atlantic Ocean.
4. Pearl Buck, a recipient of the Nobel Prize for Literature in 1938, strived to bring understanding and peace to everyone.
5. When the Republican National Convention met in San Francisco in 1964, Margaret Chase Smith, senator from Maine, received twenty-seven delegate votes for the presidential nomination.
6. At the 1984 Democratic National Convention in San Francisco, Geraldine Ferraro became the first woman to have been nominated for the Vice-Presidency.
7. Have you ever heard of Belva Lockwood, a woman whose accomplishments paved the way for both Mrs. Smith and Ms. Ferraro?
8. In 1879, shortly after she was admitted to the bar, Belva Lockwood became the first female lawyer to have argued a case before the United States Supreme Court.
9. Although the name Belva Lockwood had not been a well-known one in 1984, she received over four thousand votes for the Presidency in 1884.
10. By the time you leave high school, you will learn many interesting facts about history.
11. If modern society was an agricultural one, more of us would know about farming and about the difficulties faced by farmers.
12. Factory work is rarely affected by weather conditions, whereas farm work has always been closely interconnected with climate and temperature.
13. How many of us possess the skills to have survived on our own without the assistance of store-bought items?
14. If you would have taken a nutrition class, you would have learned how to shop wisely for food.
15. Wacky, my pet chipmunk, was acting as if she was trying to tell me something.

16. Yesterday, Dad's car was washed and waxed by my brother.
17. According to this news article, the concert last Friday night is "a resounding success."
18. At the retirement party, our teacher was given a gift by the principal.
19. Because of the excessive amount of rain this spring, the water in the dam has raised to a dangerous level.
20. After spending the entire morning working in the garden, Jim is laying down for a rest.

## CHAPTER 26

# Correct Use of Modifiers

## FORMS OF ADJECTIVES AND ADVERBS; COMPARISON

You have learned that an adjective modifies a noun or pronoun and that an adverb modifies a verb, an adjective, or another adverb. Yet you may have trouble deciding which to use after the verb *taste, look,* or *smell,* or whether to say someone "sang good" or "sang well." These and other usage problems involving the use of adjectives and adverbs are discussed in this chapter.

### DIAGNOSTIC TEST

**Selecting Modifiers to Complete Sentences.** Number your paper 1–20. Select the correct one of the two words in parentheses in each sentence, and write it after the proper number.

EXAMPLE 1. When you feel (nervous, nervously), take a deep breath and concentrate on relaxing images.
1. *nervous*

1. As you approach the intersection, drive (cautious, cautiously).
2. Listen (careful, carefully) when Lauren speaks; you should be able to detect a faint English accent.
3. This has been the most (wonderful, wonderfullest) day of my life.

4. If Charlene appears (angry, angrily), it is because she has spent the past two hours waiting for Steve to return her call.
5. When my sister and I had the flu, Rosa was (sicker, sickest).
6. This car is roomier than (any, any other) car we ever had.
7. This is the (goodest, best) meal I've had in a long time.
8. When Mrs. Gibson hands back my algebra test, I won't feel (bad, badly); I'll feel terrible!
9. If you look at the two kittens carefully, you will see that the smaller one is (healthier, healthiest).
10. It was obvious from his response in the press conference that the candidate prepared his answers (well, good).
11. This must be the (baddest, worst) movie ever made.
12. You will drive more (steady, steadily) if you keep your eyes on the road.
13. Both books are rare, but the one bound in green cloth is the (less, least) valuable one.
14. Please don't feel (sad, sadly) about the news.
15. When Corey Howard fell off the balance beam in gym class, Mr. Russell ran (quick, quickly) to help.
16. My geometry grades were higher than (anyone's, anyone else's) in my class.
17. Which do you think is (worse, worser), finding a worm in your apple or finding half a worm?
18. When I give an oral report in English class, Mr. Talbot always tells me to speak more (slow, slowly).
19. Just thinking about giving an oral report makes my heart beat (rapid, rapidly).
20. This engine is twelve years old, but it still runs (good, well).



## ADJECTIVE AND ADVERB FORMS

Make sure that you are able to tell which is the adjective form of a word and which is the adverb form. Knowing that most adverbs end in *-ly* (*clearly, happily, eagerly*) will help you only if you also understand that not *all* adverbs end in *-ly* and that a few common adjectives end in *-ly*. Some words have the same form whether used as an adjective or as an adverb.

| ADJECTIVES | ADVERBS |
|---|---|
| a *fast* swimmer | She swam *fast.* |
| a *hard* decision | He trains *hard.* |
| a *tight* fit | Seal it *tight.* |
| a *long* pause | He pondered *long.* |
| a *late* start | It began *late.* |

ADJECTIVES ENDING IN *-ly*

*daily* lesson
*early* breakfast
*lively* discussion

**26a. Linking verbs, especially the verbs of sense (*taste, look, smell,* etc.), are often followed by an adjective. Action verbs are often followed by an adverb.**



EXAMPLES The movie seemed **endless.** [The adjective *endless* is correct after the linking verb *seemed.* It modifies the subject *movie.*]
Her voice sounds **loud.** [The adjective *loud* is correct after the linking verb *sounds.* It modifies the subject *voice.*]

Some verbs may be used as either linking or action verbs. When they are used as action verbs, the modifier that follows modifies the verb rather than the subject and is, therefore, an adverb. For example, *looked* may be used as a linking verb and as an action verb.

EXAMPLES The teacher looked **angry.** [After the linking verb *looked,* the adjective *angry* is correct. It modifies *teacher.*]
The teacher looked **angrily** at the talkers. [After the action verb *looked,* the adverb *angrily* is correct. It modifies *looked.*]

When you are not sure whether a verb is a linking verb, try substituting for it a form of *seem,* which is always a linking verb. If the substitution does not greatly change the meaning of the sentence, the verb is a linking verb and should be followed by an adjective.

EXAMPLES The bread smelled fresh. [*The bread seemed fresh* gives about the same meaning; hence, *smelled* is a linking verb in this sentence.]
We smelled the bread baking. [*We seemed the bread baking* makes no sense; therefore, *smelled* is not a linking verb in this sentence.]

**26b. In making a choice between an adjective and an adverb, ask yourself what the word modifies. If it modifies a noun or pronoun, choose the adjective. If it modifies a verb, choose the adverb.**

PROBLEM They turned the TV (loud, loudly) enough for everyone to hear.
SOLUTION They turned the TV **loud** enough for everyone to hear. [The adjective *loud* modifies the noun *TV*.]

PROBLEM Has he chosen his subject (careful, carefully)?
SOLUTION Has he chosen his subject **carefully**? [The adverb *carefully* modifies the action verb *has chosen.*]

**EXERCISE 1. Selecting Adjectives or Adverbs to Complete Sentences.** Number your paper 1–10. Select the correct one of the two words in parentheses in each sentence, and write it after the proper number. If the word modifies the subject, select the adjective; if it modifies the verb, select the adverb. Remember that a linking verb is followed by an adjective.

1. Yesterday our classroom computer was acting rather (strange, strangely).
2. After it was repaired, it ran (perfect, perfectly) again.
3. Some machines break down (continual, continually), while others almost never need repairs.
4. Parts of a machine may look (normal, normally) but may break under stress.
5. Has she been studying her lines (regular, regularly)?
6. Time, it seems, treats all of us (unfair, unfairly).
7. You have to look very (careful, carefully) to see the watermark on this postage stamp.
8. I felt (awful, awfully) after eating all that food.
9. If you enunciate (clear, clearly), people will be able to understand what you are saying.
10. I tried to explain why I was late, but my mother looked at me (skeptical, skeptically).



### *Bad* and *Badly*

*Bad* is an adjective, modifying nouns and pronouns. *Badly* is an adverb, modifying verbs, adjectives, and adverbs. Since a verb of sense—*feel, smell, taste, sound*—is followed by an adjective (not an adverb) modifying its subjects, it is standard English to say *"feel bad," "smell bad,"* etc.

The team **feels bad** about losing in the finals.

If the meat **smells bad,** don't eat it.

USAGE NOTE The expression *"feel badly"* has, through usage, become acceptable, though ungrammatical, English.

### Well and Good

*Well* may be used as either an adjective or an adverb. As an adjective, *well* has three meanings.

1. *"To be in good health"*
   He feels **well.** He seems **well.**
2. *"To appear well dressed or well groomed"*
   He looks **well** in that band uniform.
3. *"To be satisfactory"*
   All is **well.**

As an adverb, *well* tells how an action is performed and means "capably."

She spoke very **well.**

*Good* is always an adjective. It should never be used to modify a verb.

NONSTANDARD The New York Philharmonic Orchestra plays good.
STANDARD The New York Philharmonic Orchestra plays **well.**

### Slow and Slowly

*Slow* is used as both an adjective and an adverb. *Slowly* is an adverb. Except for the expressions *"Drive slow"* and *"Go slow,"* which have become acceptable because of their wide use on highway signs, you will be on the safe side if you use *slow* only as an adjective.

EXERCISE 2. **Determining the Correct Use of Bad—Badly, Well—Good, and Slow—Slowly.** Number your paper 1–10. After each number, write *C* if the italicized word in the corresponding sentence is correct. If it is incorrect, write the correct word.

USAGE

EXAMPLE 1. When I painted the house, I fell off the ladder and hurt my right arm *bad.*
1. *badly.*

1. After practicing the magic trick for hours, she now has it down *good.*
2. Despite the immense size and obvious power of this airplane, the engines start up *slow.*
3. I can hit the ball *good* if I keep my eye on it.
4. Before Uncle Chet's hip-replacement surgery, his gait was painful and *slow.*
5. After studying French for the past three years in high school, we were pleased to discover how *good* we spoke and understood it on our trip to Quebec.
6. Some of the experiments the chemistry class has conducted have made the corridors smell *badly.*
7. When I handed in my essay on ecology, I was afraid Mrs. Wells would tell me it was done *bad.*
8. Whenever I watch the clock, the time seems to go *slow.*
9. When my parents correct my little sister, they tell her not to behave *bad.*
10. Don't feel *badly* if any of these sentences have tricked you; you are not alone!



**REVIEW EXERCISE A. Determining Correct Use of Modifiers in Sentences.** Number your paper 1–10. If the italicized modifier in a sentence is correct, write *C* after the proper number on your paper. If it is incorrect, write the correct form, and after the correct form write the word it modifies.

EXAMPLE 1. He plays the piano *good.*
1. *well, plays*

1. The members of our school's volleyball team get along *good* together.
2. It is just as *good* that I didn't get the job.
3. If you speak *slow,* I can understand you.
4. I was feeling *eager* about taking a computer course.
5. The soldier was not hurt *bad.*
6. Having gone to tennis camp, he plays very *good.*

7. In Elizabethan times, people dressed *different* from the way they do today.
8. Our team beat its major rival *easy*.
9. Do you feel *well* enough to go to school?
10. After school, go home *quick* to catch the TV special.

**WRITING APPLICATION A:**
**Using Adjective and Adverb Forms Correctly**

In your writing for school and business, you should use adjective and adverb forms correctly. Your readers expect you to follow the rules of standard English usage for these modifiers. Refer to the rules on pages 554–56 whenever you need help.

NONSTANDARD Joan did *good* on the test. [*Good* never modifies a verb.]
STANDARD Joan did well on the test. [The adverb *well* modifies the verb *did* and means "capably."]

NONSTANDARD These vegetables taste *badly*. [After the linking verb *taste*, you need an adjective.]
STANDARD These vegetables taste bad. [The adjective *bad* modifies the subject *vegetables*.]

**Writing Assignment**

Write ten sentences using the following adjectives and adverbs. Proofread your sentences for correct usage of these modifiers.

1. calm
2. bad
3. badly
4. well
5. good
6. slow
7. slowly
8. happy
9. brightly
10. quickly

## COMPARISON OF ADJECTIVES AND ADVERBS

**26c.** ***Comparison*** **is the name given to the change in the form of adjectives and adverbs when they are used to compare the degree of the qualities they express. There are three degrees of comparison:** ***positive, comparative,*** **and** ***superlative.***

| POSITIVE | COMPARATIVE | SUPERLATIVE |
|---|---|---|
| strange | stranger | strangest |
| friendly | friendlier | friendliest |
| delicious | more delicious | most delicious |
| neat | neater | neatest |
| careful | more careful | most careful |
| good | better | best |

## Comparative and Superlative Forms

**(1) Most adjectives and adverbs of one syllable form their comparative and superlative degrees by adding *-er* and *-est.***

| POSITIVE | COMPARATIVE | SUPERLATIVE |
|---|---|---|
| soft | softer | softest |
| crisp | crisper | crispest |
| clean | cleaner | cleanest |
| long | longer | longest |



**(2) Some adjectives of two syllables form their comparative and superlative degrees by adding the suffixes *-er* and *-est*; other adjectives of two syllables form their comparative and superlative degrees by adding the words *more* and *most.***

| POSITIVE | COMPARATIVE | SUPERLATIVE |
|---|---|---|
| early | earlier | earliest |
| cautious | more cautious | most cautious |

If you are not sure how a word is compared, consult a dictionary.

**(3) Adjectives of more than two syllables and adverbs ending in the suffix *-ly* form their comparative and superlative degrees by means of *more* and *most.***

| POSITIVE | COMPARATIVE | SUPERLATIVE |
|---|---|---|
| efficient | more efficient | most efficient |
| skillfully | more skillfully | most skillfully |

**(4) Comparison to indicate less or least of a quality is accomplished by using the words *less* and *least* before the adjective or adverb.**

| POSITIVE | COMPARATIVE | SUPERLATIVE |
|---|---|---|
| punctual | less punctual | least punctual |
| honest | less honest | least honest |

## Irregular Comparison

Adjectives and adverbs that do not follow the regular methods of forming their comparative and superlative degrees are said to be compared irregularly.

| POSITIVE | COMPARATIVE | SUPERLATIVE |
|---|---|---|
| bad | worse | worst |
| good, well | better | best |
| little | less | least |
| many, much | more | most |



**EXERCISE 3. Writing the Comparative and Superlative Forms of Words.** Write the comparative and superlative forms of the following words. If you are in doubt about any of them, use a dictionary.

1. anxious
2. hard
3. cheerful
4. eager
5. quick
6. well
7. cold
8. stealthily
9. expensive
10. enthusiastically

## Use of Comparatives and Superlatives

**26d. In standard English the comparative degree is used when comparing *two* things, and the superlative degree is used when comparing *more than two*.**

COMPARISON OF TWO THINGS

Although both puppies look cute, the **more active** one is probably **healthier**. [not *most active* or *healthiest*]

After reading *King Lear* and *A Winter's Tale,* I can understand why the first is the **more widely** praised. [not *most widely*]

COMPARISON OF MORE THAN TWO THINGS

I selected the front row because it provided the **best** view of the chemistry experiment. [not *better*]

Of the four plays we saw in New York, I think *Death of a Salesman* was the **most moving.** [not *more moving]*

> ☞ **USAGE NOTE** In informal speech and writing, however, the superlative is sometimes used for emphasis, even though only two things are being compared.

INFORMAL Which language was hardest to learn, French or Spanish? [formal: *harder*]

In this singles tennis match, the player with the strongest serve will win. [formal: *stronger*]



**26e. Include the word *other* or *else* when comparing one thing with a group of which it is a part.**

NONSTANDARD I think Rampal plays better than any flutist. [This sentence says, illogically, that Rampal plays better than himself.]

STANDARD I think Rampal plays better than any **other** flutist.

NONSTANDARD The left fielder hit more home runs last month than any member of the team. [The left fielder is a member of the team; he could not have hit more home runs than himself.]

STANDARD The left fielder hit more home runs last month than any **other** member of the team.

**26f. Avoid double comparisons.**

A double comparison is one in which the degree is formed incorrectly by both adding *-er* or *-est* and using *more* or *most.*

NONSTANDARD This week's program is much more funnier than last week's.

STANDARD This week's program is much **funnier** than last week's.

NONSTANDARD In our high school, the most farthest you can go in math is Algebra III.

STANDARD In our high school, the **farthest** you can go in math is Algebra III.

**EXERCISE 4. Using Comparatives and Superlatives Correctly.** Number your paper 1–10. Identify and correct the errors in the use of comparatives and superlatives in the following sentences; write each corrected phrase after the proper number.

EXAMPLE 1. It seems I spend more time doing my biology homework than anyone in my class.
1. *than anyone else in my class*

1. Which is the most famous Russian ballet company, the Kirov or the Bolshoi?
2. When we have Italian food for supper, Joe eats more than anyone at the table.
3. According to the National Weather Service, Hurricane Clara did more extensive damage than any hurricane in this century.
4. Although both cars appear to be well constructed, I think that the most desirable one is the one that gets better gas mileage.
5. Which of these two hotels is farthest from the airport?
6. I know this shade of blue is a closer match than that one, but we still haven't found the better match.
7. The newscaster said that the pollen count this morning was higher than any count taken in the past ten years.
8. Anyone who has heard the school band recognizes that Rick Webb is a more accomplished musician than anyone in the band.
9. Lucia has the uncommonest hobby I've ever heard of—collecting insects.
10. In the dance marathon, Bill and Inez managed to stay awake and keep on moving longer than any couple on the dance floor.



**REVIEW EXERCISE B. Using Modifiers Correctly.** Some of the following sentences contain errors in the use of modifiers. For each correct sentence, write *C* after the proper number; rewrite each incorrect sentence correctly.

1. Yesterday's tennis game was the better tennis game that I ever played.
2. Which course suited her best, chorus or band?
3. Armand is a better typist than anybody in his class.
4. I felt badly about not getting my science project done.

5. Frank is the most fastest in the hundred-yard dash.
6. Annette told me that she will try harder on the next vocabulary test.
7. Merita felt bad about losing her American history notes.
8. Which of the four shorthand dictations was the harder?
9. Which appeals to you more, a junior college or a university?
10. I'm glad you are taking grammar study more serious.

## WRITING APPLICATION B: Using Comparisons in Your Writing

Using comparisons in your writing allows you to express similarities and differences between people, objects, places, or ideas. In formal writing and speaking, you should always follow the rules for standard English usage for comparisons.

EXAMPLES The Yorkshire terrier seemed the **more playful** of the two dogs. [*More playful* is correct; the writer is comparing two dogs.]

The **prettiest** flower is the rose. [*Prettiest* is correct because the comparison involves all flowers, not just two. *Most prettiest* would be a double comparison, which is never correct.]

### Writing Assignment

Look through the advertisements in a newspaper or magazine. Find an article of clothing, an appliance, or another item that you would like to own. Jot down the names of a few companies that manufacture this item, and list the advantages and disadvantages of each brand. Decide which you would buy. Write a paragraph explaining your choice, including at least five comparisons. When you proofread your paragraph, check for the correct use of comparisons.

USAGE

## CHAPTER 26 REVIEW: POSTTEST

**Selecting Modifiers to Complete Sentences Correctly.** Number your paper 1–20. If a sentence is correct, write *C* after the proper number; if it contains an error, rewrite the incorrect part of the sentence correctly.

EXAMPLE 1. Steve, who is the most brightest student in the physics class, is also a whiz in chemistry.
1. *the brightest student*

1. For my study break, I thought a piece of carrot cake would taste deliciously with a glass of cold milk.
2. When I was shopping in Clary's, I bought this brand of shampoo because it was the most cheap one on the shelves.
3. After listening to "The Battle of the Bands," we thought that the jazz band performed even more better than the rock group.
4. As we entered the hospital, we saw a sign that read Please Talk Soft.
5. When the treasurer presented the annual report, the statistics showed that the company had done badder this year than last.
6. They had to turn the gas down because the water in the pot boiled too quickly.
7. Megan shoots foul shots so good that she has made first-string varsity.
8. Of all the rooms in the building, this room is the most noisy.
9. The more even you distribute the work load among the members of the group, the more satisfied everyone will be.
10. "You cook so good," I said to my friend Leslie after I had tasted the meal.
11. Last night the weather forecaster on Channel 6 announced that this is the most rainy spring season the area has had in the past decade.
12. When I got my economics test back, I found I had done more badly than I had feared.
13. Although Jennifer is younger than her sister, Jennifer is the tallest of the two.
14. It is often easy to spot a new driver on the road because he tends to drive more slow than an experienced driver.
15. "You always look well in blue, Ramona," said Earl with genuine admiration.
16. This fast-food restaurant advertises that its hamburgers are more bigger than anyone else's.
17. When we visited San Fransisco, I bought the most tasty piece of sourdough bread I have ever eaten.

18. After receiving a rare coin for my birthday, I began to take coin collecting more seriously.
19. Before taking a computer course I couldn't program at all, but now I program very good.
20. Speak correct at all times!

USAGE

## CHAPTER 27

# Glossary of Usage

## COMMON USAGE PROBLEMS

### DIAGNOSTIC TEST

**Selecting Correct Expressions to Complete Sentences.** Number your paper 1–20. After each number, write the correct one of the two expressions in parentheses in the corresponding sentence. Some sentences contain more than one choice.

EXAMPLE 1. When my math teacher announced the rules for the year, she said she would not (except, accept) any papers written in ink.
1. *accept*

1. When Mrs. Hayes calls on me in chemistry class, I can't help (but feel, feeling) nervous and uncertain.
2. In this morning's news report, the announcer read (where, that) the governor's advisory committee has selected certain cities to receive additional state funds.
3. All the members of Congress (except, accept) Representative Lynde voted to retain the present tax structure for another year.
4. My grandparents have (affected, effected) all of us with their generosity, hope, and faith in the future.
5. I (couldn't, could) hardly believe my eyes when I saw a 90 on my geometry test; I must (of, have) remembered the formulas better than I thought I would.

6. As a birthday gift my aunt gave me (this here, this) dictionary, but it (don't, doesn't) have a separate section of geographical names.
7. Does this poem make an (allusion, illusion) to *The Iliad?*
8. (Being that, Because) Jennifer has never learned to swim, she is afraid to go on the boat ride.
9. Do you know that (beside, besides) Spanish she also speaks French?
10. In the middle of the nineteenth century, thousands of Irish (emigrated, immigrated) to America.
11. Do you know where the public library (is, is at)?
12. After three long years of wearing braces, I (couldn't help but feel, couldn't help feeling) pleased with the results.
13. It looks (like, as if) it will pour any minute.
14. As I waited anxiously in the airport, I still (had no, didn't have no) way of knowing if Laura May had managed to catch the flight.
15. (Since, Being that) I (didn't do nothing, did nothing) to antagonize that Doberman, I can't understand why it bit me.
16. (Can't none, Can't any) of the people in town see that the mayor is appointing political cronies to patronage jobs?
17. If you want to find additional information about Southtown, you (had ought, ought) to go to the library.
18. What (kind of a, kind of) person would assassinate the President of the United States?
19. The (Gallaghers they, Gallaghers) have worked for years to increase voter registration in (this, this here) town.
20. When Alana found that rare coin in Aunt Francine's attic, she (couldn't hardly, could hardly) believe her eyes.

---

A glossary is a list of special terms or expressions, accompanied by brief comments and explanations. On the following pages you will find a short glossary of English usage, supplementing the material in Chapters 22–26.

This particular glossary contains solutions for two different types of usage problems. First, there is the problem of choosing between two words, one of which may be less acceptable or appropriate than the other. Second, there is the problem of rejecting words and expressions that should not be used at all. You need merely look up any troublesome word in its alphabetical position in the glossary.

Problems of spelling, which are treated in Chapter 31, are not contained in the list. However, every word and problem discussed in this list is listed in the index, which begins on page 779. If the glossary does not contain the answer to a usage problem, consult the index.

To use the glossary you will need to understand the terms *formal* and *informal, standard* and *nonstandard*. Read the brief description in the Summary, or review Chapter 22, in which the terms are described in detail.

In doing the exercises in this chapter, as well as in the other parts of the book, use standard formal English.

USAGE

## SUMMARY

***Standard English***

Formal The language of speakers who carefully observe all conventions of English usage; appropriate in any situation; essential in serious writing and speaking.

Informal The everyday language of people who observe most of the conventions of English usage, suitable for all but the most formal occasions.

***Nonstandard English***

Variations in usage that are not acceptable in formal writing and are best avoided in all but the most casual writing and speaking.

---

**a, an** *Indefinite articles* refer to one of a general group.

She would like to learn how to ride **a** horse.
The mayor received **an** honorary degree.

*A* is used before words beginning with a consonant sound; *an* is used before words beginning with a vowel sound. In the examples, *a* is used before *horse* because *horse* begins with a consonant sound. *An* is used before *honorary* because *honorary* begins with a vowel sound.

**accept, except** *Accept* is a verb meaning "to take" or "to receive." *Except* may be used either as a verb or as a preposition: As a verb, it means "to leave out"; as a preposition, it means "excluding."

I will **accept** another yearbook assignment.
Do we **except** women from combat duty? [verb]
She typed everything **except** the bibliography. [preposition]

**affect, effect** *Affect* is a verb meaning "to act on," "to influence." *Effect* may be used either as a verb or as a noun. As a verb, it means "to bring about" a desired result, "to accomplish"; as a noun, it means the "result" (of an action).

Decisions of the United States Supreme Court **affect** [influence] the lives of many people.
Some of the decisions can **effect** [bring about] great social change. [verb]
In history class, did you learn what far-reaching **effects** [results] the *Brown v. Board of Education of Topeka, Kansas,* decision had? [noun]

**all the farther, all the faster** Used informally in some parts of the country for *as far as, as fast as.*

NONSTANDARD The second act was all the farther we had read in *Romeo and Juliet.*
STANDARD The second act was **as far as** we had read in *Romeo and Juliet.*

**allusion, illusion** An *allusion* is an intentional reference to something. An *illusion* is a false idea or a misleading appearance.

Flannery O'Connor makes numerous biblical **allusions** [references] in her stories.
**Illusions** [false ideas] of success haunted Willy Loman.
Skillfully applied makeup creates an **illusion** [misleading appearance] of beauty.

**alumni, alumnae** *Alumni* (pronounced ə lum′ni) is the plural of *alumnus* (a male graduate). *Alumnae* (pronounced ə lum′ne) is the plural of *alumna* (female graduate). The graduates of a coeducational school, considered as a single group, are referred to as *alumni.* Although in speech it is not considered incorrect to call a group of graduates from a women's college *alumni,* the distinction is still preserved in writing and formal speech.

They asked the **alumnae** how they felt about allowing the school to admit men.
Each year the **alumni** provide two football scholarships.
Men and women from the first graduating class attended the **alumni** reunion.

**among, between** See *between, among.*

**amount, number** Use *amount* to refer to a singular word; use *number* to refer to a plural word.

USAGE

NONSTANDARD A large amount of books have been checked out of our library.
STANDARD A large **number** of books [plural] have been checked out of our library.
STANDARD A large **amount** of work [singular] is done in the library.

**and etc.** *Etc.* is an abbreviation of the Latin words *et cetera,* meaning "and other things"; thus *and etc.* means "and and other things." Obviously, there is no need to use *and* twice.

NONSTANDARD We are studying great American novelists: Hemingway, Fitzgerald, Steinbeck, Buck, and etc.
STANDARD We are studying great American novelists: Hemingway, Fitzgerald, Steinbeck, Buck, **etc.**

**anywheres, everywheres, nowheres** Use these words and others like them (*somewhere*) without the final *s*.

Is she going **anywhere** [not *anywheres*] this summer?
Office buildings were going up **everywhere** [not *everywheres*].
**Nowhere** [not *nowheres*] was help available.
I couldn't take both band and art **anyway** [not *anyways*].

USAGE

**as, like** See *like, as.*

**at** Avoid the nonstandard construction *where . . . at.*

NONSTANDARD Where is my geometry book at?
STANDARD Where is my geometry book?

**EXERCISE 1. Selecting Correct Expressions to Complete Sentences.** Number your paper 1–10. After each number, write the correct one of the two words or group of words in parentheses in the corresponding sentence.

1. Pearl Buck is an (alumna, alumnus) of Virginia's Randolph-Macon College.
2. If your teacher has (excepted, accepted) your outline, you may start to write your paper.
3. The amount of reading you do (effects, affects) your vocabulary.
4. A large (amount, number) of scarlet fever cases have been reported.
5. We were running (as fast as, all the faster) we could.
6. He had no (allusions, illusions) about how difficult English honors course would be.

7. We could not find (a, an) hotel near the museum.
8. Do you think she will (accept, except) his excuse for handing in his research paper late?
9. She found spelling errors (everywhere, everywheres) as she began to proofread her paper.
10. Herman Melville makes many biblical (illusions, allusions) in *Moby Dick.*

**bad, badly** Strictly speaking, *bad* is an adjective and *badly* is an adverb. The distinction between the two forms should be observed in standard formal usage.

Our team's chances look **bad.** [The adjective *bad* modifies *chances.*]
The left wheel wobbles **badly.** [The adverb *badly* modifies *wobbles.*]

In informal usage, however, the expression "feel badly" has become acceptable, though ungrammatical, English.

INFORMAL He felt badly about scratching my car.
FORMAL He felt **bad** about scratching my car.

**because** In informal spoken English, a sentence beginning "*The reason is*" is often completed by a clause introduced by *because.* In formal written English, do not use *because* after *The reason is.* Instead, use *that* to introduce a clause giving the reason.

INFORMAL The reason for the eclipse is because the moon has come between the earth and the sun.
FORMAL The reason for the eclipse is **that** the moon has come between the earth and the sun.

**being as, being that** Do not use these phrases as substitutes for *since* or *because.*

NONSTANDARD Being that I am going to be late, I had better call my parents.
STANDARD **Since** I am going to be late, I had better call my parents.

**beside, besides** *Beside* means "by the side of" someone or something. *Besides* means "in addition to" or "moreover."

She placed the key **beside** [by the side of] my books.
**Besides** [in addition to] fringe benefits, the job offered a higher salary.
I am not in the mood to go shopping; **besides** [moreover], I have an English test tomorrow.

**between, among** The distinction in meaning between these words is usually observed in formal written English. Use *between* when you are thinking of two items or comparing the items within a group.

What is the difference **between** an amoeba and a paramecium?
Do you know the difference **between** a simile, a metaphor, and an analogy?

Use *among* when you are thinking of a group and are not comparing the items in the group.

The five starters had twenty fouls **among** them.

**bring, take** These two words are exactly opposite in meaning. Use *bring* to indicate motion toward the speaker; use *take* to indicate motion away from the speaker. Bring means "to *come* carrying something"; take means "to *go* carrying something."

**Bring** your typed final paper to my class tomorrow.
Please **take** the model of the Globe Theatre next door.
You may **take** my softball glove to school today, but please **bring** it home.
I will **bring** my Duran Duran tapes when I come over.



**bust, busted** Avoid these words. Use a form of either *break* or *burst*, depending on the meaning you have in mind.

NONSTANDARD The headlight on the van is busted.
STANDARD The headlight on the van is **broken.**

NONSTANDARD The pipe in the apartment above us busted.
STANDARD The pipe in the apartment above us **burst.**

**can't hardly, can't scarcely** See "The Double Negative" (page 582).

**could of, should of, would of, might of** See *of.*

**done** This word is the past participle of *do*. Like all participles, *done* requires an auxiliary, or helping, verb (*is, have, had been, will be,* etc.) when used as a verb. Never use *done* as the past form of *do*; the past form is *did.*

NONSTANDARD He done all his homework over the weekend.
STANDARD He **did** all his homework over the weekend.
STANDARD He **has done** all his homework.

**don't, doesn't** *Don't* is a contraction of *do not. Doesn't* is a contraction of *does not.* Never use *don't* after a singular noun or after *he, she,* or *it;* use *doesn't.* See page 486.

NONSTANDARD She don't like seafood.
STANDARD She **doesn't** like seafood.

**double negative** See page 582.

**effect, affect** See *affect, effect.*

**emigrate, immigrate** *Emigrate* is a verb meaning "to go away from a country" to settle elsewhere. *Immigrate* is a verb meaning "to come into a country" to settle there.

Thousands **emigrated** from Germany during the 1870's.
Most of the German refugees **immigrated** to the United States.

The nouns corresponding to these verbs are *emigrant* (one who goes away from a country) and *immigrant* (one who comes into a country).

**etc.** See *and etc.*

**except, accept** See *accept, except.*

**farther, faster** See *all the farther, all the faster.*

**fewer, less** Use *fewer* if the word it modifies is plural. Use *less* if the word it modifies is singular.

**Fewer** students are going out for football this year.
You should spend **less** time watching TV.

**good, well** *Good* is an adjective; it should not be used to modify a verb; use the adverb *well.*

NONSTANDARD Jenny sings good. [*Good* is incorrectly used to modify *sings.*]
STANDARD Jenny sings **well.** [*Well* is correctly used as an adverb.]

*Well* may be used as either an adjective or an adverb. As an adjective, *well* has three different meanings: (1) to be in good health, (2) to appear well dressed or well groomed, and (3) to be satisfactory.

Mr. Kuhn looked **well** [in good health] after his operation.
Maria looks **well** [well dressed] in her club blazer.
All is **well** [satisfactory] at the launch site.

As an adverb, *well* means "capably done or performed."

Because she sews so **well,** she seldom buys clothing.

**EXERCISE 2. Selecting Correct Expressions to Complete Sentences.** This exercise covers the usage problems discussed on pages 571–73. Number your paper 1–20. After each number, write the correct one of the two words in parentheses in the corresponding sentence.

1. The pole vaulter performed (bad, badly) in the final round.
2. A second baseman normally makes (less, fewer) putouts than a first baseman.
3. I will (take, bring) the book to the library when I go.
4. After graduating from the seminary, the missionary (emigrated, immigrated) from the United States.
5. The chores were shared (among, between) the three roommates.
6. She did (good, well) on her driver's exam.
7. He is a comedian who (don't, doesn't) get many laughs.
8. The cost of the prom will be divided (between, among) the six junior homerooms.
9. Although she had no prior training, Melissa (did, done) excellent work in her industrial arts course.
10. The quartet performed (good, well) at the audition.
11. In the nineteenth century, many Orientals (emigrated, immigrated) into the United States.
12. Although we lost the game by one point, the coach (doesn't, don't) seem annoyed.
13. (Beside, Besides) defensive end, Chang played linebacker and safety.
14. Will you (bring, take) these books to our study session tonight?
15. Someone is building an A-frame cottage (beside, besides) our beach house.
16. (Being that, Since) she has passed all the tests, she is a likely candidate for the military academy.
17. The junkyard at the edge of the city looked (bad, badly).
18. Your errors will be (fewer, less) if you proofread your paper.
19. (Beside, Besides) *The Adventures of Huckleberry Finn* and *The Red Badge of Courage,* we read *The Scarlet Letter* and *A Separate Peace.*
20. The assignment on Greek philosophers was divided (among, between) the juniors in the humanities class.

**EXERCISE 3. Determining Correct Usage of Expressions.** This exercise covers all the usage problems discussed in the glossary so far.

Number your paper 1–20. If a sentence is correct, write *C* after the corresponding number. Correct any sentence that contains usage errors.

1. It don't look as if the rain will stop this afternoon.
2. In the nineteenth century, the Grimm brothers collected a large amount of fairy tales in Germany.
3. Did you do as badly as I did at the swimming meet?
4. Sometimes I get so absorbed in a movie that I forget where I am at.
5. Would you bring your guitar when you come to visit us?
6. The drought seriously affected the lettuce crop.
7. You would make fewer spelling errors if you used a dictionary.
8. These cassette players don't work as good as they used to.
9. Please bring your belongings with you when you go.
10. You must learn to accept criticism if you want to improve.
11. After looking everywheres for my tie clip, I gave up, but I didn't care about it that much anyways.
12. Did anyone else see what happened besides you and she?
13. After Ireland rebelled against English rule in 1798, many Irish people emigrated to such far-flung countries as France and Argentina.
14. Two of the three colleges she had applied to had excepted her.
15. Although I did badly on the quiz, I did very well on the exam.
16. This is all the farther this old car can take us.
17. Literature contains many allusions to Shakespeare.
18. Beside you and me, who else is going on the hike?
19. How can we three divide a dollar equally between ourselves?
20. I didn't guess until the last chapter that the butler done it.

**had of** See *of*.

**had ought, hadn't ought** Do not use *had* or *hadn't* with *ought*.

NONSTANDARD His test scores had ought to be back by now.
STANDARD His test scores **ought** to be back by now.

NONSTANDARD She hadn't ought to have turned here.
STANDARD She **ought not** to have turned here.

**hardly** See page 582.

**he, she, they, it,** etc. Do not follow a noun with an unnecessary pronoun. This error is sometimes called the *double subject.*

NONSTANDARD The computer it is down today.
STANDARD The **computer is** down today.

**here, there** See *this here, that there.*

**illusion, allusion** See *allusion, illusion.*

**immigrate, emigrate** See *emigrate, immigrate.*

**imply, infer** *Imply* means "to suggest something." *Infer* means "to interpret" or "to get a certain meaning" from a remark or action.

The governor **implied** in her speech that she would support a statewide testing program.
I **inferred** from the governor's speech that she would support a statewide testing program.

USAGE

**in, into** In formal written English, *in* means "within"; *into* means "from the outside to the inside." In informal English the distinction is not always made.

INFORMAL He threw the scraps of paper in the litter basket.
FORMAL He threw the scraps of paper **into** the litter basket.

**kind, sort, type** In standard formal usage, these nouns agree in number with a modifying adjective: thus, *this* or *that kind* (singular); *these* or *those kinds* (plural). In writing, do not commit the error of using a plural adjective with a singular noun, as in *those kind.*

**This kind** of gas is dangerous; *those kinds* are harmless.
**These types** of reading assignments are challenging.

**kind of a, sort of a** The *a* is unnecessary.

INFORMAL What kind of a musician is he?
FORMAL What **kind of** musician is he?

**lay, lie** See pages 526–28.

**leave, let** Leave means "to go away." Its principal parts are *leave, is leaving, left, (have) left. Let* means "to permit" or "to allow"; its principal parts are *let, is letting, let, (have) let.*

NONSTANDARD Leave them stay where they are.
STANDARD **Let** them stay where they are. [Allow them to stay.]

NONSTANDARD They left Jim out early for an orthodontist appointment.
STANDARD They **let** Jim out early for an orthodontist appointment. [permitted him to go]
STANDARD He **let** the air out of the tire. [permitted the air to go out]

**less, fewer** See *fewer, less*.

**like, as** *Like* is a preposition and introduces a prepositional phrase containing an object. *As* is usually a conjunction and introduces a subordinate clause.

Placido Domingo sings **like** Caruso.
Placido Domingo sings **as** Caruso once did.

*Like* as a conjunction is commonly heard in informal speech, but it is still not acceptable in standard formal usage.

**like, as if** Phrases such as *as if,* and *as though* are used as conjunctions to introduce a subordinate clause. In standard formal usage, the substitution of *like* for one of these phrases is not acceptable, although *like* is often heard in informal speech.

INFORMAL The singers sounded like they hadn't rehearsed.
FORMAL The singers sounded **as if** they hadn't rehearsed.

**might of, must of** See *of*.

**myself, ourselves** See pages 509–10.

USAGE

**EXERCISE 4. Selecting Correct Expressions to Complete Sentences.** Number your paper 1–20. After each number, write the correct one of the two words or groups of words in parentheses in the corresponding sentence.

1. You (hadn't ought, ought not) to talk so fast.
2. I (imply, infer) from what Jeff said that the test is today.
3. (These, This) kinds of questions require more thought than (this, these) kind.
4. That sort (of, of a) chair is called Windsor.
5. You ought not to have (left, let) her drop geometry last year.
6. Did the article (imply, infer) that there would be a strike?
7. I (had ought, ought) to check out a good library book.
8. What kind (of, of a) pattern did you use for that skirt?

9. It looks (like, as if) I have lost the election.
10. Will the coach (leave, let) you skip soccer practice today?
11. Mom (hadn't ought, ought not) to carry that heavy box by herself.
12. He serves the ball exactly (as, like) the coach showed him.
13. (Those, That) kind of problem should be handled in guidance.
14. I (implied, inferred) from Father's remarks about "slovenliness" that my sister and I had forgotten to clean our room.
15. When Jay Gatsby came (in, into) the room, everyone stared.
16. Try to make your drawing (like, as) the one on the chart.
17. (Leave, Let) Rosetta explain the trigonometry problem.
18. We (had ought, ought) to be leaving soon.
19. Did Mr. Stokes (imply, infer) that my paper had to be rewritten?
20. What sort (of, of a) culture did the Phoenicians have?



**none** *None* may be singular or plural. See page 479.

**nowheres** See *anywheres, everywheres, nowheres.*

**number, amount** See *amount, number.*

**of** Do not write *of* in place of *have* in such phrases as *could have, should have, might have, must have,* etc. In everyday speech we often slur the word *have,* producing a sound that might be written *could've* or *could of.* Do not allow speech habits to lead you into spelling and usage errors.

MISSPELLED He could of had a summer job if he had applied earlier.
CORRECT He **could have had** a summer job if he had applied earlier.

MISSPELLED You ought to of taken a foreign language.
CORRECT You **ought to have** taken a foreign language.

Do not use *of* unnecessarily in such phrases as *had of* and *off of.*

NONSTANDARD If I'd of known the word *raze,* I'd of gotten an "A."
STANDARD If I **had** known the word *raze,* I would *have* gotten an "A."

INFORMAL He dived off of the side of the pool into the water.
FORMAL He dived **off** the side of the pool into the water.

**off, off of** Do not use *off* or *off of* in place of *from.*

NONSTANDARD You can get a program off of the usher.
STANDARD You can get a program **from** the usher.

**or, nor** Use *or* with *either;* use *nor* with *neither.*

On Tuesdays the cafeteria offers a choice of **either** meat loaf **or** chicken.
I wonder why **neither** Frost **nor** Ellison received the Nobel Prize.

**ought** See *had ought.*

**ought to of** See *of.*

**raise, rise** See page 531.

**reason is because** See *because.*

**respectfully, respectively** *Respectfully* means "with respect" or "full of respect." *Respectively* means "each in the order indicated."

He delivered the reprimand **respectfully** but firmly.
Gina, Laura, and Ben are taking English, Latin, and French, **respectively**.

**rise, raise** See page 531.

**scarcely** See page 582.

**shall, will** *Shall,* which was once considered the only correct form for the expression of the simple future in the first person, has been replaced by *will* in most speech and writing.

STANDARD I **shall** deliver the message at once.
STANDARD I **will** deliver the message at once.

**sit, set** See pages 529–30.

**slow, slowly** *Slow* is generally used as an adjective. *Slowly* is always used as an adverb. Although designers of highway signs use *slow* as an adverb in such expressions as *"Go slow"* and *"Drive slow,"* you will be on the safe side if you use only *slowly* as an adverb.

Melville's plots develop **slowly**.
The **slow** movement of a symphony is usually the second.

**so** Because this word is usually overworked, avoid it in your writing whenever you can.

INFORMAL I have finished writing my first draft, so I am ready to revise it.
FORMAL Since I have finished writing my first draft, I am ready to revise it.

**some, somewhat** In standard formal usage, use *somewhat* rather than *some* as an adverb.

My grades have improved **somewhat** [not *some*] in the past month.

**sort** See *kind, sort, type* and *kind of a, sort of a.*

**take, bring** See *bring, take.*

**them** Never use *them* as an adjective. Use *these* or *those.*

NONSTANDARD He assigned several of them short stories for tomorrow.
STANDARD He assigned several of **those** short stories for tomorrow.

**these kind, those kind** See *kind, sort, type.*

USAGE

**this here, that there** The words *here* and *there* are unnecessary and incorrect when following *this* and *that.*

NONSTANDARD This here essay explains a process.
STANDARD **This** essay explains a process.

**type, type of** In standard usage, do not make *type* an adjective rather than a noun by omitting a following *of.*

I prefer this type **of** shirt.

See also *kind, sort, type.*

**ways** Use *way,* not *ways*, in referring to distance.

INFORMAL Wichita is a long ways from the ocean.
FORMAL Wichita is a long **way** from the ocean.

**well, good** See *good, well.*

**when, where** Do not use *when* or *where* as a substitute for a noun in writing a definition.

NONSTANDARD A spoonerism is when you switch the beginning sounds of two words.
STANDARD A spoonerism is **a slip of the tongue** in which the beginning sounds of two words are switched.

INFORMAL A thesaurus is where you can find synonyms and antonyms.
FORMAL A thesaurus is **a book** in which you can find synonyms and antonyms.

**where** Do not use *where* in place of *that.*

I read **that** [not *where*] Demosthenes learned to speak clearly by talking with pebbles in his mouth.

**where . . . at** See *at.*

**which, that, who** *Which* should be used to refer to things only. *That* may be used to refer to either persons or things. *Who* should be used to refer to persons only.

Poe's first book, **which** was titled *Tamerlane,* is now worth thousands of dollars.
Is this the only essay **that** James Baldwin wrote?
Is Emily Dickinson the poet **that** [or *who*] wrote on scraps of paper?
Beethoven was the composer **who** [or *that*] continued to write music after he had become deaf.

**who, whom** See pages 505–506.

**would of** See *of.*



## WRITING APPLICATION: Avoiding Common Usage Problems

You should refer to the Glossary of Usage whenever you encounter a common usage problem for a particular word or expression. The Glossary of Usage will tell you whether the use of a word is informal or formal and whether it is standard or nonstandard. Remember, in your writing for school and business, you should always use formal standard English.

NONSTANDARD Being that she was tired, she decided to stay at home.
STANDARD **Because** she was tired, she decided to stay at home.

### Writing Assignment

Write ten sentences, each using one of the following words. Refer to the Glossary of Usage for guidance.

1. because
2. beside
3. besides
4. bring
5. take
6. don't
7. emigrate
8. immigrate
9. in
10. into

## The Double Negative

A double negative is a construction in which two negative words are used where one is sufficient. Most double negatives are nonstandard English.

**can't hardly, can't scarcely** The words *hardly* and *scarcely* convey a negative meaning. They should never be used with the negative *not.*

NONSTANDARD I can't hardly take another step in these new boots.
STANDARD I **can hardly** take another step in these new boots.

NONSTANDARD The film is so long that we couldn't scarcely see it in one period.
STANDARD The film is so long that we **could scarcely** see it in one period.

**can't help but** In standard formal English, avoid this double negative.

INFORMAL When I hear a march by John Philip Sousa, I can't help but tap my foot to mark time.
FORMAL When I hear a march by John Philip Sousa, I **can't help** tapping my foot to mark time.

USAGE

**haven't but, haven't only** In certain uses, *but* and *only* convey a negative meaning. Avoid using them with *not* in formal writing.

INFORMAL We haven't but one chance to win this game.
FORMAL We **have but** one chance to win this game.
FORMAL We **have only** one chance to win this game.

**no, nothing, none** These words are clearly negative. Do not use them with another negative word.

NONSTANDARD I don't have no skill in gymnastics.
STANDARD I **don't have any** skill in gymnastics.
STANDARD I **have no** skill in gymnastics.

NONSTANDARD I haven't done nothing yet about my flat tire.
STANDARD I **have done nothing** yet about my flat tire.
STANDARD I **haven't done anything** yet about my flat tire.

NONSTANDARD Can't none of the staff sort the yearbook pictures?
STANDARD **Can none** of the staff sort the yearbook pictures?
STANDARD **Can't any** of the staff sort the yearbook pictures?

**EXERCISE 5. Selecting Correct Expressions to Complete Sentences.** This exercise covers the usage problems discussed on pages 578–82. Number your paper 1–20. After each number, write the correct one of the two words or groups of words in parentheses in the corresponding sentence.

1. I read in a newspaper article (that, where) dogs are being trained to help deaf people.
2. During the playing of our national anthem, we stood quietly and (respectfully, respectively).
3. The earliest feminist author was neither O'Connor (or, nor) Welty; it was Kate Chopin.
4. Don't you have (no, a) dictionary of foreign terms to refer to?
5. Jack London must (of, have) led an adventurous life.
6. Our teacher said we were to read (this, this here) chapter.
7. If you do neither prewriting (or, nor) outlining, your essay might not be coherent.
8. I had (a, an) orange for dessert.
9. The first, second, and third American astronauts were Sheppard, Grissom, and Glenn, (respectively, respectfully).
10. She made so many mechanical errors that she (could, couldn't) hardly expect an *A*.
11. As we passed Shreveport and crossed the Texas line, El Paso seemed a long (way, ways) away.
12. There (isn't, is) scarcely room on the patio for that furniture.
13. The swings in the park are rusting (some, somewhat).
14. For advice, I go to Ms. Sanchez, (which, who) is a very understanding guidance counselor.
15. There won't be (no, any) way to find those presents I've hidden.
16. This (type, type of) short story has appealed to readers for many years.
17. Pass me (them, those) notes on the experiment, please.
18. I read (where, that) a rare species of crane has been seen here.
19. He did a flip turn and pushed (off, off of) the pool wall.
20. Since I didn't have (no, any) homework, I decided to go out to shoot some baskets.



**EXERCISE 6. Revising Sentences by Eliminating a Double Negative.** Each of the following sentences has a double negative. Revise each sentence to eliminate the double negative. Refer to the Glossary of Usage for help.

EXAMPLE 1. He hadn't no pencils on his desk.
1. *He had no pencils on his desk.*
or
*He hadn't any pencils on his desk.*

1. Tom didn't have no time to buy the books.
2. Haven't none of you seen the dog?
3. She didn't contribute nothing to the project.
4. We haven't but one day to visit the fair.
5. The colt can't scarcely stand up.
6. The lights were so dim that we couldn't barely see anything.
7. They thought that they hadn't no time to go to the post office.
8. In the mountains you can't help but feel calm.
9. Can't none of them come to the party?
10. Tom didn't do nothing to help us with the dinner.



**REVIEW EXERCISE. Determining Correct Usage of Expressions.** This exercise covers the usage problems discussed in the entire glossary. If a sentence is correct, write *C* after the proper number. If a sentence contains an error, rewrite the sentence.

1. Foreshadowing is when a writer gives a hint of what's coming.
2. She felt that she played the piano sonata bad.
3. We should of paid closer attention to the group report.
4. I wonder how many Americans recall the importance of the Minutemen, which were very brave during the Revolution.
5. We've written two essays besides a ballad and a book review.
6. A large amount of my friends contributed to the charity drive.
7. Swimming is the type of sport that requires daily training.
8. After the Glorious Revolution, there wasn't nothing more to cover in today's history class.
9. Where are Mary Cassatt's paintings at?
10. Some speakers make illusions to the "good old days."
11. I need to bring my passbook to the bank this afternoon.
12. I don't know whether to except his invitation or not.
13. In this row will sit the valedictorian, the salutatorian, and the honor students, respectively.
14. Semantics is where you study the meanings of words and the way these meanings change.
15. There weren't none of us who were finished with our final copy.

16. I think these kind of stereo speakers give a better sound.
17. I couldn't hardly remember the names of all the Presidents.
18. I infer from your research paper that Gutenberg had a great affect on the way books were printed.
19. Nobel Prizes are where awards are given in literature, medicine, chemistry, physics, and the promotion of peace.
20. Being that I prefer tapes, I don't hardly ever play my records.

## CHAPTER 27 REVIEW: POSTTEST

**Determining Correct Usage of Expressions.** If a sentence is correct, write *C* after the proper number. If a sentence contains an error, rewrite the incorrect part of the sentence correctly.

EXAMPLE 1. When our class trip was canceled, many of us felt badly.
1. *many of us felt bad*

1. The motorcade moved slow toward Main Street.
2. Because the highway was poorly marked, I didn't have no way of knowing which exit to take.
3. I inferred from what Julio said that he has excepted my apology.
4. Over eighty years ago my great-grandfather immigrated from Mexico.
5. He talked persuasively for an hour, but his words had no affect.
6. I have looked everywheres but I cannot find my camera.
7. In biology class we learned about digestion, respiration, circulation, and etc.
8. The magician billed himself as a "master of allusions."
9. Hardly no one showed up for his farewell performance, which was given a number of evenings later.
10. Beside my job as a baby sitter, I work as a hospital volunteer.
11. The enormous amount of hours I spend studying has had a beneficial effect on my grades.
12. Are you implying that you noticed nothing unusual during lunch hour today?
13. My English teacher said that I could of improved my reading comprehension score if I had spent more time reading great literature.

14. The restaurant bill was split equally between the three of us.
15. The detective said that it looked like the occupant of the house had left in a hurry.
16. The reason the book was so difficult to understand was because the writing was unclear.
17. Copy the cooking instructions off of the package and leave them beside the stove.
18. If you kept less fish in your tank, they would live longer.
19. Did you think I would of given away your secret?
20. Who else beside Jun Hsing won a scholarship?

## CHAPTER 28

# Capitalization

## RULES OF STANDARD USAGE

Correct capitalization is part of good usage. Capital letters perform three main functions in English. First, they indicate the beginnings of sentences. Together with end marks, they show where one sentence leaves off and another begins—a function performed in speech by the rise and fall of the speaker's voice. Secondly, they distinguish proper names at a glance. Thirdly, they may be used to show respect.

This chapter gives the basic rules for capitalization. In your reading, you are likely to encounter usages that differ from the rules given here. This is the case both because practices change over time and because usage varies.

MECHANICS

### DIAGNOSTIC TEST

**Recognizing Correctly Capitalized Phrases.** Number your paper 1–20. After the proper number, write the letter of the phrase in each pair that is capitalized correctly.

EXAMPLE 1. a. Smith's Grocery b. smith's grocery
1. *a*

1. a. hurricane Carol b. Hurricane Carol
2. a. Spanish language b. Spanish Language
3. a. Battle of bull run b. Battle of Bull Run

4. a. Uno card game — b. Uno Card Game
5. a. Vivian Beaumont Theater — b. Vivian Beaumont theater
6. a. Ex-Senator Preston — b. ex-Senator Preston
7. a. Labor day — b. Labor Day
8. a. Republic of Ireland — b. republic of Ireland
9. a. a Sioux battle — b. a Sioux Battle
10. a. a course in Western Art — b. a course in Western art
11. a. the church choir — b. the Church Choir
12. a. the Supreme Court — b. the supreme court
13. a. the Pacific ocean — b. the Pacific Ocean
14. a. the last day of Summer — b. the last day of summer
15. a. New Hope Hospital — b. New Hope hospital
16. a. down the street — b. down the Street
17. a. Interstate 84 — b. interstate 84
18. a. an Island in the Bahamas — b. an island in the Bahamas
19. a. an Irish sweater — b. an irish sweater
20. a. the gilded age — b. the Gilded Age

---

**28a. Capitalize the first word in every sentence.**

Most students know this rule and follow it automatically. If they do not, the reason is usually either carelessness or the inability to recognize the end of one sentence and the beginning of the next. If you find the latter fault in your writing, review Chapter 12.

EXAMPLES **E**veryone expected her to be elected.
"**W**ill you take me to school?" my sister asked.

> ☞ **NOTE** It is traditional to capitalize the first word of a line of poetry, although modern poets do not always follow this style.

EXAMPLE **A**lone, alone, all, all, alone;
**A**lone on a wide, wide sea.
**A**nd never a saint took pity on
**M**y soul in agony.

COLERIDGE, *The Rime of the Ancient Mariner*

MECHANICS

**28b. Capitalize the pronoun *I* and the interjection *O*.**

The pronoun *I* is always capitalized. The interjection *O* is used mainly as an invocation in solemn or poetic language. It should not be confused with the common interjection *oh. Oh* is capitalized only when it appears at the beginning of a sentence, and it is always followed by punctuation. *O* is always capitalized and is never followed by punctuation.

EXAMPLES May **I** go to the movie tonight?
Tell me, **O** Muse, of the man of many wiles.
Maybe, oh, maybe **I** will win a medal!

**28c. Capitalize proper nouns and adjectives.**

A *proper noun* is the name of a particular person, place, thing, or idea. Its opposite, a *common noun,* does not name any particular person or thing but refers to any and all members of a class or type. For example, ***P**atsy **M**ink* (proper noun) is a particular *woman* (common noun); ***A**sia* (proper noun) is a particular *continent* (common noun); the ***W**hite **H**ouse* (proper noun) is a particular *building* (common noun). As these illustrations show, proper nouns are capitalized in standard usage, while common nouns are not.

| COMMON NOUN | PROPER NOUN |
|---|---|
| horse | **W**hirlaway |
| boat | ***C**hallenger II* |
| building | **M**etropolitan **M**useum of **A**rt |
| movie | ***T**he **E**mpire **S**trikes **B**ack* |

A *proper adjective* is an adjective formed from a proper noun.

| PROPER NOUN | PROPER ADJECTIVE |
|---|---|
| China | **C**hinese |
| Alps | **A**lpine |
| Elizabeth | **E**lizabethan |

Proper nouns have many forms and name a great variety of persons, places, and things. Study the classification of these nouns, and learn the rules that govern their capitalization.

**(1) Capitalize the names of individual persons.**

Always capitalize the first letters of given names (*Bruce, Angela*) and surnames (*Johnson, Morgan*).

In some surnames another letter besides the first should be capitalized. For instance, in names beginning *O'* or *Mc,* the following letter should also be capitalized:

| | |
|---|---|
| O'Leary | McGee |
| O'Conner | McIntyre |

Usage varies in names beginning with *Mac:*

| | |
|---|---|
| MacKenzie | Mackenzie |
| MacDonald | Macdonald |

Usage also varies in the capitalization of *van, von, de, du,* and other parts of foreign names. Whenever possible, check such names against a reference source, such as a dictionary, or determine the personal preference of their owners.

Always capitalize the abbreviations *Sr., Jr.,* and *Esq.* when they follow a name:

EXAMPLES Robert Gregory, Sr. Martin Luther King, Jr.
J. J. Laughton, Esq.

**(2) Capitalize geographical names.**

POLITICAL UNITS: *Countries, states, counties, townships, cities* United States of America, Sweden, Peru, New Hampshire, Marion County, Hamilton County, Lawrence Township, Springfield, South Bend

LANDMASSES AND LANDFORMS: *Continents, islands, peninsulas, etc.* North America, Europe, Africa, Mackinac Island, Alaskan Peninsula, Cape Cod, Cape Hatteras, Point Sur, Isthmus of Panama

TOPOGRAPHICAL AND OTHER LAND FEATURES: *Mountains, canyons, plains, forests, parks, dams, etc.* Blue Ridge Mountains, Mount McKinley, Laurel Canyon, Great Plains, Mohave Desert, Shawnee National Forest, Giant City State Park, Morse Reservoir, Horse Cave, Mississippi Valley

*Bodies of water* Pacific Ocean, Caribbean Sea, Gulf of Panama, Galveston Bay, Lake Superior, Crab Orchard Lake, Bar Harbor, Merrimac River, Long Island Sound, Northumberland Strait

*Streets and roads* Clayton Road, Morningside Drive, Washington Boulevard, Green River Parkway, Pennsylvania Turnpike, Forest Park Highway, Route 52, Thirty-eighth Street [Notice that in a hyphenated street number, the second word begins with a lower-case letter.]

**(3) Capitalize compass directions when they are used as the names of definite sections of a country or of the world. Do not capitalize them when they merely indicate direction.**

| EXAMPLES | | |
|---|---|---|
| | the **F**ar **E**ast | **e**ast of Jefferson Street |
| | the **N**orthwest | traveling **n**orthwest |
| | the **S**outh | **s**outh of the border |

Do not capitalize an adjective indicating direction unless it is a part of the name of a political unit or a recognized region: **s**outhern Iowa, but **S**outhern Hemisphere; a **n**orthern climate, but **N**orthern Ireland.

**(4) When a common noun or adjective is part of a name, it becomes a proper noun or adjective and should be capitalized. Do not capitalize such a word unless it is part of a name.**

| EXAMPLES | | |
|---|---|---|
| | Hudson **R**iver | that **r**iver |
| | White **P**lains | the **p**lains of Nebraska |
| | Union **P**ass | a **p**ass in the mountains |

This rule also covers nouns and adjectives used in names other than those of places. Thus, a **h**igh **s**chool, Lawrence **H**igh **S**chool; the **e**ve of a holiday, New Year's **E**ve.

> ☞ **NOTE** An opposite process, by which proper nouns and adjectives lose their initial capital letter, occurs as English grows and changes. Over a long period of time, a proper noun or a word derived from it may acquire a special meaning and become part of the common vocabulary.

| EXAMPLES | | |
|---|---|---|
| | braille | From Louis Braille, its inventor |
| | herculean | from Hercules |
| | jello | from the trademark Jell-O |

This kind of change does not take place all at once. In our own time, many words are undergoing such a change, and in the case of these words either a capital or a small letter is acceptable—thus, **i**ndia (or **I**ndia) rubber, **t**urkish (or **T**urkish) towel, etc. If you are in doubt, consult your dictionary.

**EXERCISE 1. Using Capitalization Correctly.** Write the following phrases and sentences, using capital letters wherever they are required. If two versions are possible, give both.

1. the far west
2. a city north of louisville
3. the utah salt flats
4. the cape of good hope
5. chris o'malley
6. hoover dam
7. southern illinois
8. lock the door!
9. the kalahari desert
10. the northeast
11. gulf of Alaska
12. mary mcleod bethune
13. a mountain people
14. vine deloria, jr.
15. hawaiian volcanoes state park
16. a north american actor
17. san francisco bay
18. skiing on the lake
19. turn west at the crossroads
20. a tibetan yak
21. mexican gold
22. the delaware
23. east indian curry
24. decatur street north
25. fifty-sixth street

**(5) Capitalize all important words in the names of organizations, institutions, government bodies, business firms, brand names of business products, buildings, ships, planes, trains, special events, historical events and periods, items on the calendar, races, religions, tribes, and nationalities.**

> ☞ NOTE Throughout this section of the chapter, keep rule 28c (4) clearly in mind: a common noun or adjective is not capitalized unless it is part of a proper name.

MECHANICS

EXAMPLES

| | |
|---|---|
| **O**hio **S**tate **U**niversity | a **u**niversity in Ohio |
| **L**indbergh **H**igh **S**chool | a **h**igh school in St. Louis |
| **I**owa **S**tate **L**egislature | the **l**egislature in Iowa |

*Organizations and institutions* **U**nited **S**tates **A**ir **F**orce, **Y**oung **M**en's **H**ebrew **A**ssociation, **P**olk **C**ounty **B**oard of **E**ducation, **M**ud **C**reek **P**layers, **U**niversity of **C**hicago, **V**assar **C**ollege

*Government bodies* **U**nited **N**ations, **U**nited **S**tates **H**ouse of **R**epresentatives, **M**ichigan **P**ort **A**uthority, **H**ouse of **C**ommons, **V**eterans' **A**dministration

*Business firms, brand names of business products* **E. F. H**utton **C**ompany, **S**helby **F**ederal **S**avings and **L**oan **A**ssociation, **D**elaware and **H**udson **R**ailway **C**ompany, **W**hirlpool, **U**nited **P**ress **I**nternational, **C**asiotone, **D**owny

> ☞ NOTE Except in advertising displays, a common noun or adjective following a brand name is *not* capitalized: Crest toothpaste, Dial soap, Pontiac sedan.

*Buildings, ships, trains, planes* Riverfront Stadium, American United Life Building, Broad Ripple Playhouse, Fox Theater, *USS Pueblo* (ship), *Air Force One* (plane), *Denver Zephyr* (train), Hyatt Regency Hotel

*Special events* Pan American Games, Mayflower Golf Classic, Senior Awards Banquet, American Medical Association Convention

*Historical events and periods* Norman Conquest, Thirty Years' War, Yalta Conference, Middle Ages, Renaissance, the Enlightenment

*Calendar items* Saturday, April, Labor Day, National Education Week

> ☞ NOTE Do not capitalize the name of a season unless it is personified.

EXAMPLES the beginning of spring
Beautiful Lady Spring

*Races, religions, nationalities, tribes* Puerto Rican, Oriental, Presbyterian, Muslim, American, Japanese, Apache

**(6) Do not capitalize the names of school subjects, except for proper nouns and adjectives. Course names followed by a number are usually capitalized.**

EXAMPLES French, Spanish, Chinese, German
Advanced Chemistry 402, Home Economics II
science, typing, speech, Russian history, computer programming

> ☞ USAGE NOTE The name of a class may be capitalized when it specifies a particular event, e.g., Senior Trip, Sophomore Play.



**EXERCISE 2. Using Capital Letters.** Write the following words and phrases, using capital letters wherever they are required.

1. the science department
2. north atlantic treaty organization
3. st. patrick's cathedral
4. *city of new orleans* (train)
5. the federal reserve bank
6. the normandy invasion
7. classes in auto mechanics
8. the world cup
9. french cuisine
10. sioux history
11. midtown traffic
12. jones and drake, inc.
13. 7260 east forty-sixth street
14. on memorial day
15. *ariadne* (boat)
16. a holiday inn
17. the louisiana world exposition
18. early summer
19. gold medal flour
20. an american history class

**EXERCISE 3. Capitalizing Phrases Correctly.** This exercise covers all capitalization rules presented up to this point. Each of the following passages contains words that should be capitalized. Write these words in a list opposite the number corresponding to each passage. If two or more words belong in a single capitalized phrase, write them as a phrase: *Washington Monument; Victoria, B.C.; United States Air Force Academy;* etc.

EXAMPLE 1. A novel my english teacher recommends is *the red badge of courage.* The novel is about the development of a young soldier, henry fleming, fighting in the civil war.

1. *English*
   *The Red Badge of Courage*
   *Henry Fleming*
   *Civil War*

1. Regret and genuine risk are the only fillies ever to win the kentucky derby. This great race, held at churchill downs in louisville, kentucky, is also known as "the run for the roses."
2. The bill of rights grants americans the privilege of voting for their governmental officials. Presidential candidates carefully choose to campaign in states such as new york, california, and texas, which have more electoral votes in the electoral college, based on the number of their members in congress.
3. Modern universities developed from the european monastery schools of the middle ages. The oldest university in this country, founded in 1636, is harvard university in cambridge, massachusetts.

MECHANICS

4. Winter haven, florida, has one hundred lakes within its immediate vicinity. Lake howard and lake eloise are two of the largest ones and are joined, as are the others, by the chain o' lakes canal.
5. Mr. chapman, our chemistry IV teacher, took us to chicago to tour the museum of science and industry.
6. The european renaissance started in italy during the thirteenth century and lasted until the reformation in the 1500's. Several outstanding events of the renaissance were the end of feudalism, the beginning of modern science, the invention of movable type, and the revival of greek and roman culture.
7. Well-known sports figures bob mathias and wilma rudolph have recently moved to indianapolis to help the city become the national amateur sports capital. Mathias will direct the national fitness foundation, and rudolph heads the wilma rudolph foundation. New facilities such as the hoosier dome, the indiana university natatorium, the indiana university track and field stadium, and the major taylor velodrome make their jobs easier.
8. The equal rights amendment was passed by the congress of the united states in 1972, but it was never ratified. Although the supreme court decision of 1954, the equal employment opportunity act, and the equal credit opportunity act have aided in ensuring minority rights, many groups feel that the support of an equal rights amendment is needed.
9. Having grown up on the banks of the mighty mississippi river at hannibal, missouri, samuel clemens (mark twain) considered the platte river in colorado a sickly little stream.
10. Each state in the united states determines the holidays it will observe. Not all states will recognize the birthday of martin luther king, jr., as a holiday. If you live in illinois, you will observe lincoln's birthday. Other states follow the preference of congress for presidents' day, combining lincoln's birthday and washington's birthday.



**28d. Capitalize titles.**

**(1) Capitalize a title belonging to a particular person if it precedes the person's name. If a title stands alone or follows a person's name, capitalize it only if it refers to a high official or to someone to whom you wish to show special respect.**

EXAMPLES Coach Knight; Bob Knight, **b**asketball **c**oach; the **c**oach, a **c**oach; **D**irector Morgan; Mrs. Morgan, **d**irector of county libraries; the **d**irector; a **d**irector; **P**resident Tsang; Pearl S. Tsang, **p**resident of New Books, Inc., the **P**resident of the United States

Admiral Watkins; **A**dmiral James D. Watkins, **C**hief of **N**aval **O**perations; the **a**dmiral; an **a**dmiral

**S**ecretary of the **I**nterior Ickes; Harold Ickes, **S**ecretary of the **I**nterior; the **S**ecretary of the **I**nterior

**Q**ueen Elizabeth II; Elizabeth II, **Q**ueen of England; the **Q**ueen of England; the **Q**ueen or **q**ueen; a **q**ueen

the **S**peaker of the **H**ouse; the **C**hancellor; the **D**irector of the **F**ederal **B**ureau of **I**nvestigation; the **P**rince of **W**ales; the **A**ttorney **G**eneral; the **M**ayor of **N**ew **Y**ork

Some titles are capitalized when they refer to a particular person or are used in place of a person's name. This is often true when used in sentences of direct address.

EXAMPLES The **G**overnor signed the bill.
A **g**overnor is an elected official.

Are you retiring at the end of this term, **P**rofessor?
A new **p**rofessor will be appointed in his place.

> ☞ **NOTE** The word *president* is always capitalized when it refers to the head of a nation; the compound word *vice-president* is capitalized (with two capital letters) when it refers to the **V**ice-**P**resident of a nation.

MECHANICS

> ☞ **NOTE** Do not capitalize *ex-, -elect, former,* or *late* when they are used with a title: **ex**-Governor Welsh, the President-**e**lect, **f**ormer Congressman Hill, the **l**ate Senator Humphrey.

The rules governing titles of honor or position also apply, in general, to words indicating family relationships, such as *mother, father, grandmother, sister, brother, aunt.* Such words are capitalized when they precede a name: **U**ncle Ed, **C**ousin Amy. They may be capitalized when they are used in place of a person's name, especially in direct address: "Did you play tennis today, **M**other?" When used alone, they are usually not capitalized: Margo has one sister and two brothers.

> NOTE Do not capitalize a word indicating relationship when it follows a possessive noun or pronoun unless it is considered a part of the name: Mrs. Graham's son, my sister Sally, but my Aunt Catherine.

**(2) Capitalize the first word, the last word, and all important words in the titles of books, magazines, newspapers, articles, historical documents, laws, works of art, movies, and television programs.**

EXAMPLES *The Catcher in the Rye, Time,* the *Tribune,* "Interview with the President," the Declaration of Independence, National War Powers Act, Kennedy-Ives Bill, Twenty-fifth Amendment, *Star Wars, Sesame Street*

> NOTE Capitalize *a, an,* or *the* in a title only when it is the first word. When used in a sentence before the names of magazines and newspapers, these words are normally not capitalized. Long prepositions (five or more letters) are usually capitalized; shorter ones are not. Coordinating conjunctions within a title are not capitalized; other conjunctions are.

EXAMPLES *The Passions of the Mind,* "*A Visit of Charity*" [*The* and *A* are part of these titles.]
the *Canterbury Tales* [The word *the* is not part of the title.]
the *English Journal,* the *Reader's Digest, Flowers in the Attic*

**28e. Capitalize words referring to the Deity.**

EXAMPLES God, Jehovah, the Father, the Son, the Messiah, the Lord

Pronouns referring to God (*he, him,* and, rarely, *who, whom,* etc.) are often capitalized.

Faith in God rests on belief in His goodness.
For He cometh, He cometh to judge the earth.

Do not capitalize *god* when referring to the gods of ancient mythology: *Poseidon was the Greek god of the sea.*

**EXERCISE 4. Capitalizing Phrases Correctly.** Write the following items, using capital letters wherever they are required. If an item does not require any capitals, write *C* for correct after the proper number.

MECHANICS

1. the *washington post*
2. ex-senator margaret chase smith
3. *the dukes of hazzard* (TV program)
4. captain of the fencing team
5. the taft-hartley bill
6. the federal communications commission
7. for god and country
8. the late bessie smith
9. "come with me, dad."
10. judge delaney

**28f. Capitalize the parts of a compound word as if each part stood alone.**

EXAMPLES English-speaking tourists, God-given rights, pro-Japanese sympathies, anti-American propaganda, non-European culture, pre-Restoration [The prefixes are not normally capitalized; the proper adjectives are always capitalized.]

Polish American, Anglo-Indian [Capitalize both parts of a compound word made up of two proper nouns, adjectives or combining forms.]

**REVIEW EXERCISE. Capitalizing Words and Phrases Correctly.** This exercise covers most of the capitalization rules presented in this chapter. Following the number of each paragraph and the form of Exercise 3 (page 594), write lists of the words that should be capitalized in the following sentences.

1

The league of nations, an international association created after world war I, has been compared with the united nations. The league was formed in january 1920 in geneva, switzerland, under the leadership of the late president woodrow wilson of the united states. The charter of the united nations was developed at a conference held at dumbarton oaks, an estate in washington, d.c. In 1945 the dumbarton oaks proposals were put before the san francisco conference. The united nations charter was ratified on october 24, 1945.

MECHANICS

2

At the columbia university school of general studies, I took a course in modern british literature. I found t. s. eliot, the english poet who wrote much of his work in america, difficult to understand—especially the section of his long poem *the waste land* called "the fire sermon." Eliot wrote essays and plays as well as poetry; and, long after his death, his *old possum's book of practical cats* was adapted into the successful broadway musical *cats*. Andrew lloyd webber wrote the music, Eliot's daughter valerie contributed some material of her own as well as unpublished notes of her father's, and trevor nunn and richard stilgoe tied it all together.

3

All english-speaking students should know something about the history of their language. English is derived mainly from anglo-saxon, or old english, which was the language developed in britain by germanic invaders of the fifth century. English has since been influenced by many tongues: danish; latin; norman or old french; greek; and even, especially in the case of american english, american indian languages. More recently, asian languages and the terminology of science have contributed to our vocabulary.

## WRITING APPLICATION: Using Capitalization Correctly in Your Writing

In the following paragraph from Joan Didion's essay "Los Angeles Notebook," notice how effectively the author has used proper nouns to create a real sense of place. The use of capitalization points up the proper nouns.

> There is something uneasy in the Los Angeles air this afternoon, some unnatural stillness, some tension. What it means is that tonight a Santa Ana will begin to blow, a hot wind from the northeast whining down through the Cajon and San Gorgonio passes, blowing up sandstorms out along Route 66, drying the hills and the nerves to the flash point. For a few days now we will see smoke back in the canyons, and hear sirens in the night. I have neither heard nor read that a Santa Ana is due, but I know it, and almost everyone I have seen today knows it too. We know it because we feel it. The baby frets. The maid sulks. I rekindle a waning argument with the telephone company, then cut my losses and lie down, given over to whatever it is in the air. To live with the Santa Ana is to accept, consciously or unconsciously, a deeply mechanistic view of human behavior.

### Writing Assignment

Write a description of a place that made a vivid impression on you. Use proper nouns to make your description more vivid. When you proofread, pay special attention to capitalization.

## CHAPTER 28 REVIEW: POSTTEST

**Capitalizing Words and Phrases Correctly.** Most of the following sentences contain words that should be capitalized. Write these words in a list opposite the number corresponding to each sentence. If two or more words belong in a single capitalized phrase, write them as a phrase: *President Reagan, Lincoln Memorial, Gulf of Mexico,* etc. If a sentence is written correctly, write *C* after the proper number.

EXAMPLE 1. The rotary club has invited representative William Bashone to speak at tonight's annual banquet.
1. *Rotary Club*
*Representative William Bashone*

1. According to John Fowler, the company's chief executive, you should not buy just any car; you should buy a ford.
2. One of the earliest cars made by Henry Ford was the Model T; it had a four-cylinder, twenty-horsepower engine.
3. On our spring vacation we toured several states in the south.
4. Johnson's bake shop is just north of state street on route 143.
5. Before you take this computer course, you must pass algebra II.
6. Senior class day is scheduled for June 18, "rain or shine."
7. Because there was so much noise in study hall, several people received detentions.
8. In a nationally televised press conference, the president warned that he would veto any tax increase.
9. Sylvia Plath, an american writer, was married to the british poet Ted Hughes.
10. The only man in American history who was not elected to be vice-president or president, yet held both positions was ex-president Gerald Ford.
11. My mother asked me to walk to the supermarket and buy a quart container of farmingbury milk and a pound of tomatoes.
12. When we toured eastern Tennessee, we visited the Oak Ridge Laboratory, where atomic research was carried out during World War II.
13. The Spanish-american Club has planned a festival for late summer; it will be held at the north end of the city.
14. If you are looking for the best apples in the state, follow route 14 until you see the signs for Peacock's Orchard.

15. In a controversial debate on the Panama canal, the United States voted to relinquish control to the Panamanian government.
16. When my Aunt Janice visited England, she toured buckingham palace and tried to catch a glimpse of queen Elizabeth.
17. Mayor-elect Sabrena Willis will speak to the public about her proposals to upgrade the city's bilingual education program.
18. Since many do not agree with her proposals because of the additional tax burden, the auditorium in city hall will be packed.
19. When spring arrives, I find it difficult to pay attention in class.
20. Although the east room of the White house is now used for press conferences, it was once a place where Abigail Adams aired the president's laundry.

## SUMMARY STYLE SHEET

| | |
|---|---|
| Sioux **C**ity | a **c**ity in Iowa |
| Grand Canyon **N**ational **P**ark | a **n**ational **p**ark |
| **W**est Virginia | **w**estern Pennsylvania |
| the **S**outh | facing **s**outh |
| Atlantic **O**cean | an **o**cean cruise |
| Madison **A**venue | a wide **a**venue |
| Key **C**lub | a students' **c**lub |
| Ford Motor **C**ompany | an automobile **c**ompany |
| Jefferson **H**igh **S**chool | a **h**igh **s**chool |
| **H**ouse of Commons | the lower **h**ouse |
| Mark Hopkins **H**otel | a **h**otel in San Francisco |
| Korean **W**ar | a tragic **w**ar |
| Union **S**tation | a railroad **s**tation |
| Independence **D**ay | a **d**ay to celebrate freedom |
| the **J**unior **D**ance | a **d**ance given by **j**uniors |
| **E**nglish, **F**rench, **L**atin | **s**cience, **s**horthand, **g**eometry |
| World **H**istory II | a course in **h**istory |
| Adorned in flowers, **S**pring arrives. | **w**inter, **s**pring, **s**ummer, **f**all, **a**utumn |
| Honda **M**otorcycles, Inc. | motorcyle |
| **D**ean Morris | Dr. Morris, the **d**ean |
| the **P**resident of the U.S. | our company **p**resident |
| **S**enator Schwartz | the oldest **s**enator |
| Ask **M**other, **C**ousin Sue | her **m**other, Mary's **c**ousin |
| *The **W**ings of the **D**ove* | (a novel) |
| the ***S**un-**T**imes* | (a newspaper) |

**G**od in **H**is goodness
**M**ayor-**e**lect Jackson
a **M**uslim, a **N**orwegian

the **g**ods and **t**heir powers
a **m**ayor

CHAPTER 29

# Punctuation

## END MARKS AND COMMAS

In listening to ordinary speech, we do not hear sounds or words in isolation; we hear groups of words that we understand as phrases, clauses, or full sentences. The speaker conveys these groupings to us by stressing certain words, pausing where necessary, and changing the pitch of his or her voice—in short, by phrasing.

In writing, we show these pauses by using marks of punctuation. These marks imitate the rise and fall of our voices, called the inflection, and indicate the pauses or stops we would use in speaking. However, that is not all they do: the written word is capable of greater refinement than the spoken word, and it is possible to show relationships in print that speech cannot indicate. For example, the semicolon can tie two closely related ideas together. Still other marks of punctuation serve to clarify or to prevent misreading; the use of italics is one of these.

For many years, writing in English was marked by what now seems to us excessive and overly detailed punctuation. This is no longer considered good style. Too much punctuation interferes with easy reading. You should try to use punctuation only (1) because you need it to make your meaning clear or (2) because conventional usage requires it. If the wording of an idea is unclear in the first place, punctuation will not usually help. If you find yourself struggling with the punctuation of a sentence, ask yourself whether the trouble lies in your arrangement of phrases or your choice of words. Often you can eliminate the problem by recasting the sentence.

## DIAGNOSTIC TEST

**Rewriting Sentences Using End Marks and Commas Correctly.** Number your paper 1–20. Rewrite each sentence, putting in any omitted end marks or commas and correcting any errors in their use.

EXAMPLE 1. Do you think that it will rain today.
1. Do you think that it will rain today?

1. Governor Jameston, a well-known Democrat does not plan on running for another term.
2. Having already served three terms he is withdrawing to spend more time with his family.
3. His supporters look upon him as a strong courageous leader.
4. His opponents on the other hand think of him as opportunistic.
5. I've often asked myself, "Is it possible that both sides could be right"?
6. I am taking courses in English, Spanish algebra and history.
7. Geometry which I took last year was not an easy subject for me.
8. The essay, that was assigned yesterday, is due next Monday.
9. Dave Peebles known for his athletic ability is also a talented artist.
10. In fact some of his cartoons have appeared in our school newspaper the *Lincoln High School Spectator.*
11. The editor in chief of the paper Valerie Monaco writes a weekly column and her sister does most of the photography for the paper.
12. When I joined the staff of the newspaper I was taught to write short powerful headlines.
13. I learned how to do paste-ups but I never could do them neatly.
14. In fact my teacher used to say, "Ken you are all thumbs."
15. Peg asked, "Have you ever read *Animal Farm* a political satire by George Orwell"?
16. You might also enjoy the movie version which is a cartoon.
17. If it is ever shown on television don't miss it.
18. Most movies, shown on television, aren't worth watching.
19. Please send this package to Mrs. Rose Sanchez 116 East Elm Street Allentown PA 18001.
20. The letter was dated June 16 1986 and was mailed from Washington D.C.

## END MARKS

In written English, an end mark indicates the close of a sentence. If you find that you often omit end marks, review the rules, examples, and exercises on run-on sentences in Chapter 12.

**29a. A statement is followed by a period.**

EXAMPLE I enjoyed the concert last night.

**29b. An abbreviation or initial is followed by a period.**

| EXAMPLES | | |
|---|---|---|
| | U.K. | United Kingdom |
| | Sept. | September |
| | Mr. | Mister |
| | A.D. | *anno Domini* ("in the year of the Lord") |
| | W. C. Handy | William Christopher Handy |

☞ **NOTE** Abbreviations in the metric system are often written without periods. EXAMPLES: km, dl

**29c. A question is followed by a question mark.**

EXAMPLE Are you going to the football game on Saturday?

**(1) Use a question mark after a direct question only; do not use it after a declarative sentence containing an indirect question.**

CORRECT Mrs. Simmons asked whether you are going to the football game on Saturday. [declarative sentence containing an indirect question]

**(2) Orders and requests are often put in question form out of courtesy, even when no real question is intended. Such a question may be followed by either a period or a question mark, though it is wise to use the question mark as a rule.**

CORRECT Will you please complete this brief questionnaire?
Will you please complete this brief questionnaire.

**(3) A question mark should be placed inside quotation marks when the quotation is a question. Otherwise, it should be placed outside quotation marks.**

EXAMPLES When you do not want to answer a personal question, you might ask in return, "Why do you ask**?"** [The quotation is a question.]

Did Mr. Shields actually say, "You are suspended for three days**"?** [The quotation is not a question. The whole sentence, however, is a question.]

**29d. An exclamation is followed by an exclamation point.**

EXAMPLES Wow**!** [emphatic interjection]
I can't imagine that**!** [emphatic sentence]
Don't cross that line**!** [emphatic command]

**(1) An interjection at the beginning of a sentence is almost always followed by a comma.**

CUSTOMARY Really**,** you can't do that**!**
RARE Really**!** You can't do that**!**

**(2) An exclamation mark should be placed inside quotation marks when the quotation itself is an exclamation. Otherwise, it should be placed outside the quotation marks.**

EXAMPLES "Down in front**!"** yelled the crowd.
She said, "You win**"!**

**(3) Do not use an exclamation mark unless a statement is obviously emphatic.**

INCORRECT Melanie was really excited about the prom!
CORRECT Melanie was really excited about the prom**.**

MECHANICS

**EXERCISE 1. Using End Marks Correctly.** All the periods, exclamation points, and question marks have been omitted from the following sentences. Number your paper 1–10. After the proper number, write each word or letter that should be followed by an end mark. After each word, write the end mark required. If quotation marks should precede or follow the end mark, write them in the proper place.

EXAMPLES 1. Mom asked, "When did you receive the letter
1. *letter?"*
2. Terrific What a throw
2. *Terrific! throw!*

1. When do you want to take your vacation
2. I did have enough money to go to the movies

3. Wow Did you see that liftoff
4. Ms Colachino finished writing her screenplay
5. T S Eliot was a distinguished poet of the twentieth century
6. Mother wants to know why you did not buy the newspaper
7. What a downpour
8. Leave the theater immediately
9. He yelled across the field, "Hurry
10. Didn't you hear her say "I'm not coming

## THE COMMA

Commas are used as frequently as end marks. They group words that belong together and separate words that do not. They are also used in conventional ways that have little to do with meaning.

### Items in a Series

**29e. Use commas to separate items in a series.**

EXAMPLES The basketball coach recommended that I practice dribbling**,** shooting**,** weaving**,** and passing. [words in a series]

We could meet before English class**,** during lunch**,** or after school. [phrases in a series]

Before I go anywhere, I must see that my room is clean**,** that my little brother is home from the softball game**,** and that the trash has been put out. [clauses in a series]

**(1) Do not place a comma before or after a series.**

INCORRECT I enjoy, gymnastics, basketball, wrestling, and football.
CORRECT I enjoy gymnastics**,** basketball**,** wrestling**,** and football.

EXCEPTION The abbreviation *etc.* is always followed by a comma unless it occurs at the end of a sentence.
EXAMPLE Randy bought hamburger, buns, onions, etc.**,** for the cookout.

**(2) When the word *and, or,* or *nor* joins the last two items in a series, the comma before the conjunction is sometimes omitted. Follow the practice prescribed by your teacher. Never omit the final comma, however, if such an omission would make the sentence unclear.**

UNCLEAR Mother, Father and Uncle Matt went to town. [How many people went to town, two or three? Is Mother being addressed or enumerated?]

CLEAR Mother, Father, and Uncle Matt went to town.

> ☞ **NOTE** Words customarily used in pairs are set off as one item in a series: *pancakes and syrup, bread and butter, profit and loss, hat and coat, pork and beans,* etc.

EXAMPLE Breakfast at the inn consists of orange juice**,** ham and eggs**,** toast**,** and coffee.

**(3) Do not use commas when all the items in a series are linked by *and, or,* or *nor.***

EXAMPLES Jake and Caitlin and Jane all took a bus.
Jim asked me to pass the celery and olives and radishes.

**29f. Use commas to separate two or more adjectives that modify the same noun.**

EXAMPLE Lana is an intelligent**,** responsible**,** sensitive director.

> ☞ **NOTE** A comma is unnecessary before a modifier so closely associated with the noun that the two words are thought of as a single concept.

EXAMPLE She is an intelligent, sensitive young woman.

To determine whether two adjectives modify the noun equally, substitute *and* for the possible comma: *intelligent (and) sensitive young woman.* If this can be done, a comma is necessary. Also, if the order of the adjectives can be reversed, a comma is needed: *She is a sensitive, intelligent young woman.*

MECHANICS

## Commas Between Independent Clauses

**29g. Use a comma before *and, but, or, nor, for, so,* or *yet* when they join independent clauses.**

EXAMPLES The Drama Club will be putting on *Macbeth*, and I can hardly wait to audition.

Amy was nervous about computer programming, but after two weeks in the class she was doing very well.

I had to follow the recipe very carefully, for I had never tried to bake a cake before.

Rule 29g applies to compound *sentences*—not compound *verbs*, compound *subjects*, and the like. In the following examples, commas should not be used.

EXAMPLES My sister was accepted at Emory University but decided to attend the University of Virginia instead. [compound verb]

What he is saying and how he is behaving are two totally different things. [compound subject]

Television crews covered the Daytona 500 and the Indianapolis 500 races. [compound object]

> ☞ **NOTE** Rule 29g is always correct; however, writers are allowed freedom in its application. When two independent clauses joined by a conjunction are very short and closely connected in thought, the comma between them may be omitted.

EXAMPLE The phone rang and I answered it.
You can take the bus or you can walk home.

The comma should never be omitted if a sentence would be confusing or unclear without it.

NOT CLEAR The teacher called on Maria and John began to answer. [Most readers would have to go over this sentence twice before realizing that the writer is not saying *The teacher called on Maria and John.*]

CLEAR The teacher called on Maria, and John began to answer.

You are expected to follow Rule 29g in all instances in the exercises in this book.

**EXERCISE 2. Using Commas with Items in a Series and with Compound Sentences.** Number your paper 1–10. After the proper number, write the words in each sentence that should be followed by a comma, and place the comma after the word. Watch for sentences in which the inclusion or omission of a comma affects the meaning. If a sentence does not require any commas, write *C* after the number.

1. The photograph showed a happy mischievous little boy.
2. Barbara will bring potato salad to the picnic and Marc will bring the cold cuts.
3. The professional soldier had served his country in wars in Germany Korea and Vietnam.
4. We studied the following authors in English class this semester: Richard Wright Lorraine Hansberry and Margaret Walker.
5. For her weekend trip she packed shorts a top and shoes for running; a swimsuit and beach robe; coordinated slacks skirt and blouse; and one pair of shoes that would match the street clothes.
6. The committee suggested that the cafeteria serve a different selection each day that classes not be interrupted by announcements and that pep rallies always be held during sixth period.
7. Students will receive paper pencils rulers etc. at the beginning of the test.
8. April liked the ballet but Jenny thought it was boring.
9. Last winter was abnormally cold icy and snowy.
10. To participate in any athletic program, you must possess skill ambition persistence and the ability to sacrifice.

## Nonessential Elements

MECHANICS

**29h. Use commas to set off nonessential clauses and nonessential participial phrases.**

A nonessential clause or phrase[1] is exactly that: not essential. Such a clause may be used to describe something, to explain something, or to add extra information, but it can be omitted without changing the basic (essential) meaning of the sentence.

NONESSENTIAL Margaret Mead**,** who was a disciple of Ruth Benedict**,** was a noted anthropologist.

The basic meaning of this sentence is *Margaret Mead was a noted anthropologist.* The subordinate clause *who was a disciple of Ruth*

[1] Nonessential phrases and clauses are also called *unrestrictive* or *nonrestrictive*.

*Benedict* can be dropped without changing this basic meaning in any way because it simply adds a bit of information to the sentence. We call this latter clause *nonessential* because it does not restrict or limit the words that it modifies (*Margaret Mead*). Most clauses that modify proper nouns are nonessential.

Now consider the effect of the clause in the sentence that you have just read.

ESSENTIAL Most clauses **that modify proper nouns** are nonessential.

Notice what happens to the meaning of the sentence if we omit the subordinate clause; we are left with *Most clauses are nonessential.* Obviously, this is not the meaning intended by the writer. In this sentence, omitting the subordinate clause *does* change the meaning, since the clause (*that modify proper nouns*) is essential to the meaning. We call this clause *essential* because it restricts or limits the word that it modifies (*clauses*); that is, it tells us that *clauses that modify proper nouns*—and only those clauses—are almost always nonessential.

NONESSENTIAL Margaret Mead**, who is the author of *Blackberry Winter*,** wrote several books on anthropology. [*Margaret Mead wrote several books on anthropology* is the basic meaning of the sentence; therefore, commas are appropriate.]

ESSENTIAL The early experiences **that Margaret Mead had as an anthropologist** are recorded in her book *Blackberry Winter.* [*The early experiences are recorded in her book* Blackberry Winter is not the basic meaning of the sentence; therefore, no commas should be used.]

NONESSENTIAL The Homecoming Parade, **which is sponsored by the student council,** will feature twenty-three floats this year.

ESSENTIAL Anyone **who appreciates color and movement** will enjoy seeing Alexander Calder's mobiles.

Understanding the difference between essential and nonessential clauses can be a valuable help in expressing the exact meaning that you have in mind. If commas were never used, some clauses could often be interpreted as either essential or nonessential.

EXAMPLE Science fiction writers (**,**) who are concerned about machines dominating people (**,**) frequently write about computer-controlled societies.

Notice the commas in parentheses. If these commas are included in the sentence, we have one meaning; if they are omitted, we have another, and very different, meaning. When commas are used, the writer is saying that science fiction writers write about computer-controlled societies; the information in the subordinate clause merely explains *why* they do so. Without the commas, however, the subordinate clause is essential, and the meaning of the sentence is that *only* writers who are concerned about machines dominating people would write about computer-controlled societies.

## Participial Phrases

Like clauses, participial phrases may be nonessential or essential. To differentiate nonessential from essential phrases, use the same tests that you have applied to clauses. When in doubt, read the sentence without the phrase; if the sentence still has the same basic meaning, the phrase is nonessential and should be set off by commas.

NONESSENTIAL The senator**,** wanting to be popular with voters**,** did not support the proposal for a tax increase. [If *wanting to be popular with voters* is omitted, the meaning of the sentence is not changed.]

ESSENTIAL The many citizens paying already high taxes will understand the senator's reluctance to favor any tax increase. [The phrase *paying already high taxes* is necessary to make the meaning clear.]

NONESSENTIAL Rosemary Casals**,** known to many Americans**,** plays an excellent tennis game.

ESSENTIAL The tennis match played at Wimbledon took over two hours.

**EXERCISE 3. Identifying Essential and Nonessential Phrases and Clauses.** Number your paper 1–10. If the italicized phrase or clause is essential, write *E* after the proper number; if it is nonessential, write *N* to indicate that you would use commas in this sentence. None of the sentences are ambiguous; that is, the italicized groups of words *must* be either nonessential or essential.

1. All students *going on the trip tomorrow* will meet in the auditorium after school today.
2. The White River Bridge *which closed today for resurfacing* will not be open for traffic until mid-October.
3. The symphony *that Beethoven called the* Eroica was composed to celebrate the memory of a great man.
4. From the composer's letters, we know that the "great man" *whom he had in mind* was Napoleon Bonaparte.

5. Natalie Curtis *always interested in American Indian music* was an early recorder of American Indian songs.
6. The driver *who caused the wreck* was going too fast.
7. The musician *who founded the annual music festival in Puerto Rico* was Pablo Casals.
8. Semantics *which is concerned with the meanings of words* is an interesting subject of study for high-school students.
9. My car *which is seven years old* simply refuses to start on cold mornings.
10. All contestants *submitting photographs for the contest* must sign a release form.

## WRITING APPLICATION A: Using Commas with Essential and Nonessential Elements

When you use commas with a nonessential participial phrase or a clause, you signal to your readers that the phrase or clause is not essential to the meaning of the sentence.

EXAMPLE Mrs. Brown**,** who was my English teacher last year**,** is my brother's English teacher this year. [The clause *who was my English teacher last year* can be omitted from the sentence without changing the meaning of the sentence.]

You should remember not to use commas with essential participial phrases or clauses. The lack of commas signals to your readers that the participial phrase or clause is essential to the meaning of the sentence.

EXAMPLE The salesmen walking by are my friends. [The participial phrase *walking by* cannot be omitted from the sentence without changing the meaning of the sentence.]

### Writing Assignment

Write sentences according to the following guidelines.
1. Write two sentences using essential participial phrases.
2. Write two sentences using nonessential participial phrases.
3. Write two sentences using essential clauses.
4. Write one sentence using a nonessential clause.

## Introductory Elements

### 29i. Use a comma after certain introductory elements.

**(1) Use a comma after words such as *well, yes, no,* and *why* when they begin a sentence.**

EXAMPLES Yes, I heard your question.
Well, I really haven't thought about it.
No, I don't think I'll go to the movie.
Why, I can't imagine where I left my keys.

**(2) Use a comma after an introductory participial phrase.**

EXAMPLES Looking poised and calm, Jill sauntered toward the bus stop. [present participle]
Exhausted after the five-mile hike, the scouts finally sat down to rest. [past participle]

> ☞ NOTE Remember that verb forms ending in *-ing* may also be verbal nouns, or gerunds (see pages 425–28). When a gerund phrase is used as the subject of a sentence, do not mistake it for an introductory participial phrase.

EXAMPLES **Following directions** is sometimes difficult. [The gerund phrase *Following directions* is the subject of the sentence.]

**Following directions,** I began to assemble the toy. [*Following directions* is an introductory participial phrase modifying *I*.]

**(3) Use a comma after a succession of introductory prepositional phrases.**

EXAMPLES In the first round of competition at the golf tournament, I had to play one of the best golfers in the state.
At the beginning of the second quarter of the game, he scored a touchdown.

> ☞ NOTE A single introductory prepositional phrase need not be followed by a comma unless it is parenthetical [see page 616, rule 29j (3)] or the comma helps to make the meaning clear.

MECHANICS

EXAMPLES For some, tests are always easy. [Without the comma, this sentence could easily be misunderstood.]
In fact, some students actually enjoy taking tests. [parenthetical expression]

**(4) Use a comma after an introductory adverb clause.**

EXAMPLES After my father had locked the car door, he remembered that the keys were still in the ignition.
If I hadn't had a spare set of keys, we would have had to walk.

An adverb clause that follows an independent clause is usually not set off by a comma.

EXAMPLE Acres of valuable timberland in the state of Washington were destroyed when a volcano erupted in 1980.

**REVIEW EXERCISE A. Using Commas Correctly.** This exercise covers all comma rules to this point in the chapter. Number your paper 1–10. After the proper number, write the words in each sentence that should be followed by a comma; then place a comma after each of these words. If a sentence does not need a comma, write *None*.

1. Soon after you fall asleep at night you begin a series of dreams, which you may not remember when you awaken.
2. Scientists who do research on dreaming believe that most people average five dreams each night.
3. There are some dreams that are common to most people but you probably do not realize that other people have "your" dream.
4. For example a common dream experience is one in which you are running but never arrive at a destination.
5. When you wake up from a nightmare you often feel tense or frightened or exhausted.
6. A dream about falling through dark endless space can be scary.
7. Looking at a sleeper's eyelids you can tell when a dream is taking place.
8. A dream is signaled by REM which stands for "rapid eye movement."
9. Dreaming helps maintain health sanity and well-being.
10. Having learned this much scientists are continuing their research on sleep and dreaming.

## Interrupters

**29j. Use commas to set off expressions that interrupt the sentence.**

Two commas are needed to set off an expression unless the expression comes first or last in the sentence.

**(1) Appositives and appositive phrases are usually set off by commas.**

An appositive is a word, with or without modifiers, that follows a noun or a pronoun and identifies or explains it. An appositive phrase consists of an appositive and its modifiers.

EXAMPLES Claude McKay's *Banjo*, the book I have often told you about, was first published in 1929, the year the Great Depression began.

Mr. Goacher, our French teacher, has studied at the Sorbonne.

When an appositive is so closely related to the word it modifies that it appears to be part of that word, no comma is necessary. An appositive of this kind is called a restrictive appositive. It is usually one word.

EXAMPLES my nephew Jim
the American gymnast Peter Vidmar
my friend Juanita
the expression *c'est la vie*

**(2) Words used in direct address are set off by commas.**

EXAMPLES Mother, did you remember to call Mrs. Johnson?
Your essay, Maria, was well organized.
Will you answer the question, Monica?

MECHANICS

**(3) Parenthetical expressions are set off by commas.**

Many words and phrases are used parenthetically. Such expressions may serve as explanations or qualifications, but they do not affect the grammatical structure of the sentence in which they appear. The following list contains a few commonly used parenthetical expressions.

after all
as a matter of fact
by the way
consequently
for example
however
I believe (hope, think, etc.)
incidentally
in fact
in the first place
naturally
nevertheless
on the other hand
therefore

EXAMPLES By the way, did you see our football team on the sports news?
A celebrity is, of course, easily recognized by many people.
It is too late to go today, I believe.

Of course, these expressions need not be used parenthetically. When they are not, do not set them off with commas.

EXAMPLES By the way, she is in my vocal music class. [parenthetical]
You can tell by the way she sings that she enjoys the class. [not parenthetical]

> ☞ NOTE A contrasting expression introduced by *not* is parenthetical and should be set off by commas.

EXAMPLE It is the dromedary, not the Bactrian camel, that is native to North Africa.

Subrule (3) is often deliberately not followed for several reasons. First, if the meaning is clear, the commas that set off a parenthetical expression are sometimes omitted to avoid an overpunctuated sentence. Second, and of great importance, is the matter of intention. When you wish the reader to pause, to consider the expression as parenthetical, set it off; if not, leave it unpunctuated. You will always be safe, however, if you follow subrule (3).

**EXERCISE 4. Using Commas with Expressions That Interrupt.** This exercise covers the three kinds of interrupters discussed in the preceding pages. Rewrite the following sentences, inserting commas wherever they are needed. If no comma is needed, write *no comma.*

1. It's the phone that's ringing Suzanne not the doorbell.
2. Have you seen Mr. Welch our new accounting teacher?
3. Some of Eugene O'Neill's early plays moody one-act dramas of the sea established his reputation with at least one important group the critics.
4. Please listen class while Jim makes an announcement about yearbook pictures.
5. Some novels such as *Moby Dick* and *The Red Badge of Courage* are more than just the adventure stories they appear to be.
6. My neighbor Mrs. Kirby gets my mail when I am away.

7. Mark Twain was not merely a clown and entertainer but a great novelist perhaps the greatest of his time and place.
8. Mr. Beck the yearbook photographer always tries I think to place each person in the most flattering pose.
9. It is the pressure of getting work in on time not the work itself that gets on my nerves.
10. As a matter of fact your lateness is your own fault since you knew what time the bus would be leaving.

## Conventional Uses

**29k. Use a comma in certain conventional situations.**

**(1) Use a comma to separate items in dates and addresses.**

EXAMPLES The conference is scheduled for Friday**,** October 26**,** 1988.

The stockholders' meeting will be held at the new Radisson Hotel**,** 9200 Keystone Crossings**,** Indianapolis**,** IN 46240. [Notice that the ZIP code number follows the two-letter abbreviation for the state without punctuation.]

> ☞ NOTE When only the month and year are given, no punctuation is necessary.

EXAMPLE Construction of the new school will begin in April 1986.

When the items are joined by a preposition, do not use commas.

The play is at the Melrose Theater **on** Broad Avenue **in** Midland Heights.

**(2) Use a comma after the salutation of a friendly letter and after the closing of any letter.**

EXAMPLES Dear Rosa**,** Sincerely yours**,**

## Unnecessary Commas

**29l. Do not use unnecessary commas.**

A mistake in writing is the overuse of commas, and the most common example of this is separation of the subject and the verb by a comma, particularly when the subject is followed by a series of phrases or clauses.

INCORRECT The algebra teacher in the room across the hall, is yelling at her noisy class. [*Teacher* is the subject; it must not be separated by a comma from the verb *is yelling*.]

CORRECT The algebra teacher in the room across the hall is yelling at her noisy class.

☞ **NOTE** Although at first glance the comma following a nonessential clause or phrase may seem to separate the subject and verb, this is really not so, since nonessential elements in the middle of a sentence are set off by two commas, one preceding and one following each nonessential element.

EXAMPLE The school nurse, having taken my temperature, sent me home.

If you remember that a nonessential element in the *middle* of a sentence must have *two* commas, you will have little difficulty with this rule.

**REVIEW EXERCISE B. Rewriting Sentences Using End Marks and Commas Correctly.** This exercise covers end marks and all comma uses. Rewrite each sentence, inserting punctuation where necessary.

1. Ms. Scott the substitute teacher walked into the study hall demanded that everyone be quiet and start studying took a candy bar away from one student intercepted a paper headed for the wastebasket and finally got a chance to call the roll.
2. First performed on March 11 1959 on Broadway in New York City Lorraine Hansberry's play *A Raisin in the Sun* which was later made into a movie was awarded the New York Drama Critics Circle Award.
3. Although the house looked like a disaster had hit Mother said that if we all helped put away toys and books picked up all the clothes lying around dusted the furniture and vacuumed the rug it would look presentable by the time Grandmother arrived.
4. After all you could look at the map to see if there is an exit from Interstate 70 to a state road that will take us south to Greenville Illinois instead of complaining because I don't know the way.

5. On her way to work each morning she saw young people on their paper routes children waiting for school buses mail carriers beginning their deliveries and the inevitable joggers puffing along on their morning workouts.
6. City buses are a pleasant way to travel but why do they run so infrequently and when they do arrive why are they in bunches of three or four or more?
7. Covered by newspapers and magazines on the table the two hundred dollars in cash escaped the thief's attention.
8. If you are going to paint window frames the panes of glass should be covered with masking tape which will protect the glass from being spattered.
9. On a beautiful fall day it is wise to go for a walk play touch football or a little basketball or go for a drive through a lovely park for it won't be long until everything is bleak cold and dreary.
10. If I had my way I would live in a climate where it would be warm not hot in the daytime and cool in the evening all year round.

**WRITING APPLICATION B:**
**Using Commas Correctly in Your Writing**

Whenever you write, you should follow the standard rules for using commas. Your readers expect clear, unambiguous writing.

**Writing Assignment**

Think of a summer position that you would like to obtain. Write a letter to the person in charge, explaining why you think you are the best person for the position. Follow the procedure for writing a business letter, and use commas correctly. Proofread your letter for correct letter form and correct comma usage.



## CHAPTER 29 REVIEW: POSTTEST

**Rewriting Sentences Using Commas and End Marks Correctly.** Rewrite each sentence, inserting any omitted end marks or commas and correcting errors in their use. If a sentence is correct as it stands, write + after the proper number.

EXAMPLE 1. Sally asked, "Where do you want to go after the recital"?
1. *Sally asked, "Where do you want to go after the recital?"*

1. Having listened to the lecture given by the stockbroker I was still confused about the stock market.
2. Who was it who said, "I only regret that I have but one life to lose for my country?"
3. Wow I think I have finally balanced this equation correctly.
4. It wasn't raining in the morning but a low thick fog blanketed the city.
5. Through an uncanny accident of birth my twin brothers were born in different years: Jack was born on December 31 1976 and Jim was born on January 1 1977.
6. James King an eighty-nine-year-old Iroquois conducts tours of the Somers Mountain Indian Museum in Somers Connecticut.
7. Any student, who had not signed up for the contest by three o'clock, will not be eligible to participate.
8. My friend Dave, running up the stairs two at a time, yelled out the good news.
9. If this music is disturbing you don't hesitate to turn it off.
10. Yes I think suburbia not city or country living suits me best.
11. As soon as they opened the desk drawer they found the torn soiled map that they had searched for all morning.
12. "Why does the telephone ring just as soon as I sit down to work," she asked?
13. My parents are trading in their car a two-door model with a sunroof bucket seats and air conditioning.
14. "It is a virus I believe that causes this sore throat," Dr. Garcia explained.
15. Since the wallpaper is in red white and blue the room will look very patriotic.
16. I have drilled practiced trained and exercised for four days and now I am too tired to compete.
17. "Well Coach I guess I'll be ready for the game," Kit said.
18. Startled, we heard a high-pitched, whining, noise just outside the window.

19. Ticking away noisily the clock reminded everyone in the room of the need for speed accuracy and concentration.
20. "Where should the question mark be placed in a quoted sentence," Yolanda inquired?

## SUMMARY OF THE USES OF THE COMMA

29e. Use commas to separate items in a series.

29f. Use commas to separate two or more adjectives that modify the same noun.

29g. Use a comma before *and, but, or, nor, for, so* or *yet* when they join independent clauses.

29h. Use commas to set off nonessential clauses and nonessential participial phrases.

29i. Use a comma after certain introductory elements.
(1) After words such as *well, yes, no,* and *why* when they begin a sentence
(2) After an introductory participial phrase
(3) After a succession of introductory prepositional phrases
(4) After an introductory adverb clause

29j. Use commas to set off expressions that interrupt the sentence.
(1) Appositives and appositive phrases
(2) Words in direct address
(3) Parenthetical expressions

29k. Use a comma in certain conventional situations.
(1) To separate items in dates and addresses
(2) After the salutation of a friendly letter and the closing of any letter

29l. Do not use unnecessary commas.

# CHAPTER 30

# Punctuation

## OTHER MARKS OF PUNCTUATION

The basic punctuation tools have been given in the last chapter. With end marks and commas alone, you can probably punctuate most of the sentences you write, and your meaning will be clear. However, just as you have learned to express complex thoughts in complex sentences, so you can learn to use the punctuation signals given in this chapter effectively. Many of their uses will be conventional, but many will also help you to write more involved sentences clearly.

MECHANICS

### DIAGNOSTIC TEST

**Proofreading Sentences for Correct Punctuation.** The following sentences contain punctuation errors in the use of the semicolon, the colon, the dash, parentheses, brackets, underlining (italics), quotation marks, the apostrophe, and the hyphen. Rewrite each sentence, correcting the error. There is only one error in each sentence.

EXAMPLE 1. The directions stated, "When you work on this exercise, read the sentences carefully".

1. *The directions stated, "When you work on this exercise, read the sentences carefully."*

1. This job requires some facility with computers, do not apply for it unless you have had some experience with BASIC.

2. We plan on arriving in San Francisco by 8:00 P.M. moreover, our hotel reservations have already been confirmed.
3. "Are Liz and Donna's eyeglass frames alike?" Marsha asked.
4. I love everything about my new bicycle except it's color!
5. Our school has had exchange students from: Liberia, Denmark, Korea, Uruguay, and France.
6. "For tomorrow, read the chapter called The Era of Reconstruction," our history teacher said.
7. When my father comes home, he reads the New York Times.
8. Was Emilia Platero with you in the shopping mall; or did she decide to stay home and work on her research paper?
9. Here are the Nebraska ZIP codes you wanted, Martinsburg, 68750; Milligan, 68406; Newman Grove, 68758; and Saronville, 68975.
10. My cousin Nori Matsuyama, who is only twenty-five years old, is a State Department consul presently she is working as a translator.
11. This morning when I woke up, I turned over in bed and faced the alarm clock; it read 8–12 A.M.
12. Yesterday Jorge declared, "Fishing is a frustrating sport".
13. "If you want to know what I think," she stated vehemently, "You should spend more time revising your work."
14. Did Maria look in the Guide to Simple Household Repairs for information about fixing that leaky faucet?
15. The thought of weeding the vegetable garden—not to mention the flower garden overwhelms me.
16. The presidency of Franklin Delano Roosevelt 1932–1945 was the longest one in American history.
17. There was a sign in the store window that read, We are open twenty-four hours—but not all in one day.
18. Do you have trouble remembering the way to spell desiccate?
19. This is someone's else paper, not mine.
20. He said, "This language Russian is just too difficult for me."



## THE SEMICOLON

The semicolon has often been described as either a weak period or a strong comma; in other words, it is part period and part comma. The most common use of the semicolon is to indicate a close relationship between two independent clauses.

**30a. Use a semicolon between independent clauses not joined by *and, but, for, or, nor, yet,* or *so.***

EXAMPLES The rain had finally stopped**;** a few rays of sunshine were pushing their way through breaks in the clouds.
Her answer was correct**;** yours was not.

Do not use a semicolon to join independent clauses unless there is a close relationship in thought between the main ideas of the clauses.

NONSTANDARD For Stan, oil painting is a difficult medium to master; he had enjoyed taking photographs when he was younger.
STANDARD For Stan, oil painting was a difficult medium to master**.** He had enjoyed taking photographs when he was younger.

**30b. Use a semicolon between independent clauses joined by the words *accordingly, also, besides, consequently, furthermore, hence, however, indeed, instead, moreover, nevertheless, otherwise, similarly, still, therefore, thus, for example, for instance, that is,* or *in fact.***

EXAMPLES Ted plays baseball well**; in fact,** he would like to try out for a major-league team.
The snowfall made traveling difficult**; nevertheless,** we arrived at our destination safely.

When the connectives mentioned in this rule are at the beginning of a clause, the use of a comma after them is optional except for *that is, for example,* and *for instance,* which are always followed by a comma. When they are clearly parenthetical (interrupters), they are followed by a comma. The word *however* is almost always followed by a comma.

**30c. A semicolon (rather than a comma) may be needed to separate independent clauses joined by a coordinating conjunction when there are commas within the clauses.**

EXAMPLE In the seventeenth century**,** the era of such distinguished prose writers as Sir Thomas Browne**,** John Donne**,** and Jeremy Taylor**,** the balanced compound sentence using commas and semicolons reached a high degree of perfection and popularity**;** but the tendency today is to use a fast-moving style with shorter sentences and fewer commas and semicolons. [commas within clauses]

**30d. Use a semicolon between lines in a series if the items contain commas.**

EXAMPLE The president of the club has appointed the following to chair the standing committees: Jonathan Stokes**,** planning**;** Rebecca Hartley**,** membership**;** Christine Stevenson**,** financial**;** and Anita Jeng**,** legal.

## THE COLON

**30e. Use a colon to mean "note what follows."**

**(1) Use a colon before a list of items, especially after expressions such as *as follows* and *the following*.**

EXAMPLES The application for employment at the manufacturing plant asked the following questions**:** How old are you? Have you ever worked in a manufacturing plant before? What other jobs have you held? [list introduced by *the following*]

We assembled the following items for our garage sale**:** lamps, books, records, toys, sheets and towels, dishes, clothing, and patio chairs.

> ☞ **NOTE** When a list immediately follows a verb or preposition, do not use a colon.

EXAMPLES The emergency kit **included** safety flares, jumper cables, and a flashlight. [list follows the verb *included*]

Each student taking the math test was provided **with** two sharpened pencils, paper, a protractor, and a ruler. [list follows the preposition *with*]

**(2) Use a colon before a long, formal statement or quotation.**

EXAMPLE Patrick Henry concluded his revolutionary speech before the Virginia House of Burgesses with these unforgettable words**:** Is life so dear, or peace so sweet as to be purchased at the price of chains and slavery? Forbid it, Almighty God! I know not what course others may take, but as for me, give me liberty or give me death! [Note that a formal statement like this need not be enclosed in quotation marks.]

MECHANICS

> ☞ **NOTE** The first word of a formal statement following a colon is generally capitalized; however, in the case of informal statements, the first word often starts with a small letter.

**(3) Use a colon between independent clauses when the second clause explains or restates the idea of the first.**

EXAMPLES Lois felt that she had accomplished something worthwhile: she had designed and sewn her first garment.
Benjamin Franklin had many talents: he was an inventor, a writer, a politician, and a philosopher.

**EXERCISE 1. Writing Sentences Using Colons Correctly.** Write five sentences, each one using a colon between two independent clauses, in which the second clause explains or restates the main idea of the first.

**30f. Use a colon in certain conventional situations.**

**(1) Use a colon between the hour and the minute when you write the time.**

EXAMPLE 5:20 P.M.

**(2) Use a colon between chapter and verse in referring to passages from the Bible.**

EXAMPLE Proverbs 10:1

**(3) Use a colon between volume and number or between volume and page number of a periodical.**

EXAMPLES *Science Digest* 102:3 [volume and issue number]
*Science Digest* 102:89–92 [volume and page number]

**(4) Use a colon after the salutation of a business letter.**

EXAMPLES Dear Mrs. Rodriguez: Dear Madam:
Dear Sir: Gentlemen:

## THE DASH

**30g. Use the dash to indicate an abrupt break in thought.**

EXAMPLES The poor condition of this road—you can feel every bump as you ride along—makes the route inconvenient.
The real villain turns out to be—but I don't want to spoil the ending for those of you who have not yet seen the movie.

**30h. Use a dash to set off parenthetical material.**

EXAMPLE Very few people in this class—three, to be exact—have completed their projects.

**30i. Use a dash to mean *namely, in other words, that is,* and similar expressions that precede explanations.**

EXAMPLE She joined the chorus for only one reason—she loved to sing.

The dash and colon are often interchangeable in this use. A dash may be considered more emphatic than a colon. If the dash is overused, it loses its emphasis.

## PARENTHESES

**30j. Use parentheses to enclose informative or explanatory matter that is added to a sentence but is not considered of major importance.**

The material enclosed by parentheses may range from a single word or number to a short sentence.

EXAMPLES Harriet Tubman (1820–1913) is remembered for her work in the Underground Railroad.
A *roman à clef* (literally, "novel with a key") is a novel about real people to whom the novelist has assigned fictitious names.

MECHANICS

> ☞ **NOTE** Commas, dashes, and parentheses are frequently used interchangeably to set off incidental matter. Which you use becomes a matter of preference, but commas and dashes are the more common.

**(1) Be sure that any material enclosed in parentheses can be omitted without changing the basic meaning and construction of the sentence.**

IMPROPER USE OF PARENTHESES George Eliot (whose real name was Mary Ann Evans) wrote poems and several well-known novels. [The idea in parentheses would be better as a nonessential clause set off by commas.]

**(2) Punctuation marks are used within parentheses when they belong with the parenthetical matter. Punctuation marks that belong with the main part of the sentence are placed outside the closing parenthesis.**

EXAMPLES My mother frequently repeats her favorite question (**"**Is that really necessary**?"**) when my sister is home from school.

During the years of the Civil War (1860–1865)**,** brothers sometimes fought against brothers.

## WRITING APPLICATION A: Using the Dash and Parentheses Sparingly

The dash and parentheses are effective when used sparingly. Too many parenthetical expressions interrupt the flow of a sentence and irritate the reader, who may even lose the point of the sentence. Study the use of parentheses by E. B. White in the following extract, taken from "Death of a Pig":

> It was about four o'clock in the afternoon when I first noticed that there was something wrong with the pig. He failed to appear at the trough for his supper, and when a pig (or a child) refuses supper a chill wave of fear runs through any household, or ice-household. After examining my pig, who was stretched out in the sawdust inside the building, I went to the phone and cranked it four times. Mr. Dameron answered. "What's good for a sick pig?" I asked. (There is never any identification needed on a country phone; the person on the other end knows who is talking by the sound of the voice and by the character of the question.)

### Writing Assignment

Write a brief biographical sketch of a famous person; for example, an author, a scientist, a doctor, or an inventor. Use at least one set of parentheses and dashes in your sketch. When you proofread your sketch, check for the correct use of these punctuation marks.

## BRACKETS

In ordinary composition you will have practically no use for brackets. Commas, dashes, and parentheses are preferable as ways of setting off parenthetical matter.

**30k. Use brackets to enclose explanations within parentheses or in quoted material when the explanation is not part of the quotation.**

EXAMPLE The article stated that "at the time of that Democratic National Convention [in Chicago in 1968] there were many protest groups operating in the United States."

## UNDERLINING (ITALICS)

**30l. Use underlining (italics) for titles of books, periodicals, newspapers, works of art (pictures, television programs, statues, and other creative works), planes, ships, etc.**

EXAMPLES *The Old Man and the Sea*
*Reader's Digest, Seventeen*
the *St. Louis Post-Dispatch* or the St. Louis *Post-Dispatch*
*The Kiss, Starry Night, Girl Reading* [works of art]
*Queen Mary* [ship], *Century Limited* [train]

The use of quotation marks for titles is now generally limited to short compositions such as stories and short poems and to parts of books, such as chapters or articles.

EXAMPLE Did you read the article "Ten Dangerous Prescription Drugs" in *Better Homes and Gardens*?

It is sometimes necessary to call special attention to a particular word or expression. For this purpose printers use a slanting type called *italic*. In handwritten or typewritten manuscripts, underlining serves the same purpose. Thus a title printed this way:

*The Red Badge of Courage*

would look like this in a typewritten manuscript:

The Red Badge of Courage (underlined)

**30m. Use underlining (italics) for words and letters referred to as such and for some foreign words.**

EXAMPLES Should the use of *their* for *there* be considered a spelling error or a usage error?
The teacher couldn't tell whether I had written an *a* or a *c*.
Some U.S. coins were stamped with the inscription *E pluribus unum.*

**EXERCISE 2. Using Semicolons, Colons, Dashes, Parentheses, Brackets, and Underlining (Italics).** Number your paper 1–10. Rewrite each of the following sentences correctly, inserting punctuation as needed.

1. I'll come by for the two of you around 7:30 dress informally and take you to the party at Orchard Lake.
2. Do you think you can punctuate the following "As Caesar loved me, I weep for him as he was fortunate, I rejoice at it as he was valiant, I honor him but as he was ambitious, I slew him"?
3. If you use visual aids charts, maps, or graphs your audience will understand the technical information more easily.
4. The citizen who spoke before the Nuclear Regulatory Commission last month pleaded "If you allow this project the Marblehead nuclear plant to be completed, you will be creating another Three Mile Island."
5. The Little Foxes, a play by Lillian Hellman its title by the way is taken from the Song of Solomon 2:15 had a remarkable effect upon Maxine last year it may have been the reading of this play that helped her decide to major in drama at Yale next year.
6. Engineers' quests for the ideal high-fidelity speaker *ideal* means the ability to reproduce exactly whatever recorded signals are fed have led to many innovative designs for example, electrostatic panels and truncated pyramids have been offered as alternatives to the traditional box-shaped enclosure.
7. The playwright handles her material I should say her lack of material quite well however, she does not adequately fill the time between 7 30 and 10 30.
8. While reading a history book called The Rise of Nazi Germany, I had to use my dictionary to find the definitions of the following terms Anschluss, Luftwaffe, and Wehrmacht.
9. When you talk in front of an audience, remember these rules speak loudly and clearly, refrain from nervous habits and gestures, look directly at your audience, and above all, have something to say that is worth saying.
10. There was an interesting article in Omni about Arthur C. Clarke's 2001: A Space Odyssey and the similarities between the flight in that movie and our own manned space flights; the article also reviewed Clarke's 2010: Odyssey Two.

## QUOTATION MARKS

**30n. Use quotation marks to enclose a direct quotation—a person's exact words.**

DIRECT QUOTATION Coach Griffey announced, **"**The track meet is canceled because of the unusually cold weather**."**

Do not use quotation marks to enclose an indirect quotation—one that does not give a speaker's exact words.

INDIRECT QUOTATION Coach Griffey announced that the track meet was canceled because of the unusually cold weather.

Remember that *enclose* means placing quotation marks at both the beginning and the end of a direct quotation. Omission of quotation marks at the end of a quotation is a common error.

**(1) A direct quotation begins with a capital letter.**

EXAMPLE When Mrs. Emery called, she said, "**D**on't forget that your appointment is at two o'clock."

However, if the quotation is only a fragment of a sentence, do not begin it with a capital letter.

EXAMPLE In Shakespeare's *Julius Caesar,* Cassius complained that Caesar "**d**oth bestride the world like a mighty Colossus."

**(2) When a quoted sentence is divided into two parts by an interrupting expression such as *she said* or *I asked*, the second part begins with a small letter.**

EXAMPLE "I really have to leave now," said Gwen, "**s**o that I will be on time."

If the second part of a broken quotation is a new sentence, it begins with a capital letter.

EXAMPLE "I'm going to the supermarket this afternoon," said Jolene. "**W**hat time will you be home from work?"

**(3) A direct quotation is set off from the rest of the sentence by commas or by a question mark or exclamation point.**

EXAMPLES "Don't you dare throw that**!**" he yelled.
He wondered aloud**,** "Did I turn the headlights off?"

MECHANICS

> ☞ **NOTE** If the quotation is only a phrase, do not set it off by commas.

EXAMPLE When she tried to keep the crystal vase from falling off the shelf and knocked over the china plates in the process, she knew what "clumsy as an ox" meant.

**(4) When used with quotation marks, the other marks of punctuation are placed according to the following rules:**

1. *Commas and periods are always placed inside the closing quotation marks.*

EXAMPLE **"**On the other hand**,"** he said, **"**your decision may be correct**."**

2. *Semicolons and colons are always placed outside the closing quotation marks.*

EXAMPLES My neighbor said, **"**Of course I'll buy a magazine subscription**";** it was lucky that I asked her on payday.

Millay uses these devices in her poem **"**Spring**":** alliteration, slant rhyme, and personification.

3. *Question marks and exclamation points are placed inside the closing quotation marks if they belong with the quotation; otherwise they are placed outside.*

EXAMPLES **"**Will you call the doctor tomorrow**?"** I asked.
**"**Move those golf clubs**!"** yelled my mother.
Didn't he say, **"**I don't want to go**"?**
I'm sick of hearing **"**This is so boring**"!**

To avoid overpunctuating, do not use more than one comma or end mark at the end of a question.

INCORRECT Did Langston Hughes write the line "My soul has grown deep like rivers."? [two end marks—a period and a question mark]
CORRECT Did Langston Hughes write the line **"**My soul has grown deep like rivers**"?**

**(5) When a quoted passage consists of more than one paragraph, place quotation marks at the beginning of each paragraph and at the end of the entire passage. Do not place quotation marks at the end of any paragraph but the last.**

> ☞ **NOTE** A long quotation is often set off from the rest of the text so as to be easily recognizable as quoted matter. The entire passage may be indented; in printed matter it may be set in small type, and in typewritten copy it may be single-spaced instead of double-spaced. *When a quotation has been identified as such by any of these devices, no quotation marks are necessary.*

**(6) Use single quotation marks to enclose a quotation within a quotation.**

EXAMPLE "Did you understand what the boss meant when he said, 'Check the vendor number and class on all of these'?" asked Jim.

Notice the placement of the question mark. It belongs with the quotation as a whole, but not with the inner quotation; therefore, it falls inside the double quotation marks but outside the single one.

**(7) When you write dialogue (two or more persons carrying on a conversation), begin a new paragraph every time the speaker changes.**

EXAMPLE "You look very nice, Maria," said Mrs. Alvarez, "but why are you so dressed up to go to a rock concert?"

"Oh, Mother," sighed Maria, "I said I was going to a concert, but I didn't say it was a rock concert."

"I didn't know that you were aware of any other kind," replied her mother. "What kind of a concert are you going to, then?"

"You mean that foot-stomping, castanet-clicking stuff like old José Greco movies?" her brother snickered.

"Oh, be still," said Maria. "It's beautiful to watch. What do you know?"

"Nick is taking me to a flamenco concert," Maria finally admitted.

"Amazing, absolutely amazing," muttered Mrs. Alvarez, knowing that she could never have convinced Maria to attend that concert.

MECHANICS

**30o. Use quotation marks to enclose titles of chapters, articles, other parts of books or magazines, short poems, short stories, and songs.**

EXAMPLES The article "Old Poetry and Modern Music" discusses how contemporary singers use poems for lyrics; for example, Simon and Garfunkel recorded "Richard Cory," a poem by E. A. Robinson.

Last night I read "The World Was New," the first chapter in the book *Fifth Chinese Daughter* by Jade Snow Wong.

**30p. Use quotation marks to enclose slang words, technical terms, and other expressions that are unusual in standard English.**

Use this device sparingly.

EXAMPLES She reached for a high note and hit a "clinker."
If you aren't familiar with computer language, you may think that to "boot" a disk means to kick it; it actually means to insert the disk into the disk drive so that the computer will operate.

**EXERCISE 3. Using Quotation Marks and Other Punctuation Marks Correctly.** Number your paper 1–10. Rewrite the following sentences, inserting quotation marks and all other required punctuation and capitalization.

1. Time magazine always has interesting comments about celebrities in a section called People
2. Have you ever attended the Greek Festival asked Mr. Doney or didn't you know that there was such a thing
3. Our teacher quotes Willa Cather's words there are only two or three human stories, and they go on repeating themselves as fiercely as if they had never happened before.
4. How do I find out who wrote the poem Dream Deferred Jill asked her English teacher
5. The phrase frosting on the cake has nothing to do with dessert it refers to something additional that is a pleasant bonus.
6. I'm still hungry complained Donna after finishing a plate of stew that baked apple looks tempting
7. When you are confronted with any kind of tragedy, wouldn't it be better instead of asking why me to read from Psalms 23 6 which starts, surely goodness and mercy shall follow me all the days of my life
8. Perhaps Lincoln's finest memorial is the poem When Lilacs Last in the Dooryard Bloom'd in Walt Whitman's book Sequel to Drum-Taps.
9. Are you saying I don't know the answer or I don't understand the question
10. Ms. Hammer warned us that the movie was in her own words a parody of the novel furthermore she advised us not to waste our money and time by seeing it.

## WRITING APPLICATION B: Using Quotation Marks and Other Punctuation Marks with Dialogue

Dialogue can reveal your characters' personalities and move the action of the narration forward. As you read the following dialogue from Bernard Malamud's "A Summer's Reading," notice the correct use of quotation marks and other marks of punctuation. Notice also that the writer begins a new paragraph for each new speaker.

> George hesitated, then said, "I got a list of books in the library once, and now I'm gonna read them this summer." He felt strange and a little unhappy saying this, but he wanted Mr. Cattanzara to respect him.
>
> "How many books are there on it?"
>
> "I never counted them. Maybe around a hundred."
>
> Mr. Cattanzara whistled through his teeth.
>
> "I figure if I did that," George went on earnestly, "it would help me in my education. I don't mean the kind they give you in high school. I want to know different things than they learn there, if you know what I mean."
>
> The change maker nodded, "Still and all, one hundred books is a pretty big load for one summer."

### Writing Assignment

Think of a funny, embarrassing, or lighthearted incident in which you and a friend or relative were involved. Write a dialogue between you and your friend or relative. When you proofread your dialogue, check for correct use of quotation marks and other punctuation marks. Afterwards, share your dialogue with a classmate and ask your classmate to tell you if the dialogue is easy to follow.



## THE APOSTROPHE

**30q. To form the possessive case of a singular noun, add an apostrophe and an *s*.**

EXAMPLES cat's cradle — Ross's brush
principal's office — bird's-eye view

When a word of more than one syllable ends in an *s* sound, the singular possessive may be formed by adding the apostrophe alone. This omission avoids the awkward hiss of repeated *s* sounds.

EXAMPLES the witness' testimony Ms. Rodriguez' car
for conscience' sake Hercules' strength

**(1) To form the possessive case of a plural noun ending in *s*, add only the apostrophe.**

EXAMPLES the girls' gym the Joneses' car
the players' uniforms the witnesses' testimony

> ☞ **NOTE** The few plural nouns that do not end in *s* form the possessive by adding an apostrophe and an *s* just as singular nouns do.

EXAMPLES men's fashions children's toys

**(2) Personal pronouns in the possessive case (*his, hers, its, ours, yours, theirs*) and the relative pronoun *whose* do not require apostrophes.**

INCORRECT The books were her's.
CORRECT The books were **hers.**

INCORRECT The leopard can't change it's spots.
CORRECT The leopard can't change **its** spots.

INCORRECT Marjorie is the girl who's mother I met.
CORRECT Marjorie is the girl **whose** mother I met.

**(3) An indefinite pronoun (*one, everyone, everybody,* etc.) in the possessive case requires an apostrophe and an *s*.**

EXAMPLES Each one's time is recorded separately.
He seems to need everybody's attention.

> ☞ **NOTE** In such forms as *anyone else, somebody else,* etc., the correct possessives are *anyone else's, somebody else's,* etc.

**EXERCISE 4. Writing the Possessive Case of Nouns and Pronouns Correctly.** Number your paper 1–20. If the possessive case in each item in the list has been correctly formed, write *C* after the proper number. If it has been incorrectly formed, write the correct form.

1. It is her's.
2. womens' department
3. that boys' radio
4. Who's is it?
5. fly's flight
6. scissors' blades
7. mice's tails
8. childrens' program
9. oxen's yokes
10. the Green's anniversary
11. company's directors
12. a man's choice
13. leaves' color
14. It is somebody's else.
15. soldiers' rations
16. it's shiny surface
17. That is their's.
18. churches' spire
19. the McNeals' boat
20. a horses' hooves

**(4) In hyphenated words, names of organizations and business firms, and words showing joint possession, only the last word is possessive in form.**

EXAMPLES father-in-law's gloves
secretary-treasurer's signature
Sears Roebuck and Company's commercials
Roz and Denise's idea

When the second word in a group of words showing joint possession is a possessive pronoun, the first word is also possessive.

INCORRECT Brenda and my picture
CORRECT Brenda's and my picture



**(5) When two or more persons possess something individually, each of their names takes the possessive form.**

EXAMPLES Baldwin's and Ellison's writings
the doctor's and dentist's fees
Carla's and Joseph's research papers

**(6) The words *minute, hour, day, week, month, year,* etc., when used as possessive adjectives, require an apostrophe. Words indicating amount in cents or dollars, used as possessive adjectives, require apostrophes.**

EXAMPLES a week's vacation, four weeks' vacation
a dollar's worth, five dollars' worth
one cent's worth, ten cents' worth

**EXERCISE 5. Writing the Possessive Case of Nouns and Pronouns Correctly.** Number your paper 1–20. Each possessive relationship listed is expressed by means of a phrase. Change each phrase so that the possessive case of the noun or pronoun will be used to express the same relationship. Write each corrected phrase after the proper number on your paper.

EXAMPLE 1. promise of sister-in-law
1. *sister-in-law's promise*

1. party of Juan and Geraldo
2. clothes of babies
3. jobs of my brothers-in-law
4. duty of sailors
5. pay of two weeks
6. restaurant of Charlie and Barney
7. worth of ten million dollars
8. coats of the gentlemen
9. singing of the birds
10. plans of the school board
11. victory of the players
12. grades of Donna and Jim
13. delay of six months
14. testimonies of the clerk and the customer
15. hotel of West Baden
16. name of it
17. flooding of the river
18. hope of everyone else
19. opinions of the people
20. beauty of Catalina Island

**30r. Use an apostrophe to show where letters have been omitted in a contraction.**

A contraction is a word made up of two words combined into one through the omission of one or more letters.

| EXAMPLES | wouldn't | *for* | would not |
|---|---|---|---|
| | they've | *for* | they have |
| | hasn't | *for* | has not |

Notice that the apostrophe always falls at the exact place at which a letter or letters have been omitted.

☞ NOTE The most common error in the use of the apostrophe in a contraction comes from the confusion of *it's,* which means *it is,* with the possessive form *its* (*its* atmosphere), which has no apostrophe. Another common error is the insertion of the apostrophe in the wrong place: *ca'nt* for *can't*, *does'nt* for *doesn't*.

**30s. Use the apostrophe and *s* to form the plural of letters, numbers, and signs, and of words referred to as words.**

EXAMPLES There are two *r*'s and two *s*'s in *embarrassed.*
Are there three *5*'s after the decimal point?
That happened back in the 1970's.
The last exercise had more +'s than O's.
Try to combine ideas without using so many *and*'s and *then*'s.

## THE HYPHEN

Hyphens function in two ways: (1) to form compounds and (2) to divide words at the end of a line. The hyphen is a flexible linking mark. By using the hyphen, the writer can take two words or parts of words, join them with a hyphen, and make a third word that has its own concept or meaning that is different from the meaning of the original words. There are few invariable rules for the use of hyphens in compound words. The following somewhat oversimplified rules will, however, be useful.

**30t. Use a hyphen to divide a word at the end of a line.**

For rules on dividing words at the end of a line, see page 32.

**30u. Use a hyphen with compound numbers from *twenty-one* to *ninety-nine* and with fractions used as modifiers.**

EXAMPLES six hundred **twenty-five**
a **three-fourths** quorum [*Three-fourths* is used as an adjective modifying *quorum.*]
**three fourths** of the audience [*Fourths* is a noun modified by *three.*]

**30v. Use a hyphen with the prefixes *ex-, self-,* and *all-,* with the suffix *-elect,* and with all prefixes before a proper noun or proper adjective.**

EXAMPLES **ex-mayor** **mid-Atlantic**
**self-improvement** **trans-Siberian**
**governor-elect** **pre-Columbian**

**30w. Hyphenate a compound adjective when it precedes the word it modifies.**

EXAMPLES a **well-designed** engine The engine was **well designed.**
a **world-famous** skier The skier is **world famous.**

> **NOTE** Do not use a hyphen if one of the modifiers is an adverb ending in *-ly*.

EXAMPLE a **partly finished** research paper

### 30x. Use a hyphen to prevent confusion or awkwardness.

EXAMPLES **semi-invalid** [prevents awkwardness of two identical vowels]
**re-cover** a chair [prevents confusion with *recover*]
a **re-creation** of the event [prevents confusion with *recreation*]
**re-mark** the term papers [prevents confusion with *remark*]

**EXERCISE 6. Using Apostrophes and Hyphens Correctly.** Number your paper 1–25. After the proper number, rewrite each item, inserting apostrophes where they are needed and adding the necessary hyphens. Change the phrasal possessives to the possessive case. If an item is correct, write *C* after the proper number.

1. watches of Brian and Jeff
2. the plans of our mothers-in-law
3. transAlaskan
4. editorial page of the *Times*
5. Youre right, arent you?
6. one third of the class
7. Is'nt your's the red car?
8. Who are all of these *you*s and *they*s?
9. part time job
10. There are three *a*s in *alphabetical*.
11. It's their's, not our's.
12. remark the boundary lines
13. politics in the 1960s
14. a closely-knit group
15. Does'nt Charlene know it's name?
16. self appointed critic
17. idea of Sue and Lynn
18. It's after five oclock.
19. three quarter length sleeves
20. Whose going to answer the phone?
21. price list of the company
22. the dental charts of Tina and Sandy
23. proudly displayed flag
24. That's all there is to know.
25. Did'nt you see Bills new car?

**EXERCISE 7. Writing Sentences Using Hyphens Correctly.** Write five sentences according to the following guidelines. Follow the rules you have learned for the use of hyphens.

1. Write a sentence with a compound number.
2. Write a sentence with a fraction used as an adjective.
3. Write a sentence containing a word with the prefix *ex-*.
4. Write a sentence with a compound adjective preceding the word it modifies.
5. Write a sentence containing a word with *mid* before a proper noun.

**REVIEW EXERCISE. Proofreading a Paragraph for Correct Capitalization and Punctuation.** Most of the needed punctuation and capitalization has been omitted from the following passage. Rewrite the passage, making every required change that you can find. If you are in doubt about a particular punctuation or capitalization problem, don't guess; look up the rule.

> The origins of most sports are unknown try as we may we cannot say exactly when or where or how such games as baseball football and golf were first played. There is however one exception to this rule the game of basketball. Historians of sport know precisely where basketball began they know precisely when it began and perhaps the most interesting fact of all they know the name of the man who invented it Dr James Naismith in the winter of 1891–92 Dr. Naismith who was then an instructor at the ymca training college now called springfield college in springfield massachusetts had a problem on his hands. The football season was over the baseball season had not yet begun his students needed indoor exercise at a competitive sport but apparently no such sport existed working with the materials at hand naismith set himself the task of creating a new indoor sport he fastened two peach baskets to the walls at opposite ends of his gymnasium and using a soccer ball he devised the game that we call basketball today Like his equipment his rules were based on his material for example he started with eighteen available players and the first rule he wrote read as follows there shall be nine players on each side imagine eighteen players set loose on a modern basketball court

MECHANICS

## CHAPTER 30 REVIEW: POSTTEST

**Proofreading Sentences for Correct Punctuation.** The following sentences contain punctuation errors in the use of the semicolon, the colon, the dash, parentheses, brackets, underlining (italics), quotation marks, the apostrophe, and the hyphen. Rewrite each sentence after the proper number, correcting the errors. There may be more than one error in a sentence. You may have to add punctuation where it is needed, or you may have to delete punctuation that is incorrectly used.

EXAMPLES 1. We went shopping with full wallets, we came home with empty ones.
1. *We went shopping with full wallets; we came home with empty ones.*
2. Did you say "that you want to join us"?
2. *Did you say that you want to join us?*

1. Among the many items I have purchased to help me succeed in school I have found the following to be most helpful—a college dictionary, a thesaurus, and a pocket calculator.
2. Ed and Jim's essays were both titled Whats Wrong with Our City.
3. Bill Cosby is a well respected and marvelously-entertaining actor.
4. "Today we will be discussing the use of humor in The Adventures of Huckleberry Finn" Ms. Gardner said at the start of class.
5. To raise money for the American Cancer Society, the girl's soccer team and the boy's soccer team played a demonstration game.
6. "Where in the world? asked Lauren, does all this soot come from?"
7. Marilyn is an all around athlete.
8. Paula said in a desperate tone, "I know Sue's directions stated, "Turn right when you get to the gas station; "but, unfortunately, I'm not sure which gas station she meant.
9. The New York Times listed a variety of temperature readings in the United States for Tuesday September, 10, 1985; Anchorage, 49°; Sault Ste. Marie, 57°; Rapid City, 69°; Macon, 77°; Los Angeles, 83°; and Phoenix, 97°.
10. "Among the writers in America today, he Galway Kinnell has earned his reputation as an outstanding poet," noted the critic in Newsweek.
11. The Lusitania sank on May 7, 1915.
12. The most difficult chapter in that physics textbook of our's is titled Simple Machines.
13. In my opinion, Kathleen said, "Mallorys Department Store always lives up to it's motto—Satisfaction Guaranteed"!
14. William Butler Yeats 1865–1939, an Irish poet who won the Nobel Prize, was once a member of the Irish parliament.
15. When the crisp, clear days of September arrive, the beach across

MECHANICS

the street becomes deserted, then I live with the wonderful illusion that the beach is mine alone.

16. "In this home-economics course," our teacher said, "You will learn long range planning."
17. I always have trouble remembering the meaning of these two common verbs, affect ('to change' or 'to influence') and effect ('to cause' or 'to accomplish').
18. My class just finished reading The Fall of the House of Usher, a short story by Edgar Allan Poe.
19. The circus audience gave a well deserved round of applause for the perfectly-timed acrobatic stunt.
20. My driver's license wo'nt expire for another two weeks.

CHAPTER 31

# Spelling

## IMPROVING YOUR SPELLING

Poor spellers, even very poor spellers, can improve their skill through understanding the nature of words, through study, and through developing their memory. Before any improvement can take place, however, a student must first want to learn to spell correctly.

Learning to spell with accuracy is no easy task. English spelling is neither logical nor consistent. Almost every spelling rule seems to have its exceptions.

You should work on the improvement of your spelling habits through using a combination of rules and good practices. In time your stock of memorized spellings will grow large enough to meet all the ordinary needs of everyday writing, and you will be able to handle the spelling of new or unfamiliar words with confidence.

One of the most important spelling rules is *Care enough to be careful.* Care in writing and care in proofreading what you have written will eliminate errors in the spelling of simple words like *too, their, its,* which account for so many of every teacher's corrections on compositions.

The discussions, rules, and exercises in this chapter suggest a number of things you can do to improve your spelling.



### GOOD SPELLING HABITS

If you develop the following good spelling habits, you are bound to improve.

(1) Keep a list of your spelling errors.
(2) Use the dictionary as a spelling aid.
(3) Learn to spell by syllables.
(4) Learn a few helpful spelling rules.
(5) Learn to distinguish between words that are often confused.
(6) Learn lists of commonly misspelled words.

**1. Keep a list of your spelling errors.** Set aside a part of your notebook for lists of words that you repeatedly misspell and of new words that seem difficult to you. If possible, keep these lists in either one of the following two orders: (1) a rough alphabetical order, using a separate loose-leaf page for each letter so that you can easily find specific words; or (2) according to general types of spelling errors: for instance, a page each for the *ie* and *ei* rule, adding prefixes and suffixes, plurals, hyphens, troublesome silent letters, homonyms, your own special spelling demons, etc. Method two is particularly helpful because it constantly reinforces spelling rules and practices. Whenever you have time, restudy your lists as part of a campaign to overcome your personal spelling problems.

**2. Use the dictionary as a spelling aid.** The only sure way to find out how to spell a word is to consult the dictionary. If you do not find the word at once, try other spellings. Check the definition to be certain that you have located the right word rather than a homonym or a similar-sounding word. When more than one spelling is given, find and use the preferred form. To determine the preferred spelling of a word, see page 692.



**3. Learn to spell by syllables.** Short words, with the exception of a comparatively brief list of so-called spelling demons, are easier to spell correctly than long ones. Some long words, such as *notwithstanding,* break down into short, easily spelled words; others, like *satisfactorily,* break down into combinations of short syllables.

Pronouncing words correctly will also help with spelling. If you say *liberry* and *athalete* and *artic* instead of lī′brer′ē and ath′lēt and ärk′tik, the chances are that you will also misspell these words. Look up pronunciations in the dictionary. Learn pronunciation symbols.

**EXERCISE 1. Dividing Words into Syllables.** Write the syllables of each of the following words, using hyphens to separate the syllables from one another. Do this exercise without looking up the words in the dictionary. Your divisions of these words may or may not correspond exactly with the dictionary syllabication; what is important is that (1) each syllable is a single sound; (2) separately, each has the same pronunciation that it has in the entire word; and (3) all letters are included and no letters are added.

1. adversary
2. alias
3. barbarous
4. chimney
5. costume
6. deficit
7. genuine
8. incidentally
9. probably
10. temperature

## SPELLING RULES

**4. Learn a few helpful spelling rules.** The following rules are simple, useful, and important. Like most spelling rules, they have their exceptions; but the exceptions are not difficult and are easily mastered. Once you have learned these rules, they should keep you from making certain common spelling errors; in addition, the rules will assist you in determining the spelling of unfamiliar words.

### *ie* and *ei*

**31a. Write *ie* when the sound is long *e*, except after *c*.**

EXAMPLES believe, field, niece, ceiling, receive, conceit
EXCEPTIONS seize, either, neither, weird

Write *ei* when the sound is not long *e*, especially when the sound is long *a*.

EXAMPLES freight, weight, reign forfeit, height
EXCEPTIONS friend, mischief, conscience

**EXERCISE 2. Spelling ie and ei Words.** The blanks in the following words stand for the letters *ie* or *ei*. Write out the words, filling in the blanks with the correct letters. Be prepared to explain how Rule 31a applies to each word.

1. dec...ve
2. ch...ftain
3. v...l
4. h...r
5. rec...pt
6. counterf...t
7. gr...f
8. th...r
9. gr...vous
10. bel...f
11. p...rce
12. l...sure
13. perc...ve
14. sl...gh
15. bes...ge
16. shr...k
17. var...d
18. ...ght
19. cash...r
20. y...ld

## -cede, -ceed, and -sede

**31b. Only one English word ends in *-sede—supersede;* only three words end in *-ceed—exceed, proceed, succeed;* all other words of similar sound end in *-cede.***

EXAMPLES precede, recede, secede, accede, concede

## Adding Prefixes

A *prefix* is one or more than one letter or syllable added to the beginning of a word to change its meaning.

**31c. When a prefix is added to a word, the spelling of the word itself remains the same.**

EXAMPLES dis + satisfy = dissatisfy im + mature = i**mm**ature
mis + spell = misspell re + commend = re**c**ommend

## Adding Suffixes

A *suffix* is one or more than one letter or syllable added to the end of a word to change its meaning.

**31d. When the suffixes *-ness* and *-ly* are added to a word, the spelling of the word itself is not changed.**

EXAMPLES plain + ness = plai**nn**ess
casual + ly = casua**ll**y

EXCEPTIONS Words ending in *y* usually change the *y* to *i* before *-ness* and *-ly:* empty—empt**iness;** heavy—heav**iness;** busy—bus**ily;** ordinary—ordinar**ily.** One-syllable adjectives ending in **y,** however, generally follow Rule 31d: dry—dryness; shy—shyly.

MECHANICS

**EXERCISE 3. Spelling Words with Prefixes and Suffixes.** Spell out each of the words described below.

1. mis + inform
2. habitual + ly
3. il + legal
4. happy + ness
5. stubborn + ness
6. crafty + ly
7. in + animate
8. im + movable
9. dis + appear
10. dis + similar

**31e. Drop the final *e* before a suffix beginning with a vowel.**

EXAMPLES care + ing = car**ing** dose + age = dos**age**
love + able = lov**able** bride + al = brid**al**

EXCEPTIONS (1) To prevent a change in pronunciation, words ending in a soft *c* or *g* preceding a final *e* generally retain the *e* before a suffix beginning with *a* or *o*. The *c* or *g* thus retains its soft sound: noti**ce**able, pea**ce**able, coura**ge**ous. (2) Words ending in *ie* change this combination to *y* before *-ing*: lie—**ly**ing.

**31f. Keep the final *e* before a suffix beginning with a consonant.**

EXAMPLES love + ly = lov**ely** hope + ful = hop**eful**
place + ment = plac**ement** care + less = car**eless**

EXCEPTIONS truly, argument, acknowledgment, judgment

**31g. With words ending in *y* preceded by a consonant, change the *y* to *i* before any suffix not beginning with *i*.**

EXAMPLES accompany + ment = accompan**i**ment
plenty + ful = plent**i**ful
satisfy + es = satisf**i**es

BUT intensify + ing = intensif**y**ing
modify + ing = modif**y**ing

**EXERCISE 4. Spelling Words with Suffixes.** Spell out each of the following words. Be ready to state the rule for each word.

1. merry + ment
2. dilatory + ness
3. beauty + fy
4. modify + cation
5. sure + ly
6. study + ing
7. hurry + ing
8. occupy + ed
9. ally + es
10. pity + ful

MECHANICS

**31h. Double the final consonant before a suffix that begins with a vowel if both of the following conditions exist: (1) the word has only one syllable or is accented on the last syllable; (2) the word ends in a single consonant preceded by a single vowel.**

EXAMPLES swim + ing = swi**mm**ing [one-syllable word]

confer + ed = confe**rr**ed [accent on last syllable; single consonant and single vowel] benefit + ed = benefited [accent not on last syllable]

confer + ence = con'ference [accent shifted; consonant not doubled]

**EXERCISE 5. Spelling Words with Suffixes.** Spell out each of the following words. Be ready to state the rule for each word.

1. plan + ed
2. defer + ence
3. die + ing
4. achieve + ment
5. trod + en
6. shape + less
7. propel + er
8. seize + ure
9. definite + ly
10. care + ful
11. desire + able
12. rob + ery
13. sense + ible
14. nine + ty
15. lose + ing
16. argue + ment
17. control + ing
18. prepare + ing
19. fame + ous
20. create + or

## THE PLURAL OF NOUNS

**31i. Observe the rules for the spelling of nouns.**

**(1) The regular way to form the plural of a noun is to add an *s*.**

EXAMPLES dog, dogs book, books horse, horses

**(2) The plural of some nouns is formed by adding *es*.**

Add *es* to form the plural of nouns ending in *s, sh, ch, z,* and *x*. The *e* is necessary to make the plural forms pronounceable.

EXAMPLES dress, dresses dish, dishes
sandwich, sandwiches fox, foxes
bus, buses waltz, waltzes

MECHANICS

**(3) The plural of nouns ending in *y preceded by a consonant* is formed by changing the *y* to *i* and adding *es*.**

EXAMPLES country, countries fly, flies
comedy, comedies theory, theories

**(4) The plural of nouns ending in *y preceded by a vowel* is formed by adding an *s*.**

EXAMPLES monkey, monkeys journey, journeys
tray, trays buoy, buoys

**(5) The plural of most nouns ending in *f* or *fe* is formed by adding *s*. The plural of some nouns ending in *f* or *fe* is formed by changing the *f* to *v* and adding *s* or *es*.**

EXAMPLES Add *s:* *gulf, gulfs* *safe, safes*
*roof, roofs* *kerchief, kerchiefs*

*Change f* to *v* and add *s* or *es:*
leaf, leaves wife, wives
shelf, shelves knife, knives

**(6) The plural of some nouns ending in *o preceded by a vowel* is formed by adding *s;* the plural of most nouns ending in *o preceded by a consonant* is formed by adding *es*.**

EXAMPLES *o* following a vowel:
studio, studios radio, radios

*o* following a consonant:
potato, potatoes hero, heroes

EXCEPTIONS Some nouns ending in *o* preceded by a consonant form the plural in the regular way, by adding *s*. Most nouns ending in *o* and referring to music belong in this class.

EXAMPLES soprano, sopranos solo, solos
piano, pianos concerto, concertos
dynamo, dynamos silo, silos

**(7) The plural of a few nouns is formed in irregular ways.**

EXAMPLES child, children tooth, teeth goose, geese
woman, women mouse, mice ox, oxen

**(8) The plural of compound nouns written as one word is formed by adding *s* or *es*.**

EXAMPLES spoonful, spoonfuls cupful, cupfuls
leftover, leftovers strongbox, strongboxes

**(9) The plural of compound nouns consisting of a noun plus a modifier is formed by making the modified word plural.**

To determine the word that is modified in a compound word, make each of the parts plural. The modified word is the one that tells what the entire compound is or does. Thus the plural of *notary public* is *notaries public* (they are *notaries,* not *publics*); the plural of *mother-in-law* is *mothers-in-law* (they are *mothers,* not *laws*); etc.

EXAMPLES runner-up, runners-up
editor in chief, editors in chief
lieutenant governor, lieutenant governors
poet laureate, poets laureate

**(10) The plural of a few compound nouns is formed in irregular ways.**

EXAMPLES drive-in, drive-ins — six-year-old, six-year-olds
walk-on, walk-ons — tie-up, tie-ups

**(11) Some nouns are the same in the singular and the plural.**

EXAMPLES sheep, deer, trout, salmon, Japanese, fowl

**(12) The plural of some foreign words is formed as in the original language.**

EXAMPLES alumnus, alumni [masculine]
alumna, alumnae [feminine]
medium, media
phenomenon, phenomena

**(13) The plural of other foreign words may be formed either as in the foreign language or by adding *s* or *es*.**

EXAMPLES index, indices *or* indexes
appendix, appendices *or* appendixes

> ☞ **NOTE** In certain words the English plural is the preferred one, for example, *formulas,* not *formulae.* Whenever you are in doubt about which plural to use, turn to your dictionary.

**(14) The plural of numbers, letters, signs, and words considered as words is formed by adding an apostrophe and an *s*.**

EXAMPLES two *s*'s — two *4*'s
*and*'s — 0's
+'s — 1980's

**EXERCISE 6. Writing the Plural Form of Nouns.** Write the plural form of each of the following words. Be prepared to explain your spelling on the basis of Rule 31i (1–14).

1. gulf
2. penny
3. father-in-law
4. valley
5. 1700
6. solo
7. life
8. larva
9. bunch
10. 1900
11. right of way
12. try
13. corps
14. shelf
15. echo
16. elk
17. ox
18. politics
19. niece
20. turkey

**EXERCISE 7. Understanding the Spelling Rules.** This exercise reviews all the spelling rules covered up to this point. By referring to the rules on the previous pages, explain the spelling of each of the following words:

1. proceed
2. lovely
3. rodeos
4. senators-elect
5. parentheses
6. teaspoonfuls
7. biggest
8. two *c*'s
9. wheels
10. illegible
11. liberally
12. handkerchief
13. wharves
14. data (plural)
15. iciness
16. obligation (final *e* dropped)
17. conceive
18. immature
19. changeable
20. secede

## WORDS OFTEN CONFUSED

**5. Learn to distinguish between words that are often confused.** Some present spelling problems because they sound alike (homonyms) but have different meanings and, usually, different spellings. Like other students, you have probably run into difficulty with such pairs of words as *capital-capitol* and *stationary-stationery*. Most of the paired words in the following lists are frequently confused even though they are not pronounced exactly alike, for example, *later-latter*.

Some word pairs present problems that are primarily those of usage rather than meaning; these words are discussed in the "Glossary of Usage" (Chapter 27).

---

**already** previously
We have *already* studied that chapter.

**all ready** *all prepared* or *in readiness*
Are you *all ready* for the exam?

---

**altar** *a table or stand at which religious rites are performed*
This is the *altar* used in the Communion service.

**alter** *to change*
Do not *alter* your plans on my account.

---

**altogether** *entirely*
The President is *altogether* opposed to the bill.

**all together** *everyone in one group or place*
My family will be *all together* at Thanksgiving.

---

**ascent** *a rise; a climb*
The climbers' *ascent* was a slow one.

**assent** *consent*
Will they *assent* to our proposal?
Our last proposal won their *assent.*

---

**born** *given life*
Ynes Mexia was *born* in Washington, D.C.

**borne** *carried; endured*
Cynthia has *borne* her troubles better than we thought she would.

---

**brake** *a device for stopping or slowing down*
An automobile *brake* will overheat if used too often.

**break** *to shatter or come apart*
Borrow my mirror, but don't *break* it.

---

---

**capital** *a city which is the seat of government of a country or state;* also, *money used to carry on a business*

Washington is the *capital* of the United States.

The company has *capital* of $100,000.

**capitol** *building in which a legislature meets* (often capitalized)

Our Senate and House of Representatives meet in the *Capitol* in Washington.

The *Capitol* in Austin is a tourist attraction.

---

**clothes** *garments; wearing apparel*

I'd like to buy some summer *clothes*.

**cloths** *pieces of cloth; fabrics*

Use these *cloths* to clean the car.

---

**EXERCISE 8. Completing Sentences with Words Frequently Confused.** Number your paper 1–10. After each number, write the correct one of the two words in parentheses in the corresponding sentence.

1. The new dam will (altar, alter) the course of the river.
2. We have finished packing and are (all ready, already) to leave for our vacation.
3. Without saying a word, the major gave a nod of (ascent, assent).
4. What city is the (capital, capitol) of Nebraska?
5. You called us after we had (all ready, already) left.
6. Please keep your foot on the (brake, break).
7. The new expenditures will be (born, borne) by the taxpayers.
8. Did you try on those (cloths, clothes) before you paid for them?
9. The governor announced that the roof of the (capital, capitol) needs repair.
10. Your arguments are not (all together, altogether) convincing.

---

**coarse** *rough; crude; not fine*

His *coarse* language and manners kept him from getting the job.

The driveway was covered with *coarse* sand.

**course** *path of action; passage or way; study or group of studies; part of a meal*
We approve of the *course* you have taken.
Jerry's parents go to the golf *course* every Saturday.
The *course* in American history lasts a full year.
My favorite main *course* is roast chicken.

---

**complement** *something that completes or makes whole*
A good shortstop is needed to *complement* the team. [to make the team complete]
The *complement* of 30° is 60°. [the angle needed to make a complete 90° right angle]

**compliment** *praise*
Nancy's performance deserved the *compliments* that it received.
I want to *compliment* you on your original Halloween costume.

---

**council, councilor** *a group assembled for conferences or legislation;* each member is a *councilor*
The student *council* meets this afternoon.
The queen's *councilors* could not agree.

**counsel, counselor** *advice* or *to advise;* a giver of advice is a *counselor*
Only a wise *counselor* can give good *counsel.*

---

**des′ert** *a dry or barren land*
Irrigation has brought new life to the *desert.*

**desert′** *to leave or abandon*
A good soldier never *deserts* his post.

**dessert′** *the last course of a meal*
My favorite *dessert* is fresh fruit.

---

**formally** *in a strict or dignified manner; according to strict rules*
The mayor will *formally* open the new recreation center on Wednesday.

**formerly** *previously; in the past*
Mrs. Dong was *formerly* head of the history department at Lakeville High School.

---

---

**ingenious** *clever; resourceful; skillful*
Carla has an *ingenious* plan to earn some money this summer.

**ingenuous** *innocent; trusting; frank*
Ian is as *ingenuous* as a ten-year-old child.

---

**its** [possessive form of *it*]
Our city must increase *its* water supply.

**it's** [contraction of *it is*]
*It's* almost time for the bell.

---

**later** *more late; at a subsequent time*
It's true that I wasn't on time, but you were *later.*
I'll see you *later.*

**latter** *the second of two*
Dr. Edwards can see you in the morning or the afternoon, but the *latter* is more convenient for her.

---

**lead** [present tense] *to go first; guide*
We want you to *lead* us.

**led** [past tense of *lead*]
Elaine *led* the way and we followed.

**lead** [led] *a heavy metal;* also, *graphite in a pencil*
Nuclear reactors are often shielded with *lead.*

---

**EXERCISE 9. Completing Sentences with Words Frequently Confused.** Number your paper 1–10. After each number, write the correct one of the two words in each of the parentheses in the corresponding sentence.

1. Court is (formally, formerly) opened with a bailiff's cry of "Oyez, Oyez!"
2. When her painting was purchased by the museum, the artist received many (complements, compliments).
3. One of my father's favorite sayings is "What's next—(desert, dessert) or (desert, dessert) the table?"

4. The discovery and development of synthetic fibers required an (ingenious, ingenuous) mind.
5. I enjoy both chicken and steak but prefer the (later, latter).
6. One of the guidance (councilor's, counselor's) jobs is to (lead, led) students into the proper (coarse, course) of study.
7. Have you tried out the new municipal golf (coarse, course)?
8. The master of ceremonies referred to Mrs. Hawke's (ingenious, ingenuous) manner that concealed an iron will.
9. Do you know the words to the song "(Its, It's) Later Than You Think"?
10. This beverage will be an excellent (complement, compliment) to the meal.

---

**loose** *free; unfastened; not tight or firm*
That *loose* wheel on your bicycle is sure to give you trouble someday.
Clothes with a *loose* fit are stylish now.

**lose** [pronounced looz] *to suffer the loss of*
You seem to *lose* everything you borrow from me.

---

**miner** *a worker in a mine*
American *miners* lead the world in the production of coal.

**minor** *under legal age;* also, *smaller* or *less important* (as opposed to *major*)
Normally, a *minor* is not permitted to sign a legal paper.
Let's not list the *minor* objections to the plan.

---

**moral** *good or virtuous;* also, *a lesson taught by a story or event*
Good conduct is based upon *moral* principles.
The *moral* of the story is plain.

**morale** *spirit; mental condition*
Teamwork is impossible without good *morale.*

---

**peace** *calmness* (as opposed to *strife* or *war*)
Disarmament is an important step toward *peace.*

**piece** *a part or portion of something*
You've had four *pieces* of cake already.

---

---

**personal** *individual; private*
My *personal* opinion has nothing to do with the case.

**personnel** *a group of people employed in the same work or service; a staff*
Most large companies prefer to find their executive *personnel* among college graduates.

---

**plain** *not fancy; undecorated;* also, *a large area of flat land;* also, *clear*
*Plain* dresses are sometimes the most expensive.
Many Western movies are set in the Great *Plains.*
Does my explanation make things *plain* to you?

**plane** *a flat surface;* also, *a woodworking tool;* also, *an airplane*
Some problems in physics deal with the mechanical advantage of an inclined *plane.*
Use this *plane* to make the wood smooth.
We watched the *plane* circle for its landing.

---

**principal** *head of a school* [noun]; also, *chief* or *most important among several things*
The *principal* will address the entire student body tomorrow.
Florida and California are our *principal* orange-growing states.

**principle** *a rule of conduct;* also, *a basic or general truth*
The *principle* of the Golden Rule is found in many religions.
This machine operates on a new *principle.*

---

**quiet** *still; silent*
The library is not as *quiet* as it should be.

**quite** *completely* or *entirely;* also, *considerably* or *very*
Are you *quite* finished?
Anne is *quite* a courageous girl.

---

**rout** *a disorderly flight; to put to flight*
What began as an orderly retreat ended as a *rout.*

**route** *a road; a way to go*
This highway is the shortest *route* to the mountains.

---

**EXERCISE 10. Completing Sentences with Words Frequently Confused.** Number your paper 1–10. After each number, write the correct one of the two words in parentheses in the corresponding sentence.

1. Literature and composition are the (principal, principle) parts of the course.
2. Automation in the coal fields has put thousands of (miners, minors) out of work.
3. Coral has a sign that she puts on her desk in the library; it reads: "(Quiet, Quite) please. Genius at work."
4. When Kurt's (plain, plane) failed to return, the (moral, morale) of his squadron sank to zero.
5. The diver found an old chest filled with (peaces, pieces) of eight.
6. Follow the marked (rout, route) or you will surely (loose, lose) your way.
7. The (principal, principle) that underlies the company's choice of (personal, personnel) is "An educated person is usually willing to learn more."
8. The columnist described the game as a (rout, route) for our team.
9. To prevent infection, always take care of (miner, minor) cuts.
10. The accident that completely demolished the car was caused by a (loose, lose) cotter pin worth ten cents.

---

**stationary** *in a fixed position*
The new state power plant contains large *stationary* engines.

**stationery** *writing materials, especially paper*
Save your best *stationery* for important letters.

---

**straight** *not crooked or curved; direct*
If you can't draw a *straight* line, use a ruler.

**strait** *channel between two large bodies of water;* also (plural), *difficulty; distress*
The *Strait* of Gibraltar links the Mediterranean Sea and the Atlantic Ocean.
My parents have always helped me when I was in bad *straits.*

---

---

**than** [conjunction; used mainly in comparisons]
Loretta is taller *than* I.

**then** adverb meaning *at that time; soon afterward*
We lived on Garden Street until last year, and *then* we moved to our new house.

---

**there** *at that place*
I will be *there* when you arrive.

**their** [possessive form of *they*]
Did your friends bring *their* bathing suits?

**they're** [contraction of *they are*]
*They're* the ones to watch.

---

**to** [a preposition that indicates direction, degree, connection, etc.; also, part of the infinitive form of a verb]
Let's go *to* the movies.
Suddenly, a bird began *to* sing.

**too** [adverb meaning *more than enough; also*]
Is it *too* far to walk?
You, *too,* are invited to the party.

**two** *one + one*
The store has *two* flavors of ice cream: vanilla and chocolate.

---

**waist** *middle part of the body*
These trousers are too tight at the *waist.*

**waste** *useless spending; unused or useless material;* also, *to spend idly or uselessly*
The movie was simply a *waste* of time.
Don't *waste* your money on books like that.

---

**weather** *atmospheric conditions*
We had good *weather* for the picnic.

**whether** [a conjunction that expresses an alternative]
I don't know *whether* he's been delayed or *whether* he isn't coming at all.

---

---

**who's** [contraction of *who is; who has*]
*Who's* going to play the lead in the show?
*Who's* been using my typewriter?

**whose** [possessive form of *who*]
*Whose* sweater is this?

---

**your** [possessive form of *you*]
Is this *your* book?

**you're** [contraction of *you are*]
I hope *you're* able to find the missing pieces of the puzzle you have been working on.

---

**EXERCISE 11. Completing Sentences with Words Frequently Confused.** Number your paper 1–10. After each number write the correct one of the two words in each of the parentheses in the corresponding sentence.

1. (Their, There) Great Dane is taller and heavier (than, then) (your, you're) Irish wolfhound.
2. The roof of the stadium is not (stationary, stationery) but can be put up or taken down as needed.
3. If the (weather, whether) isn't (to, too) awful, we will go (to, too) the game.
4. (Your, You're) right (to, too) act is determined by (weather, whether) or not (your, you're) actions are damaging to any other people.
5. (Who's, Whose) planning to write a paper on Ida Tarbell?
6. If that is not (your, you're) car, (who's, whose) is it—(there's, theirs)?
7. The Bering (Straight, Strait) is a mere fifty-four miles wide.
8. What did (your, you're) family say when you told them about the scholarship (your, you're) going to get?
9. What styles of (stationary, stationery) did you order for the class project?
10. Half of India could be fed on the food that is (waisted, wasted) every year in the United States.

**REVIEW EXERCISE. Using Words Correctly.** Write a sentence using correctly each of the words in the preceding list, beginning on page 654. You will have seventy-four sentences in all. Follow the order of the list. For related forms of words, such as *council, councilor*, you need use only one word.

## COMMONLY MISSPELLED WORDS

**6. Learn lists of commonly misspelled words.** Frequent short spelling tests are an effective means of fixing correct spellings in your mind. On this and the following pages you will find a list of 300 commonly misspelled words. Taking no more than twenty at a time, have these words dictated to you. Study the ones you miss, and record them in your list of spelling errors. When you have studied them (divided them into syllables and practiced writing each word several times), write them again from dictation. Spelling tests should be written, not oral.

*Three Hundred Spelling Words*[1]

accidentally
accommodate
accurate
acknowledgment
acquaintance
across
aerial
aisle
all right
always

amateur
analyze
annihilate
anonymous
apologize
appearance
appreciate
approaching
appropriate
approval

arctic
argument
arrangement
assassinate
association
athletics
atomic
attach
attack
attention

auxiliary
awful
awkward
bachelor
banana
bargain
basketball
battalion
beggar
beginning

believe
benefited
bicycle
biscuit
bookkeeper
breathe
bruise
bulletin
bureau
business

calendar
campaign
candidate
caricature
catastrophe
cellophane
cemetery
ceremony
chaperon or chaperone
classroom

MECHANICS

[1] The list does not include the words listed on pages 654–62.

college
colonel
colossal
column
commission
committee
comparatively
compel
competitive
completely

complexion
conscience
conscientious
consensus
contemptible
convenience
copies
cordially
corps
correspondence

corroborate
courageous
courteous
criticism
criticize
cylinder
decide
decision
defense
definitely

dependent
descendant
descent
description
desirable
develop
dictionary
different
dining
diphtheria

disappear
disappoint
discipline
discuss
disease
dissatisfied
divided
doesn't
economical
ecstasy

efficient
eighth
eligible
embarrass
emphasize
endeavor
environment
equipped
especially
etiquette

exaggerate
excellent
exercise
exhausted
exhilaration
existence
expense
extraordinary
familiar
fascinating

fatigue
February
feminine
fiery
financial
foreign
forfeit
fourth
fragile
generally

genius
government
governor
grammar
grateful
grievance
guarantee
guard
gymnasium
handkerchief

happened
harass
haven't
height
heroes
hindrance
hoping
horizon
hospital
humorous

imitation
immediately
inconvenience
indispensable
inevitable
influence
initial
inoculate
insofar (as)
interpreted

irrelevant
irresistible
kerosene
laboratory
leisure
license
lightning
likelihood
literacy
loneliness

losing
luxurious
maintenance
maneuver
marriage
matinee
medicine
medieval
mentioned
microphone

minimum
mischievous
missile
misspelled
mortgage
movable
municipal
murmuring
necessary
negotiations

nickel
ninety
ninth
noticeable
nuclear
nuisance
occasionally
occur
occurred
omitted

opinion
opportunity
optimistic
pamphlet
parallel
paralysis
parliament
particularly
pastime
perhaps

permanent
permissible
perseverance
personally
perspiration
persuade
playwright
pleasant
pneumonia
possess

possibility
practice
preference
prejudice
privilege
probably
procedure
professor
pronunciation
propaganda

propeller
prophecy
psychology
pursue
questionnaire
realize
receive
recognize
recommend
referred

rehearse
reign
relief
repetition
representative
restaurant
rhythm
satisfactorily
schedule
scissors

seize
semester
separate
sergeant
shining
siege
similar
sincerely
souvenir
specimen

strategy
subtle
success
sufficient
suppress
surprised
syllable
sympathy
symphony
synonym

tariff
television
temperament
temperature
thoroughly
tomorrow
tournament
traffic
tragedy
transferred

twelfth
tyranny
undoubtedly
unforgettable
unnecessary
vacuum
vengeance
vicinity
villain
weird

# PART FOUR

# RESOURCES FOR WRITING AND STUDYING

# CHAPTER 32

# The Library

## ARRANGEMENT AND RESOURCES

### ARRANGEMENT OF BOOKS IN THE LIBRARY OR MEDIA CENTER

**32a. Learn the arrangement of books in the library.**

### Fiction

By this time you have already learned that novels and short stories are arranged on the fiction shelves alphabetically by the author's last name. When there are two or more books by the same author, they are arranged alphabetically by title. *Jacob's Room,* by Virginia Woolf, would come before her *Mrs. Dalloway,* and both of these would precede her *To the Lighthouse.*

When you want to find out whether your library has a copy of a particular book, look for it, by author or title, in the card catalog. If the book you want is listed in the catalog but is not on the shelves, ask the librarian about it. Another student may have borrowed it; it may be in the library being repaired; it may be on "reserve" for special class use within the library. Possibly, you can ask the librarian to put your name on the waiting list. When the book comes in or is available for circulation again, the librarian will notify you.

## Nonfiction: The Dewey Decimal System

In 1876 Melvil Dewey, an American librarian, devised the system we now use for classifying nonfiction books.[1] In this system every book is placed in a certain class and is identified by a number placed on the lower spine of the book. There are ten large subject classifications, and any nonfiction book can be fitted into one of them. Within each large class there can be an unlimited number of subdivisions. Since a decimal point plays an important part in the numbering of the books, the plan is given the name Dewey decimal system.

A valuable feature of this system is that all books on the same subject may be found together on the library shelves. Once you have learned the class number of the subject you are interested in, you can go to that section of shelves in the library and find all the books in the library on this subject grouped in one place.

The following list identifies the ten major subject classifications and their numbers. Become familiar with these classifications. Knowing them will help you save time in searching for a book.

000–099 General Works (encyclopedias, periodicals, handbooks, bibliographies, etc.)
100–199 Philosophy (includes psychology, conduct, etc.)
200–299 Religion (includes mythology)
300–399 Social Sciences (education, economics, government, law, occupations, communications)
400–499 Language (dictionaries, grammars, the study of language and languages)
500–599 Science (mathematics, chemistry, physics, astronomy, geology, biology, zoology, etc.)
600–699 Applied Science, or Technology (agriculture, engineering, aviation, inventions, manufacturing, and commercial operations)

[1] The Library of Congress system of cataloging, used in many public libraries but not commonly used in high-school libraries, classifies all books, both fiction and nonfiction. Each general subject category (Philosophy, Science, etc.) is assigned a code letter. For example, the letter *H* at the beginning of a call number designates Social Science. In addition, whole categories are often subdivided by adding a second code letter to the first. Thus the letter *P* (which designates Literature) may be followed by the letter *S* to specify American Literature. Call numbers include the letter codes, followed by a series of numbers that identify specific books within a category. For example, the title *Responses: Prose Pieces 1953-1976* by Richard Wilbur, an American author, has the Library of Congress call number PS 3545. A complete schedule of Library of Congress categories and their letter codes is usually available in the reference section of any library using this system.

| | |
|---|---|
| 700–799 | The Arts and Recreation (sculpture, painting, music, architecture, photography, sports) |
| 800–899 | Literature (poetry, plays, orations, essays in English and foreign languages. Does not include novels or short stories, which are on the *fiction* shelves.) |
| 900–909<br>930–999 | History |
| 910–919 | Travel |
| 920–929 | Biography (arranged alphabetically by last name of subject of biography) |

Each class is subdivided as the need arises. For example, the large 500–599 class is devoted to science. Each science is further classified as follows:

| | |
|---|---|
| 500–509 | General Science |
| 510–519 | Mathematics |
| 520–529 | Astronomy |
| 530–539 | Physics |
| 540–549 | Chemistry |
| 550–559 | Geology |
| 560–569 | Paleontology |
| 570–579 | Anthropology and Biology |
| 580–589 | Botany |
| 590–599 | Zoology |

This subdivision can be broken down even further. For example, Mathematics has the following categories:

| | |
|---|---|
| 510–519 | Mathematics |
| 511 | Arithmetic |
| 512 | Algebra |
| 513 | Geometry |
| 514 | Trigonometry |

When books have the same class number, they are distinguished from one another by the first letter, or by a combination of letters, of the author's name. Thus, a book on plane geometry by Limond C. Stone would have the number 513.1 and the capital letter S under the number stamped on the spine of the book: $\frac{513.1}{\text{S}}$

This number, including the first letter of the author's last name, is known as the book's *call number*. To find the call number of a book, look up the book in the card catalog.

# LOCATING INFORMATION IN THE LIBRARY

## The Card Catalog

The card catalog is usually a cabinet of drawers filled with alphabetically arranged cards. In most libraries the catalog holds at least three cards for each book in the library: at least one *author card,* the *title card,* and at least one *subject card.*

**32b. Learn the uses of the card catalog.**

### The Author Card

The *author card* has the name of the author in boldfaced type on the top line. When you look up a particular author in the card catalog, you will find a separate card for each book by that author. If a book has several authors, there is a separate card under each author's name. Cards for books *about* an author follow cards for books *by* an author.

On the next page are three card catalog cards for the same book: *The Art of Contentment* compiled by Edgar Andrew Collard. From top to bottom are the title card, author card, and subject card. The numbers in the margin identify each of the following kinds of information:

1. Title
2. Call number
3. Author
4. Number of pages
5. Subject
6. Publisher and date of publication
7. Other headings under which the book is listed (In some libraries this book might be shelved with books on other related subjects.)

### The Title Card

The *title card* has the book's exact title at the top. The quickest way to find a book in the catalog is to look it up under its title. There may be many books by the same author and hence many cards to go through if you look among the author cards. If you know the exact title, however, you have only one card to hunt for. Titles beginning with *a, an,* or *the* are listed by the word following these articles. For example, the title card for *The Invisible Man* would be found under **I**.

**Catalog Cards**

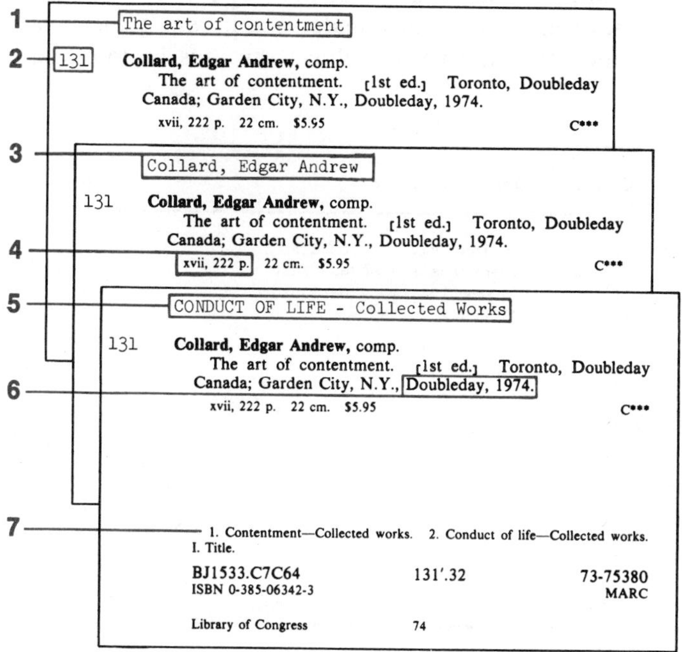


**Top to bottom: Title, Author, and Subject Cards**

## The Subject Card

At the top of the subject card, usually in capital letters, is the subject with which the book deals. Such cards are very helpful when you wish to read a number of books on the same subject but do not know any specific authors or titles.

## Information on Catalog Cards

In addition to supplying the title, author, and call number of the book, catalog cards may also cite publication facts, number of pages, and whether the book contains illustrations, diagrams, etc. Furthermore, some catalogs provide additional cards called *analytic* cards. These help you locate short stories, plays, or articles in collections of compiled works. For example, a card for either the author or the title of a short story would tell you the title of an anthology containing your subject.

In using subject cards, you will sometimes find a "see" or a "see also" card advising you to look under a different subject heading. Additional titles relating to your subject can thus be found in other places.

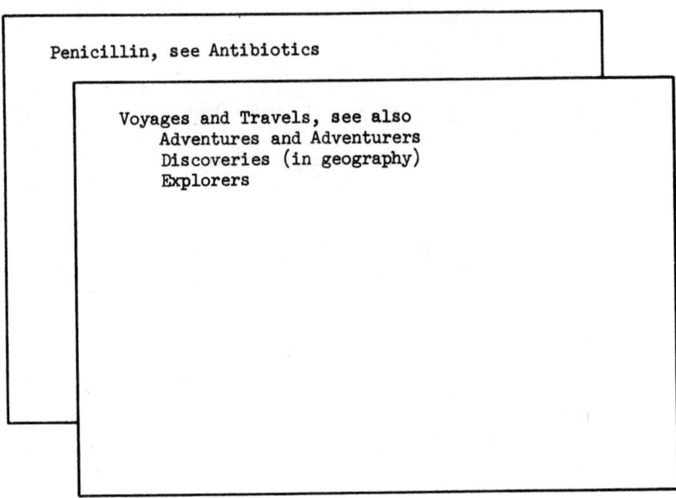


**"See" and "See Also" Cards**

**EXERCISE 1. Using the Card Catalog.** Using the card catalog in your library, write the title, author, and call number of each of the following:

1. A biography of Queen Victoria
2. A book containing either the play *Riders to the Sea* by J. M. Synge, the play *The Little Man* by John Galsworthy, or the play *The Little Foxes* by Lillian Hellman
3. A book about getting into college
4. An anthology containing at least one poem by Edna St. Vincent Millay
5. A recent book on movie-making

## The Parts of a Book

**32c.** Learn the names and the functions of the parts of a book.

### The Frontispiece

The frontispiece is a full-page illustration. It usually faces the title page.

### The Title Page

The title page gives the complete title, any subtitle, the complete name of the author or editor, the name of the publisher, and the place of publication.

### The Copyright Page

On the reverse side of the title page is the copyright page. Information on this page includes the year the book was copyrighted and the name of the copyright holder. Anyone reproducing substantial portions of the book without the permission of the copyright owner is committing a criminal offense and is liable to a suit in court.

A series of dates printed on the copyright page, such as "Copyright © 1980, 1975, 1968," means that the original copyright was obtained in 1968. In 1975 and 1980 new material was added and a new copyright secured to cover the material. The date of the last copyright is important when you are buying such books as an encyclopedia, a dictionary, or a book on science.

Sometimes a book has a large sale and is reprinted frequently. Publishers sometimes indicate on this page which printing of the book this volume represents. Do not confuse a new copyright date with a new printing date. The former tells when the book was revised; the latter, when it was merely reprinted.

### The Preface, Foreword, Introduction

These terms refer to explanatory text at the beginning of a book in which the author or a commentator speaks directly to the reader. Generally these terms are used interchangeably. However, some books may have both a preface and an introduction. In that case, the preface is usually about the particular book; the introduction is more general and may deal with the subject as a whole or the purpose of the series.

### The Table of Contents

The list of chapters, their subdivisions, and the corresponding pages make up the table of contents. Wise readers examine the table of contents before reading a book to gain an overall view of the content and organization of the work.

### Lists of Illustrations (Maps, Diagrams, Charts, etc.)

A list of illustrations, with page numbers, generally follows a book's table of contents. A very long list may be placed at the back of a book, preceding the index.

### The Appendix

The appendix, which usually appears at the end of a book, contains additional material which the author did not wish to include in the body of the book. For example, a book on American history might contain in the appendix the Declaration of Independence, the Constitution, and the Atlantic Charter.

### The Glossary

A glossary, usually at the end of the book, is a list of definitions of difficult or technical words used in the book.

### The Bibliography

Sometimes the author prepares a list of books which were consulted or which are recommended for further reading. Such lists may appear at the end of each chapter or at the end of the book.

### The Index

The index is an alphabetical list, with page numbers, of topics treated in the book. It is much more detailed than the table of contents and is useful for finding quickly the page on which certain topics are discussed.

### The Endpapers

The pages pasted inside the front and back covers of the book are the endpapers. Occasionally maps, other illustrations, or pertinent materials are found there.

**EXERCISE 2. Understanding the Parts of a Book.** Using *this textbook* as your source of information, answer the following questions.

1. On what page does the name of the author appear?
2. When was the second edition copyrighted? The first edition?
3. By what firm was this book published? Where is the firm located?
4. After reading the Preface, write in a sentence or two the primary purpose of the book.
5. What material is contained on the front endpaper?

## The *Readers' Guide*

Since most of the reference work you will do in high school deals with current rather than historical subjects, you will probably use more magazines than books in preparing a research paper.

**32d.** **Learn to use the *Readers' Guide to Periodical Literature.***

In the *Readers' Guide to Periodical Literature,* articles from more than 175 magazines are indexed alphabetically by subjects and authors. You may look up the subject in which you are interested and find articles that have been written on it and the magazines in which they appeared.

Magazine stories are listed by title and by author; the complete entry is given with the author listing only. Poems and plays are listed by author. Articles *about* moving pictures and plays are listed under the subject headings MOVING PICTURES, PLAYS AND DRAMAS, beneath the subheading **Criticisms, plots, etc.**

The *Readers' Guide* is published in paper-covered pamphlets monthly six months a year and semimonthly six months a year. Occasionally during the year a cumulative issue is published that includes the articles listed in preceding months as well as those for the current month. At the end of the year, a large volume is published containing all entries for the year. Every two years a volume covering a two-year period is published.

You must remember, however, that the usefulness of the *Readers' Guide* is limited by the availability to you of the magazines to which it refers you. When you are taking down references from the *Readers' Guide*, you should know what magazines your library has. You should know, too, whether the library has kept back issues of all these magazines or only of certain ones, and for how many years back it has the magazines.

A sample excerpt from the *Readers' Guide* is reproduced on page 678. You can probably understand most of the abbreviations used, but if you cannot, you will find a complete list with explanations in the front of the *Readers' Guide* itself.

NABOKOV, Vladimir
On revisiting father's room [excerpt from Vladimir Nabokov: a tribute; ed by Peter Quennell] D. Nabokov. por N Y Times Bk R 85:22-5 Mr 2 '80 *

NACK, William
Boxing. Sports Illus 52:81-2 Ja 21; 38+ Mr 24 '80
Future is soon. il Sports Illus 52:26-9+ Mr 10 '80
Little ray of Sunshine at Hialeah. il Sports Illus 52:20-1 Mr 17 '80
Sugar sure is sweet. il pors Sports Illus 51:92-6+ N 26 '79
Track & field. Sports Illus 52:48+ Ja 28 '80

NADELHOFFER, Heather
Math and the Messiah. M. E. Marty. Chr Cent 97:271 Mr 5 '80 *

NADER, Ralph
Corporate power in America [excerpt from introd to Big business reader; ed by Mark Green and Robert K. Massie, Jr] Nation 230:365-7 Mr 29 '80

*about*

Better than dice. D. Seligman. Fortune 101:43 Mr 10 '80 *
Multiple-choice anxiety. P. Bourgeois. il Macleans 93:39 F 4 '80 *
Nader assails ETS. R. J. Smith. Science 207: 508-9 F 1 '80 *

NADIS, Steven J.
Time for a reassessment. bibl f il por map Bull Atom Sci 36:37-44 F '80

NAEYE, Richard L.
Sudden infant death [with biographical sketch] il Sci Am 242:14, 56-62 Ap '80

NAG HAMMADI Library
Gnostic Gospels according to Pagels. J. A. Fitzmyer. America 142:122-4 F 16 '80

NAGEL, Suzanne
Suzanne Nagel, tripping the light fantastic. L. Kent. il pors SciQuest 53:20-2 F '80 *

NAHANNI National Park. See National parks and reserves—Northwest Territories, Canada

NAIL guns
Electric nail gun for the home handyman. R. Capotosto. il Mech Illus 76:64-5 Mr '80

NAILS (anatomy)
*See also*
Manicuring

NAIRN, Allan. See Brownstein, R. jt auth

NAMES, Personal
*See also*
Nicknames
Presidential candidates—Names
All about names. C. Montgomery. Good H 190: 104+ F '80
John Train is an outrageous name-dropper, who'll introduce you to Katz Meow or Iva Odor. K. McMurran. il pors People 13:41-2 Mr 3 '80
More remarkable names of real people [excerpt from Even more remarkable names] J. Train. Read Digest 116:121 Mr '80
Name calling. M. Shadick. Seventeen 39:72 Ap '80

NAMIBIA
*See also*
United Nations Council for Namibia

**Politics and government**

In white-ruled Namibia, doubts about the future. R. Knight. il U.S. News 88:64 Mr 3 '80

article by author
author entry
title of article
articles about author
illustration references
subject entry
date of issue
"see" cross reference
volume number
page reference
title and issue of magazine
"see also" cross reference
secondary subject heading

**EXERCISE 3. Using the *Readers' Guide.*** Write answers to the following questions.

1. Does your library have a list of the magazines to which it subscribes? Does the list give the dates of back numbers available? If so, for what years does the library have back numbers of either *Time* or *Atlantic*?
2. Where are the back numbers of magazines kept in your library? How do you get the particular issue you want?
3. Where are the volumes of the *Readers' Guide* kept in your library? What is the latest monthly issue?
4. You are interested in a special career and wish to read some recent articles about opportunities in this field. Consult the *Readers' Guide,* and copy the information for at least five articles that you could get in your own library on this subject.
5. The *Readers' Guide* gives you considerable information about each article listed. Copy the data given about a review of a recent television play or motion picture. Show that you understand the abbreviations by spelling out all of them.

## Information Files

### 32e. Learn the nature and proper use of the vertical file.

Another source of current information is the pamphlet, a paper-covered booklet on contemporary subjects that discusses a topic in more detail than a magazine article. It may sometimes be the size of a small book and often contains charts, diagrams, and other illustrative material. Pamphlets are published by government agencies, welfare organizations, political groups, industrial concerns, educational institutions, historical societies, etc.

Your librarian files such pamphlets, as well as interesting clippings and pictures from magazines and newspapers, in a special cabinet usually referred to as the vertical file. Consult your librarian to see whether a file folder is available on the topic you are studying.

### 32f. Use microfilm or microfiche to find information.

To save space, many libraries store some publications (newspapers, magazines, and books) or documents on microfilm or microfiche. *Microfilm* is a roll or reel of film containing photographically reduced publications. You view the film through a projector that enlarges each microscopic image to a size suitable for reading. *Microfiche* is a sheet of film, rather than a roll or reel, containing photographically reduced publications. To read the microfiche, you use a machine that, like the microfilm projector, enlarges the microscopic images to a readable size. Your librarian can tell you which publications are stored on microfilm or microfiche, where the microfilm and microfiche are located in the library, and how to use the projectors.

### 32g. Use computers to find information.

Many libraries are replacing their present book lists, catalogs, and periodical lists with a computerized system. If this is the case, you will have to use the computer to find the lists of books and periodicals in the library. Instead of looking through the card catalog or the *Readers' Guide*, you type the information you need into the computer—for example, *subject: freedom of speech*. Then the computer searches for the titles and locations of the publications on that subject and prints a list. Depending on the type of computer, you might have to read the list from the screen, or you might be able to get a printout, or printed copy, of the list of books or periodicals. The librarian will be able to tell you what kinds of computer programs your library has, where the computers are located in the library, and how to use the computers.

### 32h. Learn the location of items in your library.

To make full use of your school or public library, you should know the exact location of the principal items you wish to use. If you know exactly where to go for the information you want, you can save both the librarian and yourself a lot of time.

**EXERCISE 4. Using Your Library.** Be prepared to state where each of the following is located in your school or public library.

1. The desk where books are checked out and returned
2. The card catalog
3. The fiction shelves
4. The biography shelves
5. The science section
6. The reserved-book shelf and the new-book shelf
7. The encyclopedias
8. The vertical file
9. The back numbers of magazines
10. The *Readers' Guide*
11. The microfilm and microfiche projectors
12. The computers

## CHAPTER 33

# Reference Books

## PRINCIPAL REFERENCE BOOKS AND THEIR USES

Through its many reference books a modern, well-equipped library can give you answers to almost any question you can think of. Become familiar with the location in the library and the contents of all the reference books discussed in this chapter. Do not be satisfied with knowing only that you can get some information from an encyclopedia. You will be a more successful student if you know which reference book is the best source for the kind of information you want.

### ENCYCLOPEDIAS

Since most encyclopedias give an overall view of a subject in general articles, reading one article is usually not enough for accurate research. To find all the information that your encyclopedia has on a subject, consult the index, which is usually in the last volume.

When the Encyclopaedia Britannica expanded to thirty volumes in 1974, it introduced a new method of arrangement. The first volume became an introduction to the rest of the encyclopedia. The Micropaedia (shorter articles) occupies the next ten volumes; the Macropaedia (longer articles) occupies the final nineteen volumes. Many of the Macropaedia articles are longer than full-length books.

Most encyclopedias are kept up-to-date in two ways. First, each printing usually represents some minor revisions—political changes, deaths, etc.—and every few years a major revision is produced.

Second, most encyclopedias publish an annual volume, or yearbook, which includes major events of the year and important changes or additions to the general body of knowledge.

Investigate the encyclopedias in your school and public libraries. Among them you may find the following works, each with an annual supplement.

### Encyclopedias in Many Volumes

*Collier's Encyclopedia*
*Encyclopaedia Britannica*
*Encyclopedia Americana*
*Encyclopedia International*
*World Book Encyclopedia*

### One- and Two-Volume Encyclopedias

For brief, handy accounts of a subject, a "desk" encyclopedia in one or two volumes is adequate. Three of the better-known works of this kind are the New Columbia Encyclopedia, the Random House Encyclopedia, and the Lincoln Library of Essential Information.

## GENERAL REFERENCE BOOKS

### Yearbooks and Almanacs

*World Almanac and Book of Facts*
*Information Please Almanac*
*The International Year Book and Statesmen's Who's Who*
*Statesman's Year-book*

Although almanacs are published yearly, remember that they tell about the year preceding their date: a 1981 almanac contains information about 1980.

All four of these books are fully indexed. They contain statistical and factual information subject to constant change, like census tables, economic statistics, the results of elections and athletic and artistic competitions, the winners of all sorts of awards, and summaries of important current events. The *Statesman's Year-book* and *The International Year Book and Statesmen's Who's Who* are concerned with governments and information of particular value to governments. The

*World Almanac* is the most popular almanac and is especially valuable for its brevity; the *Information Please Almanac* is a bit less abbreviated and sometimes easier to read.

### Atlases

Although an atlas is primarily a book of maps showing political and geological divisions of the world, there is much more to be found in any atlas than the current boundaries of nations and states. Climate, food production, ethnic distribution, languages, health, kinds of industry for every continent and country are only part of the information given in a good atlas.

When seeking current geographical information, check the copyright date of a general atlas. World boundaries and political conditions change so rapidly that only a recent atlas will be of any help.

***General Atlases***

*Hammond Contemporary World Atlas*
*National Geographic Atlas of the World*
*New York Times Atlas of the World*

Some atlases show the world of the past. These historical atlases are valuable for students of history.

***Historical Atlases***

*The American Heritage Pictorial Atlas of United States History*
*Hayden's Atlas of the Classical World*
*Rand McNally Atlas of World History*
Shepherd's *Historical Atlas*
*The American Heritage Pictorial Atlas of United States History*

## BIOGRAPHICAL REFERENCE BOOKS

Many reference books in your library are devoted to the lives of people of the past and present. Like the general encyclopedias, reference books about people are sometimes available in sets or as individual volumes.

### General Biography

***Current Biography***

This is issued monthly and is concerned with outstanding personalities of our own time, whose activities are usually in the current headlines.

Published monthly in paperback, the year's issues are cumulated in one bound volume. By using the cumulative index in each issue, you can find biographies that have appeared in other issues and in other years. A separate index includes biographies from 1940 to 1980. Biographies are also indexed by professions.

***The Dictionary of American Biography***

Great Americans who are no longer living are included from all areas of the arts, sciences, politics, and industry. The articles are somewhat longer than their equivalents in ordinary encyclopedias. The complete set of fifteen volumes includes a one-volume index as well as supplementary volumes that keep the dictionary relatively up-to-date.

***The Dictionary of National Biography***

This many-volume reference work presents information about the lives of distinguished English people who are no longer living.

***The New Century Cyclopedia of Names***

This three-volume reference work lists 100,000 proper names of every description, including persons, places, events, literary works and characters, works of art, and mythological and legendary persons and places.

***Webster's Biographical Dictionary***

In one volume this book lists more than 40,000 biographies of famous men and women through the ages. Each alphabetical entry gives more information than you would find in a general dictionary, but the articles are obviously shorter than those in an encyclopedia. For quick reference, and for a guide to pronunciation of proper names, this is a helpful work.

***Who's Who***

This has long been the most frequently consulted book of facts about distinguished living British and Commonwealth persons. This one-volume work comes out annually. For distinguished persons no longer living, consult *Who Was Who.*

***Who's Who in America***

This reference work, published every two years, lists distinguished living Americans. The latest edition includes nearly 75,000 entries.

### Books About Authors

Although authors' lives are included in all biographical reference books and encyclopedias, the following books treat authors only.

*Contemporary Authors* and *Contemporary Authors, First Revision,* Gale Research Company
*The Writers Directory*
Magill's *Cyclopedia of World Authors*
*European Authors 1000–1900* by Kunitz and Colby
*American Authors 1600–1900* by Kunitz and Haycraft
*British Authors Before 1800* by Kunitz and Haycraft
*British Authors of the Nineteenth Century* by Kunitz and Haycraft
*Twentieth Century Authors* by Kunitz and Haycraft
*World Authors* by Wakeman
*Dictionary of Literary Biography*, Gale Research Company
*American Writers* by Unger

*The Writers Directory* lists briefly about 18,000 of today's writers and is published every two years. Its articles are more concise and a little more formal than those in the other books listed above. Magill's *Cyclopedia,* a popular worldwide reference book, includes pictures of the authors, as the Kunitz and Haycraft books do.

## LITERARY REFERENCE BOOKS

You have already learned something about the available biographical reference books on authors. For information about literary works, including material on plots, characters, sources, and quotations, you can consult one of the following books:

### Books of Quotations

#### Bartlett's *Familiar Quotations*

Bartlett's has been in use for over a century, with many revisions, and is the most familiar reference book of quotations. The quotations and the index occupy almost equal parts of the book. You might look up an author and read all the quotations under the author's name, or look up a key word in the quotation to discover who the author was and what the quotation was from, or what its exact wording should be. Wondering who wrote "Absence makes the heart grow fonder," for example, you might look up *absence* (or *heart,* or *fonder*) in the index. You would find "makes the heart grow fonder" in a list of cross-references giving the page number to check, and on that page of the edition you are using you would find that Sextus Propertius wrote it, in his *Elegies*.

**Stevenson's *Home Book of Quotations* and *Home Book of Proverbs, Maxims, and Familiar Phrases***

These books group quotations by subject matter instead of author so that all quotations on love or courage or learning are together. This arrangement makes the books particularly useful when you want to find appropriate quotations on a particular subject.

**Magill's *Quotations in Context***

This book of quotations includes the contexts of the quotations.

### Indexes and Collections of Poetry

***Granger's Index to Poetry and Recitations* (sixth edition)**

Occasionally you want to locate an entire poem rather than a short quotation. Under a poem's title, **Granger's Index** lists a number of books containing the work. You can then use the card catalog to locate a suggested book.

An index of authors and an index of first lines help you find the poem if you do not know the title. Two supplements cover newer collections of poetry.

The following books are only a few of the collections of poems that are found in many libraries. All three have indexes of authors, titles, and first lines.

**Stevenson's *Home Book of Verse* and *Home Book of Modern Verse***
**Van Doren's *An Anthology of World Poetry***
**Untermeyer's *Modern American Poetry* and *Modern British Poetry***

## OTHER REFERENCE BOOKS

Your library may have many other reference books on literature and other subjects. If your teacher asks you to report on any of the following books, be sure to include the title of the book, number of volumes, publication date, a brief description of contents and arrangement of material, and the principal use of the book in reference work.

### *Literature*

*American Authors and Books*
*Book Review Digest*
*Bulfinch's Mythology*
*Cambridge History of American Literature*
*Cambridge History of English Literature*
*Essay and General Literature Index*
*Guide to Great Plays* by J. T. Shipley
*Index to One-Act Plays*
*Play Index*
*Short Story Index*
*The New Century Classical Handbook*
*Oxford Companion to American Literature*
*Oxford Companion to Classical Literature*
*Oxford Companion to English Literature*

### *Grammar and Usage*

*A Dictionary of Contemporary American Usage* by Bergen and Cornelia Evans
*The Careful Writer: A Modern Guide to English Usage* by Theodore M. Bernstein

### *History and Social Studies*

*Dictionary of American History* by J. T. Adams
*The Dictionary of Dates* by Helen R. Keller
*Encyclopedia of American History* by R. B. Morris
*Encyclopedia of the Social Sciences*
*Encyclopedia of World History* by W. L. Langer
*Historical Statistics of the United States*
*Statistical Abstract of the United States*
*Webster's New Geographical Dictionary*

### *Science and Mathematics*

*Chambers Dictionary of Science and Technology*
*McGraw-Hill Encyclopedia of Science and Technology*

### *Music and Art*

*Harvard Dictionary of Music*
*The International Cyclopedia of Music and Musicians*
*McGraw-Hill Encyclopedia of World Art*
*The New College Encyclopedia of Music,* edited by Westrup and Harrison
*Oxford Companion to Music*
*Vasari's Lives of the Painters, Sculptors, and Architects* (four paperback volumes)

***Colleges and Universities***

*American Universities and Colleges*
*Barron's Profiles of American Colleges*
*College Blue Book*
*Comparative Guide to American Colleges*
*Lovejoy's College Guide*

**EXERCISE. Using Reference Books.** Indicate the reference book or books you would use to find the information requested below.

1. A list of last year's winners of the Nobel Prizes
2. The countries that border on Albania
3. The name of the poem that begins "The world is too much with us"
4. The important rivers and mountains in Nepal
5. A brief list of facts about Eleanor Roosevelt
6. A map of the Roman Empire under Augustus
7. The current presidents of M.I.T., N.Y.U., and Princeton
8. A book containing Susan Glaspell's one-act play *Trifles*
9. The definition of an unusual musical term
10. The name of a poem of which you know a familiar line

# CHAPTER 34

# The Dictionary

## CONTENTS AND USES OF DICTIONARIES

Norman Douglas, the author of *South Wind,* once wrote to his friend Muriel Draper, "Do you learn a column of the dictionary every day by heart? Well, you should." Several years later she wrote Douglas the following invitation, which wittily suggests that she had followed his advice:

> Dearest Doug:
>
> I have married, marrow, Mars, Marsala, Marseillaise, marsh, marshal, Marshalsea, marsupial, mart, martello, martial, Martin Paul Draper and live at 19 Edith Grove, grovel, grow, growl, growth, groyne, grub, grudge, gruel, gruesome, gruff, grumble, grume, grummet, grumpy, Grundyism, grunt, Gruyère, grysbok. Will you come to tea, teach, teague, teak, teal, teamster, teapot, tear, tearing, tease, teasel, technic at once (I have got some excellent wine), and stay to dine, ding-dong, ding-hey, dingo, dinosaur, dinothere, dint, diocese, dioptric, dioxide, dip—
>
> Yours—
>
> Muriel Draper

No one expects you to follow Douglas' advice literally, but you should know what kind of information a dictionary contains and how to find it. You should also know something about how dictionaries are made and what their purpose is.

The first great dictionary of the English language was compiled by Samuel Johnson in 1755. The first American dictionary, published in 1806, was also the work of one man—Noah Webster. Modern dictionaries, like *Webster's Third New International Dictionary, Webster's New World Dictionary of the American Language, The Random House Dictionary of the English Language: The Unabridged Edition,* and *The Oxford English Dictionary,* represent the cooperative efforts of hundreds of scholars and take many years to prepare. The essential method is the same, however. Dictionary makers collect all of the information they can about the way English speakers use their language and record it in a form convenient for reference.

A dictionary is a record of the usage of words—their meanings, spellings, pronunciations, histories, and forms. Its purpose is to show you how a large number of users of English have pronounced or spelled a word, what they have meant by it, and under what circumstances they have used it. This is not the same thing as telling you how to use a word—a dictionary is a record of usage, not a body of laws. Since you use words to communicate with others, it is essential that you know what words mean to other people.

## KINDS OF DICTIONARIES

### 34a. Know the kinds of dictionaries.

Excluding the many special dictionaries—dictionaries of scientific terms, foreign language dictionaries, etc.—there are two main kinds of dictionaries with which you should be familiar: the large, *unabridged* dictionary, which you will use mainly in libraries; and the "college-size" dictionary, which you should have at hand whenever you study.

### Unabridged Dictionaries

The largest dictionaries—those containing more than 300,000 words—are called *unabridged* dictionaries. *Unabridged* means that a dictionary is not a cut-down version of some larger dictionary. The best known and most available of these are

***The Oxford English Dictionary,*** Oxford University Press, New York, N.Y.

***The Random House Dictionary of the English Language: The Unabridged Edition,*** Random House, New York, N.Y.

***Webster's Third New International Dictionary,*** G. & C. Merriam Company, Springfield, Massachusetts

An unabridged dictionary has entries for about two to three times as many words as a college dictionary, and the entries are likely to be longer and more detailed, and to distinguish finer shades of meaning. For example, you will stand a better chance of finding in it a word that is unfamiliar to you but familiar to people in some other part of the world, a word that has a particular meaning in a certain part of the country, or an old or obsolete meaning of a word. *Webster's Third* and the "*OED*" (the *Oxford*) also provide actual quotations showing the use of a word.

### College Dictionaries

The most practical dictionary for everyday use is the college dictionary, which usually contains entries for between 100,000 and 160,000 words. Because a college dictionary is more frequently revised, it is more likely to be up-to-date than an unabridged dictionary. Dictionary makers, who have students in mind when they prepare college dictionaries, are careful to include useful guides to spelling, capitalization, punctuation, research paper techniques, etc. The college dictionaries listed below are reputable and well known.

***American Heritage Dictionary of the English Language,*** Houghton Mifflin Co., Boston, Massachusetts

***The Random House College Dictionary,*** Random House, New York, N.Y.

***Webster's New Collegiate Dictionary,*** G. & C. Merriam Company, Springfield, Massachusetts

***Webster's New World Dictionary of the American Language, Second College Edition,*** William Collins Publishing Company, Cleveland, Ohio

## CONTENT AND ARRANGEMENT OF DICTIONARIES

**34b. Become familiar with the content and arrangement of dictionaries.**

Most people consult the dictionary only when they want the meaning, the spelling, or the pronunciation of an unfamiliar word; however, dictionaries contain many other kinds of information. This section will point out some of these additional resources and show you how to familiarize yourself with the arrangement of your dictionary.

The following exercises apply to almost all standard dictionaries for senior high schools.

**EXERCISE 1. Finding Information in the Dictionary.** Using the dictionary with which you have been provided, write the answers to the following questions. This exercise is designed to familiarize you with the contents and arrangement of your dictionary. The table of contents of that book will help you find some of the answers.

1. What is the latest copyright date of the dictionary?
2. Is there a section on pronunciation? What is it called? On what pages does it appear?
3. Where can you find abbreviations—in the body of the text or in the back of the book? If they are in a separate section, give the name of that section and its page numbers.
4. Where do you find signs and symbols? If they are in a separate section, give the name and pages.
5. Where are spelling rules indicated, if such a section exists?
6. Where can you find the rules for punctuation and capitalization?
7. Where do you look for Jane Addams, Galileo, and Jung—in the main body of the text or in a special biographical section?
8. Where can you find the geographical location and the length of the Kabul—in the main body of the text or in a special section? Give the pages of that section.
9. Can you locate characters in fiction or in mythology? Give the pages of any special section that contains such information.
10. Where can you find the meaning of *pro bono publico, tout de suite,* and similar foreign expressions?

## DICTIONARY INFORMATION ABOUT A WORD

### 34c. Learn to use the vocabulary entries.

The words listed in alphabetical order in the main part of the dictionary are referred to as "vocabulary entries." There is, as you would expect, more information about each word in a large, unabridged dictionary than in a college dictionary.

### Spelling

When there are two acceptable spellings of a word, the more common spelling is generally given first. If the forms are of equal or nearly equal standing, they are separated by a comma or by the word *or:* **labor, labour.** If the spellings are not at all equal in frequency of occurrence, the word *also* will precede the less common spelling: **envelope,** *also* **envelop**. British preferences are often given after American spellings, set off by a comma: **analyze, analyse; peddler, pedlar; armor, armour.**

The dictionary also gives the spelling of the various forms of a word. This information is helpful when the spelling of the various forms of a word presents a problem to you. For example, if you are unsure about the past tense of *prefer, ricochet,* or *benefit,* the dictionary provides the answers with *preferred, ricocheted,* and *benefited*.

## Capitalization

Proper nouns and adjectives are usually given with capital letters in the dictionary. (Instead of capitalizing such words, *Webster's Third New International Dictionary* uses the abbreviation *usu. cap.*) If such words are sometimes used with a lower-case initial, that usage is noted.

## Syllabication

When you divide a word at the end of a line, you must divide it according to its syllables. A dictionary indicates the syllables in a word by placing a centered dot (·) or a space between them.

## Pronunciation

Dictionaries indicate pronunciation by means of accent marks, diacritical marks, and respellings that show how the words should sound. The respellings are necessary because our alphabet uses more than two hundred combinations of letters to represent the forty-two or forty-three sounds of English. Each letter or special symbol used in the respellings always stands for the same sound. The sounds represented by the various letters and other symbols in the respelling are shown on a key that usually appears at the front of the dictionary and at the bottom of every pair of facing pages. Different dictionaries use different systems of indicating pronunciation.

**stu·dent** (sto͞od′ᵊnt, sty͞ood′-), *n.* **1.** a person formally engaged in learning, esp. one enrolled in an institution of secondary or higher education. **2.** any person who studies, investigates, or carefully examines a subject. —*adj.* **3.** of, by, or pertaining to students, esp. of colleges or universities: *a student song; a student demonstration.* [late ME < L *studēnt-* (s. of *studēns,* prp.) = *stud-* (s. of *studēre* to take pains) + *-ēnt-* -ENT; r. *studiant* < MF] —**Syn. 1, 2.** See **pupil**[1].

When a word may be pronounced in more than one way, dictionaries give other correct pronunciations. The first syllable of *student,* above, may be given either the flat *oo* sound or the pointed *you* sound. There are several different methods of showing accentuation, too.

## Part of Speech

The dictionary indicates the part of speech of each word by means of common abbreviations. Notice the following example from *The American Heritage Dictionary of the English Language.*

> **stud·y** (stŭd′ē) *n., pl.* **-ies. 1.** The act or process of studying; the pursuit of knowledge, as by reading, observation, or research. **2.** Attentive scrutiny. **3.** A branch of knowledge. **4.** *Plural.* A branch or department of learning; something to be studied: *graduate studies.* **5. a.** A work resulting from studious endeavor, as a monograph or thesis. **b.** A literary work on a particular subject. **c.** A preliminary sketch, as for a work of art. **6.** A musical composition designed as a technical exercise; an étude. **7.** A state of mental absorption: *He's in a deep study.* **8.** A room intended or equipped for studying. **9. a.** One who memorizes something; especially, an actor with reference to his ability to memorize a part. **b.** The memorizing of a part in a play. *—v.* **studied, -ying, -ies.** *—tr.* **1.** To apply one's mind purposefully to the acquisition of knowledge or understanding of (any subject): *study a language.* **2.** To read carefully: *study a book.* **3.** To memorize. **4.** To take (a course) at a school. **5.** To inquire into; investigate: *study the mood of the country.* **6.** To examine closely; scrutinize: *study a diagram.* **7.** To give careful thought to; contemplate: *study the next move.* *—intr.* **1.** To apply oneself to learning, especially by reading. **2.** To pursue a course of study. **3.** To ponder; reflect; meditate. [Middle English *studie,* from Old French *estudie,* from Latin *studium,* from *studēre,* to be eager, study. See **steu-** in Appendix.*]

Here *n.* (noun) precedes definitions of the noun *study.* The abbreviations *v.* (verb) and *tr.* (transitive) precede the definitions of the transitive verb *study; intr.* (intransitive) precedes the definitions of the intransitive verb *study.* (Some dictionaries have different, full entries for each part of speech under the same word.)

## Inflected Forms

The dictionary gives other forms of a word whenever there is an important reason for this information. These forms are called *inflected* or *inflectional* forms. They may be of several kinds:

The plural of a word when formed irregularly: **crisis;** *pl.* **crises**
The feminine form of a foreign word: **alumnus;** *fem.* **alumna**
The principal parts of an irregular verb: **bring; brought; brought**

Comparative and superlative forms of an adjective or adverb if formed irregularly: **bad; worse; worst**

Case forms of pronouns: **who;** *possessive* **whose;** *objective* **whom**

## Derivation, or Etymology

Most dictionaries indicate the derivation or etymology of a word. By means of abbreviations, they show the language from which it came and what its original meaning was. With its half million words, English has drawn upon almost all modern and ancient languages. Consider the following:

*ginger* (Sanskrit)
*alibi* (Latin)
*bizarre* (French)
*paradise* (Persian)
*piano* (Italian)
*zwieback* (German)
*algebra* (Arabic)
*fjord* (Norwegian)
*tycoon* (Chinese)
*ukulele* (Polynesian)
*skunk* (American Indian)
*kimono* (Japanese)
*cravat* (Croatian)
*paprika* (Hungarian)

In addition to the derivation of words from other languages, the dictionary gives you the origin of recently coined words, hundreds of which come into the language yearly.

**free·dom** \'frēdəm\ *n* -s [ME *fredom*, fr. OE *frēodōm*, fr. *frēo* free + *-dōm* -dom] **1 :** the quality or state of being free: as **a :** the quality or state of not being coerced or constrained by fate, necessity, or circumstances in one's choices or actions ⟨the philosophical implications of the play theory are found in its opposition of ~ and necessity, of spontaneity and order —John Dewey⟩ **b** (1) **:** the status of the will as an uncaused cause of human actions **:** the absence of antecedent causal determination of human decisions (2) **:** self-realization or spiritual self-fulfillment that is not incompatible with the existence of natural causes of the will-act **:** SELF-DETERMINATION



The common English word *freedom* comes, the entry above shows, from Middle English (ME), and it got into Middle English through Old English (OE). It is one of our oldest root words. The abbreviations in your dictionary will tell you how the many other languages are identified in etymology entries. Some dictionaries list the etymology at the beginning of the entry; some list it at the end.

## Meanings

Most English words have more than one meaning. A good dictionary will provide all of the important definitions, numbering each one separately.

**growth** (grōth) *n.* **1.** the process of growing or developing; specif., *a)* gradual development toward maturity *b)* formation and development **2.** *a)* degree of increase in size, weight, power, etc. *b)* the full extent of such increase **3.** something that grows or has grown [a thick *growth* of grass] **4.** an outgrowth or offshoot **5.** a tumor or other abnormal mass of tissue developed in or on the body

Here the meanings are listed in more or less chronological order—the order of the word's etymology, from what it meant when it was first used to what it means today. Some dictionaries list meanings in the order of frequency of use, from the most common meaning to the least common meaning. Most dictionaries list extremely technical meanings of words last, no matter which order is used.

When you are looking up a word in your dictionary, read through the entire list until you find the meaning that exactly fits the context in which the word appears in your book. Many students have misused words all their lives because they settled for the first entry in their dictionaries, without realizing that there were several other meanings. The richer your understanding of all the meanings of words, the greater will be your power to understand and use language.

## Restrictive Labels

Most of the words defined in a dictionary belong to the general vocabulary of standard English. Some words, as well as some special meanings of otherwise standard words, require special treatment, and these usually appear with a restrictive label. There are three main kinds of labels: *subject* labels, which specify that a word has a particular meaning in a certain field: *Law, Med., Aeron.* (Aeronautics), etc; *geographical* labels, which indicate the area in which a particular word, meaning, or pronunciation is principally used: Brit., SW U.S. (Southwest U.S.); and *usage* labels, which characterize a word as to its level of usage: *informal, slang, nonstandard,* etc. Assigning a label such as *slang* or *informal* is necessarily a subjective judgment on the part of the definer, and not all dictionaries agree about labeling the same word.

Often a vocabulary entry in a dictionary will include synonyms for the word, and sometimes it will include antonyms. Synonyms are words which are more or less closely related in meaning to the word being defined. Antonyms are words which are opposite in meaning to the word being defined.

Here, following the abbreviation SYN., the distinctions between synonyms are explained. The synonyms are *annoy, vex, irk, bother, tease,* and *plague.* Following the abbreviation ANT., two antonyms are given: *comfort* and *soothe.*

**an·noy** (ə noi′) *vt.* [ME. *anoien* < OFr. *anoier* < VL. *inodiare* < *in odio habere* (or *esse*), to have (or be) in hate: see ODIUM] **1.** to irritate, bother, or make somewhat angry, as by a repeated action, noise, etc. **2.** to harm by repeated attacks; harry; molest —*vi.* to be annoying —**an·noy′er** *n.* *SYN.*—**annoy** implies temporary disturbance of mind caused by something that displeases one or tries one's patience; **vex** implies a more serious source of irritation and greater disturbance, often intense worry; **irk** stresses a wearing down of one's patience by persistent annoyance; **bother** implies minor disturbance of one's peace of mind and may suggest mild perplexity or anxiety; to **tease** is to annoy by persistent, irritating actions, remarks, etc.; **plague** suggests mental torment comparable to the physical suffering caused by an affliction —*ANT.* **comfort, soothe**

Besides the dictionary, there are several books of synonyms, of which the best known is *Roget's Thesaurus.* This book and other synonym dictionaries are discussed on page 699.

## Illustrations

Dictionaries illustrate many words that may not be easily visualized. *Webster's New World Dictionary,* for example, has an illustration of an *ocarina,* a small wind instrument. Many scientific illustrations are particularly helpful to students beginning their study of the sciences.

**EXERCISE 2. Finding Information in the Dictionary.** This exercise is designed to test your knowledge of the information given about words in the dictionary. With your dictionary before you, begin work at the teacher's signal. Find the answers to the following questions and write them on your paper. Although your speed indicates to some degree your efficiency in using the dictionary, accuracy is more important.

1. Which is the preferred spelling in the United States: *defence* or *defense?*
2. Copy the correct pronunciation of *pecuniary,* including diacritical marks. Be able to pronounce it correctly.
3. How many different meanings are given in your dictionary for the noun *knot?*
4. What restrictive label, if any, does your dictionary give for the word *guy,* meaning "fellow"?
5. Which meanings, if any, of the verb *bounce* have been labeled as slang?
6. How do *prophecy* and *prophesy* differ in meaning?
7. How did *gerrymander* get its meaning?
8. Who was the legendary character Guinevere?

9. From what language is the word *electric* derived?
10. What restrictive label is given the word *eftsoons?*

## Other Information in Dictionaries

### 34d. Learn to use the information entries.

In addition to giving information about words, most dictionaries give a great many facts about people and places. Such information may appear in the body of the dictionary, or it may be collected in a special section.

### Important Persons

The dictionary usually gives the following biographical data about important persons:

1. *Name:* correct spelling, pronunciation, and the first name
2. *Dates of birth and death*
3. *Nationality*
4. *Why famous*

**Wil·son** (wil′sən), *n.* **1. Edmund,** 1895–1972, U.S. literary and social critic. **2. Henry** (*Jeremiah Jones Colbath*), 1812–1875, U.S. politician: vice president of the U.S. 1873–75. **3. (James) Harold,** born 1916, British statesman: prime minister 1964–70 and since 1974. **4. John** ("*Christopher North*"), 1785–1854, Scottish poet, journalist, and critic. **5. (Thomas) Wood·row** (wo͝od′rō), 1856–1924, 28th president of the U.S. 1913–21: Nobel peace prize 1919. **6. Mount,** a mountain in SW California. 5710 ft. **7.** a city in E North Carolina. 29,347 (1970).

The biographical information in a dictionary cannot always be up-to-date for contemporary figures. A more promising source of information about contemporaries is *Who's Who* or *Who's Who in America* (see page 684).

### Important Places

In listing geographical place-names (like Mount Wilson or Wilson, North Carolina, above) the dictionary usually gives the following information:

1. *Name:* spelling, pronunciation
2. *Identification:* whether a city, country, lake, mountain, river, etc.
3. *Location*
4. *Size:* population, if a city or country; area in square miles, if a country or territory or body of water; length, if a river; height, if a mountain, etc.

5. *Importance:* If a city is a capital of a state or country, this fact will be indicated, sometimes by a star or an asterisk. The capital of a country or state will also be given under the name of the country or state.
6. *Historical or other interesting information of importance:* Thus, for Gettysburg, Pennsylvania, almost all dictionaries mention the Union victory in the War Between the States just before the Fourth of July, 1863.
7. *Governing or controlling country:* Thus, for the British Virgin Islands, a dictionary entry will say "a British possession."

## DICTIONARIES OF SYNONYMS

### 34e. Learn to use the special dictionaries.

In addition to the general dictionaries of the English language, there are many special books that are useful to anyone who does much writing. Among these are books of synonyms. Three of the best known of these books of synonyms are listed below.

Fernald, James C., ***Funk & Wagnalls Standard Handbook of Synonyms, Antonyms, and Prepositions***

This standard book lists in alphabetical order most of the words you would wish to use and gives synonyms and antonyms for them.

***The New Roget's Thesaurus in Dictionary Form***

**Roget's Thesaurus** has been the best known of the synonym books. It is now published in an inexpensive paperback edition.

***Webster's Dictionary of Synonyms***

This book of synonyms and antonyms is especially valuable for its detailed explanations of the distinctions between words of similar meaning. Like the Fernald and Roget books, it is also a handy reference volume for authors in search of a word.

**EXERCISE 3. Finding Information in the Dictionary.** Like Exercise 2, this will test your knowledge of the information given in the dictionary. At the teacher's signal, look up the answers to the following questions, and write them on your paper. Although speed is desirable, accuracy is more important.

1. Find two synonyms for the word *mercy*.
2. Write the plural of *prospectus*.

3. What is the capital of Iceland?
4. When did Queen Elizabeth I reign?
5. What was Galileo's full name?
6. What is the meaning of the abbreviation TKO?
7. What symbol is used in medicine for beginning a prescription?
8. What is the meaning of the Latin phrase *carpe diem?*
9. What is the rule for forming the plural of letters, figures, and signs?
10. Why is Trafalgar famous?

**EXERCISE 4. Finding the Etymologies of Words.** Look up the etymologies of the following words and be prepared to write or tell about them in class.

1. porcupine
2. starboard
3. laser
4. pedestal
5. boycott
6. curfew
7. infant
8. juggernaut
9. maudlin
10. sabotage

# CHAPTER 35

# Vocabulary

## MEANING THROUGH CONTEXT AND WORD ANALYSIS

An effective and large vocabulary can be one of your most valuable assets in high school, in college, and in your future vocation or profession. Studies have shown that a large vocabulary goes hand in hand with responsibility and success in the business world. Scholarship and college entrance examinations place great emphasis on vocabulary. Tests for men and women entering the armed forces also have large sections devoted to word knowledge. It is obvious, therefore, that for your immediate and future success you owe it to yourself to build as large a vocabulary as possible.

The main things you should know about words—how to find clues to meaning in context and in the formation of words—are reviewed in this chapter. But before you begin the chapter itself, take the following diagnostic test.

### DIAGNOSTIC TEST

**A. Choosing the Definitions of Words.** Number your paper 1–10. After the proper number, write the letter of the word or expression that comes closest to the meaning of the italicized word.

1. to *abrogate* a law: a. violate; b. enact; c. ignore; d. record; e. annul
2. an *astute* lawyer: a. shrewd; b. unethical; c. criminal; d. well-mannered; e. amateur

3. the *calumnies* of the political campaign: a. speeches; b. promises; c. candidates; d. agitations; e. false charges
4. living a *dissolute* life: a. exciting; b. very short; c. virtuous; d. religious; e. immoral
5. marked by *ennui:* a. enthusiasm; b. strength; c. boredom; d. sickness; e. excitement
6. a *heinous* offense: a. minor; b. infrequent; c. outrageous; d. penal; e. pardonable
7. these plants were *indigenous:* a. harmful; b. native; c. rare; d. colorful; e. hard to classify
8. to *jeopardize* our forces: a. immobilize; b. endanger; c. increase; d. surrender; e. notify
9. the *onerous* duties: a. neglected; b. daily; c. specialized; d. important; e. burdensome
10. to *plagiarize* the theme: a. copy dishonestly; b. forget; c. record; d. misunderstand; e. begin

**B. Selecting the Meanings of Words.** Number your paper 1–5. From the list below, choose the definition for the underlined word in each sentence and write the letter by the proper number. Use context clues to find the best meaning.

a. sincere remorse for wrongdoing
b. to ease the anger of
c. to abolish or annul by authority
d. being or seeming to be everywhere at the same time
e. false statements maliciously made to injure someone
f. having no motion
g. to deprive of strength or vitality

1. A group of citizens asked the governor to *abrogate* the unfair policy.
2. The candidate was shocked by the number of *calumnies* that his opponent used against him.
3. The boys showed genuine *contrition* for their part in the disturbance.
4. The progress of the deadly disease continued to *enervate* the patient.
5. Nearly half the school has succumbed to the *ubiquitous* flu.

**C.** Number your paper 1–5. Using context clues, choose the synonym for the underlined word in each sentence and write the letter by the proper number.

1. The members of the *altruistic* organization donated hundreds of working hours to charitable causes.
   a. unusual  b. unselfish  c. spontaneous  d. brave
2. The *astute* dentist immediately found the source of the pain.
   a. smart  b. unethical  c. amateur  d. polite
3. Unfortunately, the tedious speaker could not shake the students' *ennui.*
   a. enthusiasm  b. boredom  c. sleepiness  d. excitement
4. The murderer received a long prison sentence for his *heinous* crime.
   a. minor  b. infrequent  c. penal  d. outrageous
5. The county commission would hear only *secular* matters.
   a. regional  b. trivial  c. nonreligious  d. martial

---

## THE KINDS OF VOCABULARY

Your reading vocabulary and your listening vocabulary are those which you use for understanding other people. They are called the *comprehension vocabulary.* You may know that such a sentence as "She was a voracious eater" means that she had a huge appetite, or that such a sentence as "His ill-prepared and feeble effort was not a speech but rather a travesty of a speech" means that his attempt was an inferior imitation of a speech. Although these words are part of your comprehension vocabulary, they may not be part of your *use vocabulary,* which consists of the words you use in speaking and in writing. One authority has estimated that the high-school graduate has a use vocabulary of 15,000 words. You understand many more words than you use in your speaking and writing.

## CLUES TO MEANING

Children learn words by listening—to parents, older brothers and sisters, friends, teachers. Today television introduces children to the special words of science, politics, music, and art long before they see any of them in print.

Whether or not you are aware of it, all your life you will be acquiring words through the ear. Hence, one of the best ways to increase your comprehension vocabulary is to be an alert, attentive listener. Frequently the sense of the conversation will give you some idea of the meaning of the words you hear for the first time. Learning new words in this way is called "getting the meaning from the *context.*"

In addition to listening, reading is a rich source of new words. Every issue of a daily newspaper, every magazine, and every book you read will have words that are new to you. Sometimes the written context —like the heard context—will help you get some idea of the meaning of a word, but for the exact meaning there is no substitute for the dictionary. (In Chapter 34 you can quickly review the many ways in which a good dictionary can help you enlarge your vocabulary.)

**35a.** **Look for context clues to meaning.**

You have learned many thousands of words by understanding their meaning from their *context.* The *context* is the words and sentences that surround the unfamiliar word.

## Context Clues

Although a particular sentence may provide a clue to the meaning of a word in any number of ways, there are three types of clues to meaning that are especially helpful.

### Definition

Often authors will use wording that is familiar and natural to them but may not be clear to all of their readers. For the sake of clarity, therefore, they will often add a definition. Sometimes the definition may be preceded by expressions such as *in other words, or,* or *that is.* In the following examples, the definitions are italicized and the words defined are in boldfaced type.

> He was told to avoid strong **condiments,** or *seasonings,* for his food.
> Lorraine studied **ethnology,** that is, *the science dealing with the cultures of various people.*

Sometimes the definition will be in the form of an appositive or appositive phrase which will be set off from the rest of the sentence with commas. In the following sentence, you can see that *strong point* is a definition in the form of an appositive for *forte.*

> Alice's forte, her strong point, was in composing jingles.

### Synonym

Synonyms are sometimes used in a direct definition, as in the first example above. At other times they are used to replace a word rather than repeat it in the sentence or the paragraph. These synonyms, although less obvious, are also clues to meaning. In the following example, the writer uses the word *sermon* as a synonym for *homily.*

> The minister was so dedicated to preparing his homily that he refused to eat dinner until the sermon was completed.

EXAMPLE

Often a word is accompanied by an example that illustrates its meaning. Read the following sentences.

> Her acts of *benevolence* were well-known, especially her generous donations to children's hospitals.
> They were naturally *solicitous* about the child's health and were taking every precaution against a return of the disease.

In the first sentence, if you see that "generous donations to children's hospitals" is an example of *benevolence,* you can surmise that *benevolence* means "kindly or charitable acts." Similarly, if "taking every precaution against a return of the disease" illustrates a solicitous attitude, you know that *solicitous* must mean "showing care and concern."

### Comparison or Contrast

A writer may chose to compare or contrast words in a sentence. In the following example, the terms *symposium* and *conferences* are compared. This comparison helps you to discover the meaning of *symposium.*

> Registration for the symposium will be similar to that of other conferences.

Look for wording such as *like, as, similar to,* or *in the same way* to precede comparisons.

Sometimes a writer will show emphasis or the extent of a subject by setting up contrasts. You can guess the meaning of the word *metropolis* in the following sentence when you see it contrasted to the word *village.*

> Everyone from the largest metropolis to the smallest village participated in the nationwide peace effort.

Contrasting words also may be introduced by *but, not, rather than,* and *however.*

**EXERCISE 1. Using Context Clues to Determine the Meanings of Words.** Number your paper 1–10. After each number, copy the italicized word in each sentence, and write a short definition based on the clues you find in the context. You may check your definitions with the dictionary, if you wish.

1. The treatment seemed to be worsening the skin condition rather than *ameliorating* it.
2. The amount of *arable* land, that is, land that can be cultivated, is very small.
3. Mr. Anderson was unpopular because he always tried to embarrass students with sarcastic, as well as *caustic,* comments.
4. Watch for *concomitants* of a severe head cold such as a feeling of tiredness and aches in the joints and muscles.
5. *Disparaging* remarks that belittle the faculty have no place in a school campaign.
6. Because her mother was very ill, her husband had lost his job, and the children were having troubles at school, Mrs. Roberts was naturally nervous and *distraught.*
7. To everyone's surprise, Rosa did not object to the plan; instead she *acquiesced* at once.
8. The series of thefts called for *drastic* action, for example, installing an alarm system and putting iron bars on all the windows.
9. A law should not be *immutable*; rather, it should be changed when the times and the people demand it.
10. It is sometimes hard for us to imagine how life has changed in the past four hundred years; it would be a great *anachronism* to picture Columbus using a computer.

**EXERCISE 2. Using Context Clues to Determine the Meanings of Words.** The following passage, written by a naturalist, contains a variety of context clues. Study the whole passage and then write your own definitions for the italicized words. Consult your dictionary only after you have written your own definitions.

The cliché often used for the forest is "cathedral-like." The comparison is (1) *inevitable:* the cool, dim light, the utter stillness, the massive grandeur of the trunks of forest giants, often supported by great buttresses and (2) *interspersed* with the straight, clean columns of palms and smaller trees; the Gothic detail of the thick, richly carved, woody (3) *lianas* plastered against trunks or looping down from the canopy above. Awe and wonder come easily in the forest, sometimes (4) *exultation*—sometimes, for a man alone there, fear. Man is out of scale: the forest is too vast, too impersonal, too variegated, too deeply shadowed. Here man needs his fellow man for (5) *reassurance.* Alone, he has lost all significance.

The rain forest is perhaps more truly a silent world than the sea. The wind scarcely (6) *penetrates;* it is not only silent, it is still. All sound then gains a curiously (7) *enhanced* mystery. A sudden crack—what could have made it? An (8) *inexplicable* gurgle. A single, clear peal—that was a bird, probably a trogon. A whistle, impossible to identify. But mostly silence. The silence becomes (9) *infectious;* I remember sometimes trying to blend into this world by moving along a trail without rustling a leaf with my foot or popping a twig. But more often I purposely (10) *scuffled,* broke noisily through this forest where I didn't belong, tried to advertise my presence both to reassure myself and to warn the creatures of the forest that a stranger was there—I had no desire to surprise a fer-de-lance.

—MARSTON BATES

## WORD ANALYSIS

### 35b. Use your knowledge of prefixes, suffixes, and roots.

In general, English words are of two kinds: those that can be analyzed into smaller parts (*untimely, suburban*) and those that cannot (*time, face, feel*). The words of the first kind, which can be divided, are made up of parts called prefixes, roots, and suffixes. Because these parts with broad general meanings remain essentially the same in many different words, knowing something about word analysis can help you to figure out the meaning of an unfamiliar word. However, there are some difficulties that make it unwise to depend entirely on word analysis for clues to meaning. It is not always easy to tell whether a particular group of letters is really the prefix or suffix it appears to be. The *-er* in *painter* is a suffix, but the *-er* in *summer* is not. To be certain, you have to know something about the origin of the word. Moreover, the original force of a combination of word parts may no longer have much to do with the modern meaning of a word. For these and other reasons, absolute dependence on word analysis would lead you to make as many bad guesses as good ones.

There are, however, some good reasons for having a general knowledge of the way English words are formed. Word analysis helps you to understand the peculiarities of English spelling and the connection between the related forms of a particular word. (Knowing about related forms often enables you to learn four or five new words as easily as one.) In addition, word analysis gives you useful practice in taking a close look at words. Most important of all, word analysis offers you the key to the origin of English words. Since so many cultures have contributed to the vocabulary of English, the study of word origins is a fascinating one.

## How Words Are Divided

Many words that can be divided have two or more parts: a core called a *root* and one or more parts added to it. The parts that are added are called *affixes*—literally, "something fixed or attached to something else." An affix added before the root is called a *prefix;* one added after the root is called a *suffix.* A word may have one or more affixes of either kind, or several of both kinds. Only compound words like *baseball* and *post office* have more than one root. A root with no affixes at all is incapable of being divided. A word consisting of a root only is one like *stone* or *true,* to which word analysis does not apply.

| PREFIX[ES] | ROOT | SUFFIX[ES] | EXAMPLE |
|---|---|---|---|
| dis- | put- | -able | disputable |
| post- | war | | postwar |
| | sole | -ly | solely |
| | soft | -en, -ing | softening |
| il- | leg- | -ible | illegible |
| un- | self | -ish, -ly | unselfishly |
| under- | hand | -ed | underhanded |
| | bliss | -ful | blissful |

Roots are often independent words, as in the case of *war, self,* and *hand* in the table above. They are then called *free forms.* But some roots, like *-clude* in *conclude,* are not words by themselves. Such roots are called *bound forms.* Most affixes attach to bound forms.

## Prefixes

Prefixes have broad general meanings like *not, under,* and *against,* and any one of them may appear in hundreds of different words. Because prefixes often have more than one meaning, they can be hard to interpret. In general, a knowledge of prefixes will help you to know when to double consonants in such words as *misspell, overrun,* and *interrupt.* Many of the prefixes in the following list have several different spellings in order to fit with various roots.

| PREFIX | MEANING | EXAMPLES |
|---|---|---|
| ***Old English*** | | |
| a- | in, on, of, up, to | abed, afoot |
| for- | away, off, from | forget, forswear |
| fore- | before, previous | foretell, forefathers |
| mis- | bad, poorly, not | misspell, misfire |
| un- | not, reverse of | unhappy, unlock |
| ***Latin*** | | |
| ab- | from, away, off | abdicate, abjure |
| ante- | before, previous | antecedent, antedate |
| bi- | two | bisect, biennial |
| circum- | around | circumspect, circumference |
| com- | with, together, very | commotion, complicate |
| contra- | against, opposing | contradict, contravene |
| de- | from | depart |
| dis- | away, off, down, not | dissent, disappear |
| ex- | out | extract |
| in- | in, into | intrude, invade |
| in- | not, opposing | incapable, ineligible |
| inter- | among, between | intercede, interrupt |
| intra- | within | intramural, intrastate |
| non- | not | nonentity, nonsense |
| per- | through | perceive, permit |
| post- | after, following | postpone, postscript |
| pre- | before | prevent, preclude |
| pro- | forward, in place of | produce, pronoun |
| re- | back, backward, again | revoke, recur |
| retro- | back, backward | retrospect, retrograde |
| semi- | half | semicircle, semicolon |
| sub- | under, beneath | subjugate, substitute |
| super- | above, extra | supersede, supernumerary |
| trans- | across, beyond, over | transact, transport |
| ultra- | beyond, excessively | ultramodern, ultrasonic, ultraviolet |
| ***Greek*** | | |
| a- | without, lacking | atheist, agnostic |
| anti- | against, opposing | antipathy, antitoxin |

| PREFIX | MEANING | EXAMPLES |
|---|---|---|
| cata- | down, away, thoroughly | catastrophe, cataclysm |
| dia- | through, across, apart | diameter, diagnose |
| hyper- | excessive, over | hypercritical, hypertension |
| hypo- | under, beneath | hypodermic, hypothesis |
| para- | beside, beyond | parallel, paradox |
| peri- | around | periscope, perimeter |
| pro- | before | prognosis, program |
| sym- | with, together | sympathy, symphony |

**EXERCISE 3. Understanding the Meanings of Prefixes.** Copy the following words, using a slant line (/) to separate the prefix from the rest of the word. Then give the meaning of the English word. Be ready to explain the link between the meaning of the prefix and the word.

EXAMPLE 1. antithesis
1. *anti/thesis* (*direct contrast of ideas*)

1. abnegation
2. circumvent
3. hyperactive
4. intermittent
5. prospect
6. submit
7. translation
8. unnatural
9. misfortune
10. external

**EXERCISE 4. Writing Words with Prefixes.** Find and write on your paper two words that contain each of the following prefixes: *ab-*, *com-*, *dis-*, *ex-*, *in-*, *inter-*, *pre-*, *re-*. Use words other than those given as examples in the previous lists.

## Suffixes

Suffixes, you will recall, are affixes added after the root, or at the end of a word. There are two main kinds of suffixes: those that provide a grammatical signal of some kind but do not greatly alter the basic meaning of the word and those that, by being added, create new words.

The endings *-s, -ed,* and *-ing* are suffixes of the first kind; by adding them to *work* (*works, worked, working*) we indicate something about number and tense, but we do not change the essential meaning of the word. This kind of suffix is a *grammatical* suffix.

Grammatical suffixes are important in grammar, but in vocabulary we are more concerned with the second kind of suffixes—those that make new words. By adding *-ful* to *thank,* we get a different word: *thankful.* Suffixes that change meaning in this way are called *derivational* suffixes. Notice in the following examples that the addition of a derivational suffix often results in a new part of speech as well as a new meaning.

| ROOT | SUFFIX | RESULT |
|---|---|---|
| friend (n.) | -ly | friendly (adj.) |
| critic (n.) | -ize | criticize (v.) |
| prefer (v.) | -ence | preference (n.) |
| child (n.) | -hood | childhood (n.) |

Since derivational suffixes so often determine the part of speech of English words, we can classify them according to the parts of speech.

| NOUN SUFFIXES | MEANING | EXAMPLES |
|---|---|---|
| ***Old English*** | | |
| -dom | state, rank, condition | serfdom, wisdom |
| -er | doer, maker | hunter, dancer |
| -hood | state, condition | manhood, statehood |
| -ness | quality, state | greatness, tallness |
| -th | act, state, quality | warmth, width |
| ***Foreign*** (*Latin, French, Greek*) | | |
| -age | process, state, rank | passage, bondage |
| -ance | act, condition, fact | acceptance, vigilance |
| -ard | one that does (esp. excessively) | drunkard, wizard |
| -ate | rank, office | doctorate, primate |
| -ation | action, state, result | occupation, starvation |
| -cy | state, condition | accuracy, captaincy |
| -er | doer, dealer in, result | baker, diner, rejoinder |
| -ess | feminine | waitress, lioness |
| -ion | action, result, state | union, fusion |
| -ism | act, manner, doctrine | barbarism, socialism |
| -ist | doer, believer | monopolist, socialist |
| -ition | action, state, results | edition, expedition |

| | | |
|---|---|---|
| -ity | state, quality, condition | acidity, civility |
| -ment | means, result, action | refreshment, disappointment |
| -or | doer, office, action | juror, elevator, honor |
| -tude | quality, state, result | magnitude, fortitude |
| -ty | quality, state | enmity, activity |

| ADJECTIVE SUFFIXES | MEANING | EXAMPLES |
|---|---|---|
| ***Old English*** | | |
| -en | made of, like | wooden, ashen |
| -ful | full of, marked by | thankful, zestful |
| -ish | suggesting, like | churlish, childish |
| -less | lacking, without | hopeless, countless |
| -like | like, similar | childlike, dreamlike |
| -ly | like, of the nature of | friendly, queenly |
| -some | apt to, showing | tiresome, lonesome |
| -ward | in the direction of | backward, homeward |
| ***Foreign*** | | |
| -able | able, likely | capable, tolerable |
| -ate | having, showing | separate, desolate |
| -esque | in the style of, like | picturesque, grotesque |
| -fic | making, causing | terrific, beatific |
| -ible | able, likely, fit | edible, possible, divisible |
| -ous | marked by, given to | religious, riotous |

| VERB SUFFIXES | MEANING | EXAMPLES |
|---|---|---|
| ***Old English*** | | |
| -en | cause to be, become | deepen, strengthen |
| ***Foreign*** | | |
| -ate | become, form, treat | animate, sublimate |
| -esce | become, grow, continue | convalesce, acquiesce |
| -fy | make, cause, cause to have | glorify, fortify |
| -ish | do, make, perform | punish, finish |
| -ize | make, cause to be, treat with | sterilize, motorize, criticize |

**EXERCISE 5. Understanding the Meanings of Suffixes.** Copy the following words, using a slant line (/) to separate the suffix from the rest of the word. Then write a brief definition of the word.

EXAMPLE 1. beastly
2. *beast/ly* (*like a beast*)

1. identify
2. certitude
3. modernize
4. apelike
5. jealously
6. eulogize
7. eatable
8. capricious
9. peerage
10. festivity

## Roots

A root is the core of a word—the part to which prefixes and suffixes are added. To find the root, you usually have only to remove any affix there may be. For example, removal of the affixes *a* and *-ous* from *amorphous* leaves us with *-morph-,* a root meaning "form or shape." The root *-clysm-,* meaning "falling," remains after we remove the prefix *cata-,* meaning "down," from *cataclysm.*

Roots have more specific and definite meanings than either prefixes or suffixes, and a particular root appears in fewer different words. The following list contains some of the common roots in English.

| ROOT | MEANING | EXAMPLES |
|---|---|---|
| ***Latin*** | | |
| -ag-, -act- | do, drive, impel | agent, reaction |
| -am-, -amic- | friend, love | amatory, amicable |
| -aqu- | water | aquatic, aqueduct, aquarium |
| -aud-, -audit- | hear | audible, auditorium |
| -ben-, -bene- | well, good | benefit, benediction |
| -capit- | head | capital, decapitate |
| -carn- | flesh | carnal, carnivorous |
| -cent- | hundred | century, percent |
| -clud-, -clus- | close, shut | conclude, seclusion |
| -cogn- | know, be acquainted | recognize, cognizant |
| -cred- | belief, trust | incredible, credulity |
| -crypt- | hidden, secret | crypt, cryptic |

| ROOT | MEANING | EXAMPLES |
|---|---|---|
| -duc-, -duct- | lead | educate, conductor |
| -fer- | bear, yield | transfer, fertile |
| -fid- | belief, faith | fidelity, perfidious |
| -fin- | end, limit | final, indefinite |
| -frag-, -fract- | break | fragment, fragile, fraction |
| -gen- | birth, kind, origin | generate, congenital |
| -junct- | join | junction, disjunctive |
| -jud- | judge | prejudice, adjudicate |
| -jug- | join, yoke | conjugal, conjugate |
| -loc- | place | locus, locale |
| -magn- | large | magnitude, magnify |
| -man-, -manu- | hand | manicure, manual |
| -mor-, -mort- | die, death | mortuary, immortal, mortality |
| -pater-, -patr- | father | paternal, patrimony, patriarchy |
| -port- | carry, bear | transport, importation |
| -prim- | first, early | primitive, primordial |
| -punct- | point | punctuation, punctilious |
| -sci- | know, knowledge | omniscient, prescience |
| -scrib-, -script- | write | inscribe, proscribe, manuscript |
| -spec-, -spect-, -spic- | look, see | suspicious, circumspect |
| -spir- | breath, breathe | expire, inspiration, respiration |
| -tract- | draw, pull | traction, extractor, tractable |
| -uni- | one | unity, uniform |
| -vid-, -vis- | see | evident, vision |
| -vit- | life | vitality, vitamin |

***Greek***

| ROOT | MEANING | EXAMPLES |
|---|---|---|
| -anthrop- | man | anthropology, misanthropic |
| -arch- | ancient, chief | archaeology, monarch |
| -astr-, -aster- | star | astronomy, asterisk |
| -auto- | self | autonomy, automobile, autocracy |
| -biblio- | book | bibliography, bibliophile |
| -bio- | life | biology, autobiography |
| -chrom- | color | chromatic, chromosome |
| -chron- | time | synchronize, anachronism, chronometer |

| ROOT | MEANING | EXAMPLES |
|---|---|---|
| -dem-, -demo- | people | epidemic, democracy |
| -gen- | kind, race | eugenics, genesis |
| -geo- | earth | geography, geology |
| -gram- | write, writing | grammar, telegram |
| -graph- | write, writing | orthography, geography |
| -hydr- | water | hydrogen, dehydrate |
| -log- | word, study | epilogue, theology, logic |
| -micr- | small | microbe, microscope |
| -mon- | one, single | monogamy, monologue |
| -neo- | new | neologism, neolithic |
| -pan- | all, entire | panorama, pandemonium |
| -phil- | like, love | philanthropic, philosophy |
| -soph- | wise, wisdom | philosophy, sophomore |
| -zo- | animal | zoology, protozoa |

**EXERCISE 6. Learning New Words with Latin Roots.** Underline the Latin root or roots in each of the following words. Using your dictionary, write a brief definition of the word.

1. benevolent
2. conspiracy
3. cryptographer
4. distraction
5. incognito
6. induce
7. infinity
8. manipulate
9. prescription
10. unilateral

**EXERCISE 7. Learning New Words with Greek Roots.** Underline the Greek root or roots in each of the following words. Using your dictionary, write a brief definition of the word.

1. archaic
2. biodegradable
3. demographics
4. epigraph
5. geoponics
6. monochromatic

7. monogram
8. neophyte
9. panacea
10. zodiac

### *Word List*

In many of the following vocabulary words you will recognize the Old English, Latin, and Greek word parts you have just studied. Make it a habit to learn unfamiliar words from this list regularly; ten each week is a practical number.

abash
abate
abominable
abridge
abstain
abut
accentuate
accost
acquiesce
acquisition

adamant
affinity
affluent
allegory
alleviate
altercation
ambiguous
ambivalent
anagram
anecdote

antagonize
appraisal
apprise
arable
arbitrary
archives
arduous
array
askew
assail

assay
assertion
attrition
audacious
augment
auspicious
austere
autocrat
baleful
bandy

beleaguer
beneficent
bestow
betrothed
bilateral
blithe
bolster
brevity
browbeat
brunt

brusque
bulwark
bumptious
bureaucracy
camaraderie
carnage
catharsis
cede
chagrin
circumspect

cite
climactic
coalition
coherent
comely
comprehensive
concerted
congenital
conjecture
connotation

consensus
consonant
contraband
contrition
convivial
correlate
credence
debacle
debonair
decadence

deference
defile
degenerate
deign
deluge
demeanor
deprecate
derogatory
despicable
dissipate

dissolute
diverge
effete
efficacious
elation
embellish
emendation
encroach
enormity
enthrall

entity
entomology
entourage
epicure
epilogue
epithet
equestrian
erroneous
evasive
evoke

exacting
exhaustive
exodus
exonerate
expedite
expletive
extemporaneous
faction
factious
fallible

fastidious
felicitous
felony
ferocity
fidelity
filial
finality
fiord
flail
flaunt

flay
foreshadow
forgo
forte
frustrate
fulminate
furor
furtive
garrulous
gibe

gird
goad
gourmet
gradation
grandiose
guise
haggard
heinous
holocaust
hypercritical

hypochondriac
idiomatic
idyll
imbibe
immemorial
imperious
impetuous
impotent
impregnable
impromptu

impunity
inane
inception
incise
incoherent
incongruous
incredulous
indigenous
indolence
inexplicable

infer
ingratiate
inherent
innocuous
insatiable
insidious
insular
intangible
interminable
interpose

intrepid
intricacy
intrinsic
introspective
inure
invidious
invoke
irascible
laconic
laudable

lucid
lucrative
malevolent
martyr
mercenary
microcosm
misanthrope
miscreant
noncommittal
nostalgic

novice
nurture
occult
omnivorous
oracular
orient
oscillate
ostentatious
palliate
panacea

peremptory
permeate
pernicious
phalanx
philistine
platitude
plebeian
politic
populace
precipitate

predecessor
premeditated
presumptuous
pretentious
proboscis
procrastinate
prodigy
proficient
proletarian
prologue

propagate
protagonist
prototype
protract
provocation
provocative
proxy
purport
quadruped
query

quixotic
rapacious
rationalize
recalcitrant
reciprocate
recrimination
redress
reiterate
relent
remission

repartee
repugnant
resilient
rigorous
rudiment
sallow
sanction
sartorial
satiate
scapegoat

scrutinize
secular
shibboleth
shrew
sluice
solstice
somnolent
sortie
stereotype
stigma

stipend
stoic
subservient
subside
subterfuge
supercilious
supplication
surmise
symposium
synchronize

syndicate
tawdry
tenacity
tepid
terse
thwart
transient
ulterior
unremitting
vanquish

vegetate
verbose
vernacular
vilify
vivacious
vogue
waive
wily
wistful
wrest

## CHAPTER 36

# Studying and Test Taking

## WRITING TO LEARN AND TAKING TESTS

As you continue your high school studies, you will have an increasing need for skills and procedures that can make your studying more effective and your test-taking more successful.

### WRITING TO LEARN

"Writing to learn" encompasses many different writing activities—from taking notes in a lecture to preparing a written report. Writing can help you organize your thoughts, analyze a subject or a problem, and share what you have learned with others.

#### Writing the Précis

The need for making accurate and concise summaries is a constant one in daily life. Newscasters on radio and television make such summaries daily. Law students summarize hundreds of cases in the course of their legal studies. Scholars share knowledge by making abstracts, or summaries, of long research papers.

In your studies, you will be practicing the art of extracting and expressing in your own words the principal ideas from what you read. A brief summary of the main points of an article is called a *précis*. In such a composition, which should be not more than one third as long as the original, you express the central idea of the original writer in clear, concise language of your own. All illustrations, amplifications, or embellishments are omitted from the précis, which includes only bare essentials.

There are a few simple rules for making a précis:

1. Read the original paragraph or selection through attentively, to learn the general idea. Do not take notes.
2. Read it a second time, this time looking up all unfamiliar words, phrases, or allusions. You now judge the selection more carefully, noting important ideas and details.
3. List in your own words what you judge to be the essential point or points made by the author.
4. In your own words, write the first draft of the précis. Omit examples, illustrations, conversations, or repetitions.
5. Read your first draft and compare it with the original for accuracy and emphasis.
6. Eliminate all unnecessary words and change words until you have expressed concisely and clearly the main point of the selection. The précis should be no more than one third the length of the original.

Study the following example of précis writing.

> What are the real aims of study? The object of study is, in the first place, to get fast and firm possession of facts—facts of spelling, reading, mathematics, composition, history, language, geography, and the like. It is highly desirable that we should know how to spell *Chicago* and *business; Boston* and *brains;* and that we should know for all time. We want to know once for all that seven times nine is sixty-three; that Abraham Lincoln signed the Emancipation Proclamation; that an island is a body of land completely surrounded by water; and that a proper name should begin with a capital letter. Many, many minute facts, as well as certain connected bodies of truth, should be embedded in one's memory as deeply and securely as a bullet that has lodged in the heart of a growing tree. And one should master certain processes of thought, and grip a few great underlying and unchanging principles of life and conduct. [160 words]
>
> FRANCES C. LOCKWOOD

The first reading will tell you that the paragraph is about the aims of study. In your second, more careful, reading, you note that the following ideas are expressed, and you jot them down:

1. The first aim of study is to acquire facts (there are several examples given of such facts).

2. The second aim is to master processes of thought.
3. The third aim is to learn certain principles of conduct and of life.

You notice that while several illustrations of the first aim have been given by the author, none are given for the other two. In the précis you omit *all* illustrations and stick to the main ideas. The next step is to combine the three ideas you have jotted down into a single sentence, if possible.

> There are three aims of studying: to learn certain necessary facts in many areas; to learn how to think; and to learn the great rules about life and the conduct of it. [32 words]

Examining your first draft, and rereading the original, you see that you have accurately expressed the writer's ideas, but that your statement of the first and third ideas can be made more concise. In length, your précis is much shorter than one third of the original:

> The aims of study are three: to acquire needed facts; to learn how to think; to learn the universal principles of life and conduct. [24 words]

**EXERCISE 1. Writing a Précis.** Write a précis for each of these passages.

1

There are many signs of immature readers. They make fixed demands of every story and feel frustrated and disappointed unless these demands are satisfied. Often they stick to one type of subject matter. Instead of being receptive to any story that puts human beings in human situations, they read only sports stories, western stories, love stories, or crime stories. If they are willing to accept a wider range of experience, they still wish every story to conform at bottom to several strict though perhaps unconsciously formulated expectations. Among the most common of these expectations are (1) a sympathetic hero or heroine—one with whom the reader can in imagination identify while reading and whose adventures and triumphs the reader can share; (2) a plot in which something exciting is always happening and in which there is a strong element of suspense; (3) a happy outcome, that sends the reader away undisturbed and optimistic about the world; (4) a theme —if the story has a theme—that confirms the reader's already-held opinions of the world. [172 words]

LAWRENCE PERRINE

2

In any scientific inquiry the first step is to get at the facts, and this requires precision, patience, impartiality, watchfulness against the illusions of the senses and the mind, and carefulness to keep inferences from mingling with observations. The second step is accurate registration of the data. In most cases science begins with measurement. As Lord Kelvin said, "Nearly all the grandest discoveries of science have been but the rewards of accurate measurement and patient, long-continued labor in the minute sifting of numerical results." There is a certain quality of character here, and it is very significant that Clark Maxwell should have spoken in one sentence of "those aspirations after accuracy of measurement, and justice in action, which we reckon among our noblest attributes as men."

A third step is arranging the data in workable form—a simple illustration being a plotted-out curve which shows at a glance the general outcome of a multitude of measurements, e.g., the range of variability in a particular specific character in a plant or animal. The data may have to be expressed in its simplest terms, reduced perhaps to a common denominator with other sets of facts with which they have to be compared. There is a danger here of losing sight of something in the process of reduction. Thus in reducing a fact of animal behavior to a chain of reflex actions we may be losing sight of "mind"; or, in reducing a physiological fact to a series of chemical and physical facts we may be losing sight of "life."

The fourth step is [made] when a whole series of occurrences is seen to have a uniformity, which is called their law. A formula is found that fits—the finding being sometimes due to a flash of insight and sometimes the outcome of many tentatives. Newton's "passage from a falling apple to a falling moon" was a stupendous leap of the scientific imagination; the modern science of the atom is the outcome of the testing of many approximate formulations. [335 words]

J. ARTHUR THOMSON

## Writing in Other Classes

### 36a. Use writing to explore topics and concepts in science.

Writing about concepts and topics from a content-area subject, such as science (earth science, biology, chemistry, or physics), can help you understand the course material better. You can explore topics or illustrate concepts in science through several forms of writing.

Keeping a journal in which you record your reactions to course content and activities will enable you to explore your own thoughts about the course material. The journal can also be a record of your progress in the class and a source of information for your writing.

For example, you might use a journal to record each phase of an experiment you are conducting. The journal entries can include the specific procedures you follow and the results you observe. You can also discuss your reactions to each phase of the experiment, such as why specific procedures were (or were not) successful and why the results were (or were not) what you anticipated. Such journal entries can provide information you can use in a laboratory report about the experiment. In addition to discussing scientific experiments, you can use your journal to record field studies, class demonstrations, and other course activities.

You can also use your journal to explore the scientific topics and concepts your science class covers. For example, your teacher might ask you to write an entry about any of the following concepts:

1. Explain the process of oxidation.
2. Discuss why Einstein's theory of relativity was a significant scientific breakthrough.
3. Discuss three practical applications of Newton's Laws of Motion to your daily life.
4. Explain why photosynthesis cannot occur in the absence of light.

By writing about these concepts and topics, you can organize your thoughts and discover areas where your understanding is strong or weak. You can also practice applying your knowledge of the expository composition to answering essay questions or writing compositions in science courses. (See "Explanations of Complex Processes," pages 124–28.)

For your science class, you may also write book reviews about nonfiction and fiction works that deal with scientific events, periods, or figures. This kind of writing combines your scientific knowledge with your evaluation of the writer's treatment of a particular topic.

Nonfiction works to write about include biographies and autobiographies of well-known scientists, such as Paul de Kruif's biography of early scientists, *Microbe Hunters,* or Lewis Thomas's semi-autobiographical account, *The Youngest Science: Notes of a Medicine-Watcher.* You might want to write about works that explain scientific events or theories, such as Russell Freedman's *Can Bears Predict Earthquakes? Unsolved Mysteries of Animal Behavior,* or Peter Nicholls's *The Science in Science Fiction.* To write this kind of book review, you should first review information about the event or person in encyclopedias and other reference books. Then do a close reading of the work, taking careful notes about significant events and striking details in the book. Your book review should answer any of the following questions: How accurately does the book present or explain the scientific event or the scientist? How does this book add to your understanding of science? Does the author present a biased, or slanted, view of the topic—and if so, how is this bias explained? When you write your book review, include supporting details from reference works and from the nonfiction book to develop your ideas. (See also pages 133–39, writing critical reviews.)

You can also write a book review about a fictional work. This kind of book review combines your scientific knowledge with your evaluation of a work, supported by details from the work itself and from reference works. Science fiction is especially suitable for a book review in science class. For example, you might write a review of Arthur C. Clarke's classic, *2001: A Space Odyssey,* or you might compare and contrast several works by one author, such as Isaac Asimov's *Foundation* series. Read the work closely; then take notes about outstanding details or events. When you write a book review of a fictional work, answer questions like the following ones: How do the scientific concepts in this book relate to course material? How probable is the use of science and technology in this book? What evidence can you use to support your opinion? (See pages 140–47, writing essays of literary analysis.)

No matter what kind of writing you do in science, or in any other course, apply your knowledge of description, narration, exposition, and persuasion (Chapters 4, 7, and 8), as well as your knowledge of the development of paragraphs and compositions (Chapters 2, 3, and 4). Remember to use your knowledge of the writing process (Chapter 1) to improve your writing in all content-area subjects.

**EXERCISE 2. Writing in Science.** Following the writing process, prepare any of the writing activities listed below.

1. Using any one of the science concepts on page 723, or questions your teacher provides, prepare a journal entry about a topic you are currently studying.
2. For at least three days, keep a journal about an experiment, field study, or class demonstration. Then write a brief essay that discusses the separate procedures in the activity, the outcome (or the results) of the activity, and the specific ways in which this activity increased your scientific understanding. Be prepared to discuss your essay.
3. Write a book review of a fiction or nonfiction work about a scientific figure, event, or period. In your review, answer the questions listed above.

## TAKING TESTS

No matter what your plans for the years following high school, you will most likely be asked to "take some tests." The most commonly administered tests include measures of verbal fluency, reading comprehension, and/or grammar and composition.

Among the tests of this type used for college entrance, the best known are probably the *Scholastic Aptitude Test—Verbal*, or SAT—V (including the *Test of Standard Written English*), and the *English Composition Test*, or "English Achievement" test. Both are administered by the College Entrance Examination Board. Another well-known test is the *American College Testing Program* (ACT) *Assessment Test*.

Some schools and colleges do *not* require tests for admission but do administer tests for placement in courses and for guidance purposes. The military and other employers may also administer tests of English language skills for certain jobs.

Tests with the word *aptitude* in their titles are used mainly to predict future success, whether in school or on the job. They do not, on the whole, measure what you have learned in particular courses. They measure the language skills which you have been developing all your life. *Achievement* tests, on the other hand, concentrate on specific skills and information which you have learned in academic courses.

Cramming is *not* an appropriate or helpful way to prepare for tests of this nature. There are, however, a number of good test-taking practices which will help you to do your best on any examination. These may be summarized as follows:

### SUMMARY OF TEST-TAKING PRACTICES

**1. *Take a positive approach to the test*.**

a. Try to do your best even though you may be nervous. Don't panic.
b. Regard lapses of memory as normal. If you "block" on a certain question, go on and come back to it later if you can.
c. Don't expect to answer every question correctly. Some tests are built so that the average student will answer only about half the questions correctly.

**2. *Use your time wisely*.**

a. Look over the test before you start to work. Get a feel for its length and difficulty.

b. Plan your time. If you have a time limit of 20 minutes for a 40-question test, check that you are on or beyond question 21 after 10 minutes. But avoid too much clock-watching; it uses up your time and heightens anxiety.
c. Work rapidly but carefully. Answer the easy questions first. If you don't know an answer right away, leave it and go on.
d. If you have time after finishing the test, answer the questions you left out the first time. (On the ACT, you are not penalized for guessing.)

**3. *Avoid careless errors*.**

a. Pay close attention to directions. Do the sample questions even though you're sure you understand the task.
b. Read each question carefully. Be sure you know exactly what it is asking you to do.
c. Look at all the choices before you answer. In many cases the correct answer is not *absolutely* correct; it is the best among the choices.
d. Avoid careless mistakes in marking the answer sheet. Keep it lined up with the booklet if possible. The scoring machine can't tell when you were "off" by one question or one row.
e. If you change an answer, be sure you erase the first answer thoroughly. If the machine "reads" both marks, it will count the question as unanswered.

---

One of the best ways to prepare for any test is to become familiar with the types of tasks you will be asked to perform. Many test questions will be familiar, while others may be new to you. The purpose of this chapter is to show you some of these question types.

## Tests of Word Knowledge or Vocabulary

Vocabulary tests measure your understanding of the meanings of words, either in isolation or in context. Often, the relationships among words—the way they are related in meaning—will be tested. Examples of three types of vocabulary questions follow.

### Word Meanings

The simplest type of vocabulary question asks you the meaning of a word. Usually, the format is an incomplete statement to which you add one of several choices to complete the meaning. The following is a sample question of this type.

EXAMPLE **A** To whet one's appetite is to ——
a wean it
b salve it
c sharpen it
d appease it
e dampen it

Answer:[1]
**A** ⓐ ⓑ ● ⓓ ⓔ

Some questions ask for a choice between *phrases* explaining the word's meaning or use; others offer *single words* and ask you to choose a synonym of the key word.

**EXERCISE 3. Choosing the Correct Meaning.** Read the beginning of each sentence below and the choices that follow it. Choose the answer which best completes the sentence.[2]

**1** To secede is to ——

a attain
b follow
c establish
d withdraw

**2** An ingenious person is one who is ——

a impudent
b inventive
c decisive
d frank

**3** If something is superfluous, it is ——

a necessary
b shallow
c excellent
d excessive

**4** Your agreement with a decision is your ——

a ascent
b asset
c assent
d assist

[1] Answer: © *sharpen it*. When you have marked your answer sheet for ©, this is the way it will look. You will black in the circle containing the letter of the correct answer. Answers are shown this way for all sample test items throughout this chapter.
[2] Answers for this and all the following exercises will be found on page 746.

**5** Something that is done inadvertently is probably done ——

a accidentally
b imaginatively
c intentionally
d maliciously

## Synonyms and Antonyms

In a test on synonyms or antonyms you are asked to select, from four or five choices, the word *most similar* in meaning (synonym) to the word given *or* the word *most nearly opposite* in meaning (antonym). *Pay attention!* These are sometimes mixed together. There are few true synonyms or antonyms in English; the "correct" answer, therefore, is the one most nearly the same or most nearly the opposite in meaning.

Following are two sample questions in which you are to find the word *most similar* in meaning (synonym) to the underlined word.

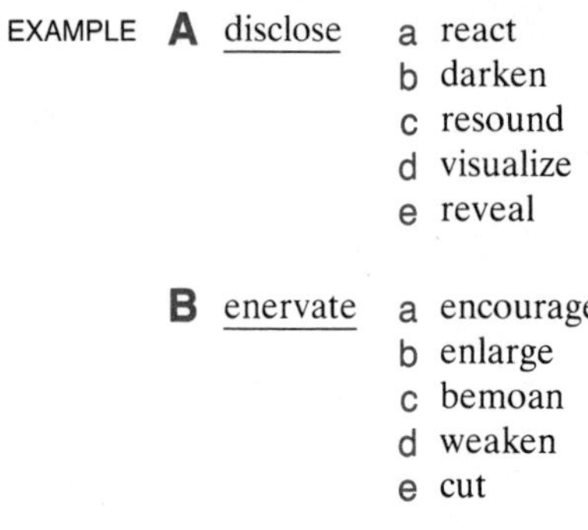

EXAMPLE **A** disclose
a react
b darken
c resound
d visualize
e reveal

**B** enervate
a encourage
b enlarge
c bemoan
d weaken
e cut

Answers:
**A** ⓐ ⓑ ⓒ ⓓ ●
**B** ⓐ ⓑ ⓒ ● ⓔ

The last question includes a common misconception of the word's meaning among the choices. Many people are confused as to whether *enervate* means to take "nerve" away or to give it; hence, *encourage* is given as an incorrect choice.

**EXERCISE 4. Choosing Antonyms.** For each of the following questions, choose the word *most nearly opposite* in meaning (antonym) to the underlined word.

**1** chaotic

a confused
b active
c orderly
d silent
e cowardly

**2** obstinate

a flexible
b persistent
c vague
d obedient
e extinct

**3** eradicate

a refine
b ratify
c endorse
d annihilate
e establish

**4** pensive

a careless
b melancholy
c sympathetic
d exuberant
e pleasant

**5** disperse

a release
b collect
c destroy
d produce
e reinforce

### Verbal Analogies

Analogies measure your understanding of the relationships among words. Here is a sample set of directions and one question.

EXAMPLE In the items below, the first and second words are related in a certain way. The third word is related in the same way to one of the four words which follow it. You are to choose the word related to the third word in the same way that the second word is related to the first.

**A** *Inch* is to *foot* as *ounce* is to ——

a weight
b meter
c yard
d pound

Answer:

In this sample question, the relationship tested is that of a unit of measurement to a larger unit in the same scale. An inch is a division of a foot. Hence, the correct answer is *pound*, since an ounce is a division of a pound.

Analogies may also be presented as in the following example.

EXAMPLE Below is a list of five pairs of related words. Choose the pair of words whose relationship is most like that of the first pair.

**A** INCH : FOOT ::

a quart : measure
b weight : peck
c ounce : pound
d mile : length
e meter : yard

Answer:
**A** ⓐ ⓑ ● ⓓ ⓔ

Again, *ounce* is related to *pound* as *inch* is to *foot*. But here you are to find the whole pair. In the first example, the first part of the second pair was given to you. If you are not familiar with analogies, it may help to turn them into sentences such as the one in the first example.

Suppose the first pair of words were *glance* and *gaze*. Both name ways of looking at something. But a *glance* is a quick look, while *gaze* has the idea of a long or thoughtful look. Which of these pairs of words, then, has the most similar relationship?

EXAMPLE **A** GLANCE : GAZE ::

a blink : scowl
b glimpse : stare
c observe : note
d skim : peek
e peruse : study

Answer:
**A** ⓐ ● ⓒ ⓓ ⓔ

Option b presents the most similar pair, since *glimpse* also implies a quick once-over and *stare* gives the notion of a long and concentrated look. Another way to check your understanding of the analogy is to compare the first and third parts, and then check to see if the second and fourth parts have the same relationship. In the original example, this check would take the form: "*Inch* is to *ounce* as *foot* is to —— ?"

**EXERCISE 5. Completing Analogies.** In the items below, the first and second words are related in a certain way. The third word is related in the same way to one of the five words which follow. Choose the word related to the third word in the same way as the second word is related to the first.

**1** *Head* is to *foot* as *cap* is to ——

a toe
b shoe
c wig
d ankle
e bottle

**2** *Sphere* is to *axis* as *circle* is to ——

a hypotenuse
b square
c radius
d circumference
e diameter

**3** *Canvas* is to *suede* as *cloth* is to ——

a leather
b cotton
c fur
d boot
e tent

In the following items, choose the pair of words whose relationship is most similar to that of the first pair given.

**4** speak : sing ::

a paint : draw
b run : walk
c prose : poetry
d move : dance
e swim : sink

**5** nose : odor ::

a mouth : speech
b ear : sound
c color : eye
d hand : hold
e foot : walk

## Reading Achievement

Your grasp of the meaning of what you read is often measured in tests for school or vocational guidance. Reading abilities are usually measured in one of the two ways described below.

### Sentence Completion

This question format could be called "fill in the blanks." Sentences are presented with one or two blanks, each indicating that a word has been left out. You are to choose the word that fits best in the sentence.

EXAMPLE **A** We laughed at the clown —— he performed funny tricks.

a but
b until
c because
d unless
e although

Answer:

The sentence clearly calls for a conjunction, but the only one that makes any sense is *because*. Questions like this look for your ability to recognize the logic and coherence of the sentence—one aspect of comprehension.

### Reading Comprehension

Reading tests are not concerned with testing whether you understand, word by word, what you have read, but rather how well you can draw conclusions and make judgments about what you read. The questions about the passage you read should not require outside information, but should be based upon the information within the passage itself. Here is a sample passage followed by three questions.

EXAMPLE Two days after his sudden death on June 9, 1870, Charles Dickens was honored in a *New York Times* obituary covering more than five of the seven long columns on the front page. The length of this article accurately reflected Dickens' position among the American reading public of a century ago, when entire households waited anxiously from month to month to discover the fate of Little Nell, or Oliver Twist, or whichever Dickensian hero figured in the novel currently being serialized for United States audiences. In later years, the novelist's reputation diminished; critics dismissed him as a "popular" writer rather than a true craftsman. His remarkably vivid characterizations were considered caricatures, even though numerous outstanding writers such as Feodor Dostoevski, Joseph Conrad, and Henry James expressed their indebtedness to "the master." But during the 1940's, writers like Franz Kafka and Edmund Wilson brought readers to a fresh awareness of Dickens' unforgettable delineations of personalities whose very names—Scrooge, for instance—have assumed an independent meaning for people around the world. Readers today are also impressed by Dickens' vision, more than 100 years ago, of what the modern city was to become. For Dickens' London was a place of smoke and filth and a decaying social fabric, rather than the rich, bustling, upper-class London of virtually all his contemporaries.

**A** The main thrust of this article has to do with ——

a modern attitudes toward Dickens
b Dickens' descriptions of London
c changes in Dickens' literary reputation
d Dickens' treatment of fictional characters

**B** Dostoevski, Conrad, and James indicated that ——

a their writing was influenced by Dickens
b Dickens wrote for a lower-class public
c they had learned about London from Dickens
d Scrooge was a caricature

**C** Apparently other British authors of Dickens' day ——

a were upper-class Londoners
b ridiculed Dickens' London
c believed Dickens an expert on city life
d pictured London as an attractive place to live

Answers:

**A** ⓐ ⓑ ● ⓓ
**B** ● ⓑ ⓒ ⓓ
**C** ⓐ ⓑ ⓒ ●

The sample questions on page 733 are fairly typical of the kinds of questions that may be asked on a reading comprehension exam. Question 1, for example, asks for the main idea of the passage. Question 2 asks for a restatement of an idea clearly stated in the passage. And question 3 asks for an inference which the reader must draw from the passage. Other types of questions often used in this type of test may ask for the meaning of a term or phrase as used in the paragraph, a recognition of the author's intent, or the identification of bias, exaggeration, value judgments, or the like.

**EXERCISE 6. Drawing Conclusions from Reading.** Carefully read the following passage. Then, read each of the questions given at its conclusion and review the passage to select an answer.

Catbirds are good neighbors; they eat small fruit, wild as well as cultivated, but they also eat insects, lots of them. Thus they earn their keep in the garden. Catbirds may be as tame as chickadees, and may sometimes even come to your hand to beg for raisins. Spring is the best time of year to listen to catbirds. However, only the male catbird sings. While his mate is brooding the eggs, the male has ample time to sing—and play the clown. A friendly bird, the male catbird has a sense of humor, or something like it. He is a mimic; he borrows music from other birds. Sometimes he merely sits in a bush, well concealed, and sings to himself, as though practicing. Other times he seeks a human companion with whom he can have a conversation. He likes company, and and he seems to need an audience. He is essentially a showoff. Try to imitate his own imitations and he will come close, and then laugh at you. The male catbird can be as musical as his cousins, the brown thrasher and the mockingbird. But he doesn't stammer, as the thrasher sometimes does. And he can break into the middle of a song to jeer at his own performance, as the mockingbird never does. He will sing part way through a robin's choicest song, then break into squawking like a barnyard hen or mewing like a cat. And after a pause he will start another song, this time perhaps that of a tanager. The catbird's songs are nearly always fragmented. Perhaps you could say he sings for his supper. You can never be sure whose song he is going to sing, but he will sing.

**1** According to the article, the male catbird is different from the mockingbird because he ——

a interrupts his own singing
b stammers during his song
c imitates the songs of other birds
d likes human companionship

**2** A factual statement about catbirds, as opposed to an opinion or value judgment, appears on ——

a lines 1–2
b lines 6–7
c lines 10–11
d lines 19–20

**3** As used in this paragraph, the word *brooding* (line 6) means ——

a sitting quietly and thoughtfully
b hovering or looming over
c sitting on or incubating
d being depressed and moody

**4** Apparently the catbird is most closely related to the ——

a chickadee
b brown thrasher
c tanager
d robin

**5** The phrase that best sums up the author's opinion of the male catbird appears in line ——

a 1
b 4
c 12
d 17

## Standard Written English

The best way for someone to "test" your ability to write standard English is to have you write. Since this is not always practical, however, multiple-choice tests have been developed to measure your knowledge of correct spelling and usage, your skill in organizing material, and your sensitivity to nuances of tone, style, and meaning. The paragraphs which follow give examples of some of the more commonly used methods of testing skills in standard written English.

### Spelling

Spelling may be tested in any number of ways. One of the most common formats consists of five words, one of which may be misspelled. You are to indicate the word spelled incorrectly or mark a choice indicating no errors. The questions usually involve basic rules of spelling and misspellings of frequently used words. Another type of question involves the misuse of homophones—words which sound alike but differ in spelling and meaning, such as *to, too,* and *two*. In this sort of test question, four phrases with different homophones are usually given, and you are asked to choose the phrase in which a homophone is used correctly or incorrectly. Study the following sample.

EXAMPLE **A** a *too* hot
b grizzly *bear*
c *peace* of pie
d tough *seas*

Answer:
**A** ⓐ ⓑ ● ⓓ

**EXERCISE 7. Identifying Misspelled Words.** For each of the following questions, choose the one word which is misspelled. If no word is misspelled, mark the answer *N* for no error.

**1** a practice
b calender
c tomato
d already
N

**2** a freight
b anchor
c pursuade
d magazine
N

**3** a efficient
b personal
c implement
d hindrence
N

**4** a *mail* a letter
b *site* a reference
c *raze* a building
d *reign* as king
N

**5** a *pare* an apple
b *tale* of woe
c *hew* wood
d *peel* of laughter
N

## Error Recognition

Error recognition questions ask you to detect or correct errors in written passages. Some questions ask you only to indicate that an error exists; others ask you to specify the type of error it is. Here are samples of three types of questions.

EXAMPLES TYPE 1.

Mark the letter of the line containing an error in spelling, punctuation, capitalization, grammar, or usage. If there is no error, mark *N* for no error.

**A** a Actually, bats are fascinating
b animals. They are the only Mammals
c living today that are able to fly.
N

Answer:
**A** ⓐ ● ⓒ Ⓝ

TYPE 2.

Mark the letter of the underlined part that must be changed in order to make the sentence correct. (Be sure to note whether underlining includes the punctuation.) If there is no error, mark answer space *e*.

**B** During the colonel period (a), many colonies had their own flags (b), the earliest of which (c) was based on the British flag. (d) No error. (e)

Answer:
**B** ● ⓑ ⓒ ⓓ ⓔ

TYPE 3.

Some of the sentences below contain errors; others are correct as they stand. For each sentence, mark your answer sheet:

a —if the sentence contains an incorrect choice of words (error in diction)
b —if the sentence is wordy (verbose or redundant)
c —if the sentence contains an overworked expression (cliché) or a mixed metaphor

d —if the sentence contains an error in grammar or structure
e —if the sentence is correct as it stands

1 Each day it was a daily occurrence to see the mail truck arrive.

2 The mass of detail is not penitent to the question at hand.

3 The young woman was fit as a fiddle as she started work.

Answers:

1 ⓐ ● ⓒ ⓓ ⓔ
2 ● ⓑ ⓒ ⓓ ⓔ
3 ⓐ ⓑ ● ⓓ ⓔ

**EXERCISE 8. Recognizing Errors in Standard Written English.** Following the appropriate set of directions, record your answers to each of the following questions.[1]

**TYPE I.** Mark the letter of the line containing an error in spelling, punctuation, capitalization, grammar, or usage. If there is no error, mark *N* for no error.

1 a Ben Franklin was an excellent student,
b but his father could not afford to send him
c to Harvard college. He dropped out of school.
N

2 a For a short time he helped his father
b make candels and cakes of soap from animal fat,
c but Ben really wanted to go to sea.
N

3 a Finally, at 12 years of age, Ben Franklin
b pledged himself to an apprenticeship the
c most common type of schooling in the colonies.
N

4 a Ben learned all there was to know about
b the printing trade from his brother James.
c He also wrote for the paper his brother published.
N

[1] The factual ideas for all these sentences came from the July 1975 *National Geographic* article on Franklin.

**5** a Although the paper was very succesful, Ben
b was unhappy. So, at 17 years of age,
c he ran away to begin a new life for himself.
N

**TYPE II.** Mark the letter of the underlined part that must be changed in order to make the sentence correct. (Be sure to note whether the underlining includes the punctuation.) If there is no error, mark *e*.

**6** Broke jobless and dirty (a), Ben landed in Philadelphia in 1723 (b). He started a business by (c) printing everything from business forms to hymnals, and he became (d) prosperous. No error. (e)

**7** Soon after he arrived in the City of Brotherly love (a), Franklin founded a four-page newspaper (b), which was published weekly, as well as (c) an almanac called Poor Richard's Almanack. (d) No error. (e)

**8** The young printer also founded (a) a political club called the Junto. (b) The members met discussing (c) the needs of the growing community. (d) No error. (e)

**9** Once a project was chosen, Franklin published (a) articles in his paper. And signatures collected. (b) Then the Junto (c) would petition the assembly (d) for action. No error. (e)

**10** By such methods, Franklin and his friends (a) attacked serious social (b) problems. Many of the institutions they established were so useful (c) that they still thrive today. (d) No error. (e)

**TYPE III.** Some of the sentences below contain errors; others are correct as they stand. For each sentence, mark your paper with one of the following letters as appropriate:

a —if the sentence contains an incorrect choice of words (error in diction)
b —if the sentence is wordy (verbose or redundant)
c —if the sentence contains an overworked expression (cliché) or a mixed metaphor
d —if the sentence contains an error in grammar or structure
e —if the sentence is correct as it stands

**11** Franklin and his friends began a public academy that later became the University of Pennsylvania.

**12** They also founded a lending library where people which had paid a small membership fee could borrow books.

**13** Before any other fire insurance company had been founded, Franklin promoted the establishment of the insurance company that survives today as the oldest fire insurance company in existence at the present time.

**14** To reduce counterfeiting, Franklin devised paper money with the imprint of a leaf, since he had observed that no two leaves were identifiable.

**15** Last but not least among Franklin's contributions should be mentioned the Union Fire Company, Philadelphia's first volunteer fire department.

## Error Correction

Error correction questions indicate the inappropriate part of the sentence and ask you to choose a suitable correction from among the choices given you. Here are some samples.

EXAMPLES **A** Eating, drinking, and *to stay up* late at night were among her pleasures.

a correct as it stands
b she liked staying up
c staying up
d to remain up

**B** *On the snow-covered branch, two sparrows, they huddled close together.*

a correct as it stands
b On the snow-covered branch, two sparrows huddled close together.
c On the snow-covered branch, two sparrows, huddled close together.
d Closely, on the snow-covered branch, huddled the two sparrows together.

Answers:
**A** ⓐ ⓑ ● ⓓ
**B** ⓐ ● ⓒ ⓓ

**EXERCISE 9. Error Correction.** Choose the letter which indicates the best correction for the underlined part of each sentence. If the sentence is correct as it stands, mark *d*.

**1** The hour was indeed late in the evening when we started back homeward toward our house.

a We started back homeward when the hour was very late.
b It was very late evening when we started home.
c We began when it was late in the evening to go home.
d Correct as it stands

**2** Rain had been falling for several hours, this having caused the streams to rise.

a which resulted in
b which was responsible for
c causing
d Correct as it stands

**3** Our road home crossed an old covered bridge over a narrow stream.

a homeward was by way of an old
b home necessitated our crossing over a
c home led us via a bridge which was an old
d Correct as it stands

**4** We couldn't but hope that the bridge was still open.

a couldn't hardly
b could scarcely
c could only
d Correct as it stands

**5** When we arrived at the river's edge, the angry waters were to be seen swirling and were carrying branches along with them as they rushed past.

a Swirling and carrying branches along with them, the angry waters were seen as they rushed past when we arrived at the river's edge.
b When we arrived at the river's edge, we could see the angry waters swirling and carrying branches along with them as they rushed past.
c Having arrived at the river's edge, the angry waters were swirling and carrying branches along with them as they rushed past.
d Correct as it stands

## Sentence Revision

This type of question requires you to mentally restate a *correct* sentence, using a given phrase. Using the phrase will require change in other parts of the sentence as well. Then you must choose, from among the choices given you, a word or phrase that will appear somewhere in the restated sentence. Study the sample given below.

EXAMPLE **A** Sentence: When night came and the temperature fell, my parents lit the fire in the bedroom.

Revision: Begin with "*Each night. . .* "

a that the temperature
b upon the temperature's
c because the temperature
d when the temperature

Answer:
**A** ⓐ ⓑ ⓒ ●

There will often be several ways the new sentence could be completed. If none of the choices given is in your revised sentence, think of another way to rephrase the sentence, and check the choices again. But be sure you do not change the meaning of the original sentence when you revise it.

**EXERCISE 10. Sentence Revision.** Mentally revise each of the following sentences according to the instruction given for each. Then choose the letter of the phrase most likely to occur in the sentence as revised.

**1** Sentence: My friend said that she hoped the bridge would hold until we got across.

Revision: Change the indirect quote to a direct quote by inserting:

a "I hoped the bridge would hold until we got across."
b "She hopes the bridge will hold until we get across."
c "I hope the bridge will hold until we get across."
d "She hopes the bridge will hold until we got across."

**2** Sentence: We finally arrived home safely. There was also a thick, swirling fog.

Revision: Rewrite these two sentences as a single sentence.

a even though
b so that
c due to the
d whereas

## Organizing Paragraphs

Another writing skill often tested is organization. The most frequent exercise designed to measure organizational ability is the scrambled paragraph. This exercise takes a paragraph and presents the sentences in random order. Your job is to figure out the order that will make a well-knit paragraph.

Here is the way the directions are likely to go:

DIRECTIONS Each group of sentences in this section is actually a paragraph presented in scrambled order. Each sentence in the group has a place in the paragraph; no sentence is to be left out. You are to read each group of sentences and decide the best order in which to put the sentences so as to form a well-organized paragraph.

Before trying to answer the questions, jot down the correct order of the sentences. Then answer each of the questions by blackening the appropriate space on the answer sheet. Remember that you will receive credit only for answers marked on the answer sheet.

A sample paragraph follows:

EXAMPLE **P** As you read, however, concentrate only on main ideas; don't try to remember everything.

**Q** If you develop an interest in what you read, you are more likely to remember the factual information in a passage.

**R** Finally, when you have completed the passage, pause to summarize the main ideas in your mind.

**S** You will have an even stronger motive for remembering those facts if you understand their importance to you.

**1** Which sentence did you put first?

a sentence **P**
b sentence **Q**
c sentence **R**
d sentence **S**

**2** Which sentence did you put after sentence **S**?

a sentence **P**
b sentence **Q**
c sentence **R**
d None of the above. Sentence **S** is last.

**3** Which sentence did you put after sentence **Q**?

a sentence **P**
b sentence **R**
c sentence **S**
d None of the above. Sentence **Q** is last.

Answers:
**1** ⓐ ● ⓒ ⓓ
**2** ● ⓑ ⓒ ⓓ
**3** ⓐ ⓑ ● ⓓ

Note the use of words such as *finally, however, even stronger*. These words refer to previous statements. You may also find clues with pronouns or adjectives that clearly refer to some noun in a previous sentence (*those* facts). Before you answer any of the questions, determine the correct order for all the sentences and write it down. Most tests, however, will not ask you to give that order all at once. They will be designed so as to give you credit for each correct relationship you detect between the individual sentences.

**EXERCISE 11. Organizing Paragraphs.** Read the following sentences carefully, and write down their correct order before answering the questions related to them. Then choose your answer for each question that follows.

**P** A perfectly normal reaction to such wrong eating is to feel let down soon after the "quick energy" is spent by the body.

**Q** The reason for eating a substantial meal—especially a substantial breakfast —is to provide energy for a full day's work.

**R** However, when one eats an insubstantial meal, the body digests the food too rapidly, and valuable energy is often wasted.

**S** When one eats high-quality foods at the same meal, energy is released to the body gradually.

**1** Which sentence did you put first?

a **P**
b **Q**
c **R**
d **S**

**2** Which sentence did you put after sentence **S**?

a **P**
b **Q**
c **R**
d Sentence **S** is last.

**3** Which sentence did you put after sentence **P**?

a **Q**
b **R**
c **S**
d Sentence **P** is last.

**4** Which sentence did you put after sentence **R**?

a **P**
b **Q**
c **S**
d Sentence **R** is last.

**5** Which sentence did you put after sentence **Q**?

a **P**
b **R**
c **S**
d Sentence **Q** is last.

*Answers to Exercises*

| Ex. 3, p. 727 | Ex. 4, p. 728 | Ex. 5, p. 731 |
|---|---|---|
| 1 d | 1 c | 1 b |
| 2 b | 2 a | 2 e |
| 3 d | 3 e | 3 a |
| 4 c | 4 d | 4 d |
| 5 a | 5 b | 5 b |

| Ex. 6, p. 734 | Ex. 7, p. 736 | Ex. 8, p. 738 | | |
|---|---|---|---|---|
| 1 a | 1 b | 1 c | 6 a | 11 e |
| 2 d | 2 c | 2 b | 7 a | 12 d |
| 3 c | 3 d | 3 b | 8 c | 13 b |
| 4 b | 4 b | 4 N | 9 b | 14 a |
| 5 b | 5 d | 5 a | 10 e | 15 c |

| Ex. 9, p. 741 | Ex. 10, p. 742 | Ex. 11, p. 744 |
|---|---|---|
| 1 b | 1 c | 1 b |
| 2 c | 2 a | 2 c |
| 3 d | | 3 d |
| 4 c | | 4 a |
| 5 b | | 5 c |

## Essay Tests

Essay questions call on your memory of facts. They also test your ability to think about and express your understanding of selected material. Because essay questions call for critical thinking and writing skills, answers can vary. However, your answer will be considered deficient if it is unfinished, not organized according to the directions, or not supported with sufficient detail.

### Preparing for Essay Tests

Prepare for an essay test by thinking of several possible questions. Then give yourself a limited time to write out a thesis statement for each of these and an outline of your answers. This is an excellent way to review the test material and to practice the skills and techniques involved in answering essay questions.

### Organizing Your Time for Writing an Essay Test

Always scan the complete test before you begin writing. Note the number and type of questions to be answered in the time allowed as well as the point value of each section. Then schedule your time.

For example, allow thirty minutes for each of two equal-value essay questions on a one-hour test. But if there were three questions, one worth fifty points and two worth twenty-five each, you would spend about thirty minutes on the fifty-point one and fifteen on each of the others.

Since all good writing involves planning, do a further breakdown of the time you set aside for each essay question. As a general rule, plan to spend about two minutes planning and one minute revising for each five minutes of actual writing.

Once you get started, use a watch or clock to help you stay on schedule. Even if you answer one question brilliantly but never get around to answering the others, you will not get a high score on the test.

### Analyzing the Question

Essay questions introduce an idea and specify how you are to discuss it. It is essential that you read the question carefully and thoughtfully until you have identified the key terms of the question and the kinds of information called for.

### Identifying Key Terms

Key terms in the question indicate the pattern of organization you are expected to use. Be aware of the kind of information and analysis called for by the pattern identified by the key terms.

*Comparison and contrast*—Key terms are *compare, contrast, show the difference, have in common, find likenesses, in what way are . . . similar/dissimilar.* The answer should include a topic sentence stating the specific points on which the subject is being compared or contrasted and details developing and illustrating these points.

EXAMPLE Question: Compare Lady Macbeth's responsibility for Duncan's murder with that of Macbeth. Refer to at least two comments or actions made by each to support your conclusion.
Key term: Compare. Answer should include a thesis that tells which character is more responsible, supported by details that show one character acting in a more decisive way than the other.

*Cause and effect*—Key terms are *analyze, explain, criticize, show why, give factors that led to, tell the effect of.* The answer should include a topic sentence identifying cause and effect and details demonstrating that the effect is the result of the named cause.

EXAMPLE Question: Analyze the conditions during World War II that led to women joining the work force in large numbers.
Key terms: Analyze, led to. Answer should include a topic sentence and two or three social or economic conditions that caused an increase of women in the work force.

*Sequence or placement*—Key terms are *list and discuss, trace, review, outline, give the steps, locate.* The answer should include a topic sentence identifying the main point that is being traced and the pattern that can be observed or the conclusion that results. A sequence or placement answer is supported by detailing events in chronological sequence.

EXAMPLE Question: Trace the involvement of American troops in Vietnam under President Johnson. Mention at least three points when the level of involvement increased.
Key term: Trace. Answer should include a topic sentence and a chronology of at least three major events that led to an increase in the number of American troops.

*Description*—Key terms are *describe, identify, give examples of, tell the characteristics of, define.* The answer should include a topic sentence giving the major characteristics of the item or concept being described and supporting sentences that detail the critical features.

EXAMPLE Question: Describe court life under Marie Antoinette and Louis XVI just before the French Revolution.
Key term: Describe. Answer should include a topic sentence and at least three activities or features especially characteristic of this time.

## Writing the Essay Answer

Think through your answer before you begin writing. Follow these steps in writing your answer.

1. Develop a thesis statement that answers the question. You may find it useful to rephrase the question as part of your statement.

For example, a thesis statement for the answer to the comparison-contrast question above might read: Although Lady Macbeth has less to do with the actual killing, she is more responsible than Macbeth for planning and urging the murder of Duncan.

2. Use the thesis as the basis for a very brief three- or four-point outline. Make sure that the outline includes points related to all the directions in the question. For the Macbeth question, an outline should include two points each for Macbeth and Lady Macbeth.

3. Use the point value of the question to decide how long your answer should be. If you have scheduled less than ten minutes, plan for one full paragraph of development and a brief introduction and conclusion. In longer essays, allow one paragraph for each main supporting point. Be sure to include specific details, examples, and references.

4. Write out your answer, using the thesis statement as an introduction.

5. Include a conclusion that summarizes your essay.

6. Allow a few minutes to proofread your essay for missing words, unclear statements, and spelling and usage errors.

7. If you do run out of time, hand in your outline with your unfinished essay so that the teacher will see that you have some grasp of the material.

**EXERCISE 12. Analyzing Essay Test Questions.** For each of the following essay test questions, list the amount of time you should schedule (include a breakdown of planning, writing, and proofreading), the key word and the pattern of organization it calls for, and the kinds of examples or support needed.

1. Question worth 25 points in a 40-minute test period.
   Define naturalism; include at least three examples of stories written in this style (give the author's names).
2. Question worth 40 points in a 60-minute exam.
   Explain the difference between an opera and a musical comedy. Include references to at least three examples of each.
3. Question worth 30 points in a 40-minute test.
   Analyze how two of the stories in this unit use a humorous treatment to effectively present a serious point about human nature.
4. Question worth 15 points in a 45-minute test.
   Review the groups who claimed territorial rights to the area now known as Florida prior to its acquisition by the United States.

**EXERCISE 13. Composing and Answering an Essay Test Question.** Following your teacher's directions, compose your own essay question on a topic you are studying in one of your classes. Assign it a point value in a test meant to take 40 minutes. Schedule the appropriate amount of time and then write a sample answer; include planning and proofreading.

# PART FIVE

# SPEAKING AND LISTENING

IV. Tango - Valse - Rag

# CHAPTER 37

# The Interview

## GETTING INFORMATION: JOB AND COLLEGE APPLICATIONS

This chapter will show you how to use the interview to gather information, how to apply for a job, and how to apply for admission to college.

## THE INTERVIEW FOR GATHERING INFORMATION

### 37a. Learn how to conduct an interview.

In preparing a research paper, a class report, or a newspaper article, you may have to interview certain people for firsthand information.

### Preparation for the Interview

In preparing for an interview, be sure to follow these guidelines:

1. ***Make arrangements well in advance.*** Mention in general terms what days and times are most acceptable to you for a meeting, but let the other person specify the exact date, time, and place.

2. ***Decide beforehand on the questions you will ask or the information you want to obtain.*** This does not mean that you cannot ask other questions during the interview. The replies you receive to your prepared questions will suggest follow-up queries.

3. ***Ask questions that require extended replies.***

DO NOT ASK Do you think juvenile delinquency is a serious problem? [This question can be answered by a simple *yes* or *no*.]

ASK INSTEAD Why is juvenile delinquency commanding the attention of so many people today?

4. ***Ask questions that are clear and straightforward.***

DO NOT ASK Will you comment on juvenile delinquency in terms of parental responsibility?

ASK INSTEAD How should parents be held responsible for delinquency?

## Participation in the Interview

Be courteous and businesslike during the interview.

1. ***Arrive on time.***

2. ***Be businesslike in your manner.*** In business, time is valuable. Nevertheless, you should not hurry. Give yourself and the other person time to think. A too-hasty interview may defeat its purpose.

3. ***Avoid argument.*** Be tactful and courteous, remembering that the interview was granted at your request.

4. ***Take notes or use a tape recorder with the other person's permission.*** Before taking notes or turning on the tape recorder, ask permission of the person with whom you are talking. If you will quote the speaker directly, read or play back the exact words for the speaker.

5. ***Follow up the interview.*** Look over your notes to refresh your memory, and arrange the material you have gathered. Send a note expressing thanks for the interview.

**EXERCISE 1. Conducting an Interview.** Conduct an interview to gather information for a report. Get your teacher's approval of the topic of your interview, and be prepared to report on it in class.

## APPLYING FOR A JOB

An employer usually requires an interview before hiring.

1. ***Arrange an appointment.*** Help-wanted ads often require that applications be submitted in writing. A letter of application should include a summary of your qualifications, a statement that you are available for an interview, and your address and telephone number. (See pages 286–87 for sample letters of application.)

2. ***Prepare a résumé.*** Take a résumé with you and hand it to the prospective employer at the time of the interview. (See page 288 for a sample résumé.)

3. ***Be careful about your appearance.***

4. ***Answer questions candidly and concisely.*** Make your answers to questions as informative as you can. For example, if you are asked whether you have ever had any business experience as a typist, you might say, "No, but at school I was a student assistant in a counselor's office and typed many official reports."

5. ***Make an impression.*** Mention anything unusual or distinctive in your background that might bear on the position you are seeking.

6. ***Ask questions.*** You may ask about hours of service, rate of pay, or chances for advancement. In your questions, show that you know something about the company or business you are applying to.

7. ***Be prepared to take tests.*** The employer may ask you to demonstrate your ability or to take aptitude, intelligence, or personality tests.

**EXERCISE 2. Enacting a Job Interview.** With one student acting as an employer and another as an applicant, enact sample job interviews for the class. Decide beforehand what sort of job is being discussed. At the conclusion of each interview, the other members of the class will offer criticism and constructive suggestions.

## THE COLLEGE ADMISSION INTERVIEW

There is no better way of finding out about a college than by visiting it. The best time to visit a college is during the fall or spring semester of your junior year. The next-best time is during the fall of your senior year. Try to visit when the college is in session.

### Preparing for the Interview

**37b. Prepare for the interview carefully.**

1. ***Know the questions you want to ask.*** Make a list of the points you would like to ask about. Here are some questions you may ask:

*Instructional program and facilities.* What additional high-school courses should I take to qualify for admission? Are there any special courses I need to meet the requirements of the college department in which I am interested? When is the orientation program for freshmen?

*Housing and dining facilities.* What housing is available to first-year students? Are first-year students required to live in college dormitories? May first-year students select their own roommates?

*Recreational facilities.* Is there a center for student activities? What intercollegiate sports are offered? Is there an intramural sports program?

*Opportunity for employment.* Does the college have a job placement bureau? Are there employment opportunities on or off campus?

*Costs.* What is the average cost of tuition, board, and lodging for a year? What is the average cost of books for first-year students?

*College regulations.* What are some of the important college regulations for all students? What special regulations are there for all students as well as first-year students? Are students allowed to use automobiles?

2. ***Consider beforehand how you will answer the questions you may be asked.*** What replies would you give to the following questions?

*High-school record.* In which subject or subjects did you receive your highest marks? What subject caused you the most difficulty? What is your rank in class? Which subject do you like best? Why? What extracurricular activities did you participate in?

*Hobbies and interests.* What are your out-of-school hobbies? What books have you read recently other than those required for school courses?

*Educational plans.* What college courses are you interested in? Why? Do you want a liberal arts or a technical education? (That is, do you want a general education in literature, history, languages, philosophy, science, and mathematics, or are you interested in specialized training to prepare for a particular career?)

## Participating in the Interview

If you write for an interview, address the admissions officer by name if possible. You will find the person's name listed in the college catalog, or your guidance counselor will give it to you. Write your own letter, following the form used for business correspondence. Reread your letter before mailing it, and correct any mistakes. Your letter represents your ability to express yourself clearly.

If necessary, ask your guidance counselor to forward a transcript of your school record to the college well in advance of the interview. If your school is unable to forward an official transcript in time, ask for an unofficial transcript to take with you or take your report cards along.

Allow at least a half day for your visit. Dress neatly and appropriately, as if you were applying for a job.

The interview is a friendly and purposeful conversation. The admissions officer wants to determine whether you are qualified for admission. You, on the other hand, want to learn whether the college suits your needs and interests.

Of course you will be nervous. However, an admissions officer is skilled in meeting young people and will put you at your ease.

Usually the admissions officer will open the interview. After some small talk about your trip, an officer may ask, "What would you like to know about this college?" Ask the questions you have prepared in advance. If you do not understand a reply, request clarification. The conversation should be businesslike, but informal and unhurried.

After you have obtained all the information you want, the interviewer will probably ask you questions. Some of these questions are listed on page 756. Your answers should be honest and complete.

Follow up your visit. Write a note of thanks to the members of the admissions staff who interviewed you or extended courtesies. This letter, like the letter requesting an interview, tells a lot about you.

## Choosing Colleges

Before applying for admission, consider many colleges. Narrow this list down before you apply. Application fees (which are often not refundable) can be expensive.

**EXERCISE 3. Enacting a College Interview.** Ask your guidance counselor to assist in presenting several sample college interviews. With the counselor acting as a college admissions officer and students acting as applicants, enact several interviews. Each interview might illustrate a particular point; for example, the importance of preparation or the bad impression created by boasting. If the guidance counselor is unavailable, your teacher or a student may assume the role of a college admissions officer. In the ensuing class discussion, point out the merits and weaknesses of each interview.

**EXERCISE 4. Reporting on an Interview.** Report to the class on an interview you have seen on television. Evaluate the skills of the interviewer and the person being interviewed. Mention any skills you think would be valuable to acquire.

## SUMMARY FOR INTERVIEWS

1. Make arrangements for an interview well in advance.
2. Decide beforehand on the questions you will ask.
3. If you are applying for a job, prepare a résumé.
4. If you are applying to a college, arrange for a transcript to be sent well in advance of the interview.
5. Dress neatly.
6. Arrive on time.
7. Be businesslike in your manner.
8. Follow up the interview with a thank-you note.

# CHAPTER 38

# Public Speaking

## LEARNING TO SPEAK EASILY AND WELL IN PUBLIC

The principles of public speaking are similar to those of social conversation, except for these differences: conversation is unprepared, informal, and random; public speaking is prepared, more formal, and purposeful. There are also many similarities between the steps in the writing process and the steps in preparing a speech. Refer to Chapter 1 as you work through this chapter.

### PREPARING THE SPEECH

Sometimes the most troublesome phase of public speaking is finding something to talk about.

**38a. In choosing a subject, consider the occasion, the interests of your listeners, and your own interests and experience.**

***The occasion may suggest a subject.*** Before you decide on a subject for a meeting, for example, find out the purpose of the meeting, the other speakers on the program, and the time allotted to your talk.

***The interests of your listeners may suggest a subject.*** Ask yourself, "What are my listeners interested in? What are their hobbies, problems, ambitions?" Talk about what concerns them.

***Your experiences may suggest a subject.*** Words will come easily to you if you are familiar with your subject. Listeners will enjoy your talk more readily because you speak from personal knowledge.

**EXERCISE 1. Choosing a Subject For a Speech.** Select a subject suitable for a talk on each of the following occasions. Explain orally the reasons for your choice.

School honor society meeting
Banquet held for a victorious school team
Commencement
Parent-Teacher Association meeting
School assembly

**38b. Limit your subject so that it can be adequately treated in your speech and so that it reflects a definite purpose.**

When preparing a speech, as in preparing a composition, you should limit your subject. For example, a broad subject like "trains" offers a world of ideas to discuss. You must limit, or narrow, this broad subject to one aspect—perhaps "my most memorable journey by train." The same principles writers use for dividing a subject into its smaller parts can help you to narrow a subject into a *topic* for your speech. Refer to pages 8–10 of Chapter 1 for suggestions.

Another way to limit your subject is by determining a definite purpose for your speech. There are four purposes of public speaking: to inform, convince, entertain, and move to action. Once you determine your purpose, always keep it in mind. Suppose that you are going to speak about television. Your purpose determines how you will limit your subject to a topic. Thus, the content of a talk on television might vary as follows:

| | |
|---|---|
| TO INFORM | Discuss the high-quality TV programs for teen-agers. |
| TO CONVINCE | Advocate that TV programs should have ratings. |
| TO ENTERTAIN | Talk about a show you liked. |
| TO MOVE TO ACTION | Urge parents to write to network presidents to develop higher-quality children's programs. |

As a beginning step, set down your purpose in a sentence and use it as a temporary title. Later you can substitute a shorter and more catchy title. Writing your title as a sentence clarifies thinking, focuses attention on the aim, and guides in the selection of material. The following are typical sentence titles:

Helen Keller overcame many obstacles throughout her life. [to inform]
Capital punishment should be abolished. [to convince]
I had my share of troubles the first time I went fishing. [to entertain]
Vote for my candidate for president of the student council! [to move to action]

**EXERCISE 2. Developing a Topic For Your Speech.** Suppose you were asked to speak to your classmates on one of the following subjects. Decide on a purpose for your talk, then limit the subject to three topics. For each topic, list three points your talk will cover.

1. Tennis
2. Hiking
3. Dancing
4. My School
5. Computers

**38c. Gather materials from your own background, from interviews with others, and from printed sources.**[1]

The first source of material should be your own thoughts and experiences. What do *you* think about the topic? What knowledge do you already have about it? Reflect, and then jot down your opinions and experiences before researching elsewhere.

After doing your own thinking, discuss the topic with others. While talking with friends and relatives, you can steer the conversation around to the topic of your speech. In conversing with others, you sharpen your thinking, acquire new ideas, and consider possible objections.

The last source of material is the library. First consult such works of reference as an encyclopedia or an annual like the *World Almanac* or *Information Please Almanac*. Articles in reference works are usually brief and touch upon highlights only, but they provide background information

Next consult the card catalog to find books on the topic. Note the date of publication of the book. Try to examine recent publications before those written years ago.

Finally, read recent magazine articles. The *Readers' Guide to Periodical Literature*, which lists magazine articles alphabetically by subjects and by authors, is an invaluable aid.

**38d. Write notes on index cards.**

You may record notes from your reading on index cards. Index cards are convenient to handle and may be arranged in any order when you prepare an outline. Start each card with a subject heading and at the bottom give the source of the information.

[1] The information-gathering strategies used in the writing process will also be helpful here. For specific instructions see pages 12–18, Chapter 1.

Native American sports
Women played a game very similar to field hockey. Players on each team held a stick with which they moved a small ball toward goal posts at opposite ends of a long field.

Daughters of the Earth
by Carolyn Niethammer p. 200.

**Model Note Card**

**38e. Outline your talk.**

The outline of a speech helps you arrange the main and supporting ideas. Write an outline after you have gathered information.[1]

**EXERCISE 3. Gathering Material for Your Speech.** Select a topic for a three-minute talk to your class. Make a list of sources you intend to consult. Use one of the following topics or choose your own.

1. How to study well
2. Why study a foreign language
3. What I like about dogs
4. My best vacation
5. Reasons to stop smoking

**EXERCISE 4. Preparing an Outline for Your Speech.** Using the topic and the sources you chose for Exercise 3, prepare an outline for a three-minute speech.

**38f. Prepare a beginning that will arouse interest and lead into the topic.**[2]

In your opening remarks you should try to capture the attention of your audience and direct them to the topic you are going to discuss. The following techniques are effective ways of beginning a talk.

[1] For instructions in outlining see pages 103–105.

[2] For specific suggestions about writing introductory paragraphs, see pages 109–10 of Chapter 4.

A STRIKING STATEMENT

More Americans have been killed in traffic accidents than in all our country's wars combined.

A QUESTION

How much weekly allowance is enough?

AN ANECDOTE

After a bitter defeat Robert Bruce, the Scottish patriot, hid in a cave. His army had been crushed and his followers had left him. He had failed again—the third time! Despondent, he watched a spider spin a web. Again and again the web broke before it was completed, and each time the spider started afresh. That spider taught Bruce a lesson!

REFERENCE TO THE OCCASION

Commencement brings back happy memories. Four years ago when we entered Louisville High School for the first time and sat in this auditorium, graduation seemed far off. Today, we look back on those four years and wonder where they have gone.

### 38g. Develop your ideas logically and persuasively.

Use the following techniques to develop your ideas.

EXPLANATION

A high-school secret society exists in a school without the knowledge or approval of school authorities. Members are elected by secret ballot and only those who belong know who the members are. Members may not disclose what happens at meetings.

STATING ADVANTAGES AND DISADVANTAGES

Let's hold a dance rather than a bake sale. A dance is more fun and less trouble to arrange. It will attract more people and be more profitable.

EXAMPLES

Boomtown High School held a successful dance last month. Townley High School will hold one next week and Centerville High the week after. Ours is the only high school in the county that does not have a dance every term.

STATISTICS

The United States has only 6 percent of the world's population, yet it consumes over half of the world's available natural gas and one third of the world's available petroleum.

REFERENCE TO AUTHORITIES

Dr. Donald H. Menzel, director of the Harvard Observatory, recently declared that interplanetary communication will be possible within the next ten years.

**38h. Restate important ideas.**

During a speech, a speaker often says the same thing in different ways. In a composition such repetition would be faulty. In public speaking, however, restatement is not repetition; it is a recasting of a thought in a different mold so that it will have an immediate impact on the listener.

**38i. Prepare a conclusion that will impress the central thought of your talk on your listeners.**

The most common conclusion is a summary of the main ideas. You may end a speech effectively with a quotation, an emotional appeal that repeats your main theme, or a thought-provoking question.

**EXERCISE 5. Analyzing the Introductions and Conclusions of Speeches.** From an anthology of speeches, read aloud the beginnings and conclusions of several talks. Discuss their effectiveness or ineffectiveness. Do the introductions arouse interest and lead into the subject? Do the conclusions drive home the main ideas?

## DELIVERING THE SPEECH

There are five methods of presenting a speech: impromptu speaking, extemporaneous speaking, memorized speaking, reading from manuscript, and a composite method.

An *impromptu talk* is organized and presented on the spur of the moment. It is delivered without preparation and relies on the speaker's general knowledge and experience.

An *extemporaneous talk* is carefully planned, but not memorized or read from a page. Usually the speaker prepares an outline, but adapts the speech to the reactions of the audience. Experienced speakers generally use the extemporaneous method.

A *memorized talk* is written and learned word by word. Memorized talks usually sound artificial.

A *speech* may be read from a *manuscript.* A speech that is read lacks naturalness of expression and prevents eye contact with the audience.

The *composite method* is a combination of two or more methods. For example, a speaker may memorize the introduction and conclusion, read a fact, and develop the main ideas extemporaneously.

### 38j. Avoid excessive nervousness.

Nearly everyone is a little tense before beginning to speak. It is a sign the body is keyed for maximum performance. *Excessive* nervousness, though, prevents coherent thinking or smooth movement. Here are some suggestions for overcoming nervousness.

1. ***Know your topic and audience thoroughly.*** Prepare well in advance of the scheduled date. Mull over your topic and think about the interests and needs of your audience.

2. ***Practice aloud.*** Use different words each time you practice. Do not try to memorize. Have your outline at hand so that you become familiar with the sequence of ideas.

3. ***Concentrate on your purpose.*** Always keep in your mind what you want your listeners to do, believe, or feel as a result of your talk.

4. ***Tell a humorous story.*** Laughter relaxes the speaker and the audience.

5. ***Welcome opportunities to speak in public.*** Stage fright diminishes with experience in speaking. As you become accustomed to talking in public, your poise and confidence will increase.

### 38k. Use nonverbal communication effectively.

Nonverbal, or unspoken, communication consists of gestures, posture, and facial expressions that relay signals between a speaker and an audience. Many of these movements are unconscious; that is, a person is not aware of making them. Nevertheless, an audience watches and interprets a speaker's movements. Excessive gesturing, for example, will usually indicate that a speaker is nervous. Stiff, wooden gestures can indicate that a speaker is unfriendly. Good speakers use nonverbal communication with precision and care.

1. ***Maintain good posture.*** Stand or sit straight as you speak. Audiences lose interest in someone whose posture is sloppy.

2. ***Maintain eye contact.*** Glance about the room. Do not stare at your note cards or at the floor. Look at your listeners. Eye contact holds attention.

3. ***Gesture naturally.*** Gestures should be appropriate. Different speakers use different gestures to express the same ideas. Common sense will dictate which gestures are appropriate for the ideas you wish to express.

Gestures should be graceful and spontaneous, arising naturally out of the urge to communicate. They should change as a speaker's ideas change.

Do not use gestures which are meaningless, awkward, flabby. Make your gestures precisely and sparingly.

Move occasionally when speaking. Move to show an important change of thought. When speaking to a small group, a shift of weight from one foot to another will suffice. Before large audiences obvious changes of position and frequent movement are necessary for visibility.

**EXERCISE 6. Analyzing a Speaker's Gestures.** Carefully watch and make notes about a speaker's gestures during an assembly or a television program. Report orally on their effectiveness.

### 38l. Speak in a conversational tempo.

Under ordinary circumstances, speak at a conversational rate. In large auditoriums it may be necessary to speak more slowly than usual. If your pace is too deliberate, however, your listeners' attention will lag.

## LISTENING TO TALKS

As a listener, you observe rules which will help you understand and remember what you hear.

### 38m. Learn how to evaluate a speech.

Listen to your classmates to learn what they have to say, to appreciate their viewpoints, and to analyze the content and delivery of their speeches. You may help them to improve and they, in turn, may help you.

The following outline for evaluation will guide your remarks. After each talk, write your evaluation on a sheet of paper and hand it to the speaker. Do not write during the speech. You should mention commendable features as well as those needing improvement.

I. Content
  A. Choice of subject
  B. Preparation and knowledge of subject matter
  C. Arrangement of material
    1. Purpose of the talk
    2. Introduction
    3. Development
    4. Conclusion
  D. Use of standard English
    1. Grammatical errors
    2. Clichés
    3. Slang

II. Nonverbal communication
  A. Posture
  B. Eye contact with audience
  C. Gestures

III. Relation of speaker to audience
  A. Direct and sincere
  B. Conversational
  C. Communicative
  D. Confident

IV. Voice, enunciation, pronunciation
V. Audience reaction
VI. General summary and evaluation

## Content

Keep these things in mind as you listen to a talk.

A. ***Choice of subject.*** If the subject was not assigned, a speaker's topic should reflect personal and listeners' interests.

B. ***Preparation and knowledge of topic.*** Note the organization of the speech, reliance on notes, familiarity with details, ability to answer questions, and skill in adapting the material to all listeners.

C. ***Arrangement of material.*** A good speech has a purpose; it also has a beginning, a middle, and an end.

1. A speaker may state the purpose at the outset of the talk or may not reveal it until the end, but no matter when the purpose is stated, listeners should easily become aware of it.

2. The introduction establishes contact between speaker and listeners. It arouses interest and states and limits the subject. Avoid trite beginnings such as "The topic I am going to discuss is. . . ." Capture the listeners' attention by a striking statement, anecdote, or reference to the occasion.

3. The topic itself or the purpose of the speaker often determines a speaker's organization. The following patterns of organization are the most commonly used:

a. *Time order.* Usually followed in a narrative speech: for example, an account of a fishing trip, or the steps in an experiment.

b. *Problem-solving order.* The statement of a problem is followed by an explanation of the solution. For example: What makes an airplane fly?

c. *Cause-and-effect order.* An exposition of the effects flowing from a specified cause. For example: Limited college facilities influence the educational opportunities of high-school graduates.

d. *Effect-to-cause order.* A result is traced to a cause. For example: The mass exodus from cities to suburbs is ascribed to one or more causes.

Arrangement is often determined by the nature of the topic or the purpose of the speaker. As a listener, consider whether the speaker arranged the material in the best possible order. What other order might have been used? Would it have been more effective?

☞ **NOTE** In persuasive or argumentative talks, a good speaker limits the number of important points to three or four. Listeners can remember three or four easily but have difficulty in keeping more than four in mind throughout a talk.

4. An effective conclusion ties the parts of a speech together. No matter which method a speaker uses in concluding—summarizing, appealing for action, quoting—listeners should be aware that their understanding of a topic has increased because they listened to the speech.

D. ***Use of standard English.*** If a grammatical error or the inappropriate use of slang distracts your attention from a speaker's message, the fault is serious. In your evaluation, mention the error and tell how it might be corrected.

### Nonverbal Communication

A. ***Posture.*** Faulty posture occurs when a speaker slumps or adopts any stance that distracts the audience.

B. ***Eye contact.*** An effective speaker looks directly into the eyes of individuals and slowly shifts the gaze around the room.

C. ***Gestures.*** Good speakers avoid distracting movements such as playing with a piece of chalk. As a listener, you should not be conscious of a speaker's gestures. They should grow out of the thought and contribute to its communication.

### Relation of Speaker to Audience

When friends converse with you, you like them to be sincere, friendly, and assured. These same qualities mark an effective public speaker.

### Audience Reaction

Very often the test of a good speech is the discussion it arouses. If, after a speaker has finished, the listeners have questions, make comments, or disagree with something, the speech was very likely a good one.

### General Summary and Evaluation

Your evaluation of your classmates' efforts and theirs of yours should be friendly, helpful, and honest.

EXERCISE 7. **Analyzing a Speech.** Listen to a speech given in your community, on television, or on radio. Report to the class on its effectiveness, using the outline on page 767.

REVIEW EXERCISE A. **Delivering a Speech.** Using the outline you prepared in Exercise 4, page 762, deliver a three-minute speech to the class. At the conclusion of the talk, your listeners will offer constructive suggestions covering content and delivery.

REVIEW EXERCISE B. **Delivering a Supporting or Opposing Speech.** Choose a bill that is before the legislature or a law that is in effect, and support or oppose it in a five- or six-minute talk. Prepare an outline. Your beginning should arouse interest and lead into your subject, your ideas should be developed logically and persuasively, and your conclusion should forcefully impress the central idea of your talk on your listeners.

**REVIEW EXERCISE C. Delivering an Expository Speech.** Choose one of the following items or one you prefer, and in a five- or six-minute speech, explain to your classmates how to use it. Your explanation should include, if possible, a demonstration of the item's use. Be prepared to answer questions once your talk is over.

1. A tennis racket
2. A pocket calculator
3. A wok
4. A slide rule
5. A small tent
6. A toothbrush
7. A thesaurus
8. A manual transmission
9. A card catalog
10. A barometer

## EFFECTIVE SPEECH

Becoming an effective speaker means knowing how to use language well in both presentation and usage. Two elements of effective speech are enunciation and the use of rhetorical devices.

### Enunciation

If your audience cannot understand what you are saying, all your preparation is wasted. The following exercises will help you improve the clarity of your speech.

**38n. Enunciate clearly.**

To enunciate clearly you must move your lips, tongue, and jaw.

**EXERCISE 8. Practicing Sound and Word Combinations.** Practice the following sound and word combinations. Read across the page.

| | | | | |
|---|---|---|---|---|
| bee-boo | bee-boo | bee-boo | bee-boo | beet, boot |
| bah-boh | bah-boh | bah-boh | bah-boh | bark, boat |
| mee-maw | mee-maw | mee-maw | mee-maw | meat ball |
| raw-bee | raw-bee | raw-bee | raw-bee | raw beet |

Exaggerate your jaw action as you practice the following sound combinations. Drop your jaw as far as you can when you say *ah.* Read across the page.

| | | | |
|---|---|---|---|
| oh-ah | oh-ah | oh-ah | oh-ah |
| so far | so far | so far | so far |
| ee-ah | ee-ah | ee-ah | ee-ah |
| street car | street car | street car | street car |

Place the tip of the tongue on the gum ridge behind the upper teeth. Lightly and agilely practice:

t-t-t d-d-d t-t-t d-d-d
tah-tay-tee-taw-toh-too
dah-day-dee-daw-doh-doo

***Slurring.*** Slurring is a common fault. When sounds are not formed crisply or when syllables are telescoped, indistinctness results.

**EXERCISE 9. Pronouncing Words Without Omitting Any Syllables.** Read aloud each word in the following list, being careful not to omit any syllables. After reading aloud, say each word in a sentence.

| | | |
|---|---|---|
| electric | mystery | grocery |
| actually | February | myths |
| average | million | precincts |

***Omitting Sounds.*** Speakers often omit essential sounds at the beginning, in the middle, or at the end of words.

**EXERCISE 10. Pronouncing the Middle and Final Sounds of Words.** Pronounce the following lists of words, giving special attention to the enunciation problem indicated for each list.

***Middle Sounds:***

| | | | |
|---|---|---|---|
| accidentally | geography | library | recognize |
| all right | government | poem | shouldn't |
| champion | jewel | poetry | wonderful |

***Final Sounds:***

| | | | | |
|---|---|---|---|---|
| child | second | chest | hollow | past |
| gold | tomorrow | last | fellow | post |
| kind | borrow | pillow | meant | left |

***Difficult Consonant Combinations.*** The *nd* combination requires a special effort to pronounce. If you omit the *d* sound in the *nd* combination, your speech will sound nonstandard.

**EXERCISE 11. Pronouncing Words with the *nd* Combination.** Make a conscious effort to pronounce the *d* in each word.

| | | | |
|---|---|---|---|
| send | band | dependable | defend |
| lend | land | round | standing |
| mend | friendly | bound | pretending |

**EXERCISE 12. Pronouncing Words with Three or More Consecutive Consonants.** A combination of three or more consonants is particularly difficult. Be overprecise as you practice these words.

*cts:* conflicts, facts, respects, restricts, tracts
*dths:* widths, breadths, hundredths
*fts:* lifts, shafts, shifts, tufts
*lds:* builds, fields, folds
*pts:* accepts, precepts, concepts
*sks:* asks, desks, disks, risks
*sps:* clasps, lisps, rasps, wasps
*sts:* adjusts, frosts, digests, insists, lists, mists, rests, tests

***Adding Sounds.*** Adding sounds is a common fault. An example is *lawr* for *law*. Avoid this error when you speak.

**EXERCISE 13. Pronouncing Words Without Adding Sounds.** Drill on the following words, being careful not to add any sounds.

| | | | | |
|---|---|---|---|---|
| athlete | draw | elm | evening | umbrella |
| burglar | bracelet | idea | film | hindrance |
| chimney | mischievous | lightning | ticklish | Westminster |

***Substituting Sounds.*** The substitution of one sound for another is a frequent fault: *ciddy* for *city; dis* for *this; tree* for *three.*

**EXERCISE 14. Pronouncing Words Without Substituting Sounds.** Practice saying the following pairs of words, taking care to distinguish between them.

| t-d | | t-th | |
|---|---|---|---|
| matter | madder | boat | both |
| metal | medal | tree | three |
| writing | riding | taught | thought |

| d-th | | w-wh | |
|---|---|---|---|
| breed | breathe | watt | what |
| dare | there | weather | whether |
| read | wreathe | witch | which |

***Mispronouncing Words with ng.*** The *ng* sound causes much confusion. You can eliminate any difficulty by learning three simple rules:

1. *All words ending in* -ng *and all words derived from them are pronounced with the final sound in* sing.

EXAMPLES bring, bringing, wing, winging
EXCEPTIONS Use the sound in *finger* in the following words: *longer, longest, stronger, strongest, younger, youngest.*

2. *The combination* nge *at the end of a word is pronounced* nj.

EXAMPLES hinge, strange, orange

3. *In all other words,* ng *is pronounced as in* single.

EXAMPLES hunger, anger, mingle
EXCEPTIONS gingham, Bingham

**EXERCISE 15. Pronouncing Words with Final *ng*.** Say the following words aloud and then use them in sentences. Pronounce the *ng* as in *sing*.

| | | | |
|---|---|---|---|
| tongue | slangy | thronging | songbird |
| ringlet | among | clingy | prongless |
| springier | fangless | harangue | twangy |

**EXERCISE 16. Pronouncing Words with *ng*.** Say the following words aloud and then use them in sentences. Pronounce the *ng* as in *finger*.

| | | | |
|---|---|---|---|
| anger | hunger | younger | fungus |
| mingle | jingle | dangle | spangled |
| linger | English | bingo | elongate |

***Transposing Sounds.*** Some mispronunciations are the result of transposing sounds, as in the list below.

| DO NOT SAY | SAY INSTEAD | DO NOT SAY | SAY INSTEAD |
|---|---|---|---|
| modren | modern | larnyx | larynx |
| prespiration | perspiration | irrevelant | irrelevant |
| calvary | cavalry | hunderd | hundred |
| childern | children | bronical | bronchial |

## Rhetorical Devices

**38o. Add variety and interest to your oral style by using rhetorical devices.**

Rhetorical devices are formal techniques of language aimed at producing speeches that are lively, forceful, and pleasing to the ear. Effective speakers use the following four rhetorical devices to add flavor to their speeches: direct questions, rhetorical questions, informal language, and climax.

***Direct Questions.*** A direct question is one that a speaker both asks and answers.

> What are the merits of the plan I propose? It is simple. It is inexpensive. It will achieve results.

A direct question can be used as a transition, leading from one division of a speech to another. It stimulates listeners to participate in a speaker's thinking. If not overused, it captures attention.

***Rhetorical Questions.*** A rhetorical question is one that requires no reply. The speaker's voice, manner, or language leads listeners to answer it in their own minds.

> What could be more exciting than a trip down the Colorado River on a rubber raft?

***Informal Language.*** In classroom talks and similar speaking situations, informality is desirable. To give your talk an air of informality:

1. Use contractions; for example, *aren't, don't, hasn't, I'm.*
2. Use short sentences.
3. Use personal pronouns. Pepper your talk with *we, you, our, ours, us.* Use *I,* too, but don't overuse it.

Notice the use of informal language in the following example:

> There are so many of us in Wakefield High that we must all observe the rules about traffic in the halls and stairways. If we don't, we can't move quickly from one place to another.

To maintain informality, speak extemporaneously. For more help with extemporaneous talks, see page 764.

***Climax.*** By piling one detail upon another in an ascending order of importance, you can drive an idea home powerfully. Notice in the following example how the speaker builds to a climax.

> You've got to love people, places, ideas; you've got to live with mind, body, soul; you've got to be committed; there is no life on the sidelines.
>
> BESS MYERSON

EXERCISE 17. **Using Rhetorical Devices in Speeches.** Make a short speech to the class, using primarily two of the devices. Good combinations are the direct question and informal language or the rhetorical question and climax.

EXERCISE 18. **Using Rhetorical Devices in Your Writing.** Write four short paragraphs illustrating each of the rhetorical devices you have just studied. You need not limit yourself to one topic, but you may find it easier if you do.

EXERCISE 19. **Analyzing the Use of Rhetorical Devices in Famous Speeches.** Analyze a speech by a famous orator such as Martin Luther King, Jr., Abraham Lincoln, or Evangeline Booth, showing what rhetorical devices were used, and, if you can, what the reason was for using that particular technique. Write down at least five examples.

REVIEW EXERCISE D. **Writing and Practicing the Pronunciation of Words.** Keep a list in your notebook of the words you find most difficult to pronounce. Using a dictionary, write next to each word its correct pronunciation. Practice saying these words aloud and use them often in everyday conversation.

REVIEW EXERCISE E. **Preparing and Delivering a Talk Using Rhetorical Devices.** Prepare and deliver a five- or six-minute talk to your classmates on a topic you have chosen. Include in your talk at least two rhetorical devices. As your classmates listen to your talk, they will write down the rhetorical devices you have used, identifying each one. At the conclusion of your talk, discuss with the class the effectiveness and appropriateness of each device.

## SUMMARY FOR EFFECTIVE PUBLIC SPEAKING

***For Speakers***

1. Choose a subject based on the occasion, your interest, or the interest of your audience.

2. Limit the subject so that it can be adequately treated in your speech and so that it reflects a definite purpose.
3. Outline the talk.
4. Prepare an interesting introduction.
5. Arrange ideas logically.
6. Restate important ideas.
7. Conclude the talk forcefully.
8. Avoid excessive nervousness.
9. Use nonverbal signals effectively.
10. Speak in a conversational tempo.

***For Listeners***

1. Evaluate talks according to:
   a. Content
   b. Nonverbal communication
   c. Relation of speaker to audience
   d. Voice, enunciation, pronunciation
   e. Audience reaction
2. Be constructive in your evaluation.

***For Effective Speech***

1. Avoid clichés.
2. Use slang only on informal occasions.
3. Enunciate clearly. Avoid slurring or other common faults.
4. Use rhetorical devices to enliven your speech.

# INDEX

# Index

## A

## B



INDEX

## C

## D



INDEX

## F



INDEX

INDEX

INDEX

## N

## P



INDEX

INDEX

## S



INDEX

INDEX

INDEX

## T



INDEX

## U



## V

## W

## Y



## Z



INDEX

# NOTES

# NOTES

# NOTES

# NOTES

B 8
C 9
D 0
E 1
F 2
G 3
H 4
I 5
J 6